WITHDRAWN

D1320328

JUNIOR COLLEGE DISTRICT

of St. Louis - St. Louis County

LIBRARY

7508 Forsyth Blvd.

St. Louis, Missouri 63105

PRINTED IN U.S.A.

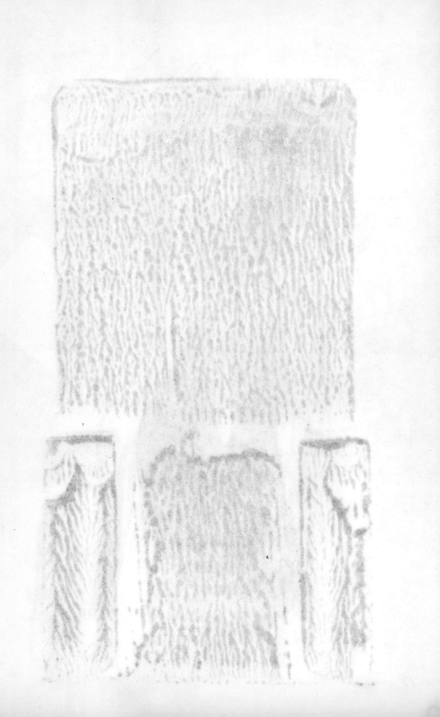

BRITISH WORKING CLASS MOVEMENTS

*

SELECT DOCUMENTS
1789–1875

BY

G. D. H. COLE AND A. W. FILSON

MACMILLAN

London · Melbourne · Toronto

ST MARTIN'S PRESS

New York

1965

First Edition 1951
Reissued 1965

MACMILLAN AND COMPANY LIMITED
St Martin's Street London WC2
also Bombay Calcutta Madras Melbourne

THE MACMILLAN COMPANY OF CANADA LIMITED
70 Bond Street Toronto 2

ST MARTIN'S PRESS INC
175 Fifth Avenue New York 10010 NY

PRINTED IN GREAT BRITAIN

PREFACE

THIS volume has been designed to serve as a companion to G. D. H. Cole's " Short History of the British Working-class Movement ", which, first published more than twenty years ago, was revised throughout and extended in the new edition of 1948. It can also be used with " The Common People ", by G. D. H. Cole and Raymond Postgate, of which a thoroughly revised edition was published in 1946. As both these volumes give book references, it has not been considered necessary to repeat them here; but references to both these books [1] have been given for each main section. The passages included in the present volume are taken from many sources. A large number have been quoted from books and pamphlets included in G. D. H. Cole's collection, now at Nuffield College, Oxford. Others come from the Place and other collections in the British Museum; from the Home Office Papers at the Record Office; from the George Howell collection at the Bishopsgate Institute, London, or from similar familiar gathering grounds. Our special thanks are due to Professor Aspinall of Reading University for allowing us to supplement our own excerpts from the Home Office Papers by quoting from his volume, " The Early English Trade Unions "; to Dr. S. R. Driver, for two documents given in his life of Richard Oastler, published under the title, " Tory Radical "; to Mrs. Barbara Hammond and to Messrs. Longmans, Green & Co. for several documents quoted from " The Skilled Labourer " and " The Village Labourer "; to Mr. A. W. Humphrey for documents quoted from his " History of Labour Representation "; to Mr. Ness Edwards, for a passage from his " History of the South Wales Miners "; to Dr. M. W. Thomas, for several extracts from his book, " The Early Factory Legislation "; to Mr. R. W. Postgate, for a passage from " The Builders' History "; and to Mr. Reg. Groves, for permission to quote a labourers' song from his " Sharpen the Sickle ".

We began work on this volume in 1937, and had prepared the greater part of the material before war broke out. We had then to lay it aside, and have only now been able to finish it. It was fully in shape before, in 1948, a series of small volumes, forming a series called " History in the Making " and covering a part of the

[1] Referred to respectively as " Short History " and " Common People ".

same ground in a substantially different way, began to be issued, and our own selections were made entirely without reference to these volumes.

We have done our best to be accurate; but in transcribing from copy in libraries, and especially in dealing with manuscript material, some errors are bound to creep in. We shall be grateful to any reader who draws our attention to mistakes of any kind.

G. D. H. C.
A. W. F.

May 1949

CONTENTS

vii

Contents

A*

ix

Contents

Contents

Contents

Contents

Contents

Contents

I

THE INDUSTRIAL REVOLUTION

INTRODUCTION

In the typical village of 1760 there was a continuous gradation of classes from the relatively rare wholly landless labourer up to the Lord of the Manor. Between these extremes, some of the poorest classes (the cottagers and squatters) divided their time between their work as labourers at wages and working for themselves either on their own small plots of land or in connection with such rights as they possessed by custom upon the waste. Some, such as the small freeholders, worked their strips with their families; while richer tenants or freeholders employed farm servants or day-labourers. The various grades of villagers had, by law or custom, widely varying rights over the common meadowland and waste. In many areas they — and still more their wives and children — carried on spinning or other domestic occupations, such as straw-hat making, in their cottages; and this supplementary source of earnings was of considerable importance in the village economy. The Enclosure Movement, however, was fast destroying the older type of village. Concentration of the ownership of land in fewer hands and the use of better implements and methods of rotation and land improvement made farming more and more a business requiring capital. Especially in view of the expenses of enclosure, small-holders were often compelled to sell out and to become labourers or to leave the countryside; while the cottagers and squatters lost their customary means of livelihood upon the commons where they had kept their livestock and cut their fuel. Moreover, the disappearance of domestic spinning and other occupations into the factories was, by the latter half of the eighteenth century, undermining the standard of living of those who depended in part on this source of income. The period was one of deepening poverty for the village labourer. Towards the end of the century the situation became still worse in view of the sharply rising level of prices after the outbreak of war. It became indispensable either to raise wages or to provide the labourers with an additional source of income. But landlords and farmers were reluctant to raise wages on account of the war prices, because it would probably be difficult to reduce them again when the exceptional conditions were over, and also because, especially during the war, prices were fluctuating very widely indeed in accordance with variations in the annual harvests. In these circumstances it became necessary not only to provide the means of subsistence for those who had lost their employment, but also to subsidise wages even for the employed labourers. Eventually Parliament legalised the Speenhamland system (1795), whereby the parish supplemented wages by an amount varying with the size of a labourer's family and with the price of corn. In the areas where this system was adopted, that is, over practically the whole of Southern England and a part of the Midlands, farmers thereafter found it most profitable to employ pauper labour and to pay a pittance wage which the parish would then supplement out of the local rates. In many areas it became necessary to qualify as a pauper in order to secure employment. In view of all these conditions there was a serious surplus of rural labour; but in face of the Settlement Acts it was very difficult for this surplus labour to migrate to the distant factory areas where employment might have been available. Broadly, what happened was that labourers from the districts nearest to the factory areas moved into the towns in search of employment, leaving their places to be filled by labourers from somewhat further off. Thus in the long run, and by a series of stages, labour was redistributed over the country; but this process took a long time, and a serious surplus of labour continued to exist in the southern counties until well after the Poor Law Amendment Act of 1834.

Meanwhile, industry had been developing at a rapid pace and had been largely changing its location. Throughout the eighteenth century the woollen and worsted trades had been growing much faster in Yorkshire than in other old centres of domestic manufacture; and in many areas, especially in the Eastern and Western counties, there had been an actual decay of weaving, accelerated later by the decline of domestic spinning due to the introduction of power-driven machinery. As the arts of iron production developed, new coalfields were opened up, and the ironworks migrated to areas where coal and ironstone were to be found together. The development of the steam-engine after Watt's improvements created a big further demand for coal and led to a concentration of the new factories near the coal mines, whereas the earlier phase of water-power had involved dispersal in search of streams suitable for turning water-wheels. Shortage of labour in the rapidly growing factory and mining areas created a situation favourable to wage-increases, which were only in part checked by the operation of the laws against combinations. Wages rose faster, from lower starting levels, in the north than in the southern half of the country as long as this shortage continued, and it was never found necessary to subsidise wages regularly under the Speenhamland system in the North of England. The sharp fluctuations of employment, however, made it necessary in some of the factory areas to use the Poor Law as a means of supplementing wages of partially employed as well as of unemployed workers, even in the factory districts.

See " Short History ", Part I, chapters 1 and 2.
" Common People ", chapters 1-6, 10 and 11.

1. THE LABOURERS

[David Davies, D.D., for many years Rector of Barkham in Berkshire, devoted much of his life to the collection of information about the condition of the labouring poor. He published much of the information in his book " The Case of the Labourers in Husbandry ", 1795. The date of his birth is unknown, but he graduated at Oxford in 1778. He died about 1819.]

From the Rev. D. Davies, " The Case of the Labourers in Husbandry " (1795), pp. 55-7.

The practice of enlarging and engrossing of farms, and especially that of depriving the peasantry of all landed property, have contributed greatly to increase the number of dependent poor.

1. The land-owner, to render his income adequate to the increased expense of living, unites several small farms into one, raises the rent to the utmost, and avoids the expense of repairs. The rich farmer also engrosses as many farms as he is able to stock ; lives in more credit and comfort than he could otherwise do ; and out of the profits of the *several farms*, makes an ample provision for *one family*. Thus thousands of families, which formerly gained an independent livelihood on those separate farms, have been gradually reduced to the class of day-labourers. But day-labourers are sometimes in want of work, and are sometimes unable to work ; and in either case their resort is the parish. It is a fact, that thousands of parishes have not now half the number of farmers which they had formerly. And in proportion as the number of farming families has decreased, the number of poor families has increased.

2. The depriving the peasantry of all landed property has beggared multitudes. It is plainly agreeable to sound policy, that as many individuals as possible in a state should possess an interest in the soil; because this attaches them strongly to the country and its constitution, and makes them zealous and resolute in defending them. But the gentry of this kingdom seem to have lost sight of this wise and salutary policy. Instead of giving to labouring people a valuable stake in the soil, the opposite measure has so long prevailed, that but few cottages, comparatively, have now *any* land about them. Formerly many of the lower sort of people occupied tenements of their own with parcels of land about them, or they rented such of others. On these they raised for themselves a considerable part of their subsistence, without being obliged, as now, to buy all they want at shops. And this kept numbers from coming to the parish. But since those small parcels of ground have been swallowed up in the contiguous farms and inclosures, and the cottages themselves have been pulled down; the families which used to occupy them are crowded together in decayed farm houses, with hardly ground enough about them for a cabbage garden: and being thus reduced to be *mere* hirelings, they are of course very liable to come to want. And not only the *men* occupying those tenements, but their *wives and children* too, could formerly, when they wanted work abroad, employ themselves profitably at home; whereas now, few of *these* are constantly employed, except in harvest; so that almost the whole burden of providing for their families rests upon the *men*. Add to this, that the former occupiers of small farms and tenements, though poor themselves, gave away something in alms to their poorer neighbours; a resource which is now much diminished.

Thus an amazing number of people have been reduced from a comfortable state of partial independence to the precarious conditions of hirelings, who, when out of work, must immediately come to their parish. And the great plenty of working hands always to be had when wanted, having kept down the price of labour below its proper level, the consequence is universally felt in the increased number of dependent poor.

2. THE STATE OF THE POOR

[Sir Frederick Morton Eden (1766–1809), one of the founders of the Globe Insurance Company, is best known for his book, " The State of the Poor ", based on extensive reports from parishes all over England, giving an account of the condition of the labouring classes during the early years of the French Wars. Eden was only thirty-one years old when he published this most impressive statistical study, which is by far the most important single source of information about working-class conditions towards the end of the eighteenth century. Eden was also an advocate of Friendly Societies and of social insurance, as well as of London improvements and the development of a public fire service.]

(a) From " The State of the Poor " : a History of the Labouring Classes in England, with Parochial Reports, by Sir F. M. Eden, 1797, Book I, chapter 3, p. 385.

In the thirty years between 1746 and 1776, Mr. Howlett thinks the inequality was more manifest. Between 1746 and 1765 wheat was only 32s. a quarter, but from the latter date to 1776 above 45s., which alone must have increased the annual expense of living by nearly four millions to counterbalance which the rise in the price of labour was little if anything more than 2d. in the shilling, e.g. labourers out of doors in the country got 10d. a day in 1737, and 12d. in 1787 ; threshers, 9d. and 12d. ; labourers out of doors near great towns, 16d. and 16d. ; and in the cloth manufacture scribblers got 14d. a day in 1737, and 15d. in 1787 ; shearmen 15d. and 18d. ; weavers' wages in the coarse trade were raised 2d. a day, but nothing in the superfine ; while women spinners got 6d. in 1737, and 7d. in 1787. I am convinced, however, that from enquiries I have made, the price of labour in most parts of England, except in the vicinity of great towns, had nearly doubled " in the last 60 years." [1]

(b) From " The State of the Poor ", by Sir F. M. Eden, 1797, Book II, chapter 2.

I most sincerely agree with those who regret that the labourer does not get more for his shilling than is usually the case ; the misfortune, however, does not arise from (what is so often most unjustly reprobated) his being obliged to purchase the few articles he has occasion for, from petty retail shops, but because either through ignorance, custom or prejudice, he adheres to ancient improvident systems in dress, diet, and in other branches of private expenditure. . . . Instead of the ill-grounded complaints, which

[1] *I.e.* from 1736 to 1796.

have so often been reiterated by writers on the Poor, that the wages of industry are in general too inadequate to provide the labourers with those comforts and conveniences which are befitting his station in the community, they would better serve the cause of the industrious peasant and manufacturer by pointing out the best means of reducing their expenses, without diminishing their comforts (pp. 491-2).

. . . .

There seems to be just reason to conclude that the miseries of the labouring Poor arose, less from the scantiness of their income (however much the philanthropist might wish it to be increased) than from their own improvidence and unthriftiness; since it is the fact, and I trust will be demonstrated in a subsequent part of this work, that in many parts of the kingdom, where the earnings of industry are moderate, the condition of the labourers is more comfortable than in other districts where wages are exorbitant. . . . It must strike every one who has at all investigated the subject of diet, that there is not only a remarkable difference in the proportion of earnings appropriated to the purchase of subsistence by labourers in the North and South of England, but that their mode of preparing their food is no less dissimilar. In the South of England the poorest labourers are habituated to the unvarying meal of dry bread and cheese from week's end to week's end; and in those families whose finances do not allow them the indulgence of malt liquor, the deleterious produce of China constitutes their most usual beverage. If a labourer is rich enough to afford himself meat once a week, he commonly roasts it, or if he lives near a baker's he bakes it, and if he boils his meat he never thinks of making it into a soup, which would be as nourishing and more palatable. In the North of England, Scotland and Wales the poorest labourers, however, regale themselves with a variety of dishes unknown in the South. . . . To begin with : *hasty pudding*, which is made of oatmeal, water and salt, about 13 oz. of meal to a quart of water, which is sufficient for a meal for two labourers. It is eaten with a little milk or beer poured upon it, or with a little cold butter put into the middle, or with a little treacle. A good meal for one person, supposing the price of oats to be 20s. the quarter, will not exceed 1d. (pp. 495-8).

. . . .

The principal advantage which the labourers in the North of England possess over their countrymen in the South consists in the great variety of cheap and savoury soups, which the use of barley and barley bread affords them an opportunity of making. The cheapness of fuel is, perhaps, another reason why the meals of the Northern peasant are so much diversified, and his table so often supplied with hot dishes (pp. 524-5).

. . . . . .

It must be confessed that the difficulty of introducing any species of food which requires much culinary preparation into the South of England arises in a great measure from the scarcity and high price of fuel. It is owing to this cause that even the labourer's dinner, of hot meat on a Sunday, is generally dressed at the baker's, and that his meals during the rest of the week consist almost wholly of bread purchased from the same quarter (p. 547).

. . . . . .

The diversity is not greater between the labourers in the North and South of England, with respect to the manner in which their food is prepared than with regard to the modes they adopt of supplying themselves with clothing. In the Midland and Southern counties, the labourer in general purchases a very considerable portion, if not the whole, of his clothes from the shopkeeper. In the vicinity of the metropolis, working people seldom buy new clothes; they content themselves with a cast-off coat, which may be usually purchased for about 5s., and second-hand waistcoats and breeches. Their wives seldom make up any article of dress, except making and mending clothes for the children. In the North, on the contrary, almost every article of dress worn by farmers, mechanics and labourers, is manufactured at home, shoes and hats excepted — that is, the linen thread is spun from the lint, and the yarn from the wool, and sent to the weavers and dyers, so that almost every family has its web of linen cloth annually, and often one of woollen also, which is either dyed for coats or made into flannel etc. Sometimes black and white wool are mixed, and the cloth which is made from them receives no dye; it is provincially called *kelt*. There are, however, many labourers so poor that they cannot even afford to purchase the raw material necessary to spin thread or yarn at home, as it is some time before a home manufacture can be rendered fit for use. It is generally acknowledged that articles of clothing can be purchased in the shops at a much lower price than those who made them at home can afford to sell them for, but that in the wearing those manufactured by private families are very superior both in warmth and durability (pp. 554-5).

. . . . . .

In consequence of the very great price of bread-corn during the whole of 1794, the distresses of the Poor were unusually great, and the sums expended on their relief beyond all former example. If, however, we except the late period of scarcity (which was such as had not occurred for near a century before) it is believed that no period during the present reign [George III] can be adduced in which the condition of day labourers was not much more comfortable than that of the same class of people in what are often called the " good old times " of former reigns. . . . (p. 560).

3. THE MANUFACTURING SYSTEM

[Robert Owen (1771–1858) was born at Newtown, Montgomeryshire, a centre of domestic textile manufacture, and thus had first-hand knowledge of conditions under the domestic as well as under the factory system. His " Observations ", from which the following extract is taken, were part of his attempt to persuade Parliament to enact a Factory Law to prevent the exploitation of child labour in the developing textile factories. His proposals, in a greatly emasculated form, provided the basis for the elder Sir Robert Peel's Factory Act of 1819. (See Section XII.)]

From Robert Owen, " Observations on the Effect of the Manufacturing System ", 1815. (Reprinted in " A New View of Society and Other Writings ", by Robert Owen, édited by G. D. H. Cole, Everyman's Library, 1927.)

Those who were engaged in the trade, manufactures, and commerce of this country thirty or forty years ago formed but a very insignificant portion of the knowledge, wealth, influence, or population of the Empire.

Prior to that period, Britain was essentially agricultural. But, from that time to the present, the home and foreign trade have increased in a manner so rapid and extraordinary as to have raised commerce to an importance, which it never previously attained in any country possessing so much political power and influence.

(By the returns to the Population Act in 1811, it appears that in England, Scotland and Wales there are 895,998 families chiefly employed in agriculture — 1,129,049 families chiefly employed in trade and manufactures — 640,500 individuals in the army and navy — and 519,168 families not engaged in any of these employments. It follows that nearly half as many more persons are engaged in trade as in agriculture — and that of the whole population the agriculturists are about 1 to 3.)

This change has been owing chiefly to the mechanical inventions which introduced the cotton trade into this country, and to the cultivation of the cotton tree in America. The wants which this trade created for the various materials requisite to forward its multiplied operations, caused an extraordinary demand for almost all the manufactures previously established, and, of course, for human labour. The numerous fanciful and useful fabrics manufactured from cotton soon became objects of desire in Europe and America : and the consequent extension of the British foreign trade was such as to astonish and confound the most enlightened statesmen both at home and abroad.

. . . . . .

These important results, however, great as they really are, have not been obtained without accompanying evils of such a magnitude as to raise a doubt whether the latter do not preponderate over the former.

Hitherto, legislators have appeared to regard manufacturers only in one point of view, as a source of national wealth.

The other mighty consequences which proceed from extended manufactures *when left to their natural progress*, have never yet engaged the attention of any legislature. Yet the political and moral effects to which we allude, well deserve to occupy the best faculties of the greatest and the wisest statesmen.

The general diffusion of manufactures throughout a country generates a new character in its inhabitants ; and as this character is formed upon a principle quite unfavourable to individual or general happiness, it will produce the most lamentable and permanent evils, unless its tendency be counteracted by legislative interference and direction.

The manufacturing system has already so far extended its influence over the British Empire, as to effect an essential change in the general character of the mass of the people. This alteration is still in rapid progress ; and ere long, the comparatively happy simplicity of the agricultural peasant will be wholly lost amongst us. It is even now scarcely anywhere to be found without a mixture of those habits which are the offspring of trade, manufactures, and commerce.

The acquisition of wealth, and the desire which it naturally creates for a continued increase, have introduced a fondness for essentially injurious luxuries among a numerous class of individuals

9

who formerly never thought of them, and they have also generated a disposition which strongly impels its possessors to sacrifice the best feelings of human nature to this love of accumulation. To succeed in this career, the industry of the lower orders, from whose labour this wealth is now drawn, has been carried by new competitors striving against those of longer standing, to a point of real oppression, reducing them by successive changes, as the spirit of competition increased and the ease of acquiring wealth diminished, to a state more wretched than can be imagined by those who have not attentively observed the changes as they have gradually occurred. In consequence, they are at present in a situation infinitely more degraded and miserable than they were before the introduction of these manufactories, upon the success of which their bare subsistence now depends.

The inhabitants of every country are trained and formed by its great leading existing circumstances, and the character of the lowest orders in Britain is now formed chiefly by circumstances arising from trade, manufactures, and commerce; and the governing principle of trade, manufactures, and commerce is immediate pecuniary gain, to which on the great scale every other is made to give way. All are sedulously trained to buy cheap and to sell dear; and to succeed in this art, the parties must be taught to acquire strong powers of deception; and thus a spirit is generated through every class of traders, destructive of that open, honest sincerity, without which man cannot make others happy, nor enjoy happiness himself.

Strictly speaking, however, this defect of character ought not to be attributed to the individuals possessing it, but to the overwhelming effect of the system under which they have been trained.

But the effects of this principle of gain, unrestrained, are still more lamentable on the working classes, those who are employed in the operative parts of the manufactures; for most of these branches are more or less unfavourable to the health and morals of adults. Yet parents do not hesitate to sacrifice the well-being of their children by putting them to occupations by which the constitution of their minds and bodies is rendered greatly inferior to what it might and ought to be under a system of common foresight and humanity.

Not more than thirty years since, the poorest parents thought the age of fourteen sufficiently early for their children to commence regular labour: and they judged well; for by that period of their lives they had acquired by play and exercise in the open air, the foundation of a sound robust constitution; and if they were not all initiated in book learning, they had been taught the far more useful knowledge of domestic life, which could not but be familiar to them at the age of fourteen, and which, as they grew up and became heads of families, was of more value to them (as it taught them economy in the expenditure of their earnings) than one half of their wages under the present circumstances.

It should be remembered also that twelve hours per day, including the time for regular rest and meals, were then thought sufficient to extract all the working strength of the most robust adult; when it may be remarked local holidays were much more frequent than at present in most parts of the kingdom.

At this period, too, they were generally trained by the example of some landed proprietor, and in such habits as created a mutual interest between the parties, by which means even the lowest peasant was generally considered as belonging to, and forming somewhat of a member of, a respectable family. Under these circumstances the lower orders experienced not only a considerable degree of comfort, but they had also frequent opportunities of enjoying healthy rational sports and amusements; and in consequence they became strongly attached to those on whom they depended; their services were willingly performed; and mutual good offices bound the parties by the strongest ties of human nature to consider each other as friends in somewhat different situations; the servant indeed often enjoying more solid comfort and ease than his master.

Contrast this state of matters with that of the lower orders of the present day — with human nature trained as it now is, under the new manufacturing system.

In the manufacturing districts it is common for parents to send their children of both sexes at seven or eight years of age, in winter as well as summer, at six o'clock in the morning, sometimes of course in the dark, and occasionally amidst frost and snow, to enter the manufactories, which are often heated to a high temperature, and contain an atmosphere far from being the most favourable to human life, and in which all those employed in them very frequently continue until twelve o'clock at noon, when an hour is allowed for dinner, after which they return to remain, in a majority of cases, till eight o'clock at night.

The children now find they must labour incessantly for their bare subsistence: they have not been used to innocent, healthy and rational amusements; they are not permitted the requisite time, if they had been previously accustomed to enjoy them. They know not what relaxation means, except by the actual cessation from labour. They are surrounded by others similarly circumstanced with themselves ; and thus passing on from childhood to youth, they become gradually initiated, the young men in particular, but often the young females also, in the seductive pleasures of the pot-house and inebriation : for which their daily hard labour, want of better habits, and the general vacuity of their minds, tend to prepare them.

Such a system of training cannot be expected to produce any other than a population weak in bodily and mental faculties, and with habits generally destructive of their own comforts, of the well-being of those around them, and strongly calculated to subdue all the social affections. Man so circumstanced sees all around him hurrying forward, at a mail-coach speed, to acquire individual wealth, regardless of him, his comforts, his wants, or even his sufferings, except by way of a *degrading parish charity*, fitted only to steel the heart of man against his fellows, or to form the tyrant and the slave. To-day he labours for one master, to-morrow for a second, then for a third, and a fourth, until all ties between employers and employed are frittered down to the consideration of what immediate gain each can derive from the other.

The employer regards the employed as mere instruments of gain, while these acquire a gross ferocity of character, which, if legislative measures shall not be judiciously devised to prevent its increase, and ameliorate the condition of this class, will sooner or later plunge the country into a formidable and perhaps inextricable state of danger.

4. THE WOOLLEN INDUSTRY

[This description of the woollen trade gives a good picture of the conditions of work under which Trade Unionism did and did not develop. Under the ' Domestic System ' in the form which it took in Yorkshire there was little tendency towards combination ; for many of the weavers worked for themselves and there were no large-scale employers against whom the main body of weavers felt it necessary to combine until the conditions had substantially changed with the beginnings of the Factory System. Accordingly, except in special skilled trades such as wool-combing, there was in Yorkshire not much combination until after 1800 ; but by 1802 we find the Yorkshire weavers united with those of Western England to prosecute an employer for disregarding the old statutes regulating conditions of labour — with the effect, however, not of securing their enforcement, but of bringing about their prompt repeal.

In Western England, on the other hand, the weavers under the Domestic System were in fact wage-earners working for large-scale merchant clothiers, with a long tradition of combination. As early as 1700 the House of Commons received a petition from the weavers of Crediton who complained that too many apprentices were being taken on. Petitions from other towns in the West followed ; but as Parliament gave no satisfaction the combination grew rapidly, and throughout the Western Counties combination reappeared on many occasions during the eighteenth century. Thereafter it died out gradually, as the woollen industry migrated more and more rapidly to the West Riding of Yorkshire, where a new type of Trade Unionism based on the factory system began to develop. The woollen industry, however, owing to technical difficulties, was relatively slow to adopt factory methods of production.]

From a Report on the State of the Woollen Manufacture of England (1806), p. 8.

. . . It may be expedient for Your Committee to state that there are three different modes of carrying on the Woollen Manufacture ; that of the Master Clothier of the West of England, the Factory, and, the Domestic system.

In all the Western Counties as well as in the North, there are Factories, but the Master Clothier of the West of England, buys his Wool from the Importer, if it be foreign, or in the Fleece, or of the Woolstapler, if it be of Domestic growth ; after which, in all the different processes through which it passes, he is under the necessity of employing as many distinct classes of persons ; sometimes working in their own homes, sometimes in those of the Master Clothier, but none of them going out of their proper line. Each class of Workmen, however, acquires great skill in performing its particular operation, and hence may have arisen the acknowledged excellence, and, till of late, superiority, of the Cloths of the West of England. It is however a remarkable fact, of which Your Committee has been assured by one of its own members, that previously to the introduction of Machinery, it was very common, and it is said sometimes to happen at this day, for the North Countryman to come into the West of England, and, in the Clothing Districts of that part of the Kingdom, to purchase his wool ; which he carries home ; where, having worked it up into Cloth, he brings it back again, and sells it in its native District. This is supposed to arise from the Northern Clothier being at liberty to work himself, and employ his family and others, in any way which his interest or convenience may suggest.

In the Factory system, the Master Manufacturers, who sometimes possess a very great capital, employ in one or more Buildings or Factories, under their own or their Superintendent's inspection, a number of Workmen more or fewer according to the extent of their Trade. This system, it is obvious, admits in practice of local variations. But both in the system of the West of England Clothier, and in the Factory system, the work, generally speaking, is done by persons who have no property in the goods they manufacture, for in this consists the essential distinction between the two former systems, and the Domestic.

In the last mentioned, or Domestic system, which is that of Yorkshire, the manufacture is conducted by a multitude of Master Manufacturers, generally possessing a very small, and scarcely ever any great extent of Capital. They buy the Wool of the Dealer; and, in their own houses, assisted by their wives and children, and from two or three to six or seven Journeymen, they dye it (when dyeing in necessary) and through all the different stages work it up into undressed Cloth.

Various processes however, the chief of which were formerly done by hand, under the Manufacturer's own roof, are now performed by Machinery, in public Mills, as they are called, which work for hire. There are several such Mills near every manufacturing village, so that the Manufacturer, with little inconvenience or loss of time, carries thither his goods, and fetches them back again when the process is completed. When it has attained to the state of undressed cloth, he carries it on the market-day to a public Hall or Market, where the Merchants repair to purchase.

5. THE COAL MINERS, 1765

[The miners have been, in modern times, the most easily organised class of workers. But we hear little of combinations in the mining industry during the eighteenth century, mainly because it was not until the end of the century that its importance became considerable except on the North-East Coast. In other coal-mining areas the development of a class of skilled miners came only towards the end of the century, when the growth of towns caused a larger demand for coal, and steam-engines began to be made in considerable numbers. Till then, coal-mining many areas was regarded as an unskilled employment, largely under the control of firms mainly engaged in the manufacture of iron. In some instances also — in the lead and tin mines of Derbyshire and Cornwall particularly — the miners were not properly wage-earners, but rented part of the seam and gambled on its richness. And in Cumberland the miners (according to John Wesley's description) seem to have lived a semi-barbarous life, lacking any of the qualities necessary for organisation. There are, however, traditions of early actions — a petition against the lack of ventilation signed by 2000 Northumberland and Durham miners in 1662, a strike in the same area for an advance of wages in 1740, and sporadic riots and strikes in South Wales. The 1765 movement, described in the document given below, is the earliest clear record of miners' organisation. Even this did not lead to any stable combination : and we hear little of the Northern miners until the great binding strike of 1810, when, after a seven-week struggle had been crushed. the owners agreed to receive delegates from each colliery for collective bargaining. In the same year (1810) the South Wales miners had a brave strike, which was doomed to failure — they had little organisation and no strike fund, and could buy nothing from the local shops, as these all belonged to the Company. Readers of Zola's " Germinal " will realise how, in a primitive mining community, the wide possessions and powers of the owner make organisation supremely difficult.]

From the *Annual Register* (1765), p. 130.

About this time last year, a gentleman or two upon a river in the neighbourhood of Newcastle, being in great want of pitmen, endeavoured to obtain these useful men by tempting them with extraordinary binding money for one year, as far as two, three and even four guineas, instead of one shilling, which was heretofore all they used to get. This encouragement made the men in the other collieries work with great reluctance all the year ; and, as the time was approaching when the above-mentioned gentlemen would be again in want, it was natural for the several coal-owners on the Tyne and Weare to consider of some method to prevent such proceedings for the future. They, therefore had a meeting, at which it was agreed, that no coal-owner should hire another's men, unless they produced a certificate of leave from their last master ; and, as no coal-owner would grant such a certificate, it was by the pitmen called a binding during the will of the master : and was, consequently, a species of slavery not to be endured in a free country.

This notion spreading like wild fire, on or about the 14th of August last, all the pitmen on the two rivers left off work, and have continued so ever since, notwithstanding the coal-owners have repeatedly declared they had no intentions of hindering them from hiring with whom they pleased, and earnestly exhorted them to return to their work till expiration of their bonds, at which time they should have a regular discharge in writing, if required. But the pitmen made sensible of their importance, in order to be revenged of their employers, rose in their demands, as often as any new proposal was made to them; so though they were in general earning from 12 to 14s. a week, they in one colliery insisted upon an advance of wages equal to 75 per cent. But the grand article they literally insisted on, was, that all their bonds be given up though some of them have till Christmas to go; which demand the coal-owners determined not to agree to; for they have always avoided binding too many at one time, lest it should be in their power to distress the trade, by refusing to work till their demands were satisfied.

Other accounts represent this affair in a different light. But all seem to agree in charging the coal-owners, in general, with very harsh usage towards the pitmen, whom, it seems, they have made a custom to bind but 11 month and 15 days, to prevent their obtaining a settlement, though this year they attempted to keep them at work for 14 month.

But whatever the causes of this disagreement might have been, the consequence of it had like to have proved fatal to that trade, so useful to the kingdom. The pitmen on the Tyne and the Weare burnt and otherwise destroyed the utensils of many coal-pits, set fire to the coals both above and below ground, and broke up the coal-ways, notwithstanding the vigilance of the soldiers placed there to prevent them; in consequence of which the waggons were stopt, the keels laid by, upwards of six hundred ships kept idle at Newcastle and Sunderland, and 100,000 men out of bread in Newcastle, Sunderland, and London, from near the middle of August last to the end of this month; when the difference between the pitmen and their employers was happily compromised, and coals fell in the port of London to 32s. per chaldron.

6. THE SEAMEN

[The following extract is taken, by permission, from Professor Aspinall's volume of selections from the Home Office Papers. This volume contains a number of other passages dealing with the combinations among the seamen, especially on the North-East Coast. These movements largely affected the coal trade between the Tyne and Wear and London. The seamen showed on more than one occasion a high capacity for combined action, though, to the best of our belief, no direct records of their combinations have survived.]

From A. Aspinall, " The Early English Trade Unions " (1949), pp. 11-13.

Thomas Powditch to William Pitt

NORTH SHIELDS, 3 *November*, 1792.

The situation of this unfortunate place begins to be so extremely alarming that I cannot refrain from making you acquainted with it. A long continuance of easterly wind had detained the ships in this port until a large fleet (about 400 sail) had accumulated. On the appearance of a change of wind from the east to the west (which is a fair wind for ships to proceed to sea) the seamen discovered a disposition to riot, and assembled in great numbers in different parts of the towns of North and South Shields, and in boats upon the river Tyne, insisting that the masters of all ships should pay four guineas wages for the voyage, although most of the people of the loaded ships had signed their articles for the usual wages (viz. 50s. for the voyage). This unreasonable demand the owners were unwilling to comply with.

The crews of each ship, when separately applied to, acknowledged themselves satisfied with the wages they had agreed for, and in excuse for leaving the ships and becoming part of the mob, said they were obliged to do so or they would be ill treated by the rest of the seamen. They proceed[ed] in boats from ship to ship and compelled the reluctant or willing seamen and officers of every ship in the harbour to leave their ships and join the mob. By this means a great number of seamen were collected; they then divided themselves into parties (forming two or three watches) under chiefs, and took possession of the port by stationing a body of seamen under one of these chiefs at the entrance of the harbour on each side of the river where it is very narrow, to prevent the ships from proceeding to sea in the nights. The hazardous situation in which some ships lay at that time (the harbour being much crowded) was the reason why their owners complied with the demands of the rioters. Their crews were then permitted to come on board their ships and take care of them, but the rioters obliged them to distinguish their ships by wearing at the masthead a jack. On the owners who had not complied, this badge of distinction had a wonderful effect by pointing out both the persons and the property of the persons who were, as they pleased to call them, the seaman's enemy. A fair wind came, and the ships distinguished by the jack at the masthead proceeded to sea amidst great acclamations and huzzas of the mob. The fear from the mob, the temptation of a fair wind, the great demand for coals at London, and no support in view were the causes, and are still the causes why the owners of the load ships complied and still comply with their unreasonable demands. A meeting of shipowners was called at the Trinity House, Newcastle, on the 14th of October, present, Mr. Brandling, Mr. Burdon, M.P., the Mayor of Newcastle, and the Town Clerk, when the trembling shipowners were prevailed upon to issue the enclosed handbill,[1] which had no other effect than to cause them to assume a more daring appearance. It then appeared (but how it happened I cannot tell) that Captain Leakey of his Majesty's ship *Racehorse* had had some talk with the mob and became a kind of mediator between them and the shipowners. Captain Leakey's interference, in my opinion, was very improper, for it surely had a great effect in confirming an opinion which they have, that the Government is afraid of provoking the lower class of people; yet I am persuaded Captain Leakey was actuated by the best of motives.

A meeting of a committee of shipowners was then held at the Trinity House (for they still continued to occupy the entrance of the harbour, permitting no ships to sail in the night and only those during the day which had complied with their demands). At this meeting nothing was determined but to call a general meeting of shipowners (for the seamen now on the arrival of every ship into the port were taken out by the rioters unless the owner or master would sign their agreement and pay their crews four guineas for the next voyage) which was held at Trinity House on Wednesday the 31st of October. (This was the first meeting I had attended, for at that time I had no ship in the harbour, now I have one.) At this meeting no magistrate, no person of authority attended, only shipowners. Whether that circumstance increased their apprehensions I cannot tell, but the experience of near thirty years had convinced them that no reliance could be placed on the magistrates of the river Tyne for the protection of their property, or on the County's magistrates for the protection of either persons or property. Deeply impressed with this truth, cast down and dejected by the insults they were daily suffering from an unrestrained mob, trembling for their little property, from which they drew the support of their families, it was

[1] Missing from Home Office Papers.

determined by a small majority once again to meet and to offer them such terms as it was impossible for the trade to bear, but such as their present unprotected state induced them to submit to if it would but preserve the peace of the port. This measure was not unresisted, as you will see by my remarks at the meeting which were warmly supported by a few spirited men, but the majority was against us.

The place appointed for the meeting to make this humiliating offer was on board his Majesty's ship *Racehorse*.

They were met on Thursday last at Shields by Captain Leakey, some shipowners and the Town Clerk of Newcastle, but their offers were rejected, and the concessions of the shipowners had no other effect on these men (now intoxicated with a power too long enjoyed) but to increase their insolence, and they still persevere in their measures, nay to some who have wished to lay their ships by, they have threatened to burn them if they do not send them to sea.

As to myself, being a person of more spirit than prudence, makes me in some degree obnoxious to the mob, and no favourite with magistrates. And although some fears for myself, family and property may cause me sincerely to wish for peace being re-established, I should not have troubled you on that account; but when I look round and see this country covered with thousands of pitmen, keelmen, waggonmen and other labouring men, hardy fellows strongly impressed with the new doctrine of equality, and at present composed of such combustible matter that the least spark will set them in a blaze, I cannot help thinking the supineness of the magistrates very reprehensible. It is possible, however, that they may think the force in this country not sufficient to authorise threatening measures, and may wish them to be amused until they can be safely resisted. If it be so, they are possessed of more wisdom than I apprehended.

P.S. Shocking to relate, the mob at this moment are driving some seamen or officers that have discovered a reluctance to comply with their mode of proceedings naked through the town before them.

7. THE SKILLED ARTISANS

[On the whole, the workers in the traditional urban skilled crafts — printers, tailors, shoemakers, braziers, pewterers, cabinetmakers, saddlers, etc. — fared better than other workers during the troublous times of the Industrial Revolution. In most cases they were not affected till later by the competition of power-driven machinery; and the increase in the numbers of the wealthy and middle classes swelled the demand for their services and put them in a strong bargaining position, of which their Trade Clubs, usually not much affected in practice by the laws against combination, were able to take advantage. Francis Place (1771–1854) had been a working breeches-maker and a Trade Unionist before he became an employer. He had a wide knowledge of the London crafts, but was sometimes apt to assume too readily that what he knew to be true of London held good for other towns.]

From the Place MSS., 27,834 f. 108 (1834).

WARTIME STRIKES IN THE SKILLED TRADES

I have now before me tables of weekly wages of journeyman tradesmen in London, who in their different trades may amount to 100,000 men, all of whom had separate trade clubs for many years, and spite of the Combination Laws, did from time to time raise their wages by means of strikes.

In these trades the ordinary wages in the year 1777 were from eighteen shillings to twenty two shillings a week — From 1777 to 1794 there were few strikes and very little advance in wages. During this the price of food rose somewhat, but the price of most other necessaries fell and wages were nearly stationary — Soon after the commencement of the war against the French Republic prices rose enormously — and in one of these trades, a very numerous trade [breeches-making], a strike took place in 1795 when the weekly wages were raised from twenty two shillings to twenty five shillings. In 1802 another strike raised the wages to thirty shillings. In 1810 another strike raised the wages to thirty three shillings, and in 1813 another strike raised the wages to thirty six shillings at which they have remained ever since. The journeymen in the other trades by their strikes raised their wages in a similar portion, though not precisely at the same periods.

8. FOOD RIOTS

[These extracts from the *Annual Register* of 1766 are typical of what happened again and again during the eighteenth century at times of food scarcity due to bad harvests or, sometimes, faulty distribution of supplies. In 1766 the conditions were especially bad, and the troubles more wide-spread than in any other year. It was not uncommon in such cases for the ' rioters ' to impound supplies from local shops and warehouses and sell them at what they regarded as a fair price.]

(a) From the *Annual Register*, 1766, Chronicle, pp. 124-5.

We hear from Newbury, that on Thursday last a great number of poor people assembled in the market-place during the time of the market, on account of the rise of wheat, when they ripped open the sacks, and scattered all the corn about, took butter, meat, cheese, and bacon, out of the shops, and threw it into the streets; and so intimidated the bakers, that they immediately sell their bread 2d. in the peck loaf, and promised next week to lower it still more. From Newbury they proceeded to Shaw-mill, there they threw the flour into the river, broke the windows of the house, and did other considerable damage there, as well as at several other mills, to the amount of near 1000l.

Letters from Devonshire inform, that besides the riots which happened at Exeter, on account of the present exorbitant price of provisions, there have been like disturbances in different parts of the same county; particularly at Uffeolm and Lemnion, where the corn-mills have been entirely destroyed by the rioters, who afterwards took upon them to seize what wheat they could meet with in the granaries of the farmers, which they carried immediately to market, and sold openly from four to five shillings per bushel, and afterwards returned to the several owners, and carried them the money which they had thus raised from the sale of their grain, together with the sacks.

(b) From the *Annual Register*, 1766, Chronicle, pp. 137-40.

There having been many riots, and much mischief done, in different parts of England, in consequence of the rising of the poor; who have been driven to desperation and madness, by the exorbitant prices of all manner of provisions; we shall, without descending to minute particulars, or a strict regard as to the order of time, in which they happened, give a short abstract of those disturbances.

At Bath, the people did a great deal of mischief in the markets before they dispersed.

They were very outrageous at Berwick upon Tweed, on account of the vast quantities of corn that had been bought up for exportation.

At Malmesbury they seized all the corn; sold it at 5s. a bushel, and gave the money to the right owners.

At Hampton, in Gloucestershire, they were opposed, some lives were lost and houses pulled down, and the military called in to quell them.

At Setbury, they seized the cheese and bacon in the warehouses, and sold out the former at 3d. and the latter at 4d. a pound.

At Bradley, near Trowbridge, they destroyed a mill, and divided the corn found in it among them.

At Leicester, and the neighbourhood, they seized three waggon-loads of cheese, and divided them among them.

At Lechdale, they seized a waggon-load of cheese, designed for London, and carried it all off; and not content with that, broke open the warehouses of the owners, and robbed them of five or six tons more.

At Oxford, the mob went to the adjacent mills, and brought off all the flour they found, and in the market place divided it.

At Exeter the mob rose, and broke open a cheese warehouse, and sold the cheese much under value; but was intimidated from proceeding to extremities, by the military; the same at Lyme, in Dorsetshire.

In the neighbourhood of Stroud, in Gloucestershire, a huckster's shop was levelled to the ground, after the occupier had killed one of the mob.

The proprietors of seven mills at Newbury, having declared that they would grind for the poor gratis, pacified the rioters.

At Redruth and St. Austle, the tinners have risen, and compelled the farmers and butchers to lower their prices.

At Kidderminster, the populace obliged the farmers to sell their wheat at 5s. a bushel.

At Stourbridge, they lowered the price of butter, meat, and wheat.

At Bewdley, they did the same.

At Gloucester, the most considerable farmers from the hills voluntarily agreed to supply the market with wheat at 5s. a bushel, and have already sold considerable quantities at that price.

At Salisbury, the risings were very serious, and much damage was expected, but by the prudent management of the magistrates, and the humanity of the farmers, who lowered the price of their wheat on the first disturbance, the danger was happily averted. Some of the ringleaders, however, were apprehended and committed to prison.

At Beckington, near Bath, a miller and his son got fire-arms to oppose the mob, and actually fired and killed a man and a boy, and desperately wounded others, which so exasperated the rest, that they set fire to the mills, and burnt them to the ground.

At Wincanton, in Dorsetshire, the rioters having been joined by the colliers did great mischief.

At Broomsgrove, in Worcestershire, the mob rose, and obliged the farmers to sell their wheat at 5s. a bushel, and the butchers their meat at two-pence-halfpenny a pound.

At Wolverhampton the same.

At Hales Owen they rose, and forced the people to sell cheese at two-pence-halfpenny, and flour for 5s. They destroyed two dressing-mills before they were dispersed.

At Coventry they rose, and were joined by the colliers from the neighbouring pits; and began by plundering the warehouses of cheese, and selling the same at low prices; and concluded by taking whatever provisions they met with by main force.

In the neighbourhood of Salisbury they rose, and having found in Bradley mill, as they said, flour, corn, ground chalk, lime, and horse-beans, they took an aversion to all bolting-mills, and accordingly destroyed seven or eight.

At Norwich a general insurrection began, when the proclamation was read in the market-place, where provisions of all sorts were scattered about by the rioters in heaps; the new mill, a spacious building, which supplies the city with water, was attacked and pulled down; the flour, to the number of 150 sacks, thrown, sack after sack, into the river; and the proprietor's books of account, furniture, plate, and money, carried off or destroyed; the bakers' shops plundered and shattered; a large malt-house set fire to, and burnt; houses and warehouses pulled down; and the whole city thrown into the greatest consternation. During this scene of confusion, the magistrates issued out summonses to the housekeepers in their respective districts, to assemble with staves to oppose the rioters; the conflict was long and bloody, but, in the end, the rioters were overpowered, thirty of the ringleaders secured and committed to prison, who, it is said, will soon be tried by a special commission.

At Wallingford they rose and regulated the price of bread, cheese, butter, and bacon.

At Thame they did the same.

At Henley upon Thames they rose, but the riot-act being read to them, they dispersed.

At Wycombe, and other places in Buckinghamshire, they rose, but were soon dispersed.

At Leicester they assembled, seized some waggon loads of cheese, and afterwards broke the windows of the county-gaol, with a view to rescue the rioters confined in it.

At Great-Colton in Warwickshire they rose, traversed the country, and did considerable damage, till being met by the military, they were encountered and dispersed, eight of them having been shot dead before they reached Kidderminster.

At Evesham in Worcestershire the mob rose, and seized some butter, and sold it at 6d. a pound. They intended to have pulled down the corn-mills there, but their ringleaders were prevailed upon to desist.

At Derby the mob encountered a party of light-horse, terribly pelted them with stones, and wounded the commanding officer: they plundered a warehouse of cheese, but thirty-four of them were apprehended, and carried pinioned to gaol. They afterwards assembled and attacked a boat on the Darwent, from which they took cheese to the value of 300l. They pay no regard to the civil magistrates, and are only in fear of the military.

At Dunnington the mob rose, and plundered a warehouse of cheese, which was defended by eighteen men with fire-arms: they were afterwards pursued by the owner, and a party of his friends, but to no purpose: the mob defended themselves by stones, drove back their pursuers, and then became pursuers in their turn. They attacked a boat upon the Darwent, from whence they took cheese to a considerable amount. The owner offered them 50l. to save his cheese, and to erect a pair of scales, and sell the whole cargo at twopence a pound; but the ringleaders cried out, *D — n his charity, we'll have the cheese for nought*.

At Aylesbury some little disturbances have happened, and a quantity of butter seized by the mob in the market there; but, by the spirit of the magistrates of the town, and the justices of the county at their quarter-sessions, the ringleaders were seized, tried, and sentenced to imprisonment, by which all further mischief was prevented.

At Pagenwell, near Stroud in Gloucestershire, a shop-keeper shot one of the mob dead, who was breaking into his house in the night, on which they set the house on fire, and burnt it to the ground.

A riotous gang of bargemen rose at Marlow in Buckinghamshire, and extorted money and provisions from the gentlemen and farmers in that neighbourhood; and having got themselves intoxicated with liquor, proceeded to Maidenhead, where, having committed some outrages, they were opposed, overpowered, and the ringleaders seized, and sent to Reading gaol.

A riotous mob assembled at Birmingham on the fair day there, and sold bread and cheese at their own prices; but being overpowered likewise by the civil magistrate's authority, their ringleaders were sent to gaol. At the same time an agreement was made with the bakers to make a sufficient quantity of household-bread, and to sell it at a penny a pound, by which means the people were pacified.

At Nottingham fair the mob seized upon all the cheese the factors had purchased, and distributed the same among them, leaving the farmers' cheese unmolested. The military were called to the aid of the civil magistracy, but, luckily, one man only was killed, and that happened to be a farmer, a bystander.

9. THE SPEENHAMLAND SCALE

[The 'Speenhamland System' of subsidising inadequate wages out of the poor rates was started by the Berkshire magistrates, meeting at Speenhamland, by Newbury, in April 1795. It was an attempt to meet the situation brought about by high prices without raising wages to meet what was expected to be a temporary emergency. But the war, and the high prices, lasted another twenty years; and the Speenhamland system, made more oppressive and more a barrier to wage-increases after 1815, lasted on till 1834.]

From J. L. and B. Hammond, " The Village Labourer, 1760–1832 " (1911), pp. 161-3.

. . . ' At the General Quarter Sessions of the Peace for this county held at Newbury, on Tuesday, the 14th instant, the Court, having taken into consideration the great Inequality of Labourers' Wages, and the insufficiency of the same for the necessary support of an industrious man and his family; and it being the opinion of the Gentlemen assembled on the Grand Jury, that many parishes have not advanced their labourers' weekly pay in proportion to the high price of corn and provisions, do (in pursuance of the Acts of Parliament, enabling and requiring them so to do, either at the Easter Sessions, yearly, or within six weeks next after) earnestly request the attendance of the Sheriff, and all the Magistrates of this County, at a Meeting intended to be held at the Pelican Inn in Speenhamland, on Wednesday, the sixth day of May next, at ten o'clock in the forenoon, for the purpose of consulting together with such discreet persons as they shall think meet, and they will then, having respect to the plenty and scarcity of the time, and other circumstances (if approved of) proceed to limit, direct, and appoint the wages of day labourers.' [1]

. . . Resolved unanimously ' that the present state of the poor does require further assistance than has been generally given to them.'

. . . The text of the second resolution runs thus : ' Resolved, that it is not expedient for the Magistrates to grant that assistance by regulating the wages of Day Labourers according to the directions of the Statutes of the 5th Elizabeth and 1st James : But the Magistrates very earnestly recommend to the Farmers and others throughout the county to increase the Pay of their Labourers in proportion to the present Price of Provisions; and agreeable thereto the Magistrates now present have unanimously Resolved, That they will in their several divisions, make the following calculations and allowances for the relief of all poor and industrious men and their families, who, to the satisfaction of the Justices of their parish, shall endeavour (as far as they can), for their own support and maintenance, that is to say, when the gallon loaf of second flour, weighing 8 lbs. 11 oz. shall cost one shilling, then every poor and industrious man shall have for his own support 3s. weekly, either produced by his own or his family's labour or an allowance from the poor rates, and for the support of his wife and every other of his family 1s. 6d. When the gallon loaf shall cost 1s. 4d., then every poor and industrious man shall have 4s. weekly for his own, and 1s. 10d. for the support of every other of his family.

' And so in proportion as the price of bread rises or falls (that is to say), 3d. to the man and 1d. to every other of the family, on every penny which the loaf rises above a shilling.' [2]

[1] *Reading Mercury*, April 20, 1795.   [2] *Ibid*. May 11, 1795.

II
POLITICAL MOVEMENTS TO 1789

INTRODUCTION

IF we except such affairs as food-riots and occasional mob activities in London and elsewhere, it was in the Wilkes movement (1763–1771) that the working classes had their earliest experience of political activity. This ' tribune of the people ' led what he called the ' middling and inferior classes ' in the first organised demand for the reform of Parliament. His skirmishes with the autocratic rule of the King and his Tory ministers were followed up by an attack on the entire system of corruption and privilege, which made both the election of members to Parliament and their attitude inside the House of Commons a mere parody of representation of the people. Popular enthusiasm flared vigorously from 1769 to 1771, and left behind it valuable lessons in political organisation. The struggle of the American Colonists, especially the Declaration of American Independence (1776), brought new life to the agitation for civil and religious liberty in Great Britain ; and speedily many members of the middle classes, who had been left untouched by a bare democratic appeal, were roused by the increasing burdens of taxation and by depression of trade to blame the expense of the war on the corrupt oligarchy, whose unimaginative handling of the situation had caused the conflict which they were now disastrously mismanaging. A well-organised campaign outside parliament was helped by sympathisers inside ; and when the Whigs came to power in 1782 Burke's Civil Establishment Bill considerably weakened the King's power to buy seats for his followers and to purchase their continued loyalty. The concession of a substantial instalment of ' economical reform ', without electoral reform, satisfied a large part of the Reformers' following, especially among the county freeholders. But within a few years the celebration of the centenary of the ' Glorious Revolution ' of 1688 partly revived the Radical movement.

See " Short History ", Part I, chapter 3.
" Common People ", chapters 7, 8, and 12.

1. WILKES AND LIBERTY

[John Wilkes (1727–1797) became a popular hero first on account of his attacks on the King and the Tories in his satirical paper, *The North Briton* (1763). Out of his arrest for ' seditious libel ' on account of an article in the famous ' Number 45 ' arose the struggle over the legality of ' general warrants ', in which he was the central figure. Expelled by the House of Commons and declared ineligible for election, he was repeatedly re-elected by the County of Middlesex, but was prevented from taking his seat, the Commons at one point declaring his defeated opponent, Colonel Luttrell, to have been duly returned. Out of these contests arose the Society of the Supporters of the Bill of Rights — the first radical political society in modern England. It was founded in 1769 by John Horne Tooke and other supporters of Wilkes, and put forward the first programme of Radical Reform. The Society was split in 1771 by a quarrel between Wilkes and Tooke, and soon disappeared ; but Wilkes, having been allowed to take his seat in Parliament in 1774, in 1776 introduced a Reform Bill providing for a drastic redistribution of parliamentary seats. The popular cry, ' Wilkes and Liberty ', was taken up all over the country during the years of his struggle with the King and the Parliament. During this period the Society of the Supporters of the Bill of Rights drew up the following instructions to be used as a test of the political merits of candidates for Parliament.]

Society of the Supporters of the Bill of Rights.

A TEST FOR PARLIAMENTARY CANDIDATES, 1771

1. You shall consent to no supplies, without a previous redress of grievances.

2. You shall promote a law, subjecting each candidate to an oath against having used bribery, or any other illegal means of compassing his election.

3. You shall promote, to the utmost of your power, a full and equal representation of the people in parliament.

4. You shall endeavour to restore annual parliaments.

5. You shall promote a pension and place bill, enacting, that any member who receives a place, pension, contract, lottery-ticket, or any other emolument whatsoever from the Crown, or enjoys profit from any such place, pension, etc., shall not only vacate his seat, but be absolutely ineligible during his continuance under such undue influence.

6. You shall impeach the ministers who advised the violating

the right of the freeholders in the Middlesex election, and the military murders in St. George's Fields.[1]

7. You shall make strict enquiry into the conduct of judges, touching juries.

8. You shall make strict enquiry into the application of the public money.

9. You shall use your utmost endeavours to have the resolution of the house of commons expunged, by which the magistrates of the city of London were arbitrarily imprisoned, for strictly adhering to their charter and their oaths; and also that resolution, by which a judicial record was erased to stop the course of justice.[2]

10. You shall attend to the grievances of our fellow subjects in Ireland, and record the complaints they may bring to the throne.

11. You shall endeavour to restore to America the essential right of taxation, by representatives of their own free election: repealing the acts passed in violation of that right since the year 1763 : and the universal excise so notoriously incompatible with every principle of British liberty, which has been lately substituted in the colonies, for the laws of customs.

2. THE AMERICAN WAR

[The Revolt of the American Colonists won widespread sympathy in England, even in the country districts where political affairs had been little thought of previously. The demand for political reform, which since 1771 had been expressed almost exclusively in Parliament, gained popular support again after the Declaration of American Independence (1776). And the Radicals began to frame a more definite creed for the movement. John Cartwright published in his " Take Your Choice ! " (1776) the essence of the Radical Programme for the next seventy years — Universal Suffrage, Annual Parliaments, Vote by Ballot, Payment of Members and Equal Electoral Districts. In the same year Dr. Price in his " Discourse on Civil Liberty ", written in welcome of the American Revolution, gave a lead to the Radical Dissenters in their struggle against the political autocracy, which denied them religious liberty. And the

[1] When Wilkes was in prison, a crowd which had assembled in the neighbouring ' St George's Fields ' was shot down by soldiers on guard (1768) : they killed six of the crowd and then followed one of their suspects, but missed their quarry and murdered an entirely innocent man by mistake.

[2] This paragraph refers to incidents in the fight over the publication of Parliamentary debates. See R. W. Postgate, " That Devil Wilkes ", p. 199.

chief manifesto of the Americans to the English public was the " Common Sense " of Tom Paine — who was later to be the inspiration of the British Radical movement. These works may have touched only the small, though growing, band of Reformers, but they laid the foundation of their future strength.]

From W. Cobbett, " The Life and Adventures of Peter Porcupine ", 1796.

As to politics, we were like the rest of the country people in England; that is to say, we neither knew nor thought any thing about the matter. The shouts of victory, or the murmurs at a defeat, would now-and-then break in upon our tranquillity for a moment; but I do not remember ever having seen a newspaper in the house; and, most certainly, that privation did not render us less industrious, happy or free.

After, however, the American war had continued for some time, and the cause and nature of it began to be understood, or rather misunderstood, by the lower classes of the people in England, we became a little better acquainted with subjects of this kind. . . .

My father used to take one of us with him every year, to the great hop-fair at Wey-Hill. . . . It happened to be my turn to go thither, the very year that Long-Island was taken by the British. A great company of hop merchants and farmers were just sitting down to supper as the post arrived, bringing in the Extraordinary Gazette, which announced the victory. A hop-factor from London took the paper, placed his chair upon the table, and began to read with an audible voice. He was opposed, a dispute ensued, and my father retired, taking me by the hand, to another apartment, where we supped with about a dozen others of the same sentiments. Here Washington's health, and success to the Americans, were repeatedly toasted, and this was the first time, as far as I can recollect, that I ever heard the General's name mentioned.

3. " TAKE YOUR CHOICE ! "

[Major John Cartwright (1740–1824) came to be regarded as the ' Father of the Reform Movement ', active almost till his death; in a variety of organisations — particularly the Society for Constitutional Information and the Hampden Clubs — he preached incessantly the views he expressed in " Take your Choice ! " (1776).]

(*a*) Extracts from John Cartwright's " Take Your Choice ! ", 1776. From
" Life and Correspondence of Major Cartwright ", vol. i, pp. 89-94.

" The all-wise Creator hath likewise made men equal, as well as
free ; they are all of one flesh, and cast in one mould. There are
given to them the same senses, feelings, and affections, to inform
and to influence ; the same passions to actuate, the same reason to
guide, the same moral principle to restrain, and the same free will
to determine all alike.

" There are, therefore, no distinctions to be made among men, as
just causes for the elevation of some above the rest, prior to mutual
agreement. How much soever any individual may be qualified for,
or deserve any elevation, he hath no right to it till it be conferred
on him by his fellows. There is, perhaps, more occasion to advert
to this distinction between desert and authority, obvious as it is,
than may be commonly imagined, as all elevation depends upon
common consent ; so it may, consequently, whenever found inconsistent with the common good, be by common consent abolished.
Hence we find that it is liberty, and not dominion, which is held by
divine right."—P. 3.

" Though a man should have neither lands, nor gold, nor herds,
nor flocks ; yet he may have parents and kindred, he may possess a
wife and an offspring to be solicitous for. He hath also by birthright
a property in the English constitution : which, if not unworthy such
a blessing, will be more dear to him than would be many acres of the
soil without it.

" These are all great stakes to have at risk ; and we must have
odd notions of justice, if we do not allow that they give him an
undoubted right to share in the choice of those trustees, into whose
keeping and protection they are to be committed."—P. 20.

" I would not hastily dissent from a received opinion, especially
one supported by great authorities ; but yet my own conceptions
of truth oblige me to believe, that personality is the sole foundation
of the right of being represented ; and that property has, in reality,
nothing to do in the case. The property of any one, be it more, or
be it less, is totally involved in the man. As belonging to him and
to his peace, it is a very fit object of the attention of his representative
in parliament, but it contributes nothing to his right of having that
representation."—P. 22.

" Whenever the first principle of any reasoning is false, we are navigating without a compass, and can have no criterion of rectitude as we go along, but must be for ever liable to error and abuse. Had we never departed from the true principle of considering every member of the community as a free man, we had done right. But when we would once form an arbitrary definition of freedom, who shall say what it ought to be ? Ought freedom rather to be annexed to forty pence, or forty shillings, or forty pounds per annum ? Or why not to four hundred or four thousand ? But indeed, so long as money is to be the measure of it, it will be impossible to know who ought or who ought not to be free. According to my apprehension, we might as well make the possession of forty shillings per annum, the proof of a man's being rational, as of his being free. There is just as much sense in the one as the other."—P. 37.

" The more I have myself contemplated the subject, and drawn comparisons between parliaments of different durations, the more confirmed have I always been in giving the preference to an annual one, provided it were fairly chosen. Indeed I never could arrive at any other satisfactory conclusion ; but here I find every satisfaction which the case requires or admits of."—P. 84.

(*b*) From " Life of Major Cartwright ", vol. i, p. 95.
Letter to Major Cartwright

" NEWINGTON GREEN, *April* 2, 1776.
" DEAR SIR,

. . . . . .

" I am, however, afraid that it will not be easy to get any number of great men, though favourable in their opinions, to such a scheme as yours, to be active and zealous in carrying it into execution ; nor have I much hope that any great reformation will take place in this country till some calamity comes that shall make us feel more, and awaken us more to reflection.

. . . . .

" I am, dear Sir,
" Your most obedient and humble Servant,
" RICHARD PRICE."

4. THE YORKSHIRE REFORMERS

[At the end of 1779 the Rev. Christopher Wyvill (1740–1822), a considerable landowner in Yorkshire, organised a ' very numerous and respectable meeting of the Gentleman Clergy and freeholders of Yorkshire, who agreed to a petition against the increase of national expenditure and against " exorbitant " emoluments, sinecure places and unmerited pensions '. The movement spread rapidly and a meeting of Deputies from different counties was held in London : in addition to ' economic ' reforms, political demands, chiefly for shorter Parliaments and more equal representation, were now included in their programme, which was conceived mainly in the interests of the squires and smaller freeholders against the great landowners and the moneyed men, as the proposal for additional county members shows. The campaign continued with some success in 1781 and with even greater success in 1782, when Burke's Civil Establishment Bill abolished some of the sinecures, made public administration cleaner and more efficient, and prevented the King from using the Civil List to give jobs to his followers. Wyvill continued to agitate for political reforms, but supporters faded away. This was a middle-class, and in some ways a reactionary, movement (for the county freeholders were very far from holding Radical views), but its methods — the Conventions and the Plan of Association — became the stock-in-trade of later working-class movements. Wyvill later took a prominent part in the movement for Catholic Emancipation. The six volumes of " Wyvill Papers " which he collected are an important source of information for early Reform movements.]

From the Report of the First Meeting of Deputies, 1780. " Wyvill Papers ", vol. i, p. 436 (1794).

A motion being made, and the question put, it was resolved,

That this meeting do recommend to the several Committees, to persevere unremittingly in support of The Petitions, and of such measures as tend to reduce the unconstitutional influence of the Crown, and for that purpose to unite the members in a General Association.

Resolved, that obtaining a law for taking the suffrages of the people, in such a mode as to prevent both expense in elections and the operation of undue influence therein, is necessary towards securing the freedom of Parliament.

Resolved, that it be recommended to our several committees to adopt the following propositions, as parts of their general Plan of Union and Association; and to endeavour to obtain the objects of such propositions, by application to and under the authority of Parliament, viz

Resolved,

1st. That a diligent examination be made into all the branches of the receipt, expenditure, and mode of keeping and passing accounts of public money, in order to obtain the Plan of Reform requested by the Petitions of the People.

Resolved,

2nd. That these be sent to the House of Commons, in addition to the present Representatives of Counties, a number of members not less than one hundred; to be chosen in due proportion by the several counties of the Kingdom of Great Britain.

Resolved,

3d, That the members of the House of Commons be annually elected to serve in Parliament.

Resolved,

4th, That it be most earnestly recommended to the Freeholders of the different counties, and to the Electors of the cities and boroughs, throughout the Kingdom, to support, at the ensuing general election, such Candidates to represent them in Parliament, as shall, previous to the election, by signing the Association or otherwise, have satisfied them, that they will support the above important regulations in Parliament, or so much thereof as shall not be obtained in the present Parliament.

5. THE WESTMINSTER COMMITTEE

[This Report of 1780, drawn up for the London Constitutional Society, includes all the six points of the People's Charter of 1837 — Universal Suffrage (4), Annual Parliaments (3), Vote by Ballot (9), Equal Electoral Districts (2), Payment of Members (14), No Property Qualifications for Members (16). But, in almost complete contrast to the Charter, the Westminster Programme is mainly an essay in political theory, and was not inspired by social grievances. It was drawn up by a sub-committee under the chairmanship of T. Brand Hollis, heir of the Republican Thomas Hollis. The sub-committee reported to the main committee of the Society for Constitutional Information, of which the chairman was Charles James Fox. Its Report was approved and was ordered ' to be circulated to the several Committees of the counties, cities, and boroughs of this kingdom '.]

From the ' Report of the Sub-Committee of Westminster ', May 1780. Wyvill Papers, vol. i, p. 240.

Plan for taking the Suffrages *of the* People, at the Election of Representatives to serve in Parliament.

1. THAT each county be divided into as many districts as it is intitled to elect Representatives, each district chusing one Representative.

2. That the division of The County into districts be constituted in such a manner, that each district contain nearly an equal number of males competent to vote in elections ; . . .

3. That the elections of Representatives to serve in Parliament be held annually through England and Wales, upon the first Tuesday in July ; that the election commence between the hours of eight and eleven, and be finally closed before sunset of the same day.

4. That all the male inhabitants of this Country (aliens, minors, criminals, and insane persons excepted) be admitted to vote at the election of Representatives subject only to the forms, provisions, and regulations specified in this report.

(5. a plan for the more equal distribution of representatives among the different counties.)

(6, 7, 8 technical details of election organisation)

9. That the poll of each district be taken by ballot . . .

13. That all members of the Commons' House of Parliament, before taking their seats, declare upon oath, that they do not hold any office or emolument at the will of the Crown, or its servants, or any Lord of Parliament ; that they will give due attendance to business, and act with all fidelity to the people, in the discharge of their important trust.

14. That all Members serving in Parliament be entitled to reasonable wages, according to the wholesome practice of ancient times.

15. That all election causes be finally decided by Jury, before the Judges of Assize.

16. That every person, competent to give his suffrage as an elector, be also esteemed qualified to be elected to serve his country in Parliament.

6. THE SOCIETY FOR PROMOTING CONSTITUTIONAL INFORMATION, 1780

[This Society (founded in 1780) was an organisation of well-to-do men who believed that by publishing and distributing tracts they would persuade the people to demand the restoration of the ancient democratic constitution, which the ruling caste had perverted. Their ideas did not touch a wide public, but the influence of their work was felt in later years.

The leading figures were Major Cartwright and Horne Tooke, and the membership included many peers and other well-known men (such as Thomas Day, author of " Sandford and Merton ").]

From the preface to a volume of Tracts issued by the Society in 1783.

SOCIETY FOR PROMOTING CONSTITUTIONAL INFORMATION

The design of this society is to diffuse throughout the kingdom, as universally as possible, a knowledge of the great principles of Constitutional Freedom, particularly such as respect the election and duration of the representative body. With this view Constitutional Tracts, intended for the extension of this knowledge, and to communicate it to persons of all ranks, are printed and distributed GRATIS, at the expense of the society. Essays, and extracts from various authors, calculated to promote the same design, are also published under the direction of the society, in several of the Newspapers : and it is the wish of the society to extend this knowledge throughout every part of the United Kingdoms, and to convince men of all ranks, that it is their interest as well as their duty, to support a free constitution and to maintain and assert those common rights, which are essential to the dignity and to the happiness of human nature.

To procure short parliaments, and a more equal representation of the people, are the primary objects of the attention of this society, and they wish to disseminate that knowledge among their countrymen, which may lead them to a general sense of the importance of these objects, and which may induce them to contend for their rights, as men, and as citizens, with ardour and with firmness.

The communication of sound political knowledge to the people at large must be of great national advantage ; as nothing but ignorance of their natural rights, or inattention to the consequences of those rights to their interest and happiness, can induce the majority of the inhabitants of any country to submit to any species of civil tyranny. Public freedom is the source of national dignity, and of national felicity, and it is the duty of every friend to virtue and mankind to exert himself in the promotion of it.

By the laws of the Constitutional Society it is unlimited in its numbers. All questions in the society are determined by ballot, and all ballots are taken by the President, or presiding member.

Gentlemen desirous of becoming members are to be admitted by ballot, and to subscribe from one to five guineas per annum.

GREAT BRITAIN AND THE
FRENCH REVOLUTION

INTRODUCTION

MEN of all classes were deeply moved by the events in France. It was a time in which

> apostasy from ancient faith
> Seemed but conversion to a higher creed.

Numerous Reform societies were founded, ranging from the aristocratic and largely parliamentary Society of the Friends of the People to the London Corresponding Society, which was the first independent political organisation of a distinctively working-class character. The British Reform societies proceeded to exchange Addresses with the Jacobin Clubs (the branches of the revolutionary movement in France); and there was constant communication between the Reform societies in different parts of Great Britain. This movement reached its climax in the British Convention, which met in Edinburgh late in 1793, attended by delegates from the Scottish and from a few English Reform societies, including the London Corresponding Society. But the Revolution in France bred enemies as well as friends to Reform in Great Britain. Price's " Discourse on the Love of Our Country ", expressing the welcome of the Radical Dissenters to the French Revolution, provoked Burke's indictment in his " Reflections "; and Burke was in turn answered for the reformers by Paine in his " Rights of Man ". These works, and the tremendous controversy which they aroused, created in the minds of the governing classes a panic fear of revolution in Great Britain. An association was founded, probably on the initiative of the Government, to spy out and suppress Radical organisations; magistrates up and down the country made it as difficult as possible for the Reformers to meet and talk; State Trials for sedition became frequent, and in some of them mere evidence of an admiration for Tom Paine was enough to ensure bias in both judge and jury. The

British Convention itself was broken up by the Government; and a new series of trials arising out of it began in Scotland, followed by still more extensive prosecutions in England. Even the aquittal of the London leaders in 1794 and the courageous persistence of, in particular, the London Corresponding Society, could not save the movement from destruction. The Reign of Terror in France, magnified by reactionary propaganda in Great Britain, had frightened a large section of the public and disillusioned many of the more moderate Reformers. Moreover, after the outbreak of war between France and England (February, 1793), war-time patriots regarded British Reformers as no better than French agents, bent on treason. In 1795 Parliament passed despotic Acts against democratic liberties; and the dwindling groups of Reformers, threatened with prosecution by the State, and with popular hostility, resorted in some cases to semi-revolutionary plotting which had no hope of success. The rise of the United Irishmen, the naval mutinies of 1797, and the Irish rebellion of 1798 heightened the Government's fear of revolution, though in fact their connection with the Reform movement in Great Britain was tenuous. Finally, an Act of 1799 banned by name all the important Reform societies which were still in existence, and some that were not, and brought this phase of the movement to an end.

There was some revival of the agitation for Reform during the later years of the war, especially when the European blockade and the rupture with the United States interfered seriously with commerce and industry. Cobbett went over to the Radicals, after his break with the Ministry of All the Talents in 1806, and in the last years of the war Major Cartwright resumed his interrupted crusade for Reform. Francis Place and others started the Reform caucus which captured Westminster, one of the very few constituencies possessing a wide franchise in the Unreformed Parliament. Reform societies began again to be founded up and down the country, and *Cobbett's Weekly Political Register* exercised a wide influence among the more Radical sections of the farming and middle classes. But no widespread Reform campaign resulted until the war was at an end and the country had to face the financial and economic problems of the post-war period.

See " Short History ", Part I, chapter 2.
" Common People ", chapters 9 and 13.

1. THE REVOLUTION SOCIETY

[There were numerous societies founded to celebrate the ' Glorious Revolution ' of 1688. The London Society, which had been very prominent in the centenary celebrations (November 4, 1788), met on the next anniversary to pay its homage to the French Revolution. Though Burke regarded this meeting as little better than treason, its proceedings were in fact respectable and unrevolutionary. Dr. Richard Price (1723–1781), a leading Nonconformist divine, already celebrated both as moral philosopher and as economist and also as a prominent supporter of the cause of American independence, preached a sermon on " The Love of Our Country ", which was a firm but mild plea for democracy and religious equality; and the Congratulatory Address to the National Assembly in France was written as from a country which had established its fundamental liberties and had no further need of revolution.]

(*a*) From a Congratulatory Address sent by the London Revolution Society to the National Assembly in France, 1789.

" The Society for Commemorating the Revolution in GREAT BRITAIN, disdaining national partialities and rejoicing in every triumph of liberty and justice over arbitrary power, offer to the National Assembly of FRANCE their congratulations on the Revolution in that country, and on the prospect it gives to the two first kingdoms in the world, of a common participation in the blessings of civil and religious liberty.

They cannot help adding their ardent wishes of a happy settlement of so important a Revolution, and at the same time expressing the particular satisfaction, with which they reflect on the tendency of the glorious example given in FRANCE to encourage other nations to assert the unalienable rights of mankind, and thereby to introduce a general reformation in the governments of EUROPE, and to make the world free and happy."

(*b*) From Dr. Richard Price's " Discourse on the Love of Our Country " (1789), p. 23.

This society [1] has, very properly, in its Reports, held out these principles, as an instruction to the public. I will only take notice of the three following :

First; the right to liberty of conscience in religious matters.

Secondly; the right to resist power when abused — And

Thirdly; the right to choose our own governors; to cashier them for misconduct; and to frame a government for ourselves.

---

[1] *I.e.* The Revolution Society.

2. THE RIGHTS OF MAN

[Burke's onslaught on the French Revolution and the English Reformers inspired a host of writers and pamphleteers to reply. Much the most influential answer was made by Tom Paine in his " Rights of Man ". Paine (1737–1809), born in Thetford, Norfolk, went to America where he fought for the Colonists against England and inspired them by his writings, especially " Common Sense " (1776), and served as Foreign Secretary to the Continental Congress ; came back to England, published " Rights of Man ", and was convicted of sedition in his absence, having fled to France on the advice of William Blake, the poet and artist. In France he was elected a member of the National Convention but found himself soon in prison as a ' moderate ' — for he strongly opposed the execution of the King. His last years were spent in the United States. He was also a notable inventor, and designed one of the earliest iron bridges. Paine was an ardent social reformer, some of whose proposals for social legislation have a remarkably modern ring. He was also a thoroughgoing democrat with an intense conviction that all men are equal and should be politically free. He had an unbounded belief in the virtues of Representative Government based on Universal Suffrage and popular sovereignty, and he produced in the second part of his " Rights of Man " (1791) a plan of social reforms in which he answered the needs of the people as only a man of the people could. The direct simplicity of his thought and style gave an amazing popularity to his writings. He was the inspiration of the working-class reformers of this period ; and, in addition, his works on Secularism (" The Age of Reason "), on the National Debt (" The Decline and Fall of the English System of Finance"), and on the land question (" Agrarian Justice "), had considerable influence on the later history of the working-class movement.]

(a) From Thomas Paine, " Rights of Man ", Part I (1790), pp. 3-4. (Edition edited by H. B. Bonner, 1937.)

There never did, there never will, and there never can, exist a parliament, or any description of men, or any generation of men, in any country, possessed of the right or the power of binding and controlling posterity to the " *end of time* " or of commanding for ever how the world shall be governed, or who shall govern it ; and therefore all such clauses, acts or declarations by which the makers of them attempt to do what they have neither the right nor the power to do, nor the power to execute, are in themselves null and void. Every age and generation must be as free to act for itself *in all cases* as the ages and generations which preceded it. The vanity and presumption of governing beyond the grave is the most ridiculous and insolent of tyrannies. Man has no property in man, neither has any generation a property in the generations which are to follow.

(*b*) From Thomas Paine, " Rights of Man ", Part II (1791), pp. 127, 153, 154, 163, 166, 174.

I do not believe that monarchy and aristocracy will continue seven years longer in any of the enlightened countries in Europe. If better reasons can be shewn for them than against them, they will stand; if the contrary, they will not. Mankind are not now to be told that they shall not think or they shall not read; and publications that go no further than to investigate principles of government, to invite men to reason and to reflect and to shew the errors and excellencies of different systems, have a right to appear. If they do not excite attention, they are not worth the trouble of a prosecution, and if they do the prosecution will amount to nothing, since it cannot amount to a prohibition of reading. This would be a sentence on the public instead of on the author, and would also be the most effectual mode of making or hastening revolutions.

.   .   .   .   .   .

Simple democracy was society governing itself without the aid of secondary means. By ingrafting representation upon democracy, we arrive at a system of government capable of embracing and confederating all the various interests and every extent of territory and population; and that also with advantages as much superior to hereditary government, as the republic of letters is to hereditary literature.

.   .   .   .   .   .

It is impossible to conceive a system of government capable of acting over such an extent of territory, and such a circle of interests, as is immediately produced by the operation of representation. France, great and populous as it is, is but a spot in the capaciousness of the system. It is preferable to simple democracy even in small territories. Athens, by representation, would have outrivalled her own democracy.

That which is called government, or rather that which we ought to conceive government to be, is no more than some common centre, in which all the parts of society unite. This cannot be accomplished by any method so conducive to the various interests of the community as by the representative system. It concentrates the knowledge necessary to the interest of the parts, and of the whole. It places government in a state of constant maturity. It is, as has already been observed, never young, never old. It is subject neither to nonage nor dotage. It is never in the cradle nor on crutches. It admits not of a separation between knowledge and power, and is superior, as government always ought to be, to all the accidents of individual man, and is therefore superior to what is called monarchy.

. . . . . .

Government is not a trade which any man, or any body of men, had a right to set up and exercise for his own emolument, but is altogether a trust in right of those by whom the trust is delegated, and by whom it is always resumable. It has of itself no rights; they are altogether duties.

. . . . . .

A constitution is the property of a nation, and not of those who exercise the government. All the constitutions of America are declared to be established on the authority of the people. In France, the word nation is used instead of the people; but in both cases a constitution is a thing antecedent to the government, and always distinct therefrom.

. . . . . .

Government is nothing more than a national association; and the object of this association is the good of all, as well individually as collectively. Every man wishes to pursue his occupation, and to enjoy the fruits of his labours and the produce of his property in peace and safety, and with the least possible expence. When these things are accomplished, all the objects for which government ought to be established are answered.

(c) From Thomas Paine, " Rights of Man ", Part II (1791),[1] pp. 227-8.

I shall now conclude this plan with enumerating the several particulars, and then proceed to other matters :—

The enumeration is as follows :—

First—Abolition of two millions poor-rates.

Secondly—Provision for two hundred and fifty thousand poor families.

Thirdly—Education for one million and thirty thousand children.

Fourthly—Comfortable provision for one hundred and forty thousand aged persons.

---

[1] This is an extract from Paine's plan of social reform, which included children's allowances up to 14 years, and old age pensions from 50 years with an increase at 60.

Fifthly—Donation of twenty shillings each for fifty thousand births.

Sixthly—Donation of twenty shillings each for twenty thousand marriages.

Seventhly—Allowances of twenty thousand pounds for the funeral expenses of persons travelling for work, and dying at a distance from their friends.

Eighthly—Employment at all times, for the casual poor in the cities of London and Westminster.

By the operation of this plan, the poor laws, those instruments of civil torture, will be superseded, and the wasteful expence of litigation prevented. The hearts of the humane will not be shocked by ragged and hungry children, and persons of seventy and eighty years of age, begging for bread. The dying poor will not be dragged from place to place to breathe their last, as a reprisal of parish upon parish. Widows will have a maintenance for their children, and not be carted away, on the death of their husbands, like culprits and criminals; and children will no longer be considered as encreasing the distresses of their parents. The haunts of the wretched will be known, because it will be to their advantage, and the number of petty crimes, the offspring of distress and poverty will be lessened. The poor, as well as the rich, will then be interested in the support of government, and the cause and apprehension of riots and tumults will cease. Ye who sit in ease, and solace yourselves in plenty — and such there are in Turkey and Russia, as well as in England — and who say to yourselves, " Are we not well off ? " have ye thought of these things ? When ye do, ye will cease to speak and feel for yourselves alone.

3. THE LONDON CORRESPONDING SOCIETY

[Thomas Hardy (1752–1832), a shoemaker, born in Scotland,[1] and the other members of the London Corresponding Society (1791–1799) were respectable working-men and small shopkeepers who had been moved by the hardness of the times and the hopes raised by the French Revolution to join in the demand for political reforms — especially Universal Suffrage and Annual Parliaments. They were organised on the Wesleyan model of ' classes ', and in their classes (or divisions, as they were called) political

[1] See his " Memoir of Thomas Hardy, By Himself ", 1832, and the report of his trial for treason in 1794, of which there are several versions.

subjects were discussed. They published the resolutions and addresses decided on at their general meetings. They kept up a constant correspondence with other Reformers and sent delegates to the British Convention. Until the middle of 1796 the Society showed more initiative and courage than any other, but in its last years, under stress of persecution, it developed into a semi-conspiratorial clique, in touch with and hoping to imitate the revolutionary ' United Irishmen '. It was finally suppressed by law in 1799.

The aims of the L.C.S. were political, with no explicit desire to change the economic system, but its members had a firm belief in the economic importance and the rights of labour. (See the quotation below from Thelwall, one of its leading lecturers.)]

(*a*) From " An Address to the Nation from the London Corresponding Society, on the Subject of a Thorough Parliamentary Reform", (1793), pp. 1-8.

FRIENDS AND FELLOW COUNTRYMEN,

Gloomy as is the prospect now before us, and unpleasing as is the talk to bring forth into open day the calamitous situation of our Country : We conceive it necessary to direct the public eye, to the cause of our misfortunes, and to awaken the sleeping reason of our Countrymen, to the pursuit of the only remedy which can ever prove effectual, namely ; — *A thorough Reform in Parliament, by the adoption of an equal Representation obtained by Annual Elections and Universal Suffrage.* — We do not address you in the confidence of personal importance — We do not presume upon the splendor of exalted situation ; but as Members of the same Society, as Individuals, zealously labouring for the welfare of the Community ; we think ourselves entitled to a share of your attention.

．　　．　　．　　．　　．　　．

Here it is proper to remind you of the false and calumnious aspersions, which have been so industriously circulated since November last : At that time of general Consternation, when the cry of danger to the Constitution was raised and extensively propagated ; when the alarm of *Riots and Insurrections*, was founded by Royal Proclamations and re-echoed by Parish Associations ; Reform was branded by the name of Innovation, and whoever dared to affirm, that the House of Commons ought to be restored to that state of independence in which it was settled at the Revolution ; and that unnecessary Places and Pensions ought to be abolished, was stigmatized as a leveller and an enemy to his King and Country.

．　　．　　．　　．　　．　　．

Our Petition to parliament was received — read — and ordered to lay on the Table — the principle contained therein : " That no man shall be taxed, but by the consent of himself, or his Representative freely chosen by himself." Neither was, nor could be denied to be a *Principle* of our Constitution ; but its effects *could* at that time be evaded by those whose interest it was to perpetuate abuses at the expence of the public.

British gold, now subsidizes armies of Continental Slaves, and the blood of half Europe is pledged for the destruction of France ! Supplies of every kind are sent from hence ! Commerce is nearly stopped ! Failures innumerable take place ! Manufacturers are ruined ! Artizans are starving ! Provisions rise in price ! the Revenue decreases, and fresh Taxes are wanting ! for fresh supplies of blood, the Liberties of our Country are invaded ! the Seaman is forcibly torn from his family ! the Peasant kidnapped from the plough ! and the starving Labourer is compelled to sell his Life and his Liberty for Bread — If such, O much oppressed Britons ! are the effects of a Four months' War, what are you to expect when it shall have lasted as many years ?

To obtain a compleat Representation is our only aim — contemning all party distinctions, we seek no advantage which every individual of the community will not enjoy equally with ourselves — We are not engaged in Speculative and Theoretical schemes ; the motive of our present conduct is the actual sense of injury and oppression ; We feel the weight of innumerable abuses, to which the invasion of our rights has given birth, and which their restoration can alone remove.

But sensible that our efforts, if not seconded by the Nation at large, must prove ineffectual, and only needlessly expose us to the malevolence of the public plunderers ; we conjure you, by the love you bear your country, by your attachment to freedom, and by your anxious care for the welfare of your posterity, to suffer yourselves no longer to be deluded by artful speeches, and by interested men ; but to sanction with your approbations, our constitutional endeavours, and pursue with union and firmness the track we have pointed out : Thus countenanced by our country, we pledge ourselves, as you will perceive by the following resolutions, never to recede or slacken, but on every occasion to redouble our zealous exertions in the cause of Constitutional Freedom.

RESOLVED UNANIMOUSLY

I. That nothing but a fair, adequate and annually renovated Representation in Parliament, can ensure the freedom of this country.

II. That we are fully convinced, a thorough Parliamentary Reform, would remove every grievance under which we labour.

III. That we will never give up the pursuit of such Parliamentary Reform.

IV. That if it be a part of the power of the king to declare war when and against whom he pleases, we are convinced that such power must have been granted to him under the condition, that it should ever be subservient to the national advantage.

V. That the present war against France, and the existing alliance with the Germanic Powers, so far as it relates to the prosecution of that war, has hitherto produced, and is likely to produce nothing but national calamity, if not utter ruin.

VI. That it appears to Us that the wars in which Great Britain has engaged, within the last hundred years, have cost her upwards of *Three Hundred and Seventy Millions*! not to mention the private misery occasioned thereby, or the lives sacrificed; therefore it is a dreadful speculation for the people of this country to look up to; That the Cabinet have engaged in a treaty with a foreign Prince, to be supplied with troops for a long period of years, and for a purpose unknown to the people of England.

VII. That we are persuaded the majority, if not the whole of those wars, originated in Cabinet intrigue, rather than in absolute necessity.

VIII. That every nation has an unalienable right to chuse the mode in which it will be governed, and that it is an act of Tyranny and Oppression in any other nation to interfere with, or attempt to controul their choice.

IX. That peace being the greatest of blessings, ought to be sought most diligently by every wise government, to be most joyfully accepted when reasonably proffered, and to be concluded most speedily when the object of the war is accomplished.

X. That we do exhort every well wisher to his country, not to delay in improving himself in constitutional knowledge.

XI. That those men who were the first to be seized with a panic, should be the last whom prudence would entrust with the management of a war.

XII. That Great Britain is not Hanover!

XIII. That regarding union as indispensably necessary to ensure success, we will endeavour to the utmost of our power, to unite more closely with every political Society in the nation, associated upon the same principles with ourselves.

XIV. That the next general Meeting of this Society, be held on the first Monday in September, unless the Committee of Delegates shall find it necessary to call such meeting sooner.

XV. That the foregoing Address and Resolutions be signed by the Chairman and by the Secretary, and that *Twenty Thousand Copies* of them be printed, published and distributed [gratis.]

MAURICE MARGAROT, Chairman.

THOMAS HARDY, Secretary.

Monday, July 8, 1793,
CROWN AND ANCHOR TAVERN,
STRAND.

(*b*) From the Place MSS., 27,812 f. 75. [1793]. Instructions of the London Corresponding Society to their Delegate to the British Convention.

ARTICLES OF INSTRUCTION TO CITIZEN A. A.

Delegate from the London Corresponding Society to the ensuing Convention at Edinburgh for the purpose of obtaining a thorough parliamentary Reform.

1st. He shall on no Account whatever depart from the original Object and Principles, namely the obtaining Annual Parliaments and Universal Suffrage by rational and lawful means.

2nd. He is directed to support the Opinion that representatives in Parliament ought to be paid by their constituents.

3rd. That the Election of Sheriffs ought to be restored to the People.

4th. That Juries ought to be chosen by Lot.

5th. That active means ought to be used to render every man acquainted with the Duty and Rights of a Juryman.

6th. That the Liberty of the Press must at all events be supported and that the publication of political truths can never be criminal.

7th. That it is the Duty of the People to resist any Act of Parliament repugnant to the original principles of the Constitution, as would be every attempt to prohibit Associations for the purpose of Reform.

8th. That this Society considering all party names & Distinctions as hostile to the general welfare, do absolutely restrict their Delegate from assuming or accepting of that Nature.

9th. This Society further requires their Delegate to be punctual and frequent in his correspondence with this Society.

(c) From John Thelwall, " The Rights of Britons " (1795), p. 43.

[John Thelwall (1764–1834) entered politics through the famous Coachmakers' Hall Debating Society, one of the numerous clubs where men were learning to discuss public affairs. He won a great reputation as a lecturer and speaker, at first on politics, later as a professional elocutionist. Thelwall was tried and acquitted, with Thomas Hardy, in 1794. (See Charles Cestre, " John Thelwall : a Pioneer of Democracy ".)]

But it is property, we are told, that ought to be represented, because by property government is supported. What ! Does property mean the navy ? Does property fill the ranks of armies ? O ! that this cruel contest, which is desolating Europe, were indeed but a war of property ! that Government required no support but from the funds of opulence ! and that the blood of our fellow-beings might stream no more.

Let us not deceive ourselves ! Property is nothing but human labour. The most inestimable of all property is the sweat of the poor man's brow :— the property from which all other is derived, and without which grandeur must starve in the midst of supposed abundance. And shall they who possess this inestimable property be told that they have no rights, because they have nothing to defend ? Shall those who toil for our subsistence, and bleed for our protection, be excluded from all importance in the scale of humanity, because they have so toiled and bled ? No ; man and not moveables is the object of just legislation. All, therefore, ought to be consulted where all are concerned ; for what less than the whole ought to decide the fate of the whole ?

(d) From " Revolutions without Bloodshed, or Reformation preferable to Revolt " (1794).

[This anonymous pamphlet, issued in 1794, is a good sample of the popular propaganda of the years immediately following the French Revolution.]

It having been industriously asserted that the happiness and prosperity of the people would not be at all increased by a Reform of the Representation, it has been thought proper to publish the following enumeration of those changes which in all probability might be thereby produced.

I.

The CLAIMS OF THE PEOPLE might be more duly attended to, and their RIGHTS restored.

II.

Taxes might be proportioned to the abilities of those upon whom they are levied, and not made to fall heavier on the *poor* than on the *rich*.

III.

The present system of Excising almost all the *necessaries of life*, as soap, candles, starch, beer, etc., etc., might be abolished.

IV.

The POOR LAWS AND LAWS OF SETTLEMENTS might be amended, and a poor man not be liable to be sent to prison for moving out of his own parish to seek employment.

V.

The GAME LAWS might be abolished, and the farmer be no longer obliged to permit his rich and insolent neighbour to trample his fields in pursuit of an animal, which, though fed by the produce of his own grounds, the farmer himself dares not kill, but under the penalty of fine and imprisonment.

VI.

Workmen might no longer be punished with imprisonment for uniting to obtain an increase of wages, whilst their masters are allowed to conspire against them with impunity.

VII.

LAW SUITS might become less tedious and expensive, and ruin no longer be the consequence of suing for justice.

49

VIII.

Some proportion might be preserved between Crimes and Punishments, and the starving purloiner of a few shillings not suffer the same punishment as a murderer.

IX.

The CLERGY might be provided for by an income more regularly proportioned, and levied in a more agreeable and respectable mode. A part of the vast revenues of the Bishops might relieve our numerous starving curates.

X.

The RICH might be prevented from swelling their excessive incomes by MONOPOLISING the necessities of life, and even the farms by which they are produced.

XI.

Some NATIONAL ESTABLISHMENT might yield to the *Children of the Poor* such instruction as might enable them to *earn their living*, and form a just notion of their *rights* and *duties* as members of society.

XII.

CONSTANT EMPLOY might be secured to the *industrious*, and due PROVISION be made for the *aged* and *disabled*.

XIII.

Families that are comparatively starving might be exempted from contributing towards the enormous sums squandered on *unmerited* SALARIES and PENSIONS.

XIV.

The UNFORTUNATE TRADESMAN, ruined, perhaps by some swindler of rank, might not be consigned to the horrors of a dungeon, because oppressed by the heavy hand of misfortune.

XV.

A poor and industrious man might no longer be prevented from getting his living by the various inclusive Franchises, Privileges and Charters of different Trades and Corporations, shutting him out from exercising perhaps the only trade he is capable of, and perhaps from the only spot where he might hope for success.

XVI.

A more *equal distribution* of the LAND TAX might take place, and some comparatively small streets inhabited by tradesmen, not contribute more than a large and extensive parish, occupied chiefly by the gentry and nobility.

XVII.

The POOR RATES might be levied by a more equitable rule than the *quantity of rent*, by which the industrious farmer and mechanic, on account of their extensive premises, are made to pay as much as their idle and opulent neighbours.

XVIII.

The *blessings of peace* might not be again exchanged for the MISERIES OF WAR, with the wicked but vain hope of rivetting chains on *thirty millions* of men, who had resolved to be free.

XIX.

Young men might no more be TREPANNED from their friends to perish in the fields of infamy and murder.

XX.

Our SAILORS might not be dragged like felons into a service they dislike, and made accomplices in slaughter.

XXI.

A more equitable plan might be adopted for the SUPPORT of the SOLDIERY than *quartering* both men and horses on one class of the people (*Publicans*) alone.

XXII.

DIFFERENCE OF OPINION on RELIGIOUS MATTERS might not exclude men from enjoying the same benefits with their Fellow-Citizens.

XXIII.

No apprehension need then be entertained of a SUBVERSION OF THE GOVERNMENT being intended, because a dozen halberds and as many musquets, had been made for the legal defence of as many individuals.

XXIV.

The EXPENSES of the NATION might not then exceed, as they now do, the enormous sum of 80,000l A DAY — 3,000l AN HOUR — or 50l A MINUTE.

Such are the changes which might take place were that reform of Parliament to be accomplished which the Duke of Richmond and Mr. Pitt *once* recommended, and which those patriots who have been exiled from their ungrateful country, or are languishing in *Bastiles*, without power of obtaining a trial, have so constantly and intrepidly laboured to effect. Consider, Fellow-Citizens, whether these changes be desirable — if they be, then ask yourselves *if they* are to be expected from a House of Parliament whose journals bear the assertion, THAT THE SEATS IN THAT HOUSE ARE BOUGHT AND SOLD LIKE STANDINGS FOR CATTLE IN A FAIR — from an Assembly which, instead of being composed, as its name imports it should be, of the real representatives of the COMMONS of this kingdom, is disgraced by a band of men sent there by an ESTABLISHED System of Private PATRONAGE :— 306 out of 513 of its members being appointed by the TREASURY and 162 individual PEERS and rich BOROUGH MONGERS. TRAITORS! TRAITORS! TRAITORS!

4. THE SOCIETY FOR CONSTITUTIONAL INFORMATION

[This Society, revived in March 1791, adopted a more lively tone under Major Cartwright's leadership. Even when we make allowances for the exciting atmosphere in which the following address was delivered, its optimism and enthusiasm give a picture of the inspiration men derived from the French Revolution in its early days.

The S.C.I. was a model on which many provincial societies were formed, particularly where the leaders were of the middle class. In Manchester, for instance, the middle-class ' Constitutional Society ' was more or less the ' Manchester S.C.I.' — though the London Society did not have local branches ; it met in the house of its chief member, Thomas Walker,[1] a prominent Manchester merchant, while his warehouse was reserved for the Reformation Society, a working-class organisation with which it collaborated on friendly terms, much as the Constitutional Society in London did with the London Corresponding Society.]

From " An Address by John Frost [2] and Joel Barlow,[3] Members of the Society for Promoting Constitutional Information ".

From " A Collection of Addresses transmitted by certain English Clubs or Societies to the National Convention of France ", Second Edition, 1793.

Citizens of France, we are deputed by a Patriot Society in London, called The Society for Constitutional Information, to congratulate you in its name upon the triumphs of Liberty. Before the epoch of your Revolution, this Society employed itself but too long upon this important object, with little hope of success. Judge from thence of the transports of its gratitude, when, *thanks to the wonderful efforts of the French nation, it has beheld the Empire of Reason extend and strengthen itself, and assure the virtuous men, by securing the happiness of their fellow-creatures, a recompense to their future labours. Innumerable societies of the same sort are forming themselves at this moment in every part of England.* The minds of all receive from this circumstance a general impression which leads them to fathom the abuses of Government, and to seek the means of remedying them — MEANS AS SIMPLE as the abuses are intricate. *After the example given by France* REVOLUTIONS will become easy. *Reason is about to make a rapid progress*, and IT WOULD NOT BE EXTRAORDINARY IF IN A MUCH LESS SPACE OF TIME THAN CAN BE IMAGINED THE FRENCH SHOULD SEND ADDRESSES OF CONGRATULATION TO A NATIONAL CONVENTION OF ENGLAND.

[1] See No. 9 of this section.
[2] John Frost (1750–1842), not to be confused with the Newport Chartist of the same name, was an active member of Cartwright's Constitutional Society in 1780, and took a leading part in the formation of the London Corresponding Society. He was imprisoned for sedition in 1793.
[3] This was Joel Barlow (1754–1812), the American poet, who was living in Paris after a residence in London. He was a close friend of Tom Paine.

5. THE SOCIETY OF THE FRIENDS OF THE PEOPLE

[The Society of the Friends of the People (founded in 1792) closely anticipated the spirit of the Whig Ministry of 1830 in its policy and class composition. Lord Grey of the Reform Bill was one of its members. They felt that some reform was good and necessary, if only as the best means of avoiding revolution. (But this address, written after the Reign of Terror had begun, does not suggest their initial friendship to the French Revolution.) The Society was composed mainly of aristocratic politicians with a purely parliamentary outlook and a distrust of popular enthusiasm. Their main achievement was the organisation of a Petition for Reform, which, however, won little support either inside or outside the House of Commons.]

From an Address of the Society of the Friends of the People, May 31, 1794.

We had seen the sudden overthrow of the ancient and powerful Monarchy of France by the force of opinion, when the People, irritated by a long course of suffering, were, by the refusal of timely redress, driven, at last, to extremity and despair :— We had seen, and were in the daily course of seeing with affliction, the dreadful consequences of a sudden Revolution, upon whatever principles, or from whatever causes. We sought, therefore (mistakenly perhaps, but honestly and conscientiously) to avert from our country, by such means as appeared to us to be safe and effectual, the calamities inseparable from such convulsions. At a moment when a spirit of liberty was seeking by untried ways to invent constitutions, we invited our countrymen to look back to their own ; to restore and to cherish it ; conceiving it to be highly improbable, that the contagion of revolution could reach this island, as long as the true principles and securities of our genuine Government, in spirit and in substance as well as in forms, should be presented to the People.

6. THE BRITISH CONVENTION, 1793

[Two ' Conventions ' had already met in Scotland, and the British Convention itself grew out of a third one. Only a few delegates came from England, the London Corresponding Society being well represented. The main motive was to co-ordinate the work of the Reformers and to give publicity to their demands, but (as later in the Chartist Convention of 1839) there was always in the background the idea of claiming to act as a new government, the People's Government. The word ' Convention ' was meant to have a challenging tone. It was as a sequel to this Convention that the Government launched the Scottish Treason Trials of 1793.]

(*a*) The Development of the Convention. From the Second Report of the Committee of Secrecy (1794), p. 42.

During the three first Days the Convention appears, from its Minutes, to have chiefly employed itself on Matters of Form ; but having on the 22nd November, 1793, changed its Title to that of " The British Convention of Delegates of the People, *associated to obtain Universal Suffrage and Annual Parliaments*," they, in almost every Particular, assumed the Stile and Mode of Proceeding adopted by the National Convention of France. They divided themselves into Sections — Committees of Organisation, Instruction, Finance, and Secrecy ; denominated their Meetings Sittings ; granted Honours of Sittings ; made honourable Mention in their Minutes of patriotic Donations ; entered their Minutes as made in the First Year of the British Convention ; instituted Primary Societies, Provincial Assemblies and Departments ; received from their Sections a Variety of Motions and Reports — some of which have the words " Vive la Convention " prefixed to them, and end with " Ça ira " — and some dated " *First Year of the British Convention, One and indivisible.*"

(*b*) The Final Resolutions of the Convention (November 28, 1793). From the Second Report of the Committee of Secrecy (1794), p. 43.

Resolved, That the following Declaration and Resolutions be inserted at the end of our Minutes, viz :—

That this Convention, considering the calamitous consequences of any Act of the Legislature which may tend to deprive the Whole or any Part of the People of their undoubted Right to meet, either by themselves or by Delegation, to discuss any Matter relative to their Common Interest, whether of a public or private Nature, and holding the same to be totally inconsistent with the First Principles and Safety of Society, and also subversive of our known and acknowledged Constitutional Liberties, do hereby declare, before God and the World, that we shall follow the wholesome Example of former Times, by paying no Regard to any Act which shall militate against the Constitution of our Country, and shall continue to assemble and consider of the best Means by which we can accomplish a real Representation of the People, and Annual Elections, until compelled to desist by superior Force.

And we do resolve, That the First Notice given for the Introduction of a Convention Bill, or any Bill of a similar Tendency to that passed in Ireland in the last Session of their Parliament;

Or any Bill for the Suspension of the Habeas Corpus Act, or the Act for preventing Wrongous Imprisonment, and against undue Delays in Trial in North Britain;

Or in case of an Invasion; or the Admission of any Foreign Troops whatsoever into Great Britain or Ireland;

All or any one of these calamitous Circumstances shall be a Signal to the several Delegates to repair to such Place as the Secret Committee of this Convention shall appoint; and the First seven Members shall have Power to declare the Sittings Permanent, shall constitute a Convention, and Twenty-one proceed to Business.

The Convention doth therefore resolve, that each Delegate, immediately on his Return Home, do convene his Constituents, and explain to them the necessity of electing a Delegate or Delegates, and of establishing a Fund, without Delay, for any of these Emergencies, for his or their Expense; and that they do instruct the said Delegate or Delegates to hold themselves ready to depart at One Hour's Warning.

7. *HOG'S WASH*, OR *POLITICS FOR THE PEOPLE*

[Daniel Isaac Eaton (1752–1814), Radical bookseller and journalist, published in 1793–1794 a journal, first called *Hog's Wash* and later *Politics for the People*, which has a good claim to be regarded as the first Radical journal written from a working-class standpoint. The name *Hog's Wash* was given to it in satirical reply to Burke's phrase ' the swinish multitude '. Eaton was three times tried and acquitted in 1793–1794, twice for publishing Paine's writings and once for a satire on the King in his paper. In 1795–1796 he was again twice indicted, and in the latter year fled to America, where he remained until 1800. On his return his property was seized, and he was imprisoned for fifteen months. On his release he resumed his bookselling and publication of Radical and Deistic writings; and in 1812 he was again sentenced for issuing the third part of Paine's " Age of Reason ". He was also made to stand in the pillory — which caused a public demonstration in his favour. He was tried again in 1813–1814 for publishing " Ecce Homo ", translated from d'Holbach's " Historie Critique de Jésus-Christ ", but was never brought up for judgment. In *Hog's Wash* he bitterly attacked the Government's war policy, and war in general, calling the French war ' a war of combined kings against the people of France '.]

(a) From Daniel Isaac Eaton, *Hog's Wash*, or *Politics for the People*, October 12, 1793.

A sure way to prevent the threatened invasion by the French.

> If we fight and tax on for a year or two more,
> The French, I dare say, will ne'er touch on our shore,
> For fear of the charge of maintaining the poor.

(b) From *Hog's Wash*, or *Politics for the People*, November 9, 1793.

FROM "THE VILLAGE ASSOCIATION."

BE ye, therefore, unceasingly employed in endeavouring to procure a fair and equal representation, in parliaments of a proper duration. When that is obtained, your other grievances may soon be expected to cease. A due equilibrium may be preserved between the respective parts of the constitution — Our gracious sovereign will be happy in lessening the burthens of his loving subjects — Limitation may take place in the *making* of Lords — Wars may be less frequently thought necessary — The swarms of pensioners and sinecure placemen may be diminished — Taxes may be lightened — The national debt may be *actually* reduced — The land tax equalized — The Poor laws amended — The Game laws abolished — The Excise laws rendered less odious — The Statute laws corrected — The partial and oppressive laws against workmen meliorated — The proceedings at Common law rendered more compatible with common sense and equity — The severity of the criminal laws lessened — The infant poor may be educated in some grand national establishment — Youth may be protected, instead of being dragged into hard and degrading servitude — The aged poor may be maintained — The Clergy more equally and agreeably provided for — The Test acts annihilated — These are some of the many blessings, which most probably would succeed to that Reform of Parliament, which it is your duty to demand, and your right to obtain.

(c) From *Hog's Wash*, or *Politics for the People*, Part II, No. 1, 1794.

THE PATRIOT'S OATH.

I SWEAR to support the good of my country, in preference to all that is dear to me besides — To watch over those who have the management of its affairs, and, according to my station in society, use all my influence to reward its friends, and punish its enemies. I swear to revere its laws; but I will always execrate the abuse of them — I will love the King, as long as the happiness of the People is his ultimate aim ; — *no longer*. If he is badly advised, I will declare myself inimical to his measures. Since reform is so notoriously wanted, both in Church and State, I will sooner die than not demand it. No bribe of place or pension shall make me swerve from my stedfastness. I swear, according to my capacity, to understand for myself the politics of my country, that I may know the honesty or knavery of every statesman. I will know the truth, and keep myself independent of every party ; and, finally, I swear, that no custom or authority shall make me embrace corruption as expedient, or wink at an unequal representation of the people, which no artifice can justify, and which is itself repugnant to the rights of Englishmen, and common sense.

8. THE RADICALS AND THE FRENCH WAR

[The Radical societies throughout the country took up a strong attitude of opposition to the war against France. The following resolutions, carried by the Sheffield Radicals on February 28, 1794, are a fair sample of the views of most of the Radical bodies.]

From *Hog's Wash*, or *Politics for the People*, Part II, No. 8, March 1794.

PEACE AND REFORM
SHEFFIELD, *Feb.* 28, 1794.

At a public meeting of the Friends of Peace and Reform, held in an open piece of ground in West-street, in Sheffield, consisting of at least *five thousand persons*, called by public advertisement, to attend to the delivery of a serious lecture, to sing an hymn composed for the occasion, and to conclude with the passing of such resolutions as the present juncture of affairs seems to call for : William Camage being called to the chair, the following resolutions were voted without a dissenting voice.

1. That WAR, the wretched artifice of courts, is a system of *rapine and blood*, unworthy of rational beings, and utterly repugnant to the mild and benevolent principles of the Christian religion.

2. That if the *present* war be a war of *combined kings* against the *people of France*, to overthrow that liberty which they are struggling to establish, it is, in our opinion, a war of the most *diabolical* kind.

3. That when public fasts and humiliations are ordered with the *same* breath, which commands the shedding of *oceans of human blood* — however they may answer the purposes of *State policy* — they are *solemn prostitutions of religion*.

4. That the landing of Hessian troops in this country (a ferocious and unprincipled horde of butchers) without consent of Parliament, has a *suspicious* and *alarming* appearance, is contrary to the spirit of our Constitution, and deserving of the marked indignation of every Englishman.

5. That it is high time to be upon our GUARD, since these armed *monsters*, may in a moment be let loose upon us; particularly as the erection of *barracks* throughout the kingdom, may only have been an introductory measure to the filling them with foreign *mercenaries*.

6. That the high and freeborn minds of Britons, revolt at the idea of such a *slavish system*, and cannot be so far broken as to kiss the hand which would chain them to its will.

7. That *Peace* and *Liberty* are the offspring of heaven, and that life without them is a burden.

8. That the thanks of this meeting are due to Earl Stanhope, for his motion and spirited speech for acknowledging the French Republic, and restoring PEACE to our distressed country; for his motion and able speech in behalf of the persecuted and suffering patriots, Messrs. Muir, Palmer, Skirving and Margarot, in which he nobly stood alone; and also for the whole of his truly animated and benevolent exertions in support of the injured RIGHTS OF THE PEOPLE.

9. The thanks of this meeting are also due to Mr. Sheridan, for his nervous and eloquent speeches in the cause of injured patriotism, and in support of the Constitution; and also to every other Member of Parliament who has nobly stood forward at this important crisis, in support of the Constitutional Liberties of Englishmen.

10. That if any thing had been necessary to have convinced us of the total inefficacy of *argument* against a *ministerial majority*, the decisions which have lately taken place in Parliament, would have fully confirmed our opinion.

11. That, therefore, the People have no remedy for their grievances, but a REFORM IN PARLIAMENT — a measure which we determine never to relinquish, though we follow our brethren in the same glorious cause to BOTANY BAY.

W. CAMAGE, Chairman.

9. THE MANCHESTER REFORMERS

[Next to London, Manchester was the principal centre of Radical agitation in England during the years following the French Revolution. As we have seen, the lead was taken by a Constitutional Society, mainly middle-class in composition, and a Reformation Society, mainly working class, both set up in 1790. The principal figure in the movement was a merchant, Thomas Walker (1749–1817), who was tried in 1794 for sedition, after an indictment for treason had been dropped. He was defended by Thomas Erskine, and was triumphantly acquitted, after Erskine had exposed the spy, Thomas Dunn, on whom the entire case for the prosecution rested. The case ended with Dunn being himself indicted for perjury. Walker was lucky, both in being able to afford the best defence and in the prejudice which then existed against the use of spies and *agents provocateurs*. It seems clear from the trial that the charges of drilling and of preparation for an armed rising brought forward by Dunn had no foundation. The resolutions of the Reformation Society are interesting as coming from a body which was mainly composed of artisans. Walker, in the book which he published in connection with his trial, cited them together with the opposing declarations of the Church and King Club — a fair specimen of the anti-revolutionary societies that were founded in many places to combat the Reformers.]

(*a*) From " The Whole Proceedings on the Trial of an Indictment against Thomas Walker and Others, for a Conspiracy ", 1794.

[From the Opening Speech by the Prosecuting Counsel — Mr. James.]

It was about the period I mentioned, or shortly after, I mean in the month of December, which followed close upon the promulgation of this detestable decree, that the society on which I am about to comment, and ten members of which are now presented in trial before you, was formed.[1] The vigilance of those to whom the administration of justice and the immediate care of the police of the country is primarily entrusted, had already prevented or dispersed every numerous assembly of persons which resorted to public-houses for such purposes ; it therefore became necessary for persons thus disposed to assemble themselves to do so, if at all, within the walls of some private mansion. The president and head of this society, Mr. Thomas Walker, raised to that bad eminence by a species of merit which will not meet with much favour or encouragement here, opened his doors to receive a society of this sort at

[1] The Manchester Constitutional Society was instituted in October 1790 ; the Reformation Society in March 1792 ; the Patriotic Society in April 1792.

Manchester, miscalled the Reformation Society : the name may, in some senses, indeed import and be understood to mean a society formed for the purpose of beneficial reform ; but what the real purposes of this society were you will presently learn, from their declared sentiments and criminal actings. He opened his doors, then, to receive this society ; they assembled, night after night, in numbers, to an amount which you will hear from the witnesses. Sometimes, I believe, the extended number of such assemblies amounting to more than a hundred persons. There were three considerable rooms allotted for their reception. In the lower part of the house, where they were first admitted, they sat upon business of less moment, and requiring the presence of smaller numbers ; in the upper part, they assembled in greater multitudes, and read, as in a school, and as it were to fashion and perfect themselves in every thing that is seditious and mischievous, those writings which have been already reprobated by other juries sitting in this and other places, by the courts of law, and, in effect, by the united voice of both houses of parliament. They read, amongst other works, particularly, the works of an author whose name is in the mouth of every body in this country ; I mean the works of Thomas Paine ; an author, who, in the gloom of a French prison, is now contemplating the full effects and experiencing all the miseries of that disorganizing system of which he is, in some respect, the parent — certainly, the great advocate and promoter.

(b) From Thomas Walker, " A Review of some of the Political Events which have occurred in Manchester during the Last Five Years ", 1794, pp. 17-18.

MANCHESTER CONSTITUTIONAL SOCIETY
INSTITUTED OCTOBER, 1790

RESOLUTION I. That in every civil Community, the legitimate authority of the *Governors*, can only be derived from the consent of the *Governed*.

II. That the happiness of the people governed ought to be the sole end and aim of all civil government.

III. That public honours and emoluments can only be due for services conferred on the State.

IV. That every person, from the highest to the lowest, appointed to and accepting of any office or trust for the benefit of the Community, is ultimately responsible to the people for the complete discharge of the duties of it.

V. That *Actions* only, and not *Opinions*, are the proper objects of civil jurisdiction.

VI. That no Law or Statute can be fairly made, which is not enacted by and with the consent of a majority of the people, given either expressly by themselves, or by means of a full, fair, and adequate Representation.

VII. That the People of Great Britain are not fully, fairly, and adequately represented in Parliament; and that the defective state of the Representation of this country, and the extended duration of Parliaments, require a speedy and effectual reform, and are objects to which the attention of this Society ought to be particularly directed.

THE CHURCH AND KING CLUB,

Held at the house of Mr. Jonathan Foster, the Weaver's Arms, on Cockpit-Hill, Manchester, think it necessary, openly, in the following Declaration, to state their reasons for publishing their Principles.

DECLARATION.

This Society beholds with infinite concern the many dangerous plots and associations that are forming in different parts of this kingdom, for the avowed purpose of disseminating discord, and for subverting the order of one of the most beautiful systems of government, that the combined efforts of human wisdom has ever yet been able to accomplish.

When we see such *deadly wounds* aimed at our glorious constitution, we consider it the duty of all good citizens, publicly to step forward, and express their abhorrence of the malevolent and most wicked intentions of those disappointed men, who are audaciously clamorous for a reform in parliament, but whose real object is to excite civil commotion in this our *happy* and well-governed state.

We are far from believing, should they ever effect their purpose, (which Heaven forbid!) that the change would be for the better, but must always regard those persons as the bane of civil society, who have given so many proofs of an innate propensity for power, and of that restless ambition which has long been their most distinguished characteristic.

PRINCIPLES OF THE CHURCH AND KING CLUB.

It is a principle of this Society, to revere the Constitution and obey the King, according to the Laws of that Constitution.

It is a principle of this Society, to reprobate the wild theories and seditious doctrines respecting the Rights of Man, which have been lately promulgated by the enemies of our most excellent constitution in church and state, as they are subversive of all civil authority; and that, if they were put in practice, would tend to nothing but anarchy and confusion, which is contrary to all order.

It is a principle of this Society, that the Constitution of this country was renovated and fixed at the time of the glorious Revolution.

It is a principle of this Society, that the Constitution has not since that time been essentially departed from.

It is a principle of this Society, that the Legislature of this country ought ever to consist of King, Lords, and Commons.

It is a principle of this Society, that all other modes of legislation, than by King, Lords, and Commons, has always been found, by experience, repugnant to the genius of Englishmen.

It is a principle of this Society, that the Establishment in Church and State, is not to be altered but by the Legislature itself; consequently any other mode would be attended with extreme danger.

It is a principle of this Society that it is requisite in every good governed state, that there must exist an established Church, and that no one is to bear any office, either in church or state, but such as will conform, and be in communion with that church.

It is a principle of this Society, that the Corporation and Test Acts are the great bulwarks of our constitution in church and state, therefore ought never to be repealed.

It is a principle of this Society, that Toleration in religious matters is to be extended to Dissenters of every denomination.

Finally, it is the fixed determination of this Society, at all times and in all places, to avow and maintain the above principles to be truly constitutional.

Signed by Order of the Society.

W. NIGHTINGALE, President.

MANCHESTER, *June 23*, 1792.

(*c*) From Thomas Walker, " A Review of some of the Political Events which have occurred in Manchester during the Last Five Years ", pp. 47-8.

REFORMATION SOCIETY.[1]

The Manchester Reformation Society, finding that the meaning of the word Equality has been much misrepresented by their enemies, (who have asserted that the people wanted an equal Partition of Property) and this Society being chiefly composed of manufacturers, mechanics and labourers, who have been principally accused of wishing to divide the property of their neighbours amongst them, think it their duty, as men, to step forward, and flatly to deny this false accusation : they do therefore unanimously declare,

I. That what they want is Equality of Rights, and not of Property.

II. That by the word Equality, they understand, that a man (let him be ever so poor, provided he is a good citizen,) has as just a claim to an equal Partition of Rights, Liberties and Privileges, as the richest.

III. That the idea of *Equally* dividing Property is absurd and ridiculous, for was property *equal* one hour, it would be impossible to prevent its being *unequal* the next.

IV. That every Government which gives Rights and Privileges to vicious people, because they are opulent, and lets poor deserving merit starve and sink into oblivion, is not adapted to preserve the happiness and welfare of the people. A Government so constructed is consequently bad, and ought to be reformed.

V. That as all men come into the world alike, and go out alike ; the sun arises upon all and the rain falls equally on all ; we wish to see the *slave* rise to the dignified character of man, and let the most haughty tyrant *know* that he is but a man.

VI. That we should not have thought it necessary to declare our sentiments on this occasion to the public, had not our enemies (those contemptible Apostates, who formerly pretended to be the friends of Liberty and Equality, but whose tongues have been tyed by a long list of places and pensions) misinterpreted our meanings, and thereby attempted to make us appear, in the eyes of the world, as men who ought not to be trusted.

Signed, by order of the Society,

SAMUEL TENNANT, Secretary.

[1] The probable date of this declaration is 1792.

10. THE LOYAL ASSOCIATIONS

[The Association to preserve Liberty and Property against Republicans and Levellers was founded in November 1792, by John Reeves (1752?–1829), the historian of English Law, who also acted as Secretary under the name of ' J. Moore '. There is reason to suspect that he worked, to some extent, under Government auspices. His views were of the ' extreme right ' ; in fact he stressed the importance of the monarchy so much that in 1795 he was prosecuted (but acquitted) for a libel on the House of Commons. A mass of correspondence poured in from every part of the country, containing congratulations, pieces of information against seditious persons, and accounts of local loyalist activities. The Declarations of loyal associations were more or less standardised — a profession of great loyalty, a resolution to discover and suppress sedition, and, almost invariably, a threat to close public-houses frequented by reformers. (As Magistrates were very often members of these associations, the last threat would be only too easy to carry out.) These local associations were mainly spontaneous, but the London Association gave them encouragement and coherence. There is a collection of Reeves MSS. in the British Museum (Add. MSS. 16, 919-16, 931) ; the first five volumes of letters addressed to the Association cover only the period from November 21–December 31, 1792. This voluminous correspondence is a sign of the fears felt by the gentry.]

(*a*) Declaration of the Association to preserve Liberty and Property against Republicans and Levellers (1792). From *Debrett's Parliamentary Register*, vol. xxxiv, p. 26.

We do hereby resolve and declare as follows :—

First — That the persons present at this meeting do become a society for discouraging and suppressing seditious publications, tending to disturb the peace of this kingdom, and for supporting a due execution of the laws made for the protection of persons and property.

Secondly — That this society do use its best endeavours to explain those topics of public discussion which have been so prevented by evil designing men, and to show, by irrefragable proof, that they are not applicable to the state of this country, that they can produce no good, and certainly must produce great evil.

Thirdly — That this society will receive with great thanks all communications that shall be made to it for the above purposes.

Fourthly — That it be recommended to all those, who are friends to the established law, and to peaceable society, to form themselves, in their different neighbourhoods, into similar societies for promoting the same laudable purposes.

Fifthly — That this society do meet at this place or elsewhere every Tuesday, Thursday and Saturday.

Sixthly — That these considerations and resolutions be printed in all the public papers and otherwise circulated in all parts of the kingdom.

(*b*) From the Reeves MSS. in British Museum, 16,921 f. 73 [1792].

Borough of Great Yarmouth. } At a Court of Mayoralty held in and for the said Borough, the 8th day of Dec., 1792.

EDMUND LACON, ESQ., MAYOR.

The Magistrates having received Information that certain Persons are in the Habit of frequently assembling at several Public Houses, within this Borough, and there forming Clubs and Associations, and reading libellous Publications, and holding seditious Discourses, tending to deceive, and render the Unwary discontented in their Stations, and to disturb the Public Peace, think it proper to give Notice to all Publicans and Ale-House-Keepers in this Borough, that it is expected from them strictly to observe the several Rules and Conditions contained in their Licences; and that if any such illegal Meetings are held at their Houses, their Licences will not in Future be renewed.

11. THE TRIAL OF THOMAS MUIR

[Thomas Muir of Huntershill (1765–1798), university graduate and advocate, was not an unusual type in the Reform movement of Scotland, where the franchise was even more restricted than in England. Personally, Muir seems to have been a brilliant and striking figure, and his name was long remembered in the Reform movement. He was sentenced to fourteen years' transportation after a trial conducted by Lord Braxfield, which displayed judicial bias at its worst. In 1796 he was rescued from Botany Bay by an American vessel, but was subsequently shipwrecked, captured by American Indians, and finally wounded in an engagement between English vessels of war and a Spanish frigate, on which he was being sent to Europe. He died of his wound after reaching France, where he was given a public welcome.

The Treason Trials connected with the French Revolution began in Scotland, where the tradition of Government repression had been well established since Jacobite days and discontent was much more widespread among the educated classes than in England.]

From the summing-up by Lord Braxfield in the trial of Thomas Muir. From " State Trials ", vol. xxiii, p. 229.

The question then, gentlemen, for your consideration is simply this : On the whole of the proof led, when taken in connexion, do you think the panel guilty of sedition or not ? Now in examining this question, there are two things which you should attend to, which require no proof. The first is, that the British Constitution is the best in the world ; — for the truth of this, gentlemen, I need only appeal to your own feelings. Is not every man secure in his life, liberty, and property ? Is not happiness in the power of every man, except those perhaps, who, from disappointment in their schemes of advancement are discontented ? Does not every man enjoy unmolested the fruits of his industry ? And does not every man sit safely under his own vine and his own fig tree, and none shall make him afraid ? The other circumstance, gentlemen, which you have to attend to, is the state of this country during last winter. There was a spirit of sedition and revolt going abroad which made every good subject seriously uneasy. I observed the reflection of the master of the Grammar School of Glasgow, who told Mr. Muir, he conceived that proposing reform then was very ill-timed ; I coincide in that opinion, and leave it for you to judge, whether it was perfectly innocent or not in Mr. Muir, at such a time, to go about among ignorant country people, and among the lower classes of the people, making them leave off their work, and inducing them to believe that a reform was absolutely necessary to preserve their safety and their liberty, which had it not been for him, they never would have suspected to have been in danger. You will keep this in remembrance, and judge whether it appears to you, as to me, to be sedition.

12. THE COMMITTEE OF SECRECY, 1794

[In 1794 a committee, whose proceedings were to be secret, was appointed by the House of Commons to investigate the strength and intentions of the Reform movement. The two Reports of this ' Committee of Secrecy ', as it was called, are valuable, not as a factual record, but as an indication of the exaggerated fears of the Government and the ruling classes. There is little evidence to support the Committee's assertion that the English Reform groups up and down the country were acting in secret revolutionary concert, or, apart from the Sheffield letter (Extract (c), p. 68), that they were plotting a violent revolution. The Reports were, however, accepted as accurate by the upper-class public, and the Government felt able to be relentless in its prosecutions.]

(*a*) From the First Report of the Committee of Secrecy (1794), p. 42.

From a Review of these Transactions your Committee feels it impossible not to conclude, that the Measures which have been stated are directed to the object of assembling a Meeting which, under the Name of a General Convention, may take upon itself the Character of a General Representative of the People. However at different periods the Term of Parliamentary Reform may have been employed, it is obvipus that the present View of these Societies is not intended to be prosecuted by any Application to Parliament, but on the contrary, by an open attempt to supersede the House of Commons in its Representative Capacity, and to assume to itself all the Functions and Powers of a National Legislature.

(*b*) From the First Report of the Committee of Secrecy (1794), p. 44.

When in addition to these Considerations, the Committee reflect on the leading Circumstances which they have already stated, of the declared Approbation, at an early Period, of the Doctrine of the Rights of Man, as stated in Paine's Publications; of the Connection and Intercourse with French Societies, and with the National Convention; and of the subsequent Approbation of the French System; and consider that these are the Principles which the Promoters of a Convention evidently make the Foundation of all their Proceedings; they are satisfied that the Design now openly professed and acted upon aims at nothing less than what is stated in His Majesty's message, and must be considered as a Traitorous Conspiracy for the Subversion of the established Laws and Constitution, and the Introduction of that System of Anarchy and Confusion which has fatally prevailed in France.

(*c*) From the Second Report of the Committee of Secrecy (1794), p. 2.

SHEFFIELD, *April* 24, 1794.

FELLOW CITIZENS,

The barefaced aristocracy of the present administration has made it necessary that we should be prepared to act on the defensive against any attack they may command their newly armed minions to make upon us. A plan has been hit upon; and if encouraged sufficiently will, no doubt, have the effect of furnishing a quantity of pikes to the patriots, great enough to make them formidable. The blades are made of steel, tempered and polished after an approved form. They may be fixed into any shafts; but fir ones are recommended, of the girth of the accompanying hoops at the top end, and about an inch more at the bottom. The blades and hoops, more than which cannot be properly sent to any great distance, will be charged one shilling. Money to be sent with the order. As the institution is in its infancy, immediate encouragement is necessary.

Struck through in ⎱ Orders may be sent to the Secretary of the Sheffield
the original. ⎰ Constitutional Club.

(*d*) From the Second Report of the Committee of Secrecy (1794), p. 15.

From what has been stated it appears, that the Design of arming, as far as it has as yet proceeded, has been conducted with great Secrecy and Caution, and at the same time with a great Degree of Uniformity and Concert in Parts of the Kingdom remote from each other. The weapons principally provided seem to have been peculiarly calculated for the purposes of sudden Violence, and to have been chosen in Conformity to the Example of what has recently passed in France. The Actual Progress made in the Execution of the Design, during the short Period of a few Weeks, sufficiently shews what might have been expected, if the Societies had proceeded, without Interruption, in Increasing the Number of their Members, and the Fund for providing Arms.

13. THE TREASON TRIALS OF 1794

[The Treason Trials of 1794, in which the leaders of the London Corresponding Society and some members of the Constitutional Society were indicted for Treasonable Conspiracy, were the sequel to the Reports of the Committees of Secrecy. The acquittal of Thomas Hardy and John Horne Tooke by the London jury, and the dropping of the cases against the remaining prisoners after these acquittals, appeared at the time to be a great triumph for the Radical cause. The outcome did not, however, prevent the Government from proceeding successfully against many Radicals in other parts of the country, as it had done in Scotland; and even in London the fears aroused by the trials and the Government's attitude led to the break-up of the Constitutional Society and to many secessions from the Corresponding Society, which was driven underground and turned into a conspiratorial body by the repression.]

From "The Trial at Large of Thomas Hardy for High Treason", October 28 to November 5, 1794. Reported by John Newton, 1794.

Extracts from Lord Chief Justice Eyre's Charge to the Grand Jury.

. . . It is a matter of public notoriety, that there have been

Associations formed in this country, as well as in other parts of the kingdom, in order to effect a change in the constitution of the commons house of parliament, and to obtain annual parliaments; and to some of these Associations, other purposes, hidden under the veil, purposes the most traitorous, have been imputed : and that some of these associations have been supposed to have actually adopted measures of such a nature, and to have gone to such excesses, as will amount to the crime of high treason. . . .

Gentlemen, I shall not now state to you, that Associations and assemblies of men, for the purpose of obtaining a reform in the interior constitution of the British parliament, are simply unlawful; but, on the other hand, I must state, they may, if I may say so, degenerate and become unlawful in the highest degree, even to the enormous extent of the crime of high treason. Gentlemen, to prove this, let us imagine to ourselves this case : A few well-meaning men conceive, that they and their fellow-subjects labour under some grievance. They assemble peaceably to deliberate on the means of obtaining redress. The number increases, the discussion grows animated, eager, and violent. A rash measure is proposed, adopted, and acted upon. Who can say where this will stop, and that those men who originally assembled peaceably, shall not finally and suddenly, perhaps, involve themselves in the crime of high treason ? It is impossible to say how far an impetuous man may precipitate such assemblies into crimes of unforeseen magnitude and danger. But let it be considered, that bad men may also find their way into such assemblies, and use the innocent purpose of their association as a stalking horse to their purposes of a very different complexion. How easy for such men to practise on the credulity and enthusiasm of honest men, lovers of their country, loyal to their prince, but perhaps eagerly bent on some speculative improvement in the frame and interior mechanism of the law. If we suppose bad men to have once gained an ascendency in an assembly of this description, popular in its constitution, and viewing popular objects, it will be easy for such men to implicate such an assembly in the most dreadful excesses. Thus far am I speaking in general, merely to illustrate this proposition; that men who assemble to procure a reform in parliament, may involve themselves in the guilt of high treason. The notoriety of these associations leads me to suppose, that the project of a Convention of the people, to be assembled under the advice and direction of some of those societies, or of delegates from them, will be the leading fact, which will be laid before you in evidence, respecting the conduct and measures of these associations; a project which, perhaps in other times, would be hardly thought worthy of much consideration; but in these our days, when it has been attempted to put in execution, in a distant part of the united kingdom, and the example of a neighbouring country before our eyes, it has become deservedly an object of the jealousy of the law. . . .

. . . I presume I have sufficiently explained to you, that a project to bring the people together in a Convention, in imitation of those National Conventions of France, in order to usurp the government of the country; and also one step taken towards bringing it about, would be a case of no difficulty. It would be the clearest high treason. It would be compassing and imagining the king's death, and not only his death, but the death and destruction of all order, religion, law, all property, all security for the lives and liberties of the king's subjects.

That which remains to be considered, is the project of a convention, having for its objects to effect a change in the mode of representing the people, and obtaining annual parliaments. . . . In deciding on the complexion and quality of this project of convention, you will lay down one principle, which is never to be departed from — that alterations in the representation of the people in parliament, or in the law for holding parliaments, can only be effected by the authority of king, lords, and commons, in parliament assembled.

This being taken as a foundation, it seems to follow as a necessary consequence, that a project of a convention, which should have for its object the obtaining a parliamentary reform, and that object only but the attaining it without the authority of parliament, and steps taken upon it, would be high treason in all the actors of it. For this is a conspiracy to overturn the government.

. . . Gentlemen, whether the project of a Convention, which has for its object the collecting together a power which should over-awe the Legislative Body, but not suspend it, and should extort a Parliamentary Reform — whether this will amount to High Treason, and to the specific High Treason of compassing and imagining the King's death, is a more doubtful question.

. . . I go on to state to you as clear, that the project of a Convention, having for its sole object a peaceable application to the wisdom of Parliament, by petition for a Parliamentary Reform, and leaving it to Parliament to exercise their own discretion on the subject, cannot of itself be ranked among this class of offences.

Gentlemen, you now proceed on these several articles of inquiry.

If you find that the parties that shall be accused before you, have been pursuing lawful ends by lawful means, or have been only indiscreet, or, at the worst, if criminal, that they have not been criminal to extent of High Treason, then say, the bills that shall be presented to you are not true bills. But if any of those persons shall appear to you to have engaged in that traiterous and detestible conspiracy already described; or if, without any formal design to go to the full length of that conspiracy, they have acted a part to bring about an alteration in the House of Commons, without the authority of Parliament, by an usurped power, and have taken upon themselves the function of Legislation, and conspired to subvert the existing Laws and Constitution, you will then do that which belongs to your office to do.

In the third view of the case of these persons, if you find them involved and proceeding on a design to collect people together against the legislative authority of the country, for the purpose of overawing the Parliament, but not suspending its functions, and so compelling the King, Lords, and Commons, in Parliament assembled, to enact laws for holding Annual Parliaments, etc. perhaps it may be admitted, in respect of the extraordinary nature, the dangerous extent, and the very criminal complexion of such a conspiracy, that this case, which I state as new and doubtful, should be put into a judicial course of enquiry, that it may be known whether it does or does not amount to High Treason. . . .

14. THE NAVAL MUTINIES OF 1797

[To many the naval mutinies of 1797 at Spithead and the Nore seemed an additional proof that the French and their allies, the wicked Jacobins in England, were plotting to ruin England. It is probably true that the ideas of liberty, which had been in circulation since the French Revolution, influenced at least some of the leaders of the mutinies; and some of the mutineers may have come from homes or districts where the Reformers had been strong; certainly, too, there were numerous Irishmen in the Fleet, including some followers of Wolfe Tone, the Irish revolutionary leader. But there is no evidence at all that either Wolfe Tone's " United Irishmen " or any of the English Reform societies had any hand in organising the mutinies; and the sailors were unquestionably anti-French. The mutinies were spontaneous : there was no deep plot.

The story of the United Irishmen and the Rebellion of '98 lies outside our field unless we accept, with the 1799 Committee of Secrecy, the story that they were planning to land a force in England and stage a revolution with the London Corresponding Society. The fears of French influence in Ireland and a consequent attack on England through Ireland had long been a cause of the Government's desire to stamp out all traces of ' sedition ' in England.]

THE MUTINY AT THE NORE

Manifesto of the Delegates to their Countrymen : Address handed to Lord Northesk on June, 6, 1797. From " Revolution from 1789 to 1906 ", by R. W. Postgate, 1923.

THE DELEGATES OF THE DIFFERENT SHIPS AT THE NORE ASSEMBLED IN COUNCIL, TO THEIR FELLOW-SUBJECTS :—

COUNTRYMEN,

It is to you particularly that we owe an explanation of our conduct. His Majesty's Ministers too well know our intentions, which are founded on the laws of humanity, honour and national safety — long since trampled underfoot by those who ought to have been friends to us — the sole protectors of your laws and property. The public prints teem with falsehoods and misrepresentations to induce you to credit things as far from our design as the conduct of those at the helm of national affairs is from honesty or common decorum.

Shall we who have endured the toils of a tedious, disgraceful war, be the victims of tyranny and oppression which vile, gilded, pampered knaves, wallowing in the lap of luxury, choose to load us with ? Shall we, who amid the rage of the tempests and the war of jarring elements, undaunted climb the unsteady cordage and totter on the topmast's dreadful height, suffer ourselves to be treated worse than the dogs of London Streets ? Shall we, who in the battle's sanguinary rage, confound, terrify and subdue your proudest foe, guard your coasts from invasion, your children from slaughter, and your lands from pillage — be the footballs and shuttlecocks of a set of tyrants who derive from us alone their honours, their titles and their fortunes ? No, the Age of Reason has at length revolved. Long have we been endeavouring to find ourselves men. We now find ourselves so. We will be treated as such. Far, very far, from us is the idea of subverting the government of our beloved country. We have the highest opinion of our Most Gracious Sovereign, and we hope none of those measures taken to deprive us of the common rights of men have been instigated by him.

You cannot, countrymen, form the most distant idea of the slavery under which we have for many years laboured. Rome had her Neros and Caligulas, but how many characters of their description might we not mention in the British Fleet — men without the least tincture of humanity, without the faintest spark of virtue, education or abilities, exercising the most wanton acts of cruelty over those whom dire misfortune or patriotic zeal may have placed in their power — basking in the sunshine of prosperity, whilst we (need we repeat who we are ?) labour under every distress which the breast of inhumanity can suggest. The British seaman has often with justice been compared to the lion — gentle, generous and humane — no one would certainly wish to hurt such an animal. Hitherto we have laboured for our sovereign and you. We are now obliged to think for ourselves, for there are many (nay, most of us) in the Fleet who have been prisoners since the commencement of the War, without receiving a single farthing. Have we not a right to complain ? Let His Majesty but order us to be paid and the little grievances we have made known redressed, we shall enter with alacrity upon any employment for the defence of our country; but until that is complied with we are determined to stop all commerce and intercept all provisions, for our own subsistence. The military have had their pay augmented, to insult as well as to enslave you. Be not appalled. We will adopt the words of a celebrated motto [*Dieu et mon droit*] and defy all attempts to deceive us. We do not wish to adopt the plan of a neighbouring nation, however it may have been suggested ; but we sell our lives dearly to maintain what we have demanded. Nay, countrymen, more : We have already discovered the tricks of Government in supplying our enemies with different commodities, and a few days will probably lead to something more. In the meantime,

We remain, Dear Countrymen,

Yours affectionately,[1]

15. REPRESSIVE LEGISLATION, 1795–1800

[Between 1795 and 1800 a powerful series of repressive Acts crushed the Radical and working-class movements. In 1795 two were passed ; one (36 Geo. III, c. 7) made it a treasonable offence to invite the population to hatred or contempt of the Crown or Government, the other (see (*a*) below) was directed against the right of public meeting. The panic

[1] This text is that prepared for printing (Wilson's copy). Lord Northesk's ends : " Your loving Brothers, Red for Ever ".

aroused by the naval mutinies of 1797 produced not only Acts dealing specifically with mutineers (37 Geo. III, c. 70 & c. 71), but also the Unlawful Oaths Act (see (*b*) below), under which the Tolpuddle Martyrs were convicted thirty-seven years later. In the following year the Newspaper Act (38 Geo. III, c. 78) checked the written expression of popular discontent, partly by a system of registration which made it easy for the Government to punish the printers and publishers of sedition, and partly by imposing a high Stamp Tax on newspapers, which made them too dear to have a wide circulation. Then, after the Irish Rebellion of 1798, when the Government half-feared that the French might attack from Ireland and be assisted by the reformers in England, a final Act was passed to suppress the remaining reform societies (see (*c*) below). The Combination Acts of 1799 and 1800 rounded off this wholesale attack on popular liberties (see next section). Except for the two Acts of 1795 there was little organised opposition to this repression, and even then little was done once the Bills had been passed by Parliament.]

(*a*) From an Act for the more Effectively Preventing Seditious Meetings and Assemblies, 1795. (36 Geo. III, c. 8.)

WHEREAS assemblies of divers persons, collected for the purpose or under the pretext of deliberating on publick grievances, and of agreeing on petitions, complaints, remonstrances, declarations, or other addresses to the King, or to both houses, or either house of parliament have of late been made use of to serve the ends of factious and seditious persons, to the great danger of the publick peace, and may become the means of producing confusion and calamities in the nation: be it enacted. . . . That no meeting, of any description of persons, exceeding the number of fifty persons (other than and except any meeting of any county, riding, or division, called by the lord lieutenant, custos rotulorum, or sheriff, of such county . . . or any meeting of any corporate body), shall be holden, for the purpose or on the pretext of considering or preparing any petition, complaint, remonstrance, or declaration or other address to the King, or to both houses, or to either house of parliament, for alteration of matters established in church, or state, or for the purpose or on the pretext of deliberating upon any grievance on church or state, unless notice of the intention to hold such a meeting, and of the time and place, when and where the same shall be proposed to be holden, and of the purpose for which the same shall be proposed to be holden, shall be given, in the names of seven persons at the least, being householders resident within the county, city or place where such meeting shall be proposed to be holden. . . .

. . . .

IV. And be it enacted, That if any persons, exceeding the number of fifty, being assembled contrary to the provisions hereinbefore contained and being required or commanded . . . to disperse themselves, and peaceably to depart to their habitations, or to their lawful business, shall, to the number of twelve or more, notwithstanding such proclamation made, remain or continue together by the space of one hour after such command or request made by proclamation, that then . . . the offenders therein shall be adjudged felons and shall suffer death, as in the case of felony without benefit of clergy.

. . . .

XII. *And whereas certain houses, rooms or places, within the cities of LONDON and WESTMINSTER, and in the neighbourhood thereof, and in other places, have of late been frequently used for the purpose of delivering lectures and discourses on and concerning supposed publick grievances, and matters relating to the laws, constitution, and government and policy of these kingdoms, and treating and debating on and concerning the same; and under pretence thereof lectures on discourses have been delivered, and debates held, tending to stir up hatred and contempt of his Majesty's royal person, and of the government and constitution of this realm as by law established:* be it therefore enacted . . . that every house, room, field, or other place where lectures or discourses shall be delivered, and publick debates shall be had on or concerning any supposed publick grievances . . . unless the opening or using of such house, room, field, or place shall have been previously licenced in manner hereinafter mentioned, shall be deemed a disorderly house or place, and the person by whom such house, room, field or place shall be opened or used for the purpose aforesaid, shall forfeit the sum of one hundred pounds for every day or time that such house, room, field or place shall be opened or used as aforesaid, to such person as will sue for the same, and be otherwise punished as the law directs in cases of disorderly houses. . . .

(*b*) From an Act for more Effectually Preventing the Administering or Taking of Unlawful Oaths, 1797. (37 Geo. III, c. 123.)

WHEREAS divers wicked and evil-disposed persons, have of late attempted to seduce persons serving in his Majesty's services by sea and land, and others of his Majesty's subjects, from their duty and allegiance to his Majesty, and to incite them to acts of mutiny and sedition, and have endeavoured to give effect to their wicked and traitor-

ous proceedings, by imposing upon the persons whom they have attempted
to seduce the pretended obligations of oaths unlawfully administered:
be it enacted . . . that any person or persons who shall, in any matter
or form whatsoever, administer or cause to be administered, or be
aiding or assisting at, or present at and consenting to, the administering or taking of any oath or engagement, purporting or intended to
bind the person taking the same to engage in any mutinous or
seditious purpose; or to disturb the publick peace; or to be of any
association, society, or confederacy, formed for any such purpose; or
not to inform or give evidence against any associate, confederate, or
other person; or not to reveal or discover any unlawful combination
or confederacy, or not to reveal or discover any illegal act done or
to be done; or not to reveal or discover any illegal oath or engagement which may have been administered or tendered to or taken by
such person or persons, or to or by any other person or persons, or
the import of any such oath or engagement; shall, on conviction
thereof by due course of law, be adjudged guilty of felony, and may
be transported for any term of years not exceeding seven years;
and any person who shall take any such oath or engagement, not
being compelled thereto, shall, on conviction thereof by due course
of law, be adjudged guilty of felony, and may be transported for any
term of years not exceeding seven years.

(c) From the Corresponding Societies Act, 1799. (39 Geo. III, c. 79.)

Be it enacted . . . that from and after the passing of this Act,
all the said Societies of United Englishmen, United Scotsmen,
United Irishmen, and United Britons, and the said Society commonly
called the London Corresponding Society, and all other Societies
called Corresponding Societies, of any other City, Town or Place,
shall be, and the same are hereby utterly suppressed and prohibited, as
being unlawful Combinations and Confederacies against the Government of Our Sovereign Lord the King, and against the Peace and
Security of His Majesty's liege subjects.

16. THE RADICAL REVIVAL, 1806–1807

[The revival of Radicalism began in 1806, with the advent of the
Ministry of All the Talents, which raised in many men hopes both of an
end to the war and of reforms of the ' Pitt system '. Cobbett at first
shared in these hopes; but very soon he realised that they would be

disappointed, and went into opposition to his former friends, offering himself as Radical candidate for Honiton in an address in which he gave a pledge subsequently reiterated by many Radical candidates. In the event Cobbett withdrew in favour of Lord Cochrane, who was defeated on this occasion, but won the seat at the ensuing General Election. The same year, Francis Place and a group of Westminster tradesmen and artisans set on foot the Westminster Radical movement, which thereafter occupied a leading position in the development of working-class Radicalism. The Westminster Radicals did not win in 1806; but the following year they succeeded in electing Sir Francis Burdett and Lord Cochrane (who had left Honiton) for the two seats. Westminster was one of the few boroughs which had a wide ' scot and lot ' franchise, so that most of the skilled workers were able to vote.]

(*a*) From *Cobbett's Weekly Political Register*, June 7, 1806.

As to professions, Gentlemen, so many and so loud, upon such occasions, have they been; so numerous are the instances, in which the foulness and shamelessness of the apostacy have borne an exact proportion to the purity and solemnity of the vow; so completely, and with such fatal effect, have the grounds of confidence been destroyed, that, it is now become necessary, upon all occasions like the present, to give a pledge, such as every man can clearly understand, and such as it is impossible to violate without exposing the violator to detection and to all the consequences of detected hypocrisy and falsehood; and such a pledge I now give in declaring, that, whether you elect me or not, I never as long as I live, either for myself, or for, or through the means of, any one of my family, will receive, under any name, whether of salary, pension or other, either directly or indirectly, one single farthing of the public money; but, without emolument, compensation, or reward of any kind or in any shape, will, to the utmost of my ability, watch over and defend the property, the liberties and the privileges of the people, never therefrom separating, as I never yet have, the just and constitutional rights and prerogatives of the crown.

．　．　．　．　．　．

But, Gentlemen, as it is my firm determination never to receive a farthing of the public money, so it is my determination equally firm, never, in any way whatever, to give one farthing of my own money to any man, in order to induce him to vote, or to cause others to vote, for me; and, being convinced, that it is this practice of giving, or promising to give, money, or money's worth, at elections, being convinced, that it is this disgraceful, this unlawful, this profligate, this impious practice, to which are to be ascribed all our calamities and all the dangers that now stare us in the face, I cannot refrain from exhorting you to be against all attempts at such practices, constantly and watchfully upon your guard.

(*b*) From the Place MSS., 27,850 ff. 19-20 [1806].

WESTMINSTER POLITICS, 1806

. . . My indignation was greatly increased when I saw the servants of the Duke of Northumberland, in their showy dress liveries, throwing lumps of bread and cheese among the dense crowd of vagabonds they had collected together. To see these vagabonds catching the lumps, shouting, swearing, fighting, and blackguarding in every possible way, women as well as men, all the vile wretches from the courts and alleys in St. Giles and Westminster, the Porridge Islands, and other miserable places ; to see these people representing, as it was said, the electors of Westminster, was certainly the lowest possible step of degradation, except, indeed, if it be possible, to hear it said, as it was said, that ' the electors of Westminster had been treated by the bounty of the Duke.' Some who mingled in the mob were ashamed of the proceedings, and as the mob pressed round the butts which contained the beer, suggested that the best way would be to knock in the heads as they stood up on end. This was done immediately. The heads were beaten in, and the coal-heavers ladled the beer out with their long-tailed, broad-brimmed hats ; but the mob pressing on, the butts were upset, and the beer flowed along the gutters, from whence some made efforts to obtain it. It may be possible to imagine something like the disgraceful scene, but it is not possible either to describe it or to excite in the reader the almost uncontrollable feelings of a spectator. I was not the only one who felt indignation. Almost every man I knew was much offended with the whole of the proceedings and with all who were concerned in them.

(*c*) From the Place MSS., 27,838 ff. 19-20 [1807].

THE WESTMINSTER ELECTION OF 1807

Our attempt became the scorn and contempt of Whigs and Tories, not a single morning paper could be said to be with us, most of them were pointblank against us. They were all either for Whigs or Tories, not one for the people. They derided us no little, and laughed us to scorn. What a parcel of people who were nobody, common tailors, and Barbers and snobs, to presume to carry Westminster. We were laughed at for our folly, and condemned for our impudence and dishonesty, in exciting people to tumults under a pretence of making an election, when we knew we had no chance of success. We cared but little for this, we were resolved to put an end if possible to all tumult and violence, to all treating, to all carousing, to bribery and perjury. . . .

On Thursday, May 7, the Election commenced.

The time between Monday and Thursday was spent in making preparations and procuring assistance by inlisting volunteers. Some rooms, not very convenient rooms, were taken at a Gin Shop called the Britannia Coffee House, for which we paid down £45. This and the printing Books for the Poll Clerks, for the Inspectors, and for the Committee, left us but little money to commence the election. It had been usual to pay every check clerk, and every clerk in the committee rooms a guinea a day. This we reduced to half a guinea a day for each of the check clerks and each of the committee clerks. Two constables were paid, 5/- a day each. Inspectors on the Hustings had been paid from two to five guineas a day. These we supplied as well as we could with volunteers; to whom we paid nothing. Canvassers had been paid from one to five guineas a day. These we found in volunteers and paid nothing. Attornies had always received large sums; and counsel on the hustings from ten to twenty guineas a day; we resolved to employ neither, to get what gratuitous assistance we could and to make that do. The High Bailiff had for many years made a large sum by elections. We resolved that the present High Bailiff should make nothing of us. . . . Our desire was to make a public,[1] and at the same time to put an end to all the disgraceful practices which had prevailed. I had a room to myself on the third floor in the house in which the committee sat, and no one except Mr. Brooks the Treasurer was to have access to that room save upon business with me. Every sort of information was sent to me, I had Lemaitre and Richter to assist during such times as they attended; all literary matters were wholly performed by us. All orders came from me during the day and in the evening I reported to the General Committee. Mr. J. Clayton Jennings became our orator on the hustings, he always came to the committee rooms before going to the Hustings, to learn the particulars which it was necessary for him to know, and he filled his office with much good sense and discretion. Nothing meaning expense could be

[1] ? Word left out in original.

ordered, unless by a sub-committee appointed for the purpose or by the Treasurer on leave given by the General Committee and no order could be given at all, but, upon a printed check, signed by those authorised to sign, and countersigned by the Treasurer. Every such order contained quantities and prices, or named services to be performed. . . .

On the morning of the election several of my coadjutors were very much depressed, we had no money, no means of making a display, nobody had joined us, the Tories despised us and the Whigs derided us. It was the being laughed at that produced the worst effect of all . . . those who could well have borne to have been abused could not bear to be laughed at.

TRADE UNIONISM TO 1815

INTRODUCTION

TRADE UNIONISM as a national movement was a product of the Industrial Revolution. But long before this, combinations of the employed had become a familiar feature of English life. Sporadic, and usually short-lived, combinations had appeared from an early date, some even in the Middle Ages; and by the eighteenth century they were becoming more numerous, stable, and effective, at any rate among the skilled artisans in a number of urban crafts. As yet, only a small section were capable of organising themselves. The vast mass who earned their living on the land, the many thousands in the personal service of the rich, and the unskilled ' mobs ' of the cities — these together formed a much larger section of the wage-earning classes than to-day, and there could be no prospect of organisation among them, though there might be rioting, especially in periods of exceptional scarcity. Moreover, some wage-earners, at any rate in market-towns and villages, had subsidiary occupations — perhaps a plot of land to supplement what they earned by following a trade; and some could still reasonably expect to become masters or at any rate semi-independent producers. The ' labouring poor ' formed a very heterogeneous class; there were among them, however, life-long wage-earners, skilled craftsmen who were building up Trade Unions with a continuous existence.

In many of the skilled trades the growth of capitalist enterprise had made it harder to climb the ladder from apprentice to master; so the journeymen, growing conscious that they had no hope of advancement, used their Trade Clubs — which often began primarily as Friendly Societies — more and more as Trade Unions to defend or better their conditions. In the woollen industry, combinations appeared in the West of England, where the merchant capitalists were gaining control of the manufacture and reducing the weaver to the status of a wage-earner under the domestic system. As early as 1718 a Royal Proclamation was issued against the weavers' unlawful clubs, combinations, etc., which were alleged to have evolved an elaborate organisation strong enough to dictate terms to the employers through strikes and the use of violence. The weavers, working scattered over whole counties under large-scale merchant employers, could not hope to make their combinations effective unless they joined forces over a wide area. Unlike the urban artisans, they could not hope to bargain on a narrow local basis; for the merchant could easily play off one local group against another. Accordingly such combinations as the weavers managed to create usually extended over a whole county, and sometimes over a still wider area. But, unlike the local Trade Clubs of the artisans, they were unable to maintain a continuous existence. They were ephemeral bodies, disappearing with the emergency that called them into being. Nevertheless they were frequent, and at times powerful. On the other hand, we hear comparatively little of combinations in large-scale enterprises. The miners, as far as we know, had no permanent organisation in any of the coalfields. In the engineering and iron industries Trade Unions developed among the specialist workers (such as scissor-smiths and nail-makers and later among the millwrights), but not among the less skilled. The urban artisans, on the other hand, were for the most part little affected by the factory system till long after it had superseded the older methods in the textile trades; and their local Trade Clubs actually grew stronger as the demand for skilled labour rose in consequence of the general advance in production. The methods of organisation, however, altered for them also. In the eighteenth century both groups habitually sought the protection of authority for their claims.

Since the Elizabethan Statute of Artificers there had been a tradition that the State should regulate labour conditions: and, when the weaver or artisan had a grievance he sooner or later appealed to Parliament or to the law for help — against low wages, long hours, truck payments, or, above all, the non-observance of the apprenticeship regulations of the Elizabethan statute. The town artisans, for the most part, confined themselves to purely local Trade Clubs, and looked to the State to enforce the regulations of apprenticeship rather than to determine wages. The weavers, on the other hand, working under more competitive conditions and for a wider market, aimed more at wage regulation than at the control of apprenticeship, though limitations of the number of apprentices also figured on occasion among their demands. At first, Parliament often listened to the workers' case with sympathy, granting some of their claims but, at the same time, limiting their right to combine in the future.

But from the middle of the century the policy of Parliament was changing. The masters' argument that regulations were unnecessary and harmful now carried more weight than the labourers' appeal for protection : trade after trade was ' freed ' from restrictions.

With this change the State attitude towards combinations became more and more hostile. As long as the principle of State protection had been considered natural, combinations to appeal for or to enforce such regulations could plead some justification. But the weakening of that principle led to an increase in the hostility of Parliament and of the law to all combinations. Then a crop of war-time strikes in the skilled trades and the general fear of the working class aroused by the French Revolution helped to create the atmosphere in which the Combination Acts (1799–1800) were passed. The hostility to Trade Unions was crystallised in a single statute which banned them all and simplified the procedure for prosecution.

These laws were savagely administered in the new industrial districts of the North and held back the progress of Trade Unions among the factory workers. But in many trades their effect was inconsiderable. The skilled artisans did not abandon or always conceal their combinations ; indeed, some employers were prepared to accept the principle of collective bargaining : the journeymen cabinetmakers, for instance, were able to frame in agreement with the employers an elaborate scale of prices, which was published. The attempt to secure State protection was continued. Some trades united to pay a lawyer to prosecute masters who employed ' illegal men ' (*i.e.* men not duly apprenticed) ; but, when they won, no costs were awarded in their favour, and, when they lost, heavy costs were awarded against them. The weavers and framework knitters employed by the merchant clothiers and hosiers in the Midlands and the South also found it possible to combine in defence of their standard of life, with no considerable obstruction from the Combination Laws. But this policy was soon to meet with a final defeat. The attempt to enforce old, long-neglected statutes by legal action led merely to the repeal of these statutes. In 1808 a third Minimum Wage Bill was, like its predecessors in 1795 and 1800, decisively rejected. In 1811 Lord Ellenborough (in Rex *v.* Justices of Kent) ruled that in the newer trades (such as engineering) the justices had a purely discretionary power to fix wages : justices, of course, were unlikely to make any use of this power. Finally, in 1813–1814, the wage and apprenticeship clauses of the Statute of Artificers were repealed, the principle of protection was finally disowned, and labour was left to find its price in the competitive market.

Peaceful agitation had consistently failed; but, largely on account of the Combination Acts, strike movements were not frequent. However, there were a number of strikes in the skilled trades, a great mining strike in 1810, and two strike movements in the textile industry (1808 and 1812), and the machine-wrecking Luddite Movement, the most dramatic of all. (See Section V.)

See " Short History ", Part I, chapter 4, section 1.
" Common People ", chapter 14.

1. TRADE UNIONS AND THE LAW BEFORE 1799.

[The legal position of Trade Unions in eighteenth-century England is still obscure, as we have not enough records of local cases. A distinction seems to have been made between combinations to enforce apprenticeship laws or wage regulations and independent combinations to raise wages or reduce hours. The former were not prosecuted, the latter were attacked in several ways. The 1548 Bill of Conspiracies of Victuallers and Craftsmen (see (*a*)) was a general statute against such combinations. In practice it was not much used, and during the century Parliament passed a series of statutes prohibiting combinations in particular trades, these prohibitions being usually coupled with regulations concerning apprentices, truck payments, and, occasionally, hours of work. It was also often argued that combinations were in restraint of trade and therefore illegal at common law (this idea underlies the Bill of Conspiracies). In addition, the theory that combinations were criminal on grounds of public policy had been hinted at in early cases (such as Rex *v.* the Journeymen Tailors of Cambridge, 1721), and was explicitly used to convict the Journeymen Printers in the 1798 trial (see (*e*)). The Combination Acts of 1799 and 1800 (see p. 90) did not therefore introduce a new principle when they banned combinations. Their primary purpose was to make prosecution simpler by applying the procedure of summary jurisdiction in the ordinary magistrates' courts, as a supplement to the more expensive and dilatory procedure of indictment for conspiracy before a superior court.]

(*a*) From A Bill of Conspiracies of Victuallers and Craftsmen, 1548. (2 & 3. Edw. VI. c. 15.)

Forasmuch *as of late . . . artificers, handicraftsmen and labourers have made confederacies and promises, and have sworn mutual oaths not only that they should not meddle one with another's work, and perform and finish that another hath begun, but also to constitute and appoint how much work they shall do in a day, and what hours and times they shall work, contrary to the laws and statutes of this realm, and to the great hurt and impoverishment of the King's majesty's subjects:* For reformation thereof it is ordained and enacted . . . that . . . if any artificers, workmen or labourers do conspire, covenant, or promise together, or make any oaths that they shall not make or do their works but at a certain price or rate, or shall not enterprize or take upon them to finish that another hath begun, or shall do but a certain work in a day, or shall not work but at certain hours and times, that then every person so conspiring, covenanting, swearing or offending, being lawfully convict thereof by witness, confession or otherwise, shall forfeit for the first offence ten pounds to the King's highness; and if he have sufficient to pay the same, and do pay the same within six days next after his conviction; or else shall suffer for the same offence twenty days imprisonment, and shall only have bread and water for his sustenance : And for the second offence shall forfeit twenty pound to the King, if he have sufficient to pay the same, and do pay the same within six days next after his conviction, or else shall suffer for the second offence punishment of the pillory; and for the third offence shall forfeit forty pound to the King, if he have sufficient to pay the same, and also do pay the same within six days next after his conviction, or else shall sit on the pillory and lose one of his ears, and also shall at all times after that be taken as a man infamous, and his saying, depositions or oath not to be credited at any time in any matters of judgment.

(*b*) Proclamations against Combinations of Woollen Weavers, 1718. From *Notes and Queries*, September 21, 1867. (Quoted from the ' Historical Register ', 1718.)

February 4, 1718. A proclamation was published against unlawful Clubs, Combinations, etc., Reciting that whereas complaint had been made to the Government that great numbers of Woolcombers and Weavers in several parts of the Kingdom had lately formed themselves into lawless Clubs and Societies which had illegally presumed to use a Common Seal, and to act as Bodies Corporate, by making and unlawfully conspiring to execute certain Bylaws or Orders, whereby they pretend to determine who had a right to the Trade, what and how many Apprentices and Journeymen each man should keep at once, together with the prices of all their Manufactures, and the manner and materials of which they should be wrought; and that, when many of the said Conspirators wanted work, because their

Masters would not submit to such pretended Orders and unreasonable Demands, they fed them with Money, till they could again get employment, in order to oblige their Masters to employ them for want of other hands; and that the said Clubs by their great numbers, and their correspondence in several of the trading towns of the Kingdom, became dangerous to the publick peace, especially in the Counties of Devon and Somerset; where many Riots had been committed, private Houses broken open, the Subjects assaulted, wounded and put in peril of their lives, great Quantities of Woollen Goods cut and spoilt, Prisoners set at Liberty by Force; and that the Rioters refused to disperse notwithstanding the reading of the Proclamation required by the late Riot Act. For these causes this Proclamation enjoined the putting the said Riot Act, and another Act made in the Reign of Edward VI (intitled ' The Bill of Conspiracy of the Victuallers and Craftsmen ',) in Execution against all such as should unlawfully confederate and combine for the purposes above mentioned in particular, or for any other illegal Purposes, contrary to the Tenour of the aforesaid Acts.

(c) An Act to prevent unlawful combinations of workmen employed in the woollen manufactures, and for better payment of their wages, 1726. (12 Geo. I. c. 34.)

Whereas great numbers of weavers and others concerned in the woollen manufactures in several towns and parishes in this kingdom, have lately formed themselves into unlawful clubs and societies, and have presumed, contrary to law, to enter into combinations, and to make by-laws or orders, by which they pretend to regulate the trade and the prices of their goods, and to advance their wages unreasonably, and many other things to the like purpose ; and whereas the said persons so unlawfully assembling and associating themselves have committed great violences and outrages upon many of his Majesty's good subjects, and by force protected themselves and their wicked accomplices against law and justice; and it is absolutely necessary that more effectual provision should be made against such unlawful combinations, and for preventing such violences and outrages for the future and for bringing all offenders in the premisses to more speedy and exemplary justice; may it therefore . . . be enacted . . . That all contracts, covenants or agreements, and all bylaws, ordinances, rules or orders, in such unlawful clubs and societies, heretofore made or entered into, or hereafter to be made or entered into, by or between any persons brought up in or professing, using or exercising the art and mystery of a woolcomber or weaver, or journeyman woolcomber or journeyman weaver, in any parish or place within this kingdom, for regulating the said trade or mystery, or for regulating or settling the prices of goods, or for advancing their wages, or for lessening their usual hours of work, shall be and are hereby declared to be illegal, null and void to all intents and purposes; and further, that if any woolcomber or weaver, or journeyman woolcomber or journeyman weaver, or other person concerned in any of the woollen manufactures of this kingdom shall . . . be knowingly concerned in any contract, covenant or agreement, by law ordinance, rule or order of any club, society or combination by this act declared to be illegal, . . . every person so offending being thereof lawfully convicted upon the oath or oaths of one or more credible witness or witnesses, before any two or more justices of the peace . . . upon any information exhibited or prosecution within three calendar months after the offence committed . . . [shall be liable to three months' imprisonment].

[Further provisions deal with the following matters :
(a) Quitting service before the time for which hired, to be committed.
(b) Spoiling the work, to pay double the value, etc.
(c) Clothiers, etc., to pay wages in money.
(d) Justices on complaint to issue warrants for levying wages, etc.
(e) Clothiers paying wages in goods, etc., forfeit £10.
(f) Appeal to the quarter sessions.
(g) Assaulting or threatening masters, etc., a felony.
(h) Breaking into a shop to cut any serges, etc., a felony.
(i) This act to extend to combers and framework knitters.]

(d) From 'Rex v. the Journeymen Tailors of Cambridge', 8 Mod. 10 (1721).

Fifthly this indictment ought to conclude contra formam statuti ; for by the late statute 7. Geo. I. c. 13. journeymen taylors are prohibited to enter into any contract or agreement for advancing their wages, etc. And the statute of 2 and 3. Edw. 6. c. 15., makes such persons criminal.

It was answered, that the omission in not concluding this indictment contra formam statuti is not material, because it is for a conspiracy, which is an offence at common law. It is true, the indictment sets forth, that the defendants refused to work under such rates, which were more than enjoined by the statute, for that is only two shillings a day; but yet these words will not bring the offence, for which the defendants are indicted, to be within that statute, because it is not the denial to work except for more wages than is allowed by the statute, but it is for a conspiracy to raise their wages, for which these defendants are indicted. It is true, it does not appear by the record that the wages demanded were excessive; but that is not material, because it may be given in evidence.

The Court : This indictment need not conclude contra formam statuti, because it is for a conspiracy, which is an offence at common law. So the judgment was confirmed by the whole court quod capiantur.

(e) " The Trial of the Journeymen Printers," 1798. From E. Atkinson, " An account of the rise and progress of the dispute between the masters and the journeymen printers exemplified in the Trial at Large ", p. 49.

Mr. Recorder's summing up of the evidence.

Gentlemen of the Jury. The charge imputed to the present defendants by the law of this country, is a very heinous crime and is properly so considered, because the consequences of it must be very fatal to society; nothing can be more fatal to society, nothing can be more injurious to society, *than men meeting privately* to do injury to large bodies of men, therefore it has at all times been considered by the law of this country, as a very serious offence. In the present instance, it not only affects the peace of society but also the commerce of the country, and for that reason is punished by very severe penalties. When, on the one hand therefore, you find the interests of society affected by it, and on the other, severe penalties attached, it becomes a very serious case for the consideration of a Jury.

The learned counsel has gone very much into the nature of the propositions made by the men to the masters, and has given you to understand that they are good and wise propositions, and that they would not do wrong upon those propositions. Now, the law is decidedly the reverse of that, for, even if you believe that they united together to do a good and useful act, the mode which they take to execute their purpose is by a conspiracy, and that, in all the books, is held to be a conspiracy. You have had a speech from the Counsel, as if he had been addressing the House of Commons, at the bar of that House, upon the merits of the question. I forbear at all to go into the question, whether it is a fair or reasonable proposition; and as to the question, whether it has been an improper prosecution, and brought from improper motives. It has been proved on all hands, that a great part of the journeymen have struck;

I therefore, do not think, that the prosecution brought by the masters, is to be reprobated under these circumstances; but I wish you to try the cause with all the temper you can, neither taking a prejudice in favour of the masters or of the men; while they conduct themselves peaceably and with good order in society, they are both valuable; journeymen are as necessary to the public in the trade as masters; and therefore as long as they conduct themselves with propriety on the one side, and on the other, they deserve to be respected; if they do not, but go to the length of offending the laws, they must take the consequence. The only question is whether these five men have offended the law in the way that I have stated, namely, that they have conspired to injure and obstruct the trade of their masters.

In the first count is contained a special charge, which, I must say, the evidence does not prove, but, I think, the evidence does prove the general count; and if that is made out to your satisfaction it will be an offence for which they are answerable.

Gentlemen, I shall state shortly the points to which your attention ought to be directed. I think it appears by the evidence, that after the 7th of April, when the agreement was at an end, and they refused to come to terms, a great part of the men struck; now, if they did strike, that was certainly an act which tended to impoverish the trade; and if so, the next question is, whether, in consequence of any proceeding which took place by Atkinson, or any of the defendants at the bar, that took place which is stated in the evidence; for upon this indictment, supposing any one of them to have acted in concert with the other, the crime is made out against them. You will likewise consider how far the defendants are equally implicated, and find your verdict accordingly.

2. THE COMBINATION ACTS OF 1799 AND 1800.

[The Master Millwrights in their petition to the House of Commons in 1795 — it was in the course of the debate on this that the first Combination Act was conceived — had complained ' that the only method of punishing such delinquents [*i.e.* strikers] under the existing laws, is by preferring an indictment, at the sessions or assizes, after the commission of the offence, but, before that time arrives, the offenders frequently remove into different parts of the country ' . . . so that the time and money necessary to discover and bring them to trial was more than could be afforded. The Combination Acts met this grievance by providing for immediate trials by summary jurisdiction before the local magistrates.

In the course of a debate on an ensuing Bill for banning combinations in the engineering trades William Wilberforce advocated a general measure of prohibition. His suggestion was taken up by Pitt and the 1799 Combination Act (39 Geo. III, c. 81) was hurried through Parliament. So many petitions were received against the Act, after it had been passed, that a committee was appointed to investigate the position and prepare an amending Bill. The new Act of 1800 made some minor, but valuable, modifications. Cases had to be tried before two magistrates — not, as in the 1799 Act, before ' one or more ', and the magistrates were not to be manufacturers in the trade in which the dispute had taken place. The arbitration clause was added in the 1800 Act, but this addition had no practical effect. An attempt to add a clause for the defence of friendly societies was defeated, but, even so, many Trade Unions succeeded in carrying on as Friendly Societies and so evading the law. Parliament had recently passed (in 1793) the first Act for the encouragement and regulation of Friendly Societies (Rose's Act); and there was certainly no intention of suppressing these bodies, as such. They were regarded, when properly conducted, as valuable instruments of self-help, which would enable the poor to provide for old age and burial, and so keep down the poor rates and encourage thrift.]

From The Combination Act, 1800. (39 & 40 Geo. III, c. 100.)

WHEREAS it is expedient to explain and amend an Act, passed in the thirty-ninth year of His present Majesty, intituled " An Act to prevent unlawful combinations of Workmen " ;

BE IT THEREFORE ENACTED that from and after the passing of this Act all contracts, covenants and agreements whatsoever, in writing, at any time or times heretofore made or entered into, by or between any journeymen manufacturers or other workmen within this kingdom for obtaining an advance of wages of them or any of them, or any journeymen manufacturers or workmen, or other persons in any manufacture, trade or business, or for lessening or altering their or any of their usual hours of time or working, or for decreasing the quantity of work (save or except any contract made or to be made between any Master and his Journeyman or Manufacturer for or on account of the work or service of such journeyman or manufacturer with whom such contract may be made), or for preventing or hindering any person or persons from employing whomsoever he, she or they shall think proper to employ in his, her or their manufacture, trade or business, in the conduct or the management thereof, shall be and the same are hereby declared to be illegal, null and void, to all intents and purposes whatsoever.

AND BE IT FURTHER ENACTED that no journeymen workmen shall at any time after the passing of this Act make or enter into, or be concerned in the making or entering into any such contract, covenant or agreement, in writing or not in writing, as is hereinbefore declared to be an illegal covenant, contract, or agreement; and every journeyman and workman who, after the passing of this Act, shall be guilty of any of the said offences, being thereof lawfully convicted, upon his own confession or the oath or oaths of one or more credible witness or witnesses, before any two Justices of the Peace for the county, riding, division, city, liberty, town or place where such offence shall be committed (which oath either of such Justices is hereby authorised and empowered to administer in such case, and in all other cases where an oath is to be taken before any Justices of the Peace in pursuance of this Act) within three calendar months next after the offence shall have been committed, shall, by order of such Justices, be committed to and confined in the Common Gaol within his or their jurisdiction, for any time not exceeding three calendar months, or at the discretion of such justices shall be committed to some house of correction within the same jurisdiction, there to remain and to be kept to hard labour for any time not exceeding two calendar months.

AND BE IT FURTHER ENACTED . . . That every journeyman or workman or other person . . . who shall by giving money, or by persuasion, solicitation, or intimidation, or any other means, wilfully and maliciously endeavour to prevent any unhired or unemployed journeyman or workman . . . from hiring himself to any manufacturer, or tradesman, or person conducting any manufacture, trade, or business, or who shall for the purpose of obtaining an advance of wages, or for any other purpose contrary to the provision of this act, wilfully and maliciously decoy, persuade, solicit, intimidate, influence, or prevail, or attempt to endeavour to prevail, on any journeyman or workman or other person hired or employed, in his work or service or employment, . . . or who, being hired or employed, shall, without any just or reasonable cause, refuse to work with any other journeyman or workman employed or hired to work therein [will for these offences be punished as in the case above]. . . .

XVIII. And whereas it will be a great convenience and advantage to masters and workmen engaged in manufactures, that a cheap and summary mode be established for settling all disputes that may arise between them respecting wages and work, be it further enacted . . . in all cases that shall or may arise within that part of Great Britain called England, where the masters and workmen cannot agree respecting the price or prices to be paid for work actually done in any manufacture, or any injury or damage done or alledged to have been done by the workman to the work, or respecting any delay or supposed delay in finishing such work in a good and work-manlike manner, or according to any contract; and in all cases of dispute or difference, touching any contract or agreement for work or wages between masters and workmen in any trade or manu-facture, which cannot be otherwise mutually adjusted and settled by and between them, it shall and may be, and it is hereby declared to be lawful for such masters and workmen between whom such dispute or difference shall arise as aforesaid, or either of them, to demand and have an arbitration or reference of such matter or matters in dispute; and each of them is hereby authorised and empowered forthwith to nominate and appoint an arbitrator for and on his respective part and behalf, . . . and the award to be made by such arbitrators within the time herein-after limited, shall in all cases be final and conclusive between the parties; but in case such arbitrators so appointed shall not agree to decide such matter or matters in dispute . . . then it shall be lawful for the parties or either of them to require such arbitrators forthwith and without delay to go before and attend upon one of his Majesty's justices of the peace . . . [whose decision shall be final].

3. THE COTTON TRADE IN 1812.

[This long-drawn-out dispute in the cotton trade shows very clearly what were the objectives and methods of the Trade Unions in the early nineteenth century. Even the factory operatives were continuin₍ the policy initiated under the economic condition of the period before the growth of the Industrial Revolution. The limitation of apprentices seems still their first aim. Having discovered that Parliament will pass neither a minimum wage Bill nor any new Bill protecting their status, they try legal action, and are again thwarted. As a last resort they strike, but the forces of the State will not tolerate this. Before recognition was won for the principle of collective bargaining, Trade Union organisation was used less for direct negotiation than for enlisting the aid of a third party. But the extensive unity achieved in this strike over a wide area was a sign that the workers were coming to rely more on their own strength.]

From the Report of the Committee on Artizans and Machinery (1824), Minutes of Evidence, pp. 59-63.

Mr. Alexander Richmond, called in ; and examined.

Have you been acquainted, for any length of time, with the manufacturing people of Scotland ? — I have had a very general acquaintance with all the manufacturing districts of Scotland ; a good deal in England ; and in Ireland for upwards of twenty years.

Have you been yourself a manufacturer ? — Yes, first as an operative, afterwards as a manufacturer, commission agent and merchant.

In what parts of Scotland have you been engaged ? — Principally in Glasgow.

During the time you were at Glasgow, had you any connection with combinations of workmen who were united on the score of wages ? — I was connected for four or five years with several applications that were made to Parliament first, which afterwards ended in a prosecution before the courts in Scotland, for the establishing a rate of wages.

What was the date of application ? — In 1811. There was an application made to Scotland alone, but in 1809, jointly with Lancashire ; which led to a long investigation by a Committee [1] of the House at that period. The late Mr. Whitbread,[2] and several other members, recommended an association on the part of the workmen, to attempt it through that medium ; that led to a connection through the whole of the cotton, and that part of the silk trade compounded with cotton, both of Scotland and England, and latterly Ireland was introduced into the association ; they made another attempt, for the purpose of getting an apprentice bill, after the association was somewhat matured, in 1811, which was the last attempt at legislative interference made by the trade ; that also failed, though there was a Committee of the House of Commons appointed upon that occasion again.

[1] This Committee was ' unanimously of the opinion, that the Proposition stated in the said petitions relative to the fixing a minimum price of labour in the cotton manufacture, is wholly inadmissible in principle, incapable of being reduced to practice by any means which can possibly be devised, and if practicable, would be productive of the most fateful consequences '. . . .

[2] Samuel Whitbread (1758–1815), a prominent Whig politician and a leading figure in the progressive humanitarianism of his day, made three unsuccessful attempts to pass a minimum wage Bill — in 1796, 1800, and 1808.

What was the object of the association then ? — It was principally pointed at restricting the admission of apprentices into the trade, fixing a certain period of apprenticeship : as the evil was considered to originate from the abundance of hands in the trade.

Were you one of the delegates appointed by the workmen in Glasgow ? — Yes ; on the failure of the last application to Parliament, the association turned its attention to some Acts of Parliament that were discovered, empowering the justices of the peace to affix rates of wages, with a view to raising the wages ; the fact was, fluctuation was a greater evil perhaps, than the lowness of the rate ; previous to that period, fluctuations, to the extent of thirty per cent, took place in the course of a month, in the price of labour ; an attempt was made to get an extra-judicial arrangement with the masters : the masters were divided in opinion on the point, some of them were for regulation, others opposed it ; after several ineffectual attempts to come to an arrangement with that part of the masters who opposed it, part of the masters being in the interest of the operatives, at last a process was entered before the quarter sessions.

What measures did the men take ? — An application was made to the sheriff at the county of Lanark, conjointly with the magistrates of the city of Glasgow, to call a meeting of the trade generally, for the purpose of getting two committees appointed, for the purpose of coming to an arrangement ; committees of the separate interests.

A committee of Masters and a committee of operatives ? — Yes ; those two committees met in the presence of the magistrates ; I formed one of the committees on the part of the operatives' interest as it was considered, and after a number of discussions we could not come to any terms ; in fact, the masters would not recognise the principle of fixing the wages at all, and then we had recourse to the proceedings upon some Acts of Parliament passed previously to the Union, but confirmed by an Act passed in the reign of George the Second, as far as I recollect, which has been acted upon repeatedly in England, on a small scale ; we were opposed in the legal part of the proceedings ; they disputed the relevancy of the action, and the competency of the court to interfere at all ; the court found themselves competent and the action relevant ; then the case was appealed to the court of session, and they affirmed the judgment of the quarter sessions, and remitted the case back for the justices to go into the merits of it ; a table of rates was drawn out, and founded upon the proceedings in the action raised, which we wished to have affirmed ; then the justices proceeded into the merits of the case ; it was to ascertain, whether the rate demanded was reasonable or not; the opposite party then deserted the case, they would not meet us in the proof; they were aware we demanded nothing but what was reasonable, and we had to go into a proof that continued upwards of two months; two witnesses were to swear to each particular fabric, and as there were a very great number of fabrics, it required a very long time. I believe it is the only case of the kind that ever took place in the empire, and I will state to the Committee the result. There were about 130 witnesses examined in all.

Was that before the court in Edinburgh? — It was before the court of quarter sessions that we went into the proof: I may state at the same time, that a case was raised in Cumberland, for the purpose of trying the question in England also; the quarter sessions of the county of Cumberland also found themselves competent to take up the question which was also carried by the masters, by writ of Mandamus, into the court of King's Bench, but it was considered better to allow the Scotch case to be tried first, before proceeding further in the English, and on the failure of the Scotch case, it was altogether abandoned; . . .

Will you state how the process proceeded? — The justices of the peace found the rate demanded reasonable; it was amended in some instances, and the masters immediately refused to pay the rate. Our counsel in the process had consented, for the purpose of obviating the difficulties and getting over the objections that might be made against the expediency, to withdraw the imperative part of the prayer; the prayer of the petition originally founded upon, prayed, that they might be compelled to pay the price, but it was only a declaratory decision, as the imperative part was withdrawn, for the purpose of preventing the difficulty; we then, as the masters refused to pay, tried every method of getting an extra-judicial decision. The present Lord Justice Clerk had been a member of the Committee of the House of Commons in 1809, and appeared decidedly opposed to the principle of interference and we conceived from the sentiments of the court, that though they had decided the law, if we went on the expediency of the case, we might very likely lose, and we determined therefore to try the experiment of striking work.

Were the masters, during the whole of this process, acting together against you? [1] — For the purpose of making a specimen, there were

---

[1] It is worth remembering that there is no record of a successful prosecution against masters for combination between 1800 and 1824, though in England such combinations were illegal under the Combination Acts, and probably at common law.

only forty masters of the leading houses made parties to the action, including a Specimen of all the branches of the trade; about sixteen to eighteen hundred of the workmen of those houses were made the pursuers in those cases.

What number of masters might there be? — There were only a portion of the masters that were parties to the action that directly opposed the leading interests, but the whole body of masters, with a few exceptions, ultimately opposed the principle of the thing; the intention of the operative interest was, to get an interference of sanction of the magistracy, and they would have been agreeable for the masters to have come forward and shown, that the trade was not able to afford the rates. We repeatedly requested them to come forward, and shew that the profits would not afford them.

The masters did not oppose the operatives, when they came to the question of the comparison of the wages of those men with those in other branches? — No; they would not attempt to invalidate the proofs, nor meet us on the proof, that the trade could not afford these wages.

Then you determined to strike? — We then determined to try the effect of a moral effort, and it was the most extensive ever made in this country. We struck, the whole kingdom: we struck nearly forty thousand looms; it continued for six weeks, without any steps whatever being taken by the masters to accommodate.

For what district? — From Aberdeen to Carlisle; we were in correspondence with the whole cotton trade in England, but the effort was confined to Scotland in the first instance.

What was the expense of the process you have mentioned? — The action was entered in January and continued till November; on the 10th of November 1812, we got the final decision. We required a week for striking the blow, as we intended it should be simultaneous; and in one day we struck, near thirty thousand, and the others followed as soon as the intelligence reached them.

What was the money expended by the operatives up to the time of the striking? — About 3,000l.

What was the organisation you had? — It extended through the whole trade in the three kingdoms; Lancashire, Cumberland, and Lanark, Renfrew, and Ayr shires, Perth, Stirling, etc. and the North of Ireland. I may state generally, that in all matters which depended upon the workmen, for twenty years I have known the trade, the Scots have decidedly taken the lead in the matters of general intelligence, and the workmen have been able always to take the lead, in preference to the population of England connected with the cotton manufacture; hence, in this instance, Glasgow was the focus of the business.

What was the result of this strike? — About three weeks after the effort commenced, there was a direct interference, on the part of the government, to suppress it, by the apprehension of all the parties concerned.

What do you mean by the apprehension of all the parties concerned? — There was a committee of five, who had conducted the process during the whole period, and we were all apprehended and committed to gaol.

You were one of the five? — I was.

Under what law were you apprehended? — There was no specific law. There was a case I might have mentioned, but as it applies directly to the combination, I will introduce it here. In 1811 a combination had taken place amongst the cotton spinners; and in a case that was aggravated by assault, that was tried at the Glasgow circuit, the present Lord President Hope, who then presided, stated that it was an aggravation of the crime of combination, that there was a clear remedy in law, as the magistrates had full power and authority to affix rates of wages, or settle disputes; that was the ground on which we entered the action in 1811. In the face of this, after having acted upon it on this principle the mere act of striking work in a body was construed as an infringement of the combination law; and after having acted upon the authority of Lord President Hope, we were convicted, of what law I am yet at a loss to know. We were held to bail, and indicted; the result of the interference was a failure. The moment the masters saw the interference made on the part of the government, though everything had gone on with perfect peace and quietness, the masters saw that submission would necessarily have to be the result on the part of the operatives; and though they had at the same time made them overtures for an arrangement, the moment that took place, they drew off.

You consider that the interference of the government, by arresting the committee, prevented the masters coming to reasonable terms with the men? — I had occasion to know that distinctly, through the medium of the sheriff of the county. I was the first of the party admitted to bail, and my colleagues being kept in prison two or three days. An overture was made to me through the sheriff of the county, at the request of several of the leading houses in the trade, whether any modification would be allowed from the rate returned from the justices. I had returned for answer, that I had not the most distant doubt, that anything that could be pointed out that was at all reasonable, would be at once acceded to on the part of the operatives, and that we were ready to meet them; but this was just at the time the interference took place, and they never made another overture upon the matter. The result was submission on the part of the operatives; they were obliged to give in, and after that, we were prosecuted and sentenced to various periods of imprisonment, from four to eighteen months.

Are you able to state on what law? — There is no statute law in Scotland; [1] the indictment went on the common law; the Court of Justiciary possesses both a legislative and a judicial power; for in that court the case was completely new, there was never any one of the same description, and they made it take a retrospective effect.

4. THE ENFORCEMENT OF THE COMBINATION LAWS

[The following extracts from the Home Office Papers are taken by kind permission of Professor A. Aspinall from his volume, " The Early English Trade Unions " — which consists of extracts from this most valuable source. They are intended to illustrate the attitude of the Government to the problem of enforcing the laws against combination. Although they are all taken from a few years and from correspondence relating mainly to a single area (Manchester and district), it would be easy to cite parallel passages from letters written at other dates or with reference to other areas.]

(*a*) Viscount Sidmouth to William Johnson Edenson, Borough-reeve of Manchester. March 28, 1816. [H.O. 43/24/377-81.]

I have the honour to acknowledge the receipt of the Memorial addressed to me by the merchants, manufacturers and inhabitants of the towns and neighbourhood of Manchester and Salford, upon the subject of the unlawful combinations at present existing amongst the working classes generally throughout the kingdom; and I beg to acquaint you that after having bestowed upon [it] the fullest considera-

---

[1] Only three trials for the crime of combination had taken place in Scotland before 1800, and the 1799–1800 Acts were completely inoperative there, as they were not so drafted as to fit in with the Scottish legal system. But, with the development of industry and the rise of industrial unrest, judges in Scotland as well as in England were disposed to regard combination as a crime at common law, and though no use was made of the Combination Acts, the Government and the employers had enough legal weapons to fight Trade Unions.

tion, I judged it advisable to consult with his Majesty's Attorney and Solicitor-General with the view of being assisted with their advice and opinion upon the prayer of the petitioners, ' that his Majesty's Government will introduce and promote such amendments of the present laws as are best calculated to remedy the evils complained of.' This subject had previously been brought under the consideration of his Majesty's Law Officers, and they have recently had a consultation by my express desire with a committee of gentlemen much interested, and maturely deliberated upon and discussed every project or suggestion communicated by them for providing the remedy sought for. They have stated to me that they are deeply impressed with the great importance of the subject, and fully sensible of the alarming extent to which the combinations of workmen in different branches of trade and manufactures have been carried, and of the dangerous consequences which they threaten to the manufactures, the public interest, and the deluded individuals themselves who are engaged in them; but they report at the same time that they cannot recommend the adoption of any of the measures that have been proposed, or think themselves warranted in expressing an opinion in favour of any new powers for suppression of the evil. Great danger and mischief arise from the combination of numbers to effect an illegal purpose, but, whenever this case exists and is capable of being satisfactorily proved, it amounts, by the law as it now stands, to a criminal misdemeanour of great enormity, and would not fail to be visited on a satisfactory conviction by punishment of considerable severity.

The Attorney and Solicitor-General further state that they do not think that it is necessary to increase the degree of such severity by any new law, nor do they believe that any proposition for such law would be favourably received by the Legislature; and although it has appeared to some that the power to punish individuals convicted of offences against the Combination Act, is not sufficient, and that benefit might be derived from extending the punishment, yet they cannot recommend a proposal to give larger powers to single magistrates acting in a summary way without a jury, nor do they think a proposal to that effect would succeed.

The great practical inconvenience which is felt, arises from the difficulty of proving the necessary facts to convict offenders; but a rule of evidence different in this case from any other, cannot be recommended, nor would it be proper to suggest that less should be required than would be thought necessary to warrant a conviction for any other species of misdemeanour. Indeed it is obvious that the more heinous the offence, in that exact proportion the evidence should be satisfactory; and still less would it be proper to suggest a departure from the usual course and nature of proof, in a case of summary proceeding by a magistrate.

The law as it stands at present, would, they are of opinion, be found sufficient, if duly enforced, and they do not see any remedy for this most enormous evil but that which would doubtless arise from an active, vigilant and well-regulated system, adopted and constantly acted upon by the masters in their various branches of trade and manufactures, to detect conspiracies and to prosecute by indictment such as could be affected by competent testimony; and much might be done by encouraging persons worthy of trust to collect, and from time to time to communicate in the most confidential manner the objects and meetings and correspondence of the conspirators, which would afford an opportunity of making examples in certain proper cases, to be carefully selected, and which in process of time might be expected to produce the most beneficial consequences, by dissolving the combinations, by infusing into the minds of its members a great degree of jealousy and distrust of each other, and which would break up that confidence in their fidelity which at present binds them together.

I beg to assure you that I fully concur in the sentiments of his Majesty's Law Officers, and I confidently trust they will prove satisfactory to all the gentlemen who have signed the Memorial before-mentioned.

(*b*) Henry Hobhouse [1] to the Rev. W. R. Hay, Manchester. Confidential. July 28, 1818. [H.O. 79/3/186-89.]

. . . I am not aware of any reason to doubt that the present discontent arose exclusively from commercial causes, but there is strong ground to believe that the political malcontents have been endeavouring to convert them to their own wicked purposes, and it is of great importance to ascertain to what extent they have succeeded, and by what means so large a body of mechanics has been subsisted without any visible means of livelihood for so long a period. . . .

(*c*) Henry Hobhouse to the Rev. W. R. Hay, Manchester. Private. July 30, 1818. [H.O. 79/3/195-97.]

. . . Even if the views of the unemployed workmen were originally unmixed with politics, it is too much to expect that they should

[1] Hobhouse was Under-Secretary of State for the Home Department.

remain so, when they are daily and nightly exposed to the harangues of such men as Drummond, Bagguley, etc. It would therefore be an important measure if the magistrates could find sufficient ground for taking those demagogues into custody. . . .

(*d*) Henry Hobhouse to James Norris. August 4, 1818. Private. [H.O. 79/3/208-10.]

. . . You cannot be more fully impressed than Lord Sidmouth is, with the propriety of the magistrate forbearing to interfere in questions between master and servant so long as the peace is unbroken, but it is impossible for the Secretary of State to contemplate with indifference the danger likely to result to the public weal from the existence, in such a population as that of the south-eastern part of Lancashire, of large bodies of men without the visible means of subsistence, and exposed to the harangues of the disaffected demagogues, who are known to be ever alive to the means of doing mischief in that quarter of England. And of course, when such a state of things exists, Lord Sidmouth is anxious to obtain frequent and authentic information of what passes, although the magistrates may not have been called into action. . . .

(*e*) Henry Hobhouse to James Norris. August 9, 1818. Private. [H.O. 79/3/221-22.]

. . . I should derive great satisfaction from hearing that a case can be made under the Combination Act against Bagguley, Drummond and Johnston. Their conviction would have a doubly good effect since it would remove them for a while from the scene of action, and would expose to the world the leaders of the conspiracy.

It is much to be wished that the masters in general would follow the example of Mr. Houldsworth. Greater good would be effected by proving that the law when put in force is capable of repressing the mischief than by any other means. This doctrine Lord Sidmouth is very anxious to see inculcated in every shape. . . .

(*f*) Henry Hobhouse to the Rev. W. R. Hay. August 11, 1818. Private. [H.O. 79/3/229-30.]

. . . Everybody here concurs with you in feeling the injury which has been done at Manchester by the backwardness of the masters. How is it possible for any Government to protect men who will not protect themselves? This is the text which ought to be preached on at Manchester for the next three months. . . .

(*g*) Henry Hobhouse to James Norris. August 12, 1818. [H.O. 79/3/230-31.]

. . . I am happy to find that at Stockport several convictions have taken place under the Combination Act, and their good effect is apparent. . . .

(*h*) Henry Hobhouse to Major-General Sir John Byng. Private and confidential. August 14, 1818. [H.O. 79/3/239-40.]

. . . Matters have certainly been better managed at Stockport than at Manchester. The masters have been more firm, and the convictions under the Combination Act have done great service. The doctrine I have inculcated is that the first object is to shew to the workmen that the law is strong enough, if it be but properly enforced, but this principle has not been acted upon in Manchester, where the manufacturer seems to rely more on your sword than on any other weapon. . . .

(*i*) Henry Hobhouse to James Norris. August 19, 1818. [H.O. 41/4/150-51.]

Having submitted for the consideration of the Solicitor-General (the Attorney-General being absent from London) the points mentioned in your letter of the 14th inst. as to the right of the magistrates to disperse the persons assembled about the mills in the manner therein described, and also as to their right to disperse persons assembled at meetings such as that lately held on Kersall Moor, I have now the honour to acquaint you that it is the Solicitor-General's opinion that if the persons assembled about the mills or on Kersall Moor conduct themselves peaceably and quietly, and there are no circumstances attending the meetings of actual force or violence, or having an apparent tendency thereto, the magistrates will not be justified in interfering to disperse them.

(*j*) Henry Hobhouse to William Marriott. August 19, 1818. Private. [H.O. 79/3/254-56.]

. . . On the present occasion the master spinners appear to have acted with very little discretion towards their men. I can of course form no judgment whether the claims of the men are either wholly or partially reasonable. But when they were first preferred, or indeed, before, the masters ought to have taken that point into their unbiased consideration, and have taken their resolution as to the line which it became them to adopt. From a resolution so formed, they ought not to recede. But I fear none such has ever been formed, but the men have been set at defiance without considering the justice of their pretensions. After they have been so long resisted, it would be mischievous that they should finally succeed. Government and the magistracy must ever discountenance combination, but they have much to complain of those who give rise to the combination by relying on the support of the law instead of considering the justice of the demands made on them.

(*k*) Henry Hobhouse to J. Lloyd. August 21, 1818. Private. [H.O. 73/3/261.]

. . . You cannot please me better than by turning your attention to the Friendly Societies, by which I have no doubt the system which is the bane of your country is in a great degree supported. . . .

(*l*) Henry Hobhouse to T. S. Withington. August 21, 1818. Private. [H.O. 79/3/261-62, 266-67.]

. . . I am happy to learn that an indictment for a conspiracy has been found on the prosecution of a master spinner at Heaton Norris. I wish there had been a few more such prosecutions. I am sure that they would have greatly tended to the dissolution of the conspiracy.

(*m*) Henry Hobhouse to J. Lloyd. August 24, 1818. Private. [H.O. 79/3/264-65.]

. . . All the information I receive tends to shew a serious intention to creating [*sic*] a combination among the journeymen in all trades, and it is very important to procure evidence on this subject, as a prosecution must be resorted to if possible. I have seen a paper printed by Wilson of Manchester, expressly owning this object. . . .

(*n*) Henry Hobhouse to William Marriott. August 24, 1818. Private. [H.O. 79/3/268-69.]

. . . The great thing wanting in your town and neighbourhood is that the masters should bring forward evidence (of which they must possess abundance) to enable the magistrates to put in force the Combination Act. I am glad to hear that there was one indictment for a conspiracy found at the Assizes. If there had been ten instead of one, it might have gone a good way to settle the business.

(*o*) Henry Hobhouse to the Chief Justice of Chester. August 25, 1818. Private. [H.O. 79/3/275-76.]

I am persuaded you will forgive me for offering a suggestion which would be quite unnecessary if you had the same means of information which I have.

The system of combination among the journeymen in the vicinity of Manchester, including Stockport and the adjacent parts of Cheshire, has gone to a length of which you have no idea. It extends not merely to a conspiracy in each trade of the journeymen against their masters, but a scheme is actually in progress for forming a combination among the mechanics in *all* trades to afford reciprocal aid to each other. Whether you will have any indictments for a conspiracy or not, I cannot tell; but I am persuaded that a luminous exposition of the law on that subject, such as would come with effect from you, could not fail to be useful to the public; and if you should feel it right to add a word or two on the duty of detecting and counteracting such conspiracies, they would be well applied to the existing circumstances; for the magistrates are placed under the greatest difficulty in acting, for want of evidence being brought before them through the timidity of the masters. . . .

(*p*) Henry Hobhouse to James Norris. February 24, 1819. Private. [H.O. 41/3/253-54.]

. . . Any depression in the rate of weavers' wages is greatly to be lamented, because it administers fuel to the latent sparks of discontent; but it is a subject upon which you are well aware that no relief can be afforded either by the executive or the legislative branches of the Government. . . .

5. THE SKILLED CRAFTS

[*The Gorgon* [1] featured a series of articles describing different Trade Clubs. This account of the tailors, written by Francis Place, who had himself been both an independent journeyman breeches-maker and a master, describes one of the most efficient and successful unions in a highly developed stage, but it was this type of organisation which had been followed for many years in the skilled trades.

[1] *The Gorgon* (1818-1819), edited by John Wade, was a very able and interesting weekly, which almost alone of the reform journals of those years devoted a large part of its space to Trade Union news and ideas.

An essential purpose of the clubs of the skilled artisans was to act as Friendly Societies ; and this form of activity, being continuous, served as a basis for Trade Union action in case of need. The tailors, among others, had used their organisation for trade purposes from an early date : they were continually criticising the increase in the number of apprentices as an attack on their privileged status, and even in 1720 [1] they combined for an advance in wages and a reduction of hours. During the French Wars (1793–1815) they were very successful in maintaining their standard of life by strike action.

The second extract gives an account of the early organisation of the London Compositors, and shows their success in carrying on collective bargaining in spite of the Combination Laws. This, however, did not prevent five compositors from being sentenced to two years' imprisonment for conspiracy in 1798, or protect the compositors of *The Times* from a similar fate in 1810. (See Webb, " History of Trade Unionism ", p. 78.)]

(a) Tailors' Houses of Call and their Organisation. From *The Gorgon*, October 3, 1818.

The organisation of the tailors is nearly as follows :

They are divided into two classes, called Flints and Dungs,— the Flints have upwards of thirty houses of call, and the Dungs about nine or ten ; the Flints work by the day, the Dungs by day or piece. Great animosity formerly existed between them, the Dungs generally working for less wages, but of late years there has not been much difference in the wages, the material difference being the working by the piece or day, instead of the day only ; and at some of the latest strikes both parties have usually made common cause.

It is of the Flints principally we mean to speak, not only because they are the largest body, but because they always take the lead. Each house of call has a book or books in which the men out of work have their names set down, and with some exceptions, they go to work when sent for, in the order in which their names stand. . . . Every man is obliged to do a day's work for a day's pay, and the day's work is regulated by the quantity an ordinary hand can do in twelve hours. He must also do his work in a workmanlike manner, or he will be dismissed the house on complaint being thrice made against him. No man is allowed to do more than a day's work in twelve hours, or to work more than twelve hours in a day, while any man remains unemployed, but when there are no men unem-

[1] See F. W. Galton, " The Tailoring Trade ", a collection of documents, valuable for the early history of Trade Unionism.

ployed, he may work over-hours; he may also at those times receive more than a day's pay for a day's work, which at other times he must not do. They have several other regulations for preserving order and decorum, and preventing injustice either to one another, or to their employers: and also for preventing their employers doing injustice to them. They have a double subscription, one for a benefit club to maintain them in sickness and when superannuated, the other a mere trifle for supporting the combination.

They have also occasionally a much larger subscription for the purpose of maintaining their own members, who cannot be employed when trade is dull, and to these they usually allow about eight or nine shillings a week. The money for this purpose is raised by a rate of payment, levied on those who have employment according to the number of days in the week they are employed. . . .

Each house of call has a deputy, who on particular occasions is chosen by a kind of tacit consent, frequently without its being known to a very large majority who is chosen.

The deputies form a committee, and they again choose in a somewhat similar way a very small committee, in whom, on very particular occasions, all power resides, from whom all orders proceed, and whose commands are implicitly obeyed; and on no occasion has it ever been known that their commands have exceeded the necessity of the occasion, or that they have wandered in the least from the purpose for which it was understood they were appointed.

(*b*) From " The London Scale of Prices for Compositors' Work: agreed upon, April 16th, 1810, with Explanatory Notes, and the Scales of Leeds, York, Dublin, Belfast, and Edinburgh " (2nd edition).

. . . The first regular and acknowledged compositors' scale for the payment of piece-work is by one writer stated to have been agreed to at a general meeting of masters, who assembled in the month of November 1785, to consider eight propositions submitted to them in a circular from the whole body of compositors, with a view to advance the price of labour. That part of the trade, however, who were most materially interested in the adjustment of the price of labour, namely, the compositors, do not appear to have been present when these propositions were discussed, or to have been permitted to offer any arguments in their favour; but the masters assumed the right to set a price upon the labour of others, although a short time afterwards they repelled with indignation an attempt of the booksellers to interfere with their practices and profits.

We are informed by another writer that the scale was not formed at a general meeting of masters, but by a committee, who, " after much labour and considerable discussion," agreed to a scale of prices, which, although it has at different times been amplified and altered to suit the various circumstances of the times, and the different kinds of work as they occurred, has served as the basis of every other scale, up to the present time.

It is not essential, at this period, to know whether the scale was agreed to by a general meeting of masters, or by a committee ; but the merit of forming the basis of the scale for regulating the price of the compositor's labour, certainly belongs to the journeymen, who, on the 6th of April, 1785, submitted to the masters eight propositions for this purpose, five of which were agreed to, and three rejected by them, after they had been laid before them upwards of seven months.

The five propositions, therefore, adopted by the masters on Nov. 26, constituted the scale of 1785, by which the price per 1000 from english to brevier, was declared to be four-pence half-penny ; . . .

The above prices for book and news work prevailed, without any attempt at alteration, until the year 1793, when the compositors, on the 14th of February, addressed a circular to the masters, requesting that the heads and direction lines (which had hitherto been set up without any allowance being made for them) and the em and en quadrats, or whatever was used at the beginning or end of the lines, might be reckoned in the square of the page.

This application appears to have given the first occasion for the masters to confer with the journeymen respecting the price to be paid for their labour ; for we learn " that the committee of masters, having held a conference with a deputation from the compositors at large, *agreed to recommend* to the master printers to comply with the first request." The second request, however, was refused, and no allowance was made for the indention of matter to suit the convenience of the masters, until thirteen years after this application, when a clause was specially introduced into the scale, to remedy this act of injustice.

. . . .

We have now reached the period when the Compositors of London had become convinced of the inadequacy of their scale of prices to regulate the wages of labour in a trade where the charges were not only various and complicated, but being in many instances only based upon custom, were liable to imposition on both sides; and accordingly we find that, for their mutual assistance and defence, the journeymen, in 1801, established a Society with the design of " correcting irregularities, and endeavouring to promote harmony between the employers and employed, by bringing the modes of charge from custom and precedent into one point of view, in order to their being better understood by all concerned."

The result of this union of the journeymen was manifested at the expiration of three years, when the compositors succeeded in forming a committee, consisting of an equal number of masters and journeymen, who were duly authorised by their respective bodies to frame regulations for the future payment of labour. This committee, who had only the preceding meagre scale as the basis of their labours, toiled diligently to remedy the various evils they had felt, and finally succeeded in producing a scale composed of twenty-seven articles, calculated, in their opinion, to meet every emergency; and, whatever may be said of its present inadequacy, every impartial person must admit that it reflects much honour on its framers, and is, indeed, a rare example of diligence, talent, and knowledge, which it is not likely will ever be equalled, or, in aptitude and general clearness, ever surpassed.

. . . . . .

In this brief history of the Scale of Prices, no notice has hitherto been taken of the wages paid to compositors on the establishment; and in this place it therefore becomes necessary to state that in 1774 persons so situated received 20s.; — in 1785, from 21s. to 27s.; — in 1793, 30s.; — in 1805, 33s.; — and in 1810, 36s.

. . . . . .

6. THE STATUTE OF ARTIFICERS, REPEAL OF WAGES AND APPRENTICESHIP CLAUSES, 1813–1814

[This statute of 1562 had attempted to stabilise and make uniform over the whole country the labourer's position in society, treating him as a useful member of the servant class, whose liberties might be curtailed, but whose standard of life should be protected by the State. The two clauses on Wages and Apprenticeships, which are quoted below, played a large part in the history of Trade Unionism; for the policy of the early combinations centred round this tradition of State protection of labourers' recognised rights. But with the development of English trade and industry, particularly in the eighteenth century, the employers found these restrictions on their freedom increasingly irksome : they held that a seven-year apprenticeship was quite unnecessary in many trades, and they explained that what made themselves prosperous or poor brought national prosperity or distress. The wage provisions of the statute had fallen into disuse by the latter part of the eighteenth century ; but the apprenticeship provisions remained in force in most of the urban crafts, though with the spread of industry outside the corporate towns they had come to apply to a much smaller proportion of the workers. The long, losing fight of the workers was ended with the Repeal of the Wage clauses (1813) and the Apprenticeship clauses (1814).]

From the Statute of Artificers, 1562. (5 Eliz. c. 4.)

XV . . . Be it enacted . . . that the Justices of the Peace . . . [and other officials] shall before the tenth day of *June* next coming, and afterward shall yearly . . . assemble themselves together : and . . . calling unto them such discreet and grave persons of the said county or the said city or town corporate, as they shall think meet, and conferring together, respecting the plenty or scarcity of the time and other circumstances necessarily to be considered, shall have authority . . . to limit, rate and appoint the wages, as well of such and so many of the said artificers, handicraftsmen, husbandmen or any other labourer, servant or workman, whose wages in time past hath been by any law or statute rated and appointed, as also the wages of all other labourers, artificers, workmen or apprentices of husbandry, which have not been rated. . . .

.   .   .   .   .   .

XXXI . . . After the first day of *May* next coming it shall not be lawful for any person . . . , other than such as now do lawfully exercise any art, mystery or manual occupation, to . . . exercise any craft now used within the realm of *England* or *Wales*, except he shall have been brought up therein seven years at the least as apprentice in manner abovesaid nor to set any person on work in such mystery, art or occupation being not a workman at this day, except he shall have been apprentice as is aforesaid, or else having served as an apprentice will become a journeyman or be hired by the year upon pain that every person willingly offending shall forfeit for every default forty shillings for every month.

V

THE LUDDITES

INTRODUCTION

MACHINE-WRECKING for one purpose or another was by no means new. The Spitalfields weavers had wrecked machinery even in the seventeenth century, and wrecking had frequently recurred, both accompanying strike action and independently. But these had been isolated instances, symbolical acts of terrorism, while the Luddites alone carried out a systematic campaign of machine-wrecking. In this period (up to 1815) there were three Luddite movements — in the Midlands, in Yorkshire, and in Lancashire and Cheshire. They were only partially interconnected: the grievances and motives were different, so that, apart from the difficulties and dangers of communications, it is improbable that there was much unity between the three groups. In the Midlands, machinery was wrecked not because it saved labour, but because certain new machines were used to produce goods of an inferior quality, which, it was believed, had brought discredit on the industry and loss of trade, and so had caused the deepening poverty of the knitters. In Yorkshire, on the other hand, the motive was certainly to prevent the spread of the shearing-gigs, on the ground that they displaced labour. In Lancashire and Cheshire opposition to the new labour-saving steam looms was mixed with protests against the rise in food prices. In all districts secret drilling, midnight raids by masked men, and a grim spirit of conspiracy encouraged the ruling-class belief that revolution was being plotted. There was no such plot, for though the source of the Luddite discontent and anger was general, the aims of the movement were limited and particular. The Government met the Luddites with a well-organised system of spying, and passed an Act which made machine-wrecking punishable by death. Peace was restored with a savage hand; but later outbreaks occurred as part of the general post-war unrest.

Luddism makes a vivid story, but, as far as its methods are concerned, it lay outside the main currents of the development of Trade Unionism.

See " Short History ", Part I, chapter 4, section 1.
" Common People ", chapter 15.

1. THE MIDLAND LUDDITES

[A House of Commons Committee, reporting on the Framework Knitters' Petition in 1812, said that ' all witnesses attribute the decay of the trade, more to the making of fraudulent and bad articles, than to the War or any other cause '. This was the main source of discontent, as the detailed threats in their Declaration show, but it was not their only grievance. As long previously as 1753 Parliament had repealed the regulations governing apprenticeship, etc., among the framework knitters ; and neither Parliament nor the law courts gave them again the protection they had asked for. The market had become flooded, especially since the turn of the century ; the revived Framework Knitters' Company fought a test case (1804), but was awarded only 1s. damages, frame rents were raised in 1805, their 1787 wage agreement was not renewed in 1807, and wage reductions followed. Trade was lost by the dispute with America. The knitters' wages were falling in a time of rising prices, and even their pittance was reduced by the system of truck payments and by numerous frauds in the way of unpublished price-lists and reductions for imperfect work. Everything seemed against them, and no peaceful policy had succeeded. On top of it all the new ' fraudulent and bad articles ' were deepening the depression and seemed to destroy hope of any recovery. Their anger was directed against the machines, which manufactured such goods, if they belonged to employers who had proved unwilling to listen to any other argument. The machine-wrecking lasted, in three spells, from March 11, 1811, to January 13, 1812, and stopped for the time being the manufacture of ' cut-ups ', the most vicious of the new fraudulent articles. A Union was formed which concentrated on peaceful bargaining ; but, when it failed to win a rise in wages, a fourth outbreak of wrecking occurred in 1814. It was easily suppressed and, at the same time, the Nottingham Union of the Framework Knitters collapsed.]

The Declaration of the Framework Knitters, Home Office Papers, 42/119.

BY THE FRAMEWORK KNITTERS

A DECLARATION

Whereas by the charter granted by our late sovereign Lord Charles the Second by the Grace of God King of Great Britain France and Ireland, the Framework knitters are empowered to break and destroy all Frames and Engines that fabricate articles in a fraudulent and deceitful manner and to destroy all Framework knitters' Goods whatsoever that are so made and whereas a number of deceitful unprincipled and intriguing persons did attain an Act to be passed in the Twenty Eighth Year of our present sovereign

Lord George the Third whereby it was enacted that persons entering by force into any House Shop or Place to break or destroy Frames should be adjudged guilty of Felony and as we are fully convinced that such Act was obtained in the most fraudulent interested and electioneering maner [*sic*] and that the Honorable [*sic*] the Parliament of Great Britain was deceived as to the motives and intentions of the persons who obtained such Act we therefore the Framework knitters do hereby declare the aforesaid Act to be null and void to all intents and purposes whatsoever as by the passing of this act villainous and imposing persons are enabled to make fraudulent and deceitful manufactures to the discredit and utter ruin of our Trade. And whereas we declare that the aforementioned Charter is as much in force as though no such Act had been passed. . . . And we do hereby declare to all Hosiers Lace Manufacturers and proprietors of Frames that we will break and destroy all manner of Frames whatsoever that make the following spurious articles and all Frames whatsoever that do not pay the regular prices heretofore agreed to [by] the Masters and Workmen — All print net Frames making single press and Frames not working by the rack and rent and not paying the price regulated in 1810, Warp frames working single yarn or two coarse hole — not working by the rack, not paying the rent and prices regulated in 1809 — whereas all plain silk Frames not making work according to the gage — Frames not marking the work according to quality, whereas all Frames of whatsoever description the workmen of whom are not paid in the current coin of the realm will invariably be destroyed. . . ,

Given under my hand this first day of January 1812.

God protect the Trade   Ned Lud's Office
Sherewood Forest.

2. THE YORKSHIRE LUDDITES

[The shearing machines, which the Yorkshire Luddites destroyed, had already caused riots in Wiltshire. They were introduced into Yorkshire in 1810 and by the end of 1811 had displaced enough labour to produce a deep feeling of resentment. In 1812 secret organisations, meeting in the dark and acting with sudden violence, carried out raids against the shearing gigs and created an atmosphere of insurrection. But spies and repression soon disintegrated an unstable movement which demanded absolute secrecy and mutual confidence. The following letter may or may not be genuine; but, whether or no, it throws light on the movement.]

A copy of a letter sent to a Huddersfield Master, 1812. Home Office Papers, 40/41.

Sir,

Information has just been given in, that you are a holder of those detestable Shearing Frames, and I was desired by my men to write to you, and give you fair warning to pull them down, and for that purpose I desire that you will understand I am now writing to you, you will take notice that if they are not taken down by the end of next week, I shall detach one of my lieutenants with at least 300 men to destroy them, and further more take notice that if you give us the trouble of coming thus far, we will increase your misfortunes by burning your buildings down to ashes, and if you have the impudence to fire at any of my men, they have orders to murder you and burn all your Housing. You will have the goodness to go to your neighbours to inform them that the same Fate awaits them if their Frames are not taken down, as I understand there are several in your neighbourhood Frame Holders, and as the views and intentions of me and my men have been so misrepresented, I will take this opportunity of stating them, which I desire you will let all your Brethren sir know of, I would have the Merchant Master Drapers, the Government and the Public know that the grievances of such a number of men is not to be made sport of [sic], for by the last returns there were 2782 sworn Heroes bound in a Bond of necessity, either to redress their grievances or perish in the attempt, in the army of Huddersfield alone, nearly double sworn men in Leeds, by the latest Letters from our Correspondents, we learn that the Manufacturers of the following Places are going to rise and join us in redressing their wrongs viz Manchester, Wakefield, Halifax, Bradford, Sheffield, Oldham, Rochdale and all the Cotton Country, where the Brave Mr. Hanson will lead them on to victory, the weavers in Glasgow and many Parts of Scotland will join us, the Papists in Ireland are rising to a Man, so that they are likely to find the soldiers something else to do than idle in Huddersfield, and then woe be to the Places now guarded by them, for we have come to the easier way of burning them to ashes, which will most assuredly be their Fate either sooner or later — the immediate cause of us beginning when we did was that Rascally Letter of the Prince Regent to Lords Grey and Grenville which left us no hope of a change for the better, by his falling in with that damned set of Rogues Perceval & Co to whom we attribute all the miseries of our country but we hope for assistance from the French Emperor in shaking off the Yoke of the Rottenest, wickedest and most Tyrannical Government that ever existed, then down comes the Hanover Tyrants and all our tyrants from the greatest to the smallest, and we will be governed by a just Republic, and may the Almighty hasten those happy times is the wish and prayer of Millions in this Land, but we wont only pray but we will fight, the Red Coats shall know when the proper times come, we will never lay down our arms till the House of Commons passes an act to put down all the machinery hurtfull [*sic*] to the Commonality [*sic*] and repeal that to the Frame Breakers — but we petition no more, that wont do, fighting must,

Signed by the General of the Army of Redressers

NED LUDD

Clerk.

3. A LUDDITE OATH

[There was no standard Luddite oath, but most of the copies we have of Luddite oaths, genuine or faked, are on the lines of the one given below. The ruling classes had a particular fear of secret societies and oaths, mainly because they were the fruits of a despair in methods of peaceful agitation. Oaths taken by members of the societies seem to have been in general scrupulously observed, except by spies sent in by the Government or local magistrates.]

From F. Peel, " The Risings of the Luddites ", (3rd edition, 1895), p. 12.

I, A. B., of my own voluntary will, do declare and solemnly swear, that I never will reveal to any person or persons under the canopy of heaven, the names of the persons who compose this secret committee, their proceedings, meetings, places of abode ; dress, features, complexion or anything else that might lead to a discovery of the same, either by word, deed, or sign, under the penalty of being sent out of the world by the first brother who shall meet me, and my name and character blotted out of existence, and never to be remembered but with contempt and abhorrence ; and I further now do swear, that I will use my best endeavours to punish by death any traitor or traitors, should any rise up among us, whenever I can find him or them, and though he should fly to the verge of nature, I will pursue him with unceasing vengeance. So help me God and bless me to keep this my oath inviolable.

VI

THE POST-WAR CRISIS

INTRODUCTION

THE general discontent of the people in the last few years of the French Wars had found very little organised expression, partly because of a confident hope that peace would bring prosperity. Instead a crisis of appalling severity came upon nearly all sections of industry, trade, and agriculture. A bewildered country laid much of the blame on the Tories, since they had been in office for an almost uninterrupted spell of thirty years; it seemed likely that the strength of the anti-ministerial feeling would combine the middle and working classes under Whig leadership in a movement against the Government and for some moderate measure of reform.

But before any such alliance could be developed, the Corn Law of 1815 caused bread riots and angry demonstrations in different parts of the country. In May 1816 agricultural Luddism broke out in the Eastern Counties and spread rapidly. Some attempt was made to rally the disorganised clamour behind a movement for political reform. The Hampden Club (founded in 1812) democratised its constitution and at last found an audience : Thomas Cleary, its secretary, and Major Cartwright went out on missionary tours and helped to organise the petition presented to the House of Commons in April and May of 1816. From London a call was issued for a nation-wide campaign of petitions, which delegates were to bring to a Convention in January, 1817.

Meanwhile in the middle classes sympathy for the Reform movement had ebbed away. The repeal of the Income Tax in March 1816 had removed one of their most deep-felt grievances, and at the same time the riots had frightened them. Robert Waithman, an influential, and very typical, spokesman of the middle-class reformers, declared at the end of November 1816 that ' There were three classes, who were in fact the decided enemies of Reform — those who lived on the national purse — the timid, whose fears had been excited as to the consequences which might arise from Reform — and the inflammatory and riotous who were its bitterest foes ', and then in December 1816 the Spencean Riots in the Spa Fields, London (an absurd attempt to seize power), finally shattered the hopes of a class alliance among the reformers. When the Hampden Club Convention met in January 1817 it could represent only a section of a divided and weakening movement.

Cobbett had tried to turn the movement into peaceful channels when, in November 1816, with the special twopenny edition of his *Register*, he appealed directly to the working class; he had urged them to abandon violence and to find the cause of their distress not in individual employers or the employing class, but in the political system and those who profited by it. But, before his work could have effect, the Government had initiated a policy of repression. A Committee of Secrecy, appointed after an attempt had been made on the Regent's life, issued in February a report full of vague premonitions of possible insurrections. The Government, acting on the report, passed a series of ' Gagging Bills ' (in March 1817),— Habeas Corpus was suspended, the regulations of the Mutiny Acts of 1797 were revived, an Act was passed for the safety and preservation of the royal family and the Government, and severe restrictions were placed on public meetings, especially where delegates were elected to a conference (this being a method of evading the Corresponding Societies Act of 1799).

The Reform movement collapsed : Cobbett, partly for private reasons, fled to America, and in 1817, instead of the optimistic clubs and meetings of 1816, came the abortive march of the Blanketeers in March and the Derbyshire Insurrection in June. The Government's policy of repression was checked by the revelation that the insurrection had been the work of one of their own paid spies : juries began to acquit prisoners, and in London Wooler and Hone struck successful blows for the freedom of the press. In January 1818 the suspension of Habeas Corpus was not renewed and peace reigned for a while in the political world.

But later in the same year a recurrence of economic difficulties brought a fresh crop of societies, usually called ' Political Protestants ' or ' Union Societies '. Mass drilling became a common feature of their activities, to prepare for revolution (according to the authorities) or (according to the reformers) to ensure that their demonstrations should be orderly and well organised. The climax of this period was the huge rally at St. Peter's Fields, Manchester, in 1819, where the massacre of ' Peterloo ' was staged. The country was horrified, but not the Government or Parliament, which promptly passed the notorious ' Six Acts ', destroying most of what remained of English political liberties. Repression produced a sullen peace, broken in 1820 by a futile plot to assassinate the Cabinet (the ' Cato Street Conspiracy ') and a series of riots in Scotland.

After George III's death the quarrel between King George IV and his Queen Caroline gave rise to a curious and brief revival of Radicalism. The people sided fervently with the Queen, if only because they hated the King, and a powerful movement in her support swept the country, the lower and middle classes being united under Whig leadership. The interest of the episode lay in the new alliance which foreshadowed the campaign for the Great Reform Bill. But its effect was short-lived, and, for the most part, the Reform movement was quiet for the years 1821–1827 : only small sections of the people were touched by the county meetings, which in 1821–24 were, largely under Cobbett's influence, demanding Reform, or by Lord John Russell's desultory enthusiasm for the subject in Parliament, or Richard Carlile's triumph in the cause of a free press. The working classes were busy with Trade Unionism and Co-operation. So in 1826 Carlile could speak of ' the futile political clamour of the Radical Reform era ', as though it were a childhood complaint which the people had left behind them.

During this period of severe unemployment Robert Owen put forward his ' Plan ' for replacing poor relief by a system of ' Villages of Co-operation ', modelled on his New Lanark establishment. There were big strikes in Lancashire and elsewhere ; and attempts were made to form a General Union of all workers in Nottingham, Manchester, and London. The Government, in dealing with the troubles, made extensive use of spies, including the well-known Oliver, who was mainly responsible for provoking the ' Derbyshire Insurrection ' of 1817.

See " Short History ", Part I, chapter 4, section 2.
" Common People ", chapters 16-19.

1. SIGNS OF UNREST

[Samuel Bamford, the Lancashire weaver-poet (1788–1872), who was imprisoned in 1817 and again after ' Peterloo ', was a moderate in politics and a strong opponent of violence. His " Early Days " (1849) and " Passages in the Life of a Radical " (1840–1844) are an important source for the history of the years after 1815. He also wrote " The Weaver Boy "

(1819) and " Homely Rhymes " (1843), and a book on " The Dialect of South Lancashire ", including some of Tim Bobbin's verses.]

(*a*) From Samuel Bamford, "Passages in the Life of a Radical" (2nd edition, 1840), p. 6.

It is a matter of history, that whilst the laurels were yet cool on the brows of our victorious soldiers on their second occupation of Paris, the elements of convulsion were at work amongst the masses of our labouring population; and that a series of disturbances commenced with the introduction of the Corn Bill in 1815, and continued with short intervals, until the close of the year 1816. In London and Westminster riots ensued, and were continued for several days, whilst the bill was discussed; at Bridgeport there were riots on account of the high price of bread; at Biddeford there were similar disturbances to prevent the exportation of Grain; at Bury, by the unemployed, to destroy machinery; at Ely, not suppressed without bloodshed; at Newcastle-on-Tyne, by colliers and others; at Glasgow, where blood was shed, on account of the soup kitchens; at Preston by unemployed weavers; at Nottingham, by Luddites, who destroyed thirty frames; at Merthyr Tydville, on a reduction of wages; at Birmingham by the unemployed; at Walsall, by the distressed; and December 7th, 1816, at Dundee, where, owing to the high price of meal, upwards of one hundred shops were plundered. At this time the writings of William Cobbett suddenly became of great authority; they were read on nearly every cottage hearth in the manufacturing districts of South Lancashire; in those of Leicester, Derby, and Nottingham; also in many of the Scottish manufacturing towns. Their influence was speedily visible; he directed his readers to the true cause of their sufferings — misgovernment; and to its proper corrective — parliamentary reform. Riots soon became scarce, and from that time they have never obtained their ancient vogue with the labourers of this country.

(*b*) From *The Black Dwarf*,[1] February 5, 1817.

The Magistrates and Inhabitants of Leeds have published a Declaration, in which they say —

" We behold with detestation, wicked attempts to produce disaffection to the established form of Government, by exciting popular assemblies, promoting political clubs, and thus setting the ignorant and uninformed, in judgment over their rulers. — Men,

---

[1] For *The Black Dwarf*, see p. 143.

of abandoned character, and desperate fortune, taking advantage of our commercial difficulties, and the unfavourableness of the seasons, sow discontent among the labouring classes of the community — vilify the high Authorities of the State — dare to use openly language of intimidation, and to disparage the very charity so liberally extended to the poor, during this period of unavoidable pressure. The difficulties, under which we labour, are attributed by them to the corruption and mismanagement of Ministers; and General Suffrage and Annual Parliaments (evils deprecated by the judicious of all parties) are held out as the only correctives; yet these would, in truth, lead to the subversion of the Constitution, and to that disturbed state of public affairs, which has produced the most calamitous effects in a neighbouring nation.

We contemplate with peculiar horror the organized system, which the seditious have contrived, for the furtherance of their designs, by the extensive circulation of inflamatory tracts and pamphlets : of these some are blasphemous parodies on the venerated forms of our Holy Religion, and which tend to root out of the minds of the unwary all fear of God, honour of the King, and reverence of the Laws.

Against these wicked conspiracies, we consider it the duty of A L L his Majesty's faithful subjects to unite, and to quell the spirit of Rebellion, by opposing to it the firm and dauntless front of Loyalty."

(c) From *The Black Dwarf*, February 26, 1817.

The Report presented to the House of Commons gives *unwittingly* a solution of the whole affair, so satisfactory, that even their own prejudices and interests could not avoid the statement. After stating various means had been employed to spread disaffection, they say the success " had been confined to the principal manufacturing districts, WHERE THE DISTRESS IS MORE PREVALENT."

Here, ye worthies of the state, then is your own CONFESSION, that the DISTRESS is the cause of the success of the disaffected. And who created the DISTRESS ? Why, YOURSELVES. And who then are the TRAITORS ? and deserve the vengeance of the laws ? They proceed to say — " Few, if any, of the higher orders, or even the middle classes of society, and scarcely any of the agricultural population, have lent themselves to the more *violent* of these projects." What the more *violent projects* are, is not known even by the ministry themselves; but whatever these projects may be, it is quite clear that their only aim is " *relief from distress*." The ministers say, but " *few, if any*, of the higher orders, are implicated."

They should have said NONE; for they know the HIGHER ORDERS are not distressed. But they want to implicate those who FEEL for the distresses of others, as THEREFORE wishing to destroy the state; and the — " FEW, IF ANY," are meant to designate those men of property and rank, who are honest enough to confess that the patience of slaves is not to be expected from the descendants of Englishmen, who have lived, and dare die FREEMEN.

2. COBBETT TURNS TO THE WORKING CLASS, 1816

[William Cobbett, until 1816, had paid no particular attention to the distress of the urban working class. Since his conversion to Radicalism he had espoused the cause of the rural workers, but had also sought for an audience among any and all whom he regarded as victims of the ' Pitt system ' of heavy national debt and a rising burden of taxation to pay the interest on it. But his ' Squire Jolterheads ' would not listen. By 1816 he began to find that the bulk of the support for his case must come from the working classes. In November of that year he wrote the first of his " Addresses to the Journeymen and Labourers " and published it simultaneously in the ordinary edition of his *Weekly Political Register* at 1s. 0½d. and in a special 2d. edition — which came to be known by his enemies as ' *Cobbett's Twopenny Trash* ' — a name which he eagerly accepted. This cheap edition proved such a success that he decided to make it a regular feature. The importance of this policy was twofold: Cobbett became primarily a working-class leader and not merely an interesting and powerful journalistic figure in the Radical world, and, secondly, he gave a tremendous impetus to the development of working-class journalism. Other journalists had, like Cobbett, written as friends of the working class, but not directly to them. But now papers and pamphlets, often printed by a hand-press, were poured forth, helping Cobbett in his declared purpose of educating the working class in political knowledge. It was Cobbett and his followers who helped to prove the futility of disorganised violence, and sowed the seeds of the great reform campaign of 1830–1832.]

(*a*) Cobbett announces the second edition of the *Weekly Political Register*, 1816.

Political Register 16 Nov. 1816.[1]

The *Register*, No. 18, which was reprinted on an open sheet, to be sold for *two-pence* by retail, having been found to be very useful, it is my intention to continue that mode of proceeding. . . .

---

[1] See also p. 300.

The Register in its *usual form* and at its *usual price* I shall continue . . . while the country was in a state of comparative insensibility I was less anxious about being read. . . . But *now* the scene is changed. *Now* events are pressing upon us so fast, that my *Register*, loaded with more than half its amount in *stamp* and other expences incidental to the stamp, does not move about *sufficiently swift* to do all the good that it might do. I have, therefore resolved to make it move *swifter*. . . .

(*b*) From an ' Address to the Journeymen and Labourers ', *Cobbett's Weekly Political Register*, November 2, 1816.

FRIENDS AND FELLOW COUNTRYMEN,

Whatever the Pride of rank, of riches or of scholarship may have induced some men to believe, or to affect to believe, the real strength and all the resources of a country, ever have sprung and ever must spring, from the *labour* of its people ; and hence it is, that this nation, which is so small in numbers and so poor in climate and soil compared with many others, has, for many ages been the most powerful nation in the world : it is the most industrious, the most laborious, and therefore, the most powerful. Elegant dresses, superb furniture, stately buildings, fine roads and canals, fleet horses and carriages, numerous and stout ships, warehouses teeming with goods ; all these, and many other objects that fall under our view, are so many marks of national wealth and resources. But all these spring from *labour*. Without the Journeymen and the labourers none of them could exist ; without the assistance of their hands, the country would be a wilderness, hardly worth the notice of an invader.

As it is the labour of those who toil which makes a country abound in resources, so it is the same class of men, who must, by their arms, secure its safety and uphold its fame. Titles and immense sums of money have been bestowed upon numerous Naval and Military Commanders. Without calling the justice of these in question, we may assert that the victories were obtained by *you* and your fathers and brothers and sons in co-operation with those Commanders, who, with *your* aid have done great and wonderful things ; but, who, without that aid, would have been as impotent as children at the breast.

With this correct idea of your own worth in your minds, with what indignation must you hear yourselves called the Populace, the Rabble, the Mob, the Swinish Multitude ; and with what greater indignation, if possible, must you hear the projects of those cool and cruel and insolent men, who, now that you have been, without any fault of yours, brought into a state of misery, propose to narrow the limits of parish relief, to prevent you from marrying in the days of your youth, or to thrust you out to seek your bread in foreign lands, never more to behold your parents or friends ? But suppress your indignation, until we return to this topic, after we have considered the *cause* of your present misery and the measures which have produced that cause.

The times in which we live are full of peril. The nation, as described by the very creatures of the government, is fast advancing to that period when an important change must take place. It is the lot of mankind, that some shall labour with their limbs and others with their minds ; and, on all occasions, more especially on an occasion like the present, it is the duty of the latter to come to the assistance of the former. We are all equally interested in the peace and happiness of our common country. It is of the utmost importance, that in the seeking to obtain those objects, our endeavours should be uniform, and tend all to the same point. Such an uniformity cannot exist without an uniformity of sentiment as to public matters, and to produce this latter uniformity amongst you is the object of this address.

As to the *cause* of our present miseries, it is the *enormous amount of the taxes*, which the government compels us to pay for the support of its army, its placemen, its pensioners, etc. and for the payment of the interest of its debt. That this is the *real* cause has been a thousand times proved ; and it is now so acknowledged by the creatures of the government themselves. . . .

We have seen that the cause of our miseries is the *burden of taxes* occasioned by wars, by standing armies, by sinecures, by pensions, etc. It would be endless and useless to enumerate all the different heads or sums of expenditure. The *remedy* is what we have now to look to, and that remedy consists wholly and solely of such a *reform* in the Commons' or People's House of Parliament, as shall give to every payer of *direct taxes* a vote at elections, and as shall cause the Members to be *elected annually*. . . .

But, this and *all other good things*, must be done by a *reformed parliament.*— We must have *that first*, or we shall have nothing good ; and, any man, who would, *before hand* take up your time with the detail of what a reformed parliament ought to do in this respect, or with respect to any changes in the form of government, can have no other object than that of defeating the cause of reform, and, indeed, the very act must show, that to *raise obstacles* is his wish.

Such men, now that they find you justly irritated, would persuade you, that, because things have been perverted from their true ends, there is *nothing good* in our *constitution and laws*. For what, then, did Hampden die in the field, and Sydney on the scaffold ? And, has it been discovered, at last, that England has *always* been an enslaved country from top to toe ? The Americans, who are a very wise people, and who love liberty with all their hearts, and who take care to *enjoy* it too, took special care not to part with any of the great principles and laws which they derived from their forefathers. They took special care to speak with reverence of, and to preserve Magna Carta, the Bill of Rights, the Habeas Corpus, and not only all the body of the Common Law of England, but most of the rules of our courts, and all our form of jurisprudence. Indeed, it is the greatest glory of England that she has thus supplied with sound principles of freedom those immense regions, which will be peopled, perhaps, by hundreds of millions.

I know of no enemy of reform and of the happiness of the country so great as that man, who would persuade you that we possess *nothing good*, and that *all* must be torn to pieces. There is no principle, no precedent, no regulations (except as to mere matter of detail), favourable to freedom, which is not to be found in the Laws of England or in the example of our Ancestors. Therefore, I say we may ask for, and we want *nothing new*. We have great constitutional laws and principles, to which we are immoveably attached. We want *great alteration*, but we want *nothing new*. Alteration, modification to suit the times and circumstances ; but the great principles ought to be, and must be, the same, or else confusion will follow.

3. THE SPENCEAN PHILANTHROPISTS

[The distress caused by the Enclosure Movement led many to blame contemporary evils on the power of the landlord. Thomas Spence has come down to us as the best representative of Agrarian Reform. The details of his plan were vague and varying, but the general outline was clear. In a state of nature, said Spence, ' property in land and liberty among men ' were equal : a social contract was made for the mutual preservation of rights, but the usurping landlords have left men to live as strangers on the land which is theirs by right. His solution was that the inhabitants of each parish should assert their lost rights and form themselves into a corporation ; land would be public property, rented in small lots to tenants, who would bid at a public auction ; rents would be paid into the parish treasury and used to pay the needs of government. The political system of the new world was extremely obscure ; we are told little more than that the duties of government would be undertaken by full meetings of parishes, in committees or in a parliament, where each member would represent a group of neighbouring parishes.

Thomas Spence (1750–1814), was born in Newcastle in circumstances of great poverty, and educated himself with a quite wide but ill-digested reading of literature. He first put forward his plan in 1775, but won so little attention that he moved to London in 1792, partly to find a new audience. He became a member of the London Corresponding Society and was imprisoned for selling Tom Paine's " Rights of Man ", but his main activity was propaganda for the plan by chalk and charcoal notices, by personal arguments, handbills, broadsheets, pamphlets, and a newspaper (*Pigs' Meat*, 1795–1796). The 1801 Committee of Secrecy thought Spence was a seditious menace and he was imprisoned again. In spite of this publicity Spence lived his last years in obscurity. One of his subsidiary interests was a new phonetic alphabet.

For a long time Spence carried on the propaganda for his plan single handed. In 1801 there seems to have been some informal group of Spenceans, and by 1807 there was a Spencean Society in existence. In 1814, after Spence's death, the ' Society of Spencean Philanthropists ' was founded. An attempt was made to organise on the lines of the London Corresponding Society, but its membership was never large. An impracticable plan was formulated for the seizure of power in London, but soon came to grief in the Spa Fields Riot of December 1816. The Government, whether from genuine or feigned panic, gave considerable prominence to the Spenceans and represented them as a revolutionary menace. They were suppressed in 1817 as a sequel to the report of a Committee of Secrecy, which made them out to be much more important than they were. One of the leading Spenceans, Arthur Thistlewood, was later executed for his part in the Cato Street Conspiracy, 1820.]

(*a*) From Thomas Spence, " The Restorer of Society to its Natural State ", 1801. Letter 1.

LONDON, *July* 19, 1800.

. . . Thus Societies, Families, and Tribes being originally nothing but Banditties they esteemed War and Pillage to be honourable, and the greatest Ruffians seize on the principal shares of the spoils as well of Land as Movables, introduced into the World all the curst varieties of Lordship, Vassalage, and Slavery as we see it at this Day.

Now Citizen, if we really want to get rid of these evils from amongst Men, we must destroy not only personal and hereditary

Lordship, but the cause of them, which is Private Property in Land. For this is the Pillar that supports the Temple of Aristocracy. Take away this Pillar, and the whole Fabric of their Dominion falls to the ground. Then shall no other Lords have dominion over us, but the Laws, and Laws too of our own making; for at present it is those who have robbed us of our lands, that have robbed us also of the privilege of making our own Laws : so in truth and reality we are in bondage, and vassalage to the landed interest. Wherefore let us bear this always in mind, and we shall never be at a loss to know where the root of the Evil lies.

Then what can be the cure but this ? Namely, that the land shall no longer be suffered to be the property of individuals, but of the parishes. The rents of this Parish Estate, shall be deemed the equal property of Man, Woman, and Child, whether old or young, rich or poor, legitimate or illegitimate. But more of this hereafter.

I remain, yours, etc.

(*b*) From Thomas Spence, " The Restorer of Society to its Natural State ", 1801. Letter 5.

LONDON, *Sept. 20th*, 1800.

CITIZEN,

The unprecedented dearness of provisions, sets every head on devising how to find a Remedy. And as people impute much of the mischief to the manner Gentlemen now follow of letting their Lands in large Farms, they talk of having Laws made to reduce Farms again to a moderate size. But this is reckoning without their Host. This is like the mice tying a Bell about the Cat's neck. Whose to do it ? Are not our Legislators all Landlords ? And are they going to make Laws to restrict themselves in the management of their property ? Believe it not. They find those rich Tenants both give them more rent, and pay more certainly than poor Men could. Neither bad seasons, nor accidents among Cattle, affect them. They are still able in spite of every mischance to pay, and also to hoard and keep up what they have, till they can get a price to their mind. All this the Landlord knows is for his advantage and makes him look on the increasing profits of the Farmer with pleasure, as he will be sure to advance his rent in proportion at the expiration of his Lease. These Landed Legislators therefore rejoice when Markets are high, and will open and shut the Ports, and give Bounties out of the national purse for the exportation of grain, rather than the Farmers shall be hurt.

It is childish therefore to expect ever to see Small Farms again, or ever to see anything else than the utmost screwing and grinding of the poor, till you quite overturn the present system of Landed Property. For they have got more completely into the spirit and power of oppression now than ever was known before, and they hold the people in defiance by means of their armed associations. They are now like a warlike enemy quartered upon us for the purpose of raising contributions, and William the Conqueror and his Normans were fools to them in the Art of fleecing. Therefore anything short of total Destruction of the power of these Samsons will not do. And that must be accomplished not by simple shaving which leaves the roots of their strength to grow again. No: we must scalp them or else they will soon recover and pull our Temple of Liberty about our Ears.

We must not leave even their stump in the Earth, like Nebuchadnezzar though guarded by a band of Iron. For ill destroyed Royalty and Aristocracy, will be sure to recover and overspread the Earth again as before. And when they are suffered to return again to their former Dominion it is always with ten-fold more rage and policy, and so the condition of their wretched subjects is quickly rendered worse as a reward for their too tender resistance.

In plain English nothing less than complete Extermination of the present system of holding Land in the manner I propose will ever bring the world again to a state worth living in.

But how is this mighty work to be done? I answer it must be done at once than at twice or at an hundred times. For the public mind being suitably prepared by reading my little Tracts and conversing on the subject, a few Contingent Parishes have only to declare the land to be theirs and form a convention of Parochial Delegates. Other adjacent Parishes would immediately on being invited follow the example, and send also their Delegates and thus would a beautiful and powerful New Republic instantaneously arise in full vigour. The power and resources of War passing in this manner in a moment, into the hands of the People from the hands of their Tyrants, they, like sham Samsons would become weak and harmless as other Men. And being thus as it were scalped of their Revenues and the Lands that produced them their Power would never more grow to enable them to overturn our Temple of Liberty.

Therefore talk no more of impossibilities. How lately have we seen Unions of the People sufficiently grand and well conducted to give sure hopes of success? Abroad and at Home, in America,

France, and in our own Fleets, we have seen enough of public spirit, and extensive unanimity in the present generation to accomplish Schemes of infinitely greater difficulty than a thing that may be done in a Day, when once the public mind is duly prepared. In fact it is like the Almighty saying ' Let there be light and it was so.' So the People have only to say ' Let the Land be ours,' and it will be so. . . .

(c) A handbill of the Spenceans. From the Place MSS., 27,809 f. 93. Undated (? 1816).

SPENCE'S PLAN

For Parochial Partnership in the Land,
is the only effectual Remedy for the
Distress and Oppression of the People.

The landholders are not proprietors in chief; they are but the *stewards* of the Public.

For the LAND is the PEOPLE'S FARM..

The expenses of the government do not cause the misery that surrounds us,

but the enormous exactions of these " *unjust Stewards* ".

Landed monopoly is indeed equally contrary to the benign spirit of Christianity, and destructive of the independence and morality of mankind.

" The profit of the earth is for all " : yet how deplorably destitute are the great mass of the people !

Nor is it possible for their situation to be radically amended but by the establishment of a system, founded on the immutable basis of nature and justice.

Experience demonstrates its necessity : and the rights of mankind require it for their preservation.

To obtain this important object, by extending the knowledge of the above system, the Society of SPENCEAN PHILANTHROPISTS has been instituted. Further information of its principles may be obtained by attending any of its sectional meetings, where subjects are discussed, calculated to enlighten the human understanding and where also the regulations of the society may be procured, containing a complete development of the Spencean system. Every individual is admitted, free of expense, who will conduct himself with decorum.

The meetings of the Society began at a quarter after Eight in the Evening, as under

First Section   Every Wednesday at the Cock, Grafton Street, Soho.
Second „   „ Thursday „ „ Mulberry Tree, Mulberry Court,
                                           Wilson St. Moorfield.
Third   „   ·   „ Monday   „ „ Nags Head, Carnaby Market.
Fourth „   „ Tuesday „ No. 8, Lumber Street, Mint, Bor-
                                           ough.

∵ Read " Christian Policy the Salvation of the Empire; " price
one shilling and sixpence, published by T. EVANS, 8 Newcastle
Street, Strand ; and sold by all booksellers.

SPENCEAN RIOTS

(*d*) From the First Report of the Committee of Secrecy (1817), p. 4.

. . . It has been proved, to the entire satisfaction of your
Committee, that some members of these Societies, acting by delegated
or assumed authority, as an executive committee of the whole,
conceived the project and endeavoured to prepare the means of
raising an Insurrection, so formidable from numbers, as by dint
of physical strength to overpower all resistance.

The first step towards the accomplishment of this object was by
the individual exertion of the members of the committee, to discover
and foment the prevalent distresses and discontents in the Metropolis
and its vicinity. Returns were made of those, who they thought were
to be relied upon for daring and hazardous enterprizes.

The design was by a sudden rising in the dead of the night, to
surprize and overpower the soldiers in their different barracks,
which were to be set on fire ; at the same time (plans having been
arranged, and some steps taken, with a view to the accomplishment
of that object) to possess themselves of the artillery, to seize or destroy
the bridges, and to take possession of the Tower and the Bank. In
furtherance of this design, a machine was projected for clearing the
streets of cavalry. A drawing of this machine fully authenticated,
and also a manuscript sketch or plan of various important parts
of the Tower, found with the drawings of the machine, have been
been laid before your committee.

The design was however relinquished a short time before its
intended execution. It was thought more prudent previously to
ascertain what force the Conspirators could actually call together,
and this it was agreed could best be done by convening a public
meeting, for the ostensible purpose of obtaining a redress of grievances
in a legal way. The map of London was inspected, and Spa Fields
were selected as the most eligible spot, from their vicinity to the

Bank and the Tower. Advertisements were accordingly prepared, and written placards circulated, of the most dangerous and inflammatory nature; of one of which the following is a copy.

" BRITONS TO ARMS !

" THE whole Country waits the signal from London to fly to Arms ! Haste, break open Gunsmiths and other likely places to find Arms ! Run all constables who touch a man of us : no rise of Bread : no Regent : no Castlereagh, off with their heads ; no Placemen, Tythes, or Enclosures ; no Taxes ; no Bishops, only useless lumber ! Stand true or be Slaves for ever."

N.B. Five thousand of these Bills are up in the Town, and printed ones, with further particulars, will appear in due time."

At this time, if not before, the intended Insurrection assumed the symbols of the French Revolution ; a committee of public Safety, consisting of 24, was agreed upon, including the names of several persons, extremely unlikely to lend themselves to such a cause. A tricolor Flag and Cockades were actually prepared ; the flag was openly carried and displayed at the first meeting which took place in the Spa Fields on the 15th of November. No acts of violence were however encouraged on that day, though some few instances of plunder occurred after the assembly dispersed, but care was taken to adjourn the meeting to the 2nd of December, by which time it was hoped that the preparations for insurrection would be fully matured. Not a moment was lost in advertising the next meeting, and great assiduity was employed in circulating the intelligence through all the great manufacturing towns in the country, by means of placards and handbills ; endeavours were used to raise subscriptions ; the expense hitherto incurred in forwarding the object of the conspiracy, and in supporting such inferior members of it as had relinquished their trades and occupations in order to devote their whole time to the furtherance of the cause, having been hitherto principally defrayed by one individual of the committee. Plans for the seduction of the Soldiers were now adopted and pursued with unremitting activity ; appeals were made to excite their sympathy, and induce them not to act against the insurgents ; attempts were made to inflame their hopes by promises of rank and reward, and to alarm their jealousy by the absurd fiction of the actual landing of a considerable foreign army, for the purpose of controlling them.

Barracks were again reconnoitred with a view to attack. The

manufacture of tricolor-ribbon was encouraged, with a view of rendering it familiar to the eyes of the Public.

Visits were repeated to those quarters of the Town, where the distress was considered as the most prevalent; and warehouses along the River, as well as shops in other places, which were known to contain Arms, Combustibles and Clothing, were examined and noted down, with the view of seizing those articles on the proper occasion.

Plans were also formed for seducing the sailors on the River, by offers of advancement to high rank under the new government, and for seizing and equipping such ships as were accessible. Immediately previous to the day of meeting, Arms were provided for the immediate use of some of the persons most actively engaged. This provision was deemed sufficient for the beginning of the Insurrection, as they felt confident that if it should be successful for two hours, as many Arms might be produced as would be necessary, from the depôts and gunsmiths' shops, which had been reconnoitred with that view.

Your Committee have further received undoubted information that a large quantity of Pike heads had been ordered of one individual, and 250 actually made by him, and delivered and paid for. It was was also undoubtedly intended to liberate the prisoners in the principal gaols in and about the Metropolis, in the hope of their concurrence and assistance in the intended Insurrection. Addresses were introduced into some of those prisons, and recommended to be communicated to others, in which the persons confined were invited, in the name of the Tri-colored Committee, to rally round the Tri-colored Standard, which would be erected on Monday December the 2d, and to wear Tri-colored Cockades themselves. It was promised that the Prisoners should be liberated by force, and arms were stated to be provided for them, and they were directed to be ready to assist in overpowering the turnkeys.

4. ROBERT OWEN AND THE POST-WAR CRISIS

[Robert Owen (1771–1858) from shop assistant had become part-owner and manager of the New Lanark Cotton Mills, where he won a widespread reputation as a successful man of business and a philanthropic employer with original ideas. In his " New View of Society " he outlined his approach to the problems of government. At that time he laid most emphasis on his theories about the formation of character. ' The old collectively [he said] may train the young collectively to be ignorant and miserable or to be intelligent and happy.' He advocated a system of Welfare Capitalism, with national education and a national public works scheme for the unemployed. In 1815 he was eagerly pushing forward a generous measure of factory reform, but when his fellow-manufacturers proved bitterly hostile to it he began to turn his attention more to the general problem of the post-war crisis. As a result, he produced a very able theory of the crisis; he found the immediate cause of the distress in the depreciation of labour through the introduction of machinery. The war had hastened on the process of industrialisation, but now the war-time demand was over and the bottom had fallen out of the market. In consequence even more men were thrown out of employment, to be replaced by the cheaper method of machinery. Unlike Cobbett and many other leaders of the working class, Owen firmly believed that machinery would benefit mankind, as soon as man was master of it. So he based his New Plan for solving the unemployment problem on the need to maintain the industrial system. He proposed a series of mainly self-sufficient communities, in which the unemployed could live under semi-co-operative conditions and be governed on Owen's principles of character formation. He hoped that the plan would be put into effect by philanthropists, the Government, or local authorities. But while he won some sympathy from royal dukes, archbishops, and the Cabinet, he could not get any promise of action from them. And the political reformers suspected the scheme both on account of the barrack-like nature of the buildings proposed, and because they regarded it as calculated to sidetrack the demand for political Reform. ' Leave us alone, Mr. Owen ', was a typical answer to his approaches. Owen, undeterred, kept on with his agitation. Before long, however, by an attack on all existing systems of religion, he helped to alienate the support of his aristocratic and episcopal sympathisers. At the same time he broadened out his scheme till he put forward his plan of communities as an ideal system of society, and not merely as a solution for the problem of unemployment. In the " Report to the County of Lanark " (1820) he based his plan on the view " That manual labour, properly directed, is the source of all wealth, and of national prosperity ". This, together with the greater attractiveness of his communities in their elaborated form began to appeal to the working classes (see p. 207). The working-class Owenites, at any rate, felt that if they were to set up a community for themselves they could be sure of a rational and happy life. Owen's message was welcomed by an audience he had very little addressed.]

(*a*) Owen at New Lanark. From " The Life of Robert Owen ", by himself (1857), vol. i, pp. 78-9, 80-81, 86-8.

. . . I entered upon the government of New Lanark about the first of January 1800.

I say " government ", — for my intention was not to be a mere manager of cotton mills, as such mills were at this time generally managed; but to introduce principles in the conduct of the people, which I had successfully commenced with the workpeople in Mr. Drinkwater's factory; and to change the conditions of the people, who, I saw, were surrounded by circumstances having an injurious influence upon the character of the entire population of New Lanark.

I had now, by a course of events not under my control, the groundwork on which to try an experiment long wished for, but little expected ever to be in my power to carry into execution.

On commencing my task I found it full of formidable obstacles. The former managers had acquired their own views of managing. They had old notions and habits, all directly opposed to mine, and from these parties I expected little assistance. The people were surrounded by bad conditions, and these bad conditions had powerfully acted upon them to misform their characters and conduct. I soon perceived that there would be much to undo and much to do, before I could obtain the results which I intended to accomplish. The people had been collected hastily from any place from whence they could be induced to come, and the great majority of them were idle, intemperate, dishonest, devoid of truth and pretenders to religion, which they supposed would cover and excuse all their shortcomings and immoral proceedings. My first object was to ascertain all the errors against which I had to contend, and as I investigated each department, I thought there would be no termination to the changes required. I soon found that a *reconstruction* of the whole establishment would be necessary for my views, and for the pecuniary success of the concern. I therefore commenced cautiously laying the groundwork for the intended changes, and I wished to make the old superintendents of the different departments my agents for this purpose. But I soon found that they were wedded to their own notions and ancient prejudices, and that for new measures it was necessary to have new men; for the old ones preferred to leave their situations, rather than be engaged in a work of such reform as I contemplated, which they said was impracticable. And to them it was so; for they had no conception of the principle on which I proposed to act, and by which I intended to govern the population. It is from this same ignorance that the public now think my views impracticable.

. . . Knowing by this time the influence of circumstances over human nature in every part of the world, my first attention was to discover the evil conditions existing among the people, and how in the shortest time they could be superseded by better. There were two ways before me, by which to govern the population. First, by contending against the people, who had to contend against the evil conditions by which, through ignorance, they were surrounded; and in this case I should have had continually to find fault with all, and to keep them in a state of constant ill-will and irritation — to have many of them tried for theft, — to have some imprisoned and transported, and at that period to have others condemned to death, — for in some cases I detected thefts to a large amount; there being no check upon any of their proceedings. This was the course which had ever been the practice of society. Or, secondly, I had to consider these unfortunately placed people, as they really were, the creatures of ignorant and vicious circumstances, who were made to be what they were by the evil conditions which had been made to surround them, and for which alone society, if any party, should be made responsible; and, instead of tormenting the individuals, — imprisoning and transporting some, hanging others, and keeping the population in a state of constant irrational excitement, — I had to change these evil conditions for good ones, and thus, in the due order of nature, according to its unchanging laws, to supersede the inferior and bad characters, created by inferior and bad conditions, by superior and good characters to be created by superior and good conditions. And this is now the course which for the happiness of all should be universally adopted in practice.

This latter mode required a knowledge of human nature, and of the science of the influence of circumstances over it, with illimitable patience, forbearance, and determination. But *with these conditions* certain ultimate success would inevitably follow. While the first mode could not ensure success if persevered in to the end of time, — and so long as it is continued must keep society in never-ending varied confusion, counter-action, and opposing feelings.

But from what source could the knowledge of human nature, the science of the influence of the circumstances over it, with illimitable patience, forbearance, and determination, be obtained? — seeing that these qualities combined had remained unknown during the past history of the human race. This is the great secret worth knowing, and which has been so long hidden from the world.

From one source only could the secret be derived; — that is, from the discovery of the knowledge " that the character of each of our race is formed by God or nature and by society; and that it is impossible that any human being could or can form his own qualities or character ".

This knowledge I had now acquired by the gradual teaching of nature, through experience and reflection, forced upon me by the circumstances through which I had passed; and it was now to be ascertained whether it had given me the patience, forbearance, and determination to proceed successfully in my task, — for I had decided to govern the New Lanark population according to these new views, — that is, on the second mode stated. For this purpose I had to lay my plans deep and wide, and to combine them with measures to ensure profits from the establishment sufficient to satisfy my commercial partners, and at first not to do too much, so as to alarm their prejudices or those of the public. . . .

The workpeople were systematically opposed to every change which I proposed, and did whatever they could to frustrate my object. For this, as it was natural for them to dislike new measures and all attempts to change their habits, I was prepared, and I made due allowance for these obstructions. My intention was to gain their confidence, and this, from their prejudices to a stranger from a foreign country, as at this time the working class of the Scotch considered England to be, was extremely difficult to attain. My language was naturally different from their Lowland Scotch and the Highland Erse, for they had a large mixture of Highlanders among them. I therefore sought out the individuals who had the most influence among them from their natural powers or position, and to these I took pains to explain what were my intentions for the changes I wished to effect. I explained that they were to procure greater permanent advantages for themselves and their children, and requested that they would aid me in instructing the people, and in preparing them for the new arrangements which I had in contemplation.

By these means I began slowly to make an impression upon some of the least prejudiced and most reasonable among them; but the suspicions of the majority, that I only wanted, as they said, to squeeze as much gain out of them as possible, were long continued. I had great difficulty also in teaching them cleanly habits, and order and system in their proceedings. Yet each year a sensible general improvement was effected.

The retail shops, in all of which spirits were sold, were great nuisances. All the articles sold were bought on credit at high prices, to cover great risks. The qualities were most inferior, and they were retailed out to the workpeople at extravagant rates. I arranged superior stores and shops, from which to supply every article of food, clothing, etc. which they required. I bought everything with money in the first markets, and contracted for fuel, milk, etc. on a large scale, and had the whole of these articles of the best qualities supplied to the people at the cost price. The result of this change was to save them in their expenses full twenty-five per cent., besides giving them the best qualities in everything, instead of the most inferior articles, with which alone they had previously been supplied.

The effects soon became visible in their improved health and superior dress, and in the general comfort of their houses.

This measure tended also to weaken their prejudices against me. But it was long before the majority of the people could be convinced that I was earnestly engaged in measures to improve their permanent condition. At length an event occurred which overcame their prejudices, and enabled me to gain their full confidence. We were now (1806) receiving a large amount of our supply of cotton from the United States, and in consequence of diplomatic differences between their government and ours, the United States laid an embargo on their own ports, and no cotton was allowed to be exported, and it was not known how long this embargo might continue, or to what ultimate consequences it might lead. The prices of all kinds of cotton immediately advanced so rapidly and so high, that the manufacturers of the article were placed in a dilemma. The master spinners had to determine whether to stop their machinery and discharge their workpeople (which most of them did), or to continue to work up the material at the high price it had attained, and run the risk of a great and sudden fall in the price of the raw material and of their manufactured stock, should the embargo be removed. Some adopted the one course, and some the other.

We were now spinners on a large scale, and to proceed in our operations was most hazardous. To discharge the workpeople, whom I then had more than half trained to my wishes, and who, if I discharged them from our employment, would have suffered great privations, would be, as it appeared to me, cruel and unjust. I therefore concluded to stop all the machinery, retain the people, and continue to pay them their full wages for only keeping the machinery clean and in good working condition. I continued to do this as long as the embargo was maintained. It was four months before the United States government terminated the embargo, and during that period the population of New Lanark received more than seven thousand pounds sterling for their unemployed time, without a penny being deducted from the full wages of anyone.

This proceeding won the confidence and the hearts of the whole population, and henceforward I had no obstructions from them in my progress of reform, which I continued in all ways, as far as I thought my monied partners would permit me to proceed, and indeed until their mistaken notions stopped my further progress.

(*b*) Owen and Post-war Relief. From Robert Owen, " Report to the Committee of the Association for the Relief of the Manufacturing Poor ", March 1817.

. . . The immediate cause of the present distress is the depreciation of human labour. This has been occasioned by the general introduction of mechanism into the manufactures of Europe and America, but principally into those of Britain, where the change was greatly accelerated by the inventions of Arkwright and Watt.

The introduction of mechanism into the manufacture of objects of desire in society reduced their price; the reduction of price increased the demand for them, and generally to so great an extent as to occasion more human labour to be employed after the introduction of machinery than had been employed before.

The first effects of these new mechanical combinations were to increase individual wealth, and to give a new stimulus to further inventions.

Thus one mechanical improvement gave rise to another in rapid succession ; and in a few years they were not only generally introduced into the manufactures of these kingdoms, but were eagerly adopted by other nations of Europe, and by America.

Individual wealth soon advanced to national prosperity, as that term is generally understood ; and the country, during a war of twenty-five years, demanding exertion and an amount of expenditure unknown at any former period, attained to a height of political power which confounded its foes and astonished its friends.

. . . But peace at length followed, and found Great Britain in possession of a new power in constant action, which, it may be safely stated, exceeded the labour of *one hundred millions* of the most industrious human beings, in the full strength of manhood.

. . . Thus our country possessed, at the conclusion of the war, a productive power, which operated to the same effect as if her population had been actually increased fifteen or twentyfold ; and this had been chiefly created within the preceding twenty-five years.

The rapid progress made by Great Britain, during the war, in wealth and political influence, can therefore no longer astonish : the cause was quite adequate to the effect.

Now, however, new circumstances have arisen. The war demand for the productions of labour having ceased, markets would no longer be found for them ; and the revenues of the world were inadequate to purchase that which a power so enormous in its effects did produce : a diminished demand consequently followed. When, therefore, it became necessary to contract the sources of supply, it soon proved that mechanical power was much cheaper than human labour ; the former, in consequence, was continued at work, while the latter was superseded ; and human labour may now be obtained at a price far less than is absolutely necessary for the subsistence of the individual in ordinary comfort. . . .

Under the existing laws, the unemployed working classes are maintained by, and consume part of, the property and produce of the wealthy and industrious, while their powers of body and mind remain unproductive. They frequently acquire the bad habits which ignorance and idleness never fail to produce ; they amalgamate with the regular poor, and become a nuisance to society. . . .

Under this view of the subject, any plan for the amelioration of the poor should combine means to prevent their children from acquiring bad habits, and to give them good ones — to provide useful training and instruction for them — to provide proper labour for the adults — to direct their labour and expenditure so as to produce the greatest benefit to themselves and to society ; and to place them under such circumstances as shall remove them from unnecessary temptations, and closely unite their interest and duty.

These advantages cannot be given either to individuals or to families separately, or to large congregated numbers.

They can be effectually introduced into practice only under arrangements that would unite in one establishment a population of from 500 to 1,500 persons, averaging about 1,000. . . .

In order to offer some practical idea of the expenses that would be incurred in founding such an establishment for 1,200 souls, the following items are submitted [see p. 139].

This sum, being divided by 1,200, gives a capital to be advanced of 80*l.* per head ; or, at 5 per cent. per annum, 4*l.* each per year.

Thus, at so small an expense as a rental of 4*l.* per head, may the unemployed poor be put in a condition to maintain themselves ;

and, as may be easily conceived, quickly to repay the capital advanced, if thought necessary.

. . . . . .

The money necessary for founding establishments on the principle of the plan now proposed, may be obtained by consolidating the

---

SCHEDULE *of* EXPENSES *for forming an Establishment for*
1,200 MEN, WOMEN, AND CHILDREN
If the land be purchased,

1,200 acres of land, at 30*l*. per acre	£36,000
Lodging apartments for 1,200 persons	17,000
Three public buildings within the square	11,000
Manufactory, slaughter-house, and washing-house . .	8,000
Furnishing 300 lodging-rooms, at 8*l*. each . . .	2,400
Furnishing kitchen, schools, and dormitories . . .	3,000
Two farming establishments, with corn-mill, and malting and brewing appendages	5,000
Making the interior of the square and roads . . .	3,000
Stock for the farm under spade cultivation . . .	4,000
Contingencies and extras	6,600
	£96,000

---

funds of some of the public charities; by equalising the poor rates and borrowing on their security. The poor [rates], including those belonging to public charities, should be made national.

. . . . . .

When these arrangements shall be adopted and carried into execution, (and sooner or later they must be, in order to permanently relieve the national distress,) new and extraordinary consequences will follow. The real value of the land and labour will rise, while all the productions of land and labour will fall; mechanism will be of more extensive worth and benefit to society; every encouragement may be given to its extension; and its extension will go on *ad infinitum*, but only in aid of, and not in competition with, human labour.

5. THE HAMPDEN AND UNION CLUBS

[The formation of the Hampden and Union Clubs in 1812 was a sign of a revived interest in reform or, perhaps, a revived hope of winning support, mainly in middle-class circles, when discontent at the long war and the political domination of Toryism had prepared the way for a renewal of the Reform movement. The Union for Parliamentary Reform was founded more or less at the same time, but was never active, and the Hampden Club was of importance only after the end of the war. Hampden Clubs were founded in a number of provincial towns, as well as in London, and the movement became much more widespread after 1815.]

(a) From F. D. Cartwright, " Life of Major Cartwright " (1826), vol. ii, p. 24. Resolutions at first public meeting of the Hampden Club, April 18, 1812.

Another club for the same [1] object had also been some time in contemplation, of which Mr. Northmore was the founder, and the first printed proposal for its institution appeared 1st of May, 1811, with sixteen names annexed. Its first public meeting took place at the Thatched House Tavern, 20th April, 1812, Walter Fawkes, Esq., in the chair. It was then

" *Resolved*—That a society be now instituted, which shall have for its object the securing to the people the free election of their Representatives in the Commons House of Parliament.

" That such society be called the Hampden Club.

" That by the laws and statutes of this realm the subject has settled in him a fundamental right of property, and he is not compelled to contribute any tax, or other charge, not set by common consent in Parliament.

" That according to Sir Edward Coke, the members of the House of Commons ought to be general inquisitors of the realm for the maintenance and execution of the laws, and for the redress of divers mischiefs and grievances.

" That according to the first statute of Westminster, anno 3. Edw. 1. A.D. 1275, because electors ought to be free, no great man (haut homme), or other by force of arms, nor by malice, shall disturb any from making free election.

" That according to the celebrated declaration of King William for restoring the laws and liberties of England, article 18th, ' all elections of parliament men ought to be free, to be made with an entire liberty, without any sort of force, or the requiring the electors to choose such persons as shall be named to them.

" That according to the constitutional position of the late Lord Camden, ' taxation and representation are inseparable '.

" And that Parliament should be of a continuance agreeable to the English constitution.

---

[1] Same as the Union for Parliamentary Reform.

" *Resolved*—That it appears to the members of this club, that the present corrupt practice of the government of this country, etc., differs most widely from the principles of its constitution. That this deviation from the fundamental laws of the land, and the want of identity which in this country ought to subsist between the representative and the represented, are in a great degree the cause of those evils under which this nation is suffering; and that, therefore, a reform of the representation in the Commons House of Parliament is alike necessary to the constitutional independence of the Crown, the liberties of the people, and the safety of the country.

" That the members of the Hampden Club pledge themselves to use every exertion in country meetings, and in all other meetings warranted by the constitution, in conjunction with their countrymen, to induce the House of Commons to take this important subject into their early and serious consideration, and restore to the country her real constitution and ancient laws.

" That it is the determination of this Club to confine their resolutions and exertions strictly to the procuring a reform in the representation of the people."

(*b*) From F. D. Cartwright, " Life of Major Cartwright " (1826), vol. ii, p. 377.

At a meeting held at the Freemasons' Tavern, on Wednesday, 10th June, 1812

EDWARD BOLTON CLIVE, ESQ. in the Chair

Resolved unanimously :

I. That an association denominated the " Union for Parliamentary Reform ", according to the constitution, is now established.

II. That the basis or constitution of this Union is expressed in the three following propositions, namely,

1. Representation — the happiest discovery of political wisdom — is the vital principle of the English Constitution, inasmuch as it is *that alone*, which in a state, too extensive for personal legislation, constitutes political liberty.

2. Political Liberty being a common right, *representation* co-extensive with direct *taxation*, ought, with all practicable equality, to be fairly and honestly distributed throughout the community, the facility of which cannot be denied.

3. The *constitutional* duration of a Parliament cannot exceed one year.

(c) From *Cobbett's Weekly Political Register*, February 15, 1817.

Letter to the People of Hampshire.

. . . In the meanwhile I hope we shall not slacken in our efforts. Nothing but a radical Reform of the parliament can, I am convinced, save our country from utter ruin. In pursuing this object, it is necessary, that our Petitions be in *decorous language*, in order that those who present them may meet with no obstacle in doing it. And I advise my countrymen to have nothing to do with any *Political Clubs*, any secret *Cabals*, any *Correspondencies*; but to trust to *individual exertions* and *open meetings*. In speaking of the *Hampden Club* lately, I could only mean the one in London. There are very worthy and zealous men, belonging to such Clubs; but, I shall be very difficult to be made believe, that they are thus employing themselves in the best and most effectual way.

6. THE MARCH OF THE BLANKETEERS, 1817

[The march of the Blanketeers from Manchester was the first Hunger March. It was organised with the help of the spinners' organisations in Lancashire and, possibly, of the London Reformers as well. The march was broken up before it had got far, and some of the men kept five months in prison without a trial, although there was a doubt whether even their arrests were legal. One man succeeded in reaching London and presented his copy of the petition to Viscount Sidmouth. This petition complained of increasing rents and taxation, of the expenses of the late war, of the corn laws, of the libel laws and the suspension of *Habeas Corpus*, all of which they blamed on the unrepresentative character of the House of Commons : they asked the Regent, therefore, to dismiss his ministers.]

From *The Courier*, March 12, 1817.

Macclesfield Courier Office. March 10, [1817]

On Sunday morning, the Magistrates of Manchester, deeming it necessary to strengthen the military force in that neighbourhood, in consequence of the declared intent of some thousands of the population, to proceed in person to Carlton House, with a Petition to the Regent, forwarded expresses to the several troops of the Prince Regent's Regiment of Cheshire Yeomanry Cavalry, requiring their immediate aid. The same evening, five troops marched into Manchester, and the remaining three were disposed in Stockport to prevent the suspected progress of the Petitioners in that direction.

Early on Monday Morning, the streets of Manchester were crowded by thousands of whom a great part were prepared with blankets and bundles for the march to London; by the activity of the Magistrates, however, and the military at their disposal, everyone most active in haranguing the multitude, all who had the appearance and character of ringleaders, were arrested and imprisoned on the spot. This cautionary measure for the possibility of which, we are indebted to the suspension of the Habeas Corpus Act, disorganised the plans of the Petitioners to such an extent, that a few thousands only, who eluded by obscure passages, the vigilance of the soldiers, succeeded in penetrating to the bridge of Stockport, and here they were encountered by a troop of the Life Guards, and a troop of the Macclesfield squadron of the Prince Regent's Yeomanry. No attempt was made to force the bridge, but many threw themselves in to the river, and crossed it wherever it was fordable. This circumstance, added to another, that the streets of Stockport were literally wedged full of the inhabitants of the vicinity, constrained the troops to withdraw from the bridge over which, of course, the Petitioners had afterwards a free passage. In the thoroughfare of the town, however, all those who had prepared themselves with the necessaries of a march (commonly comprising a blanket, and a few days' provision), were arrested partly by the laudable activity of the Stockport police, and partly by the alertness of the military force; and were in the course of the day, dispatched, under escort, to the New Bayley Prison, at Manchester. The persons apprehended, might be 200 in number; one individual was so severly wounded, that his life was despaired of. Not more than 500, out of the many thousands assembled in the morning, penetrated so far as Macclesfield, where a troop of the Yeomanry had remained to provide against such a contingency; and we have authority, on which we can rely, for positively stating, that no more than 20 persons proceeded from Macclesfield into the adjoining county of Staffordshire.

7. *THE BLACK DWARF*

[When Cobbett fled to the United States in 1817, *The Black Dwarf* rapidly became the most influential Radical journal. Edited by Thomas Jonathan Wooler (1786–1853), who had previously edited *The Statesman*, it adopted a tone of satire, ironically praising the Government for its despotic measures, and using for this purpose a 'Black Dwarf' who sardonically described the peculiar political customs of the English to a 'Yellow Bonze' in Japan. Wooler, who wrote these articles, was soon arrested for libelling the Crown and the Government, but was acquitted on one charge, the other being dismissed after a re-trial, in which the jury failed to agree. He continued to edit his paper while he was in gaol. In 1819 he was imprisoned for eighteen months for his part in the proceedings in which Sir Charles Wolseley was chosen as 'legislatorial attorney' for Birmingham. *The Black Dwarf* lasted till 1824, and had several imitators. Later, Wooler edited *The British Gazette.*]

(a) From *The Black Dwarf*, February 5, 1817.

What are the present complaints in England ? Want of commerce. Want of trade. And who encourages both, so much as those who have large salaries, and are only employed in the means of *spending them*. Do they not spend their pensions as easily as they get them ? And is it their fault, if they do not spend more ? Will they not take all the commodities you can manufacture, that can at all tend to convenience and comfort, if you will only *trust them* ? And are they not so partial to the patronization of foreign commerce, that they will smuggle over all that they can, for the mere purpose of giving you the opportunity of taking patterns from these foreign specimens of industry ? Want trade indeed ! Create a thousand lords of the bed chamber, and double, nay, treble their salaries. Then you will have trade enough to satisfy all your consciences — yourselves, your wives, and your daughters, will be all set to work : these gracious lords will *spend all they have* among ye ; they will become husbands to your wives, and fathers to your children ; they will give life to trade — you have only to give them your money. And what can you do with it yourselves. You cannot do two things at once. No man can do it. Well then, be content to discharge your duty in that state of life into which it has pleased God to place you. You are designed to earn money, for those who have time to spend it. It would derange *your* habits, and injure your morals to become *rich*. But their habits are to spend ; and as to their morals, every body knows that *they cannot be injured*. Learn then your duty, ye hewers of wood, and drawers of water ! Buckle to the wheel of necessity, and draw your lordly superiors through the dirt. They have kindly consented to provide for all your wants. They have given you laws to keep you good members of society. They have removed far from you all the benefits of the world, lest you should be puffed up with pride, and be vain glorious, and deny the LORDS. They have taken from you all temptation to sin ; and to remedy the inherent and deep-rooted depravity of your nature, they have provided for you seventy thousand priests to pray for you, and to shew you the way to heaven. They have appointed lawyers to *secure* your property, lest ye should waste it without thought, and tax-gatherers to collect quarterly your savings, in that root of all evil — *money*. This they deposit in the treasury for your good, for when you become so numerous, that it might be feared heaven would not send provisions enough for you; or what would be the same thing, that you have no means to purchase them with, they contrive to declare some righteous and holy war, in which you are killed as fast as the glory of God, and the welfare of the state requires. And does not all this claim your gratitude? Does not this melt you into extacies, at the boundless benevolence of such generous superiors. And will you still grumble at a few lords of the bed-chamber, who thus toil for your good, and exert themselves for your welfare? No, no, you will not. You will be thankful to them for their attention to you. You will commiserate their toil, and applaud their diligence. When you meet them in the public way, you will fall down before them, and worship them, saying — " The LORD giveth, and the LORDS take away. Blessed be the ways of the *Lords*." This sentence, which is now rendered as it ought to be, from the original, contains the whole of your business, and your duty. It speaks all the law, and the prophets which concerns you. It is plain and easy. It involves no sophistry. Read it attentively, learn it, and engrave it on the tablets of your heart. It is of the *last* consequence to you, for to its acknowledgment you must come at last.

Your well wisher,

THE BLACK DWARF.

(b) From *The Black Dwarf*, April 16, 1817.

They have begun to conjure up plots of the same description as that at Manchester, throughout the country. At Leeds, at Chester, at Stockport, and most of the manufacturing places, the ministerial spirit of persecution is up, and hunting for its unhallowed prey. Nothing will appease them short of the incarceration of every man of common sense, and common honesty. They feel that such men must be their foes, and they use their power in the vain attempt to root them from society. If they intend to go on much farther, or rather if the nation suffer them to proceed, they may find a considerable portion of employment for the labouring poor in the erection of new prisons; for the old will, ere long, be full of tenants, when the distressed manufacturers are informed, that they compensate those whom they deprive of liberty, without daring to accuse of crime, by an allowance of *one guinea* per week; a sum which three fourths of the labouring population can hardly earn in four. We dare say, they will have abundance of candidates for every vacant cell, when this fact shall be properly understood throughout the country.

In every town there have been some men more active than others in promoting the cause of reform; and the ministers seem to think, if they can, by any means, just or unjust, shut up these men in prison, their purpose will be answered, and their system safe. Mr. Pitt tried the experiment before, and it answered; but the mass of the nation were then, from a variety of causes, the mere tools of that juggler of state; and it was only necessary to take away from society the few that could discern the slight-of-hand tricks, which that great master in the art of deception was playing. The case, however, is very different now. Not only a great majority, but the REAL whole of society, sees that its interests have been grossly betrayed; that a vile administration is resorting to absolute tyrany, to screen its prodigality, its peculation, its heterogeneous composition, and its imbecility of complexion.

8. OLIVER, THE SPY, 1817

[In the days before an efficient police force it was difficult for the Government to discover revolutionary plots, and, if no one was plotting revolution, very difficult indeed. A solution was found in the extensive employment of the spy or *agent provocateur*, who too often took it upon himself to hatch the plots he was later to reveal. Oliver was the most notorious of the exposed spies. He had twice toured the North, first to organise petitions for parliamentary reform, and then to organise delegate meetings for the preparation of a simultaneous series of insurrections. One of his victims, Jeremiah Brandreth, led two hundred men in a march on Nottingham. The humiliating rout of this pathetic band brought to an end what has been called ' The Derbyshire Insurrection '. Oliver's role was discovered by accident; it was made public in *The Leeds Mercury* and used in parliamentary debates. But though the Government made episodes like the ' Derbyshire Insurrection ' their excuse for repressive legislation, they did not drop the Bill suspending *Habeas Corpus*, which was passing through Parliament at the time. Of the Derbyshire insurrectionists three, including Brandreth, were executed, eleven transported for life, three transported for fourteen years, and six sent to prison.]

The Post-war Crisis

(a) From *The Leeds Mercury*, June 14, 1817.

It appears that almost immediately after the suppression of the Union Societies, established in different towns in this district for affecting a reform of Parliament, some of the most violent members associated together, in a private and clandestine manner. At these meetings it is supposed to have become a question for deliberation, whether a change in the representation might not be effected without the intervention of Parliament, and a project to effect this purpose appears to have been communicated to them by Mr. Oliver, who had been introduced to these Ultra Reformers by Mitchell (a Delegate, now in custody) as a person deserving their confidence, and not only disposed to communicate to them interesting information as to the state of the country, but able to afford them the most effectual assistance ; thus recommended, he soon possessed himself of their unbounded confidence. This person is said to have represented to these credulous men, that all the people in the metropolis were favourable to a complete change in the government, that everything was organised, and that it was absolutely settled, that on the night preceding the trial of the state prisoners (the night of the 8th June,) a general rising would take place, that as a consequence of this movement all the public offices were to be taken possession of, all the constituted authorities seized, and the state prisoners released ; and that a plan had also been arranged for securing all the military, by which means a change in the government would be effected without any effusion of blood. It was further represented to them that in order to carry into effect this bloodless revolution, it was absolutely necessary that the same plan should be simultaneously acted upon in all parts of the country ; that it was therefore necessary that on the night agreed upon, namely, on Sunday the 8th inst, all the military in every district of the kingdom should be secured in their quarters, their arms seized, and that the magistrates and other civil officers should be arrested and placed in a state of restraint, not merely that no opposition might be made to the designs of the insurgents, but that they might serve as hostages for the safety of such of their own party as might fall into the hands of the government.

(b) From *The Leeds Mercury*, June 14, 1817.

Since the first edition of our paper was prepared for the press, the highly important fact has been communicated to us, from a respectable quarter, that the plot referred to in the above statement has been got up under the instigation of an agent from London, and that the principal offender has been suffered to escape with impunity.

9. THE POLITICAL PROTESTANTS, 1818

[The ' Political Protestants ', a name adopted by numbers of local reform associations, 1818–1820, illustrate an important stage in the political development of the Northern working class. They had learnt to blame the political system for some at least of their distress, but they proposed no particular set of reforms, they set no value on democracy as such (unlike the London Radical artisans), and they complained of particular grievances which affected them, rather than of the general oppression of the ruling class. This declaration of their views shows that the influence of Cobbett was already strong. The system of classes was in part taken from the Methodists, in part a natural organisation for the working class from the time of the London Corresponding Society.]

From the Home Office Papers, 42/179.

RULES AND RESOLUTIONS OF THE POLITICAL PROTESTANTS (HULL)

We the members of this Institution, wishing not to invade the rights of any man, or set of men, are at the same time determined not to CONSENT to the invasion of our own rights. Therefore we do most solemnly protest against the scandalous wicked and treasonable influence which the Borough Merchants have established in the People's House of Commons. Being firmly convinced that if such corrupt and hateful influence had not existed, which has operated to the total subjugation of our rights in that House, and converted it into a perfect mockery of Representation, our unfortunate country would not have been cursed with a twenty-five years war — with a thousand millions of Debt — with seventy millions of annual taxes — with ruined Manufactories and Commerce — with a standing army of one hundred and forty thousand men kept up in time of peace — with two millions of Paupers, and twelve millions of annual Poor Rates — a Corn Bill, to prevent the people of England eating cheap bread ; and thousands of British Subjects perishing by hunger, and many thousands more escaping to America, to avoid such horrid misery ! — A troop of spies and informers sent out to persuade a set of poor men who were but half fed, half clad, and consequently half mad, to commit acts of outrage, that they might have the advantage of hanging them! With Gagging Bills — Dungeon Bills — Imprisonments without trial:— and lastly an infamous Bill of Indemnity, to protect our seat selling tyrants from being brought to justice for all their satanic deeds. These are the fruits of the Borough Mongering Influence.

WE, bitterly lamenting the condition of our plundered and insulted Country, have resolved to unite ourselves under the denomination of POLITICAL PROTESTANTS : for the purpose of sincerely protesting against the mockery of our indisputable right to a real Representation; and to use every means in our power, which are just and lawful, to rescue the House of Commons from the all-devouring influence of the Borough Merchants, and restore it to the people, agreeable to Magna Charta, and the spirit of the Constitution, and that nothing should ever cause us to cease in our exertions, until we are fully and fairly represented in the People's House.

We sincerely believe, that political ignorance has been the cause of all our national misery and degradation, and that nothing but a firm and extensive Union of the people to promote and diffuse a correct knowledge of our immutable rights, can possibly protect our Country either from absolute Despotism on the one hand or a dreadful Revolution on the other. WE shall, therefore, meet once a week, in small Classes, not exceeding twenty in each Class, and subscribe one penny each for the purpose of purchasing such means of information as may be required; in which way we exhort all our friends to the purity of representation to associate.

The Leaders of each Class shall hold a meeting once a month, to report the progress of the Institution; and in order to do away all ground of accusation against our proceedings, we declare that we will not have any secret transactions whatever, and that our meetings, our Books and Accounts, of every description, shall at all times be laid open for the inspection of the Magistrates or others, who may request the same.

HULL, *July* 20, 1818.

10. THE PHILANTHROPIC SOCIETY, 1818

[The Philanthropic Society was, as far as we know, the first attempt to organise Unions of different trades into one ' Trades Union '. Its origin is obscure. It was most prominent in Lancashire, where it came into being in 1818 at the close of a series of unsuccessful textile strikes and was composed mainly of textile workers. But the Home Office believed it to have originated in Nottingham, among the framework knitters, as a sequel to the driving of their organisation underground after the Luddite troubles. (See A. Aspinall, " The Early English Trade Unions ".) At about the same time the ' Philanthropic Hercules ' was founded in London by the shipwright, John Gast, to unite the London trades, composed largely of skilled artisans. Neither organisation lasted more than a few months and, probably, neither did anything except teach a lesson for the future.

The similarity of their names suggests that there may have been some link between them ; but we have no record of any connection, and, in fact, they had very different problems to face, for the artisan, an aristocrat of labour, who would refer to the traditions of the trade, was very different from the textile operative, who had to frame a policy for the new industrial struggle with the factory owner.]

(a) From the Home Office Papers, 42/181.

At a Meeting of Deputies from the undermentioned Trades from Manchester, Stockport, Ashton-under-line, Oldham, Bury, &c., &c., &c.

Calico Printers, Dyers and Dressers, Hatters, Blacksmiths, Jenny Spinners, Cotton Weavers, Bricklayers, Frishan Cutters, Colliers, Sawyers, Shoe Makers, Slubbers, Mule Spinners, Machine Makers, &c.

The following Address and Resolutions were unanimously agreed to.

At a GENERAL MEETING of TRADES convened to take into consideration the Distressed State and Privations to which the Working Class of Society are reduced, by their avaricious Employers reducing wages to less than sufficient to support nature or purchase the bare necessities for our existence with great economy and hard labour ; therefore, to render redress in such cases of distress to any Body or Party reduced as aforesaid.

RESOLUTIONS.

FIRST. That there be a Union of all Trades, called the PHIL-ANTHROPIC SOCIETY, to be held in Manchester on the second Monday in every Month, when all TRADES shall send a *Delegate*, with proper credential for admission.

SECOND. That every Trade be recommended to raise a FUND amongst themselves, for the general Benefit of all TRADES joined in this Union; and in particular any Trade that may be engaged in resisting Oppression or to alleviate distress, and to enable the labouring part of the Community to live in comfort and decency.

THIRD. That any Trade feeling the necessity of an Advance of Wages, that Trade shall be bound to give notice to a Meeting of Delegates convened for that purpose; and their concurrence being obtained, all other Trades will support them.

FOURTH. That if any Trade be under the necessity of leaving their Employ through the Oppression of their Employers, They shall first call the General Representatives together and inform them; provided that such Representatives be not overpowered with too much business at one Time, that they may be prepared for supporting the cause and provide for the same; in short, no Trade shall leave their employ without first calling the other Trades together, and then act by and with their consent in taking the most favourable time for resistance.

FIFTH. That any body of Workmen being Oppressed, or illegally used, this Society will support them in obtaining legal redress.

SIXTH. That all Printing of Notices, &c. with all Delegations, or any other necessary expences, shall be paid out of their separate Funds.

SEVENTH. That a Committee of Eleven Persons be chosen by Ballot, out of the different Trades who form this Society, and shall be regularly enrolled on the list kept for that purpose. The Committee to go out by regular rotation every month, so that the whole may be changed every three months.

EIGHTH. That in order to preserve decorum in this Society or Meeting of Representatives, no person shall be allowed to advance any Political or Religious argument, under a forfeit threepence for the first offence, and sixpence for the second, which must be paid the night it is forfeited.

NINTH. That there shall be an Auxiliary Society of the different Trades in each town, that each Trade shall have its own By-Laws, and each Auxiliary to act in conjunction with the resolutions of the Central Philanthropic Society.

TENTH. That the Representatives be empowered to alter or amend, add or diminish any Rule, or Rules for the benefit of this Society, provided it does not infringe upon or act against any Trade or division belonging to the General Philanthropic Society.

G. CAVE, PRINTER, EXCHANGE BUILDINGS, MANCHESTER.

[In Home Office Papers, 42/179, there is another manifesto of the Society with only one important difference — the omission of the very interesting ninth resolution.

The Manifesto quoted here was submitted to the Crown's legal advisers for their opinion ' as to how far it is fit subject for a Criminal Prosecution '. Their answer, surprising in view of the Combination Acts, was :]

" We have considered the accompanying paper, and we are of opinion it would not be possible to institute any prosecution for the publication of it ; indeed we very much doubt whether it could be made the subject of prosecution, and as the spirit of combination amongst the workmen in this part of the country has in some degree apparently subsided, a prosecution now instituted (and particularly if it failed) ought rather tend to revive than extinguish it.

S. Shepherd
R. Gifford
Serjeants Inn, *Oct.* 19, 1818."

(b) From *The Gorgon*, January 23, 1819.

PHILANTHROPIC HERCULES

A society under this appellation has recently been established in London ; and from the judicious principles on which it is founded, promises to be of immense utility to journeymen and mechanics. The object of this association is to provide a fund by *weekly penny* subscriptions ; which fund is, to preserve the workmen of every trade from degradation, by enabling them to resist the encroachments of avarice and oppression. Every trade which joins the Union, appoints a deputy to a general committee ; these deputies are appointed for six months, and go out in rotation. When the number of efficient members in any trade belonging to the Union exceeds one hundred, an extra deputy is appointed for every additional two hundred and fifty members. Besides the general committee, sub committees are appointed by each trade for the management of its particular concerns. Each trade retains possession of its own fund ; but returns of its amount are regularly made to the general committee, who have the power to direct its application to any purpose they deem expedient.

(c) From the Place MSS., 27,799 f. 143.

ARTICLES OF THE PHILANTHROPIC HERCULES
INSTITUTED DECEMBER 2d, 1818.

For the mutual Support of the Labouring Mechanic, and the Maintenance of the Independence of their Trade against the Infringements too generally made upon their just Rights and Rewards, by the Hands of Avarice and Oppression.

I. That this association shall consist of an indefinite number of members.

II. That this society shall consist of persons from any mechanical branch or trade who are desirous of maintaining their reputation in society, and supporting their own independence, by a just, equitable, and legal demand for their labour.

III. That every person or persons desirous of becoming a member must come voluntary, and on his or their own part, and from a just sense of his or their respectability, and who is not a companion of the low and vulgar part of the community.

IV. That this association is open to receive any persons answering the description of article the second, without any consideration of age or infirmity; and all persons joining shall pay weekly and every week into the joint stock of this association, the sum of one penny as herein-after mentioned.

V. That every mechanical trade belonging to this association shall be allowed to appoint one of their body to act as their representative with the several other trades in the regulating and managing all the concerns of the Union, and that every such person so appointed shall continue in office six calendar months, at the expiration of which another shall be elected by the body to take his place, in the way and manner hereinafter stated.

VI. That in consequence of this association having been formed by a number of Deputies from several trades, and therefore have formed rules and regulations for the election and duration of the Union.[1] One of which is, that at the expiration of six calendar months, such deputy to go out of office and another to be elected in his room; and to prevent inconvenience to the association in carrying into effect article the fifth, it is to be understood that the present number of deputies that may be collected together on the beginning of this association, is to continue in office six calendar months from the date of the Union; and at the expiration thereof, the whole shall draw lots for one half to go out, and the other half to remain for the other six months, then to go out in regular order.

VII. That from the time of every deputy joining this Union, it shall be considered the commencement of his six months, and every deputy shall, on the fifth monthly night, receive of the secretary a

[1] This sentence reads as printed here in the original. The sense is clear, though the grammar is amiss.

written order to his trade to elect and appoint another deputy in his room, which deputy shall attend with the old deputy on the sixth monthly night for to take his instructions and seat for the trade he represents.

VIII. That every trade do elect its own deputy, and send by such deputy the credentials of his election and place of abode to the general meeting of deputies which shall be entered in a book for that purpose, and that such election of deputy shall be in any way and manner as may be agreed upon by the trade, most convenient for themselves.

IX. That if any trade consider the conduct of their deputy worthy of their continued confidence, they shall be at liberty to re-elect such deputy as often as circumstances require, and on his re-election, such deputy must bring his credentials of re-election, the same as a fresh deputy, which shall be entered in the book kept for that purpose.

X. That the disproportion of numbers of any branch of trade, members of this Union, will not make any difference as to the claims of any one individual member ; as the whole body united, stand on the principles of reciprocal equality; and that no individual of any trade will dispute or insinuate improperly to the injury or repose of the Union, on account of their numbers, so as to discompose or hurt the feelings of others, whose numbers may be less, but not less in zeal or purity of conduct.

XI. That the representatives for each trade shall be in proportion to the actual number of good members, at the expiration of every six months of the deputy of the trade ; that is to say, for every hundred members or less, one deputy ; and for every two hundred and fifty members, over and above the first hundred, an extra deputy, which extra deputy shall be elected and regulated according to the eighth article. But no trade to be allowed to have more than one vote on the committee.

XII. That every deputy, regular or extra, be considered as collectors to receive the penny contributions from the several members, and to avoid as much inconvenience as possible, it is ordered that every member do either by himself or proxy, pay weekly and every week into the hands of the deputy or deputies of his trade, his penny towards the general stock, which deputy or deputies will enter the same in his book, and on every monthly night report the sum collected to the general committee, and the secretary for the time being shall enter the report into the general account book.

XIII. That in case the number of subscribers in any one branch should exceed the possibility of one man collecting or receiving the contribution, it shall be proper in that case, on the part of any number of subscribers, not less than forty, to appoint an assistant collector, who shall be duly qualified to receive each contribution and transmit the same to the committee of his own trade.

XIV. That exclusive of the general committee, every trade to appoint a private committee of their own, who shall regulate all their own concerns, [collect money [1]], put the same out to interest, and such other concerns not entrusted to the general committee.

XV. That for the better establishing the mutual as well as the general confidence of every trade that composes the Union, each trade shall retain their own collection, and whenever it amounts to a sufficient sum to put out to interest, their own private committee shall invest the money in such persons' hands as the trade may approve of, under such restrictions of securities as may be deemed sufficient by the trades, and the deputy for that trade shall report the names of the trust, and the sum put out, to the general committee, and the general secretary shall enter the same, together with the sum in the book against the trade, who makes such report.

XVI. That the whole or part of the money, so collected by the several trades, and invested by them in the hands of trustees appointed by themselves shall always be at the command and power of the general committee, who when they think it necessary to call in any part or all of the stock of the several trades belonging to the Union, the general committee shall give orders for that purpose to the general secretary, who shall write such orders and address the same to the private committee, which orders shall be signed by the deputy of the trade it is addressed to.

XVII. That all disputes between the mechanic and his employer be submitted to the joint Committee, respecting the just, legal, and customary price for his labour, a book of prices belonging to such trade shall be given in to the committee for the purpose of their guidance, which upon a fair examination, and hearing the evidence of the mechanic aggrieved shall determine as to the rectitude of the mechanic's conduct making such complaint, but should such trade have no book of prices, the committee should summon four of the oldest men, or such proficient persons, members of the society who can give every information to elucidate the dispute, and should the cause or complaint be just, then the committee shall

[1] Handbill torn here.

afford such support to the complainants as they may think just and necessary, and the funds allow. But the better to elucidate any subject of dispute that may come before the committee where there arise any doubts as to the rectitude of the differences between the working party and their employers, the secretary, if the committee think proper, be ordered to write to the employer, requesting a just reason and cause of the dispute. And the answer received to be laid before the committee who shall judge impartially on the matter contained in such letter. But should such employer not think proper to answer the secretary's letter, then the committee shall determine according to such evidence before them respecting the dispute. But no trade not members of the Union can be admitted to any of the Benefits.

XVIII. That for the quicker dispatch of all business that may be necessary to be submitted to the general committees, the complainant or complainants shall, in person or by letter, make known the grievances to the general secretary, who shall, if he considers the complaint of sufficient importance, immediately summons the joint committee for that purpose on any evening, within three days from the time of receiving such complaint. But should the Secretary have any doubts of the propriety of summoning the joint committee from the nature of the complaint, he shall consult personally the *four* senior committeemen, who, with the secretary, shall determine on the propriety of calling the committee together, if the time of the regular meeting of the committee exceeds one week.

XIX. That a person duly qualified be appointed secretary by the general committee, at such salary by the year, or otherwise, for such time and under such restrictions, as the committee shall think proper, who shall answer all letters, direct all the concerns and disputes in writing that may be brought under the consideration of the committee, and that he do attend all meetings on their monthly nights, sign all letters, memorials, and all orders of the committee, and provide all books of account, and other stationery, for the use of the society, at the society's expence, and by orders from the general committee.

XX. That should any trustee be obliged from any circumstances, to leave London, and go to reside more than twenty miles in the country, such trustee shall make known the same to the committee of his trade, who shall appoint a fresh trustee; and the whole of the monies in the name of the trustee going to the country, shall be transferred to the new trustee, appointed by the committee of that trade, and a report of the same shall be made to the general secretary.

XXI. That any member of this Union Society shall be eligible to become or continue a member of any other society of whatever name or denomination.

XXII. That at any time the committee may think proper, for the purpose of keeping the bond of Friendship and Union, and giving an opportunity to the several members to see, converse, and associate with each other, they may call a general meeting of all the members, at such time and such place, as may be determined upon, and such other regulations attending the general meeting, as may be considered for the general as well as the mutual good of the several members, notice thereof being given in any way that may be agreed on by the general committee.

XXIII. That for the better enabling the secretary to perform the duties of his office, in case of necessity he be allowed a clerk, to be also appointed by the said committee, which shall attend all meetings of the committee; and in default thereof be fined one shilling and sixpence. And that the general secretary shall inspect the accounts of the clerk, and if right, shall sign the same; and that no such accounts shall be deemed valid until so signed.

XXIV. That a strong box with three locks and three keys, be provided for the general committee, in which the current cash, bonds, and other securities of this society (the bond for the production of the said box excepted) shall be deposited, that one of the said keys shall be in the custody of the landlord for the time being, at whose house the meeting shall be held, and the other two keys in the custody of the two senior committee-men, who, at the expiration of one month, shall deliver the same to the two next committee-men in seniority; it being the intention of this society, that each of the said regular committee-men shall, in rotation and according to seniority, have possession of one of the said keys for one month; and in case the landlord shall neglect to produce his key of the said box at any meeting of the committee, or within thirty minutes after the time appoi..:ed for holding such meeting, he shall forfeit two shillings and sixpence, to be deducted and retained out of the first rent that shall become due to him for the room in which the said meeting shall be held; and if either of the said committee-men having the care of the other keys shall neglect to produce the same at the place and within the time last aforesaid, such committee-men so neglecting shall be fined two shillings and sixpence. That the committee-man having the custody of the keys of the said box, shall previous to the close of every meeting of the committee, see that all the monies, deeds, papers, vouchers, and other matters and things which ought to be deposited in the said box, be duly deposited therein, and that the said box be locked and carefully put away in some convenient and safe place; and for any default therein, that he or they be fined two shillings and sixpence.

XXV. That the said landlord shall, if required so to do by the committee, enter into bond with sureties, to be approved of by the said committee, in sufficient penalty for the production of the box and all the contents thereof, in such way and manner, at such time and place, and to such person or persons as the committee shall, by writing under the hand of the general secretary for the time being, direct or require.

XXVI. That for the purpose of the general committee having at their own immediate use funds for such purpose of emergency as may casually take place, it is ordered, that every deputy do bring from their several trades each monthly night, one quarter of their penny collection, and deposit the same in the general committee box; and that the general secretary shall give a receipt for the sum received, and enter the amount thereof in the cash-book for trades.

XXVII. That the general committee for the time being shall be in full power to alter or amend any of the articles or regulations of the General Union to such extent, for general good, as may be considered by the majority of the several trades, necessary. That before such alterations shall be considered binding, a copy be laid before the several private committees by their deputy, who shall take their opinion on the alteration, and report the same to the general committee, who shall then decide according to the returned report from the several trades on the proposed alteration, which decision shall be final.

JOHN GAST, President.

11. RADICAL DEMANDS, 1818–1819

[The article from *The Gorgon* puts the case of the Trade Unionists. *The Gorgon*, edited by John Wade and including among its principal contributors both Francis Place and the shipwrights' leader, John Gast, who was at this time the most influential of the London Trade Unionists, was the first newspaper to give much space to Trade Union affairs.

The second extract gives a series of resolutions adopted at a mass meeting of Yorkshire Radicals, chiefly workers, held on Hunslet Moor, outside Leeds, in July 1819. These resolutions are typical of what was being urged at many such meetings all over the country in the year of Peterloo — which was, in fact, one of the great series of open-air demonstrations organised by the Radicals to demand Reform.]

(a) From *The Gorgon*, November 28, 1818.

"Workmen must expect to share the difficulties of their employers and the general distress of the times."

Now we have strong objections to this sharing of difficulties on the part of workmen, first—

Because at no period, to our knowledge, was the income of a working man so great, that he could afford to lose a portion of it, without, at the same time, losing a portion of the necessaries of life.

2nd. To abridge the necessary means of subsistence of the working classes, is to degrade consequently to demoralize them; and when the largest and most valuable portion of any community is thus degraded and demoralized, ages may pass away before society recovers its former character of virtue and happiness.

3rd. The necessary comforts of one class of the community should never be abridged for any public exigency, while there remains any other class in society in the enjoyment of luxuries, which may be sacrificed without inconvenience or injury.

But our fourth, and far from weakest objection to this partnership of difficulties on the part of the working classes is, that they had no share in producing them. If they had a voice in choosing their Representatives, and the time for which Parliament continued did not exceed a year; and if, under these circumstances, the working people had been so blind to their own interests, as year after year to assist in returning men to Parliament who would be at the nod and call of any and every Minister; — if they had assisted to choose men who were ever ready to vote away the lives of the people in frantic attempts against intelligence and Liberty; — if they had assisted to choose men to vote away the money of the people in sums which, till they tried the experiment, no man would have believed possible: — if they had assisted to choose men to tax them in more ways than ingenuity itself, unaided by the Devil, could have devised; if they had assisted to choose men who not only were always ready, but always eager to suspend the Habeas Corpus Act — to pass new fangled Treason Acts, Seditious Meeting Bills, Gagging Bills,

Restriction Acts and Corn Laws ; — to pass Bills of Indemnity for traitors who had violated the laws, — who had shut men in loathsome dungeons for years, against whom they could substantiate no charge, — who had sent artful villains among innocent people to seduce them into crime ; — and lastly, if they had assisted to choose men, who by their tyrannical, intolerant and persecuting measures, drove the unfortunate Irish to despair, then let loose an infuriated soldiery upon them, to half-hang, half-roast and flog out their bowels ; — if they had assisted, we say, to return men year after year to commit, and re-commit, all, or any of these things, then indeed, they would have no cause to complain. No, if their sufferings and privations were ten thousand times greater than they are, they would not be equal to one tithe of their deserts.

(b) From Papers relating to the Internal State of the Country, Nov. 1819. No. 8, p. 9 (Parl. Papers, 1819–20, vol. iv).

RESOLUTIONS PASSED AT THE MEETING HELD ON HUNSLET MOOR NEAR LEEDS, 19 JULY, 1819

RESOLVED, 1st. That there is no such thing as servitude in nature ; and therefore all statutes and enactments that have tendency to injure one part of society for the benefit of the other, is a gross violation of the immutable law of God.

2d. That as our legislators have, in innumerable instances, manifested a cruel and criminal indifference to our truly distressed situation, and treated our petitions with contempt, we therefore make this solemn appeal to our oppressed fellow countrymen, praying them to join us in forming a National Union, the object of which is to obtain an overwhelming majority of the male population, to present such a petition as can scarcely fail to have the desired effect, and to adopt such other constitutional measures as may be deemed most expedient to procure for us the redress of our manifold grievances.

3d. That we are properly satisfied that our excellent Constitution, in its original purity, as it was bequeathed to us by our brave ancestors, is fully adequate to all the purposes of good government ; we are therefore determined not to rest satisfied with anything short of the Constitution — the whole Constitution — and nothing but the Constitution.

4th. That as we are perfectly satisfied that annual parliaments and universal suffrage constitute an essential part of our constitution, and are our rightful inheritance — we shall consider our grievances unredressed, and our indisputable rights withheld from us, until we are possessed of such annual parliament and universal suffrage.

5th. That this meeting cannot but view with regret the apathy of our should-be-leaders, that is our men of property, in not supporting our mutual rights, convinced that alienation of the rich from the poor, must, in the end, be the ruin of both; that whenever oppression or despotism militates, or is the ruin of one, it must, in the end, be the destruction of the other; we therefore entreat them, ere it be too late, to stand forward and espouse the constitutional rights of the people, by endeavouring to obtain a radical reform in the system of representation, which can alone save the trading and labouring classes from ruin.

6th. That we believe the distresses we now suffer have originated in a boroughmongering system, aided by a depreciated paper currency, which has involved the nation in one hundred thousand millions of debt, and which has increased taxation to such an extent as has nearly destroyed our manufactures and commerce; and we are perfectly satisfied that nothing but a currency convertible into specie, a rigid economy, and an equal representation, can either put an end to our sufferings, or save our country from ruin.

7th. That the saving bank scheme, which was instituted under a pretence of benefiting the working classes, when nearly three-fourths of them were out of employ, is an insult to common sense and real understanding, and ought to be considered as what it really is, — an engine to work the last shilling out of the pockets of a few old servants and retired tradesmen, to enable the bank and boroughmongers to pay the fractional parts of the dividends, and to create a sort of lesser fundholders of those who know no better than to make a deposit of their hard earnings to fill the pockets of those who are draining them of their last shilling.

8th. That, as distress has become so general and extensive, we deem it highly necessary, that deputy meetings should be appointed, and out of these deputy meetings, district meetings, to meet at any place that may be thought proper; that these meetings shall extend throughout the three United Kingdoms, and that they do consist of men discreet and wise, and out of these shall be appointed men to form a National Meeting, that the whole may be brought into one focus, in order that they may devise the best plan of obtaining a Radical Reform, upon the principle of Annual Parliaments, Universal Suffrage, and Election by Ballot.

9th. That no redress can be obtained but from ourselves; that we amply possess the means; and if we fail to adopt them with vigour, and resolutely persevere therein, we shall merit every privation we may have to endure, and deserve the detestation of posterity, to whom we shall leave a greater legacy of tyranny and oppression than ever was bequeathed from one generation to another.

10th. That should the usurpers of our rights, in order to retain their power proceed to acts of violence against the people, and even succeed in incarcerating individuals, we earnestly entreat our fellow-countrymen not to suffer their exertions to relax, but, on the contrary, persevere in the steady path of duty, looking to the end, even the salvation of our country; and our fellow-countrymen will endeavour to lighten the fetters, and enliven the dungeons of those men who are now suffering, or may hereafter suffer in the sacred cause of liberty.

11th. That we consider it to be the duty of every well-meaning subject, to stand with all his might against oppression and partial law; in doing which an individual exposes himself to destruction, but if the whole community act as one man, success must be the result.

12th. That every well-wisher to mankind cannot but consider it to be his duty to endeavour, by every means in his power, to work a thorough reformation in the political and moral state of the country; and the surest mean is to lay aside every sordid maxim of avarice, and abandon the restraints of luxury and false ambition, which are at present so fatal to the nation.

13th. That a very small number of men who have guided the councils, and have plundered the people in order to complete their fraud, have hired the offscouring of society to print and publish newspapers, who have nearly succeeded in making thousands who might have been the leaders and friends of the people, believe the present system was for our good, when they were fattening on our property, and reducing all classes of society, till they have at last brought us to a strait from whence there are no issues but through a radical reform.

14th. That the passing of corn laws in opposition to the express will of the people — the combination act, in order to prevent work-people from unitedly attempting to raise their wages in proportion to the advancement of provisions — and the imposing a duty on foreign wools, at a time when the woollen manufacture, and those employed therein, are in the most deplorable condition — appear to this meeting, proof positive, that until the Members of the Commons House are really appointed by the people at large, little improvement is to be expected in the circumstances of the people, or diminution of their distress.

15th. That as soon as an eligible person, who will accept the appointment, can be found to represent the unrepresented part of the inhabitants of Leeds, in the House of Commons, another meeting shall be called for the purpose of electing him to that situation.

12. PETERLOO, 1819

[In July 1819 Birmingham elected Sir Charles Wolseley [1] their 'legislational attorney' with instructions to demand a hearing in Parliament. Some Northern towns, which were unrepresented in the House of Commons, decided to imitate this example. In Manchester a meeting was fixed for August 9, but in the interval the organisers of the Birmingham meeting had been arrested and the Home Secretary, Viscount Sidmouth, had circularised the Lords-Lieutenant of the counties with a recommendation to follow a severely repressive policy. The Manchester election meeting was cancelled and instead a mass demonstration was arranged for August 16. Reformers marched on into St. Peter's Fields, coming from all the small villages in the neighbourhood. Their entirely peaceful meeting was broken up by a deliberate massacre. Neither the anger and indignation that followed, nor the meetings, petitions and pamphlets, could turn the Government from its set determination to kill the working-class reform movement at any cost.]

R. Carlile. Open letter to Lord Sidmouth. *Sherwin's Weekly Political Register*, August 18, 1819.

. . . About 11 o'clock the people began to assemble around the house of Mr. Johnson [2] at Smedley Cottage, where Mr. Hunt [3] had

---

[1] Sir Charles Wolseley (1773–1835) was associated for a short while with the 'Left Wing' of the Radical movement; and earlier in 1819 he had taken the chair at a great rally in Stockport, for which he was sentenced to eighteen months' imprisonment.

[2] Joseph Johnson (1791–1872) was a small master brushmaker in Manchester, a leading Radical, and a friend of Cobbett. He was imprisoned for a year for his share in the St. Peter's Fields meeting.

[3] Henry Hunt (1773–1835), known as 'Orator Hunt', was the most effective Radical speaker of the day. As a practical farmer he had many interests in common with Cobbett, but their friendship was often broken by bitter quarrels; they felt

taken up his residence; about 12 Mr. Hunt and his friends entered the barouche. They had not proceeded far when they were met by the Committee of the Female Reform Society, one of whom, an interesting looking woman, bore a standard on which was printed a female holding in her hand a flag surmounted with the cap of liberty, whilst she trod under foot an emblem of corruption, on which was inscribed that word. She was requested to take a seat on the box of the carriage (a most appropriate one) which she boldly and immediately acquiesced in, and continued waving her flag and handkerchief until she reached the hustings, where she took her stand on the right corner in front. The remainder of the committee followed the carriage in procession and mounted the hustings when they reached them. On leaving Smedley Cottage, bodies of men were seen at a distance, marching in regular military order, with music and colors. Different flags were fallen in with on the road with various mottoes, such as " No Corn Laws ", " Liberty or Death ", " Taxation without Representation is Tyranny ", " We will have Liberty "; the flag used by the friends of Mr. Hunt at the general election for Westminster, and various others, many of which were surmounted with " Caps of Liberty ". The scene of cheering was never before equalled. Females from the age of twelve to eighty were seen cheering with their caps in their hand, and their hair in consequence dishevelled; the whole scene exceeds the power of description. In passing through the streets to the place of meeting, the crowd became so great that it was with difficulty the carriage could be moved along. Information was brought to Mr. Hunt that St. Peter's Field was already filled, and that no less than 300,000 people were assembled in and about the intended spot of meeting. As the carriage moved along and reached the shops and warehouse of Mr. Johnson of Smedley, three times three were given, also, at the Police Office and the Exchange. The procession arrived at the place of destination about one o'clock. Mr. Hunt expressed his disapprobation of the hustings, and was fearful that some accident would arise from them. After some hesitation he ascended, and the proposition for his being chairman being moved by Mr. Johnson, it was carried

each other to be rivals for the leadership, and were in any case difficult colleagues at the best of times. After Peterloo, Hunt was sentenced to two years' imprisonment. In 1830, at his fifth election contest, he was elected M.P. for Preston, which was one of the few constituencies with a wide franchise. In Parliament and in the country he then became the best-known spokesman of the extreme Radicals, condemning the Whig Bill and demanding a fully democratic measure, which would include universal suffrage.

by acclamation. Mr. Hunt began his discourse by thanking them for the favour conferred on him, and made some ironical observations on the conduct of the Magistrates, when a cart, which evidently took its direction from that part of the field where the police and magistrates were assembled in a house, was moved through the middle of the field to the great annoyance and danger of the assembled people, who quietly endeavoured to make way for its procedure. The cart had no sooner made its way through, when the Yeomanry Cavalry made their appearance from the same quarter as the cart had gone out. They galloped furiously round the field, going over every person who would not get out of their way, to the spot where the police were fixed, and after a moment's pause, they received the cheers of the police as a signal for attack. The meeting at the entrance of the cavalry, and from the commencement of business was one of the most calm and orderly that I ever witnessed — Hilarity was seen on the countenances of all, whilst the Female Reformers crowned the assemblage with a grace, and excited a feeling particularly interesting. The Yeomanry Cavalry made their charge with a most infuriate frenzy; they cut down men, women, and children, indiscriminately, and appeared to have commenced a premeditated attack with the most insatiable thirst for blood and distruction. They merit a medallion on one side of which should be inscribed " The slaughter-men of Manchester ", and a reverse bearing a description of their slaughter of defenceless men, women and children, unprovoked and unnecessary. As a proof of premeditated murder on the part of the magistrates, every stone was gathered from the ground, on the Friday and Saturday previous to the meeting, by scavengers sent there by the express command of the magistrates, that the populace might be rendered more defenceless.

13. THE FREEDOM OF THE PRESS, 1817–1824

[When Cobbett fled to America in 1817, on the passing of Sidmouth's ' Gagging Acts ', there were other men left to carry on the fight in the press. T. J. Wooler (1786–1853), the editor of *The Black Dwarf* (1817–1824), and William Hone (1780–1842), journalist and pamphleteer, had both been put on trial, but Hone defended himself so wittily that there were no more London prosecutions of ' blasphemous and seditious ' parodies. In 1818 the London press was free. But after Peterloo the Government renewed its attack on liberty. Richard Carlile [1] had been reprinting Tom Paine's " Age of Reason " and had spent eighteen weeks in prison without trial for reprinting Hone's " Parodies on the Book of Common Prayer ". He was already a marked man when he published his account of Peterloo ; he had at least six indictments out against him and now his trial was hurried on. He was sentenced to three years' imprisonment and to a fine of £1500 ; his stock of books was confiscated ; his business was almost ruined, and he was left little chance of paying his fine. His wife carried on the shop till she too was arrested ; her sister took on till she followed them to the same gaol. Volunteers were numerous and the shop was manned by each in turn, as long as they were free. The Government had been prosecuting newsvendors in every part of the country ; and, in addition, there was founded in 1820 ' The Constitutional Association for opposing the Progress of disloyal and seditious Principles '. They were assisted by the long-established ' Society for the Suppression of Vice ',[2] but the courageous defiance of Carlile and his followers, helped by the honesty of the London jury, won in the end ; the prosecution societies were overcome, a further bout of Government prosecutions in 1824 failed, and the next year Carlile was let out of prison, where he had been sentenced to remain as long as he could not pay his fine.]

From Richard Carlile's *The Republican*, October 27, 1820.

TO THE PUBLIC.

In consequence of the verdict of guilty given against Mrs. Carlile for selling Sherwin's Life of Paine, and No. 9 Vol 1. of *The Republican*, She is now liable to banishment by serving in the shop according to our glorious constitution. The business will therefore be managed by Mary Ann Carlile, the sister of R. Carlile, on the behalf of the infant children, or rather on the behalf of the whole family. In case the house — Fleet Street, should again be exposed to the violence of the legal thieves, the business will be opened as near the spot as possible immediately, of which due notice will be given. As this kind of business might be said to be renewed every week, at least, it depends on the periodical publications, we can begin anywhere

---

[1] Richard Carlile (1790–1843), son of a shoemaker and exciseman, was the greatest of the early champions of the freedom of the press. The fight he carried on in these years (1819–1825) was his main achievement ; but he continued his work for the freedom of the press and of speech as a provocative editor (he was imprisoned again in 1831), as the lessee of the ' Rotunda ', which he made an unique centre of free discussion, and, always, as a tireless propagandist for secularism. In the history of working-class secularism he is the chief link between the period of Paine and the period of Holyoake.

[2] The ' Vice Society ', founded in 1802, had a long career as the staunch friend of despotism in Church and State. William Wilberforce was one of its leading members.

with half an hour's preparation, and laugh at the Vice Society, and all the influence they can use against it. If one web be destroyed, a few hours' work will spin another stronger and better than before. This is the only way of meeting the persecuting thieves, and I hope and trust that Mrs. Davison will follow the steps of Mrs. Carlile. If half a dozen persons were resolved successively to oppose the Vice Society, their prosecution would become of the greatest advantage to the propagation of good principles. I will expose every branch of my family that will listen to my advice, to the venom of this society, with the confidence that in a few months we shall triumph over them. I have to add, that Mrs. Carlile is quite as composed and unconcerned as I was last year, and I have now to call upon my sister to perform her part in the same manner. The thieves have the power to shut up 55, but they cannot prevent the opening of 56, so let them go on. Their prosecutions are my joy and comfort, particularly whilst I can see one of my family opposed to them. For my own part, I am resolved never to cease, in consequence of any laws that come short of putting to death, in the open avowal and promulgation of such opinions as I conceive to be founded in truth, and the practice of which appear to me to be conducive to the interest of society. It matters nothing to me what another man thinks. I claim the same right to think and speak, and to write what I think, and to publish what I write as he does. I will never truckle to opinions propagated by force and violence because it is *prima facie* acknowledgement that they are founded on falsehood and cannot bear the scrutiny of a rational criticism. I contend that there is no necessity for laws to regulate opinions in society ; a diversity of opinion with mutual toleration will form the most stable base of its well being. But when we see men crushing the propagation of certain opinions, because the opposite are productive of profit to them, it is no longer society, but a nest of robbers who prey upon the weaker part. However I shall hope to see the imprisonment of Mrs. Carlile and Mr. Davison produce half a dozen new shops in the same line.

DORCHESTER GAOL, *Oct.* 18, 1820.   R. CARLILE

14. THE SIX ACTS, 1819

[The notorious ' Six Acts ' were passed in the December following Peterloo ; the first was directed against military exercises and training by private bodies, but could be used against demonstrations as well. The second enabled magistrates to issue warrants for the search of private houses, if there was any suspicion that arms were being kept for illegal purposes ; the third gave magistrates the power of dealing with offenders swiftly and severely ; the fourth, modelled on an Act of 1795, restricted the right of public meeting — notice had to be given by seven householders, the audience had to be composed of local residents, and the magistrates could alter the time and place of meeting ; the fifth cut down the already limited rights of free speech by penalising ' libels ' on the ' government and constitution of the United Kingdom as by law established or either House of Parliament ' ; and the sixth made working-class journals, whether they dealt in news or in comments on news, dear for the reader and dangerous for the publisher.]

(*a*) Illegal Drilling. From 60 Geo. III, c. 1.

An Act to prevent the training of persons to the use of arms, and to the practice of military evolutions and exercise (11th December 1819).

Whereas, in some parts of the United Kingdom, men clandestinely and unlawfully assembled have practised military training and exercise, to the great terror and alarm of His Majesty's peaceable and loyal subjects, and the imminent danger of the public peace ; be it therefore enacted. . . . That all meetings and assemblies of persons for the purpose of training or drilling themselves, or of being trained or drilled to the use of arms, or for the purpose of practising military exercise, movements or evolutions, without any lawful authority from His Majesty, or the Lieutenant, or two Justices of the Peace of any County or Riding, or of any Stewartry, by commission or otherwise, for so doing, shall be and the same are hereby prohibited, as dangerous to the peace and security of His Majesty's liege subjects and of His government ; and every person who shall be present at or attend any such meeting or assembly, for the purpose of training or drilling any other person or persons to the use of arms, or the practice of military exercise, movements or evolutions, or who shall aid or assist therein, being legally convicted thereof, shall be liable to be transported for any term not exceeding seven years, or to be punished by imprisonment not exceeding two years at the discretion of the court in which such conviction shall be had ; and every person who shall attend or be present at any such meeting or assembly as aforesaid, for the purpose of being or who shall at any such meeting or assembly be trained or drilled to the use of arms, or the practise of military exercise, movements or evolutions, being legally convicted thereof, shall be liable to be punished by fine and imprisonment not exceeding two years, at the discretion of the court in which such conviction shall be had.

(*b*) From 60 Geo. III, c. 9.

An Act to subject certain publications to the duties of stamps upon Newspapers, and to make other regulations for restraining the abuses arising from the publication of blasphemous and seditious libels (30th December 1819).

Whereas pamphlets and printed papers containing observations upon public events and occurrences, tending to excite hatred and contempt of the government and constitution of these realms as by law established, and also vilifying our holy religion, have lately been published in great numbers, and at very small prices; and it is expedient that the same should be restrained: . . . be it enacted . . . that from and after ten days after the passing of this Act, all pamphlets and papers containing any public news, intelligence of occurrences, or any remarks or observations thereon, or upon any matter in Church or State, printed in any part of the United Kingdom for sale, and published periodically in parts or numbers, at intervals not exceeding twenty-six days between the publication of any two such pamphlets or papers, parts or numbers, where any of the said pamphlets or papers, parts or numbers respectively shall not exceed two sheets, or shall be published for sale for a less sum than sixpence, exclusive of the duty by this Act imposed thereon, shall be deemed and taken to be newspapers within the true intent and meaning of an Act of Parliament passed in the thirty eighth year of the reign of His Present Majesty . . . and all other Acts of Parliament in force relating to newspapers ; . . .

II. And be it further enacted, that no quantity of paper less than a quantity equal to twenty one inches in length and seventeen inches in breadth, in whatever way or form the same may be made or may be printed, shall be deemed or taken to be a sheet of paper within the meaning and for the purposes of this Act.

. . . .

IV. And be it further enacted, that all pamphlets and papers containing any public news, intelligence or occurrences, or any such remarks or observations as aforesaid, printed for sale, and published periodically, or in parts or numbers, at intervals exceeding twenty six days between any two such pamphlets, papers, parts or numbers, and which said pamphlets, papers, parts or numbers respectively, shall not exceed two sheets, or which shall be published for sale at a less price than sixpence, shall be first published on the first day of every calendar month, or within two days before or after that day, and at no other time; and that if any person or persons shall first publish or cause to be published any such pamphlet, paper, part or number aforesaid, on any other day or time, he or they shall forfeit for every such offence the sum of twenty pounds.

15. THE CATO STREET CONSPIRACY

[The Cato Street Conspiracy of 1820 was a plot among a small group of ' Spencean Philanthropists ', egged on by Government spies, to murder the members of the Cabinet at a Cabinet meeting, and to use the ensuing confusion to start a general rising in London. It was part of the reaction to the Government's measures of repression enacted the previous year; but there is no evidence that the conspirators had any substantial following : indeed the spy, Edwards, seems to have taken a large part in planning, as well as betraying, the whole affair. Arthur Thistlewood, the leader, and several of his associates were hanged.]

(*a*) From G. T. Williams, " An Authentic History of the Cato-Street Conspiracy " [1820].

On the morning of Thursday the 24th of February 1820, the metropolis was thrown into the greatest consternation and alarm by the intelligence, that, in the course of the preceding evening, a most atrocious plot to overturn the government of the country, had been discovered, but which, by the prompt measures directed by the privy council, who remained sitting the greatest part of night, had been happily destroyed by the arrest and dispersion of the conspirators. Before day-light the following proclamation was placarded in all the leading places in and about London :—

LONDON GAZETTE EXTRAORDINARY,
Thursday, February 24, 1820.

Whereas *Arthur Thistlewood* stands charged with high treason, and also with the wilful murder of Richard Smithers, a reward of *One Thousand Pounds* is hereby offered to any person or persons who shall discover and apprehend, or cause to be discovered or apprehended, the said Arthur Thistlewood, to be paid by the lords commissioners of his majesty's treasury; upon his being apprehended and lodged in any of his Majesty's gaols. And all persons are hereby cautioned upon their allegiance not to receive or harbour the said Arthur Thistlewood, as any person offending herein will be thereby guilty of high treason.

SIDMOUTH.

The above-named Arthur Thistlewood is about forty-eight years of age, five feet ten inches high, has a sallow complexion, long visage, dark hair, (a little grey), dark hazel eyes and arched eyebrows, a wide mouth and a good set of teeth, has a scar under his right jaw, is slender made, and has the appearance of a military man ; was born in Lincolnshire, and apprenticed to an apothecary at Newark ; usually wears a blue long coat and blue pantaloons, and has been a lieutenant in the militia.

The particular part of the plan of the traitorous conspirators, which had been frustrated by their arrest the previous evening, was the following ; and its atrocity, fully justified the alarming impression which the first rumours had created.

It had been ascertained by the gang, that the greater part of his majesty's ministers were to dine together at the Earl of Harrowby's, and this was considered as a favourable opportunity for effecting their entire extermination : Thistlewood was to have knocked at Lord Harrowby's door, with a letter, purporting to be a despatch, or with a red box, such as is used in all the public offices, desiring it to be delivered immediately to the cabinet ministers at dinner, without delay. The servant, it was supposed, would immediately proceed with the despatch, while Thistlewood, with another of the conspirators, entered the hall as if to wait. They were immediately to open the street-door, others were to come in with hand-grenades, which were to be thrown into the house ; and, in the confusion produced by them, all the rest of the conspirators were to rush into the dining-room, where the ministers were at dinner, and the work of assassination was to have been instantly begun.

(b) From " The Trials of Arthur Thistlewood, and Others, for High Treason ", pp. 187-8. From the Judge's summing-up.

Upon the testimony, however, which had been adduced against them, there was abundantly sufficient to induce a Jury of their country to come to a conclusion that the whole of them had taken an active part in the crimes imputed to them in the indictment. From all that had appeared in the course of these trials, as well as from much of that which they had then heard, it was plain to see, that they did not embark in their wicked designs until they had first suffered their minds to be corrupted and inflamed by those seditious and irreligious publications, with which, unhappily for this country, the press had but too long teemed. He did not make these remarks to aggravate their guilt, or to enhance the sufferings of persons in their situation. He made them as a warning to all who might hear of their unfortunate fate, that they might benefit by their example, and avoid those dangerous instruments of sedition, by which their hearts and minds were inflamed, and by which they were drawn from every feeling of morality — from every sense of obligation towards their Creator, and of justice towards society. The treason of which they were charged and found guilty, was that of compassing and imagining to levy war against his Majesty, for the purpose of inducing him to change his measures and ministers; the first step towards effecting which, was to have been the assassination of the Cabinet Ministers. They had endeavoured now to complain of the testimony of those persons who had been examined as witnesses on the part of the prosecution. Some of them were accomplices in their guilt. It had here happened, as it had upon other occasions, that the principal instruments in the hands of justice, were the partners of their wickedness; and he trusted that circumstance would have its due weight and consideration with all those who became acquainted with their situation, and with the circumstances of their trial. He hoped, that for the sake of their own personal safety, if they could not be restrained by any other consideration, that they would abstain from evil communications, and from evil connexions, such as had brought the prisoners to the unhappy position in which they stood. Some of them had avowed their intention to have taken away the lives, and to have steeped their hands in the blood of fourteen persons, to many of them unknown — a crime of a character so black, that it was hitherto without parallel in the history of this country, and he hoped it would remain unparalleled hereafter. (His Lordship here seemed considerably agitated.) It now, he said, only remained for him to pass upon them the awful sentence of the law; but before he did so, he exhorted them, he implored them, to employ the time yet left to them in this life, in endeavouring, by prayer, to obtain mercy from that Almighty Power, before whom they would shortly appear.

16. THE CASE OF QUEEN CAROLINE

[The Case of Queen Caroline finds its place in this volume because the popular protests against the treatment of the Queen furnished the occasion for a general attack on the Government and had a great effect in bringing about all over the country a revival of the Radical agitation which had been driven underground by the repressive legislation of 1817 and 1819. In face of the strength of popular feeling and of the large body of middle-class supporters of the Queen's cause, the Government did not dare to adopt repressive measures against the numerous citizens' committees and mass meetings which approved resolutions protesting against the Bill of Pains and Penalties ; and the Radicals were able to use the opportunity to ventilate popular grievances as well as to uphold the Queen against the King and the Ministers. The Addresses, which included many from women as well as from Trade Societies and general town or county meetings, were mostly drafted by leading local Radicals ; and Cobbett himself is said to have drafted a number of Queen Caroline's answers, others of more moderate tone being prepared by Brougham or Alderman Matthew Wood. The Queen's death in 1821 brought the agitation to an end ; but the organisation that had been created survived in part to serve the Radical cause.]

(*a*) From An Address to the Most Gracious Majesty the Queen from the Artisans, Mechanics, and Labouring Classes of the Town of Manchester. *Cobbett's Weekly Political Register*, September 30, 1820.

May it please your Majesty, We his Majesty's loyal subjects, the Artisans, Mechanics, and Labouring Classes of the town of Manchester, beg leave most respectfully to approach your Majesty with our congratulations on your return amongst us, in contempt and defiance of the artifices and threats of your enemies.

. . . We feel that the measure now in progress against your Majesty, is subversive of every safeguard of the rights and liberties of the people. We believe that the design in degrading and dethroning your Majesty, by the monstrous Bill which the Ministry have introduced into Parliament, and which at once creates the crime, and fixes the penalty, is to give a striking and practical instance of the absurd claim to omnipotence, which those who sit in the seats which ought to be filled by the representatives of the nation, set up over the laws and constitution of our country. . . .

Apart, therefore, from all the considerations of the grievous injustice which your Majesty will individually suffer, by such an outrage upon the laws as that by which it is now sought to deprive you of your undoubted rights, we are convinced that, upon public ground, and with reference to the general safety, we are bound to raise our voices in defence of your Majesty. . . .

The artisans and mechanics of this populous and powerful district partake with us in admiration of your determination, and in readiness to assist you in carrying it into effect by all the means which we constitutionally possess, and which we humbly tender to your Majesty's acceptance.

Your Majesty cannot be unacquainted with the severe privations and deep sufferings of this immense population; and doubtless your Majesty's benevolent heart has been wrung at the dreadful events of the fatal 16th of August. The same power which scourged us is now oppressing you; — it is not less our interest than our duty, therefore, to stand up against your Majesty's enemies, who are also the enemies of the rights and liberties of the whole people. The deep-rooted and atrocious designs of this faction must be defeated; or the nation sinks at once into utter and hopeless slavery. We declare that we would rather die than live under such a state of things as that which our enemies are preparing for us. This is our solemn and serious resolution. As far as our power can extend we will prevent your Majesty from being unjustly and unlawfully sacrificed. We have no fortunes to offer, but we hold our lives valueless when justice and freedom are in danger.

(*b*) From ' The Queen's Answer to the Manchester Address '. *Cobbett's Weekly Political Register*, September 30, 1820.

I receive with great satisfaction this loyal, affectionate, and impressive Address, from so numerous, so useful, and so efficient a part of the community as the artisans, mechanics, and labouring classes of the town of Manchester. The true honour of the country has been in' the highest degree promoted by their incomparable skill and their unrivalled ingenuity, while their persevering industry has so largely contributed towards the means of maintaining the dignity of the Throne and the power and glory of the kingdom. . . . I am happy to perceive that the industrious classes in the town of Manchester, as well as in the rest of the kingdom, regard the unconstitutional attack upon my rights as an illegal invasion of their own. The Bill of Pains and Penalties, which threatens my degradation, weakens the security of that sacred tenure by which every Briton is protected in his liberty, his property, and his life. He who venerates a free Constitution will indignantly repel the introduction of arbitrary power in any of its varied forms.

We naturally compassionate the severe privations and deep sufferings, even of the idle and the dissolute; but how much more forcibly is our sympathy excited by such privations and sufferings, when they are accumulated upon the industrious, laborious, frugal, and virtuous part of this exemplary community ! My mind has indeed been often agonized by the recollection of that dreadful day, to which the industrious classes of Manchester particularly allude ; but while we cannot but know that the same hand has been our common oppressor, let us, as far as we are able, bury the past in oblivion; and trust that, though these things have been, they will be no more ! Let us endeavour to calm the perturbed passions and to heal the bleeding wounds of our distracted and lacerated country ; and, for myself, though my afflictions have been many in number and long in continuance, I shall think them all amply compensated if they should, at last, prove the means of contributing towards the harmony, the prosperity, and the happiness of the kingdom.

(c) From *The Courier*, September 27, 1820. Quoted in *Cobbett's Weekly Political Register*, September 30, 1820.

The Answers delivered in the name of the Queen to factious, seditious, and even treasonable Addresses, become daily more audacious and *alarming* ! It is impossible that her Majesty can *wilfully* authorise such communications, *if she is not insane*. Some short time ago we published the copy of an Address from the Manchester Radicals for the purpose of calling public attention and reprobation to the violent language in which it was couched, and warning the Queen herself of its evil tendency. Her Majesty receives this impudent composition, and answers, or is made to answer, that she receives it *with satisfaction*. But this is a trifle to what follows. The Addressers had spoken of the *events of the 16th of August*, 1819, in terms of most virulent abuse, describing the *legal interference of the military* as a massacre. The Queen not only adopts these sentiments, but identifying herself with the rioters, says, ' We cannot but know that the *same hand* has been our common *oppressor*'. Now she had elsewhere distinctly called the King ' my oppressor'. Here, therefore, she is made to assert that to the King's personal oppression are to be attributed the unfortunate occurrences of last year at Manchester ! That a lurking incendiary traitor should pen such infamous language, is easily conceivable — but that *a wife* should so wickedly, falsely, and *outrageously calumniate her husband*, that a Queen should so openly stir up the people to rebellion, is what we cannot suffer ourselves to imagine. Why is not *the villain who devotes his pen to these diabolical purposes, dragged from his lurking-hole to the punishment he so richly merits ?* And why do not the respectable classes of society throughout the kingdom *step forward indignantly to reprobate sentiments which can have no other tendency than to shake the constitution to its centre*, and to arm the populace against law, liberty, and property . . .

VII

THE REPEAL OF THE COMBINATION LAWS

INTRODUCTION

THE Repeal of the Combination Laws was not the work of one man. George White,[1] Gravener Henson,[2] Peter Moore [3] in Parliament, Cobbett,[4] and other national figures, and a host of local leaders and organisations, all contributed to the victory. But it was Francis Place who eventually manœuvred the repeal through Parliament. Through Joseph Hume [5] he secured the appointment of a Committee of Enquiry in 1824, packed it with sympathisers, and ' managed ' its proceedings. Its final report advocated repeal. The House of Commons carried out its recommendations, passing an Act which assumed that combinations were criminal at common law as being in restraint of trade and legalised them for a wide range of objects, but hindered strike action by specifically reaffirming the penalties on the use of ' threats ' or ' intimidation '— vague phrases in a law court. Place believed that if combination were made legal, the workers would soon find they had little power to oppose the ' Iron Law of Wages '. He prophesied greater industrial peace, and so the Act passed quietly through the House of Commons. But the working class was quick to bring secret Unions into the open, to form new ones, and to use old and new for a forward industrial movement. The alarm caused by the outbreak of strikes led to a fresh Committee of Investigation, which the friends of the Trade Unions were not able to pack. Defence associations in different towns—embryo trade councils — organised a strong opposition to the reactionary proposals of the employers. In consequence, the amending Act of 1825 was

[1] George White was a Clerk of Committees in the House of Commons.

[2] Gravener Henson was a bobbin-net maker of Nottingham ; he had been prominent in the various movements of the framework knitters.

[3] Peter Moore, M.P. for Coventry, had brought forward a Bill, drawn up by White and Henson, before Place and Hume had fully prepared themselves. Moore was invited to serve on Hume's Committee in order to get his measure side-tracked and thus to clear the way for Place's proposals.

[4] See the *Political Register*, August 30, 1823.

[5] Joseph Hume (1777–1855), the leading exponent in Parliament of Benthamism and ' public economy ', was also the constant friend of the Trade Unions and a supporter of factory legislation.

not so hostile as it would have otherwise been. Even so, it left Trade Unionists open to charges of conspiracy if they exceeded certain defined limits of collective bargaining, and made strike action more difficult than ever by threatening penalties against ' intimidation, molestation or obstruction ', etc. However, the principle of collective bargaining had been won, and the way was open for the Trade Unions to advance.

> *See* " Short History ", Part I, chapter 5, section 2.
> " Common People ", chapter 20.

1. THE EFFECT OF THE COMBINATION LAWS

[The following resolutions, adopted by Joseph Hume's Committee of 1824 as a basis for the proposed legislation concerning combinations, were carefully drafted to make freedom of combination appear a logical and necessary part of the general freedom of contract favoured by the economists of the time. The Committee also wished to emphasise the failure of legal repression as a means of preventing combinations, and the unequal incidence of the law on employers and workmen. The resolutions should be read in conjunction with the section dealing with Trade Unionism under the Combination Acts. The full Report of the Committee contains much valuable evidence upon the working of Trade Unionism while it was forced to operate largely, though not wholly, in secret.]

The Effect of the Combination Laws. From the Report of the Committee on Artisans and Machinery, 1824, pp. 589-91.

ON COMBINATION LAWS.

1.

THAT it appears, by the evidence before the Committee, that combinations of Workmen have taken place in England, Scotland and Ireland, often to a great extent, to raise and keep up their wages, to regulate their hours of working, and to impose restrictions upon their masters, respecting apprentices or others whom they might think proper to employ; and that, at the time the Evidence was taken, Combinations were in existence, attended with Strikes or suspension of work; and that the Laws have not hitherto been effectual to prevent such Combinations.

2.

THAT serious breaches of the peace and acts of violence, with strikes of the workmen, often for very long periods, have taken place, in consequence of, and arising out of the Combinations of workmen, and been attended with loss both to the masters and the workmen, and with considerable inconvenience and injury to the community.

3.

THAT the masters have often united and combined to lower the rates of their workmen's wages, as well as to resist a demand for an increase, and to regulate their hours of working; and sometimes to discharge their workmen who would not consent to the conditions offered to them; which have been followed by suspension of work, riotous proceedings, and acts of violence.

4.

THAT prosecutions have frequently been carried on, under the statute and the common law, against the workmen, and many of them have suffered different periods of imprisonment for combining and conspiring to raise their wages, or to resist their reduction, and to regulate their hours of working.

5.

THAT several instances have been stated to the Committee, of prosecutions against masters for combining to lower wages, and to regulate the hours of working; but no instance has been adduced of any master having been punished for that offence.

6.

THAT the laws have not only not been efficient to prevent Combinations, either of masters or workmen; but, on the contrary, have in the opinion of many of both parties, had a tendency, to produce mutual irritation and distrust, and to give a violent character to the Combinations, and to render them highly dangerous to the peace of the community.

7.

THAT it is the opinion of this Committee that masters and workmen should be freed from such restrictions, as regards the rate of wages and hours of working, and be left at perfect liberty to make such agreements as they may mutually think proper.

8.

THAT, therefore, the statute laws that interfere in these particulars between masters and workmen, should be repealed; and also that the common law, under which a peaceable meeting of masters or workmen may be prosecuted as a conspiracy, should be altered.

9.

THAT the Committee regret to find from the evidence, that societies, legally enrolled as benefit societies, have been frequently made the cloak, under which funds have been raised for the support of Combinations and Strikes, attended with acts of violence and intimidation; and without recommending any specific course, they wish to call the attention of the House to the frequent perversion of these institutions from their avowed and legitimate objects.

10.

THAT the practice of settling disputes by Arbitration between masters and workmen, has been attended with good effects; and it is desirable that the laws which direct and regulate Arbitration, should be consolidated, amended and made applicable to all trades.

11.

THAT it is absolutely necessary, when repealing the Combination Laws, to enact such a law as may efficiently, and by summary process, punish either workmen or masters, who by threats, intimidation, or acts of violence, should interfere with that perfect freedom which ought to be allowed to each party, of employing his labour or capital in the manner he may deem most advantageous.

2. FRANCIS PLACE AND THE COMBINATION LAWS

[Francis Place has left in manuscript a full account of his work, in conjunction with Joseph Hume and George White (the Clerk to Committees of the House of Commons), to secure the repeal of the Combination Laws. The story is told, mainly in Place's own words, in Graham Wallas's " Life of Francis Place " (1898), chapter 8.]

(*a*) From " Observations on Huskisson's Speech ", by F. P. (Francis Place) (1825), p. 21. (Quoted from Graham Wallas, " The Life of Francis Place " (1898), pp. 199-200.)

" If keeping down wages in some cases, by law, was a national good ; if the degradation of the whole body of the working people by law was desirable ; if perpetuating discord between masters and workmen was useful ; if litigation was a benefit ; if living in perpetual violation of law was a proper state for workmen and their employers to be placed in, then the laws against combinations of workmen were good laws, for to all these did they tend."

(*b*) From the Place MSS., 27,798 ff. 12-14. (Quoted from Graham Wallas, " The Life of Francis Place " (1898), pp. 203-4.)

In 1814, therefore, I began to work seriously to procure a repeal of the laws against combinations of workmen, but for a long time made no visible progress. As often as any dispute arose between masters and men, or when any law proceedings were had, and reported in the newspapers, I interfered, sometimes with the masters, sometimes with the men, very generally, as far as I could, by means of some one or more of the newspapers, and sometimes by acting as a pacificator, always pushing for the one purpose, the repeal of the laws.

I wrote a great many letters to trade societies in London, and as often as I heard of any dispute respecting the Combination Laws in the country I wrote to some of the parties, stated my purpose, and requested information. Few condescended to notice my applications, and scarcely any furnished me with the information I wished to have ; but many of the country papers inserted the articles I sent to them, and these must have produced some effect, though no signs of any appeared. Working-men had been too often deceived to be willing to trust to any one who was not well known to them. Habitually cunning, and suspicious of all above their own rank in life, and having no expectation of any mitigation, much less of a chance of the laws being repealed, they could not persuade themselves that my communications were of any value to them, and they would not therefore give themselves any trouble about them, much less to give such information as might, they thought, be some day used against them. I understood them thoroughly, and was neither put from my purpose nor offended with them. I was resolved to serve them as much as I could. I knew well enough that if they could be served in this as in many other particulars, it must be done without their concurrence, in spite of them.

The papers I continued to write for the daily and weekly press were not wholly thrown away; there was, after some time, an evident reluctance in many places to enforce the laws against the workmen; and some who did enforce them no longer met with the general support which had formerly been given to such proceedings.

(c) From the Place MSS., 27,798 ff. 20-24. (Quoted from Graham Wallas, " The Life of Francis Place " (1898), pp. 211-16.)

On the 12th February, Mr. Hume made his motion, and obtained his Committee. It was with difficulty Mr. Hume could obtain the names of twenty-one members to compose the Committee; but when it had sat three days, and had become both popular and amusing, members contrived to be put upon it, and at length it consisted of forty-eight members.

When the Committee met for business, Mr. Hume found himself in a very difficult situation; he had been so assiduously employed in various other matters, that it had been impossible for him to give attention to the details of this. He was much annoyed and embarrassed; no one assisted him, and some put obstacles in his way. I offered to attend the Committee as his assistant, but the jealousy of the members prevented this; they ' would not be dictated to ' — that is, they would not have the business put in a plain way by the only man who had made himself master of it in all its bearings, because he was neither a member of the honourable House, nor even a gentleman. Thus does pride and ignorance, in all situations, from a Committee of the honourable House to a chandler's shop in an alley, show itself much in the same way, always absurd, always pitiful, very generally mischievous. Happily nothing can subdue Mr. Hume's perseverance, and, like almost every man who perseveres in a right course, he almost always finds himself firm upon his legs at the end of his labour. Mr. Hume wrote a circular letter announcing the appointment of the Committee, and inviting persons to come and give evidence; copies of this were sent to the mayors and other officers of corporate towns, and to many of the principal manufacturers. Some one country paper having obtained a copy, printed it, and it was presently reprinted in all the newspapers, and thus due notice was given to everybody. Meetings were held in many places; and both masters and men sent up deputations to give evidence. The delegates from the working people had reference to me, and I opened my house to them. Thus I had all the town and country delegates under my care. I heard the story which every one of these men had to tell. I examined and cross-examined them; took down the leading particulars of each case, and then arranged the matter as briefs for Mr. Hume; and, as a rule, for the guidance of the witnesses, a copy was given to each. . . . Thus he was enabled to go on with considerable ease, and to anticipate or rebut objections.

.   .   .   .   .

The workmen were not easily managed. It required great pains and patience not to shock their prejudices, so as to prevent them doing their duty before the Committee. They were filled with false notions, all attributing their distresses to wrong causes, which I, in this state of the business, dared not attempt to remove. Taxes, machinery, laws against combinations, the will of the masters, the conduct of magistrates, these were the fundamental causes of all their sorrows and privations. All expected a great and sudden rise of wages, when the Combination Laws should be repealed; not one of them had any idea whatever of the connection between wages and population. I had to discuss everything with them most carefully, to arrange and prepare everything, and so completely did these things occupy my time, that for more than three months I had hardly time for rest.

. . . Mr. White and I had put the bills into form with the fewest words possible. Mr. Hume, however, suffered the Attorney-General to employ Mr. Anthony Hamond, a barrister, to draw the bills; he took our MSS., and pretty specimens of nonsense he made of them! He had all the necessary documents, some suggestions in writing, and the bills themselves as perfectly drawn as we could draw them; but he knew not how to use them. This caused considerable perplexity. We attacked his draft, and afterwards the printed bills. He paid but little attention to us, but it so happened that when the bills were once printed he considered himself as having performed all that he was likely to be remunerated for, and he gave himself no further concern about them. We now got them into our hands, altered them as we liked, had MS. copies made and presented to the House. No inquiry was made as to who drew the bills; they were found to contain all that was needful, and with some assiduity in seeing members to induce them not to speak on the several readings, they passed the House of Commons almost without the notice of members within or newspapers without.

3. THE ACT OF 1824

[The Combination Act of 1824 not only repealed the Act of 1800 and the other Acts forbidding combinations in particular trades, but also abrogated the common law doctrine by which combination was treated as unlawful conspiracy. It thus gave a very wide legalisation to Trade Unions, with no attempt to restrict their scope ; but at the same time it cast into a general form the provisions of common and statute law which made punishable any kind of violence, threat, or intimidation as a means of coercing either employers or workers to act as the combination desired. This clause (V) could have been used in the courts with effect against the Trade Unions even if it had not been replaced by the still more stringent provisions of the Act of 1825.]

From the Combination Act of 1824, 5 Geo IV, c. 95.

An Act to repeal the Laws relative to the Combination of Workmen ; and for other purposes therein mentioned (21st June, 1824).

Whereas it is expedient that the laws relative to the combination of workmen and to fixing the wages of labour, should be repealed ; and that certain combinations of masters and workmen should be exempted from punishment ; and that the attempt to deter workmen from work should be punished in a summary manner ; be it therefore enacted. . . . That from and after the passing of this Act, so much of a certain Act passed in the thirty-third year of King Edward the First, intituled who be conspirators and who be champertors, as relates to combinations or conspiracies of workmen or other persons to obtain an advance or to fix the rate of wages, or to increase or alter the hours or duration of the time of working, or to increase the quantity of work, or to regulate or controul the mode of carrying on any manufacture, trade or business or the management thereof, or to oblige workmen to enter into work ; and also . . . together with all other laws, statutes and enactments, now in force throughout or in any part of the United Kingdom of Great Britain and Ireland, relative to combinations to obtain an advance of wages, or to lessen or alter the hours or duration of the time of working, or to decrease the quantity of work, or to regulate or controul the mode of carrying on any manufacture, trade or business or the management thereof ; relative also to combinations to lower the rate of wages, or to increase or alter the hours or duration of the time of working, or to increase the quantity of work, or to regulate or controul the mode of carrying on any manufacture, trade or business, or the management thereof ; relative also to fixing the amount of the wages of labour ; relative also to obliging workmen not hired to enter into work; together with every other act and enactment enforcing or extending the application of any of the acts or enactments repealed by this act, shall be and the same are hereby repealed, save and except in as far as the same may have repealed any prior act or enactment.

II And be it further enacted that journeymen, workmen or other persons who shall enter into any combination to obtain an advance or to fix the rate of wages, or to lessen or alter the hours of duration of the time of working, or to decrease the quantity of work, or to induce another to depart from his service before the end of the time or term for which he is hired, or to quit or return his work before the same shall be finished, or not being hired, to refuse to enter into work or employment, or to regulate the mode of carrying on any manufacture, trade or business, or the management thereof, shall not therefore be liable or subject to any indictment or prosecution for conspiracy, or to any other criminal information or punishment whatever, under the Common or the Statute Law.

. . . . . .

V And be it further enacted, that if any person, by violence to the person or property, by threats or intimidation, shall wilfully or maliciously force another to depart from his hiring or work before the end of the time or term for which he is hired, or return his work before the same shall be finished, or damnify, spoil or destroy any machinery, tools, goods, wares or work, or prevent any person not being hired from accepting any work or employment; or if any person shall wilfully use or employ violence to the person or property, threats or intimidation towards another on account of his not complying with or conforming to any rules, orders, resolutions, or regulations made to obtain an advance of wages, or to lessen or alter the hours of working, or to decrease the quantity of work, or to regulate the mode of carrying on any manufacture, trade, or business, or the management thereof; or if any person, by violence to the person or property, by threats or by intimidation, shall wilfully or maliciously force any master or mistress manufacturer, his or her foreman or agent, to make any alteration in their mode of regulating, managing, conducting, or carrying on their manufacture, trade, or business; every person so offending, or causing, procuring, aiding, abetting, or assisting in such offence, being convicted thereof in manner hereafter mentioned, shall be imprisoned only, or imprisoned and kept to hard labour, for any time not exceeding two calendar months.

VI And be it further enacted, that if any persons shall combine and commit any of the crimes listed in section 6, each and every person so offending, or causing, procuring, aiding, abetting or assisting in such offence, being convicted thereof in manner hereinafter mentioned, shall be imprisoned only, or imprisoned and kept to hard labour, for any time not exceeding two calendar months ; . . .

VII For the more effectual prosecution of offenders against this act, be it further enacted, that on complaint and information upon oath before any one or more Justice or Justices of the Peace, of any offence having been committed against this act within his or their respective jurisdictions, such Justice or Justices are hereby authorised and required to summon the person or persons charged with any such offence against this act to appear before any two Justices at a certain time and place to be specified, such place to be as near to the place where cause of such complaint shall have arisen as may be.

VIII Provided always, and be it further enacted, that no Justice of the Peace, being also a master, or the father or son of any master, in any trade or manufacture, shall act as such Justice under this act.

4. THE ACT OF 1825

[The Act of 1825, passed at the instance of employers and others during the wave of strikes that followed the repeal of the Combination Laws in 1824, made more stringent the provisions against violence, threats, and intimidation. It introduced the key words ' molest ' and ' obstruct ', which were used to disallow picketing, and specifically hit at the use of combination to enforce the ' closed shop '. It also narrowed greatly the range of legalisation accorded to the Trade Unions, by laying down in Section IV that the right of combination should apply only to matters of wages and hours of labour — thus excluding such matters as the limitation of the number of apprentices or the reservation of certain jobs for apprenticed workers only. The Act of 1825 did, however, within these limits, maintain the rights of combination against common law prosecutions for conspiracy.]

From the Combination Act of 1825, 6 Geo. IV, c. 129.

(The first two sections repeal previous statutes dealing with Combinations.)

III And be it further enacted, that from and after the passing of this act, if any person shall by violence to the person or property, or by threats or intimidation, or by molesting or in any way obstructing another, force or endeavour to force any journeyman, manufacturer, workman or other person hired or employed in any manufacture, trade or business, to depart from his hiring, employment or work, or to return his work before the same shall be finished, or prevent, or endeavour to prevent, any journeyman, manufacturer, workman or other person, not being hired or employed, from hiring himself to, or from accepting work or employment from any person or persons; or if any person shall use or employ violence to the person or property of another, or threats or intimidation, or shall molest or in any way obstruct another for the purpose of forcing or inducing such person to belong to any club or association, or to contribute to any common fund, or to pay any fine or penalty, or on account of his not belonging to any club or association, or not having contributed or having refused to contribute to any common fund, or to pay any fine or penalty, or on account of his not having complied or of his refusing to comply with any rules, orders, resolutions or regulations made to obtain an advance or to reduce the rate of wages, or to lessen or alter the hours of working, or to decrease or alter the quantity of work, or to regulate the mode of carrying on any manufacture, trade or business, or the management thereof; or if any person shall by violence to the person or property of another, or by threats or intimidation, or by molesting or in any way obstructing another, force or endeavour to force any manufacturer or person carrying on any trade or business, to make any alteration in his mode of regulating, managing, conducting or carrying on such manufacture, trade or business, to limit the number of his apprentices, or the number or description of his journeymen, workmen or servants; every person so offending or aiding, abetting or assisting therein, being convicted thereof in manner hereinafter mentioned, shall be imprisoned only, or shall and may be imprisoned and kept for hard labour, for any time not exceeding three calendar months.

IV Provided always, and be it enacted, that this act shall not extend to subject any persons to punishment, who shall meet together for the sole purpose of consulting upon and determining the rate of wages or prices, which the persons present at such meeting or any of them, shall require or demand for his or their work, or the hours or time for which he or they shall work in any manufacture, trade or business, or who shall enter into any agreement, verbal or written, among themselves, for the purpose of fixing the rate of wages or prices which the parties entering into such agreement, or any of them, shall require or demand for his or their work, or the hours of time for which he or they shall work in any manufacture, trade or business, or who shall enter into any agreement, verbal or written, among themselves, for the purpose of fixing the rate of wages or prices which the parties entering into such agreement, or any of them, shall require or demand for his or their work, or the hours of time for which he or they will work, in any manufacture, trade or business ; and that persons so meeting for the purposes aforesaid, or entering into any such agreement as aforesaid, shall not be liable to any prosecution or penalty for so doing ; any law or statute to the contrary notwithstanding.

VIII

LABOUR ECONOMICS AND CO-OPERATION
IN THE 1820s

INTRODUCTION

In the 1820s there grew up suddenly a school of writers who attempted to supply a theoretical basis for the economic and social action of the working classes. In addition to Owen's " Report to the County of Lanark " (1821), where he first clearly formulated his conception of labour value, there appeared during these years the principal writings of Thomas Hodgskin, William Thompson, and the other writers more commonly grouped together as the ' Labour Economists ', or ' Anti-capitalist Economists '. These writers were strongly influenced by Ricardo, whose " Principles of Political Economy " first appeared in 1817. Upon Ricardo's theory that the amount of labour was the normal measure of value, they built the ' Socialist ' conclusion that the entire produce of labour ought to belong to the labourer as the sole real creator of wealth. If labour alone creates wealth, the poverty of the labourers, despite the rapid advance in productive efficiency, must be due to the share appropriated by the profit-maker, and the solution must lie in the elimination of profit-making by means of mutual co-operation among the labourers. The writers of this school differed considerably among themselves. Hodgskin, for example, was content in " Labour Defended " (1825) and in " Popular Political Economy " (1827) to assert the labourers' right to the whole product without laying down any system of social organisation designed to bring about the change; whereas William Thompson, in " The Principles of the Distribution of Wealth Most Conducive to Human Happiness " (1824), " Labour Rewarded " (1827), and " Practical Directions for the Establishment of Communities " (1830), combined a similar demonstration of the labour theory of value with an exposition of Owenite doctrines and a formulation of definite proposals for carrying them into effect. Much of the enthusiasm for Co-operative communities and societies for Co-operative production was stimulated by these writers; but they also helped to provide a foundation for the class-conscious Radicalism of the

189

National Union of the Working Classes and other similar movements. At the same time Owen's Co-operative theories were being developed first by George Mudie and then by Dr. William King, of Brighton, as well as by Thompson, whose work links together the anti-Ricardian and Owenite groups.

See " Short History ", Part I, chapter 5, section 1. Chapter 6, section 2. " Common People ", chapter 20.

1. CO-OPERATIVE SOCIALISM

[Robert Owen became, in spite of himself, the prophet of the early Co-operative movement. Starting as a ' welfare capitalist ' he put forward social ideas and schemes, which took on more and more the character of a proposal for a totally new social system. This development of his ideas soon frightened the ruling class but appealed to the working class. In their hands Owenism acquired new forms and became the basis of the Co-operative movement, as well as, for a time, of Trade Unionism. As a social philosopher Owen taught the essentially socialist idea that vice and unhappiness are produced by bad conditions, and demanded a higher standard of life, universal education, and a tolerant friendliness of man to man. As an economist he declared that labour is the source of all value, a theory which influenced strongly the development of Co-operative production and, in a general way, the growing confidence of the working class in its own importance and strength. As a practical reformer he proposed the establishment of largely self-sufficient Co-operative Communities, or Villages of Co-operation, in which, the working class came to feel, men would be free, equal, and prosperous.

Owen hoped that his scheme would be put into practice by the ruling class ; he had little belief (until about 1830) in the capacities of the working class to achieve their own emancipation. In 1825, discouraged by his failure to get his plan adopted in England, he founded the colony of New Harmony in America to try out his ideas. By 1828 he was forced to recognise defeat, and he returned to England.

Meanwhile his views had found an English audience. For in 1821 some working printers and their friends, under the leadership of George Mudie, founded the ' Co-operative and Economical Society ' and started *The Economist*. In addition to its propagandist activities the Society ran a small Co-operative settlement on Owenite lines. The London Co-operative Society (1824) succeeded it as the main propagandist body schemes for Co-operative communities became frequent and the London Co-operative Society started the Co-operative Community Fund Association (1826) to raise the necessary money, always the greatest difficulty facing these schemes. In 1827 the L.C.S. decided to build up an additional fund by organising a trading store and accumulating the profits which they would get by the elimination of the middleman. In the same year the famous Brighton Society was started by Dr. King. For the next year or two the trading store was the main feature of Co-operation ; the objects were partly to collect funds for a community, partly to anticipate the benefits of economy and comradely self-help, which they expected to enjoy in their Co-operative community of the future. This was the missionary period. The central body was the British Association for Promoting Co-operative Knowledge (1829) ; in this and in all other societies discussions, debates, and lectures were a regular feature. In the provinces as well as in London several Co-operative papers were published, Dr. King's *Co-operator* being by far the most important.]

(*a*) Labour the Source of Value. From " A Report to the County of Lanark ", 1820. (Reprinted in " A New View of Society, and Other Writings by Robert Owen ". Everyman's Library.)

The Evil for which your Reporter has been required to provide a remedy, is the general want of employment, at wages sufficient to support the family of a working man beneficially for the community. After the most earnest consideration of the subject he has been compelled to conclude that such employment cannot be procured through the medium of trade, commerce, or manufactures, or even of agriculture, until the Government and the Legislature, cordially supported by the Country, shall previously adopt measures to remove obstacles, which, without their interference, will now permanently keep the working classes in poverty and discontent and gradually deteriorate all the resources of the empire.

Your Reporter has been impressed with the truth of this conclusion by the following considerations :—

1st.—That manual labour, properly directed, is the source of all wealth, and of national prosperity.

2nd.—That, when properly directed, labour is of far more value to the community than the expense necessary to maintain the labourer in considerable comfort.

3rd.—That manual labour, properly directed, may be made to continue of this value in all parts of the world, under any supposable increase of its population, for many centuries to come.

4th.—That, under a proper direction of manual labour, Great Britain and its dependencies may be made to support an incalculable increase of population, most advantageously for all its inhabitants.

5th.—That when manual labour shall be so directed, it will be found that population cannot, for many years, be stimulated to advance as rapidly as society might be benefited by its increase.

· · · · · ·

The amount of this new productive power cannot, for want of proper data, be very accurately estimated; but your Reporter has ascertained from facts which none will dispute, that its increase has been enormous; — that, compared with the manual labour of the whole population of Great Britain and Ireland, it is, at least, as *forty to one*, and may be easily made as 100 *to one*; and that this increase may be extended to other countries; that it is already sufficient to saturate the world with wealth, and that the power of creating wealth may be made to advance perpetually in an accelerating ratio.

It appeared to your Reporter that the natural effect of the aid thus obtained from knowledge and science should be to add to the wealth and happiness of society in proportion as the new power increased and was judiciously directed; and that, in consequence, all parties would thereby be substantially benefited. All know, however, that these beneficial effects do not exist. On the contrary, it must be acknowledged that the working classes, which form so large a proportion of the population, cannot obtain even the comforts which their labour formerly procured for them, and that no party appears to gain, but all to suffer, by their distress.

Having taken this view of the subject, your Reporter was induced to conclude that the want of beneficial employment for the working classes, and the consequent public distress, were owing to the rapid increase of the new productive power, for the advantageous application of which, society had neglected to make the proper arrangements. Could these arrangements be formed, he entertained the most confident expectation that productive employment might again be found for all who required it; and that the national distress, of which all now so loudly complain, might be gradually converted into a much higher degree of prosperity than was attainable prior to the extraordinary accession lately made to the productive power of society.

· · · · · ·

One of the measures which he thus ventures to propose, *to let prosperity loose on the country*, (if he may be allowed the expression,) *is a change in the standard of value.*

· · · · · ·

THAT THE NATURAL STANDARD OF VALUE IS, IN PRINCIPLE, HUMAN LABOUR, OR THE COMBINED

MANUAL AND MENTAL POWERS OF MEN CALLED INTO ACTION.

And that it would be highly beneficial, and has now become absolutely necessary, to reduce this principle into immediate practice.

It will be said, by those who have taken a superficial or more partial view of the question, that human labour or power is so unequal in individuals, that its average amount cannot be estimated.

Already, however, the average physical power of men, as well as of horses, (equally varied in the individuals,) has been calculated for scientific purposes, and both now serve to measure inanimate powers.

On the same principle the average of human labour or power may be ascertained; and as it forms the essence of all wealth, its value in every article of produce may also be ascertained, and its exchangeable value with all other values fixed accordingly; the whole to be permanent for a given period.

Human labour would thus acquire its natural or intrinsic value, which would increase as science advanced; and this is, in fact, the only really useful object of science.

.   .   .   .   .   .

This change in the standard of value would immediately open the most advantageous domestic markets, until the wants of all were amply supplied; nor while this standard continued could any evil arise in future from the want of markets.

.   .   .   .   .   .

(b) Villages of Co-operation. From ' A Letter Published in the London Newspapers of July 30th, 1817 '. (Reprinted in " The Life of Robert Owen " (1858), vol. i a, pp. 68-70.)

. . . Q. *Having turned your attention to the subject, to what causes do you attribute the distress existing among the poor and working classes ?*

A. To a misapplication of the existing powers of production in the country, both natural and artificial, when compared to the wants and demands for those productions. Much of our natural power, consisting of the physical and intellectual faculties of human beings, is now not only altogether unproductive, but a heavy burden to the country : under a system, too which is rapidly demoralising it; while a very large part of our artificial or mechanical agency is employed to produce that which is of little real value to society, and which, in its act of production, entails innumerable evils of the most afflicting kind, at the present time, upon the producers, as well as upon a very large part of society ; and, through them, upon the whole of our population.

Q. *Does your experience enable you to suggest a more advantageous application of these productive powers ?*

A. It induces me to say, that they may be applied more advantageously, for society, and for the individuals ; that they may, with ease, be so directed as to remove speedily the present distress of the labouring poor, and gradually to carry the prosperity of the country to a point much higher than it has ever yet attained.

Q. *How can this be done ?*

A. By forming well-digested arrangements to occupy the apparent surplus of the labouring poor, who are competent to work, in productive employment, in order that they may maintain themselves first, and afterwards contribute to bear their proportion of the expenses of the State.

Q. *Do the means exist by which employment could be given to the unoccupied of the working classes ?*

A. It appears to me that the country possesses the most ample means to attain this object, if they were called into action. Those means consist of land unemployed ; land imperfectly cultivated ; money employed unprofitably ; manual powers of labour idle, demoralising, and consequently generating every kind of evil in society ; artificial or mechanical agency almost unlimited, and which might be made available for the most important purposes. These are the means, which, if properly combined and put into action, would soon relieve the country from poverty and its attendant evils.

Q. *How can they be put into action ?*

A. By bringing them all into useful and profitable combinations, so as to create limited communities of individuals, on the principle of united labour and expenditure, having their basis in agriculture, and in which all should have mutual and common interests.

Q. *What are your reasons for recommending such a combination of human powers ?*

A. The knowledge that I possess of the very superior advantages which each person could derive by this means, beyond any application of his own exertions for his own exclusive purposes.

Q. *What are these superior advantages ?*

A. Communities of 500 to 1,500 persons, founded on the principle of united labour and expenditure, and having their basis in agriculture, might be arranged so as to give the following advantages to the labouring poor, and through them to all the other classes — for every real benefit to the latter must come from the former. All the labour of the individuals under this system would be naturally and advantageously directed; first to procure for themselves abundance of all that was necessary for their comfortable subsistence; next, they would obtain the means to enable them to unlearn many, almost all indeed, of the bad habits which the present defective arrangements of society have forced upon them : then, to give only the best habits and dispositions to the rising generation, and thus withdraw those circumstances from society which separate man from man, and introduce others, whose entire tendency shall be to unite them in one general interest that shall be clearly understood by each. They will afterwards be enabled to cultivate the far more valuable, the intellectual part of their nature ; that part which, when properly directed, will discover how much may yet be put into practice to promote human happiness.

(c) The Contrast. From a Letter Published in the London News-papers of August 9, 1817. (Reprinted in " The Life of Robert Owen by Himself " (1858), vol. i *a*, p. 89.)

We will very hastily and sketchily sketch the contrast.

In the Manufacturing Towns,— the poor and working classes now usually live in garrets or cellars, within narrow lanes or confined courts.

In the Proposed Villages,— the poor and working classes will live in dwellings formed into a large square, rendered in every way convenient, and usefully ornamented.

In the Manufacturing Towns,— they are surrounded with dirt, enveloped in smoke, and have seldom a pleasant object on which to fix their eye.

In the Proposed Villages,— they will be surrounded by gardens, have abundance of space in all directions to keep the air healthy and pleasant ; they will have walks and plantations before them, within the square, and well cultivated grounds, kept in good order around, as far as the eye can reach.

In the Manufacturing Towns,— parents are oppressed with anxiety to secure the means of subsistence for themselves and children.

In the Proposed Villages,— in consequence of the principle of mutual cooperation being understood and practiced to its full extent, the necessaries and comforts of life are enjoyed by all in abundance.

In the Manufacturing Towns,— each family has the care and trouble of going to market to supply their individual wants, and under every disadvantage.

In the Proposed Villages,— the same trouble will provide for 1000 as is now required for one family ; and all articles will be procured on the best terms.

In the Manufacturing Towns,— each family must have domestic arrangements for cooking, etc, and one person must be wholly occupied in preparing provisions etc, for a family of ordinary numbers.

In the Proposed Villages,— the best provisions will be cooked in the best manner, under arrangements that will enable five or six individuals to prepare provisions for 1000.

In the Manufacturing Towns,— the parents must toil from ten to sixteen hours in the day to procure the wretched subsistence which they obtain for themselves and children and very often under circumstances the most unfavourable to health and natural enjoyments.

In the Proposed Villages,— the parents will be healthfully and pleasantly occupied not more than eight hours in the day.

In the Manufacturing Towns,— in bad times, and which frequently occur, the parties experience a distress not easily to be described.

In the Proposed Villages,— in the event of sickness, the utmost attention and care will be experienced ; every one, both from principle and interest, will be active and have pleasure in rendering the situation of the invalid as comfortable as possible.

In the Manufacturing Towns,— the early death of parents leaves the children orphans and subject to every evil.

In the Proposed Villages,— the early death of parents leaves the children in all respects well provided for and protected.

In the Manufacturing Towns,— the children are usually sickly and, as well as their parents, ill-clothed.

In the Proposed Villages,— the children will be ruddy and healthy, and, as well as their parents, neat, clean and properly clothed.

In the Manufacturing Towns,— the young children are much neglected and hourly acquire bad habits.

In the Proposed Villages,— the children will be well looked after, prevented from acquiring bad, and taught good, habits.

In the Manufacturing Towns,— the education of the children is neglected.

In the Proposed Villages,— the children all well trained and well informed.

In the Manufacturing Towns,— the children sent early in life to some one trade or manufacture, usually of a very unhealthy nature, and at which they must attend from ten to sixteen hours per day.

In the Proposed Villages,— the children gradually instructed in gardening, agriculture, and some trade or manufacture, and only employed according to age and strength.

In the Manufacturing Towns,— the children trained under ignorant persons, possessing many bad habits.

In the Proposed Villages,— the children will be trained by intelligent persons, possessing only good habits.

In the Manufacturing Towns, — scolding, coercion, and punishments, are the usual instruments of training.

In the Proposed Villages,— kindness and good sense will be the only instruments of training.

To proceed with the contrast would be endless ; the mind of the reader will easily supply the remainder : suffice it therefore to say—

That the Manufacturing Towns are the abode of poverty, vice, crime and misery.

While the Proposed Villages will ever be the abode of abundance, active intelligence, correct conduct, and happiness.

2. THE LABOUR THEORY OF VALUE

[Thomas Hodgskin (1783–1869), a naval officer during the Napoleonic Wars, and subsequently a journalist, was one of the founders of the London Mechanics' Institute and of *The Mechanics' Magazine*, and one of the first writers to formulate a theory of labour exploitation based on the labour theory of value. His principal works on Economics are "Labour Defended" (1825), "Popular Political Economy" (1827), and "The Natural and Artificial Rights of Property Contrasted" (1832). He was on the staff of *The Morning Chronicle* and later of *The Economist*. See Thomas Hodgskin, by Elie Halévy (in French) (1903), and G. D. H. Cole's edition of "Labour Defended" (1922).]

(*a*) From Thomas Hodgskin, "Labour Defended" (1922 edition), pp. 83 ff.

. . . Wherever division of labour exists, and the further it is carried the more evident does this truth become, scarcely any individual completes of himself any species of produce. Almost any product of art and skill is the result of joint and combined labour. So dependent is man on man, and so much does this dependence increase as society advances, that hardly any labour of any single individual, however much it may contribute to the whole produce of society, is of the least value but as forming a part of the great social task. . . . Wherever the division of labour is introduced, therefore, the judgment of other men intervenes before the labourer can realise his earnings, and there is no longer any thing which we can call the natural reward of individual labour. Each labourer produces only some part of a whole, and each part having no value or utility of itself, there is nothing on which the labourer can seize, and say : " This is my product, this will I keep to myself." Between the commencement of any joint operation, such as that of making cloth, and the division of its product among the different persons whose combined exertions have produced it, the judgment of men must intervene several times, and the question is, how much of this joint product should go to each of the individuals whose united labours produce it ?

I know no way of deciding this but by leaving it to be settled by the unfettered judgments of the labourers themselves. . . .

. . . The knowledge and skill of the master manufacturer, or of the man who plans and arranges a productive operation, who must know the state of the markets and the qualities of different materials, and who has some tact in buying and selling, are just as necessary for the complete success of any complicated operation as the skill of the workmen whose hands actually alter the shape and fashion of these materials. Far be it, therefore, from the manual labourer, while he claims the reward due to his own productive powers, to deny its appropriate reward to any other species of labour, whether it be of the head or the hands. The labour and skill of the contriver, or of the man who arranges and adapts a whole, are as necessary as the labour and skill of him who executes only a part, and they must be paid accordingly.

I must, however, add that it is doubtful whether one species of labour is more valuable than another ; certainly it is not more necessary. But because those who have been masters, planners, contrivers, etc., have in general also been capitalists, and have also had a command over the labour of those who have worked with their hands, their labour has been paid as much too high as common labour has been under paid. The wages of the master, employer or contriver has been blended with the profit of the capitalists, and he may probably be still disposed to claim the whole as only the proper reward of his exertions. On the other hand, manual labourers, oppressed by the capitalist, have never been paid high enough, and even now are more disposed to estimate their own deserts rather by what they have hitherto received than by what they produce. This sort of prejudice makes it, and will long make it, difficult even for labourers themselves to apportion with justice the social reward or wages of each individual labourer. No statesman can accomplish this, nor ought the labourers to allow any statesman to interfere in it. The labour is theirs, the produce ought to be theirs, and they alone ought to decide how much each deserves of the produce of all. While each labourer claims his own reward, let him cheerfully allow the just claims of every other labourer; but let him never assent to the strange doctrine that the food he eats and the instruments he uses, which are the work of his own hands, become endowed, by merely changing proprietors, with productive power greater than his, and that the owner of them is entitled to a more abundant reward than the labour, skill and knowledge which produce and use them.

. . . If by combining the journeymen were to drive masters, who are a useful class of labourers, out of the country, if they were to force abroad the skill and ingenuity which contrive, severing them from the hands which execute, they would do themselves and the remaining inhabitants considerable mischief. If, on the contrary, by combining they merely incapacitate the masters from obtaining any profit on their capital, and merely prevent them from completing the engagements they have contracted with the capitalist, they will do themselves and the country incalculable service. They may reduce or destroy altogether the profit of the idle capitalist — and from the manner in which capitalists have treated labourers, even within our own recollection, they have no claim on the gratitude of the labourer — but they will augment the wages and rewards of industry, and will give to genius and skill their due share of the national produce. They will also increase prodigiously the productive power of the country by increasing the number of skilled labourers. The most successful and widest-spread possible combination to obtain an augmentation of wages would have no other injurious effect than to reduce the incomes of those who live on profit and interest, and who have no just claim but custom to any share of the national produce.

(b) From Thomas Hodgskin, " Labour Defended " (1922 edition), pp. 107-9.

. . . That the capitalist can control the existence and number of labourers, that the whole number of the population depends altogether on him, I will not deny. But put the capitalist, the oppressive middleman, who eats up the produce of labour and prevents the labourer from knowing on what *natural* laws his existence and happiness depend, out of view — put aside those social regulations by which they who produce all are allowed to own little or nothing — and it is plain that CAPITAL, or the POWER TO EMPLOY LABOUR, and CO-EXISTING LABOUR are ONE; and that PRODUCTIVE CAPITAL and SKILLED LABOUR are also ONE ; consequently capital and a labouring population are precisely synonymous.

In the system of Nature, mouths are united with hands and with intelligence ; they and not capital are the agents of production ; and, according to her rule, however it may have been thwarted by the pretended wisdom of law-makers, wherever there is a man there also are the means of creating or producing him subsistence. If also, as I say, circulating capital is only co-existing labour, and fixed capital only skilled labour, it must be plain that all those numerous advantages, those benefits to civilisation, those vast improvements in the condition of the human race, which have been in general attributed to capital, are caused in fact by labour, and by knowledge and skill informing and directing labour. Should it be said, then, as perhaps it may, that unless there be profit, and unless there be interest, there will be no motives for accumulation and improvement, I answer that this is a false view, and arises from attributing to capital and saving those effects which result from labour ; and that the best means of securing the progressive improvement, both of individuals and of nations, is to do justice, and allow labour to possess and enjoy the whole of its produce.

(c) From William Thompson, " Labor Rewarded " (1827), pp. 31-2.

[William Thompson (*d.* 1833), an Irish landowner and a follower of Bentham who became a convert to Owenism, published in 1824 his chief work, " An Inquiry into the Principles of the Distribution of Wealth

Most Conducive to Human Happiness ". This was followed by his "Labor Rewarded" (1827), in which he put forward Co-operation as an alternative to Hodgskin's militant policy of working class combination to absorb profits into wages, and by his "Practical Directions for the Establishment of Communities" (1830), written for the Owenite Co-operative movement. He also advocated women's rights in "An Appeal of One-Half the Human Race" (1825).]

Were justice and beneficence consulted, instead of antipathy, in awarding the rewards of labor under the system of unequal remuneration, the largest shares of reward, as before mentioned, would be given as a compensation to those who underwent the most severe or repulsive toil. But to such labourers, simply because they are the most helpless, does competition with its unequal remuneration, uniformly afford the smallest shares. Better means in the earlier stages of society being unknown, competition with its unequal remuneration, — prizes for the few, blanks, want, and misery for the many ; prizes for the idle, blanks for the industrious, — mutual antipathy for all — has called forth the activity of industry. But in the pursuit of industry and activity, beneficence and happiness have been forgotten. The end has been sacrificed to the means. Inequality of remuneration erected into a God by the successful patrons of brute force, or "higglers in the market", has been consecrated and worshipped by public opinion, by law, by superstition. When will the industrious perceive that, as competition neither can make, nor professes to make, more than a few, the successful, happy, and that at the expense of the vast majority, it is their imperative interest to seek out for a system of industry, the honest object of which shall be to promote equally the happiness of all, by giving to all abundantly and equally the means of acquiring happiness ?

Whether then we refer to laborers of the same class, or to different species of laborers, there appears no just reason for difference of remuneration. It but aggravates the misery of the wretched, and gives superfluity, vanity, and antipathy, to the more happy, at their expense. As to different classes of laborers, those which supply the necessaries of life and are therefore the most useful, are now almost uniformly the worst rewarded ; while those classes which provide superfluities, extravagancies, luxuries, particularly if novelties, are the most amply rewarded. As to the same class of laborers, the scheme of unequal remuneration by task-work, produces at the same time excessive toil, and brings down to the lowest the remuneration of labor. It may be that skill, utility, and great demand, may happen to coincide : but this is purely accidental. Apprenticeships, corporations, guilds, and latterly, free unions amongst the industrious themselves of a particular trade, are the circumstances which now give a factitious elevation to the remuneration of particular classes of laborers ; while the great mass of the industrious remain at that *competitive* point of remuneration which enables the laborers to live out their average round of years, and to leave behind them a new race to continue the routine of unattractive, unrequited, toil. Those classes of trades or subdivisions of classes which are the best remunerated, (for the same class is not always even in the same country in all places equally remunerated,) are the mere *aristocracy* of trades, possessing no superior utility, skill, or good disposition, with no more pretensions to superior merit than any other aristocracies, but frequently partaking of the vices of all aristocracies, full of unsocial antipathies to those less remunerated than themselves, and spending in short-lived gratifications productive of preponderant evil, that superior, but still pitiful, remuneration out of the products of their labor, which the chance of circumstances enables them to procure above the mass of their brethren.—P. 31.

It may be here objected, that these two objects above advocated, " securing to labor the whole products of its exertions, and giving equal remuneration to all the laborers," would be incompatible with each other. If the best producers took all they produced, how could the remuneration be equal ? — Under individual competition, it is true, these objects would be incompatible with each other ; but not under other arrangements. Though labor might be secured in the *right* to the whole products of its exertions, it does not follow that labor might not, in order to ensure a vast increase of production and enjoyment to every one, as well as mutual insurance from all casualties, *voluntarily agree before production* to equality of remuneration — should such agreement be demonstrated to be productive of such effects. What laws cannot directly effect, the progress of enlightened self-interest, of reason and benevolence, may accomplish. —P. 37.

We have seen that, in any state of society ever so little advanced from barbarism, it is almost impossible to ascertain what portion of the produce of combined labor — and all labor to be economical must be combined out of the minute subdivisions of its various branches — has been the work of any individual laborer, and of course that it is impracticable to award to the individual, separately, the products of his labor. What cannot be done individually, we shall see may be done *collectively*; and it is clearly our duty to make the nearest approach we can, consistently with reproduction, to the securing to all the entire use of the products of their labor.—P. 37.

But we are not to suppose, as did the simple French people at the time of their (as yet) abortive revolution, as do now the equally simple American people, that the mere naming, by the industrious classes, of men to make public regulations to promote their happiness, would necessarily secure that object, or would even in any material degree secure to them the use of the products of their labor.—P. 43.

Laborers must become capitalists, and must acquire knowledge to regulate their labor on a large united scale, before they will be able to do more than dream of enjoying the whole products of their labor. Added to knowledge, the Industrious Classes must also acquire *power*, the whole power of the social machine in their own hands, in order to render their knowledge available, on a national scale, and with an immediate effect, for promoting the impartial and equal happiness of all.—P. 73.

Hopes too sanguine, it is to be feared, have been excited amongst the industrious of the direct efficacy of union to increase wages. —P. 75.

The highest price which Free Competition will enable Unions of the industrious to obtain for their labor, is not anything like the products of their labor, but that rate of remuneration which will permit the capitalists in their line of industry to reap the same profits that other capitalists in the same line, or in other equally hazardous lines, reap from their capital. . . .

Hence it is evident that the benefit of these voluntary unions to the industrious classes, are almost entirely limited to times of ordinary or extraordinary prosperity of their trades. In a declining state of trade, particularly when the decline is not limited to a particular branch, voluntary unions to guard against the evils of the underbidding of the industrious against each other, or to support those losing employment, must be inoperative.—P. 78.

It is in this way, by promoting the acquisition of capital amongst the industrious themselves, that Unions must operate in order to make any real advance towards securing to the industrious the products of their own labor. Till the industrious become capitalists as well as laborers, each possessed of that portion of capital which is requisite to make his labor productive, they must pay, and pay dearly, the full competition price, to those who may have got into their hands the land on which they live, and which by their labor produces their food, the materials on which they work, the buildings, tools, and machines, by means of which they work, for the use respectively of all these articles.—P. 87.

The whole cost of the buildings and machinery should be divided into shares, according to the number of people they were capable of employing; and every individual paying the amount of a share should become a capitalist-laborer, and would thus enjoy an increased part of the products of his labor. The same facilities for independence should of course be opened in every department to women as to men; no person being permitted to purchase more than one share. As these Trades-Manufactories would thus come to be possessed by *joint-stock companies of the laborers themselves*, other buildings and always improved machinery should be erected with their funds by the Unions, to keep up a constant refuge for the honest and industrious losing their employments. These establishments of capitalist-laborers would be something *approaching* (and but approaching) to an efficient check on the exactions of mere capitalists. They would prove that capital can be accumulated without the aid of capitalists.—P. 88.

What remedy, then, presents itself to these Trades-Manufactories for self-support, against the evils of depression or loss of trade? *Let them purchase*, or rent with the stipulation for future purchase, *enough of land in their neighbourhood, to raise their own food, and to eat it at first cost.* Let a general account be kept of the manufacturing and agricultural industry; let every agriculturist be taught the manufacturing branch, and let every manufacturer be taught to aid in agricultural operations; let the remuneration of all, whether employed in agriculture, manufacture, or superintending, be equal.—P. 90.

Thus, [with] every step that one of these Trades-Manufactories, or Associations of Capitalist-Laborers, advances in the career of supplying, by the labor of co-associates, their own wants, a proportionate advance is made in securing to themselves the whole products of their labor.—P. 91.

Now, supposing that by means of Unions through all trades and all species of labor through every part of the country, such Associations manufacturing and agricultural as here described, were gradually formed, what would they ultimately become but *Communities of Mutual Co-operation*? What does every step of improvement in their progress accomplish, but remove some of the evils of isolated exertion and Individual Competition? If it be so desirable by means of Unions, of Insurances, of prudential checks as to increase of numbers, of Mechanics' Institutions, of a Fixed System of Currency, of Free Trade in all departments, of cheap and just judicial Establishments, of the abolition of Forcible Taxation, of real, unmixed, Representative Institutions, to root out gradually, in the course of centuries, for the whole people, the multifarious evils of Individual Competition, intermixed and supported as they are in every department by Force and Fraud; how much more desirable must it be to accomplish by far the greater part of all these objects, peaceably, at once? and to reduce to insignificance the pressure of those which will remain, and which must all ultimately vanish before the information and the influence of the Industrious Classes, thus become capitalist-laborers, and enjoying the whole products of their labor?—P. 94.

(*d*) From William Thompson, " Appeal of One Half the Human Race, Women, against the Pretensions of the Other Half, Men, to retain them in Political, and thence in Civil and Domestic, Slavery " (1825), pp. 199-200 and 205-6.

Not so under the system of, Association, or of Labor by Mutual Co-operation.

This scheme of social arrangements is the only one which will complete and for ever insure the perfect equality and entire reciprocity of happiness between women and men. Those evils, which neither an equality of civil and criminal laws, nor of political laws, nor an equal system of morals upheld by an enlightened public opinion, can entirely obviate, this scheme of human exertion will remove or abundantly compensate. Even for the partial dispensations of nature it affords a remedy. Large numbers of men and women co-operating together for mutual happiness, all their possessions and means of enjoyment being the equal property of all — individual property and competition for ever excluded — women are not asked to *labor* as much in point of strength of muscle as men, but to contribute what they can, with as much cheerful benevolence, to the common happiness. All talents, all faculties, whether from nature or education, whether of mind or muscle, are here equally appreciated if they are spontaneously afforded and improved, and if they are necessary to keep up the common mass of happiness.

Under such arrangements, women may have equal improvement and use of all their faculties with men : under these circumstances, they may derive as much of happiness from every source — of the senses, of intelligence, and sympathy — as men, according to the peculiarities of organisation of each : under these circumstances, all may be perfectly equal in rights, duties, and enjoyments, according to their capabilities of acting, suffering, and enjoying. If men from an average superiority of strength, be able to add more to general happiness in the way of increasing the products of labor, where would happiness, where would men be found, were it not for the peculiar pains, privations and cares which women suffer in nourishing and rearing the infancy of the whole race ? Against the almost doubtful advantage, in the present state of improved chemical and mechanical science and art, of mere superiority of animal strength on the part of men, in increasing their utility or contributions to the common happiness, may not the unquestionable usefulness of the employment of that part of the time of women which is consumed in preserving the race be opposed ? Which is more indispensable for human happiness, that a few more broadcloths or cottons should be every year produced, or that the race itself should be every year increased and kindly and skilfully nurtured? Wherever the principle of Association prevailed, justice would prevail, and these mutual compensations — as nurturing infants against strength — would be fully admitted; no person cheerfully exerting his or her means, whatever they might be, for the common benefit, would be punished for the scantiness of those means, still less for the pains or privations attending their developement. In this, as in all the other arrangements of Mutual Co-operation, the punishments of nature, whether arising from decrease of enjoyments or from positive pain, would not only perhaps be found sufficient for all useful purposes, but would rather demand compensation than factitious increase.

3. THE CO-OPERATIVE AND ECONOMICAL SOCIETY, 1821

[The ' Co-operative and Economical Society ' was founded by George Mudie in 1821. As part of its propagandist activities *The Economist*, the first Co-operative journal, was founded. This declared itself to be ' a periodical paper explanatory of the new system of society projected by Robert Owen Esq : and of a plan of association for improving the condition of the working classes during their continuance at their present employments '. The Society launched the venture in Co-operative living described in this document in the hope of anticipating some of the benefits of a fully Owenite England. *The Economist* survived only fourteen months, and we hear little more of this Co-operative experiment. Mudie subsequently edited *The Political Economist and Universal Philanthropist* (1825), *The Advocate of the Working Classes* (1826–1827), and *The Gazette of the Exchange Bazaars*. He also took part in the Owenite community at Orbiston, in Scotland.]

From *The Economist*, March 2, 1822.

To the Working and Other Classes :

New and grand Cooperation, affording ample security for your comfortable and abundant subsistence; for your support during sickness or loss of employment, and in old age, for the education and moral training of your children; their instruction in useful knowledge and productive industry; and their permanent support for life, in the event of the death of their parents.

The CO-OPERATIVE AND ECONOMICAL SOCIETY of London, established for the above purposes in January 1821, have now reduced to practice the principles of their association, and are making very satisfactory progress toward their complete accomplishment.

The means by which the society effects its objects, the advantages which it already enjoys or purposes to accomplish and the nature of its constitution, are as follows :

MEANS

I The families contribute to a common fund for providing the necessaries of life, at wholesale prices and at the best markets, in proportion to the number of individuals in each family respectively, according to the following scale :—

A man, his wife, and five children,		1.2.6. per week.
Do.	do.	four do.	1.0.3.
Do.	do.	three do.	18.0½.
Do.	do.	two do.	17.1.
Do.	do.	one child,	16.3½.
Do.	do.	no children.	14.5.

The above scale of expenses is exclusive of rent and clothing; but includes all other outgoings, and the training and education of the children.

II The families breakfast, dine etc. together at the general tables; and in the evenings amuse themselves with conversation, reading, lectures, music etc. in the public room. The individuals, however, are at perfect liberty, at all times, to take their meals, and to spend their leisure hours, in their private apartments.

III The domestic duties of the females are performed under a system of combination, which greatly lessens the labour, and enables the females either to be profitably employed, or to command a considerable portion of leisure for rational pursuits and innocent recreations. Thus, the cooking for the whole of the families being performed at once and at one fire, occupies comparatively but a small portion of time, and is done in a much superior manner to what is possible for small individual families; and a proportionate advantage is gained in all other departments of housewifery, such as cleaning, washing, getting up linen, etc. etc. This economy of time also enables a proper number of females to be spared from their usual avocations, and to take under their constant superintendence, *without a moment's intermission*, in and out of doors, the whole of the children,— securing for them the best possible attention to their health, comfort and morals.

IV Such of the females as are not required for the discharge of the duties of housewifery, and for the care of the children, are employed, during a moderate portion of the day, in such profitable work as can be obtained, for the benefit of the society at large. The elder children are also employed during six hours daily, for the common benefit, and will be carefully instructed in the principles of Christianity, and in one or more branches of useful industry. The remainder of their time is occupied with their education, and such sports, under the care of their superintendants, as are suitable to their age. When a child is employed six hours daily, the parents of that child are reduced on the scale of expenses for living, in the proportion of one child less than the actual number of their family.

V The fund to be accumulated from the profitable employment of the females and children, from the surplus accruing from the scale of expenses of living, and from the dealing of the society, will be employed in providing profitable work for the members on their own and the society's account, — in trade, — and, as soon as possible, a sufficient sum will be invested in buildings, for the residence of the members. The whole of the congregated society, by means of the capital acquired from the various sources of accumulation, will be gradually employed on its own account, in the proceeds of which each congregated family will have an equal interest, and by means of which the society will be enabled to insure its members against the consequences of loss of employment from sickness or any other cause, and their families from the usual distress and wretchedness consequent upon the death of the parents. The orphans of the society will be in all respects treated in the same manner as the children of the surviving members. The profits of the society will also enable the expenses of living to be gradually reduced, or the clothing and rent of the members to be provided for out of the fund.

VI The society already employs its own shoemakers and tailors, and will speedily be enabled to perform all its own work within itself. The society also can now promptly execute, for the public, in the best and cheapest manner, orders for carving and gilding, transparent landscape window blinds, paintings on velvet, boot and shoemaking, gentlemen's clothing, and dressmaking and millinery.

4. THE BRIGHTON *CO-OPERATOR*

[Dr. William King (1786–1865), at one time Fellow of Peterhouse College, Cambridge, became the 'poor man's doctor' in Brighton. He took a leading part in the foundation and work of the Brighton Mechanics' Institution (1825–1828), some of whose members became the nucleus of the Co-operative Associations founded there in 1827. In connection with this movement he founded *The Co-operator* (1828–1830), which became the most influential Co-operative journal, and acquired a national influence. *The Co-operator* has been reprinted by the Co-operative Union with an Introduction and Notes by T. W. Mercer.

Some Co-operators argue that Dr. King has a greater claim than Owen to be called the father of Co-operation. He certainly did more than Owen for the direct encouragement of local Co-operative stores. King's position was : We see that men produce enough to keep themselves and others, who do not work, as well ; yet many go hungry. Indeed as long as we work for others and give them a profit, this will happen. To work for ourselves we need capital ; so we must club together, set up a trading store, then, with its accumulated profits, we can put members to work and later buy land for the building of a co-operative community. He argued that co-operation of this type would benefit all classes : it was not a combination of ' the poor against the rich, nor of workmen against masters '.

His advocacy of the value of stores and the advice he gave for their management were a powerful factor in the spread of the movement.]

From *The Co-operator*, No. 1 (May 1, 1828), p. 3.

At present we work one against another, — when one of us gets work, another loses it; and we seem natural enemies to each other.

The plain reason of this is because we work for others, not for ourselves. Let us therefore begin to work for OURSELVES, and not entirely for others. Again, — at present, in working for others, we get for ourselves only a small part, some say, one eighth, some, one fourth of the produce of our work. If, in any way, we could work for ourselves, we should get the whole. How is this to be done ? As we have no capital, we are obliged to find a master to give us employment, and we must work for common wages.

This is true — it is CAPITAL we want ; and now let us consider how this capital is to be raised. We shall find that it is by no means an impossibility. Union and saving will accumulate it.

Many of us belong to Friendly Societies, which have accumulated a large capital, by small weekly deposits ; many of us have saved sums of money in the Savings' Banks ; the thing, therefore, is very possible, for it has already been done in one way, and may therefore be done in another. We must form ourselves into a Society for this especial purpose ; we must form a fund by weekly deposits ; as soon as it is large enough, we must lay it out in various commodities, which we must place in a common store from which all members must purchase their common necessaries, and the profit will form a common capital again to be again laid out in the commodities most wanted. Thus we shall have two sources of accumulation — the WEEKLY SUBSCRIPTION, and the PROFIT on articles sold. Suppose 200 persons thus unite, and subscribe each, a shilling a week, and by purchasing at their own store, produce profit of £20 a week, they will accumulate at the rate of £30 a week, or £1560 a year. This capital, by being judiciously turned over, will accumulate even faster than at the rate here mentioned, and may be employed in any way the Society may think most advisable.

The Society will be able now to find work for some of its own members, the whole produce of whose labour will be common property, instead of that small part of which we spoke. As the capital accumulates still farther, it will employ all the members, and then the advantages will be considerable indeed. Every member of the Society will work, there will be no idlers. All the property will be common property, there will be no Pauperism or Crime. When any of the members are ill, they will live and have medical attendance at the common expense.

When the capital has accumulated sufficiently, the Society may produce any manufactures they please, and so provide for all their wants of food, clothing and houses. The Society will then be called a Community.

5. THE BRITISH ASSOCIATION FOR PROMOTING CO-OPERATIVE KNOWLEDGE

[While Dr. King was active in Brighton, a group of converts to Robert Owen's doctrines was at work in London. This group included many who were later prominent in the Reform and Trade Union struggles and in the Chartist movement. Of those mentioned, James Watson (1799–1874) had been one of Richard Carlile's shopmen. He became store-keeper for a time to the London Co-operative Society, took an active part in the National Union of the Working Classes, published and edited *The Working Man's Friend* (1832-1833), and helped in drawing up the People's Charter. He became well known as a Radical and Secularist bookseller and writer. William Lovett (1800–1877), the author of the following extract, was first active in the Cabinet Makers' Union, of which he became President. He succeeded Watson as storekeeper to the L.C.S., and was Secretary of the B.A.P.C.K. Active in the Reform struggle, he was also Secretary to the ' Victim Fund ', first raised to maintain the dependants of those imprisoned for offences against the Newspaper Tax, and later enlarged to provide for other victims of oppression. He took the main part in drawing up the Charter, and became Secretary to the first Chartist Convention. His autobiography (" Life and Struggles of William Lovett," 1876) is well known. John Cleave (1792–? 1847) was a follower of Cobbett as well as a Co-operator and a Chartist. After Cobbett's death he founded the Cobbett Club. He edited *The Police Gazette* and other Radical journals. George Foskett was one of the founders of the Metropolitan Trades' Union and of the N.U.W.C. Robert Wigg was an Owenite. Philip Orkney Skene and George Skene were also leading disciples of Owen and very active in the London Co-operative movement. Millard and Powell were also London Owenites — the latter, we believe, a journalist on *The Morning Chronicle*. Hethering-ton will be described on p. 218. Benjamin Warden was the leader of the Saddlers' Union, first Chairman of the Metropolitan Trades' Union, and a prominent figure in the foundation of Co-operative stores and work-shops in the London area after 1830. John Minter Morgan (1782–1854), known as the ' Christian Owenite ', wrote " The Revolt of the Bees "

(1826), "Hampden in the Nineteenth Century" (1834), and other Owenite works. John Gray (1799–? 1850) is best remembered for his "Lectures on Human Happiness" (1825) and his "Social System" (1831). He combined Owenism with monetary theories.]

Manuscript account given by Lovett to Place (1835). From the Place MSS., 27,822 f. 17.

The National Union of the Working Classes and others sprung out of another association entitled the British. Association for promoting Cooperative Knowledge. . . . The British Association was formed on the 11th May 1829 principally by a number of persons who belonged to a society just established in Red Lion Square, called The London Cooperative Trading Association. The object of which was to accumulate a capital for Cooperative purposes, by dealing amongst themselves and their acquaintances, and reserving the profits of the retail dealer. This Trading Association subsequently removed to Jerusalem Passage Clerkenwell, and then it was that the British Association was projected. The persons most conspicuous in forming this association were James Watson, Wm. Lovett, John Cleave, George Foskett, Robert Wigg, Philip and George Skene, Wm. Millard, Thomas Powell, and subsequently Henry Hetherington and Benjamin Warden. Those persons having read and admired the writings of Owen, Thompson, Morgan, Gray and others, resolved to be instrumental, to the extent of their abilities, in disseminating their works throughout the country. They also sought, in the propagation of those principles, to avoid the course Robt. Owen had steered, which they conceived had materially impeded his progress; that of insisting on principles, strongly opposed to the prejudices of the multitude; and condemning, though in his usual philanthropy, the Radical Reformers. By which proceedings they were led to consider him as a person inimical to their interests, and accordingly they attended his meetings and carried resolutions counter to his own. The persons above named therefore during Mr. Owen's visit to America, resolved to take up such parts of his system as they conceived would be appreciated by the majority of the Working Classes; and be the means of uniting reformers of every grade. Taking especial care to leave the subjects on which great differences of opinion existed to time and opportunity; or when men having experienced the benefits resulting from a part of his system, they might be led to investigate the whole. They held their *Committee Meetings weekly*, and meetings of their members and the public quarterly; they made arrangements by which those who had to address the public, had some time for preparing themselves, by which means the meetings were more interesting and effective. Their reports were published quarterly and distributed throughout the country, and as affording, some proofs in favour of their policy, together with the novelty of their plans (as they forcibly impressed on the working classes the importance of trading Associations) [we should note] that in less than six months from their commencement they had been the means of forming upwards of two hundred of those associations, extending from one extremity of the kingdom to the other. They had their committee of correspondence giving advice and assistance and promulgating their cooperative views. Persons in remote parts of the kingdom hearing of their projects, and requiring information, were supplied with books on the subject; and in this manner more was done in the space of twelve months to disseminate Mr. Owen's peculiar views, than perhaps he had done himself during his long career. This society was also intrusted by benevolent individuals with considerable sums of money to apply to cooperative purposes, which they did in the employment of several Spitalfields Weavers; eventually they opened a bazaar at 19, Greville Street, Hatton Garden, for the purpose of disposing of the produce, and for facilitating exchanges between the societies in town and country. This part of their arrangements owing to mismanagement was a failure. They had not been more than twelve months in existence when Mr. Owen returned from America; he commenced by condemning them as altogether opposed to his system and it was not till after a visit to Manchester at one of his delegate meetings that he was induced to acknowledge their importance. Many of his most zealous disciples bowing to his first decrees had in the interim seceded from their societies which had led to their breaking up; in addition many of those who were strict religionists had been terrified from supporting the British Association on account of many of its members attending and supporting Mr. Owen's Sunday morning lectures. Eventually the funds ceased to come in, meetings could not be got up, printing could not be any longer paid for, and dissensions respecting Mr. Owen's views led to the breaking up of an association that did much good, and if it had continued, bid fair to do more than any association of working men about this period. It may be well to observe that many of those trading associations it had been instrumental in forming are still in existence, especially in the North of England, though the major part are broken up.

IX

THE REFORM MOVEMENT, 1827–1832

INTRODUCTION

IN 1827 the mass campaign of O'Connell for Catholic Emancipation came to show Reformers the power which the people can give its leaders. English Reformers supported O'Connell, and societies such as the ' Friends of Civil and Religious Liberty ' linked the Irish and British struggles. The London Radical Reform Association (1829) arose out of the agitation, and continued fighting for the Repeal of the Union (of Ireland and England) and Parliamentary Reform long enough to bridge the gap between Catholic Emancipation and the final Reform campaign. In December 1829 Cobbett started his Northern Tour, bringing life and vigour to a key area. In January 1830 Thomas Attwood founded the Birmingham Political Union, whose importance lay mainly in its emphasis on organisation. The movement of the years 1816–1820 had consisted of small societies, which were rarely united, or even of informal groups. But now organisation became far less loosely knit. In London new societies were founded and journals were started. And soon unions were founded in the provinces on the model of the Birmingham Political Union.

The attempted *coup d'état* by Polignac in France and a strong rumour that Wellington had been an accomplice made Reform a sudden issue in the General Election of August 1830. In November, Earl Grey (the Whig Leader) came out in favour of Reform : and when the Duke of Wellington (the Prime Minister) made an uncompromising reply, popular feeling drove the Ministry out of office. Grey became Premier in November, and in March 1831 Lord John Russell introduced a measure which proposed to make a clean sweep of the rotten boroughs, to redistribute seats in Parliament more in accordance with population, and to enfranchise the middle, but not the working, class : this was wrecked in the House of Commons. The subsequent General Election gave the Whigs a majority, and their second measure passed through the House of Commons only to be defeated in the House of Lords in October. Meanwhile the

Whigs had antagonised large sections of the working class; Trade Unionism in the North and the agricultural labourers in the South found them no less repressive than the Tories; Carlile, Carpenter, and Hetherington, the leading figures in the new struggle for the freedom of the press, were prosecuted; and above all, deep suspicions of treachery were aroused by the exclusion of the working class from the franchise in all the proposed Whig measures. The National Union of the Working Classes, with their many contacts in the various Political Unions in the provinces, and Henry Hunt, now M.P. for Preston, led the struggle for a thoroughly democratic Bill.

When, after the defeat of the second Bill in the House of Lords in October, the Whigs seemed strangely disinclined to fight and very reluctant to demand additional peers, a general spirit of disillusionment followed. The riots in Derby, Nottingham, and, particularly, Bristol, seemed to threaten a revolution. But from now on the National Political Union, founded on the day of the rejection of the second Bill, began to take control of the situation. Its function was to drive the Whig leaders forward, promising them popular enthusiasm, and promising to control it. Their policy of supporting the Bill as the best obtainable, and refusing to accept anything less, prevailed over the Radical desire to condemn it as useless. A powerful campaign was organised, constitutional but extra-parliamentary; and the threat of less constitutional methods was held in reserve. In May the House of Lords in Committee carried a hostile amendment to the third Bill. The King refused to create the necessary number of additional peers and Grey resigned. Wellington tried to form a Ministry, but failed. Grey came back with the power to create peers, but there were enough abstentions on the third reading to let the Bill go through (June 1832). The House of Commons had at last been reformed. But it had not been democratised. The staple demands of working-class Reformers — the Ballot and Annual Parliaments, and, above all, Universal Suffrage — had not been granted. The Reform Act was a middle-class victory: but the working class had at least approached nearer to independent political action than ever previously, and had for the first time begun to frame a philosophy of political power for their own class. The demands which the moderates had refused to satisfy formed the programme of the Chartists four years later.

See " Short History ", Part I, chapter 5, section 3.
" Common People ", chapter 21.

1. CATHOLIC EMANCIPATION AND THE
ENGLISH REFORMERS, 1827–1829

[Daniel O'Connell's campaign for Catholic Emancipation had an indirect but important influence on the English Reform movement. His Catholic Association (founded 1823) won popular support to a degree which was then unique. Its ' Penny Rent ', its mass meetings, and its essentially popular appeal, its vigour, enterprise, and eventual success, taught the English Reformers what power an organised people can have against the Government. Considerable help was given by the English working class, partly from an instinctive sympathy with the oppressed, which had already become a tradition in the movement, and partly because, through Cobbett and other writers, the struggle for Catholic Emancipation was viewed as a fight against the Church of England, the source of so much economic injustice and political despotism. It is uncertain how far their help contributed to the Catholic triumph, but it is certain that their work was of great value to their own cause. The Friends of Civil and Religious Liberty, and its successor, the Association for Radical Reform (1829), linked together the issues of Irish freedom and English Reform. Radicals in London had found a meeting-ground where they could collect their forces for a renewed struggle.]

A Petition. From " An Account of a Meeting of the Friends of Civil and Religious Liberty ", February 12, 1827, p. 14.

To the Honourable the House of Commons, in Parliament assembled, We, the undersigned, Catholics and Protestants, beg leave to represent to your Honourable House, that we are deeply impressed with the manifold blessings that must flow from a just and legal exercise of Civil and Religious Liberty. Your Petitioners submit to your Honourable House, that it is the inalienable right of every man to worship God according to the dictates of his conscience ; that human restraints and penalties imposed by the Legislature upon any class of Christians for adhering to religious principles conscientiously adopted, and not affecting the peace of society, are intolerant, unjust, and unnatural ; your Petitioners therefore pray, that all laws imposing religious tests to qualify for civil office, and penal restrictions regarding conscience, may be totally abolished.

Your Petitioners view with poignant regret the present most unexampled state of misery and ruin into which this once happy country is plunged ; the greatest part of the working classes are without the means of employment, without food and without raiment ; while their employers are approaching, and many of them have already reached a state of bankruptcy ; yet at the same time they behold the same disregard to the miseries of the People amongst those classes who are maintained by pensions, taxes, and sinecures, which preceded the appalling and direful horrors of the French Revolution.

Your Petitioners are sensible that the cause of this distress is not of recent origin, but must be traced to the long and ruinous wars in which this country has been engaged; to carry on which an enormous debt has been contracted, and an overwhelming weight of taxation required, to pay the interest thereof; to which must also be added a profuse and unnecessary grant of unmerited pensions, useless sinecures, and other emoluments, distributed to a few particular influential families, who are thereby enabled to escape those heavy burdens and inflictions which now bow down the bulk of the People. Another and the chief cause of the present alarming crisis your Petitioners are of opinion, is the attempt to return from an unlimited use of Bank note currency to the real circulating medium of gold and silver, by which a change has been effected in the value of property, because unaccompanied by a reduction of the debt and taxes and the national expenditure, equivalent to the advance in the value of money.

With a view, therefore, to remedy the evils which afflict this country; evils which, if not timely removed, will reduce her to the lowest scale in the rank of nations, your Petitioners must earnestly entreat your Honourable House to take into consideration and pass measures which shall have for their object,

First,—an adjustment of the National Debt — that is, such an adjustment as shall consult the advantage of the fundholder, and be consistent with the safety and interests of the country.

Secondly,—a total abolition of all sinecures and unnecessary offices; a reduction of all pensions, except such as are held for age or infirmity, or loss of limb in the service of the State, or by the widows and children of those who have fallen in battle; also an equalisation of all salaries, pensions, contracts, and debts, according to the increase in the value of money, decrease in the price of commodities.

Thirdly,—a restoration of Church property to the purposes to which it was originally appropriated, viz. one third for the support of the clergy — one third for building and repairing places of worship — and the remaining one third for the Poor; by which measure the land and trade will be relieved of an intolerable and oppressive burden, now exceeding eight millions of pounds sterling annually, a sum equalling in amount the whole of the taxes when his late Majesty ascended the throne of these realms.

Fourthly,—a complete and Constitutional Reform of your Honourable House, which will secure to every man in the United Kingdom not incapacitated by physical defects or moral ineptitude, a voice in the making of those laws by which his life and property may be affected.

And your Petitioners will ever pray, etc.

2. WORKING CLASS ATTITUDES TO THE REFORM BILL, 1831

[While no important section of the working-class movement denied that the Whigs' Bill was inadequate, a large section did agree, reluctantly perhaps, that it would be wise strategy to support it. The two following documents sum up the main arguments for and against a policy of support. Henry Hetherington's *Poor Man's Guardian* was the most influential working-class newspaper of the period, apart from *Cobbett's Register*. It became a forum for the discussion of the case.

Henry Hetherington (1792–1849), Radical, Owenite, and later Chartist, was one of the foremost figures both in the struggle for the freedom of the press and in organising the working classes during the Reform agitation. Bronterre O'Brien (1805–1864) was his editor. *The Poor Man's Guardian* was published unstamped, in defiance of the Newspaper Tax; and both Hetherington and many of his salesmen were repeatedly imprisoned for violation of the law, until in 1834 Lord Lyndhurst decided that the *Guardian* was not, after all, a newspaper within the meaning of the Act.

William Carpenter (1797–1874) was another Radical journalist. He was imprisoned in 1831 for issuing his *Political Letters* (1830–1831) without a stamp. He wrote a number of political books and also theological and grammatical works.]

(*a*) Against supporting the Bill. From *The Poor Man's Guardian*, September 24, 1831.

. . . Meetings are everywhere holden — and petitions are preparing in every quarter, to promote its allowance, — but by whom are these meetings convened and by whom attended, — by whom are such petitions signed? — Why, by your hypocritical, time-serving property-loving " *middle-men* "; or if some few of the poor neglected millions — the oppressed working classes *do* sanction them, be assured that they are persuaded to do so by the arguments of those on whom they depend, and which they dare not question. Need we now repeat the opinion which from the very first moment we formed of this delusive and dangerous measure, and which deep consideration and all the fulsome and party reasoning brought forward in support of it have only tended to confirm? Yes, friends and fellow-countrymen, we protest that this measure is a mere *trick* to strengthen against your rightful claims the tottering exclusiveness of our " blessed constitution ". It is clear, *we* GAIN nothing by it; but it is said, that these middlemen, whom this measure admits into a share of the legislature, will be more inclined to hear our appeal for justice, and will return a majority favourable to it; think it not; — why, already — before even they have gained their own admittance — do they not shut the doors of parliament against you? For will they *tolerate* our *mention* even of " *Universal Suffrage* ", etc.? Yes, we thank them for their candour — do they not plainly tell you, even while they solicit your " sweet voices " to swell *their own* cry for *their own* reform, — do they not plainly tell you, that they like not *universal suffrage?* — do they not scout the very mention of equality? — and is not " property ", which you have not, the very pivot on which all their thoughts and wishes turn? . . .

(*b*) For the Bill. From *The Poor Man's Guardian*, December 3, 1831.

[Extract from a letter from W. Carpenter.]

1. In a country like England, where the government has been for ages based upon unjust distinctions; and has attached to itself a large and necessarily influential body of people, in the shape of civil employers, soldiers, loan-mongers, bankers, stock holders, excisemen, pensioners, and all who do business upon credit, no very sweeping measure of Reform can be carried at the onset. Gradual changes are the only ones that can possibly be effected.

2. The theoretical reasoning in the former proposition is borne out by the fact that the majority of the population, and especially of those classes who have always modified, and always must modify, the measures of government, are at present opposed to any further change.

3. That however just the claims of the lower class of labourers therefore is, they have not the power, *at present*, to obtain them; and justice to themselves, as well as to society at large, requires that they should abstain from everything that would produce a rupture which could only terminate in evil, and loss to all.

4. The Bill *admits* the necessity of Reform, on *general theoretical* principles, and as a *concession* to *popular opinion*. This once recognised leads necessarily to every desired change in the government. *Utility* takes the place of *antiquity*; and the *public will* that of *state-precedents*.

5. The Bill concedes, *to some extent*, the right of representation on the basis of *population*; and this concession once made, in however trifling a degree, *must* be carried onward to its *full extent*.

3. COBBETT AND REFORM, 1831

[No Radical leader had so widespread an influence as William Cobbett. Up to 1815 his appeal had been mainly to the farmers and agricultural labourers and to the middle-class readers of his *Political Register*, which was much too expensive to be bought by workmen. But in 1816 he had produced his cheap twopenny *Register*, and had set out to appeal directly to the industrial workers in the factory and mining areas. The cheap *Register* secured an unprecedented circulation, and Cobbett's influence became enormous. His appeal rested fundamentally on his intense sympathy for the sufferings of the poor and his power to identify himself with those whom he addressed. His hatred of the new industrial capitalism — ' the lords of the loom and the spinning-jenny ' — endeared him to the industrial workers of the North. In London many of the working-class Radicals wanted a Reformed Parliament as a prelude to a new society based on the control of the new industrial forces ; but Cobbett — as these ' Fourteen Propositions ' show — always attacked actual grievances, on the ground that they were destroying the ' good old times '. This appeal to the past undoubtedly strengthened his hold upon an industrial population which had not yet settled down to the new conditions of factory employment, and was still at heart largely a peasantry uprooted from the soil.]

From William Cobbett, " Manchester Lectures " (1831), p. 2.

COBBETT'S FOURTEEN PROPOSITIONS

1. To put an end to all pensions, sinecures, grants, allowances, half-pay and all other emoluments now paid out of the taxes, except for such public services as, upon a very scrupulous examination, shall be found fully to merit them ; and to reduce all salaries to the American standard.

2. To discharge the standing army, except such part of the ordnance and artillery as may be necessary to maintain the arsenals and sea-ports in a state of readiness for war ; and to abolish the military academies, and dispose of all barracks and other property now applied to military uses.

3. To make the counties, each according to the whole number of members of Parliament, maintain and equip a body of militia, horse as well as foot and artillery, at the county expense, and to have these bodies, as they are in America, mustered at stated periods;

so that at any time, a hundred thousand efficient men may be ready to come into the field if the defence of the kingdom require it.

4. To abolish titles of every description; to leave to the clergy the churches, the church-yards, the parsonage houses, and the *ancient* glebes; and, for the rest, leave them to the voluntary contributions of the people.

5. To take all the rest of the property, commonly called church-property; all the houses, lands, manors, tolls, rents, and real property of every kind, now possessed by bishops, chapters, or other ecclesiastical bodies, and all the misapplied property of corporate bodies of every sort; and also the property called crown-lands, or crown-estates, including that of the Duchies of Cornwall and Lancaster; and sell them all, and apply the proceeds to the discharge of the Debt which the late parliaments contracted with the fundholders.

6. To cease during the first six months after June, 1832, to pay interest on a fourth part of the debt; second six months to cease to pay interest on another fourth; and so on for the other two fourths; so that no more interest, or any part of the debt, would be paid after the end of two years.

7. To divide the proceeds of all the property mentioned in paragraph No. 5, and also in paragraph No. 2, in due proportion, on principles of equity, amongst the owners of what is called *stock*, or, in other words, the *fundholders*, or persons who lent their money to those who borrowed it in virtue of acts of the late parliaments, and to give to the fundholders, out of the taxes, nothing beyond these proceeds.

8. To make an equitable adjustment with respect to the pecuniary contracts between man and man, and thereby to rectify, as far as is practicable, the wrongs and ruin inflicted on thousands upon thousands of virtuous families by the arbitrary changes made by acts of the late parliaments, in the value of the money of the country.

9. To abolish all *internal taxes* (except on the land), whether direct or indirect, including stamp-taxes of every description; and to impose such a postage-charge for letters as to defray the *real expenses* of an economical and yet efficient post-office establishment, and no more; so that the postage would be merely a *payment* for the conveyance of letters, and not a tax.

10. To lay just as much custom-house duty on importations as shall be found conducive to the benefit of the navigation, commerce, and manufactures of the kingdom, viewed as a whole, and not to lay on one penny more.

11. To make effectual provision, in every department, for the maintenance of a powerful navy; to give such pay and such an allotment of prize-money to the seamen as to render impressment wholly unnecessary; to abolish the odious innovation of *naval academies*, and re-open the door of promotion to skill and valour, whether found in the heirs of nobles, or in the sons of the loom or of the plough; to abolish all military *orders*, and to place the navy next in honour to the throne itself.

12. To make a legal, fixed and a generous allowance to the King, and through him, to all the branches and members of his family; to leave to him the unshackled freedom of appointing all his servants, whether of his household or of his public ministry; to leave to him the full control over his palaces, gardens and parks, as landowners have over their estates; to take care that he be not worried with intrigues to purloin from him that which the people give him for his own enjoyment; so that he may be, in all respects, what the chief of a free people ought to be, his name be held in the highest honour, and his person held sacred, as the great guardian of the people's rights.

13. To make a more accurate valuation of all the houses, lands, mines, and all other real property, in each county in the whole kingdom; to impose a tax upon that property, to be paid quarterly, and in every county on the same day, and in such manner as to cost in the collection, or rather, payment, not more than *four hundred pounds* a year in any one county; to make the rate and amount of this tax vary with the wants of the State, always taking care to be amply provided with means in case of war, when war shall be demanded by the safety, the interest, or the honour of the kingdom.

14. To cause the PROTESTANT HIERARCHY to be legally repealed and abolished in Ireland; and to cause the Parliament of the whole kingdom to hold its sessions, and the king to hold his court IN IRELAND once in every three years; and to cause the same to take place in the city of YORK once in every three years, and also in the city of SALISBURY, once in every three years.

4. THE NATIONAL POLITICAL UNION, 1831

[The National Political Union was founded immediately after the House of Lords had rejected the second proposed Reform Bill in October 1831. It was an anxious period for the Reformers. The Government lacked determination because they feared the popular enthusiasm which they needed. The N.P.U. was founded by Francis Place and some middle-class Radicals, with some artisan support, for the purpose of arousing and at the same time controlling, the popular sentiment. They knew that an extreme Bill — with Universal Suffrage, for instance, — would alienate the moderates and let the reactionaries step in with a mild and useless measure, while this in turn might well provoke revolutionary disturbances. The extreme Radicals naturally suspected the Union: they demanded support for Universal Suffrage and Annual Parliaments. Their threatening attitude forced a concession from the N.P.U., which reserved a number of seats on its committee specifically for working-class people. Largely through the wire-pulling of Francis Place the elected working men were moderates, so that the N.P.U. was able to continue its policy, while it could claim to be now a union of all classes. The extreme wing was left isolated and the Union succeeded in rallying the main body of the people round ' The Bill, the whole Bill and nothing but the Bill '.]

(a) Objects of the National Political Union. From ' Objects and Rules of the National Political Union ', 1831. Place MSS., 27,791 f. 184.

OBJECTS OF THE UNION

1. To obtain a full, free, and effectual Representation of the People in the Commons House of Parliament.

2. To support the King and his Ministers against a corrupt Faction, in accomplishing their great measure of Parliamentary Reform.

3. To watch over and promote the interests, and to better the condition of the INDUSTRIOUS AND WORKING CLASSES.

4. To obtain the abolition of all taxes on knowledge, and to assist in the diffusion of sound moral and political information.

5. To join every well-wisher to his Country, from the richest to the poorest, in the pursuit of these important objects.

6. To preserve Peace and Order in the country, and to guard against any convulsion, which the Enemies of the People may endeavour to bring about.

(b) ' Address of the National Political Union to the People of England,' 1831. From the same.

FELLOW COUNTRYMEN,

On the renewal of the parliamentary struggle for the recovery of our rights, it becomes us to consider in what attitude, we can best watch the conflict, aid the victory, and secure the benefits of that victory when it shall be obtained.

We doubt not that the King and his Ministers are true to us. It is also necessary that we should be true to ourselves. Unless we are, they cannot help us. *Our* inertness would be weakness. Their strength to effect a Reform of Parliament mainly consists in the display of our determination that Parliament *shall* be reformed.

At that determination it is evident you have arrived. A long course of misrule has accumulated evils till they have ceased to be endurable. The sacred right of legislating for the country has been notoriously an article of traffic for private gain. The emoluments of office, whether civil, military or ecclesiastical, have been converted into a provision for the junior members of the Aristocracy, and for their servile dependents or needful tools. By the corn laws the staff of life has been changed into a rod of oppression. Restriction and monopoly have robbed labour of its freedom, and therefore of its just recompense. The expense, delay and uncertainty of the law are a denial of justice. The useful classes of society have been depressed more and more, that the idle might fatten on their spoils. The diffusion of information, on our own most important concerns and interests, has been abridged by taxation; by taxation which was obviously designed less to increase the revenue than to keep the People in ignorance. A corrupt House of Commons was the engine, in the hands of a Faction, for the infliction of these evils upon a suffering nation. Your patience, often misrepresented, often insulted, and always presumed upon, at length began to be wearied out and the uncalled for declaration of the Duke of Wellington in November 1830, that there should be no reform, called forth your decision no longer to be governed without Reform. You have pronounced the death-warrant of a system of misrule which disgraces the Aristocracy, impoverishes the Commonalty, and demoralizes all Classes.

That sentence *must* be carried into execution. Not by outrages upon individuals; not by resistance to the constituted authorities; not by violation of the laws; acts which can only injure the Common Cause, which are eagerly desired and treacherously prompted by its enemies, and which must inevitably and justly recoil upon their perpetrators. The means must be peaceful, honourable, and useful, as the end. We must efficiently support a King, an administration and a House of Commons, which have pledged faith with the people to see them righted. We must evince the necessity, on which they alone can act, of putting an end to the present anomalous state of things, and saving the Country from the domination of a body of men who are in avowed hostility to the dearest convictions and strongest desire of the nation.

You have done much, but you must do more, or all your past exertions and sacrifices may be unavailing. You have expressed your opinions; and scarcely has the expression been complete before you have been told to your faces that your opinions had changed and your ardour cooled. Express them permanently. Declare them by action; peaceful and legal action. Form yourselves into Unions, whose continued existence shall be a practical demonstration that your determination is unchanged and invincible. Parish, town and county meetings can only be held at intervals. Their influence is almost as ephemeral as their existence. Unions are a daily and hourly declaration of the nation's will. They let the enemy see *that we have nailed our colours to the mast.*

The National Political Union is founded on the conviction, expressed in the first two resolutions unanimously adopted by the public meeting held in Lincoln's Inn Fields on the 31st of October last, " that the interests of the people are most effectually promoted by well-organised and comprehensive Associations ", and " that it is highly desirable, at the present moment, that a Union should be formed of all real reformers, who wish to see the middle and working classes fairly represented ". Its objects are defined in the declaration, which follows this address. They are simply the plan of Reform introduced by His Majesty's Ministers, and the means and measures which are needful to render that Reform expedient for the purposes of good government. . . .

(c) From John Wade, " British History Chronologically Arranged ", 1839.

October 31, 1831. Meeting of the London Political Union at the Crown and Anchor, and, by adjournment, in Lincoln's Inn Fields, Sir F. Burdett in the chair. It was agreed to form a national union with branch societies, each having a delegate at the central council. At a subsequent meeting, some discord arose on a proposal that part of the council should consist of representatives from the working-classes. The chairman opposed this, because it assumed a distinction of classes to exist, having separate interests. The proposal, however, was adopted; after this, and on the alleged ground of an appearance of permanency in the union, Sir Francis withdrew his name from the association. A resolution was proposed in favour of universal suffrage, which not being supported by the middle class, the work-people formed a political union among themselves.

5. THE BIRMINGHAM POLITICAL UNION, 1830

[Birmingham was a town of the small master rather than of the great industrialist. Its political life was dominated by men who felt friendlier to the artisan and the shopkeeper than to the landlord and financier. In addition, the Dissenters formed there an influential body of Radical opinion. It is not surprising, therefore, that a movement of the middle and working classes, united for Parliamentary Reform, should have been launched in Birmingham.

The leader of the Union, Thomas Attwood,[1] and some of his chief lieutenants were primarily currency reformers. Attwood demanded as an alternative to the gold standard an easy credit system based on paper money under which the amount of credit would depend on the available supply of productive power. A reformed Parliament would, it was felt, surely understand the financial needs of the business community. The reforms proposed were, in consequence, extremely moderate; the Bill favoured at the first public meeting of the Union in May 1830 did not include Universal Suffrage, Annual Parliaments, or the Ballot. The control of the Union was unquestionably in middle-class hands. However, the founding of the Union, and the emphasis laid on the need for organisation, gave a great impulse to the movement all over the country, and provided a model for several other societies. Directly and indirectly the Union played a highly important part in the Reform campaign. Its leading figures were later prominent in the early phase of Chartism, when they attempted with only a brief success to revive the class alliance for a new non-revolutionary reform movement.]

'The Declaration of the Birmingham Political Union' (1830), p. 7. From Authorised Copy of the Resolutions passed at the meeting held at Birmingham on the 25th January, 1830.

Nor is this state of things much to be wondered at, when the present state and composition of the Commons' House of Parliament are considered. That honourable House, in its present state, is evidently too far removed in habits, wealth and station, from the wants and interests of the lower and middle classes of the people, to have any just views respecting them, or any close identity of feeling with them. The great aristocratical interests of all kinds are well represented there. The landed interest, the church, the law, the monied interest,— all these have engrossed, as it were, the House of Commons into their own hands, the members of that honourable

---

[1] Thomas Attwood (1783–1856), a banker's son and a banker himself, had from 1811 been a prominent figure in the political life of Birmingham, particularly when public feeling was roused over a grievance. He was the founder and always the leader of the B.P.U.: his power made Cobbett nickname him 'King Tom'.

House being all immediately and closely connected with those great interests. *But the interests of Industry and of Trade have scarcely any representatives at all!* *These*, the most vital interests of the nation, the source of all its wealth and of all its strength, are comparatively *unrepresented*; whilst every interest connected in any way with the *national burthens* is represented in the fullest degree! If any few individual members of the House of Commons should happen to be concerned in trade, it may be truly said that such members are in general, far more concerned in interests hostile to trade, than in trade itself. They are, too often, rich and retired capitalists, who have, perhaps, left *one tenth* of their wealth in trade, and have withdrawn the other *nine tenths* from active occupation. It is, therefore, of but little consequence to *them* whether trade flourishes or not. It is possible, indeed, that upon some occasions, these rich and retired capitalists may look with indifference on the sufferings of their competitors in trade; and after having availed *themselves* of the facilities of *credit*, to accumulate their own fortunes, they may possibly contemplate without pain the removal of these facilities from others, and their hopeless and unavailing struggles to follow in the same career.

Undoubtedly, it is essential to the national welfare that this state of things should be changed. The " Citizens and Burgesses " of the House of Commons should, in general, be real " Citizens and Burgesses "; men engaged in trade, and actively concerned in it; and leaving their fortunes and prosperity in life committed in it.

6. THE NATIONAL UNION OF THE WORKING CLASSES AND OTHERS, 1831

[The National Union of the Working Classes and Others was a product partly of the London Owenite movement, partly of left-wing political Radicalism. Its members were strongly influenced by Paine, by the struggles for the freedom of the press, and by the Association for Radical Reform, which had been founded after the agitation for Catholic Emancipation.

The Union, which was organised on the system of discussion classes with general meetings in the Rotunda,[1] soon became the forum for the

---

[1] The Rotunda, the meeting place taken over by Richard Carlile in 1830, became the open forum of the working-class movement, economic as well as political. Its lecturers included Owen, Cobbett, Hunt, Daniel O'Connell, and the future Chartist, Feargus O'Connor. The left wing of the political movement made it their headquarters during the Reform campaign, and ' the Rotunda ' was repeatedly attacking the cowardly Whigs and their useless Reform Bill.

intelligent artisan of London. The Labour Theory of Value spread by the Owenite elements led them to a political conception of class society and a demand for a share in state power by their class. In consequence, they formed the left wing of the Reform movement and opposed the middle-class Reform Bill. In addition to the Reform question, their discussions and activities embraced foreign politics, Ireland, the Unstamped Agitation, and any act of injustice or oppression that came to their notice. The Union eventually faded away when the Owenite Co-operative and Trade Union movement became the centre of working-class activity.]

(*a*) Objects of the National Union of the Working Classes. From *Penny Papers for the People*, May 27, 1831.

1. The objects of the NATIONAL UNION are, — First, To avail itself of every opportunity, in the progress of society, for the securing, by degrees, those things specified in the preceding Declaration of the Rights of Man.[1]

2. To obtain for every working man, unrestricted by unjust and partial laws, the full value of his labour, and the free disposal of the produce of his labour.

3. To support, as circumstances may determine, by all just means, every fair and rational opposition made by societies of working men (such societies being part of the Union), against the combination and tyranny of masters and manufacturers; whenever the latter shall seek, unjustly, to reduce the wages of labour, or shall institute proceedings against the workmen; the character of which proceedings, in the estimation of the Union, shall be deemed vexatious and oppressive.

4. To obtain for the nation an effectual reform in the Commons House of the British Parliament: the basis of which reform shall be annual parliaments, extension of the suffrage to every adult male, vote by ballot, and, especially, NO PROPERTY QUALIFICATION for members of Parliament; this Union being convinced, that until intelligent men from the productive and useful classes of society possess the right of sitting in the Commons House of Parliament, to represent the interest of the working people, justice in legislation will never be rendered unto them.

5. To inquire, consult, consider, discuss, and determine, respecting the rights and liberties of the working people, and respecting the just and most effectual means of securing all such rights.

[1] This Declaration of Rights was in the main a statement strongly influenced by Tom Paine, of man's rights to political liberty and equality; but a new note was also sounded — the worker's claim to the full enjoyment of the produce of his labour.

6. To prepare petitions, addresses and remonstrations to the crown, and both Houses or either House of Parliament, respecting the preservation of public rights, the repeal of bad laws, and the enactment of a wise and all-comprehensive code of good laws.

7. To promote peace, union and concord among all classes of people, and to guide and direct the public mind, into uniform, peaceful and legitimate operations; instead of leaving it to waste its strength, in loose, desultory, and unconnected exertions.

8. To collect and organise the peaceful expression of public opinion, so as to bring it to act upon the Houses of Parliament, in a just and effectual way.

9. To concentrate into one focus a knowledge of moral and political economy, that all classes of society may be enlightened by its radiation; the NATIONAL UNION feeling assured, that the submission of the people to misrule and oppression, arises from the absence of sound moral and political knowledge amongst the mass of the community.

10. To avoid all private or secret proceedings, all concealment of any of the views or objects of the Union, and to facilitate for all persons invested with legal authority, a full, free, and constant access to all the books, documents, regulations, and proceedings of the Union.

(b) From *Cobbett's Weekly Political Register*, August 17, 1833.

. . . It appears, as well from the written reports delivered in by Popay [1] to M'Lean, and by him delivered to the commissioners, as from the evidence of the petitioners themselves, that this constitution and these arrangements are as follow : 1. That the title of the association is, " The National Political Union of the Working Classes "; 2nd. That the Central Committee or body of managers, meet at a place in Theobald's-road; 3rd. That the body, or the whole of the members of the association, divide themselves into classes, after the manner of the Wesleyan Methodists; 4th. That each class has, after the manner of those Methodists, what is called a " leader ", who collects the contributions, pays the expenses, and manages the business of the class; 5th. That the class-meetings are confined to the members of the union, exclusively; but, two or more classes very frequently meet at some place, and then the meetings are called public meetings; and to these meetings any person whatever might be admitted. . . .

[1] Popay was a police spy.

7. THE GRAND NATIONAL HOLIDAY

[William Benbow (1784– ?) came from Manchester, where he took an active part in the Radical movement during the years after 1815. He then moved to London, where he became connected with the group round Arthur Thistlewood, and was imprisoned — which is perhaps why he was not involved in the Cato Street affair of 1820. On his release he acted for a time as Cobbett's publisher, but their connection was ended early in 1821 by a quarrel. Thereafter Benbow became a regular pamphleteer, bookseller, and coffee-house keeper, and a leader of the extreme wing of the London working class. He was very active in 1831 in the National Union of the Working Classes, and in January 1832 issued the pamphlet here quoted. He had been advocating the ' Grand National Holiday ' earlier in speeches at the Rotunda and elsewhere ; and he started in 1832 a short-lived journal, *The Tribune of the People*, devoted to the advocacy of his plan. As we shall see, his ideas reappeared both in the Owenite Trade Union movement of 1833–1834 and later in the ' Sacred Month ' of the Chartists. From 1837 to 1839 Benbow toured Lancashire with a horse and cart, holding open-air meetings and hawking his pamphlet. He was arrested in August 1839, a few days before the date fixed for the beginning of the ' Sacred Month '. After long delays he was tried in April 1840, and sentenced to sixteen months' imprisonment for sedition. He rejoined O'Connor's section of the Chartist movement on his release ; but from 1841 he disappears from history. The date of his death is unknown. His pamphlet is reprinted, with a long commentary by A. J. C. Rüter, in the 1936 volume of the *International Review for Social History*.]

From William Benbow, " Grand National Holiday, and Congress of the
Productive Classes ", 1832, pp. 8-13.

. . . We are the people, our business is with the people, and to transact it properly, we must take it into our own hands. The people are called upon to work for themselves ! We lay down the plan of operation ; we despair of all safety, we despair of liberty, we despair of equality, we despair of seeing ease, gaiety, pleasure, and happiness becoming the possessions of the people, unless they co-operate with us. We chalk down to them a plan ; woe to them if they do not follow in its traces !

The holiday signifies a *holy* day, and ours is to be of holy days the most holy. It is to be most holy, most sacred, for it is to be consecrated to promote — to create rather — the happiness and liberty of mankind. Our holy day is established to establish plenty, to abolish want, to render all men equal ! In our holy day we shall legislate for all mankind ; the constitution drawn up during our holiday, shall place every human being on the same footing. Equal rights, equal liberties, equal enjoyments, equal toil, equal respect, equal share of production : this is the object of our holy day — of our sacred day, — of our festival !

The grounds and necessity of our having a month's Holiday, arise from the circumstances in which we are placed. We are oppressed, in the fullest sense of the word ; we have been deprived of every thing ; we have no property, no wealth, and our labour is of no use to us, since what it produces goes into the hands of others. We have tried every thing but our own efforts ; we have told our governors, over and over again, of our wants and misery ; we thought them good and wise, and generous ; we have for ages trusted to their promises, and we find ourselves, at this present day, after so many centuries of forbearance, instead of having our condition bettered, convinced that our total ruin is at hand. Our Lords and Masters have proposed no plan that we can adopt ; they contradict themselves, even upon what` they name the source of our misery. One says one thing, another says another thing. One scoundrel, one sacrilegious blasphemous scoundrel, says " that over-production is the cause of our wretchedness." Over-production, indeed ! when we half-starving producers cannot, with all our toil, obtain any thing like a sufficiency of produce. It is the first time, that in any age or country, save our own, *abundance* was adduced as a cause of *want*. Good God ! where is this abundance ? Abundance of food ! ask the labourer and mechanic where they find it. Their emaciated frame is the best answer. Abundance of clothing ! the nakedness, the shivering, the asthmas, the colds, and rheumatisms of the people, are proofs of the abundance of clothing ! Our Lords and Masters tell us, we produce too much ; very well then, we shall cease from producing for one month, and thus put into practice the theory of our Lords and Masters.

Over-population, our Lords and Masters say, is another cause of our misery. They mean by this, that the resources of the country are inadequate to its population. We must prove the contrary, and during a holiday take a census of the people, and a measurement of the land, and see upon calculation, whether it be not an unequal distribution, and a bad management of the land, that make our Lords and Masters say, that there are too many of us. Here are two strong grounds for our Holiday ; for a CONGRESS of the working classes.

Before a month's holiday can take place, universal preparations must be made for it. It should not take place neither in seed-time nor in harvest-time. Every man must prepare for it, and assist his neighbour in preparing for it. The preparations must begin long before the time which shall be hereafter appointed, in order that every one may be ready, and that the festival be not partial but universal.

Committees of management of the working classes must be forthwith formed in every city, town, village, and parish throughout the united kingdom. These committees must make themselves fully acquainted with the plan, and be determined to use the extremest activity and perseverance to put it into execution as speedily and effectually as possible. They must call frequent meetings, and shew the necessity and object of the holiday. They must use every effort to prevent intemperance of every sort, and recommend the strictest sobriety and economy. The working classes cannot lay in provisions for a month; this is not wanted, but every man must do his best to be provided with food for the first week of the holiday. Provisions for the remaining three weeks can be easily procured. . . .

We suppose that the people are able to provide provisions and funds for one week; during this week they will be enabled to enquire into the funds of their respective cities, towns, villages and parishes, and to adopt means of having those funds, originally destined for their benefit, now applied to that purpose. . . .

" The cattle upon a thousand hills are the Lord's." When the people's voice, which Lord Brougham proclaims to be the voice of God, and surely we need no higher legal authority, calls for its own, demands the cattle of the thousand hills, who dares withhold the cattle of the thousand hills? During our holiday the people may have need of this cattle : let them order it to the slaughter-house, and their herdsmen and drovers will obey them. . . .

When all the details of the above plan are put into execution, the committee of each parish and district, shall select its wise men to be sent to the NATIONAL CONGRESS. A parish or district having a population of 8,000, shall send two wise and cunning men to Congress, a population of 15,000 four, a population of 25,000 eight, and London fifty wise and cunning men. . . .

The object of the Congress : that is what it will have to do. To reform society, for " from the crown of our head to the sole of our foot there is no soundness in us." We must cut out the rottenness in order to become sound. Let us see what is rotten. Every man that does not work is rotten ; he must be made to work in order to cure his unsoundness. Not only is society rotten; but the land, property, and capital is rotting. There is not only something, but a great deal rotten in the state of England. Every thing, men, property, and money, must be put into a state of circulation.

8. THE REFORM BILL STRUGGLE IN THE COUNTRY

[On October 8, 1831, the House of Lords rejected the Reform Bill by a majority of 41 (158 for, 199 against). At once serious disturbances broke out in various parts of the country, especially Nottingham and Derby and, a little later, Bristol. There was talk of forming an armed National Guard, on the French model, for the preservation of order; and some of the Radicals retorted with proposals for an armed ' Popular Guard '. The National Union of the Working Classes attempted to call a meeting to demand, among other things, the abolition of hereditary privilege; but the Government prohibited the meeting, and on November 21 issued a proclamation against the Political Unions, declaring some of them illegal and cautioning persons against joining them. The proclamation outlawed ' political unions composed of separate bodies with various divisions and sub-divisions under leaders and with a graduation of ranks and authority '. The Unions one and all refused to regard the prohibition as applicable to themselves and remained active. The N.U.W.C. called a National Convention in December 1831, and drew up a Bill of its own: the N.P.U. suffered some secessions, but continued its activities for ' the whole Bill, and nothing but the Bill '. When the Lords attempted, in April 1832, to whittle down the new Bill introduced by the Grey Ministry and the King rejected Lord Grey's demand that enough peers should be created to ensure the Bill's passage, the popular demonstrations speedily convinced the Tories of the impracticability of forming a Ministry to carry through a modified Reform Bill, and Grey soon resumed office. There was no violence on this occasion comparable with that of the previous autumn; but few doubted that there would have been even more widespread disturbances had not the House of Lords given way.]

(a) From John Wade, " British History Chronologically Arranged ", 1839. *October 7, 1831.*

. . . The bill being thus thrown out, the question — *what will the lords do?* — which had been earnestly and anxiously asked during the preceding months, was answered. It produced a strong and indignant feeling through the country. Some of the London newspapers were arrayed in mourning, and several noble lords who had opposed the bill were assaulted by the populace. At Derby they broke open the town gaol, and demolished the property of the anti-reformers of the place. At Nottingham there was considerable rioting, which ended in the destruction, by fire, of the ancient castle there, the property of the duke of Newcastle. His grace had become unpopular, and unintentionally given a great impulse to reform by his hasty declaration, in respect of his dependent voters, at Newark, that he had " a right to do what he pleased with his own." These excesses and a few burnings in effigy were the first outbreaks of popular rage; but, in general, there was confidence in the ultimate success of the bill, and a disposition on the part of the people and the political societies, now in action, to support the government and preserve the peace.

(*b*) From John Wade, " British History Chronologically Arranged ", 1839.

October 29, 1831. RIOTS IN BRISTOL — This city suddenly became the scene of dreadful excesses on the public entrance of Sir Charles Wetherell, the recorder. Sir Charles had been a strenuous opponent, in the house of commons, of the reform bill. The riots began on Saturday, continued through the whole of Sunday, and were only got under on Monday morning, when the corporation, the military, and the citizens awoke from the stupor into which they appear to have been thrown by this unexpected outbreak of popular fury. The whole of Bristol was on the verge of destruction; the mansion-house, custom-house, excise-office, and bishop's palace, were plundered and set on fire; the toll-gates pulled down; the prisons burst open with sledge hammers, and their inmates, criminals and debtors, set at liberty amidst the exulting shouts of the populace. During the whole of Sunday the mob were the unresisted masters of the city. Forty-two offices, dwelling-houses, and warehouses were completely destroyed, exclusive of public buildings. The loss of property was estimated at half a million. The number of rioters killed, wounded or injured, was about 110. Of about 14 or 16 who lost their lives, three died from the shots or sword-cuts of the military; the rest were mostly the victims of excessive drinking, in the rifled cellars and warehouses, which produced either apoplexy upon the spot, or disabled them from escaping from the flames that they had themselves kindled.

(*c*) Handbill. From the Place MSS., 27,791 f. 303 [1831].

" NATIONAL GUARD " AND " POPULAR GUARD "

We understand that it is in contemplation among the " middle-men " to establish a " NATIONAL GUARD ", seeing how successful and immediate a power it has been in France to suppress the PEOPLE, and to protect the established institutions of property. Friends, Brethren, and Fellow-countrymen, such a *Guard* would ensure your political thraldom, unless you have a *counter*-force. No time is to be lost — you too must form your millions into a GUARD, — " A POPULAR GUARD " : keep yourselves prepared : abstain from gin drinking, and lay by as much as possible out of your scanty earnings for the purchase of a musket and accoutrements — we can dispense with the "*fine dress*". We say no more at present ; but enough to shew our *Whigs* that, at any rate, we see through their cunning and will *endeavour* to overmatch it.

(*d*) From John Wade, " British History Chronologically Arranged ", 1839.

November 7, 1831. Meeting of the political union of the working-classes at White Conduit House, Thomas Wakley, chairman, post-poned. The notice convening this assembly, besides demanding universal suffrage, vote by ballot, and annual parliaments, declared, " That all property, *honestly acquired*, is sacred and inviolable ; that all men are born equally free and have certain natural and inalienable rights ; that all *hereditary distinctions of birth* are unnatural and opposed to the equal rights of man, and ought to be abolished " ; and they further declared that they would never be satisfied with any law that stopped short of these principles. An intimation from the police magistrates and from Lord Melbourne, that a meeting for these objects was not only illegal and seditious, but, perhaps, treason-able, led to its abandonment.

November 21. Proclamation issued declaring certain affiliated political unions unlawful, and cautioning persons against entering into such combinations.

(*e*) From John Wade, " British History Chronologically Arranged ", 1839.

May, 1832.

. . . Out of doors, the country was in a very alarming state of unanimity. The tide set all in one direction. Against the bill there was neither moral nor physical force. About its ultimate success no one affected to doubt ; that was deemed certain because the nation had willed it. The newspapers were almost entirely on the popular side, and kept up a raking fire against the " Oligarchy " and " usurping Boroughmongers." At London, Birmingham, Manchester and other large towns simultaneous meetings were held to petition the house of commons to stop the supplies. In the metropolis, placards were everywhere exhibited, enjoining the union of all friends to the cause — an enforcement of the public rights at all hazards — and a general resistance to the payment of taxes, rates and tithes. The political societies were in active communication, and at their meetings in the leading daily journals projects for *organizing* and *arming* the people were openly discussed and recommended. In case of need, the population of the large towns was ready to be precipitated on the metropolis. But this extremity was rendered unnecessary. The firm and generous devotion of William IV. to " an extensive reform ", whether carried by Whigs or Tories, deprived the hostile section of the aristocracy of the sole fulcrum, by which, with the least chance of success, it could hope to resist the universal sentiment. . . .

9. THE REFORM ACT OF 1832

[There is too little space for quoting more than the most significant provisions of the Act. In addition to the clauses quoted below, the following were the main matters covered :

Clauses 5-10. Revision of Borough boundaries ; reduction of Weymouth and Melcombe Regis to two members jointly ; requirements of Welsh Boroughs.

Clause 11. Returning Officers for new Boroughs.

Clauses 12-16. Yorkshire to have six county members, two for each Riding ; Lincolnshire to have four ; certain other counties to be divided, or to have three members ; the Isle of Wight to have one member.

Clauses 17-18. Inclusion of certain towns which are counties of themselves in adjoining counties and limitation of voting rights of freeholders for life.

Clauses 21-26. Detailed provisions regarding county voters.

Clauses 27-35. Detailed provisions regarding borough voters.

Clauses 37-60. Preparation and scrutiny of lists of voters.

Clauses 61-74. Provisions concerning polling. Limitation of expenses (71).

Clauses 75-82. Miscellaneous provisions, largely transitional.

Schedules A-L. Lists of Places and Forms prescribed.]

ANNO SECUNDO GULIELMI IV. REGIS.
C A P. XLV.

An Act to amend the Representation of the People in *England* and *Wales*.

[7th *June* 1832]

' WHEREAS it is expedient to take effectual Measures for correcting divers Abuses that have long prevailed in the Choice of Members to serve in the Commons House of Parliament, to deprive many inconsiderable Places of the Right of returning Members, to grant such Privilege to large, populous, and wealthy Towns, to increase the Number of Knights of the Shire, to extend the Elective Franchise to many of His Majesty's Subjects who have not heretofore enjoyed the same, and to diminish the Expence of Election ; ' be it therefore enacted by the King's most Excellent Majesty, by and with the Advice and Consent of the Lords Spiritual and Temporal, and Commons, in this present Parliament assembled, and by the Authority of the same, That each of the Boroughs enumerated in the Schedule marked (A.) to this Act annexed, (that is to say,) *Old Sarum, Newtown, St. Michael's or Midshall, Gatton, Bramber, Bossiney, Dunwich, Ludgershall, St. Mawe's, Beeralston, West Looe, St. Germain's, Newport, Blechingley, Aldborough, Camelford, Hindon, East Looe, Corfe Castle, Great Bedwin, Yarmouth, Queenborough, Castle Rising, East Grinstead, Higham Ferrers, Wendover, Weobly, Winchelsea, Tregony, Haslemere, Saltash, Orford, Callington, Newton, Ilchester, Boroughbridge, Stockbridge, New Romney, Hedon, Plympton, Seaford, Heytesbury, Steyning, Whitchurch, Wootton Bassett, Downton, Fowey, Milborne Port, Aldeburgh, Minehead, Bishop's Castle, Okehampton, Appleby, Lostwithiel, Brackley*, and *Amersham*, shall from and after the End of this present Parliament cease to return any Member or Members to serve in Parliament. *[margin: Certain Boroughs to cease to send Members to Parliament]*

II. And be it enacted, That each of the Boroughs enumerated in the schedule marked (B.) to this Act annexed, (that is to say,) *Petersfield, Ashburton, Eye, Westbury, Wareham, Midhurst, Woodstock, Wilton, Malmesbury, Liskeard, Reigate, Hythe, Droitwich, Lyme Regis, Launceston, Shaftesbury, Thirsk, Christchurch, Horsham, Great Grimsby, Calne, Arundel, St. Ives, Rye, Clitheroe, Morpeth, Helston, North Allerton, Wallingford*, and *Dartmouth*, shall from and after the End of this present Parliament return One Member and no more to serve in Parliament. *[margin: Certain Boroughs to return One Member only.]*

New
Boroughs
ereafter to
turn Two
Members.

III. And be it enacted, That each of the Places named in the Schedule marked (C.) to this Act annexed, (that is to say,) *Manchester, Birmingham, Leeds, Greenwich, Sheffield, Sunderland, Devonport, Wolverhampton, Tower Hamlets, Finsbury, Mary-le-Bone, Lambeth, Bolton, Bradford, Blackburn, Brighton, Halifax, Macclesfield, Oldham, Stockport, Stoke-upon-Trent,* and *Stroud,* shall for the Purposes of this Act be a Borough, and shall as such Borough include the Place or Places respectively which shall be comprehended within the Boundaries of such Borough, as such Boundaries shall be settled and described by an Act to be passed for that Purpose in this present Parliament, which Act, when passed, shall be deemed and taken to be Part of this Act as fully and effectually as if the same were incorporated herewith; and that each of the said Boroughs, named in the said Schedule (C.) shall from and after the End of this present Parliament return Two Members to serve in Parliament.

New
Boroughs
ereafter to
eturn One
Member.

IV. And be it enacted, That each of the Places named in the Schedule marked (D.) to this Act annexed, (that is to say,) *Ashton-under-Lyne, Bury, Chatham, Cheltenham, Dudley, Frome, Gateshead, Huddersfield, Kidderminster, Kendal, Rochdale, Salford, South Shields, Tynemouth, Wakefield, Walsall, Warrington, Whitby, Whitehaven,* and *Merthyr Tydvil,* shall for the Purposes of this Act be a Borough, and shall as such Borough include the Place or Places respectively which shall be comprehended within the Boundaries of such Borough, as such Boundaries shall be settled and described by an Act to be passed for that Purpose in this present Parliament, which Act, when passed, shall be deemed and taken to be Part of this Act as fully and effectually as if the same were incorporated herewith; and that each of the said Boroughs named in the said Schedule (D.) shall from and after the End of this present Parliament return One Member to serve in Parliament.

Right of
voting in
Counties
xtended to
pyholders.

XIX. And be it enacted, That every Male Person of full Age, and not subject to any legal Incapacity, who shall be seised at Law or in Equity of any Lands or Tenements of Copyhold or any other Tenure whatever except Freehold, for his own Life, or for the Life of another, or for any Lives whatsoever, or for any larger Estate, of the clear yearly Value of not less than Ten Pounds over and above all Rents and Charges payable out of or in respect of the same, shall be entitled to vote in the Election of a Knight or Knights of the Shire to serve in any future Parliament for the County, or for the

Riding, Parts, or Division of the County, in which such Lands or Tenements shall be respectively situate.

XX. And be it enacted, That every Male Person of full Age, and not subject to any legal Incapacity, who shall be entitled, either as Lessee or Assignee, to any Lands or Tenements, whether of Freehold or of any other Tenure whatever, for the unexpired Residue, whatever it may be, of any Term originally created for a Period of not less than Sixty Years, (whether determinable on a Life or Lives, or not,) of the clear yearly Value of not less than Ten Pounds over and above all Rents and Charges payable out of or in respect of the same, or for the unexpired Residue, whatever it may be, of any Term originally created for a Period of not less than Twenty Years (whether determinable on a Life or Lives, or not,) of the clear yearly Value of not less than Fifty Pounds over and above all Rents and Charges payable out of or in respect of the same, or who shall occupy as Tenant any Lands or Tenements for which he shall be *bona fide* liable to a yearly Rent of not less than Fifty Pounds, shall be entitled to vote in the Election of a Knight or Knights of the Shire to serve in any future Parliament for the County, or for the Riding, Parts, or Division of the County, in which such Lands or Tenements shall be respectively situate : Provided always, that no Person, being only a Sub-Lessee, or the Assignee of any Under-Lease, shall have a Right to vote in such Election in respect of any such Term of Sixty Years or Twenty Years as aforesaid, unless he shall be in the actual Occupation of the Premises.

Right of voting in Counties extended t Leasehold and Occupiers Premises o certain Val above Charges.

. . . . . .

XXVII. And be it enacted, That in every City or Borough which shall return a Member or Members to serve in any future Parliament, every Male Person of full Age, and not subject to any legal Incapacity, who shall occupy, within such City or Borough, or within any Place sharing in the Election for such City or Borough, as Owner or Tenant, any House, Warehouse, Counting-house, Shop, or other Building, being, either separately, or jointly with any Land within such City, Borough, or Place occupied therewith by him as Owner, or occupied therewith by him as Tenant under the same Landlord, of the clear yearly Value of not less than Ten Pounds, shall, if duly registered according to the Provisions herein-after contained, be entitled to vote in the Election of a Member or Members to serve in any future Parliament for such City or Borough. . . .

Right of voting in Boroughs to be enjoy by Occupi of Houses, etc., of the annual Val of 10l.

. . . . . .

As to
Receipt of
Parochial
Relief.

XXXVI. And be it enacted, That no Person shall be entitled to be registered in any Year as a Voter in the Election of a Member or Members to serve in any future Parliament for any City or Borough who shall within Twelve Calendar Months next previous to the last Day of *July* in such Year have received Parochial Relief or other Alms which by the Law of Parliament now disqualify from voting in the Election of Members to serve in Parliament. . . .

X

TRADE UNIONISM AND UNREST, 1820-1834

INTRODUCTION

TRADE UNIONISM met with many difficulties in the years that followed the French Wars. The Combination Acts were still in force, the final repeal of the Elizabethan Statute of Artificers (1813–1814) had left many sections bewildered and helpless, and now a deep, widespread depression blocked the way for any Trade Union advance.

The factory operatives were becoming the most important section of the working class ; the home workers were being driven by the Industrial Revolution into hopeless poverty, and in some trades the skilled artisans were in retreat, defending their privileged status against the spread of the new industrial system.

The miners and factory workers had to face a bitter hatred of Trade Unionism ; the refusal of many employers to recognise the principle of collective bargaining led to frequent riots in times of strike action, to the defeat and persecution of the workers and the temporary break-up of their organisations.

No considerable progress could be made until the repeal of the Combination Acts (1824–1825) had legalised Trade Unions. Many ' Friendly Societies' then came into the open as Trade Unions, and new Unions were formed in great numbers. In London The Metropolitan Trades' Committee published *The Trades Newspaper*, 1825, the first paper owned by Trade Unions, and in the Manchester district a second attempt was made in 1826 to form a General Trades' Union of the North. The forward movement which seemed likely to arise during the boom of 1824–1825 [1] was postponed by a slump till 1829. Then big national Unions were founded — such as the Spinners' in 1829, the Potters' in 1831, and the Builders' in 1831 or 1832 — with a set determination to rally the whole trade in a drive for better conditions. The great improvement in the internal organisation of trades made it possible for John Doherty's National

---

[1] The Steam Engine Makers' and Journeymen Steam Engine Makers' Societies were founded during this period.

Association for the Protection of Labour (1831) to win a wider support than any of the earlier attempts to form general Trades Unions. Even so, its life was short.

In town and country alike the temper of the working class was rising. The agricultural labourers attempted to force home their demand for something nearer a living wage by riots and rick-burning, and were savagely suppressed. John Doherty, one of the best Union leaders of the time, declared (January 1832) that far the most common topic of conversation for the operative was ' the appalling question of whether it would be more advantageous to the poor to attack the lives or the property of the rich '. They felt, added Doherty, that the wage increases won by the rick-burners provided a sound argument in favour of violence. Among others the miners of South Wales and Durham had bitter struggles in building up their Unions and using them; in both cases the temper of the men and the obstinacy of their employers produced riots and violence.

The agitation for the Reform Bill absorbed the energies of many Trade Unionists, and, after it was passed, a further industrial push was made. The inspiration of this new, semi-revolutionary phase of Trade Unionism came largely from Robert Owen. The Operative Builders' Union had been captured by Owenites (1833), and a Builders' Guild was set up as a first step towards workers' control of industry. A great impetus was given to strikes for higher wages; the Society for Promoting National Regeneration was founded (1833) in the factory areas to demand an eight-hour day; a number of Trade Unions employed their members in Co-operative production, often using Robert Owen's Labour Exchanges or other Co-operative Societies for the marketing of their wares. Men hoped that somehow, by violent struggle or otherwise, they would in a short while be building a new society with prosperity and justice for all.

The Grand National Consolidated Trades Union was founded in 1833, with the object of uniting the working class for a short and, in Owen's view, a peaceful struggle, which he expected would inaugurate the millennium within a few months. But the G.N.C.T.U. was never able effectively to rally behind it even the whole of the Trade Union movement as it then existed; nor could it have hoped to succeed in its ambitious projects even if the organised workers had been solidly united in its support. The Trade Unions of the North for the most part stood aloof, though the textile workers rallied to the Society for National Regeneration, which, with its demand for the eight-hour day, to be won by industrial action, was also under Owenite influence. The Builders, Spinners, and Potters, and also the Leeds, Huddersfield, and Bradford District Union, mainly based on the Clothiers' Union, which had been carrying on a bitter struggle with the employers throughout the Yorkshire woollen area, refused to merge their identity in the G.N.C.T.U. This body, in effect, consisted mainly of numerous small local Trade Clubs of craftsmen and of a mass of newly organised workers of all types who flocked into it, and flocked out of it as easily as soon as its difficulties began to accumulate. In general, the G.N.C.T.U. found its strongest backing among Trade Clubs of skilled craftsmen in trades not yet greatly affected by the Industrial Revolution. It never succeeded in organising either the main body of factory workers in Lancashire, Yorkshire, and Scotland, or the miners and metal-workers, who were little affected by Owenite ideas. Owenite Trade Unionism has been described as an anticipation of Guild Socialism; and so it was among the builders, for reasons connected with the rapid development of the contract system in the growing industrial towns. Elsewhere it combined a stimulus to Co-operative production with an appeal to a large body of hitherto unorganised workers who were in reaction against the political disappointments of 1832 and hopeful of taking advantage of the rapidly improving trade conditions of 1833 and 1834. It was, however, clearly out of the question for a body organised on such a basis to achieve any real strength or power of resistance to organised opposition. Strong national Unions had to come into existence before there could be any real possibility of building up an effective combination of all trades. The defeat of the G.N.C.T.U. was inevitable; and after this defeat came a long period of transition, during which the Trade Unionists slowly built up a new type of organisation based on more limited objectives and aiming principally at the immediate defence and improvement of the conditions of the workers under the capitalist system.

See " Short History ", Part I, chapter 6.
" Common People ", chapter 22.

1. TRADE UNIONS AFTER 1825

[The repeal of the Combination Laws in 1824–1825 was followed by the foundation of many Trade Unions, including many which had previously existed underground or under the guise of Friendly Societies, but were at length able to come into the open and to adopt published Constitutions and Statements of Policy. The London Society of Compositors was one of these. Prior to 1826 the compositors had been organised in a number of local Trade Clubs, which had come together from time to time to conduct joint movements through temporary committees. The Act of 1825 was at once followed by the establishment of a permanent Trade Union covering the entire metropolitan area.]

From " The Jubilee Volume of the London Society of Compositors ", 1898. Address issued by the Committee of the General Trade Society of Compositors of London, May 1, 1833.

ADDRESS.

In the year 1826, several active and intelligent individuals, convinced of the inefficiency of the then existing institution to protect the rights of the trade, and anxious to secure the wages of the journeyman from any such unjust reduction as had been made upon reprints, deliberated on the practicability of forming a society which, by being suited to the views and conditions of all, might be worthy of *general* support, and combine at once the energies and the talents of the trade. After having maturely considered the subject, they called a general meeting of the trade, to which they submitted the plan they had prepared for the establishment of a society, to be called The London General Trade Society, which, after discussion, received the sanction of the meeting, consisting of about fifteen hundred persons. . . .

To those who are ignorant of the proceedings of the London General Trade Society from its establishment in 1826 to the present period (1833), it is considered advisable to state that, since its commencement, not one member has quitted it on account of its mismanagement, its tardiness, inefficiency, or illiberality — its numbers have always been increasing — its receipts have been augmenting every year, and never has it been found necessary to withdraw its money from the public funds, although it has always paid its full proportion of all trade expenses, and has invariably been the foremost to reward those who have been injured in their attempts to maintain the rights of the trade.

The proceedings of the Society are openly conducted — no secret and partial investigations — no party decisions have ever stained its records — no wasteful expenditure or embezzlement of its receipts can ever take place — its accounts are publicly audited every quarter — its acts, its funds, its laws, are under the control of its members, who can at all times investigate or take part in the direction of its affairs. Its constitution is at once so simple and vigorous, yet so admirably framed to meet every circumstance that may arise, that it is enabled to afford the best advice in all cases of dispute with employers; it gives the most prompt assistance to all who need it — no tedious delays, no useless formalities fetter its proceedings, but it grants to its members immediate pecuniary aid and legal assistance, whenever such support and advice are required.

Since, then, it must be admitted by all, that those who live by their labour ought to unite to secure to themselves the just wages of labour, and since experience has shown that the disposition of masters in general is to grant the lowest possible remuneration for labour; and knowing, also, that without union amongst men, it is always in the power of employers to deprive their workmen of even a proper share of the common necessaries of life — it is a duty which every man owes to himself and to his family, to take such steps as shall secure to him the proper reward of his industry. This just reward, however, cannot be obtained by individual exertion — it is union alone that can effect it. The only security to the workman from injustice, oppression, and pauperism, is a well-conducted Trade Society; . . .

. . . It is only considered necessary, in conclusion, to remark that the efficiency of the London General Trade Society is not weakened by a variety of objects and a diversity of interests — it is truly a Trade Society, since it has but óne object in view — namely, the protection of the wages of labour; and those who desire to reap the just reward of their industry, to correct the evils arising from the illiberality and avarice of selfish employers, and secure for themselves a never-failing shelter from powerful and wealthy disputants, should, without further delay, enrol their names on the list of its members.

2. THE METROPOLITAN TRADES' UNION

[It is probable that ever since the Philanthropic Hercules the leading Trade Unionists of London had worked together through a more or less regularly meeting 'Metropolitan Trades' Committee', which, as we saw, issued its own newspaper in 1825. The Metropolitan Trades' Union of 1831 was a further attempt to strengthen and clarify their co-operation. It had a loose connection with John Doherty's National Association for the Protection of Labour.]

Opening Circular of the Metropolitan Trades' Union. From *Penny Papers for the People*, March 26, 1831.

IMPORTANT MEETING
OF THE WORKING CLASSES.

On Wednesday last the Committee appointed to prepare a Circular, to be transmitted to every society of Working Men in London, defining the objects of a proposed Metropolitan Trades' Union, made their report to a very full meeting of Delegates, Mr. Warden in the Chair, when the following Circular was unanimously adopted.

CIRCULAR.

FELLOW WORKMEN,

There is an old English proverb which declares that ' God helps those who help themselves ', and if ever a time existed in which those who have nothing to depend on but their labour should attend to their concerns it is at present ; . . .

Well, then, fellow workmen, the first great evil that stands in the way of bettering our condition, is, that we, the working people of England, are UNREPRESENTED ! totally destitute of political influence in the Great Council of the Nation ! . . . Are you content to remain the degraded victims of such an unjust system ? Shall we go on petitioning — vainly petitioning — like pusillanimous beggars — for some trifling relief, when, by a determined and united effort on our parts, we might excite the respect and insure the sympathy and support of millions of our fellow-countrymen ? We earnestly hope not. Let us henceforth adopt and practise a new principle ; — instead of every man being for himself exclusively, let us, in future, be ALL for EACH, and EACH for ALL. To do this, the intelligence and energy of the working classes must be concentrated ; and it is, therefore, proposed THAT A METROPOLITAN TRADES' UNION be formed. Its first object, to obtain, for all its members, the right of electing those who make the laws which govern them, unshackled and uninfluenced by any Property Qualification whatsoever. Its second object, to afford support and protection, individually and collectively, to every member of the METROPOLITAN TRADES' UNION ; to enhance the value of labour by diminishing the hours of employment ; and to adopt such measures as may be deemed necessary to increase the domestic comforts of working men.

3. THE GENERAL UNION OF THE SPINNERS, 1829

[The factory Unions of the North benefited most from the repeal of the Combination Laws. But the slump at the end of 1825 postponed the full enjoyment of their opportunities till 1828. Then the failure of two important strikes among the spinners of Stockport and Manchester taught them the need for better organisation. In December 1829, under the influence of John Doherty,[1] a conference was held at Ramsey, Isle of Man, with delegates from England, Ireland, and Scotland. The Grand General Union of all the Operative Spinners in the United Kingdom was set up. In England a policy was pursued of attacking employers one by one for an advance in wages and giving help to each set of workers in turn, until the strain of the Ashton strike at the end of 1830 crippled the Union's finances. The second delegate meeting in December 1830 recognised that their plans had been made on too ambitious a scale and loosened the ties between the Union of the three countries. The Union was, except in name, always an English one, and even the English section seems to have broken up in 1831. The Scots had their own powerful Union, which lasted till it was destroyed by the conviction of its leaders in 1837.]

Resolutions of the Delegates from the Operative Cotton Spinners who met at the Isle of Man (December 1829). From the Home Office Papers, 40/27 [1829].

1. That 500 copies of the proceedings of these meetings be printed and each district supplied with as many copies as may appear necessary, always taking care to prevent unnecessary or improper publicity being given.

(2. That this meeting adjourns till nine o'clock on Monday morning next.)

3. That one Grand General Union of all the Operative Spinners in the United Kingdom be now formed for the mutual support and protection of all.

4. That each nation shall manage its own affairs, always subject to the decisions and authority of a general or annual meeting of the delegates from each district who choose to send representatives to such meeting.

---

[1] John Doherty (1797 or 1799–1854) first appears as prominent in the 1825 agitation to maintain the repeal of the Combination Laws in the previous year. In 1829–1832 he was the most powerful Unionist in the North, working, as a convinced Owenite, to widen and strengthen the organisation which the working class would need in its coming struggle. The record of his organising activity, the journals which he edited, and the few articles we have from his pen leave us with an impression of his great ability. He also took an important part in the Ten Hours' Movement.

5. That every member of this Association shall contribute the sum of one penny a week to the general fund, over and above the local levy, or expence of each District, and that all persons receiving benefit from either a local or the general fund, shall contribute the same sum.

6. That all male piecers capable of spinning be caused to pay one penny weekly, to the general fund as members of this association, and that in cases of strikes all such as remain out shall receive the same allowance as the spinner, and that Mr. Johnstone and Mr. Doherty be appointed to prepare an entrance ceremony for the admission of piecers as members.

7. That the sum of 10/- a week be paid to every member of this association when they are on strike against a reduction of wages.

8. That 10/- a week be paid to members when contending for an advance of wages the same as when resisting reductions, but that no district or part of a district be allowed to strike for an advance without first having obtained the consent and authority of the other districts.

9. That no person be allowed to turn out either for an advance or against a reduction of wages, without the consent and authority of the whole districts, and that no more be allowed at any time to come out than what can be supported with the stipulated sum on any consideration whatever.

10. That any district wishing to strike against any real or supposed grievance shall first write to their national committee, and they to the other national Committees and also to each of their own districts, stating the alledged ground of complaint and call upon each to send in their opinions as to the propriety or otherwise of the proposed strike.

11. That a card with certain devices hereafter to be agreed upon be prepared to which each honourable member shall be entitled when wishing to remove from one district to another and which will entitle him to the respect and esteem of the Confederation but that no aid or countenance be given to strangers who do not produce such card (There should be a penalty on recommending strangers or others who cannot produce this card).

12. That should any member or members of this Association be proscribed by masters for their activity and exertions in promoting the welfare of the trade their case shall be stated by the proper authorities of the district to which he or they belong to the national

committee and they to the other national committees and to every other district and call upon them to contribute as much as they please either weekly or in one separate sum.

13. That Mr. Doherty remain here to finish the report of the proceedings and that they may be printed in the Isle of Man.

14. That no spinner shall allow a piecer to spin on any account whatever after the 5th of April 1830 except such as may hereafter be provided for, and they only while the spinners are in the wheel-houses or wheelgates walking to and fro with the wheels and attending to the work.

15. That each district in case of a partial strike shall support there [*sic*] own men so long as they can do so by paying 1/- per man per week, over and above their local contributions but that when they cannot pay the men on strike the stipulated sum by this subscription they shall then apply through the proper organs to the other districts for aid.

16. That a return of the names of the spinners and piecers paying in each district be made, for the purpose of having a list of all the spinners in the United Kingdom printed, and each district supplied with a copy and that they be numbered 1, 2, 3, &c. beginning at Manchester. Districts to take precedency according to their numbers, and that Mr. Doherty attach the numbers to the names, which numbers shall continue in force as long as the parties live. As members die or leave the trade their numbers shall be filled up at the annual meetings.

17. That the next annual meeting be held on Whit Monday at the Isle of Man.

18. That no person or persons be learned or allowed to spin after the 5th of April 1830 except the son, brother or orphan nephew of spinners, and the poor relations of the proprietors of the mills, and those only when they have attained the full age of 15 years; such persons being instructed or allowed to spin only when the spinner is in the wheelhouse following the wheels and attending to the work. Any person acting contrary to this shall be fined for the first offence in the sum of half a guinea, for the second one guinea, and for the third to be expelled from the society and have his name exposed throughout the whole trade.

19. That any person who may take work as a spinner at any rate below what is considered a fair and legal price shall be fined £5 and continue a regular paying member of all fair dues and demands for one year before he be entitled to the benefits of the trade and

any member causing one under his control to do so shall be fined in one half that sum and be exposed throughout the whole trade.

20. That persons on being admitted members of the Society after the first Saturday in February 1830 shall pay 10/- as an entrance fee, after the first Saturday in March £1, and after the 5th of April £2.

21. That all fines and entrance fees go to the fund of the district in which they occur.

22. That the national committee shall have power to examine the books of any district which they may suspect of making false returns for the purpose of preventing fraud.

23. That a monthly correspondence be kept up through the Secretary with each district after the appearance of the report and continue till the next annual meeting, and that the names of those persons in each district who commit any offence against the interests of the trade shall be stated in the district monthly letters to the secretary in order that such men may be known, exposed and detested, as their baseness and criminality deserve. Each district to pay the postage of its own letters.

24. That female spinners be urged to become members of an association to be formed exclusively for themselves, and that an entrance ceremony be prepared for them suited to their circumstances, and that they pay into and receive from their own fund such sum or sums as they may from time to time agree upon and they receive all the aid of the whole confederation in supporting them to obtain men's prices, or such remuneration for their labour as may be deemed sufficient under general or particular circumstances.

25. That an address be prepared by Mr. Doherty to the operative spinners of the United Kingdom calling upon them to come boldly and manfully forward and support the attempt that is now being made to prevent any further depreciation of the value of their only property their Labour, by repeated and unnecessary reduction of their wages and that 2000 copies be printed for distribution beside the 500 that will be attached to this report agreeable to a previous resolution.

26. That each district be called upon to ascertain how many subscribers can be obtained amongst their own members, for a monthly publication to be devoted entirely and exclusively to the business of spinning and to promote the welfare of the trade the price to be from 2d. to 3d. per number. That such names be sent in forthwith to Mr. Doherty and if there appear a sufficient number to cover the expence he shall be empowered to prepare and publish

such a work, to be entitled ' The Operative Spinners' Monthly Advocate or Register of their Affairs '.

27. That it is not the intention of this Association either directly or indirectly to interfere with, or in any way injure the rights and property of employers or to assume or exercise any control or authority over the management of any mill or mills, but, on the contrary, will endeavour as far as in us lies to uphold the just rights and reasonable authority of every master, and compel all the members of this association to pay a due obedience and respect to their respective masters, and all their confidential servants in authority under them, our only object being to uphold the best interests of our common country by averting all the horrid train of direful calamities, which have already made too much progress amongst us and which are inseparable from cruel poverty, ignorance, degradation, pauperism and crime, and to obtain for our families the common comforts and conveniences of life.

28. That each district now present lay before their respective bodies the necessity of an early application to Parliament for an amended act relative to the hours of labour of young persons employed in cotton factories and that the provisions of the existing laws should be extended to persons of 21 years of age and that their opinions on the same be sent in, in writing to Mr. Doherty as early as possible.

29. That Mr. Doherty be appointed secretary to this association till the next annual meeting.

30. That the best thanks of this meeting be given to Mr. Thomas Foster for his most valuable assistance at these meetings, and for the sacrifices which he must have made in coming here at his own expence to promote the welfare of our common cause.

31. That the best thanks of this meeting be given to Mr. Doherty for his exertions to promote the well being of the working classes generally but of the operative spinners in particular and that he receive the sum of £3 for preparing the report.

32. That the best thanks of this meeting be given to the Chairman for his very proper and dignified conduct in the Chair.

4. THE NATIONAL ASSOCIATION FOR THE PROTECTION OF LABOUR, 1830

[Even before the Spinners' Union had begun to decline, Doherty was busy on an even greater project — the National Association for the

Protection of Labour, a General Trades' Union. Unlike its predecessors, the N.A.P.L. did succeed in winning the support of a wide variety of workers, including some miners, potters, blacksmiths, mechanics, and millwrights, in addition to the textile operatives, who were the dominating section. Lancashire and the Midlands were its strongest centres, but it also made some headway in Yorkshire and even reached South Wales. It ran two papers: first, *The United Trades Co-operative Journal*, and then *The Voice of the People*, over 3,000 copies of which, it was said, were sold at 7d. each. The main work of the N.A.P.L. was to encourage and organise Trade Unions, to give help in time of struggle, and to take a leading part in the Short Time Committees which were agitating for factory reform. The Association broke up early in 1832. Doherty had quarrelled with the executive and was publishing *The Poor Man's Advocate*, which was devoted to factory conditions and the need for new factory laws.]

(*a*) From *The United Trades Co-operative Journal*, July 10, 1830.

NATIONAL ASSOCIATION
FOR THE PROTECTION OF LABOUR.

RESOLUTIONS AND LAWS

Agreed to by the meeting of Delegates held in Manchester, on Monday, Tuesday and Wednesday, the 28th, 29th and 30th of June, 1830.

Resolved, 1. That the miserable conditions to which, by repeated and unnecessary reductions of wages, the working people of this country are reduced, urges upon this meeting the imperative necessity of adopting some effectual means for preventing such reductions and securing to the industrious workman a just and adequate remuneration for his labour.

2. That to accomplish this necessary object a Society shall be formed consisting of the various organised Trades throughout the kingdom.

3. That this Society be called " The National Association for the Protection of Labour ".

4. That the general laws and government of this Society be formed and conducted by a general Committee, consisting of one delegate from every 1000 members.

5. That such general Committee shall meet every six months, and decide upon all subjects affecting the interests of the Association.

6. That a Provisional Council, consisting of seven persons, returned from as many districts, meet once a month, at Manchester, and be empowered to watch over the interests of the Association between each meeting of the general Committee, one of such Council

to retire every month, and another appointed in his stead from a different district.

. . . .

14. That the funds of this Society shall be applied only to prevent reductions of wages, but in no case to procure an advance. Any trade considering their wages too low may exert themselves to obtain such advance, as they may think necessary and can obtain it by their own exertions.

. . . .

17. That no trade can be admitted members of this Association that is not regularly organised and united to itself.

(*b*) From " On Combinations of Trades ". (Anon. published by J. Ridgway (1831), p. 54.)

As unions are only formed where the rate of wages affords something to lose, so it is only the upper workmen of each trade who combine.[1] The apprentices or assistants follow the fortunes of those whose places they hope one day to occupy, but they neither subscribe to, nor take any part in the confederacy. The advance, when procured, is not beneficial to them, and their condition under a turn out is always worse than that of their more provident superiors. These persons bear a proportion to the journeymen sometimes of four or five to one, and the modes by which they are not only kept in subjection to, but absolutely enlisted into the service of the Union would be curious to analyse. . . .

5. THE NORTHERN MINERS

[The story of the struggles of the miners on the North-East Coast has been told by J. L. and Barbara Hammond in " The Skilled Labourer ", chapters 2 and 3 ; and an extract dealing with the dispute of 1765 has been given earlier in the present volume. There were many subsequent disputes ; and upon the repeal of the Combination Laws the colliers formed in 1825 a United Association of Northumberland and Durham, which issued a statement of grievances in a pamphlet entitled ' A Voice from the Coal Mines '. A further pamphlet, ' A Candid Appeal to the Coalowners and Viewers ', appeared the following year, when the Association made an unsuccessful attempt to open negotiations with the owners. In

[1] There are exceptions to this proposition. The articles of an apprentice Union are given in the appendix [not included here].

1831 the colliers made a renewed attempt to improve their conditions, which had been worsened in the meantime. The Mayor of Newcastle attempted to mediate; but terms could not be agreed on, and the men struck. The owners then made concessions, and work was resumed; but a number of owners soon attempted to break the Union by bringing in blacklegs from the lead mines. When the yearly 'binding time' came round many owners refused to re-engage men known to be connected with the Union, and there was an extensive stoppage. In the end the men's resistance was broken, and the Union collapsed. Its leader, Thomas Hepburn (*d.* 1873), was also active in the Reform struggle, and was an organiser of great competence. He was victimised, and, after trying in vain to make a living as a hawker, was forced to renounce the Union as a condition of employment.]

The Miners of the North. A Letter from Lord Melbourne. From the Home Office Papers, 1832. (Quoted from J. L. and B. Hammond, " The Skilled Labourer " (1919), pp. 44-5.)

WHITEHALL, *July* 16, 1832.

SIR,—I am commanded by his Majesty to call your most serious and immediate attention to the state of the colliery districts in the county of Durham.

It appears that, for some time past, extensive and determined combinations and conspiracies have been formed and entered into by the workmen, for the purpose of dictating to their masters the rate of wages at which they shall be employed, the hours during which they shall work, the quantity of labour which they shall perform, as well as for imposing upon them many other regulations relating to the conduct and management of their trade and concerns.

In pursuance of this system, and in furtherance and support of these demands, which are as unwise and injurious to the authors of them as they are violent and unjust in themselves, tumultuous assemblages of people have been gathered together, to the great danger of the public peace, at which the most seditious and inflammatory discourses have been delivered, and the most illegal resolutions adopted.

The natural consequences of such proceedings have shown themselves in outrages of the most atrocious character, in menaces and intimidation, in the injury and maltreating of peaceable and industrious labourers, so as to endanger their lives, — and in the commission of murder in the face of open day.

In these circumstances I am commanded by his Majesty to express his confident expectation, that all who hold the commission of the peace will act with the promptitude, decision, and firmness

which are so imperatively required, and that they will exert themselves for the prevention and suppression of all meetings which shall be called together for an illegal purpose, or which shall, in the course of their proceedings, become illegal; for the detection and punishment of all unlawful combination and conspiracy, as well as of all outrage and violence; and for the encouragement and protection of his Majesty's peaceable and well-disposed subjects. — I have the honour to be, sir your humble servant,

MELBOURNE.

6. THE LABOURERS' REVOLT

[There were no Trade Unions behind the revolt which spread through the Eastern and Southern agricultural counties in the winter of 1830–1831. The Labourers' Revolt seems to have been a spontaneous movement of protest against intolerable conditions, especially those connected with the administration of the Poor Laws — the ' roundsman ' system, and the cutting down of allowances under the Speenhamland scales. Rick-burning was at first the main symptom ; but presently there were marches to solicit relief from farmers and landowners (often in the name of a mythical ' Captain Swing '), and some unpopular poor-law overseers were roughly handled. The labourers demanded the abolition of tithes, the payment of a living wage, and sometimes the disuse of labour-saving machines. The Whig Government, eager to prove its devotion to the causes of property and law and order, responded with savage repression. Special Commissions were sent to try the rioters in the counties which had been the chief centres of trouble. Nine were hanged, 457 transported, and nearly as many more imprisoned for varying terms. These drastic measures ended the revolt, and were the prelude to the New Poor Law of 1834.]

(*a*) ' Causes of the Fires '. From Cobbett's *Twopenny Trash*, November 1830.

Amongst all the crimes that men committed against their neighbours, that which the law calls ARSON, and which is *a malicious setting fire to their buildings or their stacks*, is a crime always held in great and just abhorrence, and always punished *with death* ; and so necessary has this punishment been deemed to the safety of society, that children not more than ten years of age have been put to death for it ; because it is a crime so easily committed, committed with so much secrecy, and in the commission of which a very young person may be the instrument of grown-up persons. It is a truly

abominable crime, because the commission of it may cause innocent persons to perish in the flames; and, at the very least, it may, in a moment, ruin whole families, reducing them from competence to beggary.

When, therefore, we hear of acts of this description being almost nightly committed *in England*, our first feeling is that of *resentment against the parties*; but, when we have had a little time to reflect, we are, if we be not devourers of the fruit of the people's labours, led to ask, What can have been *the cause* of a state of things so unnatural as that in which crimes of this horrid sort are committed by hundreds of men going in a body, and deemed by them to be a sort of *duty* instead of *crimes*? When we put this question we are not to be answered with the assertion, that the crimes arise from the *vicious disposition* of the working people; because then we ask, *what it is* that has made them so vicious? No; this cannot be the cause. The people are of the same make and maker that they always were; the land is the same, the climate the same, the language and the religion the same; and, it is very well known, that schools and places of worship and the circulation of the Bible and of religious books have all been prodigiously increasing for many years, and are now more on the increase than ever. There must, therefore, be some *other cause*, or causes, to produce these dreadful acts in a people the most just, the most good-natured, and the most patient, in the world. I know this *cause*; or, rather, these causes; I know also that there is an effectual *remedy* of this great and melancholy evil; and I need not say, that it is my duty to state them both with perfect frankness; a duty I shall perform as briefly and with as much clearness as I am able.

(*b*) From W. Carpenter's *Political Letters*, No. 8 (' Facts and Observations '), November 18, 1830, p. 8.

FIRE ! FIRE ! FIRE ! TAXES AND TITHES IN DANGER
Cry of the aristocracy.

The fires in Kent, which lately caused so much show of alarm among the " higher orders " (as they call themselves), have extended into the county of Surrey : several corn and hay stacks have been fired, as if by magic. On Saturday last, the whole town of Guildford was thrown into a state of dreadful excitement, by the burning of an old, empty, insulated, cowshed, the materials of which would not have sold for twenty shillings, and a heap of bean-haulm and other rubbish, the property of the worthy mayor of that place.

with them in heart and mind, though not always in act. It will frighten Lord Grey, but he ought to know it that, amongst the tradesmen, even of the metropolis, *ninety-nine out of a hundred are* on the side of the labourers. It is not that they *approve of the destruction of property*; but they think that these means, desperate and wicked as they are *in their nature*, will tend to produce THAT GREAT CHANGE which all, who do not live on the taxes, are wishing for. . . .

Thus, then, we have the whole affair before us. Retrograde movements are impossible. The millions have, at last, broken forth; hunger has, at last, set stone walls at defiance, and braved the fetters and the gallows; nature has, at last, commanded the famishing man to get food. All the base and foolish endeavours to cause it to be believed, that the fires are the work of *foreigners*, or of a *conspiracy*, or of *instigation* from others than labourers, only show that those who make these endeavours are conscious that they share, in some way or other, in the guilt of having been the real cause of the mischief. But, if any could surpass, in point of baseness and folly, these endeavours to cast the blame on foreigners, it would be the monstrous baseness and folly of imputing the risings of the labourers and the fires TO ME! This has been done, in one shape or another, in almost every newspaper in England; and, if I were not regarded by these miscreant writers as a man *for whom there is no protection from the law*, the base wretches would tremble for the consequences. I despise the miscreants and their efforts more than anything on earth, except their baser *employers*. I will say this, however, that, if I were possessed of the power of, while sitting here in London, causing the destruction that is now going on, and if I deemed it right to render evil for evil, I should be *fully justified in exercising that power*. For what injury, what evil, what destruction, have not this ARISTOCRACY and this CLERGY inflicted, or endeavoured to inflict on me? And, when I recollect what I have suffered at their hands, and in consequence of their machinations, I must be a hypocrite indeed to say, that I do not rejoice at their troubles. When they thought they had me down for ever, their exultation was boundless; and, oh! how *shameless*! For twenty long years have I warned them of this very danger; and when I meet with scorn and punishment where I ought to have found attention and marks of gratitude, more than once I have said, and particularly to the parsons of Hampshire, " Ye have set at nought all my *counsel*, and would none of my *reproof*; I also will laugh at your calamity, and *mock* when your fear *cometh*."

7. THE SCOTCH CATTLE

[The South Wales miners were engaged throughout this period in a continual bitter struggle with the coal- and iron-masters who dominated the then remote Welsh valleys. About 1830 the miners had formed a Friendly Society of Coal Mining, which had attempted to link up with John Doherty's National Association for the Protection of Labour. The following year there were serious riots in Merthyr : the colliers marched on the town and occupied it, disarming the soldiers who had been brought in to protect the magistrates and later driving back and partly disarming reinforcements of cavalry from Cardiff and Swansea. Further troops were sent for, and the colliers were finally defeated, and their leaders imprisoned. Dick Penderyn, their chief organiser, was executed ; and the Trade Union was broken up by the refusal of the masters to employ any man who would not give up his membership. These reprisals drove the movement underground. It assumed the form of a secret terrorist organisation, the ' Scotch Cattle ', which set on foot a policy of violence directed against truck shops, workers who accepted cut wages, and other offenders against the claims of labour. The Union revived in 1834, only to be beaten again by the same methods ; and the ' Scotch Cattle ' thereupon renewed their terroristic activities, as they did yet again after 1842. Their ' sign manual ' was the rough drawing (in red) which appears at the foot of the extract.]

' Scotch Cattle ' Movement. From Home Office Papers, translated from the Welsh. (N. Edwards, " The History of the South Wales Miners ", p. 30.)

" To all colliers, Traitors, Turncoats and others. We hereby warn you the second and last time. We are determined to draw the hearts out of all the men above-named, and fix two hearts upon the horns of the Bull ; so that everyone may see what is the fate of every traitor — and we know them all. So we testify with our blood."

Hoarfrost Castle April 19, 1832.

[Hoarfrost Castle, April 19, 1832.]

8. CO-OPERATIVE PRODUCTION

[From 1830 till 1834 there was a considerable amount of Co-operative production, almost entirely among the skilled artisans, who could more easily collect the capital required and who did not need outside technical or administrative help. The average Trade Unionist, as this report from Leicester shows, favoured Co-operative production as a means of strengthening his hand in time of strike action. Many of the leaders also regarded it as a prelude to workers' control of industry. In the ambitious (but short-lived) Potters' scheme, some thought chiefly of employing the unemployed, while some hoped to drive the masters out of the industry. Co-operative production never played the large part which Owen and the ' Grand National ' assigned to it — the basic industries were hardly touched, the schemes were mostly short-lived, and many of them were rather incidental to strike action than carried on with belief in their lasting success.]

(a) From ' The Report of the Committee of the North West of England United Co-operative Company ' (opened December 12, 1831), recorded in " Proceedings of the Third Co-operative Congress held in London on 23 April, 1832 " (and succeeding days).

Your Committee have much satisfaction in reporting to this congress, that after having surmounted many difficulties, they have brighter prospects before them ; and the most sanguine hopes of effecting the great objects for which they were established — viz., that " of establishing a medium of exchange for co-operative productions, and thus connecting in a close bond of union, the societies of all parts of the kingdom ". Your Committee, however, cannot but regret, that many societies, who by their delegates engaged to trade with the Company, from various causes, have not yet performed their engagements ; but they anticipate, that the causes which have prevented them, will speedily subside. This, however, has been the reason that your Committee could not carry several of the laws into effect, among the rest, that " of each trustee visiting Liverpool each week in rotation ". In order to save expence [sic] they have appointed one of their number, who lives nearest, to visit the store and transact the necessary business, and report from time to time to his colleagues ; and on matters of importance to call them together.

(b) From *The Pioneer*, March 29, 1834, p. 271.

SIR, I stated, some few weeks ago, that the members composing the Trades' Union of Leicester had begun to manufacture for themselves. The principal reasons why the operatives have taken this step is, they have long felt convinced that so long as men are taken on the funds, and kept in idleness, so long the employers will care nothing for a Union; but, find employment for the men, and it will very soon bring the masters to their senses. We have a good assortment of all sorts of worsted and cotton stockings; coloured worsted; white and brown cotton do., for the females in Union; black worsted, white and brown cotton stockings of every description, well fashioned, in quality very superior; also, men and women's white cotton gloves, with the letter U in the middle of the hand; the gloves are beautifully figured on the back of the hand. Two rooms are open at Mr. Chappell's, sign of the Trades' Union, as a depository for materials, and the sale of manufactured Union Goods wholesale and retail. We have a good Unionist turned out of work by his employer, who has begun to manufacture blacking of good quality, the lesser pots sixteen for one shilling; and we sincerely hope the members composing the great consolidated Union will give us all the encouragement they possibly can. Direct for Thomas Hartopp, Joseph Hurst, or Benjamin Norfolk, at Mr. Chappell's, sign of the Trades' Union, Bone-street, Leicester. Yours etc.

THOMAS HARTOPP.

LEICESTER, *March* 18, 1834.

9. EQUITABLE LABOUR EXCHANGES

[When Owen returned to England in 1829 he showed little enthusiasm for the stores; ' mere buying and selling ' was no part of his scheme. However, his interest was aroused by the development of Co-operative production. From 1831 the series of half-yearly Co-operative congresses offered Owen a platform for speeches on ' The New System of Society '. The Labour Exchanges were the fruit of this period of Co-operative production by Trade Unionists. The British Association in 1830 and a William King (not the Brighton King) early in 1832 had made unsuccessful attempts to carry on an Exchange system based on the London Co-operative movement. Then, rather against Owen's advice, the National Equitable Labour Exchange was started by the Owenites in September 1832. The pricing of the goods deposited was managed on two principles, first, that labour is the source of value and should determine price, each article being priced at so many hours' labour, and the labour of skilled craftsmen being counted as a multiple of that of unskilled workers, according to the prevailing wage differences. But it soon became clear not only that some goods were being priced too low and some too high, so that the cheap ones were rapidly purchased and the dear ones were left unsold, but also that, as Co-operative production existed only in a few trades, the Exchanges were overstocked with some goods and altogether unprovided with others their clients wanted : the Exchange could then not function properly as an exchange, if it could offer only a narrow range of goods. For a time, however, the ' Labour Notes ' for five hours, etc., circulated quite freely, even among local tradesmen. A branch was set up in South London and Exchanges were opened in Birmingham and Liverpool. A dispute with the landlord forced the London Exchange to find new premises in January 1833, and in July the management passed from Owen to the ' National Association of the United Trades of Great Britain and Ireland ' — in fact, a federation of the London Trade Clubs of skilled artisans (such as tailors, shoemakers, etc.). By the end of the year Owen had lost interest in the Exchange, being absorbed by his new enthusiasm for the Builders' Guild. In May 1834, when the whole Owenite movement was beginning to collapse, the Committee controlling the London Exchange ended its operations without consulting the members. The Birmingham Exchange wound up with a surplus, which it handed over to the Cottage Hospital. The Liverpool Exchange had become involved in an attempt by the Owenites to establish a Co-operative Wholesale Trading Society, which also collapsed in the general disaster of the Trade Union and Co-operative movements.]

(a) From *The Crisis*, June 30, 1832, p. 59.

Now hundreds of thousands of persons of all the various trades in existence, rise every morning without knowing how or where to procure employment. *They can* EACH *produce* MORE *than they have occasion for themselves*, and they are EACH IN WANT OF EACH OTHERS' SURPLUS PRODUCE.

The Agriculturalist can produce more wheat, oats, potatoes, bacon, cheese etc, than he can consume, and he requires, and is daily consuming — clothing, implements of husbandry, furniture etc., etc. The producers of these various articles are in want of his surplus produce, and of the surplus produce of each other ; the tailer being in want of shoes, the tinman in need of clothes, etc. etc.

The usual course pursued by these different persons to obtain the produce of each other has been, to convert their stock into money, by disposing of it to a moneyholder, or middle-man ; but should there be a scarcity of money, or the middle-man not feel inclined to take the produce offered, the producer must make a considerable sacrifice to obtain it, by giving a greater portion of his produce before he can get possession of the articles he requires ; thus being entirely dependent upon the middle-man — who always obtains a profit by retaining a part of the produce for himself, on every article that passes through his hands, to the manifest injury of the producer, who parts with his own produce at a disadvantage, and obtains that of another at an advanced price.

Now there is no necessity for this middle-man, producers can do without him — they merely want to come in contact with each other, and they can exchange their respective produce to their mutual advantage, and to the advantage of the general consumer, who may not be a producer, but has to exchange his money for their produce.

Thus, they will be able to obtain all the necessaries of life, and money also, when it may be needful.

They have only to fix upon a place where all their surplus produce can be deposited, to be exchanged for produce of similar value, and immediately the wants of the different parties can be supplied — and this too, on the equitable principle of *labour for equal value of labour.* . . . The place thus selected should be called an EQUITABLE BANK OF EXCHANGE.

(*b*) From *The Crisis*, June 30, 1832, p. 60.

All *wealth* proceeds from *labour and knowledge.*

And *labour* and *knowledge* are generally remunerated according to the *time employed.*

· Hence it is proposed, to make TIME *the standard, or the measure of wealth.* . . .

To return to the standard of value; it is known that the wages of the various trades differ from *ten shillings*, to *one shilling per day*. The average of these may be called *five shillings* per day — the great majority of all the most useful trades in the metropolis will be found only a trifle more or less than this average.

The time employed by the different trades, and called a *day*, is also various; it is desirable to reduce these varieties to one standard and for this purpose it is proposed that *ten hours shall constitute a day's labour*, and *each day* be valued at five shillings, making the *standard of labour, sixpence per hour.*

Now we know that all vocations which receive at the present time less wages than this standard will most readily accede to the principle, but the difficulty is whether those who are now receiving wages at, or more than this standard, will work on equal terms for those who do not receive this amount. But, if they consider that no union of trades can be complete without an entire circle of them can be formed, and in that case, the services of those who do not receive this amount, will be as necessary to that end as their own, it will be to their interest to consent to the measure.

Of course the above remark only applies to the labour of men, and not to that of females and children, whose labours must be remunerated according to their utility. . . . Labour, or time, added to the cost of materials, constitutes the commercial value of an article when completed for sale.

As it is not easy in practice to ascertain immediately the cost price of raw materials in hours, or the time and labour it has taken in passing through the various processes of growth and manufacture, the market price will for the present be the best by which to regulate its value.

It is proposed that notes representing the time or value of labour in the various articles to be exchanged, shall be the circulation medium to represent the amount of wealth deposited in the new Banks of Exchange.

This medium will have *three properties united* without which it cannot be just or beneficial, or fit for the purpose. These properties—

1st. The power of being *increased* precisely as real wealth is *increased*.

2ndly. The power of being *diminished* exactly as real wealth is *diminished*.

3dly. Of being *unchangeable* in its value.

Labour or Time being the only true standard of value, these notes alone can possess the above *three properties*.

The intrinsic value of an article is the labour or time necessary to produce or obtain it — and, in order to have that value correctly represented, a circulating medium ought to be employed for the exchange of these productions; which will represent accurately the labour or time required to produce them. *And such will be the properties of the New Note.*

(c) From *The Crisis*, June 7, 1834.

To the Editor of *The Crisis*,

Sir,—I beg leave, through the medium of your columns, to call the attention of the subscribers to the Labour Exchange-rent, and that of the friends of the Social System generally, to the present condition of the Institution in Charlotte-street. I would recall to their recollection the great outlay of money and labour which has been bestowed on that Institution; and although the results have not equalled the high expectations with which we set out, yet much has been done, and it would be unfair to say that all the labour and expense have been fruitless. By an advertisement in this week's *Crisis* (No. 8) I perceive that " all issues of notes on deposits have ceased ", and that " arrangements have been made for manufacturing according to the system of the Union ". I must confess that I do not quite understand this notice; I only clearly understand from it, that all the active operations of the National Equitable Labour Exchange Association are at an end, and that some other arrangements for some other and a different kind of business are in preparation. Now, I beg leave most deferentially to suggest to the committee the propriety of calling together, by advertisement and other public announcements, the original rent-payers, and those who by their money and exertions, contributed so much to the successful operations which were indisputably at one time carried on upon those premises. I think the committee are bound to take the sense of the constituency before they embark in any undertaking, other than that they were elected to conduct; I do not know that they have the power to sanction the converting of those premises to any new project, without consulting those in whom the present proprietorship of those premises exists, " the rent subscribers ". . . .

WILLIAM PEEL.

10. THE OPERATIVE BUILDERS, 1833–1834

[The Operative Builders' Union was founded in 1831 or 1832 as a federation of existing building unions. The seven main sections (Stonemasons, Plasterers, Plumbers and Glaziers, Carpenters, Bricklayers, Slaters, and Painters) retained considerable independence, but the final authority was the Grand Lodge — the ' Builders' Parliament ' — which met twice a year, and executive power lay with the Grand Committee which was appointed by the Grand Lodge.

The subsequent career of the Union arose from the peculiar conditions prevailing in the building trade. It had been usual for anyone who wanted a building erected to approach either directly or through an architect a member of each of the crafts required and make a separate contract, one for plumbing, one for painting, and so on. A painter would engage other painters and be to some extent a master, but he in turn might be engaged by one of his former employees, who had been given another contract, while there were some who had acquired a definite status as small masters, and were not themselves employed. This system gave the builders a sense of independence, which strongly influenced their theories of Trade Unionism. Recently the practice of ' general contracting ', whereby a major employer or ' contractor ' would arrange to find all the necessary labour, had spread from London to the leading provincial towns. It was against this ' general contracting ' that the Union launched its first attacks. Helped by the small masters, the operatives won initial successes. They became too confident of their strength, while the small masters were secretly deserting them. The masters were ready for the widespread Lancashire strike movement of 1833 and soon ' presented the Document '— demanding a promise to abandon Trades Unionism as a condition of employment. This attack was met by a solid strike. Meanwhile, Owenite principles had been making headway among the builders, and in September 1833 the ' Builders' Parliament ' of 500 delegates was persuaded, with the help of friendly Owenite architects, to set up a ' Builders' Guild ', which was to start Co-operative building schemes as a prelude to taking over the entire industry. The goal was a system of ' Workers' Control ', with the existing masters serving in the role of executive employees, where the Unions were prepared to accept them. The Builders' Guild immediately went into action on two fronts ; plans drawn up by the well-known architect, Joseph Aloysius Hansom, the inventor of the 'hansom' cab, for the Union Institute or Guildhall in Birmingham were adopted, and at the same time every encouragement was given to an aggressive industrial policy. But neither their organisation nor their finances could stand the dual strain. Early in 1834 men drifted back to work on the employers' terms and a halt was called to the building of the Birmingham Guildhall. The Union could not long survive the collapse of the Grand National Consolidated Trades Union in August 1834, and broke up into its component sections early in 1835.]

(*a*) From the Manifesto of the Operative Builders' Union, 1833. (Reproduced in R. W. Postgate's " Builders' History ", p. 463, from the Owen correspondence in the Co-operative Union Records, Manchester.)

. . . Seeing no prospect of any improvement in our condition, being also conscious that our most valuable materials are ignorantly wasted by being senselessly scattered throughout the four quarters of the world and that our industry and skill and unlimited powers of invention are now most grossly misdirected; we without any hostile feelings to the Government or any class of persons, have been compelled to come to the conclusion that no party can or will relieve us from the tremendous evils which we suffer and still greater which are coming upon us, until we begin in good earnest to act for ourselves and at once adopt the recommendation of Sir Robert Peel, " to take our own affairs into our own hands ".

We have decided to follow this advice and with this view we have formed ourselves into a National Building Guild of Brothers, to enable us to erect buildings of every description upon the most extensive scale in England, Scotland and Ireland.

By the arrangement and organisation which we have adopted we shall accomplish the following important results,

1st—We shall be enabled to erect all manner of dwellings and other architectural designs for the public more expeditiously, substantially and economically than any Masters can build them under the individual system of competition.

2nd—We shall be enabled to withdraw all our Brethren of the National Builders' Guild and their Families from being a burden upon the public, for they will be supported in old age, infancy, sickness or infirmity of any kind from the general funds of the Guild.

3rd—None of the Brethren will be unemployed when they desire to work, for when the public do not require their services they will be employed by the Guild to erect superior dwellings and other buildings for themselves, under superior arrangements, that they, their wives and their children may live continuously surrounded by those virtuous external circumstances which alone can form an intelligent, prosperous, good and happy population.

4th—We shall be enabled to determine upon a just and equitable remuneration or wages for the services of the Brethren according to their skill and conduct when employed by the public.

5th—We shall also be placed in a position to decide upon the amount of work or service to be performed, each day, by the Brethren, in order that none may be oppressed by labour beyond their powers of body or mind.

.   .   .   .

8th—We will form arrangements to enable all other classes of Producers of Real Wealth to unite with us to obtain equal advantages for themselves, their children and their children's children to the end of time.

(*b*) ' To the Master Builders of England '. From *The Pioneer*, September 14, 1833.

. . . We know that you have attributed to the unions a desire to level every existing establishment, and a disrespect to every existing form — that you have associated union and disorder together, and you have been alarmed at a figure of your own creation. Will you not be surprised when we announce to you, that the union has only one object, and that is, the protection of every interest in the state and your interest in common with the rest : and that your interests will be, upon the laws of the union, more safe and permanently secured, than upon any ground that has hitherto existed ? There is not a master builder in England who may not associate himself with the union, and from such association date his freedom from care, and that responsibility and liability to loss which has disturbed every mind, under circumstances such as the master builders have been obliged to endure. . . .

We invite you to come forward at this eventful time, and offer yourselves as directors or agents to the workmen, and fix for yourselves a per centage of profit on whatever is undertaken under your guidance, and upon the capital you may advance. We invite you to consider yourselves as members of one great family, and to make the interests of that family your primary end, and to do away with the rivalry which has hitherto produced so much discord. We know that you have no other road to safety, and that justice will incline you to come to this.

(c) Form of Declaration suggested by an Operative Builders' Union branch. From *The Pioneer*, September 14, 1833.

To the Editor of *The Pioneer*

I send you enclosed a copy of a Form of Declaration of Independence, which it appears to me would be well to be adopted by the members of the Lodges of the Trades' Unions generally.

FORM OF A DECLARATION OF INDEPENDENCE

We, the delegates of several lodges in the Building Trades, elected for the purposes of correcting the abuses which have crept into the modes of undertaking and transacting business, do hereby give you notice that you will receive no assistance from the working men in any of our bodies, to enable you to fulfil an engagement which you have entered into, unless you comply with the following conditions.

Aware that it is our labour alone that can carry into effect what you have undertaken, we cannot but view ourselves as parties to your engagement, if that engagement be ever fulfilled ; and as you had no authority from us to make such an engagement, nor had you any legitimate right to barter our labour at prices fixed by yourself, we call upon you to exhibit to our several bodies your detailed estimates of quantities and prices at which you have taken the work ;

and we call upon you to arrange with us a fixed per centage of profits for your own services in conducting the building, and in finding the material on which our labour is to be applied.

Should we find upon examination, that you have fixed equitable prices, which will not only remunerate you for your superintendence, but us for our toil, we have no objections, upon a clear understanding, to become parties to the contract, and will see you through it ; — after having entered yourself a member of our body, and after your having been duly *elected* to occupy the office you have *assumed*.

(*d*) From " Brief History of the Operative Building Trades Union ", 1833.

THE DOCUMENT, 1833.

We, the undersigned . . . do hereby declare that we are not in any way connected with the General Union of the Building Trades and that we do not and will not contribute to the support of such members of the said union as are or may be out of work in consequence of belonging to such union.

11. THE GRAND NATIONAL CONSOLIDATED TRADES UNION

[At a delegate meeting held in London in October 1833, a draft plan for a General Union of the Productive Classes, drawn up by Robert Owen, was discussed, and arrangements were made for a conference in Barnsley the following March. But in February, a conference in London, convened apparently on Owen's initiative, set up the Grand National Consolidated Trades Union, framed its constitution, and elected its executive.

None of the four major Unions of the time — the Builders, the Potters, the Spinners, and the Clothiers (the Leeds, Huddersfield and Bradford District Union) — agreed to join, and in fact the Grand National lacked the backing of the majority of the organised workers, as far as its industrial aims were concerned. Whatever the ordinary members had in mind as the prime objective of the Union, Owen and a large number of its leading figures hoped to use it for the introduction of a new society, based on the principle of Co-operative production by the Unions. But while Owen envisaged a peaceful movement of collaboration with the masters, James Morrison (*d.* 1835) [1] and James Elishama Smith (1801–1857) [2] adopted

---

[1] One of the Builders' leaders, and editor of *The Pioneer*, the Trades Union journal.

[2] Editor of the Owenite journal, *The Crisis*, and later of *The Shepherd* and of *The Family Herald* : known in later life as ' Shepherd Smith ' and an active religious revivalist : at this earlier date author of remarkable Socialist articles in *The Crisis* and *The Pioneer*.

a Syndicalist viewpoint, demanding workers' control and expecting a struggle to obtain it. The leaders of the movement wanted ' peaceful methods for a season '. But the rank and file pressed for immediate action, local strikes, and the great Derby Turn-out (a lock-out in which the masters demanded that the men should renounce the Union), which had begun in the autumn of 1833, used up all available funds and exposed the inefficiency of the organisation. The prosecution of the Tolpuddle Martyrs in March 1834 shook again the foundation of Trade Union rights, and for a while a brief spell of great unity was enjoyed, and the Unions outside the ' Grand National ' collaborated in defence of the prisoners. Collapse ultimately came, less through legal prosecutions than from the determined opposition of the employers, the weakness of internal organisation, and quarrels between Owen and his chief lieutenants. Owen became increasingly alarmed at the class-war tone of many of the Union's pronouncements, and wound up *The Crisis*. He also deprived *The Pioneer* of its position as the organ of the ' Grand National '. Finally, in the hour of defeat, he dissolved the organisation in August 1834, and formed a new association for Co-operative and Socialist propaganda, based on local Owenite groups and Co-operative bodies rather than on the Trade Unions.]

(*a*) The Owenite Programme. From a speech by Robert Owen, *The Crisis*, October 19, 1833.

The members of this Union have discovered that competition in the sale of their productions is the chief and immediate cause of their poverty and degradation, and that they can never overcome either as long as they shall conduct their affairs individually, and in opposition to each other.

They are, therefore, about to form national companies of production ; each trade or manufacture to constitute one grand company or association, comprising all the individuals in the business throughout Great Britain and Ireland ; but each trade and manufacture to be united to all the others by a general bond of interest by which they will exchange their productions with each other upon a principle of equitable exchange of labour for a fair equal value of labour ; and all articles, upon a principle of economy and general advantage, will be produced of the best quality only.

The next step in gradation will be the union of the master traders and manufacturers with the operatives and manual producers ; and when these two parties shall fully understand the value of this union, the Government will not only feel the necessity of uniting with them, but it will also discover the advantages to the whole empire of this national bond of union.

(*b*) Universal Suffrage. From leading articles in *The Pioneer*, May 31 and June 7, 1834.

The Poor Man's Guardian says that at last we are beginning to advocate Universal Suffrage. Beginning — we never advocated any other doctrine; we have been advocates for universal suffrage ever since the Pioneer had a being. Universal suffrage is the fundamental principle of a Trades Union, where every brother is understood to have a voice in the management of the common affairs of the trade. But it is a universal suffrage which begins with the elements of government and not, like the democratic principle of the Guardian and his friends, with the universal business of political legislation. At the moment the working classes are too ignorant of political economy, etc. to have an immediate claim for an equal share in the management of state affairs. . . . The Unions are of all other modes the only mode by which universal suffrage can safely be obtained, because it is obtained by practice, or, in the language of the trade, by serving an apprenticeship. Nothing but experience can conduct any system of policy with success, and experience of government is better acquired by commencing with the management of simple business in which we are skilled by partial success, than in launching into an ocean of business, without a chart to guide or a gale of wind to lend us an impulse. . . . Besides, such is our opinion of the growing power and growing intelligence of a Trades Union, that we are thoroughly convinced that when it is sufficiently organised, and conducted in an orderly and business-like manner, it will gradually draw into its vortex all the commercial interests of the country, and, in so doing, it will become by its own self-acquired importance, a most influential, we might almost say dictatorial, part of the body politic. When this happens, we have gained all that we want; we have gained universal suffrage; for if every member of the Union be a constituent, and the Union itself become a vital and influential member of the state, it instantly erects itself into a House of Trades, which must supply the place of the present House of Commons, and direct the commercial affairs of the country, according to the will of the trades who compose the association of industry. . . .

The house for particular trades is a real House of Commons, composed of tradesmen only — not a single individual being there who is not or has not, been a producer, skilled in some species of handicraft, and delegated by his own Union to represent their interests in Parliament. Thus, the shoemakers' Union would send a number of representatives, proportioned to the number of individuals employed in the trade; the carpenters, tailors, builders, &c. a similar proportion, so that in this House of Trades there should be an assemblage of all productive knowledge ready for use, as occasion required, and not, as now, to be called in for the benefit of the legislators, who presumptuously sit down to pass laws upon trade and commerce, without having a practical man amongst them, and without the technical skill to understand the evidence of a practical man when he is called before them. In this House of Trades we should have all knowledge necessary for the conduct of the separate divisions of productive industry. But how can we get such a House of Trades, without a Trades Union? If the various trades do not unite, how can they ever send their delegates to represent them? They never can; universal suffrage without Trades Unions would be universal hubbub. . . .

Having got universal suffrage and a House of Trades, by means of Trades Unions, let us now see how we should make up the other house. Let that be composed of the delegates of all the rest of the community; let the rich and the noble unite themselves as they think proper and find representatives for themselves to act in concert with the trades — the one party to assist and act as a check upon the other. . . .

(c) From the Rules of the Grand National Consolidated Trades Union, 1834. From a copy in the Goldsmiths' Library, University of London.

Rules and Regulations of the Grand National Consolidated Trades Union of Great Britain and Ireland, instituted for the purpose of the more effectively enabling the working classes to receive, protect and establish the rights of industry.

GENERAL PLAN AND GOVERNMENT

I. Each Trade in this Consolidated Union shall have its Grand Lodge in that town or city most eligible for it, such Grand Lodge to be governed internally by a Grand Master, Deputy Grand Master, and Grand Secretary, and a Committee of Management.

II. Each Grand Lodge shall have its District Lodges, in any number, to be designated or named after the town or city in which the District Lodge is founded.

III. Each Grand Lodge shall be considered the head of its own particular trade, and to have certain exclusive powers accordingly; but in all other respects the Grand Lodges are to answer the same ends as the District Lodges.

IV. Each District Lodge shall embrace within itself all operatives of the same trade, living in smaller towns or villages adjacent to it, and shall be governed internally by a president, vice-president, secretary, and a committee of management.

V. Each District Lodge shall have (if necessary) its Branch Lodge or Lodges, numbered in rotation; such Branch Lodges to be under the control of the District Lodge from which they sprung.

VI. An unlimited number of the above-described Lodges shall form and constitute the Grand National Consolidated Trades Union of Great Britain and Ireland.

VII. Each District shall have its Central Committee, composed of a Deputy, or Deputies, from every District Lodge of the different trades in the district; such Central Committee shall meet once in every week to superintend and watch over the interests of the Consolidated Union in that District, transmitting a report of the same, monthly, to the Executive Council in London, together with any suggestions of improvements they may think proper.

VIII. The General government of the G.N.C.T.U. shall be vested in a Grand Council of Delegates from each of the Central Committees of all the Districts in the Consolidated Union, to be holden every six months, at such places as shall be decided upon at the preceding Council; the next meeting of the Grand Council of the Consolidated Union to be held on the first day of September, 1834, and to continue its sitting so long as may be requisite.

IX. During the recess of the Grand Council of Delegates, the government of the Consolidated Union shall be vested in an Executive Council of five; which executive will in future be chosen at the Grand Delegate Council aforesaid.

X. All dispensations or grants for the formation of new Lodges shall come from the Grand Lodge of each particular trade, or from the Executive Council. Applications to come through the Central Committee of the District or by memorial, signed by at least twenty operatives of the place where such new Lodge is proposed to be founded.

XI. The Executive Council shall act as trustees for all funds provided by the Consolidated Union, and for the adjustment of strikes, the purchasing or renting of land, establishing provision stores, workshops, etc.; or for any other purpose connected with the general benefit of the whole of the Union.

XII. All sums for the above purposes to be transmitted from the

Lodges to the Executive Council through some safe and accredited medium.

XIII. District and Grand Lodges shall have the control of their own funds, subject to the levies imposed on them by the Executive Council.

XIV. The ordinary weekly subscription of members to be three-pence each member.

XV. No strike or turn-out for an *advance* of wages shall be made by the members of any Lodge in the Consolidated Union without the consent of the Executive Council; but in all cases of a *reduction* of wages the Central Committee of the District shall have the power of deciding whenever a strike shall or shall not take place, and should such Central Committee be necessitated to order a levy in support of such strike brought on by such reduction of wages, such order shall be made in all the Lodges; in the first instance, in the District in which such reduction hath taken place, and on advice being forwarded to the Executive they shall consider the case, and order accordingly.

· · · · · · ·

XXI. In all cases of strikes or turn-outs, where it is practicable to employ members in the making or producing of such commodities or articles as are in demand among their brother Unionists, or any other operatives willing to purchase the same, each Lodge shall provide a workroom or shop in which such commodities and articles may be manufactured on account of that Lodge, which shall make proper arrangements for the supply of the necessary materials; over which arrangements the Central Committee of the District shall have the control, subject to the scrutiny of the Grand Lodge Committee of the trade on strike.

(*d*) ' Senex ' [J. E. Smith] on Wage Slavery. From *The Pioneer*, June 14, 1834.

. . . Your present object must be to change your wages into a fair share of profits of the productive concern in which you are employed. This is the object of Trades Unions, if they have any rational object at all — and I do not see why it is not at once openly avowed. I would banish the word wages from the language, and consign it with the word slavery, to historians and dictionaries. Wages is a term of purchase; it means the piecemeal purchase of your blood, and bones, and brains, at weekly payments; it is the present name for the Saturday's market price of man, woman and child !

12. THE YORKSHIRE TRADES' UNION

[The Yorkshire Trade Unionists had been following a course of their own during the years covered by, first, John Doherty's and then Robert Owen's attempts to form a ' General Union '. Both Doherty's N.A.P.L. and Owen's ' Grand National ' were organised quite openly, whereas the Clothiers' Union, centred at Leeds, was a secret society. This course had been forced on the Yorkshiremen by the action of the employers, many of whom from 1825 had entered into a bond to discharge all known Trades Unionists and their children. This anti-Union movement had begun in the worsted trade, and had led to a great stoppage in 1825, in which the workers were defeated. When Richard Oastler launched, in 1830, his crusade against ' Factory Slavery ', the Yorkshire workers threw themselves into the ' Short Time Movement ', which was carried on openly, but also kept their secret Trade Union organisation. The Yorkshire Trades' Union, from 1831 onwards, was engaged in a series of bitter struggles with the employers in the woollen and worsted trades, who continued their endeavours to break it by means of the ' bond '. The Union, on its side, set out to organise workers in other trades and outside Yorkshire ; and in 1833–1834 there was much confusion between its organising efforts and those of the ' Grand National ', some local groups being unaware of the difference, and not knowing which they had joined. With the rise of the ' Grand National ', the Yorkshire masters redoubled their efforts to destroy ' the Trades' Union ', and a great lock-out in 1834, coinciding with the rise and fall of the ' Grand National ', ended in the defeat of the workers and in the disappearance of the Yorkshire Trades' Union — though many of its constituent units survived as independent local societies. The only full account of the movement is in G. D. H. Cole's " Attempts at General Union ", published in 1939 at Amsterdam as a monograph in the " International Review for Social History ".

The Yorkshire Trades' Union and its constituent societies, like many other Unions which had grown up during the period of repression, used Initiation Ceremonies and administered oaths of secrecy. The Ceremony used by the Woolcombers' Union, which was a part of it, is here reproduced.]

(*a*) From " The Character, Objects and Effects of Trades' Unions " (1834), p. 42. (Reproduced in " Attempts at General Union, 1829–34 ", by G. D. H. Cole, " International Review for Social History ", 1939.)

OATH TAKEN BY A MEMBER OF A " YORKSHIRE UNION "

" I do, by Almighty God and this Loyal Lodge, most solemnly swear that I will not work for any master that is not in the Union, nor will I work with any illegal man or men, but will do my best for the support of wages ; and most solemnly swear to keep inviolate all the secrets of this Order; nor will I ever consent to have any money for any purpose but for the use of the Lodge and support of the trade; nor will I write, or cause to be wrote, print, mark, either on stone, marble, brass, paper or sand, anything connected with this Order, so help me God, and keep me steadfast in this my present obligation ; and I further promise to do my best to bring all legal men that I am concerned with into this Order; and if ever I reveal any of the rules may what is before me plunge my soul into eternity ".

(b) Initiation Ceremony, Enacted on the Reception of Members into the Wool-Combers' Union.[1] From " The Character, Objects and Effects of Trades' Unions ", 1834.

DRAMATIS PERSONAE

OUTSIDE TILER, a member of the Union who keeps guard on the outside of the room in which the members are assembled.

INSIDE TILER, ditto, on the inside.

PRINCIPAL CONDUCTOR, the person who conducts to the Lodge those who are to be initiated into the mysteries of the Union.

PRESIDENT, VICE-PRESIDENT, WARDEN, SECRETARY, MEMBERS OF THE UNION, WORKMEN ABOUT TO BE MADE MEMBERS.

Members say the following prayer

O God, who art the author of peace and lover of concord, defend us in this our undertaking, that we may not fear the power of our adversaries, through the merits of Jesus Christ, our Lord. Amen.

Outside Tiler knocks at the door

INSIDE TILER : Who comes here to disturb the peace and harmony of this our most worthy and honourable order ?

PRINCIPAL CONDUCTOR (from without) : I am not come here to

---

[1] The text here given is taken from a hostile source, being quoted from the anti-Trade Union pamphlet entitled " The Character, Objects, and Effects of Trades' Unions ". The pamphlet gives the following explanation : " The scene is usually the first floor of a tavern, which is doubly planked throughout, and the interstices filled with wood shavings in order to prevent any one overhearing the ceremonies. The time is 8 or 9 o'clock in the evening, at which hour the above-named *dramatis personae* with the exception of the principal conductor, and those who are about to enter the Union, are supposed to be collected together for the performance of the following drama. On one side of the apartment is a skeleton, above which is a drawn sword and a battle-axe, and in front stands a table, upon which lies a Bible. The principal officers of the Union are clothed in surplices.

disturb the peace and harmony of this your most worthy and honourable order. I am a brother, with strangers who wish to be admitted into your most worthy and honourable order.

INSIDE TILER : Most worthy President, Vice-, Secretary, and brothers all, a brother stands at the door with strangers, who wish to be admitted into this your most worthy and honourable order.

PRESIDENT : In the name of the Lord, admit him.

> *Enter Principal Conductor, followed by the strangers with their eyes bandaged. Members salute, and then sing a hymn*

PRINCIPAL CONDUCTOR :

Strangers, within our secret walls we have admitted you,
Hoping you will prove honest, faithful, just and true,
If you cannot keep the secrets we require,
Go hence, you are at liberty to retire.
Are your motives pure ?

STRANGERS : Yes.

PRINCIPAL CONDUCTOR : Do you declare they are ?

STRANGERS : Yes.

PRINCIPAL CONDUCTOR : Then, brethren, to initiate these strangers we will now proceed,
And our most worthy master may proceed to read.

> *Members sing a hymn*

WARDEN : Stand, ye presumptuous mortals, strangers' steps I hear,
And I must know your trade and business here.
By my great power, there's nothing can from vengeance stay us,
If you come here intending to betray us.

PRESIDENT : Most worthy guardian of our sacred laws,
They're wool-combers, and wishful to protect the united cause.

WARDEN : Then all is well.

VICE-PRESIDENT : Strangers, you're welcome, and if you prove sincere,
You'll not repent your pains and labour here.
We have one common interest, and one common soul,
Which should by virtue guide and actuate the whole.
Our trade requires protection, by experience sad we know ;
Our duty is to prevent recurrence of our former woe.
Our commonwealth was like some savage land,
Where the weaker slaves, and strongest bear command,

Where tyrants rule with uncontrolled sway,
And degraded subjects do their will obey.
Such was our domestic lot, our suffering and our care
Enraged our minds with sadness and despair.
And when we'd united and our rights obtained,
We found that only half our point was gained,
Our interests were so many and so various,
The tenure of our rights so frail and so precarious,
That had we not invented Lodges our protection to ensure,
All, all would have come to nought, as it had done before.
Strangers, the design of all our Lodges is love and unity,
With self-protection founded or the laws of equity,
And when you have our mystic rights gone through,
Our secrets all will be disclosed to you.
We deem you worthy our friendship, trust and confidence to share,
See that you make the prosperity of our cause your constant care.
Let your tongue be always faithful, your heart conceal its trust,
Woe, woe and dishonour attend the faithless and unjust.
Guards, give the strangers sight.

> *The bandages are removed from the eyes of the strangers, and they are placed opposite the skeleton.*

PRESIDENT : (*pointing to the skeleton*) :
Strangers, mark well this shadow, which you see,
It is a faithful emblem of man's destiny.
Behold that head, once filled with pregnant wit,
These hollow holes once sparkling eyes did fit ;
This empty mouth nor lips nor tongue contains,
Of a once well furnished head, see all that now remains.
Behold this breast, where a generous heart once moved,
Filled with affection, loving and beloved,
Mark well these bones, the flesh hath left its place ;
These arms could once a tender wife embrace.
These legs in gay activity could roam,
But, alas ! the spirit's dead, the life is gone.
O death ! O death ! Thy terrors strike us with dismay.
Only the spirit just, which hath left its empty clay,
Can set thee at defiance and in triumph say,
O death, where is thy sting ?   O grave, where is thy victory ?
The sting of death is sin — are we not sinners all ?
Then upon us one day the heavy stroke of death must fall.

VICE-PRESIDENT : Strangers, hear me ; and mark well what I say,
Be faithful to your trust, or you may rue this day.
You are now within our secret walls, and I must know if you can keep a secret.

STRANGERS : Yes.

VICE-PRESIDENT : And will you do it ?

STRANGERS : Yes.

VICE-PRESIDENT :

Then amongst us, you will shortly be entitled to the endearing name of brother,
And what you hear or see here done, you must not disclose to any other ;
We are uniting to cultivate friendship as well as to protect our trade,
And due respect must to all our laws be paid.
Hoping you will prove faithful, and all encroachments on our rights withstand,
As a token of your alliance, — give me your hand.

And now, shouldst thou ever prove deceitful, remember thy end, remember. Guards, put these strangers into darkness, and conduct them to our most worthy master, to be further instructed in this our most worthy and honourable order.

> *The eyes of the strangers are again bandaged, and they are then made to walk several times round the room, while the members stamp on the floor with their feet. They are then led to the table, upon which the Bible is placed ; the right hand of each is placed upon the sacred volume : the bandages are then removed from their eyes, and they take the following oath :*

I, A. B., woolcomber, being in the awful presence of Almighty God, do voluntarily declare that I will persevere in endeavouring to support a brotherhood, known by the name of the Friendly Society of Operative Stuff Manufacturers, and other Industrious Operatives, and I solemnly declare and promise that I will never act in opposition to the brotherhood in any of their attempts to support wages, but will, to the utmost of my power, assist them in all lawful and just occasions, to obtain a fair remuneration for our labour. And I call upon God to witness this my most solemn declaration, that neither hopes, fears, rewards, punishments, nor even death itself, shall ever induce me directly or indirectly, to give any information respecting any thing contained in this Lodge, or any similar Lodge connected with the Society; and I will neither write nor cause to be written, upon paper, wood, sand, stone, or any thing else, whereby it may be known, unless allowed to do so by the proper authorities of the Society. And I will never give my consent to have any money belonging to the Society divided or appropriated to any other purpose than the use of the Society and support of the trade, so help me God, and keep me steadfast in this my most solemn obligation; and if ever I reveal either part or parts of this most solemn obligation, may all the Society I am about to belong to, and all that is just, disgrace me so long as I live; and may what is now before me plunge my soul into the everlasting pit of misery. Amen.

VICE-PRESIDENT : Guards, put these strangers into darkness. Rise and stand. (*To the strangers*).

> *The strangers having been blindfolded, the members sing a hymn, and then salute. The strangers are then led out. Members then say the following prayer:*

O God, who art the author of peace, etc. (*same as at the commencement*).

PRESIDENT : In the name of King Edward the Third [1], I declare this Lodge to be now duly closed, and so it is.

God save our noble King,
William the Fourth let's sing,
Brethren, ere we depart, let us join hand and heart
In this our cause;
May our next meeting be blest with sweet harmony,
Honour, and secrecy in the Mechanic's cause.

Exeunt

(c) A Letter from the Home Office. From *The Poor Man's Guardian*, September 14, 1833. (Reproduced from " Attempts at General Union, 1829–34 ", by G. D. H. Cole, " International Review for Social History ", 1931).

". . . I am directed by Viscount Melbourne to acknowledge the receipt of your letter of the 17th of August, together with the memorial of the merchants, manufacturers, etc., of the West Riding of the County of York, and to express his Lordship's regret that the great importance of the subject to which his attention is called thereby, as well as the general pressure of public business, has prevented him from sending an earlier reply.

[1] Because the woollen manufacture was supposed to have been introduced in Edward III's reign.

As his Lordship has often before expressed it in Parliament, he considers it unnecessary to repeat the strong opinion entertained by his Majesty's ministers of the criminal character and the evil effects of the Unions described in the Memorial, upon the interests of the masters, the workmen themselves, and the country in general.

Many of the acts mentioned are in themselves actual breaches of the law, and no doubt can be entertained that combinations for the purposes enumerated are illegal conspiracies, and liable to be prosecuted as such at common law.

In reply to the request of advice and council, his Lordship has only to observe that proceedings of this nature can only be successfully encouraged by concession and weakness. You may rely that the Government will take the most prompt and efficient measures to repress disorder, to punish crime, and to secure the effectual execution of the law; but the local knowledge and experience of the memorialists themselves will better suggest to them the precise measures which they should adopt, and the course which it will be most expedient for them to pursue."

13. THE NATIONAL REGENERATION SOCIETY

[Meanwhile, the Lancashire workers, though some of them threw in their lot with the ' Grand National ', had been largely occupied with the Society for National Regeneration, founded in 1833, with John Doherty, Robert Owen, William Cobbett, and John Fielden, the Radical cotton spinner of Todmorden, among its principal supporters. Instead of seeking the Ten Hours' Day from Parliament, the factory workers were urged to take matters into their own hands by a concerted refusal to work for more than *eight* hours. The leaders of the Ten Hours' Movement were strongly opposed to this step, which was based largely on disappointment with the provisions of the Factory Act of 1833. The National Regeneration Society shared the fate of the rest of the Owenite movement, and no more was heard of its projects after 1834.]

Resolutions of the Society for Promoting National Regeneration, November 25, 1833. From *The Pioneer*, p. 109.

It was unanimously resolved

1. That it is desirable that all who wish to see society improved, and confusion avoided, should endeavour to assist the working classes to obtain " for eight hours work the present full day's wages ",

such eight hours to be performed between the hours of six in the morning and six in the evening; and that this new regulation should commence on the 1st day of March next.

2. That, in order to carry the foregoing purposes into effect, a society should be formed, to be called " The Society for Promoting National Regeneration ".

3. That persons be immediately appointed from among the workmen to visit their fellow-workmen in each trade, manufacture, and employment, in every district of the kingdom, for the purpose of communicating with them on the subject of the above resolutions, and of inducing them to determine upon their adoption.

4. That persons be also appointed to visit the master manufacturers in each trade, in every district, to explain and recommend to them the adoption of the new regulation referred to in the first resolution.

.   .   .   .   .   .

15. That Messrs. Oastler, Wood, Bull, Sadler, and others, be urgently requested to desist from soliciting parliament for a ten hours bill, and to use their utmost exertions in aid of the measures now adopted to carry into effect, on the 1st of March next, the regulation of " eight hours work for the present full day's wages ".

14. THE TOLPUDDLE MARTYRS

[Late in 1833 George Loveless, a labourer and Methodist preacher, with a small group of followers formed a Friendly Society of Agricultural Labourers at Tolpuddle, in Dorsetshire, encouraged thereto by a visit from travelling delegates from an unspecified ' Trade Society ' — possibly one of the numerous offshoots of the secret Yorkshire Union, which had been sending its emissaries far and wide, or possibly the still embryonic ' Grand National '. Loveless made use of some sort of Initiation Ceremony recommended by these delegates ; and his Society seems to have established some connection with the ' Grand National '. The magistrates, hearing of what had been done through a spy, posted up placards threatening those who joined the Society with transportation, and arrested Loveless and five others, who, after a thoroughly unfair trial before a biased judge and jury, were sentenced under the Act of 1797 forbidding ' unlawful oaths ' and, by order of the Whig Government, were rushed out of the country before the national protest movement which speedily followed had had time to gather force. Despite the widespread protests, organised by a ' London Dorchester Committee ' with William Lovett at its head,

[*continued on page 286*

(a) The Tolpuddle Martyrs: Placard. From "The Book of the Martyrs of Tolpuddle, 1834-1934" (T.U.C. General Council, 1934), p. 12.

CAUTION

Whereas it has been represented to us from several quarters, that mischievous and designing Persons have been for some time past, endeavouring to induce, and have induced, many Labourers in various Parishes, in this County, to attend Meetings, and to enter into Illegal Societies or Unions, to which they bind themselves by unlawful oaths, administered secretly by Persons concealed, who artfully deceive the ignorant and unwary, —

WE, the undersigned Justices think it our duty to give this PUBLIC NOTICE and CAUTION, that all Persons may know the danger they incur by entering into such Societies.

ANY PERSON who shall become a Member of such a Society, or take any Oath, or assent to any Test or Declaration not authorized by Law—

Any Person who shall administer, or be present at, or consenting to the administering or taking any Unlawful Oath, or who shall cause such Oath to be administered, although not actually present at the time—

Any Person who shall not reveal or discover any Illegal Oath which may have been administered, or any Illegal Act done or to be done—

Any Person who shall induce, or endeavour to persuade any other Person to become a Member of such Societies,

WILL BECOME

GUILTY OF FELONY,

AND BE LIABLE TO BE

TRANSPORTED FOR SEVEN YEARS

ANY PERSON who shall be compelled to take such an Oath, unless he shall declare the same within four days, together with the whole of what he shall know touching the same, will be liable to the same Penalty.

Any Person who shall directly or indirectly maintain correspondence or intercourse with such Society, will be deemed Guilty of an Unlawful Combination and Confederacy, and on Conviction before one Justice, on the Oath of one Witness, be liable to a Penalty of TWENTY POUNDS, or to be committed to the Common Gaol or House of Correction, for THREE CALENDAR MONTHS; or, if proceeded against by Indictment, may be CONVICTED OF FELONY, and be TRANSPORTED FOR SEVEN YEARS.

Any Person who shall knowingly permit any Meeting of any such Society to be held in any House, Building, or other Place, shall for the first offence be liable to the Penalty of FIVE POUNDS; and for every other offence committed after Conviction, be deemed Guilty of such Unlawful Combination and Confederacy, and on Conviction before one Justice, on the Oath of one Witness, be liable to a Penalty of TWENTY POUNDS, or to Commitment to the Common Gaol or House of Correction, FOR THREE CALENDAR MONTHS; or if proceeded against by Indictment may be

CONVICTED OF FELONY

AND TRANSPORTED FOR SEVEN YEARS

C. B. WOLLASTON	HENRY FRAMPTON
JAMES FRAMPTON	RICHD. TUCKER STEWARD
WILLIAM ENGLAND	WILLIAM R. CHURCHILL
THOS. DADE	AUGUSTUS FOSTER

JNO. MORTON COLSON

COUNTY OF DORSET
Dorchester Division

February 22d, 1834.

G. Clark, Printer, Cornhill, Dorchester.

the Government refused to take any action to undo the sentences until the great Trade Union movement had been crushed. Only in 1838 was a free pardon issued by the Government, and not till 1839 did the last of the men get back to England. A fund was then raised by the Trade Unions to settle them on farms ; and they took some part in the Chartist movement, but subsequently (except James Hammett) emigrated to Canada.

The sentence passed on the Tolpuddle Martyrs was a severe blow to the Trade Union movement. Although the ' Grand National ' at once discontinued all ceremonies of initiation, the fear of the law drove many workers out of the movement and helped to ensure its collapse.]

(*b*) From George Loveless, " Victims of Whiggery " (1837), p. 5.

About the years 1831–2, when there was a general movement of the working classes for an increase of wages, the labouring men in the parish where I lived (Tolpuddle) gathered together, and met their employers, to ask them for an advance of wages, and they came to a mutual agreement, the masters in Tolpuddle promising to give the men as much for their labour as the other masters in the district. The whole of the men then went to their work, and the time that was spent on this affair did not exceed two hours. No language of intimidation or threatening was used on the occasion. Shortly after we learnt that, in almost every place around us, the masters were giving their men money, or money's worth, to the amount of ten shillings per week — we expected to be entitled to as much — but no — nine shillings must be our portion. After some months we were reduced to eight shillings per week. This caused great dissatisfaction, and all the labouring men in the village, with the exception of two or three invalids, made application to a neighbouring magistrate, namely, William Morden Pitt, Esq. of Kingston House, and asked his advice ; he told us that if the labourers would appoint two or three, and come to the county hall the following Saturday, he would apprise the chief magistrate, James Frampton, Esq. (whose name I shall not soon forget) and at the same time our employers should be sent for to settle the subject. I was one nominated to appear, and when there we were told that we must work for what our employers thought fit to give us, as there was no law to compel masters to give any fixed sum of money to their servants. In vain we remonstrated that an agreement was made, and that the minister of the parish (Dr. Warren) was witness between the masters and the men ; for this hireling parson, who at that time said, of his own accord, " I am witness between you men and your masters, that if you will go quietly to your work, you shall receive for your labour as much as any men in the district; and if your masters should attempt to run from their word I will undertake to see you righted, so help me God ! " — so soon as reference was made to him, denied having a knowledge of any such thing.

From this time we were reduced to seven shillings per week, and shortly after our employers told us they must lower us to six shillings per week. The labouring men consulted together what had better be done, as they knew it was impossible to live honestly on such scanty means. I had seen at different times accounts of Trade Societies; I told them of this and they willingly consented to form a friendly society among the labourers, having sufficiently learnt that it would be vain to seek redress either of employers, magistrates or parsons. I inquired of a brother to get information how to proceed, and shortly after, two delegates from a Trade Society paid us a visit, formed a Friendly Society among the labourers, and gave us directions how to proceed. This was about the latter end of October 1833. On the 9th of December, 1833, in the evening, Edward Legg (a labourer) who was witness against us on our trial, came and desired to be admitted into the Society; by what means he was introduced there I cannot say; but well do I know that James Hammett, one of the six that he swore to, was not there.

Nothing particular occurred from this time to the 21st of February, 1834, when placards were posted up at the most conspicuous places, purporting to be cautions from the magistrates, threatening to punish with seven years' transportation any man who should join the Union. This was the first time that I heard of any law being in existence to forbid such societies. . . .

[We were arrested on the 24th of February and were taken for our trial on the 15th of March.]

As to the trial, I need not mention but little; the cowardice and dastardly conduct throughout are better known by all that were present than could be by any description that I can give of it; suffice it to say, the most unfair and unjust means were resorted to in order to frame an indictment against us; the grand jury appeared to ransack heaven and earth to get some clue against us, but in vain; our characters were investigated from our infancy to the then present moment; our masters were inquired of to know if we were not idle, or attended public houses or some other fault in us; and much as they were opposed to us, they had common honesty enough to declare that we were good labouring servants, and that they never heard of any complaint against us, and when nothing whatever could be raked together, the unjust and cruel judge, Williams, ordered us to be tried for mutiny and conspiracy, under an act of 37 Geo III Cap 123, for the suppression of mutiny among the marines and seamen, a number of years ago, at the Nore.

15. THE DISSOLUTION OF THE ' GRAND NATIONAL '

[Owen, though he inspired the ' Grand National ', was not at the outset a member of it. He joined it only when the sentence on the Tolpuddle Martyrs presented a decisive challenge to the entire Trade Union movement. He then took a leading part in the protest against the sentences, and attempted to hold the Union together. But by August it had become evident that the ' Grand National ' was breaking up ; and Owen, without securing the assent of the membership, announced its dissolution. A section of the leadership attempted to carry on the Union ; but by 1835 both the ' Grand National ' and the Yorkshire Trades' Union had been finally broken.]

(*a*) From *The Crisis*, May 3, 1834.

THE FUTILITY OF PARTIAL STRIKES

Strikes after strikes in thick succession rise. Last week our attention was engaged by a formidable strike at Oldham, and by the termination of the long continued strike of Derby, whose fatal issue might almost have deterred the working classes from ever after engaging in such unequal contests with their employers, before their Union was sufficiently complete to have a long strike and a strong strike and a strike all together. The evil of all these engagements is, that they are partial ; they are merely skirmishes, which may for a season annoy the enemy, but never can accomplish anything conclusive, for the benefit of industry at large. . . . There is another method of procuring salvation than this starvation system of partial striking ; but that method cannot be employed without a full number of the trades, and perfect unity of action. . . .

By a general union they [the working classes] might provide themselves with every species of power ; and by a general strike they might bring their superiors to any terms of accommodation. But these petty strivings are like petty thefts. . . . [Partial strikes] are unjust to other departments of the trade, merely because they are abstracting from a portion to divide amongst a portion ; they are making laws for one trade and not for all trades.

(*b*) Dissolution of the ' Grand National ' and formation of the British and Foreign Consolidated Association of Industry, Humanity, and Knowledge. From *The Crisis*, May 17, 1834.

OFFICIAL DOCUMENT
TO THE UNIONS OF GREAT BRITAIN AND IRELAND.

LONDON, 20th August, 1834.

The Grand National Consolidated Trades Union of Great Britain and Ireland having experienced much more opposition from the employers of industry, as well as from the Government, than its promoters anticipated, deemed it prudent to call an especial meeting of delegates from all parts of England, to consider what would be the wisest course to adopt to save honest industry from the most injurious and unjust oppression, and to put an end to the unnatural feelings of hatred and hostility which have arisen through the ignorance alone of both parties, between masters and operatives from one end of the kingdom to the other. . . .

Among other conclusions, which, with the reasons for them, will be hereafter given to the public, they came to the following :

1. That the name of the Union should be changed from that of the " Grand National Consolidated Trades Union " to that of the " British and Foreign Consolidated Association of Industry, Humanity and Knowledge ".

2. That the interests and objects of the producers of wealth, and of all the industrious ought to be the same, and that if the subjects bearing on this conclusion were fairly and fully developed, it would be demonstrated that the employers and the employed have precisely the same interest.

.   .   .   .

7. That the business of this association shall be directed under one mind, to insure unity of design and promptness of execution, but that the person exercising this high trust, and his immediate official assistants shall be at all times responsible to the Great Metropolitan Council of the Association.

16. THE JOURNEYMEN ENGINEERS

[The skilled engineering craftsmen played no large part in the Trade Union excitements of the early 1830s. The rapid advance of engineering techniques had led in the 1820s to the establishment of a number of

Societies, the most important being the Steam Engine Makers, which began at Liverpool in 1824, and the Friendly Union of Mechanics, which seems to have been started in Manchester at about the same time, and was subsequently known as the ' Old Mechanics ', or, in full, as the Journeymen Steam Engine and Machine Makers' Friendly Society. This latter Society was the nucleus round which the Amalgamated Society of Engineers was built in 1851. (See Section XVII, 5.) The Committee of Operative Engineers mentioned in this extract was a federal body linking together for joint action the London branches of the various Societies and a number of purely Trade Clubs. Such Joint Committees became common in the 1840s for the conduct of concerted movements, among which the questions of hours of labour and overtime payment, and also the opposition to piecework and to the employment of unapprenticed men on skilled work, were prominent. The employers, in other cases besides that of the London dispute of 1836, retorted by discharging the workers who attempted to enforce their claims by Union bargaining. In the dispute here recorded, the engineers got what they wanted after the strike had continued for eight months.]

From Hetherington's *Twopenny Dispatch*, August 13, 1836. A message from " The Committee of Operative Engineers ".

TO THE OPERATIVE ENGINEERS AND ALL THE LOVERS OF TRUTH AND JUSTICE IN GREAT BRITAIN AND IRELAND.

FRIENDS AND BROTHER WORKMEN—In order to prevent any misunderstanding going abroad on the subject of our strike, we beg to lay before you a full and concise statement of all the facts connected therewith.

For some time our attention has been directed towards the removal of several grievous evils that had crept into the various shops in our trade. At some shops the hours in working had been ten hours, and at others ten hours and a half per day, sometimes one body of men have been working overtime to a degree that was seriously injurious to their health, while another body of men have been out of employment, and requiring support from those men that were in work. Some shops were paying for overtime at the rate of a quarter of a day for the first two hours and time and half for all time after that, other shops only pay at the rate of regular day time.

We determined to make an effort to assimilate the hours of working per day, and the rate of paying for overtime in all the shops in the trade in London. As we expected, from the known disposition of the " long time " masters, that they would offer every opposition to salutary measures, we determined to attack them one at a time, beginning with Seaward's first. Accordingly a deputation waited on Mr. S. Seaward on the 29th of June last, requesting him to reduce the hours per day, from ten hours and a half to ten hours, and to pay for overtime at the rate of time and a quarter for the first two hours, and time and half for all hours after that; with this reasonable request he refused to comply. The deputation then informed him that it was the intention of the men generally to leave the employ on the Saturday evening following and then withdrew. About an hour afterwards a placard was posted up in the factory, of which this is a literal copy :—

NOTICE TO WORKMEN

Those workmen belonging to any combination which has for its object the forcing masters to pay them for more time than they work, except the usual allowance, which will always be continued, may take themselves off forthwith. . . .

After reading this placard, the men determined to turn out immediately, and so left the premises forthwith, determined not to return until their reasonable requests were complied with. The Messrs. Seaward's, in order to strengthen their cause, set about forming a Union amongst the " long time " masters. But in this they could only prevail upon three to join them, viz. Maudsley and Co, Miller and Co, and Pen and Son. . . .

. . . There is now [10 August] upwards of 400 men out of employment, relying on the generosity of their friends and brother workmen, and thanks to them for their generous efforts, for we have not relied on them in vain.

17. THE TRIAL OF THE GLASGOW COTTON SPINNERS, 1837

[In April 1837 there was a strike of the cotton spinners in and around Glasgow ; and arising out of this picketing took place at factories where blacklegs — known locally as ' nobs ' — were working, and some attacks were made on mills and on the homes of blacklegs. In one case a ' nob ' was shot dead ; and a member of the Cotton Spinners' Association was charged with the murder, and the leaders of the Association with conspiracy to hire him to commit the crime. During the case much evidence was cited from the early history of the Association — largely from the period when the Combination Laws were still in force. The leaders were charged with ' administering unlawful oaths '; and it seems clear that before 1824 some sort of oath had been in use, at any rate in some branches. But it is very doubtful whether any oaths were still being administered in 1837 : most of the spinners who were called in evidence, except those who came forward to give evidence in response to the offer of rewards by the authorities, denied that they had ever taken or heard of any oath connected with the Association. At the trial, the prosecution entirely failed to prove any complicity of the Association in the murder ; and this charge was withdrawn. Nevertheless, the Spinners' leaders were sentenced to seven years' transportation for conspiracy — a verdict which, despite the evidence that minor acts of violence had been at least connived at, shocked the Trade Union world and recalled the treatment meted out to the Dorchester labourers three years before. After the trial the Cotton Spinners reconstituted their Association on a basis intended to limit its activities explicitly to regular collective bargaining.]

(*a*) From the First Report of the Select Committee on Combinations of Workmen (1838), Minutes of Evidence, p. 35.

Examination of Angus Campbell.

752. Mr. *Wakley*] The first intimation that you had from your own employer of the reduction that was to take place on the Monday morning was given to you on the preceding Saturday evening ? — Yes.

753. But the notice generally to the cotton-spinners was not more than three or four days ? — Not above two days to the majority.

754. The strike took place upon the 8th. of April ? — Yes.

755. Did the masters in 1827 promise that they would make an advance of wages when trade should revive, without any request or interference on the part of the workmen ? — Yes.

756. Did they fulfil that engagement ? — No, not till 1836.

757. Mr. C. *Villiers*] Did the trade revive ? — Yes.

758. Mr. *Wakley*] When the advance took place in the autumn of 1836, was it in consequence of an application to the masters from the workmen themselves ? — Yes.

759. So that there had been no advance for nine years ? — None.

760. But an advance having taken place in the autumn of 1836, you were informed in the first week of April 1837, that the Masters were about to take off the amount that had been put on in the preceding autumn. — Yes.

761. You resisted the reduction ? — Yes.

762. And the consequence of that was a strike ? — Yes.

763. Within three weeks after the existence of the strike, did

you then agree to return to your work upon the proposals which the masters at first made ? — Yes.

764. What took place between the masters and yourselves upon that occasion ? — The workmen belonging to each factory went to their employers, and told them they were willing to work upon their terms. Every master whose men had struck said, we will not accept you upon those terms ; except you agree to a further reduction ; and presenting the men at the same time with a document specifying the nature of the reduction.

765. Do you believe, and can you state that it is the belief of the cotton spinners generally, that no strike would have taken place if the masters had all concurred in giving an intimation to the men on the same day that a reduction was to take place? — I am fully convinced of it, and I heard it from every man belonging to the Glasgow Association individually.

766. You say you are fully convinced that there would have been no strike if the masters among themselves had concurred in giving you a general notice as to the proposed reduction ? — Yes.

(b) From " The Rights of Labour Defended : or The Trial of the Glasgow Cotton Spinners, for the Alleged Crime of Conspiracy, etc. to maintain or raise the Wages of Labour, before the High Court of Justiciary, at Edinburgh, on the 10th and 27th November, 1837."

INDICTMENT
In an abridged form

The Indictment charged *generally*, That an Association was formed many years ago by the Cotton Spinners in Glasgow and vicinity, the precise period and place of its formation being unknown, " for the purpose of raising or keeping up the wages of the Operative Cotton Spinners " ; That unlawful oaths were taken by the members of the Association to keep secret the transactions thereof ; That large numbers of Cotton Spinners had been induced to join the Association, to whom illegal oaths were administered ; That the Association had at various times resolved to strike work, " in order to obtain an advance of wages, or in resistance to a reduction of wages " ; That on these occasions the members had illegally " conspired " together to intimidate, molest, and threaten the workmen acting contrary to the will of the united body ; That the united body had appointed Guard Committees to watch at the Factories under strike, to intimidate the new hands, and had used threats and committed violence ; That the Association had paid money as rewards to persons for perpetrating violence, and had aided them in escaping from justice; That the members of the Union had conspired together to send, and had sent, threatening letters to the masters of factories, or their managers, threatening them with personal violence, and to burn their premises; That Secret Committees were appointed to carry the threats into execution; And *particularly*, that a strike took place on the 8th of April, 1837, " on account of a reduction of the wages " resolved on by the masters, when a conspiracy was entered into, and various committees were appointed to overcome the resolutions of the Masters, by means of exciting terror and alarm in the minds of the Masters and Non-Unionists, by threatening them with personal violence, and destroying their premises. . . .

(c) From the Articles of the Association of Operative Cotton-Spinners of Glasgow and Neighbourhood. First Report of the Select Committee on Combinations of Workmen (1838), p. 299.

Article 1. *Designation of the Association.* This Association to be termed, the Association of Operative Cotton-Spinners of Glasgow and Neighbourhood, and to have for its only object, the supporting of prices, and enabling its members to obtain a fair remuneration for their labour. The funds of this Association shall not be applied to any other purpose than those specified in the articles.

XI

THE FREEDOM OF THE PRESS

INTRODUCTION

SOMETHING has been seen in previous sections of the repression to which the press was subject, not only under the law of libel, which could be freely used against journalists and pamphleteers who attacked the British Constitution, but also under the special laws passed to restrict the circulation of newspapers and political pamphlets by heavy taxation. Sidmouth's Gagging Acts of 1817, which heavily muzzled the press, were followed by the Six Acts of 1819, one of which was specially designed to strike at the issue of cheap ' periodical pamphlets '. The first of the great libel trials following the French Revolution was that of Tom Paine in 1792, for publishing " Rights of Man " ; and from that time onwards there had been frequent prosecutions and convictions both of the publishers and editors of Radical journals and of those who ventured to act as salesmen to the public. Reference has been made in Section VI to the prosecution of Richard Carlile, who in 1817 republished Paine's principal writings as well as other works held to be seditious or blasphemous, and to his own journal, *The Republican*. Carlile and a long succession of his shopmen were sent to gaol during the period of post-war repression ; and *Cobbett's Twopenny Register* — nicknamed ' *Twopenny Trash* ', which he had begun to publish unstamped in 1816, was among the victims of the new legislation of 1819. Thereafter, with the passing of the post-war crisis, the Government became less active in prosecuting Radical journalists and newsagents ; and Cobbett was able to publish unmolested for some years an unstamped sixpenny edition of his complete *Register*. This, however, like other unstamped journals, could not be sent through the post, as the stamped journals were. The ' unstamped ' had to be distributed in parcels by coach to local newsagents. Presently, in 1827, the Stamp Office forced Cobbett to discontinue his unstamped edition under threat of legal action. With the revival of the Reform agitation about 1829, there was a renewed outburst of unstamped journalism. Cobbett issued his monthly *Twopenny Trash*, which was just within the law because it was only monthly : Henry Hetherington decided to defy the law openly by publishing *The Poor Man's Guardian*, with a challenging title-page, every week. Repeated prosecutions both of Hetherington and his salesmen and of other Radical journalists and newsagents followed, until in 1834 Lord Lyndhurst surprised everyone by giving the verdict that *The Poor Man's Guardian* was too paltry an affair to deserve to be called a newspaper, and was therefore not liable to newspaper tax. In 1836 the Whig Government reduced the newspaper tax from 4d. (for a paper of normal size) to a flat duty of 1d. The tax was not fully repealed until 1855, and the duty on paper, against which the advocates of a free press then directed their efforts, lasted until 1861. The struggle of 1830–1834, in which Hetherington was the leading figure, holds a key position in the development of the working class movement. It was closely connected both with the rise of the National Union of the Working Classes and with the whole movement for really Radical Reform; and the group which played the leading part in it was largely identical with that which, as soon as the freedom of the press had been substantially achieved, turned its attention back to Radical politics, founded the London Working Men's Association, and drew up The People's Charter.

See " Short History ", Part I, chapter 4, section 2 ; and chapter 7, section 1.
" Common People ", chapters 18 and 19.

1. THE NEWSPAPER ACT OF 1819

[The author of the " History of the Taxes on Knowledge " was himself a participant in the later phases of the struggle which his book describes. The book was written in his old age, when he was well over eighty. It does not effectively cover the period before 1830, for which reference should be made to W. H. Wickwar's " The Struggle for the Freedom of the Press, 1819–1832 " (1928).

The Government did all it could at this time to incite the local magistrates to take action against ' seditious and blasphemous publications ', but it was reluctant to undertake prosecutions itself, save in cases of exceptional importance. The work of denunciation and prosecution was in practice largely undertaken by Wilberforce's ' Vice Society ' and similar bodies, usually known to the Radicals as ' the Bridge-street gang '.]

(*a*) From C. D. Collet, " History of the Taxes on Knowledge " (1899), chapter 3.

. . . As a climax to the restrictions on the Press came the 60 George III. cap. 9, the one of the six Acts which in its practical operation survived the other five. The preamble established for the first time a distinction between public news and remarks on news. The latter, as they were published at frequent intervals and at low prices, had come to be more dreaded than the intelligence itself. The Act was accordingly directed against " pamphlets and printed papers containing observations on public events and occurrences tending to excite hatred and contempt of the Government and Constitution of these realms as by law established, and also vilifying our holy religion ". By Section 1 " any pamphlets or papers printed periodically, or in parts or numbers, at intervals not exceeding twenty-six days between the publication of any two such pamphlets or papers, parts or numbers, where any of the said pamphlets or papers, parts or numbers respectively, shall not exceed two sheets, or shall be published for sale at a less sum than sixpence, exclusive of the duty by this Act imposed thereon, shall be deemed and taken to be newspapers ".

. . . .

Finally, what became known as the Security System was established. Section 8, under a penalty of £20, forbade any one to print or publish a newspaper, or a pamphlet, or a paper containing, etc., " which shall not exceed two sheets, or which shall be published for sale at a less price than sixpence, without first executing a bond to his Majesty, together with two or three sufficient sureties conditional that such printer or publisher shall pay any fine which may at any time be imposed on him for any blasphemous or seditious libel ".

(b) From the Home Office Papers, 41/5/43 (1819). Extract from a letter from Lord Sidmouth to the Mayor of Exeter.

It afforded me great pleasure to learn that the venders of those mischievous and detestable libels . . . were under prosecution at Exeter. I should be extremely sorry if the prosecution which you have instituted for the latter [Sherwin] was withdrawn. It is fortunate when such publications are taken up by magistrates and other persons of respectability in the places where they are sold, and a prosecution carried on by them for obvious reasons is to be preferred to one carried on by the Government; but a reluctance to take the step, and to follow it effectually, is not unfrequently occasioned by an apprehension of the expense necessarily attending it. . . . A greater service cannot be rendered to the country at this time than by activity and perseverance against the authors, printers, and publishers, including itinerant venders, of blasphemous and seditious tracts. If the friends of the Constitution throughout the Kingdom will stand forward and equal the activity of its enemies, internal tranquillity will soon be restored.

2. RICHARD CARLILE

[Richard Carlile, by his steady defiance of the law and his enrolment of a succession of helpers who took his place as salesmen of his publications while he was in prison, did a great deal to break down the enforcement of the Libel and Newspaper Laws by stirring up public opinion against the prosecutions and thus making both the Government and the magistrates more reluctant to undertake them, and juries more unwilling to convict.]

(a) From Carlile's *The Republican*, March 3, 1820.

Being fired with ardour by the political publications of the day, in the spring of 1817 I resolved to try my fortune at giving them a more extensive circulation in London. I . . . succeeded in placing them into twenty different shops in London and its vicinity that never sold them before. My plan was to carry them to the different shops for sale, as they were scarcely worth fetching, in point of profit, after Mr. Cobbett had gone to America and the Habeas Corpus [was] suspended. My ardour was not to be damped by any danger or difficulty. I persevered, and many a day traversed thirty miles for a profit of eighteen pence.

(b) From Carlile's *The Republican*, May 23, 1823.

My whole and sole object, from first to last, from the time of putting off my leather apron to this day, has been a Free Press and Free discussion. When I first started as a hawker of pamphlets I knew nothing of political principles, I had never read a page of Paine's writings; but I had a complete conviction that there was something wrong somewhere, and that the right application of the printing-press was the remedy.

(c) From Carlile's *The Republican*, May 21, 1824.

Whereas ignorant and bad men in power have ever conspired to prevent others from knowing more than themselves, and . . . have ever persecuted such other men as have desired to see the human race going on in progressive improvement :

Be it known to all that . . . between the 7th and 15th of the month of May inst., three persons were arrested from the shop, 84 Fleet Street, London. This is, therefore, to give notice that all persons who will present themselves to sell books in the said shop, free of cost in getting there, are desired immediately to forward their names that they may be regularly called upon, so as to prevent the stoppage of sale in the said shop. It is most distinctly to be understood that a love of propagating the principles, and a sacrifice of liberty to that end, as far as it may be required, AND NOT GAIN, must be the motive to call forth such volunteers; for — though R. Carlile pledges himself to do what he has hitherto done to give such men the best support in his power — should any great number be imprisoned, he is not so situated as to property or prospects as to be able to promise any particular sum weekly. . . . As the matter seems to be an experiment on the part of Lord Eldon, Robert Peel & Co., to see how far the opposition can be carried, and whether the promises to come forward and stand prosecutions will be realized, all good men are exhorted to make and communicate their resolve, and to hold themselves in readiness.

3. WILLIAM HONE

[William Hone (1780–1842) was also an important contributor to the struggle for a free press. In 1817 he began to publish his political squibs against the Government, many of them in verse and many illustrated with drawings by George Cruikshank. Hone excelled in parodies of scripture and the prayer-book (" The Sinecurist's Creed ", " The Political Litany ", etc.). He was three times prosecuted and acquitted by London juries in 1817 for these lampoons; and the published reprints of his " Three Trials " had a wide circulation. In 1820 he espoused the cause of Queen Caroline, and published numerous squibs against the King and the Ministers. The following is a good sample of his style.]

From " The Political House that Jack Built ". Printed by and for William
Hone, 1820.

These are
THE PEOPLE
all tatter'd and torn,
Who curse the day
wherein they were born,

On account of Taxation
    too great to be borne,
And pray for relief,
    from night to morn :
Who, in vain, Petition
    in every form,
Who, peaceably Meeting
    to ask for Reform,
Were sabred by Yeomanry Cavalry,
    who
Were thank'd by T H E M A N,[1]
    all shaven and shorn,
All cover'd with Orders —
    and all forlorn ;
T H E D A N D Y O F S I X T Y,
    who bows with a grace,
And has *taste* in wigs, collars,
    cuirasses, and lace :
Who, to tricksters and fools,
    leaves the state and its treasure,
And, when Britain's in tears,
    sails about at his pleasure :
Who spurn'd from his presence
    the Friends of his youth,
And now has not one
    who will tell him the truth ;
Who took to his counsels, in evil hour,
The Friends to the Reasons of lawless Power,
That back the Public Informer, who
Would put down the *Thing*, that, in spite of new Acts,
And attempts to restrain it, by Soldiers or Tax,
Will *poison* the Vermin, that plunder the Wealth,
That lay in the House, that Jack built.

4. COBBETT'S *REGISTER* AND THE STAMP DUTY

[Cobbett had been imprisoned for libel in 1810 ; but he did not court prosecution under the Newspaper Tax. He discontinued his *Twopenny Registers* when the law was stiffened up against political pamphlets ;

    [1] *I.e.* King George IV.

and though he issued thereafter an unstamped edition of the *Register* at 6d, paying pamphlet duty on it but not newspaper tax, and arguing that it was not a newspaper, but only a pamphlet liable to duty at a much lower rate, he was never actually prosecuted. Indeed, he was allowed to continue for some years unmolested, but was at length informed in 1827 that if he went on he would be charged with duty at the full rate. He then discontinued the unstamped edition, but in 1830 and 1831 issued *Twopenny Trash* side by side with the weekly *Register* as an unstamped periodical pamphlet.]

(a) From *Cobbett's Weekly Political Register*, October 26, 1816.

. . . The newspapers which are notoriously devoted to corruption are continually endeavouring to rouse and to direct the rage of the people against bakers, brewers, and butchers. The corrupt men know very well what is the real cause of the people's suffering : but their object is, first, to turn their eyes away from that real cause, and, next, to stir them up to acts of violence against tradesmen who are fellow-sufferers with themselves; because by so stirring them up an excuse is afforded for quelling them by force of arms. Let the people always bear this in mind, that nothing pleases Corruption so much as to see Troops called forth for the purpose of protecting innocent Farmers and Tradesmen against misguided violence : and that nothing is so sorrowful a sight to the friends of freedom.

I am, for my part, so deeply impressed with the magnitude of this evil that I propose to address, in my next Register, *a Letter to the Labourers and Journeymen of this Kingdom*, calculated to lay before them a perfect knowledge of the real causes of their sufferings, and to preserve the tranquillity and to restore the happiness of that country. That this intended letter may have as wide a circulation as possible it is my intention to cause it *to be published afterwards on a single open sheet of paper* and to cause it *to be sold at a very low price.* . . .

Open sheets, that is to say, a sheet of paper not folded up nor printed with an intention to be folded up, requires no stamp, and may be printed and sold without any. The whole of one of my Registers might be printed in rather close print upon the two sides of one sheet of foolscap paper. . . .

(b) From *Cobbett's Weekly Political Register*, November 16, 1816, pp. 497, 498, 509-10.

BOTLEY, *12th Nov.* 1816.

The Register, No. 18, which was reprinted on an open sheet, to be sold for *two-pence* by retail, having been found to be very useful, it is my intention to continue that mode of proceeding until *the Meeting of Parliament*, or, perhaps, until *the Reform shall have actually taken place.* . . .

Of the *shilling and a half-penny*, which is the present retail price of the Register, a very small portion is left to the *Author*. Not more, perhaps, than *two-pence half-penny*, if every expence be reckoned. I have no *advertisements*, no *paid-for paragraphs*, and I publish little but what I myself write. It is impossible to publish with the stamp cheaper than I do, unless I go quite without compensation for my labour and time. Yet this *high price* must necessarily narrow the circulation ; and, indeed, this is the obvious effect of such *heavy taxes* on the paper first, and, next, on the *stamp*. Still, as the Register was read in *meetings* of people in many towns, and one copy was thus made to convey information to scores of persons, I was somewhat satisfied ; or, at least, I thought I was doing all that it was possible for me to do. But I have recently been informed, that, at *three* public-houses in one country town, the landlords have objected to *Meetings for Reading the Register being held at their houses*, for fear they should LOSE THEIR LICENCES. . . .

. . . P.S.— The Series of *Open Sheets* will begin with No. 15 of the present Volume. No. 15 is an answer to the Question : " *What good would a Reform of Parliament do ?* " Then comes No. 16, which shews " *How the Reform might be accomplished without creating confusion.*" No. 17 contains, *An Address to the Leaders at Public Meetings*, on the proper mode of proceeding at those Meetings. No. 18 is the *First Address to the Journeymen and Labourers of England, Wales, Scotland and Ireland*. No. 19 contains an *Address to the People of Scotland* on the Meeting at PAISLEY, and also a letter to Mr. JABET *of Birmingham, proving the falsehood and insolence of his defence of Corruption*, and justifying the *indignation* of his townsmen against him. — All these are now *re-printing* and will be ready for sale and to send to the country by the 23d instant. — So that orders may, at once, be given for all, or for any, of them, and to any extent. . . .

(c) From *Cobbett's Weekly Political Register*, December 4, 1824, p. 578.

. . . Now, as to the REGISTER, there is, every week, *a pamphlet edition*, price 6d. *without a stamp*. This cannot go by post. It is, therefore, to be got *in the country* only *by coach parcel*, or from some person who sells it in some country town. But, there is also, every week, a *stamped edition*, price 1s. This goes *by post*, and is obtained *through the newsmen, as other newspapers are.* — This price of 1s. seems great; but, observe, the stamp costs 4½d. . . .

(d) From *Cobbett's Weekly Political Register*, August 21, 1830.

. . . I perceive that you want very much to be enlightened ON THE STATE OF OUR PRESS, which you appear to regard as being FREE, and which, as I am going to prove to you, is the most *enslaved* and the *vilest* thing that has ever been heard of in the world under the name of press. I say, that I am going to PROVE this; and proof consists of *undeniable facts*, and not of vague assertions. Take, then, the following facts :

1. All paper is *taxed*, and this tax, together with the expense attending it and paying of the tax in advance, and with the *monopoly* that arises out of these, makes the paper cost the double of what it would cost, if there were no tax.

2. No man dare use a printing-press, or types for printing, without a *license* from the authorities of the county in which he resides. All the presses are recorded in the archives of the counties, and the keepers of those archives are compelled to communicate the records to the Minister of the interior, who has, thus, a complete surveillance over all the presses in every part of the country.

3. Suppose you are going to begin the publication of a journal. FIRST, you must send, in writing, the *title of the journal*, and the names of the *proprietor*, the *printer* and the *editor* (or publisher), to the *commissaires du bureau des Timbres* (commissioners of the board of Stamps). SECOND, the proprietor, printer and editor, must go in person before these Commissaires, and declare, *on oath*, that they are the proprietor, printer and editor of said journal; and each of them must make declaration *on oath* of the town, street, and house, in which each of them lives; and they must all declare *on oath* the house in which the journal is to be published. THIRD, having advanced thus far, you leave these Commissaires for a little, and you, the proprietor, are obliged to go before A JUDGE, taking *two bondsmen* with you; and this Judge makes you all three enter into bonds to the amount, each of you, of *four hundred pounds sterling*, to pay the amount of four *hundred pounds*, if a fine to that amount should, *at any time*, be inflicted on the proprietor on account of libel in the said journal. FOURTH, having had the good luck to find two friends, rich enough to be able to declare *on oath*, that they possess four hundred pounds each, over and above all their

debts, and *courageous* enough to run so great a risk, and having purchased some paper to print the journal on, you are not *yet* permitted to print; but must go back to the *Commissaires du bureau des Timbres*, and have your paper *timbré*, or stamped. FIFTH, your journal sells for *sevenpence* by retail, and you, the proprietor, sell it for sixpence to the retailers, and these *Commissaires* make you pay (before you print) *fourpence for every sheet of aper*; that is to say, *for every single journal*; and, as the *tax on the paper* is a quarter of a penny, or more, you have (before you can print) *fourpence and the quarter of another penny* to pay to the Government, *out of your sixpence*, having one penny and three quarters left to pay the *paper-maker*, the *printer* and the *editor* (or publisher), and to compensate you for your *time* and your *talents*!

" Eh bien! but you will have *advertisements*, and you will get a great deal by those." FIRST, it is not *certain* that you will have any; and if you have, the *Commissaires des Timbres* must have a word with you about *them* too; but you must pay them THREE SHILLINGS AND SIXPENCE TAX for every advertisement, though it be but *one single line*; and here you see how *impartial* this Government is, for it makes the poor servant man or woman, who advertises for a place, pay just as much tax as the lord who advertises the sale of an estate worth a hundred thousand pounds! However, this *advertising* is the great source of *revenue* with our journals, except in very few cases, such as mine, for instance, who have no advertisements. Hence, these journals are an affair of *trade* and not of *literature*; the proprietors think of *the money* that is to be got by them; they hire men to write in them; and these men are *ordered* to write in a way to please the classes who can give most advertisements. The Government itself pays large sums in advertisements, many hundreds a year, to some journals. The aristocracy, the clergy, the magistrates (who are generally *clergy* too) in the several counties; the merchants, the manufacturers, the great shopkeepers; all these *command* the press, because without their advertisements it cannot be carried on *with profit*. If a man scorn to carry on this vile *trade*, and write and publish for the information of the people, then the Government takes from him, as it does from me, *fourpence farthing out of every sixpence*.

Now let us see what sort of *liberty* you have to *express* your *thoughts* upon this paper, thus loaded with imposts. The Attorney-General sees in your journal something that he *does not like*. That is enough: he, of his own authority, and without consulting any body, puts on record in the Court of King's Bench (*cour royale*) *an accusation against you*, and, without letting you know *what it is*, has you seized and *put into jail until the time for trial*, which may be, if he please, six or nine months. You are permitted to be at large until the time of trial, if you can find *two bondsmen* to give bail for your appearance to take your trial. You are not furnished with any copy of the accusation against you; without it you cannot defend yourself; and if you have it you must *pay for it*; so that from the moment he puts his hand on you your *ruin has already begun*. When you come to trial, it is not before a jury taken at hazard and by ballot, but *a special jury*; that is to say, a *jury of rich men*, who are appointed by an officer of the Government, in the following manner: from the list of these rich men of the county he names 48; the 48 names are given to you, and you are allowed to strike out 12; the Attorney-General strikes out 12; and the first 12 of the remaining 24 who come into Court are your jury. But, observe, this officer *appoints the whole forty-eight*! At the trial, the public prosecutor *begins*; you then *defend yourself*; and then he *speaks again*, and you are *not allowed to reply*. As to what may be a *crime*, or *libel*; in the first place, *truth* may be a libel; and, in fact, *any thing* may be a libel that a special jury will say is a libel, there being *no law* to define what is, or what is not, *a libel*. As to the *punishments*, they are *fine*, *imprisonment*, and *bonds*; and of these I am well qualified to give you a full description. . . .

There is something far worse even than that; for *any ill-natured neighbour may be your prosecutor, and cause you to be crammed into prison or held to bail*. England is full of *Justices of the Peace*. Almost all the *Aristocracy and Clergy*, and many of the *Naval and Military Officers*, are justices of the peace; all appointed by the government, *and dismissed at the sole will of the government*; and, therefore, wholly dependent on the government for their offices. Suppose you to publish any thing that *any Justice of the Peace may choose to consider a public libel*, he can, upon the oath of any man, that you have *published* the thing, *published* it only, SEND YOU TO JAIL AT ONCE TO WAIT UNTIL YOU TAKE YOUR TRIAL; or, he can compel you to bring men of property to be bound for your appearance to take your trial, and for your not publishing any libel or committing any breach of the peace in the mean while; and then follow all the forfeitures and all the other consequences, as in the case of proceedings by the Public Prosecutor! . . .

5. *THE POOR MAN'S GUARDIAN*

[Henry Hetherington, follower of Robert Owen and later one of the leading members of the London Working Men's Association, played the outstanding part in the renewed struggle over the Taxes on Knowledge that accompanied the Reform agitation. For a time he attempted to evade the law by publishing what was in effect a weekly periodical under a different title for each issue, claiming that each was a separate pamphlet and therefore not liable for newspaper tax. In 1831, when his salesmen were convicted in spite of this plea, he decided to publish *The Poor Man's Guardian* with the challenging heading given in the first of these extracts. The third extract gives the changed form of the title-page after Lord Lyndhurst had given judgment in 1834 that the *Guardian* was not a newspaper, and was therefore not liable to the tax. Thereafter in practice, if not in law, unstamped papers were not prosecuted, if they catered for a public which could not afford the stamped newspapers. The Reformers now attacked the stamp duty itself. In April 1836 The Association of Working Men to Procure a Cheap and Honest Press was founded, but in the following month the stamp duty was reduced from 4d. to 1d., and, though the members of the Association were not fully satisfied, they set aside for the time being their proposed agitation. It was from this circle that the foundation members of the London Working Men's Association were recruited.]

(a) From the first number of *The Poor Man's Guardian*,[1] July 9, 1831.

THE POOR MAN'S GUARDIAN

A weekly newspaper for the people, established contrary to " Law ", to try the power of Might against " Right ".

No. 1.   *Saturday July 9. 1831*   Price 1d

FRIENDS, BRETHREN, AND FELLOW COUNTRYMEN, Our " *appeal* ", as it is called — or rather the appeal of our friends — has turned out as we anticipated ; — the conviction of Messrs Birnie, Hall, and Robinson has been *confirmed* : it has been decided by their " sapient worships " that distinct and nameless papers written by the same author, and published irregularly, form only one connected paper, bearing one and the same name, and published at stated periods — or, in fine, that the papers written by the *Poor Man's Guardian*, are within the meaning of *Castlereagh's Act*. Be it so ; we wished to avoid " *the law* " as we would a very nuisance ; we wished —

---

[1] The first under this title. Earlier numbers had been issued from 1830 as " *Penny Papers for the People*, by the Poor Man's Guardian ".

though at a great inconvenience — to keep as close as possible though without actually trespassing on the common of which this act of tyranny has deprived us, — but we find it impossible; " the law " is made behind our backs — without our consent — kept secret from us — and when discovered — is unintelligible, — or, whether intelligible or not, it is to be interpreted by the paid servants of those who enforce it — and, consequently, escape from it is hopeless! Be it so, we say : we are prepared for the fight; it is a mere legal one on the part of our persecutors, but a moral one on ours ; we know that we must suffer, but we are content to do so for the benefit of our fellow-creatures ; we have before our eyes the fatal examples of all those who have ever advocated the *truth* ; but we shrink not from the worst, — be our reward the cross of agony itself, on which Christ *expiated his* " SEDITION ", and be our doctrines, like his — pure and just as they are — rejected by all mankind ; or, be they like his, only received to be distorted — even by those who profess the most to venerate them — into an authority for every species of rapacity and injustice — still we are prepared.   Better — far better not to be, than be as we are ! Yes, we buckle on our armour of patience and perseverance — we draw forth our sword of reason, — and we brave the whole host of tyranny! Defiance is our only remedy; — we cannot be a slave in all : we submit to much — for it is impossible to be wholly consistent — but we will try, step by step, the power of RIGHT against MIGHT ; and we will begin by protecting and upholding this grand bulwark and defence of all our rights — this key to all our liberties — THE FREEDOM OF THE PRESS — *the press, too, of the* IGNORANT *and the* POOR ! We have taken upon ourselves its protection, and we will never abandon our post : we will *die* rather.

The fight is begun, and we must cast off the trammels both of disguise and fear ; we cannot avoid the struggle, and we must meet it manfully ; — no more *evasion* ; we will not *trespass*, but deny the authority of our " lords " to enclose the *common* against us ; we will *demand* our *right*, nor treat but with *contempt* the despotic " law " which would deprive us of it ; we will trample it under our feet — and resist to the last any *power* that may attempt to enforce it.

To you — friends and brethren — you whose cause we are advocating — whose rights we demand — whose liberties we defend — whose interests we espouse — to you we now appeal, not to let us fight our perilous battle singlehanded ; we look to you for support ; we ask you not to incur danger or expense — we desire not the risk of interest or person — we ask you merely to purchase, with your weekly pennies, and *read*, and *mark*, and *inwardly digest*, our " *newspaper* ", to be called henceforward " THE POOR MAN'S GUARDIAN ", which will contain " *news, intelligence, and occurrences* ", and " *remarks and observations thereon* ", and " *upon matters in church and state, tending* ", decidedly, " *to excite hatred and contempt of the Government and Constitution of the tyranny of this country, as* BY LAW *established* ", and also " *to vilify the ABUSES of religion* " — and will be " *printed in the United Kingdom, for sale, and published periodically* " (every Saturday) " *in yearly parts and weekly numbers, at intervals not exceeding twenty-six days, and will not exceed two sheets, and will be published for a less sum than sixpence* " (to wit) *the sum of* ONE PENNY, " *exclusive of the duty imposed by the 38 Geo. III c 78 and the 60 Geo. III. c 9* " or any other acts whatsoever, and despite the " laws " or the will and pleasure of *any tyrant* or any *body of tyrants* whatsoever, any thing herein before, or anywhere-else, contained to the contrary notwithstanding.

(*b*) From *The Poor Man's Guardian*, June 21, 1834.

TRIUMPH OF THE PRESS ! — HURRAH !
THE GUARDIAN A LEGAL PUBLICATION.

Well, Men of England, at last we have had a real triumph. After all the badgerings of the last three years — after all the fines and incarcerations — after all the spying and blood-money, *The Poor Man's Guardian* was pronounced, on Tuesday, by the Court of Exchequer (and by a *Special* Jury too !) to be a perfectly legal publication. Upwards of 500 victims have been imprisoned for selling this paper. A host of respectable publishers have suffered in pocket and person for the same offence. Mr. Hetherington himself has endured two incarcerations of six months each, and Mr. and Mrs. Wastney are at this moment languishing in Newcastle Gaol — their business broken up and their children in the workhouse. And for what ? — For selling a paper Lord Lyndhurst has just declared to be a strictly legitimate publication. Talk of compensation for rotten boroughs and West Indian slave drivers ! What compensation are the 500 victims to have ? What compensation are poor Mr. and Mrs. Wastney to have ? They will have none ! Compensation is only for opulent robbers and slave drivers. Poverty and probity are insuperable bars against compensation.

The Whig hirelings who whilom racked their brains in finding out grievances, real or imaginary, to make a ladder for them to power and pensions — the hypocrites who out of place used to shed crocodile tears for the ignorance of the poor, and to damn the Sidmouths and Castlereaghs for excluding poor Blacky from the luxury of knowledge — those knaves who used to split the ears of the groundlings about the " palladium of our liberties," telling us " a free press was like the air we breathe ; if we have it not we die " — all these impostors were humbled in the dust by Tuesday's verdict. That verdict informed them that their 500 victims were innocent in law, as in justice, — that their persecutions were, therefore, wanton, as well as cruel acts of tyranny, and (worst of all !) that they should have no more victims. This was the lesson read to the Whigs by Tuesday's verdict — a lesson which they will never forget till the last moment of their lives.

Well then, men of England, at last we have a free People's Press. *The Guardian* may henceforward be announced without fear of fine or dungeon. Publishers may publish it, and news-vendors hawk it, without molestation from spies or informers. Colley and Currie may now go and break stones on the highways, for their occupation, like Othello's, is gone !

Radicals of England ! — brave and warm-hearted supporters, we wish we could shake hands with you all. Long and anxious have been your and our struggles in the cause. Long and anxiously have you laboured with us to establish a people's press. — You have your reward. The verdict of Tuesday establishes that the poor may henceforward have unstamped *politics*, though not unstamped *news*, as well as the rich. You may have cheap pamphlets, but not cheap newspapers. This is a point gained at any rate. It is victory No. 1. With God's blessing you will shortly have victory No. 2. By bearding the " law " we have established the legality of cheap political pamphlets. By the same process we shall, with God's blessing and the people's support, compel the rogues to give you cheap political newspapers. . . .

(c) From *The Poor Man's Guardian*, February 21, 1835.

THE

POOR MAN'S GUARDIAN,

A WEEKLY PAPER FOR THE PEOPLE

This paper (after sustaining a Government persecution of three years and a half duration, in which upwards of 500 persons were unjustly imprisoned, and cruelly treated for vending it) was,

on the Trial of an Ex-Officio Information filed by

HIS MAJESTY'S ATTORNEY GENERAL against HENRY HETHERINGTON,

IN THE COURT OF EXCHEQUER,

Before LORD LYNDHURST *and a* SPECIAL JURY,

DECLARED TO BE

A STRICTLY LEGAL PUBLICATION

Printed and Published by H. Hetherington, Savoystreet, Strand.

XII

THE FACTORY MOVEMENT, 1815–1850

INTRODUCTION

THE first so-called Factory Act was passed in 1802, on the initiative of the elder Sir Robert Peel. It was known as the Health and Morals of Apprentices Act, and dealt exclusively with the conditions of pauper apprentices in cotton mills. This system was already beginning to die out, as employers preferred using local children where they were available to incurring the full responsibility for housing pauper children sent from the workhouses in the big towns. As population increased in the factory districts, the children of adult factory workers and others became available, and the reluctance of parents to send their children into the factories was gradually beaten down by sheer necessity. Nothing was done to regulate the conditions of ' free ' children until 1819, when an agitation started by Robert Owen bore fruit in Peel's second Act, again limited to cotton mills. About the same time, helped by Nathaniel Gould of Manchester, the factory workers began their long struggle for reform of factory conditions. John Cam Hobhouse helped them to put minor amending measures on the statute book in 1825, 1829, and 1831, and then the leadership of the parliamentary movement passed for a time to Michael Thomas Sadler, on whose defeat in 1832 it was taken over by Lord Ashley, later Earl of Shaftesbury. The Act of 1833 extended regulation to other textile industries besides cotton, and started the system of factory inspection ; but the Ten Hours Bill, for which the Short Time Committees had been continuously agitating, did not become law until 1847 — and then was defeated in operation by the employers' resistance and by legal interpretation of its provisions, so that Ashley was induced to accept the Ten-and-a-Half Hours compromise Act of 1850.

See " Short History ", Part I, chapter 6, section 2 ; and chapter 7, section 2. " Common People ", chapter 23.

1. ROBERT OWEN'S FACTORY BILL, 1815

[Owen's draft Bill of 1815 was never introduced into Parliament in the form in which he drew it up; but it provided the basis for the Bill introduced by the elder Sir Robert Peel, which became law, in a considerably diluted form, in 1819. It will be seen that Owen wanted legislation applying to all textile, and not only to cotton, factories; that he wanted the minimum age for the employment of children to be ten, and regulation to extend to eighteen; that he asked for a maximum working day of 10½ hours, exclusive of 1½ hours for meals, and for the prohibition of night work for persons under eighteen; and that he proposed the appointment of inspectors (called Visitors) by the Justices of the Peace. It would have been hopeless before 1832 to ask that inspectors should be appointed by the Central Government.]

From Owen's Factory Bill of 1815. Quoted from " Life of Robert Owen " (1858), vol. i. *a*, pp. 23-6.

. . . That from and after the Fifteenth day of *April* one thousand eight hundred and sixteen, the said recited Act and this Act shall extend and be construed to extend to all Cotton, Woollen, Flax, *and other* Mills, Manufactories, or Buildings, in which *Twenty or more Persons* shall be employed *under* the age of *Eighteen Years*.

And be it further Enacted, That no Male or Female shall be employed in any such Mill, Manufactory, or Building, until he or she shall have attained the age of *Ten* years, to be ascertained by the Register of Baptism, or other satisfactory evidence.

And be it further Enacted, That no person being under the age of Eighteen years shall be employed in any such Mill, Manufactory, or Building, for more than *Ten hours and a half* in any one day, exclusive of *half an hour* for Breakfast, *one hour* for Dinner, and *half* an hour for Instruction, making in the whole, *Twelve hours and a half*; and to prevent working in the night, the aforesaid *Twelve hours and a half* shall be performed sometime between the hours of *Five* of the clock in the morning, and *Nine* of the clock in the evening : provided always, That in case any Mill, Manufactory, or Building, shall be prevented from working on account of necessary repairs, or other unavoidable accident, it shall and may be lawful for the Master or Mistress of such Mill, Manufactory, or Building, to employ any person under the age of Eighteen years, for a longer period than *Ten hours and a half* in a day, provided that no such persons shall be compelled to work in any one day more than Two hours beyond the period herein before mentioned, nor to exceed in the whole the time so lost.

And be it further enacted, That every such person shall, for the Four first years after the time of their admission into any such Mill, Manufactory, or Building, be instructed one half hour in every working day, in Reading, Writing, and Arithmetic, by some discreet and proper Person to be provided by the Master or Mistress of every such Mill, Manufactory, or Building, in some room or place to be set apart for such purpose in or near such Mill, Manufactory, or Building, or in some public School near thereto.

. . . And be it further Enacted, That so much of the said Act,[1] as directs that the Justices of the Peace for every County, Stewartry, Riding, Division, or Place, shall appoint two Persons, one of whom shall be a Justice of the Peace, and the other shall be a Clergyman of the Established Church of *England* or *Scotland*, to be Visitors of Mills, Manufactories, or Buildings, shall be and the same is hereby Repealed.

And be it further Enacted, That the Justices of the Peace for every County, Stewartry, Riding, Division, or Place, in which any such Mill, Manufactory, or Building shall be situated, shall . . . appoint the Clerk of the Peace or his Deputy in *England* or *Ireland*, or his Deputies in Scotland, or one or more persons duly qualified, and not interested in or in any way connected with any such Mills, Manufactories, or Buildings, to be Visitors of such Mills, Manufactories, or Buildings, in such County, Stewartry, Riding, Division, or Place, for the year ensuing; and the said Visitor or Visitors, or either of them, shall have full power and authority from time to time throughout the year, to enter into and inspect any such Mill, Manufactory, or Building, and the young Persons employed in such Mill, Manufactory, or Building, at any time of the day, or during the hours of employment, as they shall think fit; and such Visitor or Visitors shall report at least once in every year, in writing, to the Quarter Session of the Peace, the state and condition of such Mills, Manufactories, and Buildings, and the young persons employed in them, and whether the same are or are not conducted and regulated according to the directions of the said recited Act and this Act; . . .

And be it further Enacted, That every Master or Mistress of any such Mill, Manufactory, or Building, who shall wilfully act contrary to or offend against any of the Provisions of the said Act or this Act, shall for every such offence, (except where otherwise directed,)

[1] *I.e.* Peel's Act of 1802, dealing with pauper apprentices.

forfeit and pay any sum not exceeding Ten Pounds nor less than Five Pounds, at the discretion of the Justices before whom such Offender shall be convicted. . . .

2. THE FACTORY ACT OF 1819

[The Act passed in 1819, after prolonged negotiation between the elder Peel and representatives of the manufacturers, fell a long way short of what Owen had proposed. It applied only to cotton factories : it put the minimum age for factory employment at nine, instead of ten, and regulated conditions only up to sixteen, instead of eighteen ; it fixed working hours at 12, instead of 10½, exclusive of meal-times ; and it entirely omitted any provision for inspection beyond what had been already laid down in respect of pauper apprentices in the Act of 1802 (see previous extract).]

From Factory Act, 1819 (59 Geo. III. c. 66).

I. . . . That from and after the First Day of *January* One thousand eight hundred and twenty, (1820) no Child shall be employed in any Description of Work, *for the Spinning of* COTTON *Wool into Yarn, or in any previous Preparation of* SUCH *Wool*, until he or she shall have attained the full Age of *Nine* Years.

II. And be it further enacted, That no Person, being under the Age of *Sixteen* Years, shall be employed in any Description of Work whatsoever, in spinning Cotton Wool into Yarn, or in the previous Preparation of such Wool, or in the cleaning or repairing of any Mill, Manufactory, or Building, or any Millwork of Machinery therein, for more than *Twelve* Hours in any one Day, *ex*clusive of the necessary time for Meals ; such Twelve Hours to be between the Hours of *Five* o'Clock in the Morning and *Nine* o'Clock in the Evening.

III. And be it further enacted, That there shall be allowed to every such Person, in the course of every Day, not less than *Half an Hour* to Breakfast, and not less than *One full Hour* for Dinner ; such Hour for Dinner to be between the Hours of Eleven o'Clock in Forenoon and Two o'Clock in the Afternoon.

. . . .

VII. And be it further enacted, That every Master or Mistress of any such Cotton Mill, Manufactory, or Building, who shall wilfully act contrary to or offend against any of the Provisions of this Act, or any of the Provisions of the above-recited Act, shall for every such Offence forfeit and pay any Sum not exceeding Twenty Pounds, nor less than Ten Pounds, at the Discretion of the Justices before whom such Offender shall be convicted ; . . .

3. YORKSHIRE SLAVERY

[Richard Oastler's famous letter to *The Leeds Mercury* in September 1830 set on foot a new phase of the factory movement which had previously been connected mainly with the cotton industry, though the Yorkshire woollen operatives had been demanding the extension of the Act of 1819 to cover the woollen industry. Oastler (1789–1861), who came to be called ' the Factory King ' from his unquestioned leadership of the Yorkshire movement, was a ' Radical-Tory ', by profession a land-steward, and by connection a strong Evangelical Churchman. His activities on behalf of the factory workers and against the New Poor Law of 1834 landed him in difficulties with his employer, and in 1840 he was imprisoned in the Fleet Prison, on account of a claim against him for sums due to his employer which he alleged he had been entitled to spend. In prison he edited *The Fleet Papers* (1841–1844), which contain much autobiographical material and information about the factory movement. Later, he edited *The Home* (1851–1858). There is an admirable life of him by C. Driver, under the title " Tory Radical " (1946).

John Fielden (1784–1849), though a large employer in the cotton industry, was the lifelong friend of the factory workers and as inveterate an enemy as Oastler of the New Poor Law and of the entire Whig *laissez-faire* outlook. He supported the People's Charter, and, in Shaftesbury's absence from Parliament, introduced the Ten Hours Bill which became law in 1847.]

(*a*) From Richard Oastler's Letter to *The Leeds Mercury*, October 16, 1830. Reprinted in " Tory Radical ", by C. Driver (1946), pp. 42-4.

YORKSHIRE SLAVERY

To the Editors of the Leeds Mercury

' It is the pride of Britain that a slave cannot exist on her soil; and if I read the genius of her constitution aright, I find that slavery is most abhorrent to it — that the air which Britons breathe is free — the ground on which they tread is sacred to liberty.' *Rev. R. W. Hamilton's Speech at the Meeting held in the Cloth-hall Yard, September 22d, 1830.*

GENTLEMEN,— No heart responded with truer accents to the sounds of liberty which were heard in the Leeds Cloth-hall Yard, on the

22d instant, than did mine, and from none could more sincere and earnest prayers arise to the throne of Heaven, that hereafter slavery might only be known to Britain in the pages of her history. One shade alone obscured my pleasure, arising not from any difference in principle, but from the want of application of the general principle, *to the whole empire.* The pious and able champions of *negro* liberty and *colonial* rights should, if I mistake not, have gone farther than they did; or perhaps, to speak more correctly, before they had travelled so far as the West Indies, should, at least for a few moments, have sojourned in our own immediate neighborhood, and have directed the attention of the meeting to scenes of misery, acts of oppression, and victims of slavery, even on the threshold of our homes.

Let truth speak out, appalling as the statement may appear. The fact is true. Thousands of our fellow-creatures and fellow-subjects, both male and female, the miserable inhabitants of a *Yorkshire town*, (Yorkshire now represented in Parliament by the giant of anti-slavery principles) are this very moment existing in a state of slavery, *more horrid* than are the victims of that hellish system ' *colonial slavery.*' These innocent creatures drawl out, unpitied, their short but miserable existence, in a place famed for its profession of religious zeal, whose inhabitants are ever foremost in *professing* ' temperance ' and ' reformation,' and are striving to outrun their neighbors in missionary exertions, and would fain send the Bible to the farthest corner of the globe — aye, in the very place where the anti-slavery fever rages most furiously, her *apparent charity* is not more admired on earth, than her *real cruelty* is abhorred in Heaven. The very streets which receive the droppings of an ' Anti-Slavery Society ' are every morning wet by the tears of innocent victims at the accursed shrine of avarice, who are *compelled* (not by the cart-whip of the negro slave-driver) but by the dread of the equally appalling thong or strap of the over-looker, to hasten, half-dressed, *but not half-fed*, to those magazines of British infantile slavery — *the worsted mills in the town and neighborhood of Bradford*!!!

Would that I had Brougham's eloquence, that I might rouse the hearts of the nation, and make every Briton swear, ' These innocents shall be free ! '

Thousands of little children, both male and female, *but principally female*, from seven to fourteen years of age, are daily *compelled* to *labour* from six o'clock in the morning to seven in the evening, with only — Britons, blush while you read it ! — *with only thirty minutes allowed for eating and recreation.* Poor infants ! ye are indeed sacrificed at the shrine of avarice, *without even the solace of the negro slave*; ye are no more than he is, *free agents*; ye are compelled to work as long as the *necessity* of your needy parents may require, or the cold-blooded avarice of your worse than barbarian masters *may demand*! Ye live in the boasted land of freedom, and *feel* and mourn that *ye are slaves*, and slaves without the only comfort which the negro has. He knows it is his sordid, mercenary master's interest that he should *live*, be *strong* and *healthy*. Not so with you. Ye are doomed to labour from morning to night for one who cares not how soon your weak and tender frames are stretched to breaking! You are not mercifully valued at so much per head; this would assure you at least (even with the worst and most cruel masters) of the mercy shown to their own labouring beasts. No, no! your soft and delicate limbs are tired and fagged, and jaded, at only *so much per week*, and when your joints can act no longer, your emaciated frames are cast aside, the boards on which you lately toiled and wasted life away, are instantly supplied with other victims, who in this boasted land of liberty are HIRED — not sold — as slaves and daily forced to hear that they are free.

.   .   .   .   .   .

The blacks may be fairly compared to beasts of burden, *kept for their master's use*; the whites, to those *which others keep and let for hire*. If I have succeeded in calling the attention of your readers to the horrid and abominable system on which the worsted mills in and near Bradford is conducted, I have done some good. Why should not children working in them be protected by legislative enactments, as well as those who work in cotton mills? Christians should feel and act for those whom Christ so eminently loved, and declared that 'of such is the Kingdom of Heaven.' — I remain, yours, etc.,

A BRITON

FIXBY HALL, NEAR HUDDERSFIELD, *Sept.* 29, 1830.

(*b*) From John Fielden, "The Curse of the Factory System" (1836), pp. iii–iv.

PREFACE

When I consented to become a Member of Parliament, it was not with a view of joining party men or aiding in party movements; but, in order to assist, by my vote, in doing such things as I thought would benefit the labouring people as well on the land as in the factory and at the loom. I have, all my years of manhood, been a Radical Reformer, because I thought Reform would give the people a power in the House of Commons that would secure to them that better condition of which they are worthy.

There is no natural cause for our distresses. We have fertile land, the finest herds and flocks in the world, and the most skilful husbandmen ; we have fine rivers and ports, and shipping unequalled ; and our ingenuity and industry have given us manufactures which ought to complete these blessings. I am a manufacturer ; but I am not one of those who think it time we had dispensed with the land. I think that these interests are all conducive to the prosperity of the nation ; that all must go together, and that the ruin of either will leave the others comparatively insecure.

But, with all our means of prosperity, and, if we believe the high authority which reminds us of it every session of Parliament, with all the prosperity that we *have*, I cannot believe it necessary that the manufacturers should work their labourers in the manner that they do. The proposition, therefore, of my Lord Ashley, to diminish the excessive labour of those who work in factories, is one for which I cordially thank him, and in which he shall have my support. I know it to be one of bare justice and humanity. I have long thought it, and have aided those who were more active than myself in attempts to obtain it. I am concerned in a very large business myself, and as my manufacture, my home trade and my export trade, is almost exclusively of that sort in which the Americans attempt to compete with us, I must be one of the first to be ruined, if foreign competition is to ruin us.

The object of the following pages is to show that the workpeople have been and are cruelly treated ; that they have not idly asked for protection, but that humanity and justice require it ; that we shall do ourselves no harm by granting it to them ; but always avowing, that I would cast manufactures to the winds, rather than see the workpeople enslaved, maimed, vitiated, and broken in constitution and in heart, as these pages will but too amply prove they now are.

JOHN FIELDEN.

LONDON, 17*th May*, 1836.

4. THE SHORT TIME COMMITTEES

[The agitation for factory legislation was carried on in the factory districts by Short Time Committees, including friendly employers and middle-class sympathisers as well as representatives of the workers. These Committees, in addition to conducting local agitations, worked in close touch with the leaders of the factory movement in Parliament, and sent deputations to interview M.P.s when factory matters were under consideration. The first of the following extracts relates to the appointment by the Whig Government early in 1833 of a Royal Commission to report on the question of further factory legislation. The factory reformers believed that this was intended as a device for shelving the matter, by getting an unfavourable report based chiefly on the masters' evidence. But Edwin Chadwick, who took the leading part in the Commission, was convinced by the evidence of the need for legislation; and the Commission's Report actually served as the basis for the Factory Act of 1833, which extended regulation to the woollen and other textile industries and included provision for the appointment of inspectors under Home Office authority. The second extract shows how the Short Time Committees tried to ignore the Commission and to press on their own Ten Hours Bill, which went a long way beyond what Parliament conceded in the Act of 1833.]

(*a*) From the First Report of the Select Committee on Combinations of Workmen (1838), p. 256 (examination of John Doherty).

Mr. Pringle) Will you state generally for what purposes the combination took place ? — There were several objects of the Spinners' association; the main object was to prevent reductions of wages; and next, if it be possible, and we hope it will be certain, to procure an Act of Parliament to lessen the hours of labour in factories. That point, I believe, in fact I know, during the whole of my connexion with the spinners of Manchester, has been one that has never changed. Our society has been abandoned at different periods, and our meetings given up, but we have never abandoned the hope and attempt to lessen the hours of labour by Act of Parliament.

Mr. O'Connell) You mean what is called the Ten Hours' Bill ? — Yes; 10 hours or less.

Mr. Pringle) You do not deprecate the interference of the Legislature with such a subject as that ? — No, we do not; we seek it.

To what extent, then, do you deprecate the interference of the Legislature with the interests of the workmen ? — With regard to the mode of carrying on their combinations or anything of that description.

Are there any other objects or purposes for which you associate ? — The other object of combination would be in endeavouring to prevent certain harsh treatment, to which we find we are gradually becoming more and more subjected.

Lord Ashley) You say that what is technically called the Factory Question has been the main object of your combination for many years ? — It has for more than 20 years, to my knowledge; I can state as a fact, that in 1818, when our combination was broken up, in consequence of a strike that was unsuccessful, in the year or two following that, when the men contributed nothing to the funds of the union, they contributed regularly for the purpose of procuring an Act of Parliament upon that question, and one was enacted in 1819.

Do you ever make contributions now for the purpose of carrying out that result ? — Regularly; as soon as a notice appears of the question being mooted in Parliament, a discussion takes place, and so much money is set aside to defray the expense of attending to the proceedings in Parliament, and obtaining information.

(*b*) From 'Alfred' [Samuel Kydd], "The History of the Factory Movement" (1857), vol. i, pp. 254-6.

At Manchester, Mr. Sadler and Mr. Oastler were welcomed by a public procession and dinner. The reporter for the *Leeds Intelligencer* thus described the scene he witnessed : " Soon after five (in the afternoon of Saturday the 23rd of August, 1832) Mr. Sadler and Mr. Oastler left the Shakespeare, and entered an open carriage prepared for them by the Committee, amidst the most enthusiastic cheering; the bands saluting and the flags waving. They were accompanied by Mr. John Wood of Bradford, the Rev. Mr. Bull, and Mr. Perring. Amidst this almost hurricane of applause the word was given to move forward for the place of meeting — Camp Field.

" The procession was headed by two men, bearing a flag with the representation of a deformed man, inscribed — ' Am I not a man and a brother ? ' underneath, ' No White Slavery '. Then came a band of music ; then the Committee and their friends ; then a long line of Factory children bearing a great variety of banners, decorated mops, brushes, and other utensils connected with their employment, hundreds of them singing, ' Sadler for ever, Oastler for ever ; six in the morning, six in the evening.'

" One of the children carried a whip, and a strap made into thongs, with the inscription, ' Behold and weep.' Next to this immense multitude of ' little victims,' as they were aptly designated, came the carriage with the visitors. A countless number of men followed, five or six deep, all staunch friends of the Ten Hours'

Bill, having at short intervals bands of music, banners, &c., with mottos expressive of some sentiment, opinion, or fact connected with the great cause. We cannot pretend to give a tithe of these inscriptions. We observed, ' Cursed are they that oppress the poor ; ' ' Let us unite and gain by strength our right ; ' ' Sadler and Oastler for ever ; ' ' Welcome to Sadler ; ' ' Oastler our Champion ; ' ' Sadler our advocate ; ' ' Let us unite in laying the axe to the root of infant slavery ; ' ' No White Slavery ; ' ' Death to infant oppression ; ' a figure of a deformed man exclaiming, ' Excessive toil is the burden of my soul.' One person carried a very neat model of a cotton-factory, inscribed, ' The infant's bastile.' On other banners we remarked, ' Revere Oastler, the children's friend ; ' ' The Factory system is the bane of health, the source of ignorance and vice ; ' ' The enactment of a Ten Hours' Bill will be attended with beneficent results to both master and man.' Many of these flags and banners were of costly materials, and the devices skilfully executed ; some of them were of more homely materials, but all were showy, and the effect to the eye cannot be conveyed in the most eloquent description. There were seventeen bands of music, and several hundred flags.

" In this order did the procession move through the principal streets of Manchester. The applause which greeted Mr. Sadler and Mr. Oastler was both enthusiastic and continuous. The men shouted ; the women clapped their hands, or held up their infant children, and screamed ' God bless Mr. Sadler,' ' God bless Mr. Oastler ; ' and thousands, we repeat, thousands, crowded round the carriage as it proceeded, and insisted upon shaking their benefactors by the hands, and all cried ' *Welcome to Manchester.*' Nor were the greetings confined to the crowds in the streets. The windows were filled with spectators ; even the house-tops in many instances were occupied. As to Mr. Sadler, his name was in every mouth. . . ."

(*c*) From C. Driver, " Tory Radical " (1946), pp. 553-5.

APPENDIX C

Instructions concerning the Reception of the Royal Commission issued to local Short Time Committees by the Manchester Delegates' Conference, April 26th, 1833.

Instructions to the Short Time Committee of England and Scotland, with Reference to the Commission.

I. That on the arrival of the Royal Commissioners in every Town or District, a written Protest shall be presented by the Short-Time Committee of such Town or District, in a body or by their Secretary, protesting against the proceedings of the Commission as unnecessary, partial, and delusive, agreeably to the Form (to be forwarded), or otherwise expressed as the said Short-Time Committee may see good.

II. That each Short-Time Committee shall select two or more intelligent, and discreet, and inflexible men of good character, to watch the proceedings of the said Commissioners, from their arrival in, to their departure from, any place to which they may proceed. The duty of which Select Committee shall be, most accurately to observe and note the proceedings of the said Commissioners : the Mills or places to which they proceed, the persons whom they shall examine : distinguishing whether they are employers, overlookers, or operatives ; and whether the latter are selected by or examined in the presence of, their masters or overlookers : and also to notice the time such Commissioners remain in each Mill or Factory they profess to inspect, and the number of hands employed ; and also the persons whom they principally consult, or with whom they associate or visit ; and also their conduct and proceedings in every particular, all which they shall as far as possible observe and record.

. . . . . .

V. That the said select Committee shall inform themselves whether the Commissioners shall examine the Hospitals, Infirmaries, Poor-Houses, Sunday Schools, Lying-in Hospitals, and other charitable Institutions, as well as the Cottages and Cellar-dwellings of the poor, and ascertain as far as possible the nature and results of their several examinations.

VI. That the said select Committee shall ascertain as far as possible, any alteration which shall have been made in the Ages of the Children employed in Mills and Factories, their time of refreshment, hours of labour, or wages, or whether any extra painting, whitewashing, fencing off machinery, or other improvements in the management of the said Mills or Factories, since the Bills for their regulation have been agitated, and especially since the Royal Commission has been known to be appointed : also to obtain as full and correct a list as possible of all the cripples and maimed in their neighbourhood, with their residences, etc.

VII. That the said Committee shall, if possible, inform themselves whether the infant, weakly, infirm, crippled or maimed hands shall have been removed, or the condition and temperature of the Mills, or the speed of the Engine, or the dress and condition of the Children altered and improved previous to the inspection of the said Commissioners.

VIII. That the said Committee shall inquire into, and record any cases of breaches of the existing law, gross instances of cruelty, or degradation and suffering which in the course of their duty now imposed upon them may fall under their notice, with a view to a further exposition of the state of factory labour.

. . . .

X. For the purpose of affording ocular demonstration in the persons of those employed in factory labour of the necessity for the limitation proposed by Lord Ashley, it be especially recommended to the fathers, mothers, and children of the operatives, peaceably and orderly, to assemble every evening, after the closing of the Mills, before the House or Inn, whether the said Royal Commissioners shall remain, and state to them whether or not they wish to obtain the Ten Hours Bill.

XI. That a Book shall be kept by each Select Committee of all matters and things observed or done by them, agreeably to the above directions, and that a copy of the same shall be transmitted with all reasonable speed, by the Lancashire Committees to the Central Committee in Manchester, addressed to Mr. G. Higginbottom, 14, Larendon Place, Chorlton Row, Manchester ; or by the Yorkshire Committees, to Richard Oastler, Esq. Fixby Hall, near Huddersfield. The Friends in Scotland have directed Communications to be sent to Dr. D. M'Aulay, 40, London-Street, Glasgow.

(*d*) From C. Driver, " Tory Radical " (1946), pp. 555-7.

APPENDIX D

The Address of the Operatives of England and Scotland, to All Ranks and Classes of the Land, April 1833.

FELLOW COUNTRYMEN—We appeal to you on behalf of the Ten Hours Bill, now before the House of Commons, and under Lord Ashley's care. Whatever may be the manifold causes of national distress, and of that poverty, in most cases, or that profligacy in some, which induces parents to submit their offspring to such ruinous toil, and whatever remedies it may be considered proper to apply, still, in the name of justice, let the law of England protect children without further delay from lawless and heartless avarice. We, who now address you, are operatives ourselves ; we have heard and read discussion upon discussion on this humane and righteous measure, and after calm and deliberate reflection, we unanimously conclude that it will be favourable to commerce in general, to the honest master, and the industrious man, and to the moral and political health of society. . . . By a table appended to the evidence before the select committee, it is demonstrated, that more have died before their twentieth year, where the factory system extensively prevails, than have died at their fortieth year elsewhere. But this suffices not. Insatiable as death, the rich oppressor still asserts his right, to add to his blood-guilty store, by working the British Infant beyond the time of the soldier, the farmer, nay the adult felon, and the more fortunate child of British colonial slavery.

Let Lord Ashley's name be dear to Britain's honest labourers and oppressed factory children. Let his factory bill have your support. Our request is that you will use every lawful and constitutional means to promote its legislative adoption this session. Give them no rest — pour out your petitions for us and our children at the foot of the throne, and into both Houses of Parliament. Protest, as we do, against the mill-owners' commission. We will not, except by legal obligation, try our cause before it. We challenge such a jury, appointed as it is by those who have been arraigned at the bar of their country to try their own cause, or rather to cover their guilt from public view. . . . We leave our cause in your hands, and implore our fellow-countrymen of every rank, to petition without delay for the Ten Hours Bill, and that it may be passed without reference to a partial, unjust, unnecessary, and delusive parliamentary commission, sued out on false pretences, to the abuse of his Majesty's royal prerogative, and to the hurt and grief of his loving and loyal subjects.

GEO. HIGGINBOTTOM,
Chairman.

MANCHESTER, *April* 25, 1833.

(*e*) From ' Alfred ' [Samuel Kydd], " The History of the Factory Movement " (1857), vol. i, pp. 235-6 and 239-40.

THE YORK COUNTY MEETING, 1832

There has not been held, in the whole course of English agitations, a more remarkable gathering than that which met in the Castle

Yard of York, on April 24, 1832, to demonstrate to Parliament that Yorkshire was in earnest for a Ten Hours' Bill. The nearest factory town to York was Leeds, a distance of twenty-four miles; many of the outlying districts were from forty to fifty miles from the place of meeting. The air was cold, the rain during the previous night fell in torrents, the weather was described in the Castle Yard to be " the most inclement within memory." Leeds, Bradford, Bingley, Keighley, Dewsbury, Heckmondwicke, Batley, Huddersfield, Honley Holmfirth, Marsden, Meltham, Elland, Hebdenbridge, Pudsey, Rawden, Otley, and other towns and villages were that day represented in the Castle Yard. Thousands of men foot-sore, but not faint of heart, who had walked from twenty-four to fifty miles, blessed God when their eyes that morning saw York Minster. Not only men, but factory boys and girls, mothers with infants in their arms, fifty miles from their own homes, were there to hold up their hands to heaven as an earnest of their desire to be freed from a worse than an Egyptian bondage. It was a sight to have made a man love his kind; to have seen how the stronger helped the weaker along the road to York, and from York home again; to make them share each others' food, to behold the noble spirit of self-sacrifice which made those in front wait for and often return to help onward those in the rear. Oastler and Bull were everywhere cheering and encouraging the straggling bands. Fatigue, hunger, and thirst, were borne with courage and self-denial; property of all kinds was safe as if all had been in their own parishes. The meeting was most numerously attended, the Castle Yard, which was then of very large area, having been three parts full. The estimated numbers varied, all admitted there were many thousands.

. . . . . .

The banners were in many cases very strikingly expressive. Most of them had a Scriptural phrase or allusion. Some were painted by the rude artist to represent the ' horrors ' of the mill system — such as a father carrying his little girl through a pelting storm of sleet and snow to a noted flax mill near Leeds, at five in the morning, himself in tatters, and having taken off his own remnant of what was once a coat, to cover his hapless babe, who was doomed to earn its parent's living, as well as its own, at the certain destruction of its own health and morals, and probably its very life — doomed to lie in a premature grave.

Others had inscribed ' Father, is it time ? ' a cry which is often heard the night through in the crowded and wretched dormitory of the factory working-people, and which little children, more asleep than awake (dreading the consequences of being late), were often heard to utter.

5. THE FACTORY ACT OF 1833

[The Act of 1833 provided for an extension of regulation to all types of textile factory. It prescribed a maximum working day of 9 hours for children between nine and thirteen, and of 12 hours for young persons between thirteen and eighteen, with special exceptions for silk factories. Its chief importance lay in the inclusion of other industries besides cotton, and in the appointment of salaried inspectors to enforce the law. At first there was much disappointment at the inadequacy of the regulations drawn up under the Act, and fear of it becoming a dead letter. But, limited as its provisions were, the inspectors did make a real effort to enforce them, and conditions did gradually improve.]

(*a*) The Purposes of the Act. From Leonard Horner, " The Factories Regulation Act Explained ", 1834. (Quoted in M. W. Thomas, " The Early Factory Legislation " (1948), p. 70.)

This Act has three great objects in view : *first*, to prevent children and young persons from being worked a greater number of hours than is believed to be safe for their health ; *secondly*, to give time for the children to receive a suitable education, and to insist that their education shall not be neglected ; and *thirdly*, to accomplish these ends without interfering with the generally established number of hours of daily work of adults.

(*b*) Oastler's Comment. From Richard Oastler, " The Rejected Letter ", 1836. (Quoted in M. W. Thomas, " The Early Factory Legislation " (1948), p. 71.)

. . . Finding himself very much annoyed by the innumerable petitions presented by the people to Parliament, he [Lord Althorp] told the Millowners, that the question could not be allowed to sleep, and that an Act of some sort must be passed, *in order to satisfy the demands of the people, and to put down the agitation, which was so annoying the Government*. After a good deal of ' back-stairs intriguing,' the *Millowners and the Government* concocted a Bill, and . . . we are informed that it was supported by the Millowners, *because they knew it to be impracticable*.

(c) The Benthamite View. From *The London and Westminster Review*, October 1836. (Quoted in M. W. Thomas, " The Early Factory Legislation " (1948), p. 73.)

We repeat, without watchfulness and exertion . . . the present law . . . will become a dead letter. For there are arrayed against it powerful interests which must defeat it, unless an agency be created adequate to enforce it. There is the interest of the parent, who, it is proved, cares only for the wages of his child, and who will do everything in his power to evade any provision made for its physical and moral improvement, if that improvement costs any portion, however small, of the child's wages. There is the interest of the workman on whom the care required, by the law, of the health and morals of the child imposes considerable trouble and some expense. There is the interest of the master to whom the strict observance of the regulations necessary to insure the proper instruction of the child must cause still more trouble and expense. There is the interest of the advocate for imposing restriction on adult labour who, in order to demonstrate that there is no true remedy for the evils of the factory system but the Ten-hour Bill, will do anything in his power to counteract the working of a measure, the direct and immediate object of which is limited to the regulation of the labour, the protection of the health, and the security of the education of the young. . . . There is the interest of the ally, the chief active promoter of the Ten-hour project, the operative agitator . . . who avoids the necessity of labour by taking on himself the more easy employment of declaiming.

(d) The Effects. From Leonard Horner, " On the Employment of Children in Factories ", 1840. (Quoted in M. W. Thomas, " The Early Factory Legislation " (1948), p. 74.)

The Act of 1833 has been productive of much good ; it has put an end to a large proportion of the evils which made the interference of the legislature then necessary. But it has not done nearly all the good that was intended. The failures have mainly arisen from the defects in the law itself ; not in the principles it lays down, but in the machinery which was constructed for the purpose of carrying the principles into operation. . . . There was this further source of error, that it was in some degree legislating in the dark ; a great part of the mechanism adopted was entirely of a novel description, of a kind that had never been tried in former factory acts ; and after it was set to work, much of it was found to have been ill-contrived, and some positively so bad that it obstructed, and to a great degree prevented, the attainment of the object.

6. THE SHORT TIME COMMITTEES IN THE 1840s

[The Short Time Movement continued throughout the Chartist agitation, but was resumed with increased vigour after the Trade Union defeats of 1842. In 1844, a new Factory Act limited the working hours of children to 6½ a day, but at the same time lowered the minimum age of employment to eight years. The Act introduced the half-time system, and in many respects improved and stiffened up the regulations. The operatives, however, were bitterly disappointed at the continued rejection of the Ten Hours Clause, and a considerable argument arose on the question whether, instead of continuing the parliamentary agitation for the Ten Hours Bill, it would be better to attempt to secure the limitation of the working day by direct negotiation with the employers, backed by the threat of strike action. In the event, the first of these courses was preferred, and the Ten Hours Bill became law three years later (see next extract).]

From Philip Grant, " The History of Factory Legislation ", 1866 (referring to 1844).

The delegates from Lancashire who had fought the battle in London, on their return issued a pamphlet giving an excellent report of the campaign, and concluded with the following remarks :—

" Nearly thirty years have elapsed since the late lamented Sir Robert Peel first brought the sufferings of the factory children before parliament ; ever since that period not a session has passed without something being done to improve their condition ; and each year has developed new facts and brought forth new arguments in support of the views promulgated by that estimable man. What, then, is the course now to be adopted ? Are we still to persevere with a peaceful agitation in the country, and in respectful application to parliament for redress ? Or are we to follow the advice of men in high places, and take our affairs into our own hands, and accomplish by combination that abridgement of our labour which, for the present, has been refused by parliament ?

. . . . . .

It is but justice here to observe, that some of our warmest supporters in the House of Commons are in favour of forming a union between masters and men to abridge the hours of factory labour without the aid of parliament. Should such an effort be successfully made, then all further agitation on the subject would be unnecessary ; but should it fail, we still have parliament to appeal to. In that tribunal we have now many influential friends; friends whose great aim and object is to benefit the factory operatives, and who will never fail to interest themselves in our behalf so long as we conduct our proceedings in the same spirit of peaceful and constitutional agitation which has hitherto governed the meetings in favour of short time.

Although our labours during the present session of parliament have not been crowned with success, yet we believe much has been gained by the new bill, which is now passed into a law. A new principle has been acknowledged, viz., that adult female factory labour ought to be restricted. By this enactment much good will be effected in the more distant parts of the country, where females are now worked thirteen, fourteen, and even sixteen hours a-day. Let it be known, wherever the report reaches, that after the 1st day of October next, females of whatever age cannot be worked more [than] twelve hours a-day, for five days in the week, and nine hours on the Saturday, without breaking the law.

All cases of overworking should be reported to the Chairman of the Central Short Time Committee, Red Lion Inn, London Road, Manchester. " . . .

7. THE TEN HOURS ACT

[At length, in 1847, the Ten Hours agitation, which had begun in 1819 and had been renewed in 1830 and carried on continuously from that time, achieved success in the placing on the Statute Book of the Ten Hours Act. This was not, however, by any means the end of the matter, as Shaftesbury hoped; for the Act afforded so many loopholes for evasion, and provoked so much resistance from the employers, that the struggle was almost immediately resumed. The employers pressed for relaxation, and the Short Time Committees for amendment to make the Act fully effective. In 1850 the ' Parke Judgment ', declaring lawful the use of ' relays ' of juvenile workers and thus enabling employers to keep their factories open and to work the unprotected adults as long as they pleased, knocked the bottom out of the Ten Hours Act. In face of the employers' demand for a day of 11 hours and of the Government's attitude, Shaftesbury agreed to compromise on a new Act fixing the working day at $10\frac{1}{2}$ hours. The Short Time Committees bitterly opposed this concession; but it was made in the Act of 1850. The ' relay ' system was not done away with until the further amending Act of 1853.]

Shaftesbury's Letter to the Short Time Committees, 1847. From E. Hodder, " The Life and Work of the Seventh Earl of Shaftesbury ", (1892), p. 369.

MY GOOD FRIENDS,—Although there is no longer any necessity to name you collectively and as united together for the purpose of obtaining a reduction of the hours of working in factories, I will address a few words to you . . . on questions of the highest and dearest interest.

First, we must give most humble and hearty thanks to Almighty God for the unexpected and wonderful success that has attended our efforts. We have won the great object of all our labours — the Ten Hours Bill has become the law of the land; and we may hope, nay, more, we believe that we shall find in its happy results, a full compensation for all our toils. . . .

I need not, I know, exhort you to an oblivion of past conflicts, and to hearty endeavour for future harmony. I trust that there will be no language of triumph, as though we had defeated an enemy. Let us be very thankful that the struggle is over, and that we can once more combine, not only the interests, but also the feelings, of employer and employed, in a mutual understanding for the comfort and benefit of each other, and for the welfare of the whole community. . . .

Although the final completion of this great measure has been achieved by another, I could not, after so many years of labour, take leave of it altogether without a few words to you of advice and congratulation. To no one could the lot have fallen so happily as to our friend Mr. Fielden. He joined me in 1833 in the introduction of the first Bill, and has been ever since, as you well know, your able, energetic, and unshrinking advocate.

In bidding you farewell, I do not retire from your service. I shall, at all times, hold myself in readiness to aid you in any measures that may conduce to the moral and physical welfare of yourselves and your children.

XIII

THE NEW POOR LAW

INTRODUCTION

THE New Poor Law of 1834 set out to abolish the Speenhamland System of subsidising wages and all forms of outdoor relief for the able-bodied and to substitute ' deterrent ' workhouses, in which man and wife were separated and life made deliberately rigorous. Control was vested in a central commission — ' the three Bashaws of Somerset House ' — who were quick to apply the new regulations as ruthlessly as possible. In the agricultural districts of the South they met with little resistance from the demoralised labourers, passive after the defeated revolt of 1830 and the Tolpuddle case of 1834. But when in 1836 — a year of bad trade — the Act began to be introduced into the manufacturing districts of the North, it aroused intense opposition. A mass revolt, led in particular by the Methodist J. R. Stephens and the Tory Democrat Richard Oastler, prevented the introduction of the new Act in many towns. This was a revolt against more than the Poor Law ; it was a hunger revolt against the new industrial civilisation. Feargus O'Connor, who moved north in 1837 and founded *The Northern Star*, found it easy to turn the movement into political channels and to rally the North behind the Charter in a blind hope that when the Charter was won a new life would begin.

> *See* " Short History ", Part I, chapter 7, section 1.
> " Common People ", chapter 23.

1. COBBETT ON THE POOR LAW BILL

[Whigs, Tories, and middle-class Radicals were for the most part united in support of the Poor Law Amendment Bill of 1834. The working classes, on the other hand, were solidly against it, and were supported by the ' Radical Tories ', such as Oastler and Stephens, and also by a section of Tory opinion which hated centralisation and bureaucracy, and regarded the Bill as a blow at the authority of the local Justices of the Peace. Cobbett for once found himself in alliance with John Walter, of *The Times*. Both denounced the Bill in all its stages as subversive of British traditions of local freedom, as well as gross tyranny at the expense of the workers.]

From *Cobbett's Weekly Political Register*, May 3, 1834.

I have this bill; but I will not now attempt an analysis of it, chiefly because I have not duly considered the extent of all its terrible consequences if attempted to be carried into execution. It is a sort of *Austrian* project : a scheme for bringing every thing and every body within the control, the immediate control, of the kingly part of the Government. This bill will totally abrogate all the local government of the kingdom : the gentlemen and the magistrates will be totally divested of all power, tending to uphold their character, and to secure their property, and their personal safety in the country. I have talked to twenty gentlemen, farmers and attorneys ; every man of them has said : " If this bill be attempted to be put into execution, there will be a revolution in England "; and I am so firmly persuaded of the soundness of their opinion, that I should look upon the result as something inevitable.

. . . . . .

In the country an execution of this bill is literally impossible : every parish would be plunged into confusion immediately ; men would not work, and there must be constables and jailers, or police and soldiers, stationed in every parish. The Parliament may pass the law, but it never can be executed ; it would be a mere heap of rubbishy words, flung aside, while the government of parishes would be carried on without any law at all.

2. THE CALL TO RESISTANCE

[William Cobbett died in June 1835. His last articles in his *Political Register* were largely devoted to attacking the new Poor Law Commission and calling for nation-wide resistance to the enforcement of the Poor Law Act.]

From *Cobbett's Weekly Political Register*, June 13, 1835.

For it really appears to be another " RURAL WAR ", and

threatens to be much more durable and mischievous than the last rural war; and there is this circumstance in addition, in this case; that is to say, that this new scene of trouble, of turmoil, and of boiling blood, has been caused by the Parliament itself; that Parliament duly warned by me of all the consequences. In this respect it is another PEEL's-Bill affair. The proposition is made in the year 1833; the projectors are then warned, and are besought not to adopt the measure; they persevere a great deal more eagerly on account of the warning and the prediction, as if for the express purpose of making the prophet a liar. Half-a-dozen counties are in a state of partial commotion; the jails are opening the doors to receive those who are called the rebels against the Poor-law Bill! No matter as to any other thing relative to this measure; here is the country disturbed; here are the jails filling; here are wives and children screaming after their fathers; here are these undeniable facts; and what is the cause? Not a desire to overturn the Government on the part of the people; not a desire to disobey the settled laws of the country; not any revolutionary desire; not any desire to touch any one of the institutions of the country. What is it then? Why a desire and a resolution, as far as they are able to adhere to it, to maintain the laws of their country, as they were settled at the time when the *present church of the country was established*; to maintain those laws which formed the foundation, the very fundamental principles of the Government; and which are of two hundred and forty years' standing.

3. THE RESISTANCE

[Serious resistance to the new Poor Law began only in 1837, when the Commissioners first attempted to put it into operation in the factory districts. The labourers in the areas which had been under the Speenhamland System had been too recently crushed after the 'Labourers' Revolt' of 1830 and the conviction of the Tolpuddle Martyrs in 1834 to be in a position to resist; and the Commission devoted its first efforts to getting the new system applied in the 'Speenhamland' counties, mainly in the South. When in 1837 they turned their attention to the North, at a time of trade recession, a widespread resistance soon developed, incidentally turning Chartism from a relatively small and peaceable movement into a violent mass revolt. Oastler in Yorkshire and the Rev. Joseph Rayner Stephens in Lancashire became the outstanding orators of the anti-Poor Law movement in the North.]

(a) Extract from a Speech by the Rev. J. R. Stephens on the New Poor Law, January 1838. Printed in R. G. Gammage, "History of the Chartist Movement" (1st edition, 1854), pp. 64-5.

The people were not going to stand this, and he would say, that sooner than wife and husband, and father and son, should be sundered and dungeoned, and fed on "skillee", — sooner than wife or daughter should wear the prison dress — sooner than that — Newcastle ought to be, and should be — one blaze of fire, with only one way to put it out, and that with the blood of all who supported this abominable measure. . . .

He (Mr Stephens) was a revolutionist by fire, he was a revolutionist by blood, to the knife, to the death. If an unjust, unconstitutional, and illegal parchment was carried in the pockets of the Poor Law Commissioners, and handed over to be slung on a musket, or a bayonet, and carried through their bodies by an armed force, or by any force whatever, that was a tidy sentence, and if this meeting decided it was contrary to law and allegiance to the sovereign — that it was altogether a violation of the constitution, and of common sense, it ought to be resisted in every legal way. It was law to think about it, and to talk about, and to put their names on paper against it, and after that to go to the Guildhall and to speak against it. And when that would not do, it was law to ask what was to be done next. And then it would be law for every man to have his firelock, his cutlass, his sword, his pair of pistols, or his pike, and for every woman to have her pair of scissors, and for every child to have its paper of pins and its box of needles, (here the orator's voice was drowned in the cheers of the meeting) and let the men with a torch in one hand and a dagger in the other, put to death any and all who attempted to sever man and wife.

(b) From Richard Oastler. "Damnation! Eternal Damnation to the Fiend-begotten Coarser-Food New Poor Law" (1837), p. 10.

What I am now going to say, *I have written beforehand*, in order that there might be no mistake, and that I might afterwards know what I have said. (Mr. Oastler here read from the M.S. in question) :—

"I tell you deliberately, if I have the misfortune to be reduced to poverty, That that man who dares to tear from me the wife whom God has joined to me, shall, if I have it in my power, receive his death at my hands! If I am ever confined in one of those hellish

Poor Law Bastiles, and my wife be torn from me, because I am poor, I will, if it be possible, burn the whole pile down to the ground. This will I do, if my case shall be thus tried, if I have the power; and every man who loves his wife, and who is unstained by crime, will if he can, do the same.— Further, I will not pay any tax imposed upon me, under this Act. I will ' resist ', as the Dissenters are resisting the Church Rates.''

4. THE ANTI-POOR LAW ASSOCIATIONS

[Anti-Poor Law Associations, of which the Huddersfield Association was one of the most active, having Oastler's strong support, were formed in a number of areas in the North to organise the resistance. Most of them merged later into the local Chartist organisations.]

From *The Northern Star*, March 10, 1838.

' The Address of the Anti-Poor Law Association Committee, to the rate-payers and inhabitants of several boroughs comprised in the Commissioners' Poor Law Union for the Huddersfield district.'

FELLOW RATE PAYERS.

The time has come for you to give a practical demonstration of your hatred to the new Starvation Law.

Recollect ! that the 25th of March is the day which is set apart for the election of new Guardians for the ensuing year ; therefore, it will depend upon your exertions, whether you will allow men to be elected as Guardians, who are the mere tools of the three Commissioners in carrying out their diabolical schemes for starving the poor, reducing the labourers' wages, and robbing you the rate-payers of that salutary control you have hitherto exercised over your money and your townships affairs ; or will you elect men of character and of humanity, whose high and independent spirit will scorn to submit to the three headed monster of Somerset House, and will prefer death itself, rather than sacrifice the rights of their neighbours and constituents at the bidding of three pensioned lawyers, residing in London, and living in princely splendour out of your hard-earned money.

We call upon you to awake, arise, assert your rights, and maintain your liberties, by electing men on whom you can depend, and who will not betray you in the day of trial; and we feel persuaded that all those of you who possess any love of country, any affection for your wives, your husbands, and your families, and do not wish to be separated from them, or to see poverty punished as a crime, and in whose bosom glows the smallest spark of sympathy or philanthropy — this call will not be made in vain.

Therefore for the guidance of your conduct, we beg to suggest to you the following considerations :

First.—We recommend the formation of local committees in every township, village, and hamlet, where committees have not been formed. [Some technical advice on the procedure for nomination and election follows.] . . .

Rate-payers, do your duty and select none who are in the remotest degree favourable to the hellish Act. Remember that the law is cruel, illegal, and unconstitutional — one of degradation and absolute starvation for the poor. That the real object of it is to lower wages and punish poverty as a crime. Remember also that children and parents are dying frequently in the same Bastile, without seeing one another, or knowing of one another's fate.

5. THE STRUGGLE AT TODMORDEN

[Todmorden, on the border between Yorkshire and Lancashire, was the place where Fielden Brothers had their principal mills; and under John Fielden's leadership an active resistance was put up to the Commissioners' attempts to get a Board of Guardians elected and working in the area. Despite all the Commissioners could do by full use of the powers of the law, the new Poor Law was never fully enforced in the Todmorden Union while John Fielden remained alive.]

(a) From the Fourth Annual Report of the Poor Law Commissioners (1838), pp. 47-8.

On the occasion of our issuing the usual order to the Guardians of Todmorden Union a most extraordinary course of conduct was pursued, with the view of defeating the operation of the law, by Messrs. Fielden and Co., cotton-manufacturers, the proprietors of very extensive works in some of the townships of that Union. These gentlemen suddenly dismissed from their employment the whole body of their workpeople (amounting, as we are informed, to several thousand hands), with an intimation, which was published by placard and signed by one of their firm, that they should altogether cease to afford employment to their people until the persons who were acting as Guardians should be induced to resign their offices.

This step having been accompanied by the advertisement of a public meeting to be held in the immediate neighbourhood of the meeting of the Guardians, the latter very properly took measures to avoid assembling on that occasion, and to effect an adjournment of their meeting to a subsequent day.

In the mean time, such precautionary steps were taken by the resident magistrates as effectually secured the peace of the neighbourhood, and enabled the Guardians to assemble on the day of the adjourned meeting, and to proceed, undisturbed, in carrying the order of the Commissioners into execution.

In the following week Messrs. Fielden and Co., having wholly failed in this remarkable endeavour to intimidate the Guardians in the execution of their duty, re-opened their works, and received back their work-people into employment.

(*b*) From the Fifth Annual Report of the Poor Law Commissioners (1839), pp. 31-4.

In Todmorden Union, immediately on the introduction of the new system, an attempt was made by the partners of one manufactory, as stated in our last Report, to prevent the peaceable operation of the law, by throwing the whole of their work-people at once out of employment, and closing their works. This attempt to intimidate the guardians, by endangering the peace of the neighbourhood, having been defeated by the promptitude of the magistrates, and the steady determination of the guardians, Messrs. Fielden, on the 16th day of July, re-opened their works; and on that day a printed placard was posted in and about Todmorden, purporting to be signed by Mr. John Fielden, one of the partners, and addressed to the Board of Guardians.

In this placard the following remarkable passages occur :—

" To oppose force to force we are not yet prepared ; but if the people of this and the surrounding districts are to be driven to the alternative of either doing so, or surrendering their local government into the hands of an unconstitutional board of lawmakers, the time may not be far distant when the experiment may be tried, and I

337

would warn those who provoke the people to such a combat of the danger they are incurring.

.   .   .   .   .   .

" I cannot help adding, as a point worthy of your most serious consideration, that your real difficulties may only commence when the period arrives for the relief of the poor being administered by your board, and the officers acting under it. Supplies will be required, the rates will have to be collected, and, after having disregarded the entreaties of your brother rate-payers, this may be much more difficult to accomplish than you expect, even with the threatened force at your back. You have heard that tithes could not be collected in Ireland; and if you persevere you may have the satisfaction of knowing that rates cannot be collected in England."

On the guardians proceeding to assume the administration of relief, and to demand from the overseers of the several townships the sums necessary for this purpose, the overseers of Todmorden and Langfield (the townships in which Messrs. Fielden's works are chiefly situate) adopted a course of passive resistance and disobedience to the law, in which they have persevered up to the present time. The overseers of the other townships having supplied the necessary funds, the guardians at once assumed the administration of relief to the poor in those townships; but the poor of Todmorden and Langfield have not been relieved by the Board of Guardians for want of the necessary funds.

In the meantime the powers of the law have been exerted against the overseers of the two townships making default. The overseers of Todmorden have been convicted of a first and second offence under the 98th section of the Poor Law Amendment Act, and the fines of 51*l*. in the first instance, and of 20*l*. in the second, have been levied by distress upon the goods of one of them. An appeal, which the overseers entered against the second conviction at Salford sessions, was abandoned at the moment of trial. A *mandamus* has been sued out against the same parties from the Court of Queen's Bench to compel them to pay the required sums to the guardians, and this process is still pending. The overseers of the same township have also been indicted, and found guilty of a misdemeanor, for neglecting to make and render an account of their expenditure to the auditor of the Union. This indictment the defendants removed by *certiorari* from the court of quarter sessions to the Queen's Bench, and it was accordingly tried before Mr. Baron Alderson at the late Liverpool assizes, when the learned judge overruled certain objections made by the defendants on questions of law, but gave them leave to move the Court of Queen's Bench to reverse his judgment.

Such is the present situation of the Todmorden Union as regards the enforcement of the law by legal process in the course of justice. The length of time which it requires to carry those processes through the several courts is the more to be regretted, as, under the present circumstances, there appears to be no legal provision in force for the relief of the poor in either of the two townships in question.

We regret to be obliged to add to this statement, that, besides this refusal of the necessary supplies for the relief of the poor, the other mode of resistance to the law adverted to in the above placard of the 16th July, has been adopted in this Union by a number of misguided persons, who appear to have believed that the time had arrived for opposing force to force, and that a violent resistance to the law was not only justifiable, on the part of those who were adverse to its operation, but that it might be attended with a successful result.

On the 16th November last two constables from Halifax, who were employed in executing a warrant of distress upon the overseer of Langfield, were violently assaulted and overpowered by a concourse of persons, the first assembling of which was accompanied by the ringing of a bell in one of Messrs. Fielden's factories, from which a large number of work-people issued, and took part in the riot which ensued. The two officers were stripped of their clothes, and otherwise brutally treated, and had great difficulty in escaping with their lives into the adjoining township of Stanfield; and here a further riot took place, accompanied by some destruction of property, and an attack upon the building in which the guardians were accustomed to meet.

On Wednesday, the 21st November following, the magistrates having previously issued summonses to certain persons to attend to be sworn in as special constables on the Thursday, it appears to have been deliberately determined by the parties who were disposed to resist the law by force, that the interval before the swearing in of the special constables should be taken advantage of for the destruction of the property of parties supposed to be favourable to the law.

Accordingly a large number of persons assembled in the afternoon of Wednesday, and proceeded well prepared with clubs and large pieces of timber, provided, as it afterwards appeared by the use which was made of them, for the purpose of battering and demolishing the doors and windows of the houses they attacked. The objects of this violence were the houses of the chairman and several other guardians of the Union, the clerk of the Union, and other persons supposed to be friendly to the law. A great destruction of property ensued; the obnoxious parties and their families were placed in peril, and in two instances attempts were made to set fire to dwelling-houses, which attempts fortunately failed. Mr. Crossley, one of the resident magistrates, despatched a request for military aid to the commanding officer at Burnley, but before the arrival of the troops the work of destruction had been abandoned, and the rioters had voluntarily dispersed.

Such was the state of excitement and alarm occasioned by these unfortunate proceedings, that the magistrates, in their subsequent active exertions to apprehend the rioters, deemed it expedient on two occasions to call out a military force in support of the constables while engaged in making prisoners of some of the workmen in Messrs. Fielden's mills. It has also appeared essential to the security of the neighbourhood that a combined force of infantry and cavalry should be stationed at Todmorden for the present.

More minute details of these proceedings have probably been supplied to your Lordship from other quarters, but we have thought it right to advert to them in this Report, as showing the origin and character of the opposition which has been encountered at Todmorden.

Nothing certainly could be more applicable to this case than the excellent observation made by the learned judge on the trial of some of the rioters convicted at York, to the effect, " that there were parties far more deserving of punishment, in reference to these transactions, than the misguided men who then stood before him for sentence ". An observation, to the same effect, appears to have been made by a jury at Liverpool in delivering their verdict of guilty against one of the Todmorden rioters of the 21st November ; they recommended the prisoner to the mercy of the court, on the ground that he had been " influenced by others ".

Since the military have been stationed in Todmorden tranquillity has prevailed in the neighbourhood, and the guardians have been enabled to carry on the administration of relief in all the townships of the Union, excepting only the two townships from which the necessary funds have not been supplied. It is our intention to proceed in using such means, for enforcing obedience to the law in the townships of Todmorden and Langfield, as we may find available for that purpose.

6. " THE BOOK OF THE BASTILES "

[G. R. Wythen Baxter's " The Book of the Bastiles " (1841) was a large volume made up of accounts of oppressive action taken under the new Poor Law, speeches and writings against it, and attacks on the Poor Law Commissioners. It had a wide influence ; but by the time it appeared the Commissioners had already succeeded in getting the new system into operation over nearly the whole country.]

From G. R. Wythen Baxter, " The Book of the Bastiles " (1841), Introduction, pp. iii-iv.

The *Book of the Bastiles* is composed not only for the present generation, but for posterity (and to both, surely, such a work will be useful and acceptable) — not only to excite the abhorrence of future beings for an atrocious legislative decree and its administrators, but, at the same time, to show those who shall fill our vacant places, when we shall be no longer seen, that there were not wanting men — and fine, noble-minded men too — notwithstanding the outrageous inhumanity which prevailed at the period — who, in the face of arbitrary power, persecution, death, and neglect and contempt worse to brook than death, dared be honest, dared be humane, and oppose it. In other words, the *Book of the Bastiles* is intended to certify to Englishmen, yet unborn, that the same age which produced a Brougham, a Russell, a Malthus, and a " Marcus ", nurtured and reared also, as if in extenuation, a Stanhope, an Oastler, a Fielden, and a Walter, — a General Johnson, and a Bishop of Exeter, as excellent as eloquent — benevolent — a constant opponent of the " boon ".

But the paramount reason for publishing the *Book of the Bastiles* was, the urgent necessity in the present alarming crisis — a crisis mainly attributable to the operation of such harsh, biting statutes as the New Poor-Law — of calling the attention of the upper and middle classes to the inhumanity, unchristianity, injustice, and political and social danger of the continued administration of the New Poor-Law Amendment-Act in England and Wales.

Had there been no *lettre de cachet*, the revolutionary *Marseillaise* would never have been tuned in retribution, and Louis XVI. would have died in his bed, and not on the block. Had there been no New Poor-Law, the name of Chartist would never have been heard ; nor would Birmingham have been heated with fire and fury, or Newport have run red with the gore of Britons from the hills. These are truisms that need no further parley. That Rural Police, and increased taxation, are the " Act's " necessary assistants on the Government's side, and stack-firing, and the manufacturing of pikes, its natural accompaniments on the side of the governed, are facts, alas ! equally incontrovertible. The New Poor-Law and good government and good order cannot exist together; the former must and will destroy the other two.

ib. p. x.

A few words more — the author's last — " *Baxter's last words* " — Barons of England, your halls are famous with the noble deeds of your sires of old — Gentlemen of England, ye were once generous — cruelty was not wont to be the cognizance of either. Noblemen and Gentlemen, assume what your fathers were. — Repeal the New Poor-Law — that law which they would never have suffered to be — and declare yourselves your country's saviours. Do so; and perform, by peaceful means, what, if left undone by you, will most assuredly at last be consummated by popular fire, sword, and fury. No people could long endure the barbarities of such despots as the trio of Somerset-house — they would indeed be base if they did — and least of all will those sprung from earth's best blood, the British people. From such an ignominious yoke they must

"——————— be free or die, who speak the tongue
That Shakespeare spake ; the faith and morals hold
Which Milton held : "——

7. THE SEPARATION OF THE SEXES

[" The Book of Murder ", by Marcus, published in 1839, purported to be based on an essay ' On the Possibility of Limiting Populousness ', which was said to have been written by ' One of the Three ', *i.e.* by one of the Poor Law Commissioners. Composed in the style of Malthusianism, it recommended various forms of painless infanticide as means of reducing the pauper population. Obviously written in the first instance in the spirit of bitter irony, it was believed by many Chartists, including J. R. Stephens, to have been written by someone connected with the Poor Law Commission ; and this belief was not removed by Edwin Chadwick's denials. The plausibility of the charge, such as it was, rested on the Poor Law Commission's insistence on separation of the sexes, in order to prevent paupers from having children or engaging in sexual intercourse. " The Book of Murder ", in its Chartist reissue, included a commentary, from which the second extract is taken.]

(*a*) From Marcus, " The Book of Murder ", 1839, title-page.

The
BOOK OF MURDER !

A VADE-MECUM

for the

Commissioners and Guardians

of the

NEW POOR LAW

throughout Great Britain and Ireland,

Being an Exact Reprint of

THE INFAMOUS ESSAY

on the

POSSIBILITY OF

LIMITING POPULOUSNESS,

BY MARCUS,

One of the Three.

With a Refutation of the Malthusian
Doctrine.

Oh ! grief, then, grief and shame ! If in this
Flourishing Land there should be dwellings where
The new-born babe doth bring unto its
Parents' soul, no joy ! where squallied Poverty
Receives it at the birth, and, on her withered knees,
Gives it the scanty bread of discontent.—SOUTHEY.

" Rachael weeping for her children and would not be comforted, because they were not."

PRINTED BY JOHN HILL, BLACK HORSE COURT, FLEET ST.,

And now Re-printed for the Instruction of the Labourer,

BY WILLIAM DUGDALE, NO. 37, HOLYWELL STREET, STRAND.

PRICE THREE-PENCE.

1839.

343

(*b*) From Marcus, " The Book of Murder ", pp. 7-8.

In this case, therefore, as in the case of food, and as it is in the case of every other commodity, it is evident and undeniable that the wants and necessities of the people do not furnish the measure of production; but that the amount of production is determined, not by what is requisite for supplying the wants of the people, but by the amount of profit which is attainable by the Capitalists, who neither sympathize in interests with the rest of the people, nor are even aware of all the means by which profit to themselves, and consequent employment for the people, might be attained. When true Political Economy shall have sufficiently instructed the Governments, legislative measures will of course be devised for removing the mischievous restraints upon production which now obviously exist, and which cry aloud for the application of efficient and beneficial principles of " regulation "; or when the Working classes are sufficiently instructed and sufficiently united to acquire a controul over the application of their own labour, then, indeed, their own wants will furnish the measure by which the amount of production is to be determined, and then indeed *they* will be able so to regulate the application of their own labour as always to insure for themselves the supply of a superabundance of wholesome, nutritious, and agreeable food, and always to insure for themselves comfortable and healthful homes, well furnished with all the articles of utility or convenience which human labour, and human labour alone, can produce. There is not one class of those articles, which is not now produced in greater abundance than the Capitalists think desirable; but there is also not one class of them of which it would not be necessary to produce *more* than is now produced, before the wants of the Working Classes could be supplied. The Capitalists, so long as they alone possess the power of controuling the application of human labour, will take care that a sufficiency is not produced for supplying the wants of the Working Classes. Indeed it is impossible for them to suffer a sufficiency for that purpose to be produced without entailing ruin upon themselves. The Working Classes, therefore, now distinctly see that it is impossible for them *ever* to be supplied with a sufficiency of the necessaries or comforts of life, under the *regime* of the Capitalists, and that their future well-being can only be promoted by legislative enactments, wisely devised upon true principles of Political Economy, for that purpose, or by the Working Classes themselves adopting efficient measures for acquiring a controul, or some degree of controul, over the application of their own labour.

XIV

CHARTISM TO 1839

INTRODUCTION

THE Chartist movement had four main phases. The first of these, which is covered in this section, closed in 1839 with the Newport Rising and the arrest of many of the leaders. The second phase culminated in the extensive strike movements of 1842, known as the ' Plug Plot '. The third ended with the failure to make even the embryo of a British revolution in the year of European revolutions, 1848. The fourth had no definite end; but by 1858, when the last Chartist Conference met, the movement was practically dead.

The first phase was closely bound up with the struggle against the new Poor Law in the factory districts and with the agitation for factory reform. These gave it its mass following, and converted what had begun as a constitutional movement for the reform of Parliament into a general working-class uprising against intolerable economic conditions. The constitutional movement began with the foundation of the London Working Men's Association in 1836, and with the revival in the following year of the Birmingham Political Union, which had played a leading part in the Reform struggle of 1830–1832. The Charter was drafted by the London Working Men's Association in consultation with Francis Place and a number of Radical M.P.s, and was later adopted by the Birmingham Political Union, which had put forward its own separate petition. Thereafter, the two bodies set to work to rally national support for a combined Petition, to be presented to Parliament by a delegate Convention of the Industrious Classes, which met in London early in 1839. Well before this, sharp differences had appeared between the ' moral force ' and the ' physical force ' men, the former insisting that the Convention was no more than a constitutional body with the task of presenting the Charter, whereas many of the ' physical force ' school preferred to regard it as an alternative Parliament, much more representative of the people than the middle - class Parliament created by the Reform Act. The ' physical force ' men threatened revolutionary action, or at least a general strike (the ' Sacred Month ')

345

to compel Parliament to cept the Six Points. Of course, there were many who stood somewhere between these two opinions. When Parliament, at a time of trade depression, did reject the Chartist Petition, a general strike was found to be impracticable, and of the general insurrection planned by a group of ' physical force ' Chartists, only the purely local Newport Rising actually occurred.

See " Short History ", Part I, chapter 7, sections 2-4.
" Common People ", chapter 23.

1. THE LONDON WORKING MEN'S ASSOCIATION

[The London Working Men's Association was founded in June 1836. Earlier in the year men of the skilled artisan type, who had taken a prominent part in the work of the National Union of the Working Classes, in Trade Clubs, in the Co-operative Movement, and in the Unstamped Agitation, gathered together under the leadership of William Lovett. In April the ' Association of Working Men to Procure a Cheap and Honest Press ' was founded to attack the Stamp Duty on Newspapers, but as in the following month this was reduced from 4d. to 1d., they abandoned their proposed agitation. It was from this circle, however, that the foundation members of the L.W.M.A. were recruited. At first the Association was little more than a study group to equip them for quiet propaganda : but soon they began to hold public meetings and undertake missionary work. In 1837 they drew up, in conjunction with a group of Radical M.P.s, the People's Charter, a Reform Bill setting out the ' Six Points ' and the administrative details needed to make them operative. The L.W.M.A. had much stronger international interests than most of the Chartist groups : the Address to the Canadian workers is one of a number sent to the working classes of Europe and America. (See Lovett's " Life and Struggles ", where several of the Addresses are reprinted.)]

(*a*) From the Place MSS., 27,819 f. 31 (1836).

. . . We, who this day form the association of working men to procure a cheap and honest press, have unanimously resolved :—

1. To appeal to our fellow-citizens of the other classes from time to time, and in every way we can, till the press is as it ought to be perfectly free.

2. To stimulate our own class, in every way possible to continual efforts in the holy cause of a free press.

3. To use every legal means in our power to organise working men's associations as a system of intercommunication between working men throughout the kingdom for this beneficial purpose.

4. To use all legal means of procuring and supporting cheap newspapers.

5. To take steps for disseminating instructive tracts among our brethren throughout the country.

6. To do all we can to aid and succour our brethren when under any oppression legal or illegal connected with the press.

7. And never to cease our exertions till the Press is as free to the working man as to the Chancellor of the Exchequer himself.

(*b*) From the Address and Rules of the London Working Men's Association for benefiting Politically, Socially, and Morally the Useful Classes [1836], p. 6.

OBJECTS.

1. To draw into one bond of UNITY the *intelligent* and *useful* portion of the working classes in town and country;

2. To seek by every legal means to place all classes of society in possession of their equal political and social rights;

3. To devise every possible means, and to use every exertion, to remove those cruel laws that prevent the free circulation of thought through the medium of a *cheap and honest press*;

4. To promote, by all available means, the education of the rising generation, and the extirpation of those systems which tend to future slavery;

5. To collect every kind of information appertaining to the interests of the working-classes in particular, and society in general, especially statistics regarding the wages of labour, the habits and condition of the labourer, and all those causes that mainly contribute to the present state of things;

6. To meet and communicate with each other for the purpose of digesting the information acquired, and to mature such plans as they believe will conduct in practice to the well-being of the working-classes;

7. To publish their views and sentiments in such form and manner as shall best serve to create a moral, reflecting, and yet energetic public opinion, so as eventually to lead to a gradual improvement in the condition of the working classes, without violence or commotion;

8. To form a library of reference and useful information; to maintain a place where they can associate for mental improvement, and where their brethren from the country can meet with kindred minds actuated by one great motive — that of benefiting politically, socially and morally the useful classes.

Though the persons forming this Association will be at all times disposed to cooperate with all those who seek to promote the happiness of the multitude, yet being convinced, from experience, that the division of interests in the various classes, in the present state of things, is too often destructive of that union of sentiment which is essential to the prosecution of any great object, that they have resolved to confine their members, as far as is practicable to the working classes. . . .

(c) From " An Address to the Reformers on the Forthcoming Elections ", issued by the L.W.M.A. (1837). From W. Lovett, " Life and Struggles ", pp. 118-20.

FELLOW COUNTRYMEN,— It is now nearly six years since the Reform Bill became a part of the laws of our country. To carry that measure despite the daring advocates of corruption, the co-operation of the millions was sought for and cheerfully and honestly given. They threw their hearts into the contest, and would have risked their lives to obtain that which they were led to believe would give *to all* the blessings of LIBERTY. Alas, their hopes were excited by promises which have not been kept, and their expectations of freedom have been bitterly disappointed in seeing the men, whom they had assisted to power, spurning their petition with contempt, and binding them down by still more slavish enactments — at seeing the new constituency they had raised, forgetting their protestations, and selfishly leaguing themselves with their oppressors. . . . But the people have learnt a profitable lesson from experience, and will not again be stimulated to contend for any measure which excludes them from its advantages. They now perceive that most of our oppressive laws and institutions, and the consequent ignorance and wretchedness to which they are exposed, *can be traced to one common source* — EXCLUSIVE LEGISLATION ; *and they therefore have their minds intently fixed on the destruction of this great and pernicious monopoly* ; being satisfied that while the power of law making is confined *to the few*, the exclusive interests *of the few* will be secured at the expense of the many. Seeing this, it will be well for their cause if honest Reformers throw their fears and scruples aside, and generously repose confidence in those who have no exclusive interest to protect, unjust privileges to secure, or monopolies to retain, but whose interest is in the peace and harmony of society, and in having a Parliament selected from *the wise and good of every class*, devising the most efficient means to advance the happiness of all. . . .

(*d*) From an Address to the Canadian People from the London Working Men's Association, 1837. From W. Lovett, " Life and Struggles ", p. 110.

Yes, friends, the cause of DEMOCRACY has truth and reason on its side and knavery and corruption are alone its enemies. To justly distribute the blessings of plenty which the sons of industry have gathered, so as to bless without satiety all mankind — to expand by the blessings of education, the divinely-mental powers of man, which tyrants seek to mar and stultify — to make straight the crooked paths of Justice, and to humanize the laws — to purify the world of all the crimes which want and lust of power have nurtured — is the end and aim of the democrat ; to act the reverse of this the creed and spirit of aristocracy. Yet of this latter class are those who govern nations — men whose long career of vice too often forms a pathway to their power — who, when despotic deeds have stirred their subjects up to check their villainy, declaim against ' sedition ', talk of ' designing men ', and impiously invoke the attributes of the Deity to scare them from their sacred purpose. . . .

2. THE BIRMINGHAM POLITICAL UNION

[In Birmingham in the 1830s the small master was still far more common and important than the large capitalist employer. The lack of sharp class antagonisms had made it easy to form a class alliance in the Reform Campaign of 1830–1832. In 1837 the Birmingham Political Union was revived, partly with the object of agitating for the Currency Scheme of its chief figure, Thomas Attwood ; but Parliamentary Reform was also made a part of the programme. A National Petition was drawn up, and later an appeal was made for all Reformers to unite. The B.P.U. took the initiative in uniting the Chartists and largely supplied the strategy of a National Petition, a National Convention, and the collection of a National Rent to pay the expenses. But when the movement turned into a half-revolutionary national struggle based on the mining and factory areas the Birmingham middle-class leaders lost their influence and found themselves more and more alarmed at the character of the working class agitation they had helped to create.]

From the Birmingham Petition, 1837.

That your present petitioners feel compelled to declare that the Reform so obtained has most grievously disappointed the hopes and expectations of the country. After five years of patient trial your petitioners have no reason to believe that the wants and interests of the industrious classes are better understood, or their rights and liberties better protected now, than they were in the unreformed Parliament; and your petitioners are convinced, that it is absolutely necessary to effect a further and much more extensive Reform of the Commons House of Parliament, before the industrious classes can hope to enjoy any permanent relief and protection.

That your petitioners humbly represent to your Honourable House, that during the years 1835 and 1836, a material improvement was effected in the trade of the country, the workmen in most trades had full employment and their employers enjoyed comparative ease and prosperity. No large stocks of goods, and no overtrading of any kind existed. Within the last six months, a great and lamentable change has taken place. The workmen are, to a frightful extent, unemployed, and yet, of the few goods produced, the greater part remains in the warehouses of the producer. The process of production and consumption are alike arrested. Distress and embarrassment press upon both employer and labourer; and such of them as still hold up, are rapidly exhausting the resources that hard labour and economy may, in better times, have enabled them to accumulate.

That Parliament having adopted and persevered in maintaining laws, which are calculated to make money scarce and food scarce; and perceiving that this double mischief could not fail to force the working men to seek refuge in the workhouse, have not hesitated to enact other laws, which visit poverty as a crime, and thus to accumulate punishment and degradation, as well as misery, upon the heads of the poor. . . .

Your petitioners do, therefore, most earnestly implore your Honourable House to take this petition unto your serious consideration, and they pray :—

First,—that you will forthwith proceed to consider, with a view to the repeal thereof, the law of 1819 . . . [which restored the Gold Standard].

Second,—that you will forthwith proceed to consider, with a view to repeal, the laws passed in 1815, and subsequently, for regulating the importation of foreign and colonial corn; and, generally, all laws at present in existence, which have for their object to impose a duty upon or to prohibit the importation of any of the necessaries of life.

Third,—that you would consider with a view to repeal, the

laws recently enacted, which visit poverty as a crime. Lastly, and above all things, your petitioners pray, that your Honourable House will proceed to bestow upon your petitioners, and the people at large, the following great and undeniable constitutional rights and privileges, namely—

> HOUSEHOLD SUFFRAGE
> VOTE BY BALLOT
> TRIENNIAL PARLIAMENTS
> WAGES OF ATTENDANCE FOR PARLIAMENTARY
>   REPRESENTATIVES
> ABOLITION OF PROPERTY QUALIFICATION FOR
>   REPRESENTATIVES.

3. UNIVERSAL SUFFRAGE

[Bronterre O'Brien (1805–1864) had been the virtual editor of *The Poor Man's Guardian* under Henry Hetherington. In 1836 he published his translation of Buonarotti's " History of Babeuf's Conspiracy " ; and the following year he issued *Bronterre's National Reformer*. This was followed by *The Operative* (1838–1839) ; and then O'Brien transferred his journalistic activities to Feargus O'Connor's *Northern Star*.]

From *Bronterre's National Reformer*, January 15, 1837.

UNIVERSAL SUFFRAGE.

This is, after all, the grand test of Radicalism. The man who would not give you the franchise, though he were to offer you every-thing else, ought not to be trusted. Without the franchise you can have nothing but what others choose to give you, and those who give to-day, may choose to *take away* to-morrow. Knaves will tell you that it is because you have no property you are unrepresented. I tell you, on the contrary, it is because you are unrepresented that you have no property. Every industrious man who produces more (*in value*) of the goods of life than he needs for his own or his family's use, ought to own the difference as property. You are almost all in that condition, for there are few of you who do not yield more value to society every day than society gives you back in return. Why are you not masters of the difference ? Why is it not your property ? Because certain laws and institutions, which other people make, take it away from you, and give it to the law-makers. But if *you*

351

were represented as well as *they*, you would have quite other laws and institutions, which would give the wealth to those who earned it, and consequently, the best share to the most industrious. Thus your poverty is the *result*, not the *cause* of your being unrepresented.

4. THE PEOPLE'S CHARTER : THE SIX POINTS

[The People's Charter, a programme of six demands for political reform, drawn up by William Lovett and others, advised by Francis Place and acting at the outset in collaboration with a number of Radical M.P.s, rapidly became a general rallying point for the forces of discontent. In August 1838 a huge meeting was held at Newhall Hill, Birmingham, where the leaders of the various groups came together and agreed to merge their several agitations in a united campaign for the Charter.]

From a Handbill.

THE SIX POINTS OF THE PEOPLE'S CHARTER.

1. A vote for every man twenty one years of age, of sound mind, and not undergoing punishment for crime.

2. THE BALLOT.—To protect the elector in the exercise of his vote.

3. NO PROPERTY QUALIFICATION for members of Parliament — thus enabling the constituencies to return the man of their choice, be he rich or poor.

4. PAYMENT OF MEMBERS, thus enabling an honest tradesman, working man, or other person, to serve a constituency, when taken from his business to attend to the interests of the country.

5. EQUAL CONSTITUENCIES, securing the same amount of representation for the same number of electors, — instead of allowing small constituencies to swamp the votes of larger ones.

6. ANNUAL PARLIAMENTS, thus presenting the most effectual check to bribery and intimidation, since though a constituency might be bought once in seven years (even with the ballot), no purse could buy a constituency (under a system of universal suffrage) in each ensuing twelvemonth ; and since members, when elected for a year only, would not be able to defy and betray their constituents as now.

Subjoined are the names of the gentlemen who embodied these principles into the document called the " People's Charter ", at an influential meeting held at the British Coffee House, London, on the 7th of June, 1837 :—

Daniel O'Connell, Esq., M.P.   Mr Henry Hetherington.
John Arthur Roebuck, Esq., M.P.   Mr John Cleave.
John Temple Leader, Esq., M.P.   Mr James Watson.
Charles Hindley, Esq., M.P.   Mr Richard Moore.
Thomas Perronet Thompson, Esq., M.P. Mr William Lovett.
William Sharman Crawford, Esq., M.P. Mr Henry Vincent.

5. THE NATIONAL PETITION, 1837

[The National Petition was the focal point for Chartist activities until the first Chartist Convention met in 1839. The local Chartists devoted their energies to collecting signatures for the Petition and organising meetings for the election of delegates to the Convention, which was to supervise its presentation. The Petition could be treated as a symbol of Chartist Unity — as it became at the Newhall Hill meeting — because its language avoided touching on their differences, except for the short reference to the laws ' which by making money scarce, make labour cheap ' — and even that reference was generally acceptable, though most of the Chartists did not, like Attwood and his followers, regard it as the main issue.]

(*a*) From the National Petition. Place MSS., 27,820, f. 374. [July 1838].

Unto the Honourable the Commons of the United Kingdom of Great Britain and Ireland in Parliament assembled, the Petition of the undersigned, their suffering countrymen,

" HUMBLY SHEWETH,

" That we, your petitioners, dwell in a land where merchants are noted for enterprise, whose manufacturers are very skilful, and whose workmen are proverbial for their industry.

" The land itself is goodly, the soil rich, and the temperature wholesome ; it is abundantly furnished with the materials of commerce and trade ; it has numerous and convenient harbours ; in facility of internal communication it exceeds all others.

" For three-and-twenty years we have enjoyed a profound peace.

" Yet with all these elements of national prosperity, and with every disposition and capacity to take advantage of them, we find ourselves overwhelmed with public and private suffering.

" We are bowed down under a load of taxes ; which, notwithstanding, fall greatly short of the wants of our rulers ; our traders are trembling on the verge of bankruptcy ; our workmen are starving ; capital brings no profit and labour no remuneration ; the home of the artificer is desolate, and the warehouse of the pawnbroker is full ; the workhouse is crowded and the manufactory is deserted.

" We have looked upon every side, we have searched diligently in order to find out the causes of a distress so sore and so long continued.

" We can discover none, in nature, or in providence.

" Heaven has dealt graciously by the people ; but the foolishness of our rulers has made the goodness of God of none effect.

" The energies of a mighty kingdom have been wasted in building up the power of selfish and ignorant men, and its resources squandered for their aggrandisement.

" The good of a party has been advanced to the sacrifice of the good of the nation ; the few have governed for the interest of the few, while the interest of the many has been neglected, or insolently and tyrannously trampled upon.

" It was the fond expectation of the people that a remedy for the greater part, if not for the whole, of their grievances, would be found in the Reform Act of 1832.

" They were taught to regard that Act as a wise means to a worthy end ; as the machinery of an improved legislation, when the will of the masses would be at length potential.

" They have been bitterly and basely deceived.

" The fruit which looked so fair to the eye has turned to dust and ashes when gathered.

" The Reform Act has effected a transfer of power from one domineering faction to another, and left the people as helpless as before.

" Our slavery has been exchanged for an apprenticeship to liberty, which has aggravated the painful feeling of our social degradation, by adding to it the sickening of still deferred hope.

" We come before your Honourable House to tell you, with all humility, that this state of things must not be permitted to continue ; that it cannot long continue without very seriously endangering the stability of the throne and the peace of the kingdom ; and that if by God's help and all lawful and constitutional appliances an end can be put to it, we are fully resolved that it shall speedily come to an end.

" We tell your Honourable House that the capital of the master must no longer be deprived of its due reward ; that the laws which make food dear, and those which, by making money scarce, make labour cheap, must be abolished ; that taxation must be made to fall on property, not on industry ; that the good of the many, as it is the only legitimate end, so must it be the sole study of the Government.

" As a preliminary essential to these and other requisite changes ; as means by which alone the interests of the people can be effectually vindicated and secured, we demand that those interests be confided to the keeping of the people.

" When the State calls for defenders, when it calls for money, no consideration of poverty or ignorance can be pleaded, in refusal or delay of the call. Required, as we are universally, to support and obey the laws, nature and reason entitle us to demand that in the making of the laws, the universal voice shall be implicitly listened to. We perform the duties of freemen ; we must have the privileges of freemen. Therefore, we demand universal suffrage. The suffrage, to be exempt from the corruption of the wealthy and the violence of the powerful, must be secret."

(*b*) From a speech by P. H. Muntz. From a pamphlet, " The Grand Midland Demonstration at Birmingham, August 6, 1838 ".

. . . But they must get rid of both Tories and Whigs. They must get up a general system of agitation. They must not agitate for every paltry question. And above all they must beware of the old motto, " Divide and Conquer ". They must make their stand upon the national petition, throwing aside all minor points that caused dissension (cheers). The question of the corn laws must for the time, be laid aside, as well as every other question that set the manufacturer against the farmer, the man against the master, or the landlord against the tenant. These must all be laid aside, and they must join hand and heart in one great and general effort. (Loud cheers). Let them once get a fair and just representation of the people, and they would ultimately secure the peace, the happiness, and the permanent welfare of the people (cheers). Let not the attention for a moment be withdrawn from the main point of universal suffrage. All other evils, the corn laws, the poor laws — forget all these for an instant — let nothing be thought of but the principle which will give you the power of returning such men as, when returned, will repeal, if necessary, a dozen such laws a day.

355

6. THE LONDON DEMOCRATIC ASSOCIATION

[The London Chartist leaders mostly belonged to the Moral Force School, but some of the most extreme advocates of insurrection were to be found in the London Democratic Association, which was formed in 1837 as a breakaway organisation by some members of the L.W.M.A. Their chief figure, George Julian Harney,[1] at this time modelled himself on Marat and the French Revolutionaries and had a definite political creed to support his appeal for armed action — unlike some of the Northern Physical Force leaders who too often had no theoretical background and were concerned wholly with immediate practical grievances. The L.D.A. won little attention or respect from other Chartist leaders in London, but it had considerable support among the disorganised section of the London working class, and among the Physical Force Chartists of the North.]

(*a*) From *The London Democrat*, April 20, 1839.

Men of the East and West, men of the North and South, your success lies with yourselves, depend upon yourselves alone, and your cause will be triumphant. The SIXTH OF MAY is approaching. Prepare ! Listen not to the men who would preach delay. The man who would now procrastinate is a traitor, and may your vengeance light upon his head. One word of advice. In the two or three weeks you have remaining, let me exhort you to ARM. I mean you that are yet unarmed; for oh, thank God, tens of thousands of you can now, hand to hand and foot to foot, assert your right to be free men. To you that are not so prepared I say again, ARM to protect your aged parents, ARM for your wives and children, ARM for your sweethearts and sisters, ARM to drive tyranny from the soil and oppression from the judgement-seat. Your country, your posterity, your God demands of you to ARM ! ARM !! ARM !!!

France is on the eve of revolution, Belgium pants to be free, in Germany liberty is awake, the patriots of Spain are ready to send Isabella and Carlos to the devil together, the Italian lifts his head,

[1] George Julian Harney (1817–1897) had been Hetherington's shop boy and had been imprisoned during the Unstamped Agitation. He had an intense admiration for Bronterre O'Brien and learnt from him to look to the French Revolutionaries for guidance. In the first stage of Chartism (up to 1839) he was continually demanding armed action, apparently believing that the working class could and would triumph in a revolution of street fighting. In the 'forties and 'fifties his main interest was the development of working-class internationalism, through the Society of Fraternal Democrats and subsequent organisations. In the course of this work he met Marx and Engels, who at one time hoped that he would be their effective spokesman in England. But Harney disappointed them and came to be scorned by Marx as ' Citizen Hip-hip-hurrah '.

and the exiled Pole again dreams of the restoration of his fatherland ; but Englishmen all look to you — yes still

" England's the anchor and hope of the world ".

Come, then, men of the North, from your snow-capped hills ; come, then, men of the South, from your sunlit valleys ; come to the gathering ; unite, fraternise, arm, and you will be free !

Let the one universal rallying cry, from the Firth of Forth to the Land's End be EQUALITY OR DEATH.

Yours fraternally,

GEORGE JULIAN HARNEY.

(b) From *The London Democrat*, June 1, 1839.

. . . Now I have no objection to the " People's Charter ", as a fundamental law of this country, but I have a great objection to its being considered as a panacea for all the evils under which you labour. No, my friends, the disease which is now preying on your vitals, is much too deeply seated to be affected by remedies of that kind. Your whole social system requires " revolution ", your commercial system requires " revolution ", your political system requires " revolution ", and nothing short of actual convulsion will enable you to effect a cure.

As I said in my last, you must inscribe on your banners, " the land national property ", " no usury laws ", and " no exclusive monopolies or charters ". Now these are fundamental principles, and well understood, and would immediately effect a change in the system ; but establish the " People's Charter " to-morrow, and the working man would not have one difficulty the less to contend with. I know very well that the " mountebanks ", who are now travelling the country, will endeavour to persuade you that all these things would follow the establishment of the " People's Charter ". . . .

Now this is a monstrous delusion, and the discussion of that will bring me to a consideration of the absolute impossibility of gaining either the " People's Charter " or any other *grand principle* without an " *insurrection* ". For instance, suppose that your ' leaders ' are correct in their prophecies, and that the " People's Charter " would gain everything you want, are the individuals who compose the House of Lords such nincompoops as many take them to be ? Why, good God ! it was nothing but the fear of civil war that compelled them to yield to the demand for the " Reform Bill " ; and surely they would not yield on *this point* so easily, backed as they are by all the powers and institutions of the State. But there is also a House of Commons opposed to a man against you ; and do you suppose, that under the present system, you will *ever* be able to get a majority in your favour, they at the same time believing with your leaders, that the " People's Charter " would be the means of obtaining for you less labour and more enjoyment ? Again, supposing that they do yield to your demands — the Monarchy still exists — the House of Lords still exists, and you have a House of Commons elected on the principle of universal suffrage, &c, &c, &c. Do you think that if a law, abolishing individual landed property, was to pass the House of Commons, that the other house would ever agree to it ? *Never would they.* A civil war, at least, would have to set the question at rest ; and mind you, there are many other laws (if you, the working classes, are to reap any benefit from just legislation) that would have to come before their notice, and almost all of them of equal importance too. Well then, I say, look at the difficulties that would still surround you, and the only conclusion that you *can come to*, is that insurrection at last must be had recourse to. And hence is the necessity of an insurrection, viz., that you will be enabled, in one breath, to enact what laws you please. Slow legislation won't suit your disease — a convulsive remedy will cure it. No my friends, insurrection must come ; be prepared when it does, to get what you want. After you have obtained practicable fundamental principles, then the " People's Charter " will answer your expectation, for whilst it cannot obtain for you what you want, still it will retain for you what you have got.

J. C. COOMBE.

7. *THE NORTHERN STAR*

[Feargus O'Connor (1794–1855), who had been an Irish O'Connellite M.P. till he quarrelled with O'Connell, stood unsuccessfully for Oldham on Cobbett's death in 1835, and attempted from that time on to build up a centralised Radical movement under his own leadership. In 1836 he set up a Central Committee of Radical Unions in London, and helped in founding the London Democratic Association. He started *The Northern Star* at Leeds as a weekly in November 1837, at the price of 4½d., and put himself at the head of the revolt against the New Poor Law in the North. *The Northern Star* became by far the most influential working-class newspaper : in 1839 it was selling 50,000 copies a week, and each copy had many readers — and listeners. Much of O'Connor's power rested on his control of *The Northern Star* ; but at the same time its pages were generally open to all brands of Chartist and working-class opinion, and, by recording the activities of Chartists and Trade Unionists throughout the country, it gave the movement a unity which otherwise it would have lacked.]

From R. G. Gammage, " History of the Chartist Movement, 1837–54 " (1894), pp. 16-17.

. . . Another paper was launched in the borough of Leeds under the title of *The Northern Star*. Its proprietor was the popular Feargus O'Connor, who had become the idol of the operatives in the manufacturing districts. Never was a journal started more opportunely. It caught and reflected the spirit of the times. It was not, however, with his own means alone that O'Connor succeeded in establishing the *Star*. Not less than £800 was subscribed in shares by his friends, without whose timely assistance it is doubtful whether he could, at that time, have ventured on the speculation. Those friends had faith in its success, and the result proved the reasonableness of their anticipations, for *The Northern Star* speedily stood at the head of the democratic journals. Its editor was the Rev. William Hill, an acute and clever but not a very agreeable writer. It was not, however, for its editorial department that it was so much valued. Two circumstances contributed to raise it in popular estimation. One of these was the popularity of O'Connor, a popularity which was largely due to the fact of his having a journal in which to record all his proceedings and to place his words and deeds in the most advantageous light. The other circumstance was, that the *Star* was regarded as the most complete record of the movement. There was not a meeting held in any part of the country, in however remote a spot, that was not reported in its columns, accompanied by all the flourishes calculated to excite an interest in the reader's mind, and to inflate the vanity of the speakers by the honourable mention of their names. Even if they had never mounted the platform before, the speeches were described and reported as eloquent, argumentative, and the like ; and were dressed up with as much care as though they were parliamentary harangues fashioned to the columns of the daily press. Thus men of very mediocre abilities appeared to people at a distance to be oracles of political wisdom. It must not be thought that these observations are intended to cast a slur on the real talent exhibited by the working class in this great movement ; for, however much that talent was exaggerated, it was more than sufficient to forbid its being despised.

8. THE FIRST CHARTIST CONVENTION, 1839

[The first Chartist Convention met in London in February 1839, expecting the Petition to be ready almost at once. It was not, however, ready till May; and thereafter a change of Ministry further delayed its presentation. The Convention, compelled to wait, had nothing to do but talk; and talking accentuated differences. The fundamental cleavage came over the function of the Convention. Was it merely to supervise the Petition, or was it the embryo of a provisional government? The tone of the delegates grew more and more militant with delay, and some members of the right wing seceded from the debates. In May the Convention moved to Birmingham, and thence issued its challenging manifesto, with a series of questions to the people on the forms of direct action which could be taken if the Petition were rejected. Thereafter the Convention adjourned, and the delegates toured the country, hoping to kindle a fresh and more aggressive enthusiasm. The delegates reassembled in July; the arrest of Lovett, the secretary, following on other arrests of leading Chartists, was a real challenge to their claims of strength, and they could offer no answer. They returned to London to await the debate on the Petition. In July the House of Commons rejected the Petition, and the Convention found itself faced with the necessity of action. Attwood's proposal for a second petition met with no support. The Birmingham middle-class leaders had by then completely broken away, and the Government had made many arrests among the Chartist leaders. Those who were left attempted to make the Convention a semi-revolutionary organisation of the working classes. At a poorly attended meeting it was decided to call a general strike of a month's duration — the ' Sacred Month '. But no real preparations were made, and the nature of the strike was not settled: it was left open whether it was meant merely as a strike, or as the signal for working-class revolution. The delegates soon found that, in face of the severe depression of industry, there was no adequate popular support for the strike movement; and, after much hesitation and confusion, the strike resolution was rescinded. After further fruitless talk the Convention was disbanded in September, confessing its defeat. The policy of peaceful united action between the middle classes and the working classes had been wrecked by mutual distrust and difference of attitude; and independent working-class action had failed because the workers were too weak and ill-organised, especially in face of serious trade depression, to make a successful industrial onslaught on the well-entrenched and continually growing powers of capitalism.]

(*a*) Resolutions of the Convention, to April 1839.

(i) From *The Charter*, February 17, 1839.

Proposed by Bronterre O'Brien and passed unanimously, 12th February, 1839.

That this Convention convinced that, at the present eventful crisis, it is indispensably necessary to the success of the National Petition that the people's undivided attention should be concentrated upon that question alone, to the exclusion of all others, being also convinced that the present agitation for a repeal of the Corn Laws was intended and does actually tend to divert the working classes from that permanent object; and being further of opinion that such an unconditional repeal as would alone be likely to receive the sanction of the Anti-Corn Law agitators, would be rather injurious than otherwise to the interests of the poorer classes : we, the delegates of this Convention do therefore most earnestly recommend our constituents in particular, and the unrepresented classes in general, to deprecate and oppose all and every agitation for or against a repeal of the Corn Laws, until the fate of the National Petition and People's Charter shall have been determined by the legislature, so far as the legislature is competent to determine it.

(ii) From *The Charter*, February 17, 1839.

Resolution moved in the Convention by J. P. Cobbett, 14 February 1839 and lost by 36 votes to 6.

1. Resolved. That this Convention calls itself the " General Convention of Delegates from the Industrious Classes ".

2. Resolved,— that this convention will not adopt, but will oppose and protest against any and every thing, whether in act or in word, which may arise among the members of its own body, and which may be in any degree in contempt of the law.

3. Resolved,— that the whole practical business of the delegates met in this Convention is to superintend the presentation of the ' People's Petition ', and by personal communication with members of the House of Commons, to obtain in that house as much support as possible to the prayer of that petition.

4. Resolved,— that it is no part of the business of the delegates to this Convention, in their collective capacity and as now appointed, to offer, under any circumstances whatsoever, any dictation or advice for the guidance of their constituents or of any part of the people.

(iii) From *The Charter*, March 10, 1839.

Resolution carried unanimously, 6th March, 1839.

That this Convention recommends to the delegates who may address public meetings in London and elsewhere, the propriety of acting up to the advice they have given to their missionaries, which is, to refrain from all violent and unconstitutional language, and not to infringe the law in any manner, in word or deed.

(iv) From *The Charter*, April 14, 1839.

Resolution carried unanimously, 8th April, 1839.

That this Convention will take no part, and will not recommend the radicals to take any part, in the present crisis of a factious contest for place and power between the hypocritical Whigs and the tyrannical Tories.

(v) From *The Charter*, April 14, 1839.

Resolution carried 9th April, 1839.

That the right of the people of this country to possess arms, is established by the highest legal authority beyond all doubt.

[This was proposed as an amendment to a motion that a committee be appointed to draw up a case for the opinion of counsel on the legal right to possess arms. The voting was : for the amendment 19, for the original motion 4, while 6 supported a motion for ' previous question '.]

(*b*) From *The Charter*, February 17, 1839.

He [J. P. Cobbett] had felt, however, immediately after the discussion had begun, that there was in fact no difference between them whatever. (Hear hear). They were all moral-force men, and all physical-force men. (Cheers). What did they mean by moral force ? Did it mean that they denounced all violent measures ? Did they say that their constituents had given them a petition signed by 3,000,000 of " fighting men " ? that was what was said by one of their calumniators — one of the men who denounced them for employing threats and menaces. (Hear, hear, and cheers). What we meant was, that we would show such a mass of men, conscious of the injustice of which they were the victims, and entertain such a resolve themselves for the galling oppressions under which they laboured, that the Government and the legislature, if they wished to save the country from convulsions, which would break down the very framework of society, must concede what the people demanded. (Cheers). That was " Moral force " — (Hear, hear). There could not be an exhibition of moral force without physical force. It was an act of self defence, for the safety of life and property ; and, unless the legislature should convince them that a petition was the merest farce in the world, they were all physical force men — (Cheers) — not for the purpose of destroying life and property, but of convincing the oppressors of the people that they would suffer no longer in silence. (Cheers). . . .

(*c*) From the Manifesto of the General Convention of the Industrious Classes, May 14, 1839.

We respectfully submit the following propositions for your serious consideration :—

That at all the SIMULTANEOUS PUBLIC MEETINGS, to be held, for the purpose of petitioning the Queen to call good men to her councils, as well as at all subsequent meetings of your Unions and Associations, up to the First of July, you submit the following Questions to the People there assembled :—

1. Whether they will be prepared, AT THE REQUEST OF THE CONVENTION, to withdraw all sums of money they may INDIVIDUALLY or COLLECTIVELY have placed in savings' banks, private banks, or in the hands of any person hostile to their just rights ?

2. Whether at the same request, they will be prepared immediately to convert all their paper money into gold ?

3. Whether, IF THE CONVENTION SHALL DETERMINE that a SACRED MONTH will be necessary to prepare the millions to secure the Charter of their political salvation, they will FIRMLY resolve to abstain from their labour during that period, as well as from all intoxicating drinks.

4. Whether, according to their OLD CONSTITUTIONAL RIGHT — a right which modern legislators would fain annihilate — they have prepared themselves WITH THE ARMS OF FREEMEN, TO DEFEND THE LAWS AND CONSTITUTIONAL PRIVILEGES THEIR ANCESTORS BEQUEATHED TO THEM.

5. Whether they will provide themselves with CHARTIST CANDIDATES so as to be prepared to propose them for their representatives at the next general election; and, if returned by SHOW OF HANDS, such candidates to consider themselves veritable representatives of the People — to meet in London at a time hereafter to be determined on ?

6. Whether they will resolve to DEAL EXCLUSIVELY WITH CHARTISTS; and in all cases of persecution, rally round and protect all those who may suffer in their righteous cause ?

7. Whether, by all and every means in their power, they will perseveringly contend for the great objects of the People's Charter, and resolve that no COUNTER AGITATION FOR A LESS MEASURE OF JUSTICE shall divert them from their righteous object?

8. Whether the people will determine TO OBEY ALL THE JUST AND CONSTITUTIONAL REQUESTS OF THE MAJORITY OF THE CONVENTION?

(*d*) From R. G. Gammage, " History of the Chartist Movement " (1894 edition), p. 112.

Resolution carried by the Convention on May 17th, 1839, on the motion of Bronterre O'Brien.

1st.—that peace, law, and order, shall continue to be the motto of this Convention, so long as our oppressors shall act in the spirit of peace, law, and order to the people; but should our enemies substitute war for peace, or attempt to suppress our lawful and orderly agitation by lawless violence, we shall deem it to be the sacred duty of the people, to meet force with force, and repel assassination by justifiable homicide.

2nd.—that in accordance with the foregoing resolution the Convention do employ only legal and peaceable means in the prosecution of the great and righteous objects of the present movement. Being also desirous that no handle should be afforded to the enemy for traducing our motives, or employing armed force against the people, we hereby recommend the Chartists who may attend the approaching simultaneous meetings, to avoid carrying staves, pikes, pistols, or any other offensive weapons, about their persons. We recommend them to proceed to the ground, sober, orderly and unarmed. As also to treat as enemies of the cause, any person or persons, who may exhibit such weapons, or who by any other act of folly or wickedness, should provoke a breach of the peace.

3rd.—that the marshals and other officers, who may have charge of the arrangements for the simultaneous meetings, are particularly requested to use every means in their power, to give effect to the recommendation embodied in the preceding resolution. We also recommend that the aforesaid officers do in all cases consult with the local authorities before the meetings take place.

4th.—that in case our oppressors in the upper and middle ranks should instigate the authorities to assail the people with armed force, in contravention of the existing laws of the realm, the said oppressors in the upper and middle ranks, shall be held responsible in person and property, for any detriment that may result to the people from such atrocious instigation.

(e) Resolutions of the Convention, July to August 1839.

(i) From *The Charter*, July 21, 1839.

That the House of Commons having refused to go into committee on the prayer of the National Petition, it is vain to expect redress from that House; it is therefore the opinion of the National Convention that the people should work no longer after the 12th of August next, unless the power of voting for Members of Parliament to enable them to protect their labour and their rights is previously given and guaranteed to them.

[An amendment that the Holiday should start on the 5th August was defeated by 20 votes to 5 (2 abstentions): an amendment that a committee be set up to examine the best time for starting the ' Sacred Month ' was lost by the casting vote of the Chairman. Finally, the original motion (reprinted above) was carried by 13 votes to 6 (with 5 abstentions) on the 17th of July.]

(ii) From *The Charter*, July 28, 1839.

Carried 24th July, 1839, by 12 votes to 6 with 7 abstentions.

That this Convention continues to be unanimously of opinion, that nothing short of a general strike, or suspension of labour throughout the country, will ever suffice to re-establish the rights and liberties of the industrious classes, we nevertheless cannot take upon ourselves the responsibility of dictating the time or circumstances of such a strike, believing that we are incompetent to do so for the following reasons :

1st. Because our numbers have been greatly reduced by the desertion, absence, and arbitrary arrests of a large portion of our members.

2nd. Because great diversity of opinion prevails amongst the remaining members, as to the practicability of a general strike, in the present state of trade in the manufacturing districts.

3rd. Because a similar diversity of opinion seems to prevail out of doors, amongst our constituents and the working classes generally.

4th. Because, under these circumstances, it is more than doubtful whether an order from the Convention for a general holiday would be generally obeyed, in other words, whether a strike would not prove a failure.

5th. Because, while we firmly believe that an universal strike would prove the salvation of the country, we are at the same time equally convinced that a partial strike would only entail the bitterest privations and sufferings on all parties who take part in it, and, in the present exasperated state of public feeling, not improbably lead to confusion and anarchy.

6th. Because, although it is the duty of the convention to participate in all the people's dangers, it is no part of our duty to create danger unnecessarily, either for ourselves or others. To create it for themselves would be folly — to create it for others would be a crime.

7th. Because we believe that the people themselves are the only fit judges of their right and readiness to strike work, as also of their own resources and capabilities of meeting the emergencies which such an event would entail. Under these circumstances, we decide that a committee of three be appointed to reconsider the vote of the 16th instant, and to substitute for it an address, which shall leave to the people themselves to decide whether they will or will not commence the sacred month on the 12th of August, at the same time explaining the reasons for adopting such a course, and pledging the Convention to cooperate with the people in whatever measures they may deem necessary to their safety and emancipation.

(iii) From *The Charter*, July 28, 1839.

Carried 25th July, 1839, with one dissentient.

That the Convention having provisionally appointed the 12th of August as the day for the general cessation from labour, it becomes necessary to appoint a council, which shall sit in London, and whose duty shall be to receive evidence from those delegates who shall forthwith return to their respective constituents, and also from the country at large, with a view of taking the most effectual means of giving effect to such plan as the majority of the working class shall decide upon.

(iv) From *The Charter*, August 11, 1839.

Passed by the Council of the Convention, 7th August, 1839.

That anonymous letters and strange reports have reached this council as to the formation of secret associations of persons pretending to be Chartists, and leagued together for the purposes of firing, assassination, and like diabolical objects, we beg to apprise all Chartists, that while we believe the letters and reports alluded to to be no other than base fabrications of our enemies, got up for the purpose of discrediting our sacred cause, we deem it necessary at the same time to caution them against having any connexion whatever with any party or parties suspected of being capable of realising such atrocious and diabolical schemes. We also advise them to avoid all secret organisations and societies, as the best and only means of protecting themselves from spies, incendiaries, and traitors. Our warfare against misgovernment is an open one, and shall be openly conducted.

(v) From *The Charter*, August 11, 1839.

Carried unanimously, 5th August, 1839.

Resolved,— That from the evidence which has reached this council from various parts of the country, we are unanimously of the opinion that the people are not prepared to carry out the " Sacred Month " on the 12th of August. The same evidence, however, convinces us that the great body of the working people, including most of the trades, may be induced to cease work on the 12th. inst., for one, two, or three days, in order to devote the whole of that time to solemn processions and meetings, for deliberating of the present awful state of the country, and devising the best means of averting the hideous despotism with which the industrious orders are menaced by the murderous majority of the upper and middle classes, who prey upon their labour. We, at the same time, beg to announce to the country that it is the deliberate opinion of the council, that unless the Trades of Great Britain shall cooperate, as united bodies, with their more distressed brethren, in making a grand moral demonstration on the 12th instant, it will be impossible to save the country from a revolution of blood, which after the enormous sacrifices of life and prosperity, will terminate in the utter subjection of the whole of the working people to the monied murderers of society. Under these circumstances we implore all our brother Chartists to abandon the project of a sacred month, as being for the present utterly impracticable, and to prepare themselves forthwith to carry into effect the aforesaid constitutional objects, on the 12th inst.. We also implore the united trades, if they would save the country from convulsion, and themselves and families from ruin, to render their distressed brethren all the aid in their power, on or before the 12th inst., towards realising the great and beneficent object of the holiday. Men of the trades ! the salvation of the empire is in your hands.

[Adopted unanimously, August 5, 1839, at a meeting of the Council which sat while the Convention was adjourned.]

(*f*) Dissolution of the Convention, September, 1839. From R. G. Gammage, " History of the Chartist Movement, 1837–54 " (1894), p. 156.

. . . At a sitting of the Convention on September the 6th, O'Brien made a motion that the body should dissolve, which was seconded by Dr. Taylor; eleven voted for, and eleven against the motion. Frost, the chairman, gave his casting vote for the dissolution. Those who voted for the resolution were Messrs. Bussey, Skevington, Richards, Barry, Jones, Cardo, Pitkeithly, O'Brien, Harney, Hetherington, Frost, and Dr. Taylor. Against it were Messrs. Burns, Lowery, Neesom, Hartwell, O'Connor, Wolstoneholme, Carpenter, Jackson, Smart, James Taylor, and Deegan. . . .

9. THE NEWPORT RISING

[For some time before the final dissolution of the Convention, the more decided advocates of Physical Force, as well as the Moral Force party, had lost faith in it. While it was still in session some Chartists, it is clear, had been secretly planning a general insurrection. The details of their plan, as well as its extent, remain obscure; but it is generally supposed that the seizure of Newport by the Welsh Chartists was to have given the signal for the rest of the country. On the night of November 3, 1839, John Frost led some three thousand colliers in an attempt to rescue Henry Vincent, the leading orator of the L.W.M.A., from Newport Gaol, and to seize the town. But the plot became known to the authorities; and the small force, part of which lost itself in the darkness, was easily overwhelmed by the soldiers who were holding the town.

The planned rising came to nothing, but some sort of plotting continued for another couple of months. In December, Frost and other leaders of the Newport Rising were sentenced to death; but the sentence was commuted to transportation largely owing to Chartist meetings and demonstrations of protest all over the country. There was, however, a wholesale arrest of leading Chartists: by the end of June 1840, at least five hundred were in gaol. As for the Rising itself, there had never been any real prospect of success; and if initial successes had been won, the insurgents had, as far as we know, no plans for organising their victory.]

From " The Trial of John Frost for High Treason " (1839), p. 160.

Such are the declarations alleged by the witnesses to have been made by the prisoner; whether made or not you, gentlemen, are to be the judges. It is for you to say whether you infer from such declarations, accompanied with the other statements, an intent and a mind on the part of the prisoner, by means of these preparations, to alter and effect any great and general movement among the people ; whether it was an object with him by the terror these armed men would inspire, by the force he carried with him, to seize the town of Newport and keep possession of it, or whether his intention was to make the beginning then, that there should be a further spread of such conduct, which would then be carried into effect. You are to say whether there was such an intention, or whether you are not satisfied by the evidence that such could fairly be imputed to him. The ground he takes is one of a much more moderate complexion. He says that all he intended to do was, by showing the force of the men, that they should be able to carry a measure of a more limited nature, the amelioration of Vincent's treatment. You will recollect, gentlemen, that it lies upon the Crown fully to establish the guilt of the prisoner, and, if you consider it has been established, then, however painful the duty, still it is necessary for you to fulfil it. It is a case for your consideration alone ; the Court cannot interfere with it, and, therefore, I leave it in your hands, quite convinced that you will come to that conclusion which truth and justice require.

XV

CHARTISM : LATER PHASES

INTRODUCTION

FOR six months after Frost's arrest in November 1839, there was little done beyond the organisation of protests and help for the victims. Then came a revival, first in Scotland — the Scottish Chartists were now reorganising their movement on lines of their own as an independent unity — and later among the local bodies in the English towns, mainly in London and the North. In July 1840 a Conference in Manchester, dominated by O'Connor's followers, founded the National Charter Association, which set out, more definitely than any previous body, to become the party of the working class. But there were also a number of breakaways : Christian Chartist societies were founded in Bath, Birmingham, and other towns ; Thomas Cooper, the poet, founded the Shakespearian Association of Leicester Chartists. In the spring of 1841 William Lovett, now completely estranged from the O'Connorites, founded the National Association of the United Kingdom for Promoting the Political and Social Improvement of the People, which speedily became little more than a society for promoting a system of national education. But these organisations were all unimportant : only the N.C.A. had any mass following. O'Connor, now in prison, was busy discrediting Lovett and O'Brien ; and on his release he immediately assumed the leadership of the N.C.A. Under his guidance it bitterly attacked not only the middle-class reformers, but also the artisan stratum of the working class, which he accused of lukewarmness and narrow self-interest. Preparations for a new petition and convention were pressed forward with the enthusiastic energy which O'Connor alone among the Chartist leaders was able to inspire. Throughout this period an active struggle for working-class support was proceeding between the Chartists and the Anti-Corn Law League, which had been founded as a national body simultaneously with the meeting of the Chartist Convention of 1839. Many Chartists were of course in favour of the repeal of the Corn Laws ; but others, among whom Feargus O'Connor was prominent, opposed repeal both because they believed in a ' back to the land ' movement, and because they regarded it as an attempt by the employing classes to seduce the workers from the pursuit of more fundamental reforms. Among those who favoured both Corn Law Repeal and Radical reform, there were endeavours to reconcile the conflicting elements behind a common programme. Prominent in these efforts was Joseph Sturge, the well-known Birmingham Quaker-Radical, who — in 1842 — founded the Complete Suffrage Union, in an endeavour to bring about a renewed alliance between the middle and working classes. The Complete Suffrage Union set to work to collect signatures for a reform petition of its own ; and both petitions reached the House of Commons in the early months of 1842, and were in turn rejected in April and May of that year.

After this further rebuff even O'Connor made some attempt to secure reconciliation among the conflicting groups. But the middle classes, even where they were prepared to endorse the positive demands of the Chartists, showed for the most part an irreconcilable antagonism to the name and traditions of the Charter itself. When, after the rejection of the petitions in 1842, the Chartists attempted to put themselves at the head of the great strike movement in the factory areas (sometimes known as the ' Plug Plot '), this antagonism was increased. The Complete Suffrage Union collapsed ; Lovett, who had for a time collaborated with Sturge, virtually withdrew from the agitation ; and the field was left clear for O'Connor.

The strikes of 1842 had been doomed to failure on account of the seriously depressed condition of industry. But after 1842 economic conditions began to improve. Financial conditions were stabilised by the Bank Charter Act of 1844, and the Anti-Corn Law crusade moved on, by way of Peel's partial reforms, to the complete success of the Repealers in 1846. Middle-class sympathy with Radicalism weakened as the economic system settled down ; and to a considerable extent working-class policy was also turning to new channels. The Rochdale Pioneers opened their Toad Lane store in 1844 ; and the foundations of a more stable type of Trade Unionism, as well as of the modern consumers' Co-operative movement, were being laid.

But Chartism was not yet a spent force. In the years after 1842 O'Connor evolved his Land Scheme, which he succeeded, for the time, in making an integral part of the Chartist crusade. In 1845 the Chartist Land Co-operative Society, later renamed The National Land Company, was set up by the N.C.A. It promised, by methods whose financial unsoundness became only gradually apparent, to

N*

establish its many thousands of subscribers in villages of peasant proprietors, and thus to prepare the way for the happy England which would be realised with the winning of the Charter. Land settlement became the main object of Chartist activity until the financial collapse of the scheme in 1847.

This failure turned the Chartists back to their political demands. The financial crisis of 1847, though it was fairly soon surmounted, left trade bad in the following year; and riots and demonstrations in many parts of the country encouraged the Chartists to believe that the people were ready for a new campaign. Moreover, the outbreak of revolution in many parts of Europe — the ' spectre haunting Europe ' Marx called it in the " Communist Manifesto " — roused high hopes in England among the small group of Chartists who were in contact with the foreign revolutionaries. The Society of Fraternal Democrats, which included a number of the Chartist leaders, and other groups which were in personal contact with Marx, Engels, and other continental exiles, had been for some time prophesying a wave of European revolutions in which Great Britain would share. The Chartists set to work to organise their third great National Petition. Meetings were held all over the country, and the inevitable Convention made plans for a National Assembly. But the great fiasco on Kennington Common on April 6 finally revealed the weakness of the agitation, and broke the influence of Chartism as a national movement.

The few months following the demonstration on Kennington Common present an obscure picture of muffled plotting. There seems to have been some attempt to plan an insurrection, but it is impossible to say how widespread this was, or how it was organised. Certainly there was at no time any hope of success. The only effect was to increase working-class disillusionment and to cause a large number of arrests among the Chartist leaders. Several abortive attempts were made to revive Chartism as a peaceful propagandist movement, including Lovett's People's League, and Bronterre O'Brien's National Reform League, which, for a short time, possessed some importance. Meanwhile, middle-class Radicals were again attempting to persuade the Chartists to abandon the Charter and to support schemes of more limited reform ; but even the best of these — Joseph Hume's Little Charter — won but little support either among the Chartists or in Parliament.

In 1850 Ernest Jones emerged from two years' imprisonment to find that the Chartist world was in a state of confusion. O'Connor had lost his control over the N.C.A., which was still the largest Chartist organisation. Inside the N.C.A. a split was developing between those who, like O'Connor himself, had weakened towards a policy of compromise with the middle classes, and those who still stood out for the Charter and nothing but the Charter. Jones took sides with the latter group and soon assumed the leadership. By the end of 1852 *The Northern Star* was sold, O'Connor was in an asylum, and Jones dominated the N.C.A., with his *People's Paper* as the leading organ of the movement. Most of those who disliked Jones or his policy broke away, or drifted out. Jones now attempted to make the N.C.A. a more or less Marxist working-class party. But the conditions were against him; and in spite of his untiring activity over a number of years, the N.C.A. faded away. The last conference of the Chartist rump was held in 1858; and thereafter even Ernest Jones, in his last years, accepted the necessity for a policy of class compromise, and endeavoured to work for reform in association with the middle-class Radicals.

Chartism as a movement thus died out. But it had by no means completely failed, even though it had achieved none of its declared objectives. If conditions had improved and English employers become less ruthless, this was at any rate partly due to the sympathy and the fears which Chartism had aroused. Moreover, Chartism prepared the way for other movements. From the People's Charter Union sprang the renewed agitation for the Repeal of the Taxes on Knowledge, which secured in 1861 the abolition of the last penny of the tax on newspapers. The removal of the property qualification for members of Parliament in 1867, the Reform Act of 1867, and the Ballot Act of 1872, began the process of realising the Chartist programme. Although the Society of Fraternal Democrats collapsed in 1852, the Chartist tradition of democratic internationalism was carried on by the International Committee and the International Association, which may be regarded as forerunners of Marx's International Working Men's Association of 1864. Even Ernest Jones's apparently fruitless crusades left their mark on working-class opinion. Nevertheless, the fundamental challenge of Chartism had failed; and that challenge could not be repeated until, decades later, the Socialist movement came into being, armed with an essential weapon which Chartism always lacked — the clearly formulated demand for an alternative social system.

See " Short History ", Part I, chapter 8.
" Common People ", chapters 24 and 25.

1. THE NATIONAL CHARTER ASSOCIATION

[Chartist bodies up to 1839 had been purely local, united through their common campaign for the Charter but not by any organisational links. The N.C.A. was in fact the first attempt to set up a party for the working class. Unfortunately some of the proposals put forward in the initial constitution had to be abandoned for legal reasons. The Corresponding Societies Act of 1799 still made it illegal to have societies with branches; and if the local bodies elected their own delegates to the National Executive, they became branches and therefore illegal; instead of the Chartists of a town electing their delegates to the N.C.A., the later arrangement was that they elected members to a General Council which appointed local officials and delegates. Progress was slow at first; but, especially after O'Connor's release from prison, the N.C.A. became far the most important Chartist organisation; though a great number of the original leaders kept away on account of political or personal differences with O'Connor. In May 1841 a petition was presented for the release of the Chartist prisoners with more signatures than had been collected for the first National Petition. When O'Connor came out of prison in August 1841, activity was intensified, and a new petition for the Charter was planned.]

From *The Northern Star*, August 1, 1840.

'A PLAN FOR ORGANISING THE CHARTISTS OF GREAT BRITAIN. AGREED UPON AT A MEETING OF DELE-GATES APPOINTED BY THE PEOPLE, AND HELD AT THE GRIFFIN INN, GREAT ANCOATS STREET, MANCHESTER, ON MONDAY JULY 20TH, 1840.'

DESIGNATION OF THE ASSOCIATION.

1. That the Chartists of Great Britain be incorporated in one Society, to be called " The National Charter Association of Great Britain ".

OBJECTS.

2. The object of this Association is to obtain a " Radical Reform " of the House of Commons, in other words, a full and faithful representation of the entire people of the United Kingdom.

PRINCIPLES.

3. The principles requisite to secure such a representation of the people are :—The right of voting for members of Parliament,

by every male of twenty-one years of age, and of sound mind; Annual Elections; Vote by Ballot; no Property Qualification for Members of Parliament; Payment of Members; and a division of the Kingdom into Electoral Districts; giving to each district a proportionate number of representatives according to the number of electors.

MEANS.

4. To accomplish the foregoing objects, none but peaceable and constitutional means shall be employed, such as public meetings to discuss grievances arising from the existing system; to show the utility of the proposed change, and to petition Parliament to adopt the same.

CONDITIONS OF MEMBERSHIP.

5. All persons will become members of this association on condition of signing a declaration, signifying their agreement with its objects, principles, and constitution, when they shall be presented with cards of membership, which shall be renewed quarterly, and for which they shall each pay the sum of twopence.

REGISTRATION OF MEMBERS.

6. A book shall be kept by the Executive Council, hereinafter described, in which shall be entered the names, employment and residence of the members of this association throughout the kingdom.

7. Wherever possible, the members shall be formed into classes of ten persons; which classes shall meet weekly, or at other stated periods, as most convenient; and one out of, and by, each class shall be nominated as leader, (and appointed by the executive as hereinafter ordered) who shall collect from each member the sum of one penny per week, to the funds of this association.

WARD DIVISIONS.

8. Each town, wherever practicable, shall be divided into wards or divisions, according to the plan of the Municipal Reform Act. Once in every month, a meeting of the members of the said wards shall be held, when addresses shall be delivered, and the society's business transacted. The leaders within the said wards shall attend the said monthly meetings, and give such a report of the state of

their classes as they may deem best, provided always that such report be given in temperate and lawful language.

ELECTION OF WARD COLLECTOR.

9. At the first meeting of each ward or division, a collector shall be nominated (afterwards to be appointed by the Executive, as hereinafter ordered,) to whom shall be paid the monies collected from the classes by the leaders, and the said collectors shall pay the said monies to the Treasurer (assistant) of the town or borough, at the weekly meeting of the Council.

LOCAL OFFICERS.

10. Each principal town, with its suburban villages, shall have a Council of nine persons, including an assistant Treasurer and Secretary.

DUTIES OF LOCAL TREASURER.

11. The aforesaid treasurer shall receive the monies from the Ward collectors, and all monies subscribed for the Association, in the said township and suburbs; he shall keep an exact account, and transmit the proportion (one moiety) due once a month to the General Treasurer.

DUTIES OF LOCAL SECRETARY.

12. The aforesaid secretary shall keep a minute book of all the transactions of the Town Council, and a record of all meetings connected with the society in his jurisdiction, and shall with the sanction, and under the direction of the said Council, transmit for publication such portions of the said records or minutes as may be deemed necessary.

DUTIES OF LOCAL COUNCIL.

13. The Town Council shall meet for the transaction of business once every week, and shall have the power of appropriating to the purposes of the society in their own locality a sum not exceeding one half of the subscriptions, and other monies, received in the said locality. They shall also see that the recommendations and instructions of the Executive Council are carried into effect, and they shall have full power to adopt such means as may seem to them meet,

provided such means are in conformity with the fundamental rules of the Association, and do not contravene the decisions of the Executive Council.

COUNTY OR RIDING GOVERNMENT.

14. In each County or Riding there shall be a Council, the number to be according to the circumstances and population of the said County or Riding, with a sub-treasurer and secretary.

GENERAL GOVERNMENT.

15. The general government of this Association shall be entrusted to a General Executive Council, composed of seven persons, including a Treasurer and Secretary.

DUTIES OF THE GENERAL TREASURER.

16. The General Treasurer of this Association shall be responsible for all monies entrusted to him, in such penal sum of money as may be determined upon by the Executive Council; he shall keep an exact account of all monies received and expended for the Association; and shall, once every month, publish a statement of the same in the *Northern Star*, *Scottish Patriot*, and in such other of the Chartist newspapers as may be selected by the Executive Council, and once every three months a full balance sheet, which shall first be examined by auditors appointed for the purpose by the Executive.

DUTIES OF THE GENERAL SECRETARY.

17. The General Secretary shall keep in a book an exact record of the business, monetary or otherwise, of the Executive Council; he shall receive and forward the directions of the Executive to the sub- and assistant secretaries, answer all correspondence, and perform the general duties of a Secretary, as he may be required by the Executive.

NOMINATIONS AND ELECTION OF THE EXECUTIVE COUNCIL.

18. The nomination of candidates for the Executive Council shall take place in the Counties or Ridings, each County or Riding being allowed to nominate one candidate, on the 1st day of December each year — the names of the persons so nominated shall be returned

immediately by the secretary, called sub-secretary, of the County or Riding to the General Secretary — (this year to the secretary of the Provisional Committee, who have full powers to carry this plan into effect in the best possible manner) — and a list of the whole be transmitted by him — per post — to the local (assistant) secretaries, who shall take the election of their localities on the 1st day of January following, and immediately forward the result of such election to the General Secretary, who shall lay the same before the Executive for examination, and by their order publish within one week of receiving the whole of such returns in the *Northern Star*, or *Scottish Patriot* and in any other democratic journal, a list of the majorities, and declare who are the persons duly elected. The Executive Council shall be elected for twelve months, when a new Council shall be chosen in the manner and at the period aforesaid, outgoing members being eligible for re-election.

POWERS AND DUTIES OF THE EXECUTIVE.

19. The Executive Council shall be empowered to adopt any measures for the advancement of the objects of this Association, as may be consistent with its fundamental laws, for which purpose they shall have the disposal of one half, at least, of the monies collected throughout the Society and lodged with the General Treasurer. They shall appoint all the members of the County or Riding and Local Councils, and all officers throughout the Association, in the appointment of whom, however, they shall be confined to those who may be nominated by the members resident in each place.

TIME OF NOMINATION AND APPOINTMENT OF SUBORDINATE COUNCILS AND OFFICERS.

20. To prevent any interruption to the election of the Executive Council, the nomination of County or Riding Councils shall annually take place on the 1st day of February of each year, and the appointment on the 1st day of March following.

REMUNERATION OF OFFICERS.

21. The General Secretary shall be paid for his services the sum of £2 per week, and each member of the Executive Council the sum of £1 . 10. per week, during the period of their sittings.

COMPENSATION.

22. The members of the Executive shall be entitled to compensation for loss consequent upon their acceptance of office, either by being employed as missionaries, during any recess that may happen while they continue in their official capacity, or in such other way as may be most convenient for the Association; the question of compensation to be determined by the County or Riding Councils. When members of the Executive shall be employed as missionaries, the salaries shall be the same as when employed in the Council. Coach-hire, and one half of any other incidental expenses shall be paid to them in addition, by the parties who shall request their services, or in the event of being employed by the Executive to open new districts, the same proportion of expenses shall be allowed out of the general fund.

SOME MEANS FOR THE ATTAINMENT OF THE GREAT END.

1. The people shall, wherever convenient and practicable, put into operation Mr. O'Brien's plan of bringing forward Chartist Candidates at every election that may hereafter take place, and especially select where possible those as candidates who are legally qualified to sit in Parliament.

2. The members of this ASSOCIATION shall also attend all Public Political Meetings, and there, either by moving amendments or by other means, enforce a discussion of our rights and claims, so that none may remain in ignorance of what we want, nor have the opportunity of propagating or perpetuating political ignorance or delusion.

3. It is urgently recommended that strict sobriety be observed by all Members and Officers of this Association.

4. The diffusion of political knowledge.

On this subject it was resolved

" That as the appointment of Missionaries, the publication of tracts and the employment of the power of the press for the advancement of our views, is more properly the business of the Executive Council, and will depend upon the extent to which the people may avail themselves of the plan now submitted for their adoption, the delegates would, in the meantime, enumerate as advocates of the " People's Charter " especially the Northern Star, Scottish Patriot, Northern Liberator, True Scotsman and the following cheap and talented periodicals, viz. :—The Penny Northern Star, Western Patriot, Trumpet of Wales, Advocate and Merthyr Free News, Chartist Circular, Hetherington's Odd Fellow, and Cleave's Gazette, and they would further recommend the Executive Council, as speedily as possible, to divide the country into Districts, engage Missionaries, and bring out the Press, to the utmost extent, in the cause of the people."

JOHN ARRAN, Secretary.

MANCHESTER, *July 24th,* 1840

2. THE NATIONAL ASSOCIATION

[In gaol, Lovett had written, with John Collins's help, his " Chartism " (1841), in which he planned to re-create Chartism as an educational movement. When he came out he founded the ' National Association for Promoting the Political and Social Improvement of the People ', which was to gather together men of goodwill of all classes for the establishment of a voluntary system of National Education, secular and completely free from State control. He believed now that a long period of education was needed before the Charter could be won, and that the working class was too poor and too weak to carry on a movement independent of other classes. The National Association won very little support among any class, and played almost no part in the Chartist movement, to some extent because it was blackballed by O'Connor. Only one of its schools was established, and Lovett, dropping out of politics, taught there for many years.]

From " Rules and Objects of the National Association for Promoting the Political and Social Improvement of the People ".

OBJECTS.

First. To draw unto one bond of unity, persons of all CREEDS, CLASSES, and OPINIONS, who are desirous of promoting the political and social improvement of the people.

Second. To create and extend an enlightened public opinion in favour of the principles of the PEOPLE'S CHARTER, and by every just and peaceful means secure their legislative enactment; so that the industrious classes may be placed in possession of the franchise, the most important step towards political and social reformation.

Third. To disseminate such facts and opinions in favour of the *political and social rights of women* as may lead to their enfranchisement, and the amelioration of their social condition.

Fourth. To publish from time to time such *Addresses*, *Tracts*, and *Pamphlets* as the Association may consider necessary for promoting the political and social improvement of the people; and as soon as its funds permit, to publish a *weekly* or *monthly periodical*, as the official organ of the Association.

Fifth. To form a *General Library* of the most useful works on politics, morals, the sciences, history, and general literature, for reference and circulation among the members; and as soon as practicable to establish circulating libraries to be sent in rotation, from one town or village to another for the use of similar associations that may be formed.

Sixth. To promote the legal formation of *similar associations* in different parts of the country and endeavour to create an opinion among the middle and working classes, in favour of establishing *Public Halls* and *Schools* for the people; in which their children may be properly educated and themselves mentally and morally improved.

Seventh. To promote the education of the rising generation and the political and social improvement of the people by means of *Schools*, *Lectures*, *Public Meetings*, *Discussions*, *Classes for Mutual Instruction and Meetings for Rational Amusement* after their hours of toil.

Eighth. To send, from time to time, to such localities as may require them, *Missionaries* for the purpose of lecturing, or in any way promoting the object of the Association.

3. THE COMPLETE SUFFRAGE MOVEMENT

[In 1841 an essay on ' Reconciliation between the Middle and Lower Classes ' appeared in *The Nonconformist* and was republished as a pamphlet by Joseph Sturge, a Quaker banker and corn merchant. The essay suggested that the middle class should support the working-class demand for the franchise and that the working class should in return abandon the Charter and all talk of violence. Sturge used his influence in the Anti-Corn Law League to gather middle-class support, and in April 1842 called the first Complete Suffrage Conference, which was also attended by many of the working-class Chartists opposed to O'Connor. This Conference adopted one by one all the six points of the Charter; but, when Lovett moved that the Charter itself should be adopted, the Sturge-ites showed so much anxiety that the Conference was adjourned. Meanwhile a petition based on the six points was sent to Parliament and was there heavily defeated. The Conference reassembled in December;

O'Connor, who had previously denounced the movement, was present with several of his followers. Sturge attempted to make the basis of discussion a Bill of Rights drafted for the occasion, but Lovett moved that instead they should discuss the Charter. His motion was carried and the Sturgeites left the Conference; there was a further split between the followers of Lovett and O'Connor and the movement collapsed, though the Complete Suffrage Union lingered on ineffectually till 1844. There had, in fact, been little hope of success, as the Chartist leaders who were sympathetic to its ideas had no following in the most important centres of the movement.]

(a) From the ' Address of the Council of the National Complete Suffrage Union to Political Reformers of all shades of opinions ', September 1842. From William Lovett, " Life and Struggles " (Bohn edition), p. 285.

. . . We, therefore, submit the following propositions for the consideration of the conference, which we call upon you, the Reformers of the United Kingdom, to elect :—

1. To determine on the essential details of an Act of Parliament necessary for securing the just representation of the whole adult male population of the United Kingdom of Great Britain and Ireland; such act to embrace the principles and details of complete suffrage, equal electoral districts, vote by ballot, no property qualifications, payment of members, and annual parliaments, as adopted by the first Complete Suffrage Conference.

2. To determine what members of Parliament shall be appointed to introduce the said act into the House of Commons, and in what manner other members of the house shall be called upon to support it.

3. To endeavour to ascertain how far the friends of unrestricted and absolute freedom of trade will unite with us to obtain such an Act of Parliament, provided we resolve to use our newly acquired franchise in favour of such freedom of trade, and to vote only for such as will pledge themselves in its favour.

4. To devise the best means for maintaining competent parliamentary candidates pledged to our principles; the most effectual means by which assistance may be rendered to them in all electoral contests; and also the best means for registering the electors and non-electors throughout the kingdom who may be disposed to promote our objects.

5. To consider the propriety of calling upon the municipal electors to adopt immediate measures for securing the election of

such men only to represent them in their local governments as are known to be favourable to the principles of complete suffrage.

6. To call upon our fellow-countrymen seriously to consider the great extent, to which, in various ways, they now willingly co-operate with their oppressors, and to ascertain how far they may be disposed to prove their devotion to the cause of liberty, by refusing to be used for the purposes of war, cruelty, and injustice, and particularly by the disuse of intoxicating articles.

7. To express an opinion as to the duty of the people giving their countenance and support to all those who may suffer from espousing their cause.

8. To determine the best legal and constitutional means for energetically and peaceably promoting the above objects ; for checking all kinds of violence and commotion by which the enemy triumphs; for disseminating sound political knowledge ; for spreading the principles of sobriety, peace and tolerance throughout the country, and by every just and virtuous means preparing the people for the proper exercise of their political and social rights.

9. To devise means for raising a national fund for the purpose of promoting the above objects as well as to protect all persons, who in their peaceful prosecution of them, shall become victims of unjust laws or despotic ordinances.

And in order to convince the middle classes that the working population have no ulterior object inimical to the general welfare of society, we advise that they meet in the forthcoming conference on terms of perfect equality to discuss these important propositions, feeling convinced that our principles need no other aid than their own intrinsic excellence ; having truth for their basis, and the happiness of the human family for their end, and affording the best guarantee for the security of private property, which we regard as sacred and inviolable, equally in the poor man's labour and the rich man's possessions. . . .

(*b*) From the " Report of the Proceedings at the Conference of Delegates of the Middle and Working Classes held at Birmingham, April 5, 1842, and three following days ", p. 69.

Mr. Lovett then moved and Mr. Curr seconded the following resolutions ; — " That an association be now formed to be entitled ' The *National Complete Suffrage Union* ', and that the following be its objects : — 1. The creating and extending an enlightened public opinion in favour of the following principle and details of complete suffrage — viz., the extension of the elective franchise to every man twenty-one years of age, who has not been deprived of his rights of citizenship in consequence of a verdict of a jury of his countrymen. The abolition of the property qualification for members of Parliament. The adoption of voting by ballot. The dividing the country into equal electoral districts. The payment of all legal election expenses, and a reasonable remuneration to members of Parliament — and that annual parliaments are a proper means of securing responsibility of members to their constituents.

2. To invite all persons to become members of this Union, who are favourable to the great principle of political equality — all who belong to every description of political association or society, for improving and benefiting the people — as well as persons of all creeds, classes and opinions, who are desirous of seeing their country prosperous, enlightened and free.

3. To influence members of parliament in favour of complete suffrage, to cause it to be repeatedly introduced in the House of Commons, till such time as it is enacted as the law of these realms — to support those members who introduce it with petitions, memorials, or remonstrances, and to carefully register the names of all those members of parliament who vote for or against it, so that the people may be fully made acquainted with the friends and opponents of their principles.

4. To effect an annual enrolment of all electors throughout the kingdom. Who are favourable to our objects, and in all cases of elections of members of parliament to advise or assist in the bringing forward and supporting those candidates who may be approved of, and who will pledge themselves to vote for complete suffrage.

5. To request the non-electors in every town and borough throughout the kingdom, to exercise their influence and record their names in favour of all candidates pledged to complete suffrage.

6. To oppose the return of any member of the present House of Commons who may not vote in favour of the motion which Mr. Sharman Crawford is about to introduce, unless he pledge himself to vote hereafter in favour of the principle adopted by this conference.

7. To devise the best means by which an important principle of the British Constitution, as set forth by Blackstone and others, may be enforced by the people on their rulers, should they much longer resist their just and constitutional rights — that is, the refusing to pay any aids or taxes imposed without their consent, or that of their representatives in parliament.

8. To recommend all classes of society to refuse to participate in the horrors of war, or to be used for the purposes of cruelty and injustice; and in order that our movement may be peaceably and morally conducted, to recommend sobriety and temperance.

9. To appoint as many voluntary missionaries and lecturers as may be deemed necessary, to visit different parts of the country for the purpose of generally explaining the views of this Union, for promoting its efficient organisation, for lecturing on its different objects, and for otherwise seeing that the intentions of the general body are carried into effect throughout the kingdom, according to the instructions they receive from the general council.

10. To print from time to time, such tracts and pamphlets as the Union may consider necessary for promoting its objects, and when its organisation is complete, to print a national weekly newspaper, and to support only such daily and other weekly newspapers and periodicals as may be favourable to its objects.

11. To raise a national fund for the carrying out of the above objects — 1st, by the issuing of half-yearly cards to members at 6d. each; 2dly, of annual cards to annual subscribers at 5s. and 10s. each; 3rdly, of cards to honorary members, who give a donation of £5 or upwards.

12. To adopt every just, peaceful, legal, and constitutional means for carrying the above resolutions into effect, and only such."

(c) From " Report of Proceedings at the Conference of Delegates of the Middle and Working Classes, held at Birmingham, April 5, 1842, and three following days ", p. 70.

The National Complete Suffrage Union to their Countrymen.

FRIENDS AND FELLOW-CITIZENS,—Our country's crisis has arrived; her sufferings have gone up into *his* ear, who hath pledged his truth that the rod of the oppressor shall be broken into pieces. A nation's interests are cast into the crucible; be it yours to watch the process, and conduct it to the desired result. They who take the sword shall perish by the sword; let your force be argument; your lever public opinion; and your triumph must be joyous.

Believe that vice is slavery; virtue true liberty and nobility; and that to be free, you must be self-emancipators.

The character of your time is energy and celerity; exemplify your correspondence with it; work in this good cause, as those who hear their country's call, that every man do his duty, and under the conscientious persuasion that every man has something to do, and can do it.

The fearful alternative is convulsion or regulation; as you dread the former strive in season and out of season for the latter.

Borrow an instructive lesson from your foes — the class who are, as they falsely think, interested in maintaining the ills under which our country grieves — the removal of which has originated this Union, — have always been distinguished by their systematic union and energy. By these they have triumphed; let reformers in this imitate them; thus is the present crisis to be effectually met and improved. Have class legislators generated and turned to their profit the dissensions of reformers? Let such alienations, and the very appearance of them, be in all time coming anxiously guarded against.

Having assumed as our basis the principle of universal adult male suffrage, labour for its diffusion among all classes; keep simply by the principle. Believing that union is strength, abstain from every source of mutual recrimination; bury past animosities; consign to oblivion hitherto discrepancies of sentiment; abolish, as far as may be, every term and watchword that may have been the badge of party or section; and henceforth in language simple as your aim, strive in harmony for the welfare of our common country. Draw your ammunition from the magazine of argument; take every suitable opportunity to discuss in a free and kindly spirit the things in which you may have differed from others, or among yourselves; studiously retain your temper as you would preserve yourself and persuade your opponent,

Labour to obtain an accurate registration of electors in your district — those who are of your mind, especially, as to our great movement; endeavour to obtain a list of non-electors who agree with you, and peaceably so regulate . . . their organisation, that on proper occasions, and for all profiting influences, they may furnish to all an exponent of their political opinions.

Make the conclusions of the Union the essential tests of the sentiments and measures of candidates for a seat in parliament.

Endeavour, in your respective districts, to obtain lecturers that may expound and recommend the principles and measures of the Union. Hold public meetings; form associations of your own, which though necessarily unconnected with the National Union, may promote the one great object; and by every laudable means imbue the people of every class with the tenets of the Union, and ripen the public mind for practical measures.

Above all things avoid secret and unlawful proceedings.

Cherish earnestly the happy fraternal feeling which has eminently characterised the first conference, and which furnishes, as we trust, the best augury of our future proceedings and success. Let everything be done peacefully; abstain from every appearance of the evil that might make your good be evil spoken of. Lay your account with reproach; be nothing terrified by it; live it down by your quiet and honest life, known and read of all men. Thus will you become better citizens and better men, and prove to the conviction of your bitterest enemies that as you justly demand of them your rights, you are worthy of them; that as you have energy to obtain them, your purpose is to lay them out to usury for the common weal of the country of your birth and your affections.

(*d*) From *The Birmingham Journal*, December 31, 1842.

Mr Beggs then read the following resolutions :—

1. That this conference convened in conformity with a resolution passed at the first complete Suffrage Conference, held at Birmingham, April 5th to 8th, 1842, and having for a paramount object the consideration of the necessary details of a bill, embodying the principles then agreed upon, viz.— the extension of the suffrage to all male adults, not deprived of the rights of citizenship by a verdict of a jury of their countrymen — vote by ballot — equal electoral districts — abolition of a property qualification by members of parliament — payment of members for their services — and annual parliaments,— do now declare its adoption of these principles; pledges itself to employ such means only for obtaining the legislative recognition of them as are of a strictly just, peaceful, legal and constitutional character; and will forthwith proceed to fulfil the mission with which it has been entrusted, resolved to support its chairman in preventing the introduction of any propositions not in accordance therewith.

2. That as this conference will resist the introduction of any topics not obviously relevant to its main design, so it also disclaims all interference with existing organisations, recognising as its paramount duty, the arriving, if possible, at a cordial agreement in reference to the object towards which peaceful agitation may be directed.

3. That this conference, agreeable to resolution 17, passed at the first conference, is prepared to receive and to consider all documents which may be laid before it, and which may be supposed to contain

an embodiment of the necessary details for working out the principles already recognised.

4. That the documents so to be presented to this conference be taken into consideration at the opening of our next session, by a committee consisting of the whole body of delegates; and that the committee be instructed to observe the following rules :— 1. That the bill to be presented by the Council of the " National Complete Suffrage Union " be taken as the basis of discussion. 2. That each clause as it is read shall be considered *pari passu* with the correlative clauses of the other documents. 3. That all amendments be handed up to the chairman in writing.

Mr Lovett said he rose for the purpose of suggesting to Mr Beggs, the propriety of substituting the word " Charter," in the fourth resolution, in place of the bill. (Loud and continued cheering). The Charter has been well known amongst the public; they were wedded to it, and they could not be weaned from it. It contained all that the bill professed to give them, and he thought, for many reasons, it should be the basis of any measure they might bring forward. (Renewed cheers). When he took part in the first conference, he was given to understand that it would be brought forward. Impressed with the conviction that the object of the Complete Suffrage Union was to effect a thorough union of the two great classes, and not to consult any particular class, he had taken part in their proceedings, and endeavoured to press upon them the great necessity of adopting that bold and generous course which would concentrate the masses. With an understanding that the People's Charter would be brought forward at the present conference, he postponed his intention respecting it at the first conference; and he must say, he was not a little surprised to find that it had not been so brought forward, but that in its place a bill, which, they were told, would take five hours to read, had been prepared. He thought the council had done wrong in the course they had taken, and he hoped they would retrace their steps and go at once to the consideration of the People's Charter.

. . . .

The adjourned Debate.

Mr Lovett said, he thought it would be well now if Mr Beggs would give an answer to the question that he put to him the night before. He had asked him if he would consent to allow the bill to be withdrawn.

Mr Beggs said he could not; upon which,

Mr Lovett said, he felt placed in an unpleasant situation, by the refusal of Mr Beggs and friends to withdraw the bill. He had now no other course left than to propose the following amendment :—

That the document called the People's Charter, embracing all the essential details of just and equal representation, couched in plain and definite language, capable of being understood, and appreciated by the great mass of the people, for whose government and guidance all laws ought to be written,— that measure having been before the public for the last five years, forming the basis of the present agitation in favour of the suffrage, and for seeking to secure the legal enactment of which, vast numbers had suffered imprisonment, transportation and death,— has, in the opinion of this meeting, a prior claim over all other documents proposing to embrace the claims of just representation; it is therefore resolved that we proceed to discuss the different sections of the People's Charter, in order to ascertain whether any improvements can be made in it, and what those improvements shall be; it being necessary to make that document as clear and perfect as possible.

4. THE CHARTISTS AND THE ANTI-CORN LAW LEAGUE

[The Anti-Corn Law League was founded in 1839, but did not have any considerable mass following until 1842. By then Chartist failures had driven many into other movements, among them the Anti-Corn Law League, which became a powerful rival to the National Charter Association. Chartists were not agreed on the policy they should adopt on this issue. Some were protectionists; some were free traders, but believed that Free Trade without the Charter would be valueless. Some believed the two agitations could go their own ways separately, some that Free Trade could not be won without the Charter first reforming Parliament. For the most part they adopted the views, propounded by O'Brien, that though Free Trade might be of value in a Chartist England, the League was a menace : it was meant, they said, to distract attention from Chartism, by posing as the working man's friend, and in practice the manufacturers would merely lower wages if the Corn Laws were repealed and prices fell. The attacks on the League were bitter, but the League advanced to success, and more and more Chartists dropped their hostility to Free Trade.]

(a) From *The English Chartist Circular*, vol. 2, No. 59 (1842).

Attitude to be adopted at Anti-Corn Law Meetings, as recommended by the executive committee of the National Charter Association, March, 1842.

PUBLIC ARRANGEMENTS

1st. Every Corn Law Repealer or middle class professor of Chartism, should make a public and unreserved declaration and attachment to the whole principle of the Charter, before he can take part with us in the agitation, or cooperate with us. 2nd. The Corn Law party or middle class agitators desiring to cooperate with us, should be called upon to agree to the unqualified right of speech for all our leaders at all political meetings, and the full privilege of moving amendments to all motions, whenever it may appear to the people or their advisors to be necessary.

Without the first unreserved admission, we can have no security for the sincerity of their professions, and consistency of conduct.

Without the second all important provision we can have no effective check upon the guidance of public opinion. . . .

FIRST CHARTIST RESOLUTION

That class legislation is the original and existing cause of all grievances, political, social, moral and physical; that its effects are self-evident in the discontent, poverty and bondage of all the useful classes in society; that this meeting is firmly of opinion, that the first remedy should be as comprehensive as the first cause, and therefore adopt, without alteration or deduction, the entire principles of the People's Charter.

SECOND CHARTIST RESOLUTION

That this meeting unreservedly condemns all taxes levied upon bread and other necessaries of life, that it is of the opinion that the monopoly in food depends upon the monopoly of the Suffrage, that it has no confidence in any Government appointed under the present system, and despairing of the removal of existing misery, is fully convinced that the total and entire repeal of the Corn and Provision Laws, can only be the act of a Parliament representing the interests and opinions of the whole people of Great Britain and Ireland.

(*b*) From *The Liberator*, March 24, 1842.

THE ANTI-BREAD TAX CIRCULAR

We have read with much pleasure, the following remarks, extracted from the *National Liberator*, a Glasgow Chartist newspaper.

At the present time, when the remorseless supporters of tyranny are, with the most unblushing effrontery, asserting their right to maintain their high rents and starve the people, it is, in our opinion, extremely injudicious in any meeting of working men to propose the " usual amendment ", in opposition to a demand for the total and immediate abolition of the iniquitous corn and provision laws. These odious restrictions are precious in the sight of our aristocratic agriculturists, more sacred in their consideration than the glory of their country, nay, than the temporal and eternal interests of the millions whom they oppress. How ridiculous then is it [to] hear the very class who suffer most, and whose sufferings are tantalised by those who produce them, reiterate the arguments and fallacies of their dominant and merciless oppressors. . . . Governments naturally detest every agitation opposed to their policy ; they know the force of popular excitement, they know it has frequently hurled the haughtiest and the most powerful administrations from their eminence, and even potentates from their thrones ; consequently those who assist the ' powers that be ' to crush opposition and to stifle the clamour of disaffection against any obnoxious measure, are rendering, though it may be unconsciously, a most important service to the officials of the state. It is on this ground that we regret deeply the obstruction which many of our Chartist brethren continue to give to meetings called to remonstrate against the infamous starvation laws. What good purpose can it serve ? Will it annihilate the anti-corn-law movement ? That is undoubtedly the object contemplated ; but what benefit would that confer on our cause ? None whatever. The agitation maintained by the league has, we make bold to say, been one of the most powerful auxiliaries which our own movement has had, by awakening, as it has done, hundreds of thousands to the evils of class legislation, and by giving, as its results do, broad and incontrovertible evidence to the whole country, that these monopolies will be perpetuated until the people be represented in the House of Commons. . . .

5. CHARTISM AND THE TRADE UNIONS

[In London the Chartists had a quite close contact with many of the Trade Societies ; Lovett and Hartwell, in particular, among the London leaders had been active Trade Unionists, while the Bootmakers seem to have been consistent supporters of Chartism (as of all other working-class efforts of the time), but perhaps the most significant indication of the contact was the committee of Trade Unionists, which founded *The Charter* as a working-class weekly to be supported by Trade and other working-class societies. In the North, except among the miners, there is less evidence of formal connection between the Chartists and the Trade Unions before 1842; but the masses that followed O'Connor were largely the same as those who had taken part in the great Trade Union uprisings between 1828 and 1834, and *The Northern Star* gave much space to news of Trade Union doings. Some of the Trade Unions, however, had put a definite ban, after 1834, on the introduction of politics into Trade Union meetings. In 1830 the miners on the North-East Coast were apparently contemplating a strike for the Charter, but nothing came of this, and from 1841 their main interest was Martin Jude's " Miners' Association ". The ' Plug Plot ' gave evidence of Chartist enthusiasm in mines and factories, but this was short-lived and may have often come from workers, who were not industrially organised. The National Charter Association attempted to capture the support of the Trade Unions : *The Northern Star*, which in 1844 became *The Northern Star and National Trades' Journal*, had from the first devoted considerable space to Trade Union news. But the Chartists could never point to any solid backing from the Trade Unions — this was one of their major weaknesses, especially when they entertained plans of calling a General Strike.]

(*a*) From a Letter from ' Bronterre ' (J. B. O'Brien) in *The Northern Star*, October 13, 1838.

[A correspondent who has written to me] says " I think, as the trades came out so nobly [in a recent Manchester demonstration], a letter to the trades from you in the *Star*, would be a new stimulant to useful agitation, the more especially as they joined the procession and made common cause with us in other towns, as well as in this. The following is a correct list for Manchester :—1st, tailors ; 2nd, national associated smiths ; 3rd, mechanics or machinists ; 4th, smiths and furriers ; 5th, smiths and wheelwrights ; 6th, dyers ; 7th, fustian shearers ; 8th, callenderers ; 9th, joiners ; 10th, men's boot and shoemakers ; 11th, ladies' shoemakers ; 12th, painters ; 13th, masons ; 14th, marble masons ; 15th, marble polishers and sawyers ; 16th, bricklayers ; 17th, labourers ; and 18th, spinners.

(*b*) From *The Charter*, July 21, 1839.

NEWCASTLE, *July 12th*, 1839.

TO THE SECRETARY OF THE CONVENTION

SIR,— I am instructed by the council of the Newcastle Political Union, to inform you that nearly all the colliers in the North are laid in with a stern determination on the part of the men not to commence work again until they have gained their rights. We have done all in our power to try to get them to wait for the commands of the Convention. The answer is, that they have waited long enough for aught they have to expect from their tyrants. They add, " We are prepared to commence ". In fact, they have done so ; for no sooner did the news of Dr Taylor's arrest arrive, followed by that of Messrs Collins and Lovett, than the strike commenced, and it has gone on increasing until now. There are more than 25,000 pitmen alone on strike, besides the town trades, who are in expectation of your orders daily. It is earnestly requested that the time of strike be not delayed, but that it be put in force by Monday next, or the consequences in this district will be dreadful to contemplate ; and if the Convention wish to retain the confidence of the people here, they must speedily act. In expectation of a speedy answer, I am, in haste, etc.

P.S. Since writing the above, I hear that ten more of the collieries have struck, with the aggregate amount of men, — namely, 7,000.

(c) From *The Charter*, April 28, 1842.

THE WEST LONDON BOOT AND SHOEMAKERS'
CHARTER ASSOCIATION TO THE TRADES OF LONDON

FELLOW-WORKMEN,—

Most of us have hitherto, like too many of our class, regarded *politics* as something foreign to our interests, as a word of mystical meaning which concerned the rich and influential, and only of primary interest to those who had votes to sell, or ambition to purchase them. Hence we have been content to pursue our respective avocations with unremitting industry, to regard our trade affairs as a paramount interest, and to consider those only our enemies who sought to reduce our wages or infringe on our prices ; without extending our inquiries to ascertain how far our trade, our wages, and the very feelings of our employers towards us, were dependent on, and subject to, superior influences — those of our POLITICAL *institutions*. While however we entertain the same favourable opinions of our trade associations, events have recently transpired to convince us, that we do not sufficiently direct our attention to the *source of our trade and domestic grievances*. We firmly believe brethren that our wages have been greatly supported by union, and that without our unions we should ere now be ground down to the lowest point of subsistence ; but we have recently perceived that even the very *existence of our unions* is dependent on the mere caprice or despotic will of an *irresponsible government*, which at any moment has the power to enact the most rigorous laws for our annihilation. Nay, almost every circumstance affecting our happiness, from birth to death, is dependent on this corrupt and absolute power . . . and why, let us ask, has this system of injustice been permitted so long? Simply, fellow workmen, because the *working classes conceived they had nothing to do with politics.* . . . A political movement is now making throughout the length and breadth of the land to give the working men an equality of political rights, a right in making the laws they are compelled to obey. We would therefore call on you earnestly to join, as we have done, in this struggle for freedom, to form as we have formed, a Chartist Association in connection with your own trade. . . .

6. THE CHARTIST PETITION OF 1842

[The second Chartist Convention was a less ambitious affair than that of 1839, though the second Petition had many more signatures than the first. The 1842 Convention was appointed to sit only for a limited period, and there seems to have been no talk of ' ulterior measures '. The Convention was largely occupied with an attempt to heal quarrels that had broken out inside the N.C.A., especially between O'Connor and O'Brien.]

From R. G. Gammage, " History of the Chartist Movement, 1837–54 " (1894), pp. 208-9.

Meanwhile the Executive were directing the attention of the country to the subject of another petition for the Charter, and they submitted a draft of the same for adoption. This second Petition did not, however, stop at the Charter; but, as well as stating a host of grievances, prayed for a repeal of the legislative union between Great Britain and Ireland. Here again was a bone of contention. A portion of the Scottish Chartists were opposed to the introduction of any other subject into the Petition than the Charter, and a controversy on the subject took place between Dr. M'Douall and John Duncan, one of the best and ablest of the Scottish Chartists. The majority, however, went with the Executive, and the signing of the Petition proceeded very briskly. A Convention was appointed to sit in London for three weeks, for the purpose of superintending its presentation. It consisted of twenty-five members, whose names were as follows :—Abraham Duncan, E. Stallwood, James Leach,

J. R. H. Bairstow, C. Doyle, W. P. Roberts, George White, Feargus O'Connor, N. Powell, R. Lowery, James Moir, S. Bartlett, William Beesley, J. M'Pherson, G. Harrison, P. M. M'Douall, Morgan Williams, R. K. Philp, Ruffy Ridley, W. Woodward, J. Mason, William Thomason, Lawrence Pitkeithly, J. Campbell, and J. Bronterre O'Brien. It will be seen that only six out of the twenty-five were members of the first Convention. This body met in London on the 12th of April, 1842, and received the signatures to the National Petition, which in the aggregate were stated to amount to thirty-three thousand. The Petition was presented to the House of Commons by Mr. Duncombe on the 2nd of May, on which occasion there was a large procession, which left the Convention Room and proceeded through several of the principal thoroughfares to the House of Commons. The authorities had strictly ordered that no vehicles should pass along the thoroughfares, so as in any way to interfere with the procession, which order was rigidly enforced. The concourse of people assembled on the occasion was immense ; many strangers being present from the country to witness the proceedings. Duncombe presented the Petition, which was wheeled into the House, and stated the purport of its prayer ; he then gave notice of a motion that the petitioners be heard at the bar of the House, through their counsel or agents, in support of the allegations which the Petition contained. When Duncombe brought forward his motion there was the usual quantity of speaking. Macaulay was the great opponent of the motion. He stated that he had no objection to any one point of the Charter but universal suffrage, which he described as amounting to nothing short of the confiscation of the property of the rich. He uttered during his speech the most unfounded and abominable calumnies against the working class. Duncombe's speech was noble and manly, and elicited the warm esteem of men of all parties ; but no amount of good speaking was sufficient to draw forth a response from the House of Commons, and only fifty-one members, including tellers, were found to vote in favour of his motion. That House was too cowardly or too callously indifferent to the condition of the people, to consent to meet the veritable representatives of the suffering poor face to face, and listen to an exposure of their wrongs from those who were best qualified to make it. Duncombe declared that so much was he disgusted with the conduct of the House of Commons, that if the people ever got up another petition of the kind, he would not be a party to their degradation by presenting it. . . .

7. THE PLUG PLOT

[In July 1842 a strike movement, which started among the Lancashire cotton spinners, spread to the Midlands and even to Wales and northwards into Scotland. It was called the ' Plug Plot ', because in the factory areas the strikers marched from factory to factory, removing the boiler plugs in order to bring the steam-engines to a stand. Soon meetings of strikers began to pass resolutions that ' all labour should cease until the People's Charter became the law of the land '. The Chartist leaders had not started the strike movement nor had they given it this political colouring. Indeed, O'Connor had begun by denouncing it as a plot of the Anti-Corn Law League manufacturers, who wanted a chance to close their works in face of bad trade and hoped to make political use of the distress. But when the Chartists saw the success which had followed the work of local Chartists, many hoped at last to bring about the General Strike they had attempted to promote in 1839. Trade, however, was very bad ; and the strikers were soon starved back to work. The fears aroused by the movement brought a fresh wave of arrests of leading Chartists.]

(a) From *The Northern Star*, August 20, 1842.

GREAT DELEGATE MEETING OF THE TRADES OF MANCHESTER AND THE WHOLE SURROUNDING DISTRICT

. . . There was exhibited as might have been expected a difference of opinion among the thousands who were represented by the several members of this important meeting as to the precise object to be recognised as the distinct purpose of the strike. Some, and those the majority, were instructed on the part of their constituents, to disclaim all minor and secondary objects of contention, and to declare that their resolution was fixed to uphold the strike on no other ground than as a means to obtain the Charter, for which purpose they were resolved to maintain it to the last extremity.

Others, and those principally from Stalybridge and the other localities where the strike began, were instructed that their constituents regarded it as merely a trades' strike, a question of wages, and trades' rights ; while a considerable number of places, without giving any opinion of their own, expressed by their delegates their readiness to uphold their brethren in any struggle that might be deemed advisable, and to abide therefore upon the decision of that meeting be the same what it might ; . . . Of the eighty-five delegates, fifty-eight declared for the Charter ; seven for making it a trades' contest ; nineteen to abide the decision of the meeting ; and one, the representative of the stone masons of Manchester, stated that his constituents were individually for the Charter, but that he had no instruction from them as a body, and could not therefore pledge them to any precise course of action.

(*b*) Resolution of Chartist Delegates in Conference at Manchester, August 17, 1842. From *The Northern Star*, August 20, 1842.

That whilst the Chartist body did not originate the present cessation from labour, this Conference of Delegates from various parts of England, express their deep sympathy with their constituents, the working men now on strike; and that we strongly approve the extension and continuance of their present struggle till the PEOPLE'S CHARTER becomes a legislative enactment, and decide forthwith to issue an Address to that effect; and pledge ourselves on our return to our respective localities to give a proper direction to the people's efforts.

8. THE METROPOLITAN PARLIAMENTARY REFORM ASSOCIATION

[Francis Place was among those who believed, after the rejection of the Chartist Petition of 1842, that the time had come for a further attempt to unite the working class and middle-class Radicals on the basis of a demand for Manhood Suffrage, the Ballot, the Triennial (instead of Annual) Parliaments. With this end in view, he founded the Metropolitan Parliamentary Reform Association; but he found too little support to achieve any durable success.]

From the Place MSS. 27,810 f. 152 (1842).

.   .   .   .   .   .

The extent of information amongst the people appears to warrant the conclusion that the time has come when Associations, to promote a thorough Reform of the House of Commons, may be formed, without reference to classes or parties, and free from any particular denomination, excepting that of Parliamentary Reformers. . . . The plan of the Society is as follows :—

METROPOLITAN PARLIAMENTARY REFORM ASSOCIATION
OBJECTS :—

1. To obtain for each man of twenty-one years of age the right of voting for *a* representative to serve in the Commons House of Parliament. . . .

2. That the country be divided into as many polling districts, as there may be representatives in the House of Commons.
3. That the duration of Parliaments may be shorter, but shall not be longer than three years.
4. That every elector shall be eligible to be elected.
5. That the Right of voting for a representative shall be exercised secretly by ballot.
6. That each representative of the people shall be paid for his services.

For the purpose of carrying this plan into effect generally, it is necessary that a sufficient amount of money be raised, to enable the Association to take rooms in an eligible situation for offices.

To employ a well-qualified man to act as secretary.

To employ as many assistants as may be necessary to carry on the business with precision, punctuality, and energy.

To correspond with as many individuals in every part of the country for the purposes of the society, and for the promotion of other similar societies in as many places as possible.

To devise and carry into effect a plan, by which a weekly account of the proceedings of every such society may be published, and thus to make the proceedings of all known to all, without in any way breaking the obnoxious laws which limit the intercourse of reformers in different parts of the country. . . .

9. THE CHARTIST LAND SCHEME

[O'Connor's Land Scheme was a plan to settle families on the land as peasant smallholders. After some years of initial propaganda the Chartist Co-operative Land Society (later renamed the National Land Company) was founded in 1845. The vigorous propaganda work of O'Connor collected a mass of subscribers, and in 1846 O'Connorville was founded on a site near Rickmansworth. Other estates were bought and let out in smallholdings to those subscribers who had been lucky in the ballot. But by the end of 1847 the financial difficulties facing the scheme — and the financial incompetence of its directors — had become obvious. In 1848 a Committee of the House of Commons reported that the Company was illegal, its finances in a state of chaos, and its promises impossible to fulfil; O'Connor was absolved from any suspicions of fraud, indeed he had been heavily out of pocket. This Land Scheme owed a great deal to the Owenite Communities, the last of which, Queenwood in Hampshire, had been wound up in 1845 after six unhappy years. But whereas in

Queenwood and the other Owenite Colonies the land was cultivated and its produce shared in common, each O'Connorite settler rented a separate holding, and owned what it produced.]

(*a*) From the Second Report of the Select Committee on the National Land Company (1848), p. 49.

From the Rules of the Chartist Cooperative Land Society, 1845.

OBJECTS OF THE SOCIETY

To purchase land on which to locate such of its members as may be selected for that purpose, in order to demonstrate to the working classes of the kingdom, firstly the value of the land, as a means of making them independent of the grinding capitalist; and, secondly, to show them the necessity of securing the speedy enactment of the " People's Charter ", which would do for them nationally what this society proposes to do sectionally; the accomplishment of the political and social emancipation of the enslaved and degraded working classes being the prominent object of the society.

(*b*) From the First Report of the Select Committee on the National Land Company (1848), p. 5.

CIRCULAR OF THE NATIONAL LAND COMPANY (1847)

A Happy Home for Honest Industry, National Land Company provisionally registered; shares £1 . 6s each payable by instalments of 3d, 6d, 1s. and upwards per week. The objects aimed at by this company are, the elevation of the character and social improvement of the condition of its members. The means by which the company propose to realise these objects, so laudable in themselves, and so desirable to all, are so moderate as to place them within the reach of the poorest in the community. Benefits: The advantages which this company guarantees to its members are as follows: the subscriber of two shares, or £2 . 12 . 0, entitles himself to a house, three acres of land, and £22 . 10 . 0; the subscriber of four shares, or £5 . 4 . 0, to a house, four acres of land, and £30. The annual rent-charge which will be made by the company on its allotted members for the aforesaid benefits is regulated by a principle which will, in every case, prevent its becoming a burden to those who will have to bear it. The company affords great facilities to its members to become freeholders of their dwellings and allotments, as the interest charged on the capital expended in the completion of an allotment is redeemable by a process of which every industrious and provident member may avail himself. The company presents to the public other admirable features in the circumstances, that it invests the allotees with the elective franchise, and that it causes the original amount subscribed by each member to revert to him, together with a proportionate share of any profits that may accrue from the transactions of the company when the whole of the members are located. The company have likewise a bank of deposit and redemption, which presents peculiar advantages to the working classes, either for the redemption of the rent-charge of their buildings, or for the general purposes of a savings bank. Progress : The prosperity which has marked the career of the National Land Company, since the day of its formation, has been unexampled in the annals of similar institutions. It dates its origin from the 19th of May 1845 ; and since that time to the present, it has diffused itself over England, Scotland, and Wales. It has likewise extended itself into Ireland, Belgium, and France ; and judging from its daily augmentation, it bids fair ere long to be as powerful and as effective a confederation as ever existed in the British Empire. The company now extends to 360 branches, and numbers about 13,000 members, holding 40,000 shares, who have already subscribed upon their shares upwards of £22,000. Three excellent estates have been purchased by the Company, and have been assigned to its members, and the directors are now seeking other eligible investments. Branches of the company are now formed in every town of any note in Great Britain, of which parties may become members. . . .

(c) From the Sixth Report of the Select Committee on the National Land Company (1848), p. 111.

THE SELECT COMMITTEE appointed to enquire into the NATIONAL LAND COMPANY, who were empowered to Report the Evidence taken before them, from time to time, and their opinion, TO THE HOUSE ;—

Have further considered the matters to them referred, and have agreed to the following RESOLUTIONS and REPORT :—

1. THAT the proposed additional provisions to the Friendly Societies' Acts which are incorporated in the Bill, entitled " A Bill to alter and amend an Act of the 9th and 10th years of Her present Majesty, for the amendment of the Laws relating to Friendly Societies ", will not include the National Land Company within those Acts.

2. THAT the National Land Company is not consistent with the general principles upon which the Friendly Societies are founded.

3. THAT the National Land Company, as at present constituted, is an illegal scheme, and will not fulfil the expectations held out by the Directors to the Shareholders.

4. THAT it appearing to this Committee by the evidence of several witnesses that the books of proceedings of the National Land Company, as well as the accounts of the Company, have been most imperfectly kept, and that the original balance-sheets signed by the auditors of the Company have been destroyed, and only three of those balance-sheets, for the quarters ending the 29th of September and the 25th of December 1847, and the 25th of March 1848 respectively, have been produced; but Mr Feargus O'Connor having expressed an opinion that an impression had gone abroad that the monies subscribed by the National Land Company had been applied to his own benefit, this Committee are clearly of opinion, that although the accounts have not been kept with strict regularity, yet that irregularity has been against Feargus O'Connor's interest, instead of in his favour; and that it appears by Mr Grey's account there is due to Mr Feargus O'Connor the sum of 3,298l. 5s. 3½d., and by Mr Finlaison's account the sum of 3,400l.

5. THAT, considering the great number of persons interested in the scheme, and the *bonâ fides* with which it appears to have been carried on, it is the opinion of this Committee that powers might be granted to the parties concerned, if they shall so desire, to wind up the undertaking and to relieve them from the penalties to which they may have incautiously subjected themselves.

In submitting these Resolutions to the consideration of THE HOUSE, it is the opinion of your Committee that it should be left entirely to the parties concerned to propose to Parliament any new measure for the purpose of carrying out the expectations and objects of the promoters of the Company.

1 *August* 1848.

10. THE FRATERNAL DEMOCRATS

[The Society of Fraternal Democrats, which was founded in 1845, included in its membership continental refugees as well as English Chartists. Its activities consisted mainly of meetings and manifestoes celebrating the European struggles for freedom and appealing to the English people to support and imitate them. Its immediate effect on public opinion, even Chartist opinion, was small, though the publicity it gave to foreign affairs helped to produce the Chartist revival of 1848. It has, however, some historical importance as the forerunner of the First International. Its leading figures — such as G. J. Harney — came into close contact with Marx, Engels, and other leaders of the new Socialist and Communist movements, and through them introduced into England some of the ideas of International Socialism, as well as those of Mazzini and other non-Socialist exiles.]

From " The Principles and Rules of the Society of Fraternal Democrats ", 1845.

This society composed of natives of Great Britain, France, Germany, Scandinavia, Poland, Italy, Switzerland, Hungary and other countries has for its

OBJECTS

The mutual enlightenment of its members; and the propaganda of the great principle embodied in the society's motto

" All men are brethren."

The members of this society agree to adopt the following

DECLARATION OF PRINCIPLES.

In accordance with the above declaration of the brotherhood of the human race, we renounce, repudiate and condemn all political hereditary inequalities and distinctions of ' caste '; consequently we regard kings, aristocracies, and classes monopolising political privileges in virtue of their possession of property, as usurpers and violators of the principle of human brotherhood. Governments elected by and responsible to, the entire people is our political creed.

We declare that the earth with all its natural productions is the common property of all; we therefore denounce all infractions of this evidently just and natural law, as robbery and usurpation. We declare that the present state of society, which permits idlers and schemers to monopolise the fruits of the earth and the productions of industry, and compels the working classes to labour for inadequate rewards, and even condemns them to social slavery, destitution and degradation, is essentially unjust. That labour and reward should be equal is our social creed.

We condemn the " National " hatreds which have hitherto divided mankind, as both foolish and wicked; foolish, because no one can decide for himself the country he will be born in; and wicked, as proved by the feuds and bloody wars which have desolated the earth, in consequence of these national vanities. Convinced, too, that national prejudices have been, in all ages, taken advantage of by the people's oppressors, to set them tearing the throats of each other, when they should have been working together for their common good, this society repudiates the term ' Foreigner ', no matter by whom or to whom applied. Our moral creed is to receive our fellow men, without regard to country, as members of one family, the human race; and citizens of one great commonwealth—the world. Finally, we recognise that great moral law—" Do unto thy brother, as thou wouldest thy brother should do unto thee ", as the greatest safeguard of public and private happiness.

11. THE CHARTIST PETITION OF 1848

[The bad trade which followed the financial crisis of 1847 produced a number of hunger demonstrations in the early months of 1848 : and the revolutionary movement in Europe — especially the French Revolution — was welcomed in a series of excited meetings. It seemed to many that England might follow the example of the continent. Another Chartist Petition was organised (with only five of the six points, as in deference to O'Connor's prejudice the ballot was abandoned); a convention met in London and decided that if the Petition was rejected it would call a National Assembly — virtually a threat to take over the government of the country; plans were made for a monster demonstration on Kennington Common on April 10; and the Government made counter-preparations as if this was to be the signal for an uprising. The fiasco of April 10 is the best-known incident in Chartist history. The crowd was much smaller than had been anticipated, and it was not allowed to cross the Thames in order to accompany the Petition to the House of Commons. When the Petition was examined, the signatures were found to amount to less than two millions (though O'Connor had boasted that there were over five and a half millions). The petition was rejected by the House of Commons. Then ensued a round of mass meetings throughout the country, at which delegates were elected to the National Assembly the Convention had agreed to call. The Assembly met on May 1, 1848, and there was much argument for and against an appeal to force. O'Connor opposed the calling of the Assembly as involving illegal action, and discharged Ernest Jones from *The Northern Star* for attending it. After a fortnight of futile debates, the Assembly, not knowing what action to take, decided to adjourn for six weeks. It did not meet again. During the next few months there was some abortive revolutionary plotting, especially in London; and excitement continued in the factory areas. Many more demonstrations were held; but the physical force section had no national leadership and was much too weak to attempt an insurrection.]

(a) From " Proceedings of the National Convention assembled at the Literary and Scientific Institution John St. London " (1848), p. 10.

Resolutions adopted :—

1st. That in the event of the National Petition being rejected by the House of Commons, This Convention prepare a National Memorial to the Queen to dissolve the present Parliament, and call to her council such ministers only as will make the People's a cabinet measure.

2nd. That this Convention agree to the convocation of a National Assembly, to consist of delegates appointed at public meetings, to present the National Memorial to the Queen; and to continue permanent sitting until the Charter is the law of this land.

3rd. That this convention call upon the country to hold simultaneous meetings on Good Friday, April 21, for the purpose of adopting the National Memorial, and electing delegates to the National Assembly.

4th. That the National Assembly meet in London on Monday, April 24th.

5th. That the present Convention shall continue its sittings until the meeting of the National Assembly.

(b) From *The Annual Register*, 1848, Chronicle, p. 50.

THE GREAT CHARTIST DEMONSTRATION.—. . . It was announced that no opposition would be made to the constitutional right of meeting to petition, nor to the proper presentation of the petition; the meeting would be allowed to be held, but if the assemblage should attempt to pass in its return in an organised procession, Her Majesty's Government were resolved to stop so dangerous and illegal a proceeding by force of arms.

Great preparations were accordingly made. The inhabitants generally, along the lines of thoroughfare converging to Kennington Common, kept close houses — doors and windows shut, and in some cases barricaded for stout defence. The measures of Government, devised and personally worked by the Duke of Wellington, were on a large and complete scale, though so arranged as not to obtrude themselves needlessly on the view. The Thames' bridges were the main points of concentration; bodies of foot and horse police, and assistant masses of special constables, being posted at their approaches on either side. In the immediate neighbourhood of each of them, within call, a strong force of military was kept ready for instant movement — at Blackfriars Bridge, Chelsea Pensioners, etc; at Waterloo Bridge, Horse Guards, Marines, etc; at Westminster Bridge, horse, foot and artillery. Two regiments of the line were kept in hand at Millbank Penitentiary; 1200 infantry at Deptford Dockyards, and thirty pieces of heavy field ordnance at the Tower, all ready for transport by hired steamers, to any spot where serious business might threaten. At other places, also, bodies of troops were posted, out of sight, but within sudden command, — as in the great areas of the untenanted Rose Inn Yard, at the end of Farringdon Street; in the inclosure of Bridewell Prison; and in several points of vantage immediately round Kennington Common itself. The public offices at the West End, at Somerset House, and in the City, were profusely furnished with arms; and such places as the Bank of England were packed with troops and artillery, and strengthened with sandbag parapets on their walls, and timber barricading of their windows, each pierced with loop-holes for the fire of defensive musketry.

In addition to the regular civil and military force, it is credibly estimated that at least 120,000 special constables were sworn and organised throughout the metropolis, for the stationary defence of their own districts, or as movable bodies to cooperate with the soldiery and police.

(c) The National Assembly. From R. G. Gammage, " History of the Chartist Movement " (1894), p. 329.

[Ernest Jones, supporting the adjournment of the Assembly, said :]

" He did so with peculiar feelings, because they had now heard the funeral oration for that Assembly pronounced by its own members. Several members had joined their eloquence for that purpose : there was a division amongst them. When that Assembly met, it was then that the Chartist body saw the elements of popular power gathered together and concentrated. It was then that that power might have been wielded for the mightiest objects; but amid the desertion of friends, and the invasion of enemies, the fusee had been trampled upon, and the elements of their energy were scattered to the winds of heaven. Resolutions had been received from different parts of the country, but how got up, or in what sort of meetings, he would not say, abusing, some of them, certain members of the Assembly, and others, the whole Assembly itself. Under these circumstances then, he decided within himself, that if they started again, as start they must, they must start afresh, start with new power, with new energy, with new confidence; they must start afresh from the fountain head of Democracy. As for that Assembly, they were but sixty in number. They had waited for the remaining forty delegates from the other districts. They had not gone forward with the Memorial, and that was the reason. The best thing they could now do was to dissolve, and return to their constituents. Their meeting had not been in vain; *they had gained two triumphs — first, union, and second, independence.* These were triumphs they had achieved, and which it was worth meeting to achieve."

12. HUME'S LITTLE CHARTER

[After the dissolution of the National Assembly Joseph Hume, the veteran Reformer, attempted to rally Radical opinion behind a movement for Household (instead of Manhood) Suffrage, combined with the ballot and the redistribution of seats to accord better with the population of the various districts. O'Connor, who had quarrelled with the Chartist Assembly, favoured this move. But Hume's motion was defeated in the House of Commons by 358 votes to 84.]

From Hansard's " Parliamentary Debates ", June 20, 1848, col. 879.

Mr HUME rose to bring forward the motion of which he had given notice, namely—

' That this House, as at present constituted, does not fairly represent the population, the property, or the industry of the Country, whence has arisen great and increasing discontent in the minds of a large portion of the People ; and it is therefore expedient, with a view to amend the National Representation, that the Elective Franchise shall be so extended as to include all Householders — that votes shall be taken by Ballot — that the duration of Parliaments shall not exceed three years — and that the apportionment of Members to Population shall be made more equal.'

13. THE NATIONAL REFORM LEAGUE

[Among those who attempted to revive Chartism after the failure of 1848 was J. B. O'Brien. Land Reform, Currency Reform, and Owenism had moulded O'Brien before Chartism began. And he continued to emphasise the economic basis of the working-class movement. He was avowedly a social reformer, who hoped to use a Chartist Parliament for a reconstruction of economic life. Though the National Reform League he founded came to nothing, its programme is of considerable interest, as here he gathered together the varied demands of the last twenty years.]

(*a*) From *The National Reformer*, January 16, 1847.

1st. The land of the United Kingdom must be made the public property of the whole people of the United Kingdom.

2nd. That the only rational way of doing that is, to abolish the private ownership of land altogether, make all rents payable *to* and *for* the state, make the tenant right, or right of occupancy, equal to all, and secure to every leaseholder full value for all *bona fide* improvements made by him on the soil during his occupancy.

3rd. That the only safe, peaceable, and humane way of effecting such settlement is, to restore the land gradually to the public, as the land lords die off, so as not to disturb any proprietor existing at the time of passing the law, during his or her life; and on the lapse of their estates to the nation, at their death, to secure to their heirs, assigns, or representatives, the full money value of each estate, payable by annual instalments, out of the future rents, so that even the remotest appearance of confiscation or spoliation may be avoided, and the aristocracy left without a shadow of pretext for rebelling against the law.

4th. That the National Debt, and all other public debts, be legislated for on the same principle as the land, namely, the capitals to be recognised, and payment of them guaranteed by annual instalments. But not more plundering of the taxpayers and debtor-interests, by everlasting usury and law expenses, kept up merely to feed one portion of the community in idleness at the expense of the rest.

5th. Gold and silver to be for ever abolished as currency and as standards of value, and to be treated as mere mercantile commodities, which they are. The quarter or bushel of wheat to be henceforward the recognised standard of value — its average price (measured by labour) to be the unit of account — the Bank of England, and all other privileged corporations for the issue of money, to be abolished — the Government itself to be the sole issuer of the legal tender money of the country — all mercantile paper to be issued in conformity with its denominations — such mercantile paper to be issuable upon every description of exchangeable wealth, as well as on gold and silver, but not until ample security has been given to the local administration by the issuers — such paper to be then stamped, and made a legal tender from all parties but the issuers, by whom it must always be convertible, on demand, into Government paper, or into the precious metals at the market price. And on the issuing of such mercantile paper, no privilege of any sort to be allowed — the right of issuing being made equal for all who shall comply with the law, by furnishing the required security for the solvency of the issuers.

6th. Public marts or bazaars to be established for the deposit and sale of all manner of goods and commodities on the principle of equitable exchanges. No manufacturer or depositor to appraise or sell his own goods, but all sales and exchanges to be effected by salaried officers, elected by the depositors. Such officers to appraise all goods upon delivery, and to give to depositors the money price of them in a paper currency that shall fairly represent them by expressing their value in labour or corn — such notes to be of the same denomination as the Government notes, and convertible into the same. . . .

7th. In order to enable industrious men to stock farms, and to manufacture goods on their own account, District Banks should be established, into which should be paid the rents of each district; and from those rents, loans should be made to every deserving man who could bring competent testimony as to character and fitness to be trusted with an advance. The stock and labour of every such man should be mortgaged, as it were, to the public, for the repayment of the loan, out of the future proceeds of his industry — the borrower paying barely as much interest as might suffice to support the banking institution. By this means the public property would, without loss to the public, be made instrumental in rescuing the major portion of the public from that degrading bondage to usury and employers, which, nowadays, has made perfect slaves of nine-tenths of the population. This is what we call an honest system of public credit. The banks would be public, the funds public, and the loans or accommodations would be made only to those who would turn them to honest and productive account. And no man would complain that he was mulcted or taxed to take a brother out of bondage, inasmuch as the sums advanced would be public property, and the labour and stock of the borrower held responsible for repayment. Next to the nationalisation of landed property and the establishment of an efficient currency, this system of credit would be the most effectual instrument conceivable for emancipating the industrious classes. For, who would be the hired bondsman of another, if he could till the soil, or manufacture goods, on his own account. And what properly constituted Democratic Government would refuse to establish banks, the object of which was to make freemen of its citizens ? . . .

(*b*) From a leaflet [1850] in The Goldsmiths' Library.

PROPOSITIONS OF THE NATIONAL REFORM LEAGUE, 1850.

For the Peaceful Regeneration of Society : Liberty in Right : Equality in Law : Fraternity in Interest.

The following Resolutions on behalf of the League, were unanimously passed at a crowded meeting of the National Regeneration Society, held on the 16th. of March 1850, in the large theatre of the Literary Institution, Leicester Square, London, on the motion of J. Bronterre O'Brien, seconded by Richard Hart ; they have also received the assent of the National Charter Association and the Fraternal Democrats, and have been carried at various public meetings :—

" This meeting is of opinion that in addition to a full, fair, and free representation of the whole people in the Commons House of Parliament, upon principles the same, or similar to those laid down in the People's Charter, the following measures, — some of a provisional, the others of a permanent nature — are necessary to ensure real political and social justice to the oppressed and suffering population of the United Kingdom, and to protect society from violent revolutionary changes :—

I.   A repeal of our present wasteful and degrading system of poor-laws. . . .

II.   . . . It is the duty of the Government to appropriate its present surplus revenue, and the proceeds of national and public property, to the purchasing of lands, and the location thereon of the unemployed poor. . . .

III.   . . . The Public Debt and all private indebtedness affected by the fall of prices should be equitably adjusted in favour of the debtor and productive classes, . . .

IV.   The gradual resumption by the State (on the acknowledged principle of equitable compensation to existing holders, or their heirs) of its ancient, undoubted, inalienable dominion, and sole proprietorship over all the lands, mines, turbaries, fisheries, &c., of the United kingdom and our Colonies; the same to be held by the State, as trustee in perpetuity, for the entire people, and rented to them in such quantities, and on such terms as the law and local circumstances shall determine. . . .

V. That, as it is the recognised duty of the State to support all those of its subjects, who, from incapacity or misfortune, are unable to procure their own subsistence; and as the nationalisation of landed property would open up new sources of occupation for the now surplus industry of the people (a surplus which is daily augmented by the accumulation of machinery in the hands of the capitalists), the same principle which now sanctions a public provision for the destitute poor, should be extended to the providing a sound system of National Credit, through which any man might (under certain conditions) procure an advance from the national funds arising out of the proceeds of public property, and thereby be enabled to rent and cultivate land on his own account, instead of being subjected, as now, to the injustice and tyranny of wage-slavery. . . .

VI. That the National Currency should be based on real, consumable wealth, or on the bona fide credit of the State, and not upon the variable and uncertain amount of scarce metals; . . .

VII. That . . . it is an important duty of the State to institute in every town and city, public marts or stores, for the reception of all kinds of exchangeable goods, to be valued by disinterested officers appointed for the purpose, either upon a corn or a labour standard; the depositors to receive symbolic notes representing the value of their deposits, such notes to be made legal currency throughout the country, enabling their owners to draw from the public stores to an equivalent amount, thereby gradually displacing the present reckless system of competitive trading and shopkeeping. . . .

It is not assumed that the foregoing Propositions comprise all the reforms needed in society. Doubtless there are many other reforms required besides those alluded to; doubtless we want a sound system of national education for youth, made compulsory upon all parents and guardians; doubtless, we require a far less expensive system of military and naval defence than now obtains; doubtless we require the expropriation of railways, canals, bridges, docks, gas-works, water-works, &c.; and doubtless we require a juster and more humane code of civil and penal law than we now possess. But these and other needful reforms will be easy of accomplishment when those comprised in the foregoing propositions shall have been effected."

14. THE NATIONAL PARLIAMENTARY AND FINANCIAL REFORM ASSOCIATION

[In 1849–1850, following Hume's lead, the middle-class Reformers set to work to organise a new movement on the basis of a demand for Household Suffrage, the Ballot, Triennial Parliaments, and Financial Reform designed to reduce and equalise tax burdens. The Radicals in Parliament pressed these demands, and were duly defeated on the main issues, but succeeded in 1850 in carrying a motion for the enfranchisement of £10 householders in the counties. The Government (Lord John Russell's) was induced to promise some sort of Reform Bill, but fell from office before it could be carried through. Thereafter, Reform was pushed aside by the Crimean War, and subsequently by Lord Palmerston's lifelong opposition. The middle-class Radicals' campaign thus came to nothing.]

From *The Reformers' Almanack and Political Year Book* (1850), p. 34.

. . . When we wrote last year all was apathy, the only sign of life being the commencement of the Freehold Land movement. Now we find a great organisation, with ample resources for accomplishing not only financial, but Parliamentary reform — twenty-five distinct organisations for obtaining the 40s. freehold franchise — two important conferences, both tending to the same result, on the eve of assembling — and a £50,000 fund, *in prospectu*, to work out the grand scheme. Truly the political schoolmaster must have been abroad!

Having devoted considerable space to a more particular reference to the Freehold Land question, we shall have only to allude to it incidentally, confining ourselves, for the most part, to a brief and hurried sketch of the Parliamentary and Financial Reform movement during 1849. On the eve of the assembling of Parliament in that year, there was, with the exception of the *Liverpool Financial Reform Association*, no organised body of political Reformers capable of enlisting any large amount of public support. Some months previously, a *People's League*, based on the broadest democratic basis, had been commenced under favourable auspices; but it languished for want of public support, and virtually became a *caput mortuum*.

About Christmas, in 1848, ripening public opinion found expression in numerous and effective public demonstrations in most of our large towns, but no immediate results followed. Strong as was the desire to commence a united movement for some general measure of Parliamentary reform, the object seemed scarcely practicable. Men of experience and sagacity hesitated to embark on a project which might be frustrated by the violence of faction. Retrenchment and economy were still the cry — organic change being only timidly and casually hinted at.

At length some practical steps were taken for the purpose of organising Reformers of all classes. To the metropolis — where political intelligence has always predominated, but has unfortunately hitherto been associated with extreme caution — must be assigned the credit of taking the initiative. The Financial Reform Associations of Liverpool and Manchester had paved the way for practical effort by creating an intelligent public opinion in favour of decided political changes. The leading Reformers of London undertook the responsibility of making an appeal of a more definite character to the opinion thus created. The metropolis heartily responded to their call, and a movement was commenced, which resulted in the organisation of a society, the name of which is now familiar to the ears of the British public. Amongst the " great facts " of the year 1849, not the least remarkable is the establishment of the *National Parliamentary and Financial Reform Association.*

The origin and history of the new movement merit a somewhat detailed description. On the 29th of January, 1849, a preliminary meeting of some hundred Reformers of the metropolis was convened, by the venerable Francis Place, at the Crown and Anchor Tavern — now the Whittington Club — to consider the propriety of forming a new organisation of the friends of reform. After some discussion, resolutions were adopted setting forth the necessity of the strictest economy in the national expenditure, and of a reform in the House of Commons, as the only means of ensuring it. Resolutions were subsequently adopted for forming a Financial Reform Association to carry out these objects, and co-operate with similar societies, and for promoting throughout the country a well-organised system for increasing the number of 40s. freeholders in counties, and to complete the registration of voters in counties, cities and boroughs. Sir Joshua Walmsley, who was at the time engaged in contesting the representation of Bolton, was unanimously appointed President of the Association. His restoration to Parliament seemed to infuse new vigour into the Reform movement, and invest it with the *prestige* of success. The friends of reform were already aware of his business talents, and expected important results from his judgment and energy. Expectation was not disappointed. The nucleus of a powerful organisation was speedily formed, and a list of subscriptions put forth, which showed that the sinews of war would not be wanting. On the 1st of March the Council of the new society, now duly constituted, under the title of the *Metropolitan Parliamentary Reform Association*, put forth their first appeal " to the People of London ". Its preliminary address, without entering into details, set forth in appropriate terms, the objects which it sought, and the means by which it proposed to effect them. In a short period the organisation of the society was completed, offices were taken, and a succinct statement of its objects was submitted to the public. From that prospectus we extract the following passage, descriptive of the reforms proposed :—

" Satisfied that no material diminution of the public burdens, nor any sensible improvement in the mode of their imposition, will or can take place until the House of Commons is made a more faithful reflex of the opinions, wants, and interests of the people at large, the council have determined that the means and energies of the Association shall, in the first instance, be directed to the attainment of an effectual reform of our representative system.

That Reform will consist of, 1st, such an extension of the suffrage as will confer the right to be registered as an elector upon every man of full age, not subject to any legal disability, who for twelve months shall have occupied any tenement, or portion of a tenement, for which he shall be rated, or shall have claimed to be rated, to the relief of the poor; 2ndly, the adoption of the system of voting by ballot; 3rdly, the limitation of the duration of parliaments to three years; and, 4thly, such a change in the arrangement of the electoral districts as shall produce a more equal apportionment of representatives to constituents."

From this extract it will be seen that the political principles adopted as the basis of the new society are, in effect, the same as those embodied in Mr Hume's annual motion in the House of Commons. As an auxiliary to the main agitation, THE METROPOLITAN AND HOME COUNTIES FREEHOLD LAND SOCIETY was established for the purpose of qualifying its members to vote at elections for the counties of Essex, Hertford, Kent, Middlesex, Surrey, and Sussex. . . .

15. THE FIRST TRADE UNION CANDIDATE, 1852

[William Newton, the Engineers' leader (1822–1876), stood for Tower Hamlets, a big London constituency, in 1852. There were five candidates for the two seats, two Whigs, two middle-class Radicals, and Newton. He got 1095 votes, against 7728 for the leading candidate. The Whigs were elected, leaving Newton well at the bottom. This deserves to rank as the first real working-class candidature for the House of Commons, though he was no longer working at his trade. Newton was prominent in London local politics as well as in the Trade Union movement. *The Operative* was Newton's own paper.]

(a) From *The Operative*, April 10, 1852.

. . . There is a growing conviction that the rights of labour will never be fairly advocated, nor its wrongs unsparingly exposed, till a man from the ranks of labour — a man with strong will and a clear brain — with physical energy, and a resolution to dare the sneers of the well bred, and the clamours of class factions, catches the eye of the speaker of the House, and in burning words pours forth the woes, the sympathies, the aspirations of the toilers. It is more than possible that the next Parliament will include a few real apostles of labour. The artizans of this country may, if they will, secure that result, and then day will begin to dawn upon those whom the privileged classes have hitherto kept in darkness and obscurity.

(b) From *Reynolds' Newspaper*, April 25, 1852.

ELECTION INTELLIGENCE.

Tower Hamlets.—Mr. W. Newton, whose name in connexion with the Amalgamated Society of Engineers is so familiar to the public, has issued an address to the electors of the Tower Hamlets declaratory of his determination of going to the poll. He thus expounds his political creed :—

" The first question to which I shall refer is the great question of political freedom, which is taking so strong a hold upon the minds of the people of this country. I am thoroughly impressed with the conviction that the only measure consistent with justice is the admission of every sane man untainted by crime within the pale of the constitution ; and I am perfectly persuaded that public opinion is generally tending toward a recognition of the great political truth that the basis of representation should be manhood and intelligence, instead of property and taxation, and the establishment of universal suffrage among the institutions of the country. Looking to that as the great fundamental political change upon which all others must rest, I am not insensible to minor and subsidiary measures which would of necessity accompany it. Among these are an equitable distribution of electors to representatives, facilities for protecting the voter from intimidation, by means of vote by ballot, and a considerable shortening of Parliaments; approving of which I pledge myself, should I be returned, to present myself annually before the constituency and seek an approval of my conduct. It also appears to me to be absolutely certain that with the attainment of the rights of the people other time-honoured abuses — remnants of a past age — would be raised (*sic*) to the ground. The voice of the people once fairly allowed to be heard, the separation of church and state would be secured, as also the emancipation of the Jews. Then the great dissenting bodies of this country would be freed from the mingled insult and injustice of being compelled to support with their property an ecclesiastical system opposed to their consciences, and religion would be left to that voluntary support which furnishes the best test of the sincerity of its professors, and is most consistent with its fullest and highest developement. It would be an unpardonable omission in an address of this character to pass by the topic of education. I am sensible that the subject is surrounded by difficulties of no ordinary character, but I am also unable to shut my eyes to the fact that the two great results of ignorance are poverty and crime, and that a people can never become really civilised or virtuous till some steps are taken to meet and deal with those evils. I would therefore earnestly support the enactment of a measure which should provide for that training which it is necessary all should receive without violating the principles or scruples of any community. The plan which appears to me to present the best chance of success, is one which would give to local bodies the power to conduct their own educational arrangements. Other candidates who seek the favour of representing you in Parliament, no doubt entertain views nearly in accordance with those which I have expressed — but the distinctive ground upon which I stand is the mode in which the poverty and labour of the country is to be legislated for. I believe the labour question to be that which more immediately presses for solution, and upon the satisfactory settlement of which the welfare of all classes depends. It is my opinion that when trade and manufacture leave thousands of men idle, it is as much the duty of the rulers of the country to provide employment for them, as to furnish the means of education. Our laws already acknowledge the obligation of the state to find the bare means of subsistence for those who cannot find the opportunity to support themselves by their own labour. But bare is not all that is required. The labourers of this country do not require charity, but the independence of honest labour — and while there are in this country the two great sources of all wealth — land and labour — both idle, both ready to be brought into contact, and to produce necessaries and luxuries for millions, I cannot conceive that the trading classes of this country can be fairly called upon to pay for the support of those who are both willing and able to provide for themselves."

Mr. Newton concludes by advocating the abolition of taxes on knowledge, and declaring himself a free trader in entirety.

(c) From *Reynolds' Newspaper*, May 9, 1852.

Mr William Newton rose, and was received with loud and reiterated cheers. He observed that great masses of the people, whether enfranchised or not, must of necessity exercise much political influence. There was no class that ought to possess so much power as the labouring class; the higher grades were from position and influence able to protect themselves, not so with the masses of the working orders; they were helpless. He contended that universal suffrage could alone meet the exigencies of society. There were eighty nine members in the House of Parliament who annually vote for Mr Hume's motion, and on platforms represent themselves as advocates of universal suffrage, but they shirk the question as impracticable when put to the test. He, however, pledged himself, if returned to Parliament, to try the feeling of the House by bringing forward a distinct and definite measure for the enfranchisement of the whole people. (Loud and prolonged cheers). He disapproved of the allotment of state money for the purpose of any particular religion. He would not only refuse to endow any sectarian church, but would likewise remove all invidious differences and distinctions regarding religious opinions. The Jew should be as free as the Christian. He asked, if Parliament was filled with men like Cobden, Bright, Hume, &c, would they find the means of employing the redundant labour in the country? Would they direct their whole efforts to the elevation of the working classes in the social sphere? Had they hitherto striven for this? He insisted that the possession of political power was to be aimed at for the purpose of leading to social amelioration. All legislative enactment that does not tend to increase employment for labouring men was not one of social improvement. We ought to be a happy people; there was the capability of producing happiness in this country, but there was not the will or the wisdom with our rulers to obtain it. (Loud cheers). Society had a downward tendency, and if something was not done to arrest such before long, no government would restrain the passions of down-trodden people rendered criminal and desperate by persecution and pauperism. Pauperism in England was synonymous with slavery elsewhere, excepting that the English pauper was considered as an incumbrance and worthless, whilst on the slave a certain value was fixed, and consequently he was more cared for. (Hear, hear.) The government should be required to deal with surplus labour, and so long as there was one yard of ground uncultivated that was cultivable, the land and the labour should be brought into contact. (Loud cheers). Every order of society depended upon the well condition of the working classes, and unless they were comfortable and contented, let the monarch, the aristocracy, the rich and influential look to their security. The Lord Chancellor had lately introduced a measure of reform in his court, and three masters in Chancery had been dismissed, but these persons had been pensioned, and were provided for for the rest of their lives; but how was it with labour? A man devotes the best years of his life to the perfecting himself in some calling; machinery was introduced and entirely superseded his labour, but he received no compensation for the injury inflicted upon him. He contended that society was as much bound to support the workman who was thrown out of employ by the introduction of machinery as masters in chancery who were disturbed from the lucrative offices they had so long filled. In the Parliament we for ever heard of the rights of the monarch, the rights of the aristocracy, the rights of church, the rights of the manufacturers, etc., but never the rights of labour. But if the Tower Hamlets gave him (Mr Newton) an opportunity he would introduce a new vocabulary into the senate. (Loud and enthusiastic cheering). . . .

16. ERNEST JONES AND THE LAST DAYS OF CHARTISM

[Ernest Jones (1819–1869) came from an aristocratic family, and for some time was 'in society'. But his ambition to cut a literary figure was never satisfied, and the failure of his financial speculations made him a bankrupt. In 1845 he joined the Chartist movement and became O'Connor's right-hand man. After serving two years' imprisonment (1848–1850) he came under Marx's influence and remained the chief and best exponent of the class struggle view-point until, in 1858, he began to seek an alliance with the middle-class Radicals.

The importance of Ernest Jones lies in what he attempted: for he achieved little. He lectured as a Chartist, and Chartism faded steadily away. He preached the class war and tried to found a working-class Marxist party, while the working class was turning to methods of industrial peace and to political collaboration with the middle-class Radicals. He remained personally a popular figure, and his teachings helped to keep alive ideas which came into their own in the Socialist revival of the 1880s.

In the 1880s he became the leader of the rump of the National Charter Association, those who refused to compromise with the middle class and stood for an unrelenting loyalty to the Charter itself. At a special Convention in 1852 he secured the adoption of a policy of independent class struggle and attempted to reorganise the N.C.A. as a Marxist party. He was particularly anxious to rally the Trade Unions for a forward movement, but his ' Labour Parliament ', called during the period of Trade Union solidarity just after the great Preston strike of 1853, came to nothing. At last, wearied by a sequence of such failures, he accepted in 1858 the necessity of working for half-way measures. He died in 1869, just when he seemed likely to be returned as a Radical member of Parliament for Manchester.]

(a) From *The People's Paper*, November 13, 1852.

THE SOCIAL WAR.

KIND MASTERS AND SLAVISH MEN

Welcome brutality — but Heaven preserve us from ' kind masters '. Brutal tyranny can enslave the body, but brutal kindness does worse, it enslaves the mind. . . .

Amid the mass of factory tyranny which meets us on all sides, amid the mass of murmuring and indignant misery, there is nothing more sickening to my mind, than the language and sentiments of certain portions of the working classes, who are perpetually talking of ' the mutual confidence of employers and employed ' — ' the identity of their interests ', — ' the kindness of their good masters ', — ' the excellence of their intentions ' — ' the duty to their employers ', — and other sickening and disgusting epithets, in which either ignorance or cowardice wait on human degradation. . . .

' Duty to your employers '. Your duty is, to have no employers at all, but to employ yourselves.

Now a word with reference to this identity of ' interests ' :—
It is the interest of the employer, as he confesses, to buy cheap and sell dear — but the terms ' cheap ' and ' dear ' are relative, and you

will find it is his interest to *sell cheap* and buy *cheaper*. For it is cheapness that forces a market for him in his competition with the foreigner and with his competitor at home.

Now, how can he sell cheaply ? By buying *more* cheaply. What does he buy ? Raw material *and labour* — wool, cotton, flax *and human flesh.*

Low wages, therefore is a necessity for the employer.

Working men ! are your interests identical with his ? But to *keep lowering* wages, is another of his ' interests '. Why ? Because as competition in manufacture continues increasing abroad, the market becomes more and more artificial, and must be *forced* more and more by underselling. And, of course, this must be done by lowering wages. . . .

Now what say you to ' identity of interests ' ?

My friends I'll tell you plainly how the interests really lie :

IT IS YOUR INTEREST TO RUIN THEM AND IT IS THEIR INTEREST TO RUIN YOU.

And one of these alternatives must be the result. Do not suppose that I advocate such a state of things — the alternative is horrible — *but it is inevitable.* Blame those whose system has rendered it so — do not blame us, who, out of this choice of evils, select the lesser of the two.

.   .   .   .   .   .

(*b*) The Mass Movement. Decisions of the Labour Parliament, March 7, 1854.

[This Labour Parliament (which was held at Manchester) was an attempt to unite the trade unions for mutual defence and for common action in demanding reforms. The fifty or sixty delegates present represented no important trade, except cotton : indeed, most of them claimed to represent towns rather than particular trade unions. None of them, before or after this Conference, won any particular favour in the trade-union world. It is not surprising that the movement lasted only a few months. The main proposal was for raising a fund through a weekly levy on wages, graduated according to the earnings of each member.]

From *The People's Paper*, March 11, 1854.

III. APPLICATION OF FUNDS.

That the funds collected shall be applied as follows :—

a. To support all towns and places now or hereafter on strike, or locked out, that recognise the Mass Movement now, or may hereafter do so; that equal support shall be afforded to towns in proportion to the numbers out of employ; that, on the same principle as that on which, when provisions run short on board of ship all receive alike, thus the same relief shall be given, without distinction of high or low paid trades, with those exceptions that shall hereafter be mentioned in the Constitution of the Mass Movement; that in order to provide a separate fund for liquidating the debts incurred by strikes and lock-outs during the last twelve months, and a fund for the future defence of any that may be victimised by the employers, every member on entering the Mass Movement pay one penny, and one penny quarterly thereafter.

b. That a department be opened for ascertaining and regulating the price of labour.

c. That, while the working man has an undoubted right to participate in the profits of the employer, he has a right higher still, — that of employing himself; and that, for the purpose of self-employment, as also for the purpose of more effectually regulating wages by removing the power of surplus labour from the employers' hands, the funds of the Mass Movement be further employed in the purchase of land. . . .

d. That, independent [sic] of self-employment and relief of the labour market from its surplus be still more secure your committee recommend the further application of the available funds for the establishment of cooperative factories, workshops, and stores, such to be the property of the Mass Movement. Those employed therein to receive that amount of wages regulated by the tariff for the price of labour, previously named, and one half of the net profits realised on the articles produced and sold, the other half of the profits to go to the revenue of the Mass Movement. That the chief manager of each co-operative undertaking be elected by the operatives engaged therein, subject to the approbation of the directing body. . . .

IV. LABOUR LEGISLATION

That the power of the Movement be further exerted to secure a due restriction of the hours of labour; a limitation of female labour in manufacture, as also an entire abolition of the labour of young children in mines, factories and all other sorts of labour; a cessation of the tyrannical system of discharge notes, of fines, abatements, and other unjust modes of reducing wages, of the truck system, of the silent system in factories, of the custom of locking operatives up in the same, and of all the inhuman machinery of factory oppression now in exercise against the employed in every branch of industry.

(c) From *The People's Paper*, February 13, 1858.

Report of Chartist Conference, 1858.

Mr. Ernest Jones, who was received with a thunder of applause, said one of the most important movements that had ever been organised by the Chartist body was now in course of action. Times altered, and as times altered, results altered, also, and he now begged to read the second proposition of the programme. He considered that they should meet the middle classes halfway and take what was offered, if what was offered was a reasonable proposition from the middle classes. If they only had a £5 franchise it would be throwing the preponderance into the hands of the middle classes, and widening the distance between them and other working classes. But if the working classes could get the Universal Manhood Suffrage, then they would for a time waive the other points of the charter. If they would obtain the ballot it would be sufficient for a time, and if they could get these two points, it would throw the balance of power into the hands of the working classes, and the other points would soon follow. (Cheers). He had opposed one-sided middle class movements, but he would not oppose middle class movements which were any benefit to the working class. If the middle classes did not first give the hand and first make the advance, let the Chartist body make the advance. It was competent upon them to do so. If they joined, they could go forward together ; and if not they the Chartists would go forth alone, and no time was to be lost. Now the time had come and now the opportunity had arrived. The middle classes had agreed that this movement was best. Let them hold out a friendly hand to them, and insist upon having the fair and honourable rights of the Chartist body. They were not going to abandon the Charter ; but they were going to obtain what they could towards it, at the same time agitating for the whole six points. He now called upon them to unite with the middle classes for Universal Manhood Suffrage.

Mr. Jones sat down amid loud and continued applause.

THE CO-OPERATIVE MOVEMENT, 1835–1875

INTRODUCTION

THE earlier Co-operative movement suffered a severe blow when the great Owenite Trade Union movement collapsed in 1834. Thereafter, Owenism never had a mass following; but Owenite Societies maintained their existence in most of the bigger centres, and divided their activities between propaganda for the ' Rational Religion ' and attempts to establish Owenite ' Villages of Co-operation '. Queenwood, their principal venture of this sort, ran its course between 1839 and 1846. Meanwhile, in 1844, the Rochdale Pioneers, an offshoot from an earlier Owenite Society, had set up their Toad Lane Co-operative Store, in which they combined the democratic control of the Society by the members, on the principle of ' One Member, One Vote ', with the payment of interest on share capital and of ' dividend on purchases ' made at the Store. ' Dividend ' was not a new idea, though the Pioneers may have reinvented it. At all events, the success of the Rochdale Society soon led to imitation of its methods; and the modern Consumers' Co-operative movement grew under its inspiration. The Pioneers were also mainly responsible for the creation of the first effective Co-operative Wholesale Society.

While the Rochdale Society was still feeling its way, first the Redemptionists and then the Christian Socialists re-entered the field with projects of Producers' Co-operation. These mostly broke down; but the Christian Socialists helped to secure a satisfactory legal basis for all types of Co-operation in the Industrial and Provident Societies Acts, and also gave a stimulus to Co-operative educational work. The newly founded Amalgamated Society of Engineers collaborated with them for a time in projects of Co-operative Production; and there was a big renewal of such projects, with Trade Union participation, in the later 1860s and early 1870s. These mostly broke down in the depression that set in during the later 1870s. Meanwhile, the modern series of Co-operative Congresses had begun in 1869, just after the establishment of the Trades Union Congress.

See " Short History ", Part II, chapter 2.
" Common People ", chapter 30.
G. D. H. Cole, " A Century of Co-operation ".

1. THE OWENITE SOCIALISTS

[The collapse of the ' Grand National ' in 1834 was by no means the end of Owenism, though after 1834 it was no longer a mass movement commanding strong Trade Union support. The later Owenism had two main aspects — the advocacy of a ' Rational Religion ' based on Owen's teachings and devoid of theological content and the continued attempt to establish ' Villages of Co-operation ', or ' Home Colonies ', as they came to be called. The Owenites continued to meet in annual Socialist Congresses (they officially adopted the name ' Socialists ' in 1841), and to maintain numerous local Societies for these two purposes. The establishment of the National Community Friendly Society in 1837 was designed to make possible the accumulation of funds for the founding of Owenite Communities and meanwhile to imitate the ordinary Friendly Societies in providing benefits for the members. Still later, amid the collapse of Chartism in 1848, there was an attempt to unite the remains of the Owenite movement with the followers of O'Brien in a National Rational Society combining Owenite principles with O'Brien's ' State Socialism '. (See Section XV.)]

(*a*) From Rules of the National Community Friendly Society held in the Social Institution, Salford, Lancashire [1837].

From the Preface, pp. iii and viii.

The establishment of *communities of united interests and exertions*, has for many years been an object of paramount interest to the disciples of ROBERT OWEN, and at the Congresses which have been held in various parts of England during the last seven years, many plans have been proposed and adopted with a view to the attainment of this object. Hitherto these plans have failed to produce the consummation so devoutly wished, although it is undeniable, that talent of the highest order, zeal of the most ardent nature, and very considerable experience, had been united in their formation.

The great increase, within the last year, of the number of those who perceive the truth and practicability of the new views of society, appeared to offer another favourable opportunity for collecting, and wisely employing, the necessary elements for the creation of a rational system of education, employment, and consumption among the producers of wealth, and accordingly to this subject the Congress, which has just concluded its sittings, directed the greatest portion of its time, and the most serious and attentive deliberation.

. . . . . .

It must be evident, however, that every thing depends on the producers of wealth themselves taking up the subject in good earnest, and applying all the powers of both mind, purse, and skill, to the task of their redemption from the servile and degraded position they now occupy; without such conduct on their part, the best concerted schemes for their manumission will remain a dead letter, and however excellent they may abstractly be, produce no beneficial effect upon their condition, and it is not necessary for us to enlarge upon the many reasons which now call, trumpet-tongued, upon them to be up and doing. The melancholy spectacles of wretchedness which are everywhere presented to us of thousands of willing and industrious artizans and their families, who are starving amidst a superabundance of wealth of all descriptions, form a far more powerful appeal and incentive to follow this course, than the most studied and elaborate essay or the most eloquent oration, and we trust will have the effect of stimulating all who desire happiness for themselves and families, immediately to become members of the National Community Friendly Society.

. . . . . .

(*b*) From the Rules, p. 9.

The objects of this Society shall be to raise, from time to time, by subscriptions among the members thereof, or by voluntary contributions, or donations, or loans, various stocks or funds for the mutual assistance, maintenance, and education of their wives and husbands, children or nominees, in sickness, infancy, advanced age, or other natural state or contingency; which stocks or funds shall be applied as follows :—

First, for the purchase or rental of land whereon to erect suitable dwellings and other buildings; or for the purchase or rental of dwellings or other buildings wherein the members shall by united labour support each other, under every vicissitude, including the establishment of schools for children, or any other purpose not unlawful; by these and every other means consistent with honesty and impartial justice to arrange the powers of production, distribution, consumption and education, in order to produce among the members feelings of pure charity, and social affection for each other, and practically plant the standard of peace and good will on earth towards all men.

Second, an auxiliary fund for the payment of the current expenses of the Society, and such other incidental charges as may be necessary to carry out its objects.

(c) From Propositions of the National Reform League, 1848.

[This extract embodies an attempt by O'Brien to bring together the Owenites and his own following among the Chartists.]

NATIONAL RATIONAL LEAGUE

Based upon the social system of Robert Owen and the political programme of Bronterre O'Brien.

_____

OBJECTS OF THE SOCIETY

1st. To secure the association of those persons who, being free from the evil spirit of creed, Sectarianism and Priestcraft, will respect the Authority of Reason, and reverentially accept the decrees of Conscience.

2nd. To discover Truths connected with the laws of Nature, the progress of thought or the Lives of Good Men of all ages and countries, so that they may be rendered of practical value as guides to a healthful, moral and manly life.

3rd. To assist in the regeneration of Society by aiding every organised body whose aim is to abolish superstition, ignorance, drunkenness, or political injustice, or any other of the numerous evils which now afflict society.

4th. The League proposes to attain its objects, by means of Co-operating to promote the delivery of lectures and free discussions bearing upon Land, Credit, Currency, Exchange, Science, History and Religious Freethought; by means of Schools in which the young shall be educated in Love, Wisdom and Virtue, to know the inestimable value of Truth, Freedom and to fear nothing but Vice, Serfdom and Dishonour, by means of classes for adults, and by means of publications in the form of journals, essays and volumes. . . .

2. QUEENWOOD, OR HARMONY HALL

[In 1839 the Owenites acquired the estate of Queenwood, at East Tytherly, in Hampshire, and there established Harmony Hall, as a Co-operative Community. The venture lasted until 1846, passing through many troubles during its brief existence. The major part of the funds was supplied by rich friends of Owen ; but substantial sums were raised by the Co-operative and Socialist groups all over the country, mainly in small contributions from poor people. Owen had by this time become convinced of the inability of the working classes to conduct their affairs except under middle-class supervision, and had considerably modified his ideas of community organisation. At Queenwood there were two classes of settlers — the well-to-do, who paid for accommodation but did not undertake manual labour, and the settlers sent by the local Societies, who worked for their keep. In addition, at the outset, it was felt to be necessary to employ local skilled agricultural workers for some of the work. These arrangements caused much discontent among the working-class Owenites, who wanted a democratically organised community of equals and objected to the control retained by the wealthy Owenites who had supplied most of the funds. The question was fought out at successive annual Socialist (*i.e.* Owenite) Congresses ; and in 1844 the Societies insisted on taking over the control. The Community was, however, in serious financial difficulties ; and in 1845 the trustees acting for those who had advanced the capital, closed it down. The local subscribers got back only a small part of their money, and several of the wealthier Owenites lost nearly all they had.]

From an article by G. J. Holyoake in *The Movement*, April 20, 1844.

FOR WHOM IS HOME COLONIZATION INTENDED — Let those who have imbibed the flattering notions of human equality which the Platoes and Mores have pictured, and those dreams of human perfection which the Shelleys have embodied in song, and who would learn how widely different is fact from fiction, and how remote is the dawn of humanity's brighter day from the realities of 1844 — let such read the " Development " of the plans and principles of communities by Robert Owen. In this book the profound and masterly views of society, which eminently distinguish Mr. Owen, are set forth in diagrams and figures, and though the result is strikingly calculated to damp enthusiasm, it can hardly fail to awaken that cool determination whereby progression only can be achieved, and the condition of humanity permanently improved.

The slow advance of the Tytherly experiment has been owing to the miscalculation of the working classes as to the part they are to take in its perfection. This evil can be corrected only by greater frankness than is now practised towards them. Mr. Owen, in his " Instructions to the Missionaries ", in 1839, speaks to the purpose on this point — his words are " the middle class is the *only* efficient *directing* class in society — the working class never did *direct* any permanent successful operations ". In his Egyptian Hall Lectures in 1841, he declares that " the working classes are too inexperienced even to know their real position, and that they will pass from one error to another, until, like Peter the Great, they will be *beaten* into a knowledge of the powers against which they have to contend, and of the means effectually to overcome them ". Certainly a charming fate. Mr. Owen's estimate of the conditions of the working classes is, that they are powerless, penniless and prostrate at the feet of the capitalist, at the door of the poor house, or the mouth of the grave. Since falsehood has its degrees of comparison, I suppose we must set this down as an *atrocious* truth. But if it be truth most useful is it, that it be told.

In the " Development " it is set down that the expence of each home colony will be £700,000, and that the number of active adult persons in each will be 1548. The question is, when will the working classes be able to erect one of these communities ? Why, if 1548 persons paid 1*s*. per week, they would be 173 years in establishing one !

This is the fair and sunny side of the picture. In these home colonies there are to be three classes — one of hired labourers, and one of candidates — the third is the members' class, the class in which every Socialist naturally expects that he will be. This class comprises only 360 persons. In our present branches there are not 360 persons able to pay 1*s*. per week, but if there were, they would be 747 years in erecting one of these communities ! ! The present members of the Universal Community Society of the Rational Religionists will be jolly old fellows when they enter into it.

3. THE ROCHDALE PIONEERS

[The Rochdale Pioneers, regarded as the founders of the modern movement of Consumers' Co-operation, opened their Toad Lane Store on December 21, 1844. There had been earlier attempts at Co-operative enterprise in Rochdale, and the Pioneers' Society sprang out of an Owenite Socialist group attached to Owen's Rational Society. A number of its leading members had subscribed funds towards the establishment of

Queenwood. The objects of the Society are plainly Owenite; but the founders, disappointed with the events at Queenwood, decided to concentrate their immediate efforts on establishing a retail store.

A few years after the Pioneers began business, a different group of Co-operators in Rochdale set up in 1850 a Co-operative Corn Mill, and appealed to the Pioneers for help. The mill soon got into difficulties; and the Pioneers reorganised it, mainly under their own control. Five years later they decided to launch out as textile manufacturers; but, instead of setting up a factory as a branch of the Pioneers' Society, they established a separate body, the Rochdale Co-operative Manufacturing Company, which began business in 1854, at first in hired premises, until the Company built its own mill in 1859. Of these ventures, the Corn Mill continued on Co-operative lines, its capital mainly owned by the Rochdale and other Consumers' Societies. It was finally taken over by the Co-operative Wholesale Society. The Manufacturing Society, on the other hand, was financed mainly by individual Co-operators who subscribed to its shares. At first it shared profits with its employees; but in 1862 it ceased to do this during the crisis caused by the Cotton Famine, and became an ordinary profit-making concern. The same fate overtook a number of similar Co-operative ventures founded as joint-stock companies with individual shareholders.]

(a) From G. J. Holyoake, " History of the Rochdale Equitable Pioneers ", 1857 (1st edition), p. 11.

These Pioneers, in 1844, declared the views of their Association thus :—

' The objects and plans of this Society are to form arrangements for the pecuniary benefit and the improvement of the social and domestic condition of its members, by raising a sufficient amount of capital in shares of one pound each, to bring into operation the following plans and arrangements :—

The establishment of a Store for the sale of provisions, clothing, etc.

The building, purchasing, or erecting a number of houses, in which those members, desiring to assist each other in improving their domestic and social conditions, may reside.

To commence the manufacture of such articles as the society may determine upon, for the employment of such members as may be without employment, or who may be suffering in consequence of repeated reductions in their wages.

As a further benefit and security to the members of this Society, the society shall purchase or rent an estate or estates of land, which shall be cultivated by the members who may be out of employment, or whose labour may be badly remunerated.'

Then follows a project which no nation has ever attempted, and no enthusiasts yet carried out :—

'That, as soon as practicable, this society shall proceed to arrange the powers of production, distribution, education, and government; or, in other words, to establish a self-supporting home colony of united interests, or assist other societies in establishing such colonies.

That, for the promotion of sobriety, a Temperance Hotel be opened in one of the Society's houses as soon as convenient.'

(*b*) From the Society's *Almanack*, 1860.

HINTS TO NEW SOCIETIES.

*From the Almanack for 1860, issued by the Rochdale Equitable
Pioneers' Society Limited*

1st.—Procure the authority and protection of the law by enrolment.

2nd.—Let integrity, intelligence, and ability, be indispensable qualifications in the choice of Officers and Managers; and not wealth or distinction.

3rd.—Let each member have only one vote, and make no distinction as regards the amount of wealth any member may contribute.

4th.—Let majorities rule in all matters of government.

5th.—Look well after the money matters. Punish fraud, when duly established, by the immediate expulsion of the defrauder.

6th.—Buy your goods as much as possible in the first markets; or, if you have the produce of your industry to sell, contrive if possible to sell in the last.

7th.—Never depart from the principle of buying and selling for READY MONEY.

8th.—Beware of long reckonings. Quarterly Accounts are the best, and should be adopted when practicable.

9th.—For the sake of security, always have the accounted value of the " Fixed Stock " at least one-fourth less than its marketable value.

10th.—Let members take care that the Accounts are properly audited by men of their own choosing.

11th.—Let Committees of Management always have the authority of the members before taking any important or expensive step.

12th.—Do not court opposition or publicity, nor fear it when it comes.

13th.—Choose those only for your leaders whom you can trust, and then give them your confidence.

14th.—Members to carry away their own purchases.

(c) From W. Robertson, " Rochdale Past and Present : a History and Guide ", 1876.

Our notice would be incomplete if the great and successful educational efforts of the society were not mentioned. Very early in its history a fortieth part of the profits was applied in providing a news-room and library for members and their families. The fund is managed by a separate committee. Notwithstanding that for many years the educational department was really illegal, it was continued until sanctioned by law, and it has now assumed somewhat colossal dimensions. The money spent on news-rooms (of which there are thirteen branches), libraries, lectures, classes, and other educational agencies, has, for many years past, amounted to upwards of £1,000 per annum. The society has seldom placed itself in antagonism to other tradesmen. It has won its way slowly but surely until it has become of world-wide celebrity, and it cannot be doubted but that its success has inaugurated a new era for the labouring classes of this and other countries. The anticipations of its founders are not all realised, but the hitherto attained success has no parallel in the history of industrial effort. Its capital is now nearly £200,000. It is dividing interest and profit at the rate of £40,000 per annum, and gives encouragement and assistance to the social, economical, and educational improvement of its members, and affords a model for hundreds of similar societies throughout the civilized world.

(d) From *The Rochdale Equitable Pioneers' Society Almanack*, 1864.

THE ROCHDALE DISTRICT CO-OPERATIVE CORN MILL SOCIETY, LTD.

This Society, although one of the most delicate in its infancy, has now grown to be one of the strongest and most healthy. Almost seven-eighths of the business done is with Co-operative Societies, there being about 50 who trade with it. It supplies its Members, and others who trade with it, with pure, wholesome, unadulterated flour, meal, etc. Some people have objected to the flour from this Mill, simply because, when supplied to them pure, it did not look so well to the eye when baked into bread : we know that when they have been most deceived they have been best pleased. Those who choose to adulterate for themselves can do so. The gradually increasing business has necessitated an increase in the productive power, consequently the Society added in 1862 (to its previous working plant) one 25-horse-power steam engine and 6 pairs of French stones, which are now at work helping to supply the increased demand. It has also erected in the past year 3 cottage homes. There have been delivered from the Society's Mill, Weir Street, in the last year : 58,254 sacks of flour (280 lbs. each), 6,867 loads of oatmeal (240 lbs. each), 5,638 loads of malt, 21,595 loads of other goods.

THE ROCHDALE EQUITABLE MANUFACTURING COMPANY, LIMITED.

The principal object of the founders of this Society was the equitable division of the profits arising from the manufacturing of Cotton and Woollen Fabrics. They believed that all who contributed to the realisation of wealth, ought to participate in its distribution. To this principle the Society has proved recreant, to the great regret of its originators. But " honour to whom honour is due ", and this Society is still entitled to a share. During the past year [1] its Mills have run full time for about 9 months, and the remainder 4 days a week ; and more, it has paid the same rate of wages for work done since the cotton scarcity than it did before, which is more than can be said of some Manufacturers in the same town. And we must say that the inferior qualities of cotton now worked in Cotton Mills is so much worse to get through, that it is a sufficient reduction in itself without reducing the wages.

4. CO-OPERATIVE DIVIDEND ON PURCHASES

[The Rochdale Pioneers decided to pay interest on the share capital invested by their members and, after providing for depreciation, education, and various other charges, to distribute the rest of their trading surplus in the form of a dividend on each member's purchases, at so much in the £1 (1s. 8d. was an early rate of dividend). They have often been credited with the invention of dividend on purchases ; but this device had in fact been practised by a number of earlier Societies, of which the following extract gives an example.]

---

[1] *I.e.* during the Cotton Famine.

From *The Poor Man's Guardian*, April 7, 1832, reporting a meeting of the First Western Co-operative Union, an Owenite Society in West London, of which the leader of the Saddlers' Union, Benjamin Warden, was Chairman.

An interesting discussion ensued upon the propriety of altering the laws so as to allow a percentage to every member in proportion to the amount of his dealings. The members appeared to be generally of the opinion that the adoption of the proposition would be a considerable advantage, as it would confer immediate benefit upon all those who dealt extensively at the store, and remove he discouragements which the most zealous and persevering co-operators had hitherto experienced.

It was moved, seconded, and carried by a large majority — that every member of the Union shall receive a percentage upon his or her dealings, to be paid quarterly.

The article requiring members to deal at the store to a certain amount was then expunged from the rules and regulations.

5. THE REDEMPTION SOCIETIES

[Upon the collapse of Queenwood a new attempt was made by the advocates of Owenite Co-operation to carry out their principles in a democratic way. At Leeds in 1845 and at a number of other places there were set up General Labour Redemption Societies, designed to build up out of a weekly subscription of 1d. a capital fund that could be used to acquire workshops, factories, and farms, and later to create Co-operative Communities. The Leeds Redemption Society for some years carried on a Community Settlement in Wales; and a number of Societies set up Co-operative Stores and workshops. The movement died away in the 1850s, some of the Societies being converted into Co-operative Stores and others becoming Friendly Societies.]

(a) From *The Herald of Redemption*, Leeds (1847), p. 16. (Quoted in Benjamin Jones, " Co-operative Production " (1894), vol. i. p. 102.)

This brings us to the statement of the remedy which the Redemption Society proposes for the great and acknowledged evils affecting society. . . . We intend to unite the labour of all for the benefit of all. . . . To this end we have determined to make an experiment, and give the principle of co-operation a fair trial. . . . Men of all religious denominations have attached themselves to the society. It embodies also amongst its most active workers, men professing all shades of political opinions; and it has now upwards of 600 members.

(*b*) From Address and Rules of the Bury Redemption Society. (Quoted in Benjamin Jones, " Co-operative Production " (1894), vol. i, p. 98.)

OBJECTS

To unite labourers of every grade for the purpose of carrying out and extending the practice of associative labour — (1) By forming working associations of men and women, who shall enjoy among themselves the whole produce of their labour, after the repayment of the borrowed capital (if any), with a fair rate of interest thereon. (2) By organizing both among such associations and any others of combined workmen and capitalists who may be admitted into the union, the interchange and distribution of commodities. (3) By reducing the hours of labour in all trades, or amongst the workers of any branch of industry, being members of the society. (4) To purchase and cultivate land upon the cooperative principle, and to provide for education of children, maintenance of widows and orphans, etc.

The following calculation will show the power which we have by a weekly subscription of one penny per week. In Great Britain there are 6,000,000 adult males; take of these, and of such females as choose to subscribe, 4,000,000; these will yield, at one penny per week, £20,000 weekly, or £1,040,000 a year; this, with compound interest, would amount, in sixty years, to £3,471,129,995 18s. 4d. Now this sum would buy up all the property in the kingdom. Fellow-workers, here lies our power; let us begin at once to use it, and millions yet unborn will bless us for our exertions.

(*c*) From *The Christian Socialist* (1851), vol. ii, p. 291. Article by J. M. Ludlow describing the Stockport Working Men's Redemption Society. (Quoted in Benjamin Jones, " Co-operative Production " (1894), vol. i, pp. 97-8.)

. . . At present the society has fallen to fourteen members, from forty that they once were. Two of its members are employed shoemaking, besides one binder, and one in making hats. Their premises were opened on the 20th of January last, and at their last stocktaking the stock was found to be worth £40, the capital subscribed having been £22 — which would show a profit of 100%. But I was sorry to hear that they deemed themselves obliged to give credit. All profits are to be left in the business, unless members choose to leave, when they can take out 50% of the profits made on their contributions. Their business is worth £2 to £3 a week.

6. THE CHRISTIAN SOCIALISTS

[The Christian Socialist movement, started by J. M. Ludlow, who enlisted F. D. Maurice and through him Charles Kingsley, began in 1848, inspired largely by the French movements for Co-operative Production (Buchez, Louis Blanc, etc.) and by the outbreak of the French Revolution of that year. *Politics for the People*, later replaced by *The Christian Socialist*, was its first journal. The extract is from an article of Kingsley's, written under the name of ' Parson Lot '.]

From *Politics for the People*, May 13, 1848.

Letters to the Chartists, No. 1.

. . . My only quarrel with the Charter is, that it does not go far enough in reform. I want to see you *free*; but I do not see how what you ask for will give you what you want. I think you have fallen into just the same mistake as the rich of whom you complain — the very mistake which has been our curse and our nightmare — I mean, the mistake of fancying that *legislative* reform is *social* reform, or that men's hearts can be changed by act of parliament. If anyone will tell me of a country where a Charter made the rogues honest, or the idle industrious, I shall alter my opinion of the Charter, but not till then. It disappointed me bitterly when I read it. It seemed a harmless cry enough, but a poor, bald, constitution mongering cry as I ever heard. That French cry of " Organisation of Labour " is worth a thousand of it, and yet that does not go to the bottom of the matter by many a mile.

7. THE SOCIETY FOR PROMOTING WORKING-MEN'S ASSOCIATIONS

[The Christian Socialists set up this Society in 1850. The Council of Promoters represented the suppliers of capital for the movement: the Central Board, representing the Associations, was to take over full control when the capital had been repaid or otherwise secured. For the history of the movement and of its failure, see C. E. Raven, " Christian Socialism, 1848–1854 " (1920).]

(*a*) From " Tracts on Christian Socialism ", No. 5 (1850).

THE SOCIETY FOR PROMOTING
WORKING-MEN'S ASSOCIATIONS.

CONSTITUTION.

The object of this Union is :—To carry out and extend the principles and practice of associated Labour :

1st. By forming Associations of Working-men, who shall enjoy, among themselves and their families, the whole produce of their labour ; subject to the repayment of borrowed capital (if any), with a fair interest thereon.

2nd. By organizing, both among such Associations and among any others of combined capitalists and working men who may be admitted into the Union, the interchange and distribution of commodities.

3rd. By establishing among all the Associations admitted into the Union, Institutions for the common benefit of the members, as Friendly Societies, Model Lodging Houses, Schools, etc.

4th. And by the full development of every means of brotherly help and support, which the capital, the credit, the custom, the knowledge, and the influence of the Associations can afford.

Article 1st.—The Associations shall make a periodical Allowance to their members (representing the Wages of the present competitive system), which shall be a fair day's remuneration for a fair day's work, according to the talent and industry of the individual receiving it ; and shall, as far as possible, be the same in all the Associations of the same trade, in the same place, and for the same nature and quality of labour.

2nd. The net surplus, or the profit of the present system — that is to say, what remains of the produce of the labour of an Association, after deducting the current expenses, and any sums due for re-payment of borrowed capital (if any), and the interest upon the capital employed in outfit and other standing expenses, shall be equally divided between ALL the Associates, in proportion to the time they have severally worked.

One third of the profit, at least, shall be left to increase the capital, and consequently, the number of Associates. This capital shall be equally divided among the members of the Association for the time being, and may bear interest at a rate to be fixed by the rules of the Association. Payment of the shares of this capital cannot be required, but the right to the interest may be assigned among members of the Association.

Each Association shall contribute a sum to be fixed by the Central Board towards such provident purposes as shall be, from time to time, defined by the Central Board. This sum may be raised either by weekly contributions of the Members, or by reserving a certain proportion of the profits of the Association, or by both of these methods, as the Central Board may determine in each case.

3rd. No hired workman shall be employed without giving to him the same rate of Wages as an Associate would be entitled to for similar work in the shape of Allowance, and (unless he be dismissed for misconduct), a certain sum in lieu of Profits, to be fixed by the Association, or, in case of dispute, by the Central Board.

No new Associate can be received until he has been employed as a Probationer for a period, whether consecutive or otherwise, to be fixed from time to time by each Association, with the sanction of the Central Board.

All hired workmen shall be remunerated as Probationers, and entitled, at their option, to be considered as Probationers.

The Association shall, with the sanction of the Central Board, form rules for the admission and remuneration of Apprentices, and in their default the Central Board shall form such rules.

4th. All officers shall be elected for a time to be fixed in each case, by the Laws of the Association, and shall be capable of re-election, and liable to be dismissed from their office, in such manner as is provided by the Laws of the Association. Each Association shall have a Manager who shall not be engaged in any other commercial business but that of the Association.

5th. The Central Board herein before referred to shall be composed as prescribed in " The Organisation of the Society ".

6th. The price of the articles sold by the different Associations of the same trade and place shall be regulated by those Associations, subject to the Control of the Central Board, in such a manner as to prevent either Monopoly or unfair Competition.

7th. All disputes between members of an Association shall be settled by Arbitrators, to be chosen by the parties from Members of the Society; or, in case of their differing, by an Umpire, chosen by the Arbitrators before entering on their reference.

All disputes between a Manager and his Association, or any member of it, shall be settled by Arbitrators, to be named by the parties, and in case of their differing, by an Umpire chosen in the manner above-mentioned.

All disputes between Associations shall be settled by the Central Board, with an appeal to the Council of Promoters, if one third of the members of the Central Board for the time being desire it.

8th. The accounts of each Association shall be examined and kept in order by an accountant, chosen by the Council of Promoters, and paid by the Associations.

The accounts shall be open to the inspection of the Central Board, and the Council of Promoters, and to that of all the Associates and Creditors of the Association.

Any Association may provide that the accounts shall be open to the inspection of the customers, or any of them. A statement of the accounts of each Association shall be drawn up periodically, at such intervals not exceeding six months, as the Laws of the Association provide.

9th. All the work of an Association shall, when it is possible, be done on the premises of that Association.

No work shall be done on Sundays.

The hours of daily labour must not exceed ten, excluding meal-times, unless with the assent of the Central Board, and of the Council of Promoters.

The Central Board shall from time to time make regulations as to the exchange of labour among the Associations, and as to the time which each Association shall employ in work for other Associations.[1]

10th. All Associations shall, as soon as possible after their formation, send to the Central Board a copy of their Laws, and a list of the names of their Associates, which list shall, from time to time, be corrected, so as to show the names of the Associates for the time being.

Every Associate shall be entitled to a copy of the Laws of his Association.

Every Associate shall, on his admission, sign the Laws of his Association, and shall be considered as binding himself thereby to conform in all respects to the Laws for the time being.

Each Associate is expected to pay one penny per week towards the expenses of the Central Office.

11th. None of the Associations connected with this Society shall ever be made the instruments or agents of political agitation.

[1] This law is intended to facilitate the commencement of the Central Office of Exchange and Interchange.

The Associates in their individual capacity being, however, at liberty to act as they please in this matter.

12th. No Association, so long as it remains in debt to the Council of Promoters, shall borrow money without the consent of the Council of Promoters.

13th. The execution of this Constitution is entrusted to the Central Board, with appeal to the Council of Promoters.

The Central Board, with the consent of the Council of Promoters, may, from time to time, revise the present Constitution.

REMARKS

1st. The Promoters will not interfere with the Laws of any Association, further than by this Constitution, except as advisers.

2nd. The conditions on which money can be advanced to the Associations are that, so long as any of the capital advanced by the Promoters shall be unpaid, the Promoters reserve to themselves right of veto on the appointment of the Manager, and on the regulations of the Association relating to his powers and duties. [See 2nd Tract, p. 4.]

OUR SUCCESS DEPENDS

Firstly—On every Associate being firmly impressed with the idea that his personal interest is subordinate to that of his Association and dependent on it.

Secondly—On each Association acting upon the principle, that its particular interest is subordinate to that of the Union, and dependent on it.

ORGANISATION OF THE SOCIETY

I. THE SOCIETY.

This Society consists of the Promoters and the Associates.

All business between the Society and the Associations, on the one hand, and between the Associations and the public at large on the other hand, is transacted by the Council of Promoters, who have power to nominate any Promoter as Member of the Council.

The functions of the Council are—

1st. To collect and administer all funds contributed or advanced to the Society, for the promotion of its objects.

2nd. To diffuse the principles of Co-operation, as the practical application of Christianity to the purposes of Trade and Industry. . . . The Associates are all Members of the Working Associations connected with the Society.

They are represented by a Central Board.

2. THE CENTRAL BOARD.

The Central Board consists of—

1st. The Manager of each Association; or, in case of his unavoidable absence, a Deputy to be named by him for each meeting.

2nd. One Delegate from each Association, to be chosen from time to time by that Association, for such period (not less than three months) as they shall determine on.

3rd. A Secretary, who shall be appointed and paid by the Council of Promoters.

These persons vote in the deliberations of the Central Board.

The following persons have a right to be present, and to speak, but not to vote, in the deliberations of the Central Board.

1st. The Members of the Council of Promoters.

2nd. One Member of each Association, to be changed for each meeting.

N.B. It is recommended that each Associate should attend in rotation.

3rd. Any persons invited by the Council of Promoters.

The functions of the Central Board are—

1st. To regulate all the relations of the Associations with each other; and, with the concurrence of the Council of Promoters, those of the united Associations with the public at large.

2nd. To co-operate with the Council of Promoters in forming new Associations with the public at large.

The Central Board may, from time to time, and with the approbation of the Council of Promoters, make such alterations in the Constitution of the Board, as may be required.

The Central Board shall communicate minutes of all its proceedings to the Council of Promoters, make such alterations in the Constitution of the Board, as may be required.

The Central Board shall communicate minutes of all its proceedings to the Council of Promoters, and shall give to the Council notice of the time and place, and when possible, of the objects of its meetings.

3. THE COUNCIL OF PROMOTERS.

1st. The Council shall consist of a President, twelve Ordinary Members, and an unlimited number of Honorary and Corresponding Members.

2nd. The President and the Ordinary Members of the Council for the time being shall form a Board, by which all the duties assigned by the General Constitution of the Society to the Council shall be discharged, and which shall, from time to time, fill up any vacancy in the number of Ordinary Members, and may nominate any Promoter to be an Honorary or Corresponding Member of the Council.

3rd. If the office of President becomes vacant, the Ordinary Members, for the time being, shall forthwith proceed to elect a new President.

4th. Two of the Ordinary Members, to be selected by a Rota, shall attend, if possible, every day, except Sundays, Christmas Day, or Good Friday at the Central Office.

5th. Any member, whose duty it is to attend at the Central Office may, with the approval of the President, appoint any Honorary or Corresponding Member to be his substitute in attending at the Office.

6th. A meeting of the Ordinary Members of the Council shall be held every week at the Central Office.

7th. A General Meeting, at which all Members of the Council shall have a right to attend, shall also be held at stated times, to be fixed by the Council, at the Central Office, for the purpose of conferring with persons desirous of entering into Association, and of giving information as to the proceedings of the Society.

8th. For the present the General Meetings of the Council are weekly.

9th. The President or any Ordinary Member may introduce Visitors at any General Meeting of the Council.

(b) From " Report of the Society for Promoting Working Men's Associations " (1852), p. 32.

The Society has for some time past determined to discourage advances of money to bodies of working men about to start in association, unless they have first shown some signs of preparedness for the change from their old life, and have subscribed some funds of their own. This has been done, because it has been found very necessary to have some proof that men have foresight and self-denial before they should be encouraged to associate. Working men in general are not fit for association. They come into it with the idea that it is to fill their pockets and lighten their work at once, and that every man in an association is to be his own master. They find their mistake in the first month or two, and then set to quarrelling with everybody connected with the association, but more especially with their manager, and after much bad blood has been roused, the association breaks up insolvent, has to be re-formed under stringent rules and after the expulsion of the refractory members. One illustration of these positions we shall mention, and one only, as it is useless to rip up wounds which have in many cases healed entirely. In the first nine months of our life as a society we set up three sets of shoemakers in association, supplying in two instances the whole of the funds, and in the other all but £5. None of the men were picked, we accepted them just as they came to us. We gave to them absolute self-government, merely reserving to ourselves certain rights of interference in cases of dispute or mismanagement while any capital remained due to us. Each one of the associations had quarrelled with and turned out its original manager in six months ; one, the West End Bootmakers, went to pieces altogether before nine months had gone. The other two struggled on till the beginning of the year, never paying their way, and continually quarrelling. By the joint assent of the Council and the Central Board, they were then amalgamated, and some of the worst members turned out ; but still matters went wrong, until, in May last, we were obliged by another great outbreak and threatening insolvency to take away all self-government from the associates, leaving them only in cases of tyranny an appeal to the society against their manager. . . .

Where the associations are successful the great danger which they and all who are interested in them have to guard against is exclusiveness. The associates find their own position greatly improved, and fear to endanger it by taking in new members. They are apt, therefore, to make too stringent rules as to admission, and to require payments from new members proportionate to the capital which the society has gained, and such a few of the most skilful of working men can pay out of their present wages. The effect of this will be that a great many small associations will spring up, instead of a few large ones, unless working men will look forward and take a broader and more Christian view of their work. These small associations will compete with and ruin one another.

8. THE ENGINEERS AND CO-OPERATIVE PRODUCTION

[The Amalgamated Society of Engineers was founded in January 1851, and began almost at once to consider the establishment of Co-operative factories. The Christian Socialists agreed to help ; and plans were started for taking over works in Liverpool and East London. The A.S.E. by ballot vote of its members decided to invest £10,000 in Co-operative factories. But, before more than small beginnings could be made, the great lock-out of 1852 completely swept away the funds of the A.S.E. Several small factories were, nevertheless, carried on with capital supplied mainly by the Christian Socialists, who gave invaluable help to the A.S.E. in the lock-out. The A.S.E. Council made an attempt to employ its members on Co-operative lines during the stoppage ; but, when it was over, the Union was in no condition to carry on with the ambitious projects of 1851, and the small Co-operative engineering works gradually died out.]

From *The Operative*, 23rd December, 1851.

The Council of the Amalgamated Society of Engineers Etc. direct attention to the following propositions :

That if the Central Association of Employers carry out their threat of a Masters' strike, and refuse to conduct the work of the country, it is the duty of working men to take the matter into their own hands, and begin manufacturing for the public.

That as the employers in the Engineering and Machine-making trades refuse to continue to be the medium between the producer and the consumer, there is nothing left for the working men but to put themselves in direct communication with the consumers of the products of their labour, and offer to perform the work without the intervention of their present employers.

Workmen to perform work on the premises of customers, can be obtained by application to the General Office, and as offers have already been made of capital to conduct the operations of self-employment, large jobs will be undertaken and accomplished by workmen on their own account. The public is especially invited to promote this arrangement both by a supply of work and funds, for which latter an interest of 5 per cent will be paid. The same to be invested in the names and hands of parties of public repute and independent of the workmen.

That inasmuch as many of our members have lathes and other tools in their possession, and as in a crisis of this description it is desirable that all available means should be at the disposal of the council, it is hoped that they will, as early as possible, communicate their intention of lending such tools for the benefit of those persons who may be thrown out of employment by the masters' strike. All communications to be addressed to Mr. W. Allan, 25, Little Alie Street, Whitechapel, founder.

9. THE CENTRAL CO-OPERATIVE AGENCY

[E. V. Neale, a leading Christian Socialist, who greatly helped the engineers and later became Secretary of the Co-operative Union, was the main agent in the attempt in 1851 to set up a Wholesale Agency for the supply of goods to, and the marketing of the products of, the entire Co-operative movement. The Central Co-operative Agency was a fore-runner of the Co-operative Wholesale Society; but, being set up in London, whereas the main strength of the Co-operative movement was in the North, it stood little chance of success. It was wound up in 1857.]

From the Furnival Papers, vol. i, No. 24.

Report of a Meeting for the Establishment of the Central Co-operative Agency, May 30, 1851, p. 5.

The chairman said . . . Originally there were two objects in view in establishing the institution. They hoped it would not only become a working man's shop to a greater extent than it had done, but also that it would become the centre of other institutions established in other parts of the country, and they had found to a very great extent, this had been the case in Lancashire and Yorkshire, where the matter had been taken up with much greater zeal and earnestness than in London. The advantage of a central Metropolitan Establishment to the Provincial Stores was obvious. They had been previously cheated to an enormous extent, by having spurious articles supplied to them at a high price. But the founders of that institution believed they could not only assist these Provincial Stores in getting the best goods at the fair market price, but secure the still more important object of forming a centre, by which all of them would be held together; and further, that this establishment would not only hold them together — would not only serve the mere selfish purpose of supplying cheap goods — but the higher and more important object of promoting industrial associations. (Hear, hear.) It therefore now became a question, whether they could not make that more useful and more central in future, by making the retail subordinate to the wholesale business, and by making it a place from which Local Stores might be certain, wherever established, of procuring all goods of the best quality at wholesale prices. If they succeeded in that object, they would as mentioned in the report, put it in the power of any body of men in and around London, to form societies, however small the number of members might be, in their own localities, and to supply themselves from a common centre with the best articles of grocery, or any other description of articles they might require, much more conveniently than heretofore. Instead of individual depositors coming from a great distance to make their separate purchases, the Central Agency would supply at once the requirements of each locality through the medium of such societies. The advantages of the system would be brought home, as it were, to each man's own door; and thus, in the second place, tend to make that Establishment a centre to which goods manufactured by Working Men's Societies might be consigned and redistributed in a manner that would greatly tend towards furthering the practical progress of Association.

10. CO-OPERATIVE FLOUR MILLS AND WOOLLEN MILLS

[Corn-milling was the earliest form of Co-operation in England, mills having been set up in the middle of the eighteenth century. There were further ventures during the Napoleonic Wars; and in the 1840s and 1850s the movement spread rapidly. The Leeds Co-operative Society began in 1845 as a corn mill; and the Rochdale Pioneers established a separate Corn-milling Society in 1850. Many of the mills, as Ludlow here points out, had little connection with the main Co-operative movement. Still less connection had the woollen mills here mentioned: they either died out or developed into ordinary joint-stock concerns. The extract is taken from a series of articles Ludlow contributed to *The Christian Socialist* in 1851, under the title ' Notes of a Co-operative Tour through Lancashire and Yorkshire '.]

From *The Christian Socialist*, 1851, vol. ii.

. . . From Mr. Simpson's I was taken by Mr. Scott to the Bradford Flour Mill, which however I had not time to go over. The Society, which numbers over 1,200 members, and has been about four years in existence, has built the mill for itself, and is grinding about 125 sacks a week. It is conducted on the same principle as the other flour-mill societies of Yorkshire, that of selling as nearly as possible directly at cost-price to members only; a restriction by which they, as well as other similar enrolled bodies, find themselves much hampered. I cannot help observing, that this was one of the establishments where I met with the least of encouragement and confidence, and where I had most pains in obtaining the requisite information. I should imagine, indeed, that with the exception of the one at Leeds, these Flour Mill Societies, which are very much in the hands of the middle classes, are as yet but slightly imbued with the spirit of co-operation, and rather shrink from being looked upon in their true light, as practical co-operators; and perhaps Bradford is yet among the most advanced. The number of them is much greater than is commonly supposed, chiefly in Yorkshire. Besides Leeds and Bradford, they are to be found also (frequently by the name of " Union Mills ") at Halifax, at Birstall, at Thirsk, at Whitby, at York, at Stamford, at Hull, where there are two. There are others, as our " List " shows, at Lincoln, at Birmingham, and in Devonshire at Devonport and Stonehouse.

There is another class of semi-co-operative bodies extensively founded by the middle-classes in Yorkshire, of which I regretted not being able to inspect a specimen, the Joint-Stock woollen mills of the West Riding. An account of them forwarded by Mr. Aldam to Mr. Gladstone will be found in the Appendix to the Commons' Report on Joint-Stock Companies, of 1844. The shareholders are all small clothiers, seldom exceeding forty, and they unite on the understanding that " whatever work the partners have to do, they must do it at their own mill ", at one fixed price for the same kind of goods. The business is carried on by a manager, who accounts to the partners, and these Associations of small clothiers are said to compete successfully with the large manufacturers. I am credibly informed that they are not generally registered under the Joint-Stock Companies' Act, and therefore remain out of the pale of the law, as they did seven years ago, when first brought under the notice of the Parliamentary Committee. If so, they might possibly be made available allies in the coming struggle for the amendment of the partnership laws.

Yours ever,

J. M. LUDLOW.

11. CO-OPERATIVE SOCIETIES AND THE LAW

[Most of the early Co-operative Societies had no assured legal basis, though a few were registered as Friendly Societies. The ' frugal invest-

445

ment ' clause of the Friendly Societies Act of 1846 gave them their first opportunity to acquire an effective legal status ; but the position remained unsatisfactory until the Christian Socialists helped them to get an Act specially designed to meet their needs. This was the Industrial and Provident Societies Act of 1852, which, with many amending statutes, provides the main legal basis for the movement of to-day.]

(*a*) From the Friendly Societies Act, 1846 (9 & 10 Vict. c. 27).

. . . A society may be established, under the Provision of the aid Acts, for any of the following purposes, (that is to say). . . .

4. For the frugal Investment of the Savings of the Members for better enabling them to purchase Food, Firing, Clothes, or other Necessaries, or the Tools or Implements of their Trade or Calling, or to provide for the Education of their Children or Kindred, with or without the Assistance of Charitable Donations : Provided always, that the shares in any such Investment Society shall not be transferable, and that the Investment of each Member shall accumulate or be employed for the sole benefit of the Member investing, or the Husband, Wife, Children or Kindred of such Member, and that no part thereof shall be appropriated to the Relief, Maintenance, or Endowment of any other Member or Person whomsoever, and that the full Amount of the Balance due according to the Rules of such Society to such Member shall be paid to him or her on withdrawing from the Society, and that no such last-mentioned Society shall be entitled or allowed to invest its Funds, or any Part thereof, with the Commissioners for the Reduction of the National Debt. . . .

(*b*) From the Industrial and Provident Societies Act, 1852 (15 & 16 Vict. c. 31).

. . . I. It shall be lawful for any Number of Persons to establish a Society under the Provisions of this and the said recited Act, for the purpose of raising by voluntary subscriptions of the Members thereof a Fund for attaining any Purpose or Object for the Time being authorised for the Laws in force with respect to Friendly Societies, or by this Act, by carrying on or exercising in common any Labour, Trade, or Handicraft, or several Labours, Trades, or Handicrafts, except the working of Mines, Minerals, or Quarries beyond the limits of the United Kingdom of *Great Britain* and *Ireland*, and also except the Business of Banking, whether in the said United Kingdom or elsewhere ; and this Act shall apply to all

Societies already established for any of the Purposes herein mentioned, so soon as they shall conform to the Provisions hereof.

. . . . . .

XI. Nothing in this or the said recited Act shall be construed to restrict in anywise the Liability of the Members of any Society established under or by Virtue of this Act, or claiming the Benefit thereof, to the lawful Debts and Engagements of such Society: Provided always, that no person shall be liable for the Debts or Engagements of any such society after the Expiration of two years from his ceasing to be a Member of the same.

(c) From the Industrial and Provident Societies Act, 1862 (25 & 26 Vict. c. 87).

20. In the event of a Society registered under the Act being wound up, every present and past Member of such Society shall be liable to contribute to the Assets of the Society to an Amount sufficient for Payment of such Sums as may be required for the Adjustment of the Rights of the Contributories, amongst themselves, with the Qualifications following; (that is to say),

1. No past Member shall be liable to contribute to the Assets of the Society if he has ceased to be a Member for a Period of One Year or upwards prior to the Commencement of the Winding-up:

2. No past Member shall be liable to contribute in respect of any Debt or Liability of the Society contracted after the Time at which he ceased to be a Member:

3. No past Member shall be liable to contribute to the Assets of the Society unless it appears to the Court that the existing Members are unable to satisfy the Contributions required to be made by them in order to satisfy all just Demands upon such Society:

4. No Contribution shall be required from any Member exceeding the Amount (if any) unpaid on the Shares in respect of which he is liable as a past or present Member.

12. THE CO-OPERATIVE WHOLESALE SOCIETY

[The spread of Co-operative Societies in the North of England soon created a demand for some sort of Wholesale Society, or Central Purchasing Agency. The Rochdale Pioneers for a time carried on a Wholesale Department, to serve the neighbouring Societies; and Neale's Central Co-operative Agency set up a branch in Manchester, and attempted to serve the Northern Stores. But the Northern Co-operators wanted to create their own body, centred upon the Consumers' Stores rather than on the Producers' Societies favoured by the Christian Socialists. This was difficult until 1862, when the second Industrial and Provident Societies Act made it lawful for one Co-operative Society to hold shares in another. In 1864 the Lancashire and Yorkshire Co-operators set up the North of England Co-operative Wholesale Society, which was owned by the local Consumers' Societies and paid dividends on purchases to them. Abraham Greenwood, a leading figure in the Rochdale Society, was one of the protagonists in this scheme. The Scottish Co-operators set up their own separate Wholesale Society in 1868–1869. The English Society dropped the prefix ' North of England ' in 1872, and soon spread over the whole country, including Wales and parts of Ireland.]

(a) From *The Co-operator*, March 1863.

PLAN FOR A WHOLESALE AGENCY
BY MR ABRAHAM GREENWOOD OF ROCHDALE.

(The following suggestive Paper on the important subject of a Wholesale Co-operative Agency, as distinguished from the more expensive and risky Depot, was read by the author, Mr. Abm. Greenwood, of Rochdale, at the recent Co-operative Conference held in Oldham. Mr. Greenwood has kindly revised his plan, and sent it for publication in *The Co-operator*, at the request of the Conference and Co-operators generally. We commend the matter to the attention of Committees, Secretaries, and Members; and expect to see united, prompt and prudent action thereupon.)

Before proceeding to develope a scheme of a wholesale agency, permit me in the first place, to glance at past efforts to accomplish the object we are this day met to discuss — namely, the desirability of aggregating the purchasing power of the Co-operative stores, especially of Lancashire, Yorkshire, and adjoining counties.

The first attempt in this direction was made by the Christian Socialists, conspicuous amongst whom were Edward Vansittart Neale, Esq., The Rev. F. D. Maurice, the Rev. Charles Kingsley; J. M. Ludlow, Thomas Hughes, F. J. Furnivall, Joseph Woodin and Lloyd Jones, Esqrs. I am thus circumstantial in mentioning the names of these gentlemen, that their services in the early stages of the Co-operative movement may be acknowledged: they not only wished well to, but aided nobly by their well-known talents, and no less by their pecuniary assistance, the cause of true Co-operation. They instituted the " Central Co-operative Agency ", for the purpose of counteracting the system of adulteration and fraud prevailing in trade, and for supplying to Co-operative stores a quality of goods that could be relied upon, and in the highest state of purity. The agency did not prove a success, but had to be given up, entailing great loss to its promoters. There is still a remnant of the agency left, known by the firm of " Woodin & Co., Sherborne-lane, London ".

The second effort was made by the " Equitable Pioneers " Society in 1852, by initiating a " Wholesale Department ". This department was originated for supplying goods to its members in large quantities, and also with a view to supplying the Co-operative stores of Lancashire and Yorkshire, whose small capital did not enable them to purchase in the best market, nor command the services of what is indispensable to any store — *a good buyer*, who knew the markets, and *what, how* and *where* to buy. The Pioneers' Society invited other stores to co-operate in carrying out practically the idea of a wholesale establishment, offering, at the same time, to find the necessary amount of capital for conducting the wholesale business, for which the Pioneers' Society would charge this department at the rate of 5 per cent per annum. A few stores did join, but they never gave that hearty support necessary to make the scheme thoroughly successful. Notwithstanding this counteracting influence, the wholesale department, from the beginning, paid interest not only on capital, but dividends to the members trading in this department. Had all concerned in this affair displayed shrewdness and persistence, the practicability of acting in concert in a matter of this kind would ere this have been demonstrated, and placed in the category of Co-operative " facts ". However, after a time the demon of all working-class movements hitherto — jealousy — crept in here. The stores dealing in the wholesale department of the Pioneers' Society thought that it had some advantage over them ; while, on the other side, a large number of the members of the Pioneers' Society imagined they were giving privileges to the other stores which a due regard to their interests did not warrant them in bestowing. My opinion is, that had there been no other cause of failure than those mentioned, the Central Co-operative Agency and the Equitable Pioneers' Wholesale Department must inevitably have failed, from their efforts being too soon in the order of Co-operative developement.

Failures have their lessons ; and if read aright, lead on to success. . . . Let us see if the progress of Co-operation now offers ample room for success. There were in England, when the " Central Co-operative Agency " was established, not more than ten stores, and not more than seventeen when the Rochdale Store established its " Wholesale Department ". What a contrast, indicative of Co-operative progress, these times present with those of ten or twelve years ago ! Now there are some hundreds of Co-operative stores in the United Kingdom. In the October number of *The Co-operator* of last year there are enumerated upwards of 300 stores. . . . There is no doubt therefore that there is now an ample field for a wholesale agency. . . .

(*b*) From *The Co-operator*, March 15, 1867.

From the prospectus of the North of England Co-operative Wholesale Industrial and Provident Society.

. . . .

HOW THE SOCIETY ORIGINATED

At the Co-operative Conferences convened to promote the amendment of the Industrial and Provident Societies Act, the necessity of Co-operative Societies aggregating their Purchases, so as to secure the profits of the Wholesale Trader, was constantly pressed on the attention of the assembly : legal difficulties, however, interposed a barrier to the formation of a society with that object.

The passing of the " Amended Act " in 1862 having removed the legal impediments, a *special* Conference was called to consider the advisability of organising a Federation of Societies for the purpose of Wholesale buying. Nearly all the Co-operative Societies in the North of England were represented at the Conference, which closed its deliberations by *passing unanimously a resolution to form this society.* §

OBJECTS

1st. To carry on the trade of Wholesale Tea Dealers, Grocers, and Provision Merchants.

2nd. To enhance the Profits of Co-operation, by buying the commodities required with Ready Money, in quantities sufficiently large to command the best Markets, thereby diminishing the cost of distribution, by bringing the Producer and Consumer into more immediate contact.

§ Mr Abraham Greenwood, of Rochdale, must be regarded as the principal originator of the Co-operative Wholesale Society, of which he has ever since been the President. In *The Co-operator* for March, 1863 (Vol. 3), Mr Greenwood propounded his plan for a Wholesale Agency, which, with some modifications, formed the basis of the present admirable organisation. [This note is in the original.]

3rd. To consolidate and extend the movement, by enabling small societies to purchase their goods on the most advantageous terms, thus securing them from imposition in the days of their infancy and inexperience.

The business is strictly conducted on *ready money* principles.

Goods are sold to Co-operative Societies only.

Profits divided Half-yearly, in proportion to each Society's Purchases.

CONDITIONS ON WHICH CO-OPERATIVE SOCIETIES ARE ADMITTED TO MEMBERSHIP.

Shares are issued on condition that a society take out One Share for each of its Members, and continues to hold One Share for each Member, increasing the number annually as its Members increase.

An Application for Shares must be made by Resolution, passed at a Members' Meeting, attested by the signature of the Secretary and Three Members, and executed under the Seal of the Society.

One Shilling per Share must be paid on application, on which Interest at the rate of Five per Cent. per annum is allowed.

No further call will be made ; but the Dividend and Interest of each Society will be retained, and passed to the credit of their Capital Account until their Shares are paid up.

Shares can be paid at once.

No Shares are issued to Private Individuals, this being strictly a Federation of Co-operative Societies.

On payment of One Shilling per Member, Societies are entitled to all the privileges and benefits of Membership.

The General Meetings of the Society are held Half-yearly, in the Months of *May* and *November*. At these Meetings the Balance Sheets are presented, and the Officers, Directors and Auditors elected.

Societies are entitled to be represented at these Meetings by Delegates, proportioned to the number of their Members — One Delegate being allowed for any number of Members up to 100, and an additional Delegate for every additional 200 Members.

HALF BONUS TO NON-MEMBERS

At the Fourth Half-yearly Meeting of this Society it was resolved —" That Co-operative Stores not being Members of this Society, but desirous of becoming Members, shall be allowed Half Bonus on their Purchases, the said Bonus to be carried to the Capital Account of each Society claiming to be admitted as Members under the provisions of this Resolution, until the amount is equal to a Paid-up Share for each of their Members, as provided in Rule 2." It will be seen that the only condition on which Half Bonus is granted, is — that it is allowed to remain in the funds until, by a process of accumulation, the Society claiming it holds a Paid-up Share for each of its Members.

Half Bonus is forfeited unless applied for within Six Months of the time declared.

Trade Lists and Forms of Application for Shares can be had from the Cashier.

(c) From *The Co-operative News*, November 23, 1872.

EXPANSION OF THE WHOLESALE.

At last, some of our enthusiastic correspondents will say, at last a new step in Co-operative progress is about to be realised, by the commencement of manufacturing processes on behalf of the whole of the federated stores. Our more timid friends, who have listened from time to time to orations by the leaders of society, in which co-operation has been gently patted on the back as a very good thing for working people so long as it is kept to the work of distribution, will hold their breath at the announcement that the representatives of 264 stores have resolved to try to produce some of the various goods which they keep in stock. For ourselves, while advocating the slow and sure line of policy, we have always plainly declared the fact, that the substitution of stores for the establishments of individual shopkeepers, useful and important as it is for economy, for education and morality, is still only one side of co-operation, and we incline to think that there has been ample time and experience to make safe the foundation which is to bear the whole superstructure, and that it is now time to commence the building.

Co-operative stores are now turning over £10,000,000 per annum, and the Wholesale, which does not deal in one-half of the requirements of these stores, is doing 10 per cent of that trade, whilst its connections reach only about one-half of the stores, and its partners comprise only about one-quarter of them. Now it is very desirable, in order to promote the greatest good of the greatest number, that every co-operative store should be a partner in the

Wholesale, and that the Wholesale should be able to supply all the wants of the stores. How is this to be accomplished ? Evidently the stores must be made to feel that such partnership and such trading is for their interest ! . . .

The profits divided by the Wholesale last quarter, after payment of interest, was £3,274 as compared with £2,933 in the corresponding quarter of last year. Now, if the Wholesale be expanded so as to correspond more nearly to the requirements of its customers, and if it can add the profits of the manufacturer to those of the retail and wholesale dealer, will not this prospect of extra profit be the surest possible plan of bringing in the remaining stores as shareholders and customers ? . . .

It will be asked where is the capital to come from ; how are poor working men to furnish the necessary funds ? The answer is perfectly simple. The members of the retail stores have only to authorise their committees to appropriate the necessary sum per member before declaring their next dividend, and the thing is done ; nay the stores which purchase largely from the Wholesale have only to allow their dividends to be retained in that establishment, and that will be sufficient for the present purpose. . . . The necessary money exists in plenty ; it only needs impounding like a river at its source, in order to be made useful to the whole community, instead of contributing to the profits or the pleasures of a few individuals.

We understand the resolutions of the directors of the Wholesale to be,

(a) To take 400 additional shares in the Printing Society.
(b) To purchase premises for the manufacture of biscuits.
(c) To commence a boot and shoe manufactory, and to procure suitable premises in which to conduct the Manchester trade, i.e. a regular home-trade warehouse, including articles of general drapery.
(d) To establish a blanket manufactory, or take shares in one, commenced on the federative principle.

13. THE CO-OPERATIVE CONGRESS AND THE CO-OPERATIVE UNION

[The Owenite Co-operators held regular annual Congresses in the 1830s and 1840s ; and a number of Conferences were organised in the 1850s, largely under Christian Socialist influences. But no permanent national organisation for the entire Co-operative movement came into being until 1869, when the Central Co-operative Agency (a revival of Neale's organisation of the 1850s), in conjunction with the Lancashire and Yorkshire Co-operative Conference Association, called in London a gathering which became the first of a regular annual series of Co-operative Congresses and gave birth in 1870 to a Co-operative Central Board, the embryo of the modern Co-operative Union.]

From a Circular issued by the Central Co-operative Agency, October 1868.

PROPOSED CO-OPERATIVE CONGRESS
To be held in London in February 1869.

The rapid growth of Co-operation is one of the most remarkable facts in connection with modern history.

Originating with the working classes, a system of business has been introduced, which, if rightly conducted, promises to change completely the social and industrial aspect of the country, by altering in its very essence the relationship between buyer and seller, employer and employed.

Whether this most important movement shall be so wisely conducted as to achieve a speedy and complete success, with as little disturbance and loss as possible to those interests and persons that are likely to be affected by it, is above all others a question of deep interest to the community, especially to those who, as Co-operators, are practically engaged in working out the change.

Co-operation is spreading everywhere; but its leading principles are not strictly defined — Its methods of business, either in distribution or production, as operating in the different societies are not in harmony. Its success in individual cases is doubtful where it might be certain; whilst the failures and losses, through the mistakes of ignorance or selfishness, are not only hurtful to those who enter on such experiments, but are a grave discouragement to thousands who, were it not for these, would readily enrol themselves in the ranks of Co-operation.

The success of the movement is no longer doubtful; but there are obstacles to be removed, and dangers to be encountered, which render counsel necessary amongst those who have studied the principle of Co-operation, and who have practically engaged themselves in its working.

How shall the union of the stores and other similar associations be secured, so that the weak and the strong — those of old standing and long experience, and those just entering into life — may be made mutually useful, helping each other's growth, and securing each other's success ?

What steps shall be taken to secure those further and higher developments of business connected with the wholesale, and with import and export, which the growing importance of the Co-operative movement render necessary; or such protection as those engaged in associative labour may require ?

What may be needful in the way of Propagandism ?

And, above all, how the relative claims of Labour and Capital on profits shall be adjusted, so as to secure the truest and fairest measure of advantage for both ?

A scientific developement of association will lead to a safe issue; Co-operation means united efforts for defined objects; and those efforts cannot be effectively made without a clear and thorough understanding of what is aimed at, on the part of those concerned in the movement.

In this view a meeting of gentlemen who take an interest in the various associative movements was held on the 28th. of August . . . when it was agreed unanimously to call a Congress, to meet in London in February, 1869. . . .

BUSINESS OF CONGRESS.

1. To consider what further steps can be taken to give effect to the resolution of the Manchester Congress, viz. — " To utilize the organisation of the Trade Unions for co-operative purposes ".
2. IIow to make Co-operative societies mutually helpful.
3. To consider the possibility of forming an organisation of all Co-operators and Co-operative societies, both at home and abroad.
4. What are the best means to bring the productions of Co-operative societies into the co-operative and general market ?
5. What are the best practical means to promote a knowledge and practice of true Co-operation among the people ?
6. To discuss the propriety of instituting a system of Banking, and Labour Exchange, for the purpose of aiding the developement of true Co-operation.
7. How can Co-operation be best applied to Agriculture, so as

to be a means of improving the condition of the agricultural labourer ?

8. How can Co-operative Manufacturing societies avail themselves of the Land, so as to unite agriculture with manufactures ?

14. THE REVIVAL OF CO-OPERATIVE PRODUCTION

[In the late 1860s and early 1870s there was a great revival of Co-operative Producers' Societies, sponsored in many cases by the Trade Unions. The coal miners were especially active in the starting of Co-operative Collieries ; and many Co-operative Textile Mills were also set up, as well as many 'Working class Limiteds' — that is, joint-stock companies founded with capital mainly supplied by textile workers. These latter were in many cases partly sponsored by the Consumers' Co-operative Societies, but soon lost all connection with the Co-operative movement. The urge to embark on Co-operative Production was especially strong on the North-East Coast, where, in addition to collieries, the Ouseburn Engineering Works was set up as a Co-operative venture, and an Industrial Bank was started to finance Co-operative Producers' Societies. When the boom of the early 1870s gave place to severe depression later in the decade, most of these ventures speedily came to grief, though a few managed to survive.]

(*a*) From *The Co-operator*, February 15, 1868.

PARTNERSHIPS OF INDUSTRY.

GREENING AND COMPANY, LIMITED,

Manufacturers of Iron Gates, Fences, Palisades, Espaliers, Hurdles, Tree Guards, Garden Seats, Verandahs, Vases, Fountains, Tomb Railings, Stable Fittings, Garden Rollers, Poultry Houses, Emigrants' Houses, Bridges, Corn-rick Stands, etc. Also, Wire Strained Fences, Rope Fences and Moveable Fences for Railways, Parks, Farms, Gardens, Game Preserves, Poultry Courts, Sheep Walks, etc. ; also of Wire Netting, Plant Guards and Protectors, Garden Bordering and Archways, Aviaries, Pea and Plant Trainers, Pheasantries, Hen Coops, and Garden Lounges.

For Catalogues and information, address, enclosing Stamps — MESSRS. GREENING & CO., 4, Warren-st. Manchester, & Victoria Iron and Wire Works, Salford.

TRADE   MARK

THE COBDEN MEMORIAL MILLS
SABDEN, LANCASHIRE.

Nominal Capital, £80,000 in £10 Shares. 6,000 Shares to be issued of £10 each — £60,000. 2,000 Shares to be reserved for Workpeople — £20,000. The Calls upon the Shares are £1 on Application, £1 on Allotment, £1 Quarterly, until sufficient Capital has been called for working out the enterprise. The Calls upon Co-operators' Shares will be received ' at 1/6 per week, by the Secretaries of Clubs in almost every town.

Every inducement will be given to the Servants of the Company to do their duty. They will have special facilities for taking up Shares by Weekly Subscriptions ; and one-half of the surplus profits above 10 per cent. will be divided amongst them, in proportion to the position they hold in the Company's service.

Application for Shares may be addressed to

EDWARD OWEN GREENING,
4, Warren-street, Manchester.

CO-OPERATIVE COLLIERIES — THE SOUTH BUCKLEY COAL AND FIRE-BRICK COMPANY, LIMITED — Nominal Capital, £50,000 in £10 Shares. 4,000 Shares to be issued — £40,000. 1,000 Shares to be reserved for Workpeople — £10,000.

To ensure the most profitable working of the enterprise, the remuneration of the Directors is made contingent on Profits ; and the Collieries and Brickworks will be placed under the system which has proved so successful in the case of the Whitwood and Methley Collieries in Yorkshire, where a bonus is paid to the Servants of the Company in proportion to the profits earned above 10 per cent. This arrangement has been found to induce zealous co-operation by them in the promotion of the interests of the Company ; to lessen the chances of disputes and strikes ; and to result in larger production, and greater and more regular profits than are made even by private firms.

EDWARD OWEN GREENING,
4, Warren-street, Manchester.

AGRICULTURAL CO-OPERATION—This Association supplies its members with Implements and Machines by the best

Makers, and with Unadulterated Seeds, Manures, and Manufactured Cattle Food, at cost price, upon the Co-operative system. An investment of £1 and upwards (bearing interest dividend) constitutes Membership, after election by Council. No further liability. Rules and all information post-free on receipt of two stamps, or by personal application at the Offices of the Association.

EDWD. OWEN GREENING,
Managing Director.

Offices — 29, Parliament-street, Westminster ;
4, Warren-street, Manchester.

" THE INDUSTRIAL PARTNERSHIPS' RECORD ", price 2d. monthly ; or forwarded, post-free, on the day of publication — Single copy, 2/6 per annum ; 2 copies, 4/6 do. ; 3 copies, 6/- do. ; 4 copies, 7/6 do. (No. 1 appeared on 1st March, 1867).

' " THE RECORD " is an Illustrated Monthly Paper, advocating the PARTNERSHIPS OF INDUSTRY, in which *the Profits are divided between the Workers and the Capitalists.* Amongst the Contributors are Mr. THOS. HUGHES, M.P., Mr. J. M. LUDLOW, and Mr. LLOYD JONES. A Specimen Copy will be sent on receipt of 3 stamps. It may also be had of the Publishers, F. PITMAN, Paternoster-row, and F. FARRAH, Strand, London ; and from " THE INDUSTRIAL PARTNERSHIPS' RECORD " Office, 4, Warren-Street, Manchester.

TO TRADE UNIONS.

In order to make known the principles of INDUSTRIAL PARTNERSHIPS among members of Trades Unions, grants of back numbers of *The Record* will be made to Secretaries and others who will undertake to circulate them. All applications should be accompanied by a small subscription to cover postage, etc. Apply to E. O. Greening, *The Industrial Partnerships' Record* Office, 4, Warren-street, Manchester.

CONVENIENT INVESTMENTS AT FIVE PER CENT— The Directors of the COBDEN MEMORIAL MILLS are now prepared to receive Deposits upon Interest at FIVE per Cent, secured by Mortgages, Debentures, or Promissory Notes bearing the Company's Seal. These Advances will be withdrawable at any time upon the following Notice :—

For Sums up to £20 . 14 Days' Notice | For Sums up to £100 . One Month's Notice.

For Form of Application, address — EDW. OWEN GREEN-ING, 4 Warren-Street, Manchester.

Price 1d. or Free by Post for Two Stamps. 12 pp. 8vo. " The Present Position and Prospects of Partnerships of Industry." A Paper prepared at the request of the Economy and Trade Section of the Social Science Association. By EDW. OWEN GREENING. Published by request.

(b) From Maberly Phillips, " A History of Banks, Bankers and Banking in Northumberland, Durham and North Yorkshire ", 1894.

INDUSTRIAL BANK, LIMITED. NEWCASTLE-UPON-TYNE.
Founded 1872. Failed 1876.

In 1872 a bank was projected in Newcastle under the above name. The Prospectus issued at the time will best explain the aim and purport of the promoters. It states :—

" This company is formed with the object of supplying Banking facilities to Industrial Societies, and to the trading and commercial classes generally, on the mutual principle. That principle, as applied to Assurance, is well understood, and has had a large success. After providing for a reserve fund, all profits above 10 per cent. will be equally divided between capital, and those members who are customers and whose transactions with the company have been profitable. The Company proposes to undertake all legitimate Banking business. Its operations will not be confined to Industrial Societies, although both from them and from the general public it has already received promises of a large amount of support. From a return ordered by the House of Commons to be printed on 26th April, 1871, it appears that of 1,375 Industrial Societies, which had been registered to 31st December, 1870, 749 made returns. The number of members of these 749 Societies, was 249,113 ; the Share Capital, £2,034,261, the Loan Capital, £179,128, the amount received in goods, £8,202,466. The value of buildings, fixtures, and land, £962,276 ; the capital invested with companies incorporated under the Companies' Act, £204,696 ; and the disposable net profit realized from all sources during the year, £555,435. In Northumberland there are 27 Industrial Societies which gave returns, with 12,426 members, a turnover of £384,617, and net profit amounting to £28,479. In Durham the numbers were — Societies, 42 ; members, 18,019 ; cash received for goods, £509,584 ; profits, £47,338.

. . . The Directors guarantee that the Company will commence business with the entire Capital perfectly intact, the whole of the preliminary, legal, and other expenses being covered by the fund created by the payment of 1/- per share, and any surplus therefrom will go to the formation of a reserve fund. . . . A considerable number of shares has already been applied for, but it is intended that all *bona fide* applications shall be fairly considered, regard being had to priority of date of application.

CAPITAL.

Total Capital £250,000
Cash Capital, to be paid up . . £150,000

The capital of the Company is composed of Fifty Thousand Shares of £5 each, 10,000 of which are now issued, £3 per Share to be paid as follows :—11/- on application, 1/- of which will be devoted to the payment of preliminary expenses, etc., 10/- on Allotment ; First Call of 10/- on 1st August, 1872, the remaining Calls not to exceed 10/- per Share, and one month's notice to be given of each Call.

Provisional Directors — John Hunter Rutherford, William Douglass, John Curry, Joseph France, George Fryer, Samuel Thompson, John Burnip ; Manager — Alexander Hannay ; London Agent — The Alliance Bank, Ld ; Solicitor — W. Brewis Elsdon ; Auditors — Benson, Eland, & Co. ; Secretary (*pro tem.*) — John McPherson ; Temporary Offices, 4, Royal Arcade."

The shares appear to have been freely applied for, most of the large Co-operative Societies in the district becoming holders. The doors of the bank were opened for business on Monday, July 8th, 1872, the offices being at the south side of the Pilgrim Street entrance to the Royal Arcade, the same premises that had been occupied by the Newcastle Savings' Bank. A considerable business was done, especially with the Co-operative Societies. In July, 1875, the report is as follows :—

" The directors congratulate the shareholders that notwithstanding the depression of trade during the half year, the bank has made steady progress. 301 new shares have been issued, and from the premiums £100 has been added to the reserve fund, which now stands at £1,300." A net profit was shown of £1,020, out of which it was proposed to pay a dividend of 3/- per share, or at the rate of 10 per cent. per annum.

At the meeting held in January, 1876, a dividend of 1/6 per share was resolved upon. Sundry questions were asked as to the bank's position in regard to the Ouseburn Engine Works (started and carried on for a few years upon co-operative principles), which had recently failed. The officials reported that there might be a loss, though not greater than the reserve fund would cover. But dark days were in store, and the Ouseburn Engine Works proved to be a mill-stone that dragged the ill-fated bank to the ground. Early in October, 1876, rumours were abroad regarding the stability of the " Industrial " and on the 6th of that month the following notice was posted on the doors :—" Pending the negotiations for amalgamation with the Wholesale Co-operative Society, the business of this bank will be suspended for a few days ".

The business of the bank being greatly confined to the Co-operative Societies, little public inconvenience was experienced by the stoppage.

A great number of meetings were held, complications arose between the bank, the Co-operative Wholesale Society, and the Ouseburn Engine Works. Eventually liquidators were appointed and the bank was wound up. On January 24th, 1877, a first dividend of 3/4 in the pound was paid.

15. CO-OPERATIVE BANKING

[In the same year as the Industrial Bank was founded at Newcastle-on-Tyne, the Co-operative Wholesale Society decided to set up its own Banking Department, out of which its extensive banking activities have gradually grown. At first, it received deposits only from member *societies*, and used its resources almost entirely for financing its own trading operations. Abraham Greenwood was the principal mover in its establishment, and was in charge of it from 1874 to 1898.]

From Percy Redfern, " The Story of the C.W.S.", 1913.

Resolution carried at the Quarterly Meeting of the Co-operative Wholesale Society on May 18th, 1872.

That, as a means to commence and gradually develop a banking business, authority be given to the Committee to receive loans from the members withdrawable at call, and subject to 1 per cent below the minimum Bank of England rate of interest, the sums to be used in our own business, or lent out on approved security.

XVII

TRADE UNIONISM, 1840–1868

INTRODUCTION

AFTER the great defeat of 1834, the Trade Union movement fell back upon the individual Societies which had been drawn into the successive attempts to form a 'General Union'. Some large Societies survived; but in most trades national organisation disappeared, and only local bodies remained. The Builders' Union broke up, only the stone-masons maintaining a strong national Society, though a shadow of national organisation continued among the Carpenters and Joiners. The first large-scale revival occurred in 1842, in connection with the great strike movement already described in Section XV (see Section XV, 7). During this period the miners succeeded in establishing a National Association, which lasted till the end of the 1840s, and then broke down. Meanwhile, the attempt to create a 'General Union' had been renewed in 1845, with some temporary success.

A new phase set in with the creation of the Amalgamated Society of Engineers in 1850–1851; for the A.S.E. set a new standard of stability with its high contributions and benefits, its centralisation of control, and its moderate policy. This 'new model' was imitated in other trades, e.g. by the Amalgamated Society of Carpenters and Joiners in 1861. In the meantime, considerable progress had been made in securing Trade Union recognition and rights of collective bargaining in the cotton and hosiery trades, and also in the building industry in some areas. The London Trades Council, reorganised and put on a stable basis in 1860, acted as a central agency for the movement, especially for the skilled crafts, during the 1860s, until its place was taken after 1868 by the Trades Union Congress. The miners' movement revived on a large scale in the 1860s, under the leadership of Alexander Macdonald; and there was also a revival of the agitation for factory reform. In the main, the development of Trade Unionism during this period was confined to skilled workers, who alone were able to establish durable combinations of the new type. The Reform Act of 1867, by enfranchising the skilled workers in the towns (see Section XX), added greatly to the influence of the Trade Unions on Parliament.

See " Short History ", Part II, chapter 3.
" Common People ", chapters 28-30.

1. MEETINGS OF TRADES' DELEGATES

[Although the London Trades Council dates its foundation from 1860, the organisation of the London Trades was in fact nearly continuous, at any rate from the period just after the Napoleonic Wars. Even when there was no formal ' Trades Union ' or Council in existence, there were means of summoning meetings of delegates from the various Societies when need arose, a common purpose being the organisation of help for Societies involved in strikes or lock-outs. Similar meetings of delegates were held in other towns — *e.g.* Sheffield, Manchester, Glasgow ; and these developed later into formal Trades Councils with a continuous existence. The destruction of the Grand National Trades Union in 1834 did not involve the discontinuance of these delegate meetings, which were important as links between districts as well as among the Trade Societies in each town.]

From *The Charter*, March 31, 1839. Resolution carried unanimously at a meeting of delegates from the Trades Societies in London.

That this meeting feeling that the cause of the journeymen bookbinders is the cause of all trades' societies, and seeing that if the bookbinders fail in their present struggle it may be speedily necessary for them to defend themselves against similar attempts to suppress their societies, it becomes necessary, and we hereby pledge ourselves to support the journeymen bookbinders by all the means in our power.

2. THE MINERS' ASSOCIATION OF GREAT BRITAIN AND IRELAND

[The miners had played a part in the industrial activity of the early 1830s, especially in Northumberland and Durham and in Lancashire. There was a great revival in the early 1840s, when, under the leadership of Martin Jude, the various district associations formed a national body, and engaged both in strike action and in legal conflict with the colliery owners concerning the conditions of employment, especially the yearly bond and the conditions of virtual servitude which still existed in some of the coalfields, above all in Staffordshire. The M.A.G.B. engaged the Chartist lawyer, William Prowting Roberts (1806–1871), to fight the miners' battle in the courts — which he did with great success. But the M.A.G.B. did not endure : its energies were worn out by the continual struggles of the ' Hungry 'Forties ', and by 1850 it had practically ceased to exist, though county Unions remained in a number of areas, especially the North-East Coast and Yorkshire.]

From R. L. Galloway, " Annals of Coal Mining and the Coal Trade " (2nd Series, 1898), chapter 14.

From the time of the strikes in the north of England in 1831 and 1832, the relations between the coal-owners and the pitmen continued strained, and the men were most difficult to deal with (*Child. Employ. Com.*, Append. i., p. 625). No long period elapsed before a renewal of the struggle took place. It can scarcely be doubted that the time-honoured arrangement of the yearly bond had considerably altered in character, and become somewhat unequal, after the curtailment or withdrawal of the guaranteed wage, as appears to have been done by some at least of the coal-owners ; this being one of the chief benefits the pitmen had formerly enjoyed under the bargain.

. . . . . .

In the latter part of the year 1836 the northern pitmen began to renew their agitation, a meeting being held on Saturday, October 31, at Black Fell, near Gateshead (*Min. Jour.*, iii. 123). Several meetings were also held in north Northumberland during December following, to endeavour to abolish the bondage system in that district (Latimer's *Loc. Rec.*, p. 66), but the attempt was wholly unsuccessful. After a strike of some months the pitmen resumed work in March, 1837, on the same terms as previously (*ibid.* p. 70; *Trans. N.E. Inst.*, xv., 236). . . .

The pitmen of the north of England took some part in the Chartist agitation of 1838–9. The chief organ of the movement was Feargus, or Fergus, O'Connor's paper, *The Northern Star and Leeds General Advertiser*, established in November, 1837, to promulgate the Chartist programme of universal suffrage, etc. . . .

In the autumn of 1842 a considerable amount of turbulence prevailed among the colliers in Scotland, Yorkshire, Lancashire, and Staffordshire (*Mid. Min. Com.*, First Report, p. 25), the ebullition in the latter coalfield being particularly violent. . . . On August 1, a great meeting, advertised by Arthur O'Neil, a notorious

Chartist agitator, was held at West Bromwich, attended, according to the miners' account, by 15,000 persons.[1] A few of those present carried sticks, but great precautions had been taken to anticipate disturbance, a meeting of magistrates being held in the town on the same day, and soldiers riding about with drawn swords. No demonstration took place beyond a few Chartist speakers. Resolutions to the following effect were proposed by O'Neil, and unanimously carried :—

" That the men should strike until the masters conceded the wages agreed to at the meeting.

" That they should not resume work till the masters gave 4s. a day of nine hours, allowing one hour out of them for dinner.

" That half-days, quarter-days, and buildases, were oppressive, and must be wholly done away with.

" That the truck system should be discountenanced.

" That they would no longer suffer themselves to be treated as slaves, in a country called the land of freedom."

Some other meetings were held, one at Wednesbury ; but subsequently, on account of the distracted state of the district, the holding of meetings was made illegal by Royal proclamation. The strike was carried on from four to seven weeks, and was characterised by great violence and intimidation, particularly in the Pottery district. A special Commission sat at Stafford for the trial of the offenders, many of whom were very heavily sentenced. . . .

While the associations, or unions, which had been formed among the miners in various districts, had been organised chiefly with a view to obtaining the same object — viz., higher wages and shorter hours of work — they had hitherto been of a more or less local and insulated character, and when a strike took place in one district it had the effect of driving the trade away to another. A more comprehensive scheme now began to be entertained — viz., to form a combination of miners all over the kingdom. The project is said (*Min. Jour.*, xiv., 65) to have originated with Fergus O'Connor, for the purpose of forwarding his own political views of universal suffrage. The idea was immediately acted upon, and on November 7, 1842, " The Miners' Association of Great Britain and Ireland " was established at Wakefield, with John Armstrong, president, and John Hall, secretary (*Member's Card*; Tremenheere's *Report*, 1847, p. 14).

The principal objects of the association, as set forth in article 1

[1] The civil authorities estimated the total number at 10,000, of whom only about 6,000 took part at the meeting.

of the rules and regulations, were " to unite the coal, lead, and ironstone miners of Great Britain and Ireland, with a view to equalise and diminish the hours of labour, and to obtain the highest possible amount of wages for the labour of the miner ".

On the recommendation of Mr. O'Connor, Mr. William Prowting Roberts was appointed legal adviser to the association, at a salary of £700 a year. Paid delegates were also employed to visit the mining districts and induce the workpeople to enroll themselves as members.

The pitmen of Northumberland and Durham joined the new association in large numbers, forming, indeed, its most important section. In accordance with the policy of the union, they commenced restricting their day's work in May 1843, a month after the annual binding had taken place. . . .

The association which had been formed by the miners at this time, was admitted to be the most comprehensive and complete that had ever been established. Every expedient was had recourse to, to make the combination all-embracing. When promises of higher wages and shorter hours were insufficient, threats and intimidation were not spared. Guns were discharged at night into cottage windows ; men were ill-treated at or on their way to work, their gardens destroyed, or their tools taken from them and broken ; one man was thrown over a bridge 20 ft. high, and various annoyances of a minor kind were resorted to (Tremenheere's *Report*, 1846, p. 7). . . .

The Miners' Association having attained to extensive proportions in the early part of 1844, numbering about 60,000 members (Tremenheere's *Report*, 1847, p. 14), mostly composed of the miners of Northumberland and Durham, Lancashire, and Lanarkshire (other districts also having unions of their own), a general strike was in contemplation, the avowed object of which (Fordyce's *Coal and Iron*, p. 34) was to stop all the manufactories until their demands were conceded. . . .

On March [1844] a conference of delegates was held at Glasgow, at which the question of a general strike was discussed, when the votes were given as follows :—

For the strike	. . .	23,357
Against „	. . .	28,042
For a partial strike	. .	1,528
Majority against any strike	.	3,157

Inasmuch, however, as the delegates from Northumberland and Durham represented that their organisation was complete, and that the expiration of the yearly bonds on April 5 offered a favourable opportunity of enforcing their demands, it was agreed that they might suspend work; though the other districts were not to be called upon to contribute pecuniary aid, and the Scotch miners likewise declined to join in the payment of Mr. Roberts, the solicitor.

Accordingly, when the bonds expired on April 5, nearly the whole of the persons employed below ground in Northumberland, and Durham, amounting to upwards of 22,000 men and boys (Tremenheere's *Report*, 1846, p. 6.), ceased work and entered upon the fourth great struggle with their employers since the time when they began to form themselves into unions about 1825–6.

.   .   .   .   .   .

There was a curious element of religion in the strike, on the side of the men. Many of the local preachers were its most active supporters. Prayers for its success were offered up in the chapels; and it was no uncommon thing, for a wayside crowd to join in supplicating the assistance of heaven, and to request that the men who were brought from a distance to work in a colliery — the " blacklegs " as they called them — might be injured (Tremenheere's *Report*, 1846, pp. 8, 16, 25). . . .

But not long subsequently the case of the miners began to assume a hopeless aspect. They had parted with their furniture and their clothes, and even the wedding rings of their wives, and incurred debt wherever possible. They had endured great hardships and privations, large numbers of them bivouacking in the country lanes after being ejected from their cottages. But worst of all, their places were being filled up with new workmen from the Welsh and Cumberland coal mines, some from the lead mines, others from Ireland. The pitmen had been impervious alike to kind offers, threats, and ejectments, but the policy of filling up the pits with strangers was too much for them. After continuing for a period of about nineteen and a half weeks, the strike virtually terminated about the second week in August (Latimer's *Loc. Rec.* p. 182), when the men began to return to work at their old prices. . . .

The great strike of 1844, proved the breaking up of the yearly bondage system in the north of England. For many years afterwards a monthly notice only was made use of. At a later period an attempt was made to reintroduce it, and it was temporarily adopted at a number of collieries in Durham, but it never again became the general practice.

3. THE NATIONAL ASSOCIATION OF UNITED TRADES FOR THE PROTECTION OF LABOUR, 1845

[This body was the first, after the collapse of 1834, to revive the idea of ' General Union ' on a national scale. It was intended to be, not a comprehensive Union, but a Federation of independent Societies for mutual help both in securing improved wages and conditions, or resisting reductions, and in working for industrial legislation and the recognition of the rights of collective bargaining. It favoured ' Boards of Trade ', *i.e.* joint bodies of employers and workers for the regulation of wages and conditions, and also conciliation and arbitration. Although it never commanded general support, it lasted until 1867, and was largely responsible for securing both the Molestation of Workmen Act of 1859 (see p. 551) and the Conciliation Act of 1867.

The Conference of Trade Unions which launched the N.A.U.T.P.L. decided to divide the functions proposed for it between two separate bodies, and accordingly set up side by side with it the National Association of United Trades for the Employment of Labour, which was to raise capital for settling Trade Unionists on farms or establishing Co-operative Workshops. The Chartist influence is evident in the plans for land settlement, which were contemporary with those of the Chartist National Land Company. Actually, the Association concerned itself mainly with industrial employment. In 1848 the two Associations were merged ; and thereafter little was heard of the proposals for self-employment, which were carried on mainly through the Redemption Societies until the Christian Socialists came into the field. (See pp. 432 and 434.) T. Slingsby Duncombe, M.P., President of the N.A.U.T.P.L. and its sister body, was also associated with O'Connor's Land Scheme. He had been Radical M.P. for Finsbury since 1835.]

(a) From *The Northern Star*, March 29, 1845.

Report of the Committee appointed at the Inaugural Conference of the National Association of United Trades for the Protection of Labour to consider plans of activity.

" The *immediate* measures which it appears to your committee that conference might usefully take into consideration are the following :—

1. A society to be called the Association of United Trades for the Protection of Industry.

2. A Central committee to carry out the objects of the said Association, and the formation of a fund to defray the necessary expenses.

3. The leading objects of the Association may be divisible into two departments — the first external having reference to the influence

of the Legislature on the conditions of the industrious classes; the second internal, or the efforts made by the Trades to improve their own conditions.

With respect to the first of these divisions, your committee suggests that the Central Committee should be empowered and instructed to take every opportunity, by means of petitions to Parliament, deputations to the Government and members of both houses of the Legislature, cheap publications, public meetings, and to other legal, reasonable and peaceable measures to enforce the adoption of shorter hours of labour wherever practicable. . . .

4. Another measure to which serious consideration should be directed is, the establishment of local Boards of Trade, similar to those which have so long existed in France and Belgium, composed of masters and operatives, to whom all matters affecting the regulation of wages, duration of labour, disputes etc. should be referred, and their decisions have the authority of law. . . .

5. The second division of the Association should be the collection and diffusion of information, as to the means by which the capital skill and labour of the trades can be applied for their own benefit, and especially to enable them to abstract from the labour market, and set to profitable employment, the redundant hands, who, if suffered to remain in it, would reduce the wages of the whole trade to which they belong . . . upon this most important point your committee beg to be clearly understood : they propose no definite plan, but merely throw out the suggestion as one deserving of serious consideration from the conference.

6. The Central Committee should be instructed to carefully prepare a constitution for concentrating the energies, legalising the proceedings, and giving practical effect to the growing desire for location in the land, and other measures for the profitable employment of the funds of such Unions as might be desirous of using them."

(*b*) From a Circular, 1845.

THE NATIONAL ASSOCIATION OF UNITED TRADES FOR THE EMPLOYMENT OF LABOUR IN AGRICULTURE AND MANUFACTURES.

(Provisionally registered.) — Shares £5 each, payable by Quarterly Instalments of 10s. per share.

President : THOMAS S. DUNCOMBE, ESQ., M.P.
Bankers : THE UNION BANK OF LONDON.

THIS ASSOCIATION is to be composed of Subscribers to its Funds, who agree to be governed by its Laws, and its objects are—

1.—The Purchase or Rental of Lands whereon to locate and employ the surplus labour of the Association, in such manner as shall be most conducive to their own welfare and that of the Association.

2.—The Erection or Rental of Buildings for Domestic, Industrial and Commercial purposes, in such localities as may be best suited for these respective objects, and the promotion of the general interests of the Association.

3.—The application of these Lands and Buildings so as [to] meet the corporate and individual requirements of the Members of the Association. 1. To afford to Trades in their corporate capacity the power of Leasing in perpetuity, or of purchasing in fee simple, such Lands and Buildings belonging to the Association as they may require for the location and employment of their Surplus Members; and also the power of Investing their Funds with the Association by way of Loan or Mortgage on any of the Property of the Association. 2. To divide such portions of the Estates purchased by the Association, as may be thought expedient into small Farms, to build thereon suitable Cottages and Out-houses, and to Sell and Lease the Property thus improved to individuals selected in accordance with the Laws of the Association. All Leasehold Farms may be Sold, and the proceeds re-invested in fresh Estates, to be improved and dealt with in like manner, in order that the subscribed Capital of the Association may, to the largest possible extent, promote the purchase of, and the drafting upon the Land the unemployed Members of the Association.

It is the only Institution in this country which is capable of providing for the wants and necessities of the Industrious Classes upon the principle of Self-Support.

In the first place, a ready market is found for the labour of the Mechanic and Artizan by the strongest of human ties — the Bond of Union — unity is strength, and in no instance can be seen so powerfully and with advantage, as in an Association of this nature. Every Member of the Association determinedly combines with his Fellow-man for the Protection of Industry, and not, as is erroneously supposed, for the purpose of opposing the Employer. Every man has an undoubted right to a "*fair day's wages for a fair day's work*", and the conduct of the employer towards the workman but too plainly shows that the combination is not on the part of the man towards the master, but of the employer towards the workman.

The workman is unable to stand out against the oppression of the Capitalist, except by a fair, vigorous, and unyielding union of heart and purpose, which is perfectly consistent with the Divine Law of doing unto others as we would be done unto.

The working man has yet a great deal to do in order to carry out this grand point; it is the duty of everyone to assist with his counsel, advice and means in defending the working man from oppression, and this can only be done by the means pointed out.

A very large number of men are continually employed by the Association in making up Goods for Sale, and the public can purchase them at a very small per centage above the cost price : the object being to keep men in constant employment, rather than they should submit to a reduction of Wages.

It is the duty as well as to the interest of the working man to support this Institution by every means in his power, and to encourage by his example the efforts of the industrious classes to maintain themselves in their true position without degradation, for it is only by a zealous union and co-operation that the industrious classes can successfully resist the overbearing extortion of the employer, and become their own masters.

N.B.   All applications for Goods, and lists of prices, to be made to Mr THOMAS WINTER, 11, Tottenham Court Road, London.

(c) From *The Labour League* [1] August 5, 1848.

. . . To the Members of the National Association of United Trades for the Protection and Employment of Industry, it is unnecessary for us to state in detail the objects of that association. But at the commencement of our weekly labours, and in view of the publication falling into the hands of thousands who have not seen the monthly reports previously issued by the central committee, we shall as briefly as possible, state the objects for which that association is formed, and which this periodical will advocate.

They are the following :—

1st. The protection of industry against the unreasonable aggressions of capital, by means of mediation, arbitration, and where

---

[1] This was the official organ of the Association.

necessary, pecuniary support, derived from the subscriptions of the trades composing the association, which is formed on the basis of a Mutual Assurance Society, each member receiving benefits in proportion to his payments.

2nd. The employment of that surplus labour, which constitutes the reserve in the competitive market, by means of which wages are always kept down to the lowest subsistence level. Until this is done, no effectual safeguard against the constant deterioration of the working classes will be secured. The association proposes to effect this object by applying the funds heretofore squandered in strikes to reproductive purposes, and by setting to work in their own trades, as far as possible, all those entitled to pecuniary support. In addition to this, the formation of an Employment Fund of £50,000 within two years, by means of graduated weekly payments according to wages, was resolved upon at the annual conference of the Association held in Liverpool during Whit week. The subscriptions to this fund to be invested in a bank in the name of three trustees : T. Wakley, Esq., M.P., Sharman Crawford, Esq., M.P., and John Fielden, Esq., the late member for Oldham, whose exertions in favour of the working classes have made him so universally and deservedly respected. Previous to the completion of the fund and the commencement of practical operations, it is proposed to apply to Parliament for an act to legalise the proceedings in the same way as those of railway companies, and on obtaining that act the fund will be devoted to the formation of self-supporting industrial colonies, in various parts of the country, for the benefit of the trades.

These two objects lie within the power of the trades themselves. The third object of the Association is to operate upon public opinion and upon Parliament in favour of certain changes in the condition of the trades, which cannot be obtained without legislative intervention. These are :—

" To cause the employers in trades, wherever practicable, to provide properly lighted and ventilated workshops for those employed by them, in order to do away with the middleman and sweating system, and prevent the numerous evils arising from work being done in private houses.

Regulation of the hours of labour in all trades, with a view to equalise and diffuse employment among the working classes, so that some shall not be overworked, while others are starving for want of employment.

The employment of the surplus labour of the country by the Government in useful public works, such as the reclamation of waste land, arterial drainage, improvement of harbours, deepening of rivers, etc.

Sanitary regulations of a general and comprehensive character.

The appointment of a minister of labour to superintend the carrying out and practical operation of these various measures, for the improvement of the condition of the industrious classes."

4. THE POTTERS' UNION AND EMIGRATION SOCIETY

[The Potters had been among the first Unions to recover from the defeat of 1834, and in the 1840s they had a powerful Society. It was widely believed, both in the ' Hungry 'Forties ' and later, that as wages depended on supply and demand, the only means of raising them was to create a scarcity of labour ; and a number of Trade Unions took steps actively to encourage emigration.]

(*a*) From *The Potters' Examiner*, February 24, 1844. From ' The Laws of the United Branches of Operative Potters '.

FUNDAMENTAL PRINCIPLE

Union in Strength

DEDUCTION

1st. The different branches of Operative Potters acknowledge, and believe in, this principle, by the fact that they have been, and now are, endeavouring, as far as possible, to unite, in one bond of unity, the operatives belonging to their respective branches.

2nd. This principle being acknowledged, it can only be advantageous in the ratio as large numbers of the various branches unite, whose interests are identical, practically carrying out, with a unity of sentiment and action, the objects they have in view.

3rd. It is therefore necessary, to secure the advantages of union, that the Slip-Makers, Throwers, Lookers to Ware, Turners, Handlers, Hollow-ware Pressers, Flat-Pressers, Printers, Oven-Men, Saggar-Makers, Kiln-Men, Packers, Warehouse-Men, China Potters, Painters and Gilders, form a consolidated union of their different branches, for the more fully carrying out the objects for which they, as separate societies, were organised.

The Union is anxious to avoid collisions between the employed and employer, so as to endanger a strike, or turn-out, feeling assured that they are alike injurious to both; but should a difference arise that may call for the interference of the Union, such difference shall be laid before the district board; and if not adjusted by them, the Central Board shall take such measures as may lead to an amicable agreement.

REGULATIONS AND LAWS.

Section 1. NAME.

1. This association shall be known by the name of the United Branches of Operative Potters Association and shall comprise members of the Slip-Makers, Throwers, Lookers to Ware, Turners, Handlers, Hollow-ware Pressers, Flat-Pressers, Printers, Oven-Men, Saggar-Makers, Kiln-Men, Packers, Warehouse-Men, China Potters, Painters and Gilders and all other branches in any way connected with the branches of the Potting business.

Section 2. OBJECTS.

2. To unite in the bonds of unity and friendship, the members comprising the above branches of Operative Potters, and to promote their physical, intellectual, moral and social improvement.

3. To collect every kind of information relating to the Union in general, and the above branches in particular, especially regarding the wages of labour, the habits of the labourer, and all those circumstances influencing the rate of prices and hours of employment.

4. To meet with each other for the purpose of digesting the information thus acquired, and to mature such plans as they believe will conduce to their well-being.

5. To publish their views and sentiments . . .

6. To take seriously into consideration the Unemployed; and to adopt such plans as shall be conducted to their general good and the interest of the Union.

7. To shorten the hours of labour, for the purpose of giving to all an opportunity of sharing in the existing demand for labour, and of placing the Potters in general in those independent, leisurable circumstances so highly requisite for mental and moral improvement.

8. To restrict as far as practicable, the number of Apprentices, to avoid, if possible, the growing evils of Surplus Labour.

9. To obtain a general and equitable form of agreement between employers and employed.

EMIGRATION

10. To enter immediately, into practicable operations for the formation of a United, Joint Stock, Emigration Company, consisting of an unlimited number of Subscribers, in Shares of £1 each, to be paid in weekly instalments of not less than 1s., for the purpose of placing on the land, in easy and comfortable circumstances, numbers of our unfortunate fellow-operatives; and of giving to all a more favourable opportunity of accomplishing the great object we have in view; viz., a fair and just remuneration for labour.

(*b*) From *The Potters' Examiner*, July 20, 1844.

. . . Here we have a principle to act upon : make labour scarce, and you make it powerful. Power in the hands of working potters, would soon induce them to regulate the number of apprentices to a given number of journeymen, and also the number of hours in which it would be requisite for a working man to earn his " daily bread ". These important objects would most certainly form the great moving principle of this newly acquired power. But how to obtain this power is the present great consideration.

To obtain a clear understanding of this matter, it is first requisite that we should ascertain the *cause* of our present *weakness*.

The strength or weakness of an associated trade's body depends entirely on the number of its unemployed. If this be large, no combination can ever give a society strength; but if, on the contrary, the number of the unemployed be small, power will be the consequence, even though there be no combination whatever. . . . That society, therefore, that can put into operation plans and principles for the removal of its redundant hands, is in a position to realize all that a trade's society can consistently desire; namely, a reasonable price for labour, and full employ for the whole of its hands. The potters of Staffordshire are in that position; and, agreeably to the foregoing principles, have organised a company; and have enrolled the same under Act of Parliament; and which is calculated, if properly conducted, to realize that scarcity of labour so much required by all combined trades' bodies. That company is THE POTTERS' JOINT-STOCK EMIGRATION SOCIETY — the great safety valve of the United Branches of Operative Potters.

5. THE AMALGAMATED SOCIETY OF ENGINEERS

[In 1851 the Journeymen Steam-engine Makers' Society, already the most powerful Society among the engineering craftsmen, amalgamated with a number of small Societies to form the Amalgamated Society of Engineers, on a basis of strongly centralised control of policy and finance. The new Society, with its high rates of contributions and benefits and its combination of Trade Union and Friendly Society functions, became the model for the reorganisation of a number of other skilled crafts — carpenters and joiners, ironfounders, bricklayers, etc. We have seen earlier how at the outset it interested itself in projects of Co-operative Production. (See p. 442.)]

From the Rules of the Amalgamated Society of Engineers, 1850.

Rule XIII.

1. There shall be an equalisation of the funds in each branch every twelve months, immediately after the issuing of the yearly report, according to the number of members in each branch. The Executive Council shall authorise the debtor branches to pay to the creditor branches the equalisation money due to them, within twenty-eight days after receiving the report, in such manner, form, and place, as they may think best, and with the greatest security. The Executive Council shall have full power to cause one branch to remit to another branch, from time to time, whatever sums of money they may deem necessary to meet the expenditure of such branch. . . .

Rule XXII.

1. District committee and its duties. 2. Secretary and his duties. 3. Members when entitled to benefit. 4. Extent of fund. 5. Powers of committee. . . .

1. A committee of seven members shall be appointed in each locality or district where there is more than one branch of our society, each branch as nearly as practicable, appointing an equal number, varying their branch of trade as much as possible; and when only one branch of a society exists, the ordinary branch committee shall watch over and protect the interests of the trade. They shall have power to place on the funds of the society any member who may be discharged for refusing, in accordance with their advice, to infringe any of the rules or recognised customs of the trade; or who may be discharged for carrying into operation any measure for

the benefit of the trade, which has been agreed to by the Society, and authorised by the Executive Council, such as abolition of " piecework ", of " systematic overtime ", and such other measures as are calculated to improve its condition.

2. A secretary and president shall be appointed by each local committee every quarter. The secretary shall write to the General Secretary on the 1st of every month, stating the business transacted by the committee, the number of members in receipt of 15s. per week, and the opinion of the members in their district on the measures calculated to benefit the society and the trade.

3. Any member being discharged in conformity with this rule shall be entitled to the sum of 15s. per week until he again obtains employment; and if it is proved to the satisfaction of the district committee that he has not exerted himself to get employment, or has refused to accept a situation, he shall be disentitled to further relief.

4. No committee shall expend of this fund a greater amount weekly than is contributed by the members they represent, at the rate of 5d. per month, unless by the consent of the Executive Council.

5. If any circumstance takes place in a locality which jeopardises the situation of a number of members, the local committee shall refrain from advising them until the Executive Council shall have been consulted and their opinions ascertained. The Executive Council shall have power to appoint a deputation, if necessary, to attend at the place where such circumstance has arisen, and if it be decided to proceed with the matter, they shall have power to authorise a greater expenditure than the locality would otherwise be entitled to. But if they find that the expenditure of this fund exceeds the weekly income of 5d. per member in the aggregate, they shall have power to prohibit further claims upon it until the circumstances then at issue be decided.

Rule XXIII.

1. Systematic overtime and its discontinuance. 2. Piecework, etc.

1. That in order to secure to our members a good general prospect of employment, we repudiate " systematic overtime ", as being the cause of much evil, through giving to a number the privilege of working more than a legitimate week's time, whilst doing so deprives other members of situations, producing much domestic misery and causing a great expenditure of the Society's

funds. We, therefore, authorise the Executive Council to take steps for its immediate discontinuance by ascertaining the opinions of our members and the practices of various localities in relation thereto, and issuing a general order for all districts simultaneously to adopt this resolution. Any member refusing to comply with this resolution renders himself liable to be excluded. The district committee shall decide upon all cases of exemption from this resolution, which shall be in cases of accident, etc, to machinery, requiring instant and continuous attention.

2. That the same steps be taken to abolish piecework, to destroy the practice of working more than one lathe or machine, to prevent a greater number of apprentices or admission into one trade than are likely to find employment therein — apprentices to be in proportion of one to four journeymen ; and to endeavour by all reasonable means to assimilate the number of working hours in each district, so that uniformity may pervade the trade rules, in order that on subsequent occasions, if circumstances require a further reduction of the hours of labour, such may be accomplished without one district having to make greater advances than another.

6. THE ENGINEERING LOCK-OUT OF 1852

[The formation of the Amalgamated Society of Engineers was speedily followed by a big lock-out of its members by the engineering employers in Lancashire and London, its two chief strongholds. The employers accused the Society of attempting to interfere with ' management ' by placing a ban on overtime and on the forms of piecework then prevalent in the engineering trades. The Engineers received help in their resistance both from the Christian Socialists and from the workers in other trades ; and the lock-out gave rise in London to an attempt to promote wider unity, though this had for the time no effect. The engineers were driven back to work, and were forced in many cases to sign a 'document ', renouncing Trade Union membership, on which many employers insisted as a condition of employment. Those who signed, however, regarding their signatures as having been obtained under duress, did not leave the Society, which soon emerged stronger than before.]

(a) From *The Operative*, February 7, 1852.

Declaration of the Executive Council of the Amalgamated Society.

In consequence of the demands and intentions which have been attributed to the Amalgamated Society, the Executive Council have thought it necessary publicly to declare what they have done, and publicly to deny what they have not done. They have not demanded the discharge of unskilled workmen. They have not endeavoured to throw the skilled operative, not belonging to the Society, out of work, nor have they recommended others to do so. Neither have they countenanced a system of intimidation having that object. They do not seek to fix or to equalise wages, but hold the doctrine that wages should be settled by individual agreement. They do not endeavour to prevent the introduction of machinery; but by their skill and labour perfect and multiply it.

They do not attempt to bring about any of those things; but in their Circular to the employers carefully limit themselves to the questions of overtime and piecework — To these they still rigidly confine themselves, and they conceive that the reasons for asking for the cessation of these practices are sufficient to justify them.

They look upon overtime as both a privilege and an evil. A privilege because it holds out to men an opportunity of making more money; an evil, because that money is made at the expense of their own health, strength, mental powers, and happiness, as well as the welfare and independence of others. It is not the first time in the world's history that a privilege has been an evil at once to those whom it seemed to benefit, and those whom it evidently injured, but in whatever light piecework and overtime are regarded, the members of the Amalgamated Society, by a majority of more than nine thousand to a minority of less than twenty, have expressed their wish to give them up, and abolish the systems. The reasons which prompted them to this may be shortly stated :—First, as to ' systematic overtime ', a term meant to imply time regularly worked (over and above the ten hours) from week to week, and from month to month, and in many instances the whole year round, without intermission. They know it deprives them of rational enjoyment, prevents them from using opportunities for culture, and weakens their physical powers. They feel that their well-being is not a thing to be bought and sold for so many shillings a week. They contend there is no necessity for it, because hundreds are begging to be allowed to take their share of the work. Belonging to a society as they do, their overtime earnings, or a portion of them, go to support those of their fellows whom that overtime keeps idle ; and, above all, they recognise the gross injustice of, by any voluntary act of theirs, degrading men as competent and industrious as themselves, into dependents on the funds of the Association.

With regard to piecework, they wish it to be fully understood that their objections are to the system as it is, not as it ought to be. The Executive Council will continue to oppose piecework as it now is, not as it ought to be. The Executive will continue to oppose piecework as it now is, for the following reasons :—The price is arbitrarily fixed by the masters or the middle men, and often piece masters or sweaters are introduced, who take a portion of that price themselves ; thus making the workman pay out of his wages for the cost of direction and management. If the workman should, by dint of his own expertness and working very hard, earn much more than an ordinary week's wages, the price which was arbitrarily fixed is as arbitrarily reduced for the profit of the manufacturer, who refuses to pay the price originally agreed upon. This is done with the strongest and most expert workmen, and the moderate in strength and ability are compelled to work worse than slaves for a comparatively miserable pittance. . . . The Executive Council feel that their justification might well stop here, but there are questions not entering into the general dispute which are pressed upon them, and to which they desire to give a frank answer. They are asked whether they acknowledge the right of any employer to engage who he likes, and the right of every industrious man to work at any honest calling that is open to him. They answer that they do, but at the same time they also assert their right to refuse to instruct any man in their trade, so that he might take their places at reduced wages, or force them to accept a lower price. They are asked also how they dare limit the right of the employer to take any number of apprentices. They answer that if the employer will teach *his* apprentices, he may take as many as he pleases, but they are called upon to do that, and they claim to say how many or how few they will teach. Their skill is as much theirs as the employer's establishment, his business and his capital are his, and they claim a right to dispose of it or communicate it according to rules which appear to them to be beneficial. The Executive Council of the Amalgamated Society hope that this explanation of their views and acts is sufficient to demonstrate that while they assert the right of their members, and endeavour to secure their welfare, they do not attack the just claims or peril the prosperity of any other class.

By order of the Executive Council,

Jos. Musto, *President.*

Wm. Allan, *Secretary.*

Feb. 2, 1852.

(b) From *The Operative*, March 27, 1852.

Address to the Trades by the Metropolitan Trades Conference.

. . . Our safety then lies in union, wider spread and more closely knitted — union which shall apply, not to one trade only, but to all trades — union which shall take in all existing organised societies. With such union strikes would cease with the necessity for them, and fairness would be secured by the power to assert that as a right which we are now too often compelled to sue for as a boon. For the accomplishment of this, our ideas point to a legal combination of all trade societies in a great federative union, which while leaving the organisation of each intact, shall band together the strength of all for mutual support, and the advancement of common interests.

We think also that the time has arrived when the working classes should consider the possibility of labouring for themselves and enjoying the fruits of their own toil. Wherever possible it is essential to start co-operative factories and workshops, where shall commence the accumulation of property for the worker, and in which he may secure self-employment. This subject, however, like that of a general federation, embraces principles of vast magnitude, and details of the greatest importance. They demand the thought and action, not only of the metropolitan trades, but of those of the whole country, and we therefore recommend that a general conference of labour, a true people's parliament for the whole kingdom, be assembled in London as soon as possible.

We call, then, upon our fellow workers to meet in their council rooms throughout the provinces, to consider this address, and the report of the meeting and resolutions of the conference which is inclosed. To address themselves to the matter like men worthy to be free. To form a judgement, and to let us know the result. We hope that result will be the appointment in every locality of a delegate for an imperial conference to be held in London, to consider the general questions we have indicated and the vote of the utmost that can be spared from the society's funds, for the assistance of the Amalgamated Society. Remember, workmen of England, that that society is not only fighting its own battle, but yours also. That it stands in the gap to protest both by word and deed, against social tyranny and industrial serfdom. That it is defending for all the great right to combine. That it is warding off a blow aimed, not only at itself, but at every union of workers throughout the kingdom. That it is holding out against the deprivation of every right of the labourer. That it is refusing a Declaration which would sign away the liberty of the toiler and leave him a being without rights, though capable of suffering wrongs. In the success of the Amalgamated Society, your own independence is bound up. Let that be put down, crushed, annihilated by a combination of employers, and your own turn is sure to come. Their defeat will be the signal for an onslaught, not only against combinations as they are, but the principle of combination itself. If then, you be indeed men, worthy of freedom, if you would not become as much the serfs of commerce as your forefathers were of Feudalism — if you long for social elevation — if you desire to live and die free, and to leave freedom to your children — come forward nobly, generously, wisely, in support of that society, which, suffering for the defence of its own rights, is standing between you and oppression, shielding you from degradation and forwarding the progress of labour. . . .

7. THE PRESTON LOCK-OUT OF 1853

[This was by far the biggest industrial struggle in the cotton trade since the general ' turn-out ' of 1842. It affected both spinners and weavers, and was part of a general struggle which extended over a large part of the cotton area. The Unions had been endeavouring to secure a rise in wages, which had been heavily cut in the depression of 1847, and had been supporting strikers at firms paying bad wages out of the funds of their Unions. The employers retorted with a general lock-out, refusing to re-employ workers unless they renounced Trade Union membership. They also launched prosecutions against the Union leaders, whose arrest helped to break the strike — the charges being subsequently abandoned. Funds in aid of the Preston workers were raised in many places, including London, by specially constituted Trades' Committees. There are full accounts of the affair in the " Report of the Social Science Association on Trade Societies " (1860), and in George Howell's " Labour Legislation, Labour Movements, Labour Leaders " (1902).]

(*a*) From the National Association for the Promotion of Social Science, " Report on Trade Societies " (1860), p. 224.

Preston Lock-Out.—To the British Public.—In consequence of the various misrepresentations which have so unblushingly been put forth by the " Masters' Association " ; we, the Weavers' Association, feel it to be a duty to ourselves and the public to publish the following answers :—

1st.—In the document issued yesterday by the Masters' Committee, they say, ' that the differences which in the first instance existed would have been arranged, and would not have resulted in a general stoppage of the mills, had it not been for the improper interference of strangers between the masters and their hands '. We beg to say distinctly, that no *strangers* had, either properly or improperly, interfered in the disputes between the masters and the hands, previous to a notice being given for a general stoppage.

2nd.—We repeat, that we have been ' locked out, in order to starve us into submission ', not because we objected to the advances made upon the price paid in 1852, for the great body of us were perfectly satisfied with the advances given, but because we thought fit to give our own money to support some four mills' hands that had disputes with their employers, the primary cause of our sympathy being, that these workpeople had been denied the opportunity of explaining, or coming to an arrangement with their employers. . . .

3rd.—They say, ' We at once admit that, owing to the depressed state of trade in 1847, a general reduction of wages took place '; but with respect to the promise of restoring it when trade revived, they say, ' We deny, however, that any such promise was made by the masters generally, although this might have been done by some individual firms '. We are prepared to admit that every employer in the town did not make that promise ; there were several firms, where had the hands, or any portion of them, raised the shadow of an objection to the reduction, or solicited a promise of any description, they. would have received summary ejectment ; and such a process, in the state of the labour market at the time, would have been next to starvation and death ; but the promise given at the firms where the masters allowed some little ' freedom ', was justly considered applicable to all, and consequently, to those firms where the hands did not ask, at that time, to be other than degraded slaves.

4th.—. . . You say, ' *that in a well regulated spinning and weaving establishment*, the average earnings of all classes of hands are about 10s. each '. You forget to tell us whose well regulated establishment this is ; but if all establishments where the average earnings are less than 10s. per week, are badly regulated establishments, we are prepared to prove from your own books, if you will furnish us with the facility, that the great body of establishments are anything but ' well regulated '.

5th.—We repeat that the wages paid in Preston are less than what are paid in other districts, and this is the secret cause of the determination of the workpeople to improve their condition.

. . . . . .

7th.—We beg to say, that in this struggle the masters are the aggressors ; we were (with the few exceptions referred to) satisfied with the wages given us before the ' Lock-Out ' ; we understand that we must not resume work unless we submit to a reduction of ten per cent ; we have offered to have the question settled upon reasonable terms, but ' no concession ' is the terms of our employers : they have forced us to rely for an existence upon aid from other towns, and now tell us, that we can only resume work upon condition that we will degrade ourselves in the eyes of the world, by accepting a reduction which must naturally be followed by a reduction in the wages of those who have so generously saved our children from starvation. Are these the only terms of honourable men ? Will it be the interest of the employers of Preston to see their workpeople both degraded and dishonest ? — We think not ; but if it be, we tell them that we will suffer much more before we will submit to such depravity.

In conclusion we again reiterate, that we are prepared at any time to bring this dispute to an honourable and reasonable arrangement.

By Order of the Power-Loom Weavers' Committee,

JAMES WHALLEY, *sec.*

" COMMITTEE ROOM, PRESTON,
    Dec. 28th, 1853."

(*b*) From " Balance sheet and Address of the Metropolitan Trades' Delegate Committee on the Preston Lock-Out from Nov. 24, 1853 to June 24, 1854 " (n.d.), p. 21.

In November, 1853, in consequence of representations made by the Preston Operatives, an organisation of the London Trades was effected to give efficient help to their fellow-labourers in Preston. The success which has attended the efforts of the London Delegates has exceeded all previous precedent. They have been instrumental in raising, by voluntary contributions and grants of money from societies' funds, the sum of £4,648 13s. 1d., £2,508 0s. 7d. of which sum have passed through their hands, and the remaining £2,140 12s. 6d. have been remitted by the various bodies subscribing direct to the Preston Committee. During the contest deputations from this body have visited 567 meetings of the London

Trades; notwithstanding which the expenses, including printing, secretaries' salaries, and deputations will be found to be under 5 per cent of the sum subscribed.

8. THE LONDON BUILDING DISPUTE OF 1859

[The London Building Dispute of 1859 arose out of the ' Nine Hours Movement ', which had been started by the operative stone-masons in 1853. The building workers, except the stone-masons, were organised for the most part in a large number of small local Trade Clubs and Societies, which formed from time to time local Joint Committees for common action. Such a Committee was formed in London in 1858 to press the ' nine hours ' demand, but was met with victimisation of the leaders of deputations which went to interview employers. Such action by Messrs. Trollope led to a strike, to which the Master Builders retaliated with a general lock-out, demanding the signature of a ' document ' renouncing Trade Unionism as a condition of re-employment. Finally, in February 1860, the employers withdrew the 'document ', and the men returned to work on the old terms. In this case, as in that of the Preston dispute of 1853, large collections were made for the strikers and much help was given by Unions in other trades. The London Trades Council developed as a permanent body out of the Committee formed to raise funds for the builders.]

From " Balance sheet of the late Strike and Lock-out in the London Building Trades " (1860), Preface, p. 3.

The recent struggle in the Building Trade of London is distinctly traceable to a movement for the Reduction of Hours of Labour. This movement was originated by the Operative Masons, in the year 1853. During a considerable time this agitation for fewer hours of daily toil may be said to have been confined to the ranks of this body of enterprising and intelligent mechanics, and though complete success has not yet crowned their endeavours, and the agitation after a few months vigorous prosecution has become fainter, the impulse which began in England has extended to the remotest portions of the globe, and the Masons of the United States, Canada, Australia and Tasmania are at the present moment engaged in demanding this equitable and human concession. On the 12th of January, 1858, the Carpenters and Joiners of London resolved to take part in the movement, and some short time after these were joined by the other branches of the building trade. The means employed were such as the law and custom of this country deem moral and constitutional. For the purpose of enlightening the minds of the working classes, and influencing the public opinion of the nation, trade and general meetings, lectures, discussions, letters in newspapers, and the extensive circulation of a " prize essay " were resorted to by the chosen conductors of the " Nine Hours Movement ".

Another of the means employed was repeated appeals by earnest and respectfully worded addresses, and deputations of working men, to several of the large building firms.

These appeals did not invariably, nor even generally, meet with that courteous treatment which the operative builders had a right to expect.

Sometimes their addresses were either harshly and rudely answered, or else received with silent contempt ; and worse than this, in several instances, the men composing the deputation were discharged from their employment, and thus as far as the power of the firm was concerned, deprived of the means of subsistence.

This conduct, on the part of some of the master builders, was not only grossly unjust and tyrannical towards the particular operatives thus victimised, but highly insulting to the entire body of the working classes.

But the conductors of the " Nine Hours Movement " did not for some time feel themselves in a position to resent their harsh and arbitrary proceedings in the manner dictated by their keen sense of the wrong committed.

At length, however, the moment for marking their disapprobation of the unjust dismissal of their brother workmen arrived, in a manner unsought by them, and sooner than they at one time expected.

A deputation, composed of some of Messrs. Trollope's workmen, waited upon these gentlemen, respectfully urging upon them the propriety of conceding the " Nine Hours " boon to the men in their employ.

A prominent member of the deputation was a mason, who for his part in this proceeding was immediately dismissed from Messrs. Trollope's establishment. . . .

All the masons at Messrs. Trollope's job at Knightsbridge resolved to strike until the discharged mason was re-called.

And now thought the conductors of the " Nine Hours Movement " was the time for them to mark not only their sense of the tyrannical dismissal of working men, but also to strike a blow for the success of the cause entrusted to their guardianship.

The Joiners, Bricklayers, Plasterers, Labourers, etc, united with the Masons in the " strike " against the Messrs. Trollope. These gentlemen were asked not only to receive the unjustly discharged mason again into their employment, but to reduce the hours of work from ten to nine in their establishments.

This they refused and the " strike " which began on the 21st of July, 1859, was allowed to proceed. . . .

A large and influential number of the master builders made common cause with the Messrs. Trollope, thus endorsing the unjust act of these gentlemen in discharging the working man for daring to express the desires of his fellow operatives.

But the " Master Builders " did more than come to the rescue of Messrs. Trollope's. They resolved to close their own establishments until the " strike " against Messrs. Trollope should be abandoned, and not again to open them to any operative who should not give a written pledge, not to belong to ANY society that in any way directly or indirectly interfered with the rate of remuneration, the hours of work, or any other arrangement between employer and the employed.

The written pledge thus required has since become known and even famous as the " odious document ".

It was designed, and even avowed to be a death-blow aimed at all the trades' unions or working man's clubs throughout the kingdom.

To give effect to this tyrannical resolution the building firms comprising the " Central Association " determined on a " Lock Out " of all the independent operatives in their establishments ; this cruel and remorseless measure came into operation on the 6th of August 1859. No less than 225 building establishments joined in this " Lock-Out ".

9. THE LONDON TRADES COUNCIL

[From the 1820s there had existed for many years an almost continuous Metropolitan Trades' Committee for common action among the London Trade Societies ; but after 1834 this Committee seems to have had a less continuous existence and to have come together only on special occasions to conduct a joint campaign or to organise help for a body of workers on strike or locked out. The London Building Dispute of 1859–1860 led to the establishment of a permanent body, to which the national Trade Unions with offices in London, such as the Engineers, sent delegates, as well as the purely metropolitan Societies. Until the establishment of the Trades Union Congress in 1868, the London Trades Council largely served the Trade Union movement as a central organisation both for organising help for Unions in trouble all over the country and for representing working-class grievances to Parliament and to the public.

The position of the Council was not, however, unchallenged. A section of the London trades resented its domination by the leaders of the Amalgamated Societies and gathered behind George Potter, the leader of the Builders' movement of 1859, in a rival body, the London Working Men's Association, which was mainly political in activity. (For the L.W.M.A.'s political aspect see p. 540.)]

(*a*) From the " Report of Trades Council of London ", 1862.

GENTLEMEN,

In presenting to you the second Yearly Report of the Council we would for a moment draw your attention to the circumstances which first brought it into existence. Most of you are aware that during the winter of 1859–60 delegate meetings were held weekly, for the purpose of aiding the Operative Builders of London in defeating what is properly termed the " odious document ". That document was a blow aimed at the Trades' Unions of this country, and the trades generally came forward nobly in support of those who were opposing it. The result was a complete triumph. This triumph may be attributed chiefly to the delegate meetings held week after week in Shaftesbury Hall.

At the termination of that memorable struggle it was felt that something should be done to establish a general trade committee, so as to be able, on emergency, to call the trades together with dispatch, for the purpose of rendering each other advice or assistance, as circumstances required. A committee was therefore elected to draw up a code of rules, which was done, and after being amended at a delegate meeting, was adopted, and the Trades Council established.

The first fruits of the Council was the publication of a Trades' Directory, a work of great value, though not without mistakes. Previous to this there were no means of extensive intercommunication between the trades, except through a few individuals, who had the good fortune to possess a large number of addresses to all parts of the kingdom. The publication of this Directory therefore placed in the hands of every trade the means of correspondence, and already many can testify to its usefulness. . . .

The next subject of importance which came before the Council was the employment of the sappers at the Chelsea barracks, where a dispute existed between the employer and his workmen. This was a question of great importance, not only to the building operatives, but to the whole of the workmen of this country. It was a direct interference on the part of the Government, and the Council took immediate steps to effect their removal. And here was shown the great value of a Council such as the present. There was no other body likely to take the subject up with such promptitude and probable success as our Council. They therefore called a delegate meeting, at Shaftesbury Hall, on July 30th 1861, at which meeting 50 societies were represented, sending 70 delegates, and representing a total of 50,000 men. This meeting passed resolutions condemnatory of the Government; sent a petition to Parliament, which was presented by Sir S. M. Peto, Member for Finsbury; and sent a deputation of fifteen to the Secretary for War, and received in Parliament a promise of their removal. The whole of this was effected in ten days, which shows plainly the capabilities of the Council for good, if properly supported.

The Sheffield outrages was a subject that claimed our early attention. Our Secretary wrote letters in answer to the charges brought against us, which were inserted in the *Builder*, *Daily News*, etc. Many friends thought that a delegate should have been sent down to investigate the affair; but our funds were too low to do so.

Meetings have also been held in reference to the strike in the Building Trades against the hour system. Delegates from the Council have spoken at public meetings, for the purpose of aiding the men on strike. A delegate meeting was called to consider the best means of obtaining support for the Masons in their long and arduous struggle. Appeals for support have been investigated on behalf of Masons, Bricklayers, Weavers, Coopers, Shoemakers, and others, and credentials given them to go before the trades. Correspondence has been opened with Glasgow, Liverpool, Manchester, Dublin, Bristol, Sheffield and other place, for the purposes of friendly counsel or assistance. Our continental brethren also have corresponded with us; first, the Neapolitan workmen, through Mr Congreve, the latter contributing £5 . 18 . 0 in aid of the Builders' strike against the hour system. J. B. Winstanley, Esq. of Braunstone House, near Leicester, had generously contributed between £40 and £50, through our secretary, to the Operative Builders in their present struggle.

Several gentlemen have urged upon the Council the necessity of doing something towards establishing an educational establishment, with classes, library, reading rooms, etc, and several have offered to give their services gratuitously as teachers, if a number of working men were willing to enrol themselves as students. We have been obliged to keep it in abeyance for a time, but if the trades rally round the Council they may at some future time extend their usefulness in this direction.

Your Council has also been watching the progress of the " Accident Compensation Bill ", and presented a petition in its favor, believing it will be beneficial to working men if carried. They will further endeavor to promote the progress of the Bill until it becomes a law of the realm. We hope to have the active cooperation of all societies in this matter.

We cannot close our report without referring to some matters of a political character. The Trades' Council of Glasgow and some other places came forwards as the Champions of Reform. Your Council was urged to give their support and assistance to the movement. The Council considered the matter, and resolved not to take up political questions as a Council ; but as most of the members of the Council are in favour of Reform, they determined to cooperate with other bodies, not as a Council, but as individuals. . . .

(b) From *The Beehive*, April 8, 1865.

[Report of the Adjourned Meeting of the London Trades' Delegates.]

. . . The Chairman said the meeting, which he thought was a fair representation of the London trades, would now be called upon to express an opinion upon the conduct which had been recently pursued towards Mr. Potter by some half dozen men calling themselves the London Trades' Council. (" Shame upon them ! ") They were all aware of the prompt and admirable manner in which Mr. Potter had called them together in an important emergency, and he was sure they all felt that, not only the men in the iron trades, but the trades of London, were deeply endebted to him for having come forward in the way he had done. (Cheers.) Yet a section of the London Trades' Council had cast aspersions on his character as a trader in and an abettor of strikes. (Cries of " Shame, shame ! " and groans.) He thought that such aspersions were most unjust and unfounded. (Cheers.) Mr. Potter had by his own conduct shown that he was not guilty of these charges — (Cheers) — and he called upon them to pass a resolution which would express their own appreciation of the high character of Mr. Potter, and his perfect disinterestedness and public spirit in this matter. (Cheers). . . .

Mr. G. Howell, bricklayer, one of the persons who attended the meeting at the Bell, Old Bailey, here rose and made some observations, but which were totally inaudible to the reporters amidst the confusion and uproar, and cries of " Turn him out ! " which greeted him from all parts of the meeting. Order being at last restored by Mr. Howell resuming his seat, the chairman continued . . .

10. THE MINERS' UNIONS, 1858 TO 1875

[The Miners' National Union organised by Martin Jude in the 1840s broke down in 1850, and in most of the coalfields Trade Unionism almost disappeared for a time, though purely local organisations continued in being. The renewed attempt at national organisation began about 1858 under the leadership of Alexander Macdonald, who had already organised the Scottish coalfields. The new movement did not become strong in England until the Leeds Miners' Conference of 1863 ; but thereafter it rapidly gathered force, and the miners put themselves at the head of the agitation for the amendment of the law of master and servant (see p. 552), and also pressed for improved legislation in the interests of safety and health and of fair payment of wages through the right to appoint independent check-weighmen at the collieries. Macdonald set out to unite all the coalfields in a federal National Association of Miners, but was hostile to the proposal to establish a centralised National Union. This led to a split, and the miners became divided between Macdonald's National Association and the rival Amalgamated Association of Miners, which had its chief strength in Lancashire and South Wales. The two bodies worked together in the agitation for improved mining legislation which achieved success in the Coal and Metalliferous Mines Acts of 1872. Both groups, but especially Macdonald's National Association, engaged actively in the promotion of Co-operative Collieries (see p. 457). The miners' movement flourished during the trade boom of the early 1870s ; but the struggles attending the slump of the following years destroyed the Amalgamated Association and reduced the National Association to an almost nominal existence except in Northumberland and Durham.]

(a) From *The Beehive*, December 26, 1863.

Address of the Miners' National Association, December 18, 1863.

. . . All active interference with local trade disputes relating to wages or workings is not in the province or duties of the council.

We believe it would be equally impolitic and injurious to interfere or to dictate to any class of men or masters as to how or how not they shall or may work. . . . The council do, however, recognise the duty, when well-informed on any local trade dispute, and on being satisfied that *justice* rests with the workmen, either in the matters of weighing, treatment or prices, of making the case known to the mining class generally, and they would feel, in certain cases, the necessity of recommending that support should be given in such degree as may appear requisite for the end to be obtained. . . .

(b) From *The Miner and Workman's Advocate*, January 7, 1865.

MARKET HALL, CHESTERFIELD,
    Dec. 28*th*, 1864.

Address of the National Council of Practical Miners. Dec. 28th, 1864.

TO THE MINERS OF THE UNITED KINGDOM

BRETHREN—

A conference of practical miners — men of your own order — has been held. Your representatives assembled on Monday last, and the work they have performed will appear in your organ of this week. You will see that your representatives directed their attention first to the all important question — *life*.

You can judge for yourselves whether the course they pursued was not the right one to secure preservation and prolongation of the lives of the colliers of this country. The letter which is being forwarded this day to her Majesty's secretary of State on the subject of inspection opens up the question of too long neglected protection provided by the Legislature, but which heretofore has been a farce.

Your delegates also considered, very carefully, the question of labour and wages, especially in relation to the payment of labour by weight, the desirability of weighing-machines being placed at every pit, and in every case under the supervision of a check-weighman appointed by the men.

In four days much has been done towards the emancipation of our order.

A conference, composed wholly of practical miners, has been held ; a council, composed wholly of practical miners, has been elected.

By the statement of accounts which will be published in this week's MINER, you will see how nobly the country has responded to our call, and how carefully we have regarded the trust confided in us.

It only remains for this conference to give expression to the hope that every mining district in the United Kingdom will *now* rally round the National Council of Practical Miners. Without our brethren resolve to unite to form one bond of brotherhood for the protection and support of our class so long neglected and so long oppressed, we shall continue to be an exception to the organisation that has been effected in every other trade in the kingdom.

Brethren! our duty is clear. We shall do all that in us lies to effect a perfect organisation. We shall visit every district and point out the advantages of union; but without *you* we are comparatively powerless. Join yourselves at once into lodges; form your lodges into districts; discuss every question that has a bearing upon you, as wealth producers and as citizens. Do this and you will not only emancipate yourselves, but secure respect and esteem.

We offer no antagonisms to capital. Capital and labour are, as far as interests are concerned, identical. Let the union of ALL be cemented, and a brighter day will dawn on the poor pitmen of our country.

Your representatives have also very carefully considered the state of the law as regards truck, compensation in case of death or accident, and the Masters and Servants' Act. The Dudley accident has been considered, and the Miners' Attorney-General, at the request of your late Council, attended the Conference, and will take immediate steps to ensure justice being done in the case of Dudley, and will also prepare a bill to be brought before Parliament, in the ensuing session, whereby a rich man's law — a mighty tyrant — under which British workmen get three months' imprisonment with hard labour for smoking a pipe in a pit, whilst their employers get a fine of forty shillings for allowing the pit to be full of carbonic acid gas, with death staring on every side, shall be remedied, and all men made equal before the law.

Brethren we rely on your assistance and counsel.—

Yours faithfully

on behalf of the Committee

THOMAS KIMBERLEY, President.

(c) From the Seventh Report of the Royal Commission on Trade Unions, 1867, p. 46.

Evidence of Alexander Macdonald. Answer, 15,434.

. . . Yes, I am satisfied of this, that even if without combinations of the workmen they might have been passed, yet it was on the representations of the workmen that the laws to destroy truck were passed, that it was on the representations of the workmen that all the inspection Acts were passed, and that it is owing to the representations of the workmen that education is now a portion of the statutes of this country as far as children working in mines are concerned.

(*d*) From the Eighth Report of the Royal Commission on Trade Unions, 1867, p. 14.

Evidence of John Normansell, secretary to the South Yorkshire Miners' Association.   Answer, 16,205.

. . . [The South Yorkshire Miners' Association] . . . has many objects.   First, to raise from time to time by contributions among the members funds for the purpose of mutual support.   Secondly, to assist its members in striving to obtain better legislation for the efficient management of mines, whereby the health and lives of the miners may be prolonged.   Thirdly, compensation for accidents when the employers are liable.   Fourthly, to assist all lodges and members when unjustly dealt with by their employers or agents. Fifthly, a weekly allowance to members locked out, or when driven into a strike.   Sixthly, a weekly allowance to members when injured while following their employment.   Seventhly, a grant of £8 at the death of any member caused by accident while following his employment.   Eighthly, to shorten the hours of labour, and to infuse steadier habits of working among all its members.   Ninthly, to secure the true weight of the miners' material at the pit banks, thus giving to both employers and employed their legitimate due.   Tenthly, to abolish all illegal stoppages at the pay offices, and to secure the prices and wages that the members may at all times bargain for. Eleventhly, to improve the miners' positions, morally, mentally and physically.   Twelfthly, to extend the association's principles to our less fortunate brethren by aiding all other similar associations that have for their objects the rights of labour.   Thirteenthly, a weekly allowance to the widows and orphans of members who lose their lives by accident while following their employment.   These are the benefits of the general association.   The benefits out of local lodges are, a weekly allowance to members when sick from natural causes, an allowance of £4 at the natural death of any member, an allowance of £2 at the death of a member's wife, an allowance of £1 at the death of a member's child if under 12 years of age.

(e) From the Eleventh Report of the Royal Commission on Trade Unions, 1867, p. 263.

Rules of the South Yorkshire Miners' Association. Established April 1858. Revised April 17th. 1865, and to be in force for the future government of this association.

OBJECTS.

The objects of this association are, first, to raise from time to time by contribution among the members funds for the purpose of mutual support.

2. To assist its members in striving to obtain better legislation for the more efficient management of mines, whereby the health and lives of the miners may be prolonged.

3. Compensation for accidents, where the employers are liable.

4. To assist all lodges and members when unjustly dealt with by their employers or agents.

5. A weekly allowance to members locked out or driven into a strike.

6. A weekly allowance to members injured while following their employment.

7. A grant of £8 at the death of any member caused by accident while following his employment.

8. To shorten the hours of labour, and also to infuse steadier habits of working among all its members.

9. To secure the true weight of the miners' material at the pit banks, thus giving to both employers and employed their legitimate due.

10. To abolish all illegal stoppages at the pay offices, and to secure the prices and wages the members may at all times bargain for.

11. To improve the miners' position, morally, mentally, and physically.

12. To extend the association's principles to our less fortunate brethren, by aiding all other similar associations that have for their objects the emancipation of their fellows from the grasp of capital.

The Association shall be termed and known by the name of " The South Yorkshire Miners' Association, Barnsley District ", and shall consist of members employed in and about the various collieries of the surrounding neighbourhood, — such collieries to be divided into as many lodges as may be deemed expedient, and the district shall embrace as many lodges or collieries as may be desirous of joining the association (always providing the general board of management sanctions the application). Every Lodge shall appoint its own local officers and conduct its own affairs in the manner set forth in the following rules.

(*f*) From " Minutes of the Conference of the Miners' National Association held in the Lesser Trades' Hall, Glasgow, on Tuesday, Wednesday, Thursday, and Friday, 20th, 21st, 22nd and 23rd of May, 1873 ", p. 5.

THE PRESIDENT'S [ALEXANDER MACDONALD'S] ADDRESS

He said that in a meeting such as he addressed it was not unfair to take a passing view of their existence as an association. In the year 1858, he remembered a similar conference of miners being held in Ashton-under-Lyne, which did not represent more than 4,000 persons. At that time union amongst miners was a thing totally unknown. Their friends of South Yorkshire had then just come into existence, but the result of that meeting was to cement together and create a greater bond of unity amongst the scattered fragments which constituted the Miners' Association of the period. The movement continued to increase, and columns were written, some of misrepresentation, others of abuse, others declaring that miners' unions, or unions of any kind amongst workmen, were totally worthless and would in the end prove abortive. Notwithstanding all that was said and done, the principles they had so dear at heart continued to be developed more or less until the year 1863. It was then that the Association really came into existence. From the first they were simply a federal association, allowing each district association to deal with its own affairs as it best could. They tried the process of amalgamation. They tried to see if it was possible for all to be governed — the internal as well as the general affairs of the Association — by the Executive Committee. They found by repeated experiments, and, above all, by one portion of the mining community which was there represented, the hopelessness of taking the matter out of the workmen's hands, and dealing with it in a wholesale manner. From 1863 to 1867 the association continued to increase. In 1863 they were more a rabble than an organised body — gathered together from all corners of the earth, almost without a fixed purpose, and with many opinions, some of them as diverse as the two poles. They continued, however, to hold together till 1867, when symptoms of dissension arose amongst them, and in 1869, a secession took place — that portion who seceded from the Association believing in continuing to deal with strikes and all questions. The great bodies that constituted the Miners' Association remained steadfast to the principles of federalism — to the principle that it was better to assist by voluntary action than by a general levy on the part of the executive. . . .

(*g*) From " Proceedings of the National Conference of Miners held at Saltburn-by-the-sea on the 30th and 31st August, and 1st September, 1875 ", p. 8.

The Chairman reviewed some of the incidents connected with the Miners. They were aware, he said, that the Miners' National Association was called into existence at a very stirring time in the history of the mining interests of this country — namely, in January 1863. One of the great objects of the Association was the amelioration of the condition of working miners in respect to the improvement of ventilation, the shortening of hours of boy labour, better regulations in regard to the weighing, and an improvement of the management of mines. So far as ventilation was concerned, a very great step in the right direction had been taken since the year 1863, and he was satisfied that no one would dare to dispute that that change had to a large extent if not entirely, been brought about through the influence of the Miners' National Association. (Applause). In regard to the system of weighing, although they had it in a form by the Bill of 1860, it was in a very unsatisfactory condition. Now although in a few forms it was not quite perfect, that was a state of things that applied to every law that had been passed in the United Kingdom from the earliest period of its history. So far as the improvement in the education of managers was concerned, they had made a great stride, that yet would have to be tested by time in order to show what were the effects of such a step. Still the most sanguine of men in 1863 could not have thought that they could have reached the point at which the law stood at the present day. With reference to the youths, they were aware that in 1863, although there had been legislation on the matter to some extent, a boy could be taken into the mines when ten years of age ; but a boy could not now be taken into the mine before he was twelve, or ten years of age under special circumstances, while he could now only work 54 hours a-week. These were the leading features of the beneficial changes they had effected, and it was not necessary to dilate further on them. He thought, however, that they were warranted in saying they had succeeded in the objects they started with in a manner that few bodies of working men had done. (Hear, hear). They succeeded under two conditions — the first was that their movement was exclusively confined to the working miners themselves. When the amelioration of the condition of factory workers was brought about it was by the instrumentality of a large number of outsiders. The miners' agitation was begun among members, and was maintained among themselves; and he ventured to affirm that it was an agitation in its effects for which countless thousands would yet bless the men that had taken part in it. There was another condition in connection with these changes, and it ought to be an incentive to those who follow in such a work — and that was, that all the way, step by step, they met the stern opposition of those who are called the employers of the country. It was true that there were two or three honourable exceptions; but the general body of the mine-owners of the country opposed them, there could be no doubt. These two conditions ought to be satisfactory, and to stimulate others to go forward in a similar direction. Another improvement the National Association desired to draw attention to, and that was to improve the laws respecting labour. They were quite aware that in 1863 the law of contract was in itself most vicious, and he ventured to say that it was most unrighteous that a workman who broke his contract should be liable to three months' imprisonment, and the employer could only be sued for a civil debt. As an Association they took up the matter, and the result was that there was a Select Committee of Inquiry and subsequently an Act of Parliament. They did not cease their operations; they believed the law, although amended, was still unsatisfactory, and now he was glad to say that, before their organisation merged into its new form, the law of contract between employer and employed would have become satisfactory. The laws of intimidation and conspiracy had also had their attention. The most sanguine of men could not, he thought, have anticipated that these laws could have been placed in such a satisfactory state as they are now.

(*h*) From " Amalgamated Association of Miners. Report of the Executive Committee's Proceedings, from October 23rd to November 28th, 1873 ", p. 3.

[At the meeting on the 23rd October, 1873, it was resolved]

1 : That the bills lying in the printers' hands in Cornwall be distributed among the men there, to explain matters relative to the lock-out at Burnley, and that Mr Pooley be requested to do it.

2 : That the solicitor's bill be paid for getting damages for five

men at Rhymney, who were discharged without a month's notice having been given, in consequence of not having a discharge note; and we also express our pleasure in finding the men got £8 12s. each in lieu of being so discharged.

3 : That the miners of Salop, who have been locked-out, do their best to amicably adjust the prices in changing from measuring to weighing.

4 : That the Secretary write to the man of No. 7 Lodge, Swansea Vale District, and inform him that we cannot hear his case, only by his laying the same before his district and their sending it here officially; also that the District Secretary be requested to inform us when sending the case whether the men work under notice at the colliery when he was discharged.

5 : That a circular be printed and sent to every district of this Association, informing the officials that no case will be entertained by the Executive, except the same has been submitted to the District Committee and officially sent here, signed by the officers, and the district seal attached to the credential or letter.

6 : That Mr W. Pickard having informed this Executive that Messrs. Evans & Co, of Haydock, near St. Helens, are prepared to carry out the arrangements made between certain employers and representatives of the men as to adopting the weighing system, we request Mr W. Pickard to get a deputation of the men to accompany him to see Mr Chadwick, with a view of carrying out the arrangements in changing from measure to weight.

7 : That Mr Hadley made enquiries as early as possible into the case of the men of Radley's Colliery, St. Helens, relative to adjusting prices in changing the mode of working from measure to weight; and if the men's statement be found correct as to the employers weighing coal only which is got from the wet part of the mine to find an average of weight, the men be supported according to the 11th resolution of the Executive, passed on the 3rd day of September last.

8 : That Messrs. T. Halliday and G. Pickard take the full control, under the Executive, of conducting the Burnley lock-out, and do all in their power to bring the same to a satisfactory issue.

9 : That circulars be sent to every district of the Association, drawing their attention to the resolutions of former Committee, relative to the Plimsoll Seamen's Fund, also the Parliamentary Fund; and also to the resolution of Conference, regarding the Burnley Fund, as supplementary aid for members who are defending the rights of combination, and have been locked out for four months.

10 : That Messrs. D. Evans and T. Halliday enquire into the case of the men of Caerphilly District, who are claiming support from this Association, on the grounds that their case was the same as those men who were paid when the change occurred in getting coal from the long ton to the imperial ton ; also that they try to get a fair settlement of the Wernddu dispute, while at Caerphilly.

11 : That we get legal advice on the West Cumberland District case, relative to the late secretary withholding cheques, etc, belonging to the said branch of this Association ; also as to what course to pursue in regard to the Trustee of the said district who refuses to sign papers necessary for the district to get full possession of the money, etc, belonging to the said branch.

12 : That we give the weavers of Caerphilly, Aberdare, and Merthyr the sum of £15, seeing they have been out for four weeks, and taking into consideration that they supported the miners liberally in South Wales during the great strike.

(*i*) From the " Report of the Miners' National Association Conference ", March 1874, p. 13.

[Meeting of the Councils of the Miners' National Association and the Amalgamated Association of Miners in Manchester, March 1874.]

This meeting agrees that the joint committees of the two Associations shall work in harmony together in seeking alterations in the Payment of Wages Bill ; the Master and Servants Act ; the Criminal Law Amendment Act ; the Compensation Bill, and all other Acts of Parliament that press unjustly and unfairly upon the working miners of the Country, with the understanding that each association defrays the Parliamentary expenses, in accordance with the members each represents.

(*j*) From " Proceedings of the National Conference of Miners held at Saltburn-by-the-sea on the 30th and 31st August, and 1st September, 1875 ", p. 13.

He (Mr A. Macdonald) did not want to take one half-dollar or one half-cent from any man who had acquired his money fairly ; but the present relation was that the few went riding in wealth, while the many were born to overwhelming poverty. (Cheers). They had amended the laws — or, at any rate, the laws had been amended to some extent. (Hear, hear). They must amend the social relations of the working classes still further. (Cheers). The land was passing, and had been for years, from the hands of the old aristocracy and men who gained it by stealth and by violence. (Cheers). Vast accumulations had passed into the hands of a very few. He did not say it had been stolen from labour, but it had passed into other hands, from the folly and ignorance of the masses. (Hear, hear). Their object must be to teach these masses, and when they taught them to let others understand the meaning of their teaching — that by every legal means they should do what they could to have a more equal division of that which is the product of capital and labour — a more equal division between employer and employed. (Cheers). The true way to this end was by cooperative collieries and institutions everywhere. . . .

(*k*) From " Proceedings of the National Conference of Miners, held at Saltburn-by-the-sea on the 30th and 31st August, and 1st September, 1875 ", p. 79.

The question of attending the trade Congress at Glasgow in October was next considered.

Messrs. Brown (Stafford), Cowey (West Yorkshire), and the President, spoke generally of the irregular and unbusinesslike proceedings of the last Congress at Liverpool.

Mr. Colledge felt humiliated to see the conduct of many of the delegates at the two last Congresses. He would not go again. Their President and Mr. Burt, with all their position, were both insulted.

Mr. Brittain said they should still be represented.

Mr. Cowey was disgusted with the proceedings, and Mr. Brown would not attend another Congress.

The President remarked that the scenes at the Trades Union Congress had been notorious. It was urged that their representation should be more according to numbers, which would be the only means to place a large association like the Miners' Union in its right position.

Resolution was passed that no deputation be sent to the forthcoming Congress.

11. CONCILIATION AND ARBITRATION

[From 1845 the National Association of United Trades had been pressing for legislation to establish ' Boards of Trade ' — that is, bodies for conciliation and arbitration in labour disputes. By the 1850s the number of employers who were prepared to accept such methods, and to give some recognition to Trade Unions, was increasing, though in most industries the employers were still entirely hostile both to collective bargaining and to any interference with their freedom to fix wages and conditions as they pleased. In a few cases, Conciliation Boards began to be set up ; and as the new Trade Unions became more averse to strike action with the growth of their Friendly Society activities their leaders began to press more strongly for the development of peaceable methods of settling disputes. The book on " Trades' Unions and Strikes ", written by the Bookbinders' leader, T. J. Dunning, in 1860, illustrates the new attitude.]

(*a*) From T. J. Dunning, " Trades' Unions and Strikes " (1860).

It is superfluous to say that the price of labour, like that of everything else, is determined by the quantity or supply of it *permanently* in the market ; when the supply of it *permanently* much exceeds its demand, nothing can prevent the reduction of wages ; and, conversely, when the demand for it permanently much exceeds its supply, nothing can prevent their rise. In these two extreme points all contention is hopeless. No Trade Society on the one hand, however well organised, can, or ever did, prevent the fall of wages in the first case ; nor, in the other, can, or ever did, the most stringent legislative enactment, of which there have been many instances, prevent their rise. Trade Societies, however, rarely meddle with these two extremes. Leaving them, we come to the intermediate states that admit the operation of Trade Societies ; and, indeed, which call them into existence (p. 5).

In all bargains, the buyer wishes to buy as cheap, and the seller to sell as dear, as he can ; but their interests, all being exchangers, and each, from the highest to the lowest, depending upon this principle — exchange — for his position in life and even for his daily sustenance ; all things being equal, their interest is not one of opposition, but of mutual interest ; and neither the one wishing to get as much, nor the other in wishing to pay as little as possible, can injure the other. But if, as alluded to above, either party possess an advantage over the other in the bargain, this position of mutual interest is changed into one of opposition, in which the weaker party is sure to be deprived of some proportion of what is justly due to him. In this position as bargainers for the sale and purchase of labour, stand the employer and employed. Singly the employer can stand out longer in the bargain than the journeyman ; and as he who can stand out longest in the bargain will be sure to command his own terms, the workmen combine to put themselves on something like an equality in the bargain for the sale of their labour with their employers. This is the *rationale* of Trade Societies, which is very clearly indicated by Adam Smith in his " Wealth of Nations " (p. 7).

The object intended is carried out by providing a fund for the support of its members when out of employ, for a certain number of weeks in the year. This is the usual and regular way in which the labour of the members of a Trade Society is protected, that the man's present necessities may not compel him to take less than the wages which the demand and supply of labour in trade have previously adjusted ; strikes, which we shall hereafter notice, being only resorted to on extraordinary, and, generally speaking, most unusual occasions (p. 7).

When a body of men stand out for a price which their employers refuse to give, while this dispute is pending, the position of the workmen is that of a strike. As strikes are the last resort, as they are always expensive and as they engender mutual ill-feeling, they should never be entered into without duly calculating the probabilities of success, nor until all means of amicably settling the difference have failed. It often happens that workmen have no alternative, but either to submit to a reduction tyrannically enforced, without any reasoning on the matter being allowed, or to cease from labour. Often has a strike thus been precipitated, and ruin inflicted on employer and employed, which might have been averted by a little calm reasoning on the matter. It is the same when a rise in wages is asked by the men. Both parties are apt to view each other as enemies, and in this jaundiced view, which prevails equally on both sides — aggravated by the unconciliatory tone which is sure to result from such a state of feeling — reasoning on the subject — as the subject, considering the important results to both parties which are then pending should be reasoned upon — is rendered impossible. The beginning of strife is like the letting out of water, that might be, at the commencement, easily stopped. But if there be one thing more than another which, in their turn, both parties in these circumstances often, to all appearances, agree in throwing aside, it is the conciliatory spirit which might prevent these ruinous disputes. But while strikes are always to be deprecated, because they are, for the time, a state of moral warfare, and, like all states of hostility, productive of mutual bitterness — and because they are carried on at a loss to both parties — we are, notwithstanding, clearly of opinion, from long experience of their results to journeymen both of success and defeat, that there is no proper alternative, in certain cases, than the position of a strike (p. 23).

(b) From " Report of the Select Committee on Masters and Operatives (Equitable Councils of Conciliation) 1856 ", p. 160.

Evidence of Samuel Higginbotham.

1891. Have you been engaged in Macclesfield in reference to any differences that have taken place between the masters and workmen ? — In the early part of 1849 there was a very disastrous turnout in the silk trade between the masters and the men. I had had experience as to the sad consequences of strikes previously, as in the year 1816. A deputation from the masters and the men waited upon me to know whether I would undertake the office of chairman to a Board to be established, somewhat on the principle of the Conseils des Prud'hommes. It was to be composed of 12 masters on the one side, and 12 men on the other ; and supposing that there should be a difference of opinion, the chairman, who was to be independent of trade, to have a casting vote that should be decisive upon the question. . . .

1892. Will you state what took place upon that ? — Subsequently I was introduced to the meeting, and it was agreed that there should be a meeting at Macclesfield Town Hall a few days subsequently, at which various rules and regulations to guide the board should be agreed upon ; those rules and regulations I hold in my hand. The consequence of that decision was, that we met from month to month for a series of months, to adjust a series of tariffs as to the prices to be paid for the various fabrics manufactured in the silk trade. As you may suppose, during the progress of the board there were several cases of what we call locks, and I had to give the casting vote sometimes on the masters' side, and sometimes on the workmen's side, and upon no one occasion that I can bring to my recollection was there any offensive remark, or any remark that one might feel hurt at, with one exception ; . . .

[*Ibid.* p. 167.]

Evidence of Samuel Higginbotham.

1970. What rate of wages did you fix as being proper for a large body of workmen per day or per week ? — That does not enter at all into this book.

1971. Had you not some standard to guide you as to what ought to be the earnings of an artisan ? — That does not at all enter into consideration here.

1972. Did not that come before you ? — No, because our workmen work by the piece.

1973. In fixing the wages by the piece, how much per day did you intend that an ablebodied industrious man should get ? — It was a question which never came before the Board. The question was, what should be paid for a particular article ; one man would in the same length of time, perhaps do double the work which another man would do, and twice as well.

1974. Supposing an industrious, ablebodied, and careful artisan worked by the piece, what would he be able to get by the day at your price ? — That was a question which never came under consideration.

[*Ibid.* p. 189.]

Evidence of Mr Charles McDonald, Silkweaver of Macclesfield.

1983. To your knowledge, do you consider that the establishment of that Board of 12 masters and 12 men answered the purpose for which it was established ? — It answered the purpose for which it was established ; that was to prevent strikes, or the necessity for strikes ; there was not a strike during the whole three years of its existence.

1984. In what way did it prevent strikes ? — There was an authority that both masters and men gave a certain sort of obedience to ; their decision was not law, but they gave a certain sort of obedience to it ; as long as the masters agreed to meet the men, the men were always satisfied with their decisions, and they even submitted to reductions, and were glad to do so.

. . . .

1986. If these equitable arrangements answered the purpose for which they were intended, and prevented strikes, why was not the Board re-established afterwards ; having found the benefits of it for three years, why did you not establish it again ? — My own opinion is, and it is the opinion of the manufacturers, that it was solely for want of having legal force ; some manufacturers evaded it, and there was no legal power to enforce their regulations ; when the Board was first established they agreed to a rule " That upon any direct case of a breach of the arrangements of this Board being discovered, the same shall be visited upon the manufacturer or weaver by fine and exposure, and upon a repetition double the fine in each case, the informer to receive the half of the fine ", but they had no power to enforce it, except by doing that which the Boards were established to prevent, namely by striking the hands ; they had no way of compelling a master to comply with the regulations of the Board, unless by doing the very thing they were established to prevent.

(c) From *The Bookbinders' Trade Circular*, March 19, 1858.

[The rules of the arbitration agreement between the Compositors' Society and the Master Printers' Association (1856).]

1. The object of the Arbitration Committee : to avoid referring Trade Disputes to Courts of Law.

2. That such Arbitration Committee shall consist of three masters to be nominated by the master in whose Office the dispute shall have taken place, and three journeymen, who shall not be employed in the said office, to be nominated by the journeymen, and be presided over by a barrister as chairman, who shall be appointed annually, and who, in all cases of division in which the votes of the arbitrators are equal, shall decide the question at issue by his casting vote.

3. Disputes referred to an Arbitration Committee must be adjudicated upon within two months from the day of such dispute being referred to such Committee, unless an extension of time be mutually agreed upon by the contending parties or deemed necessary by the barrister.

4. The fee of barrister and hire of rooms to be paid by the party against whom the decision may be given.

5. Either party neglecting to appoint their members of the Arbitration Committee within one month after the claim has been made in writing for the appointment of such Committee, or refusing to refer the matter in dispute to arbitration, to be considered as having received an adverse decision.

6. That the Scale of 1810, with the additions, definitions, and explanations, as arranged at a conference of Master Printers and Compositors held in 1847, form the basis of the decisions of the committees. That when the arbitrators consider the words of the Scale ambiguous, their application to the particular case in dispute doubtful, or that they have no reference to the question under consideration, ascertained established usages shall be taken as decisive ;

but when trade practices are found to be so varied as not to constitute " custom ", the award shall be based on equity and analogy.

7. That these rules shall be considered as having come into operation on the 1st. day of January, 1856, and shall continue in force until written notice to discontinue them be given by either committee ; such notice not to take effect until after three months from the time of its delivery.

(*d*) From ' An Account of the Origin and Progress of the Board of Arbitration and Conciliation in the Hosiery and Glove Trades, of which Nottingham is the centre '. (Issued by the Board.) Eleventh Report of the Royal Commission on Trade Unions (1867–1869), Appendix 1, No. V.

. . . Questions of wages, the manner in which certain classes of work should be performed, and the rate at which new classes should be paid constantly occupy the attention of the board, but in addition other matters have arisen which have an important bearing on the material and moral interests of the workmen. One of the first subjects which demanded its attention was the abominable practice of the truck system. . . . The board advertised in the public newspapers their determination to stop the system by prosecuting the offenders, and by removing the machinery from any middle-master having recourse to such practices. A prosecution was instituted in one instance, and these measures had the effect of entirely stopping this oppressive system ; if it is at all practised at present it is in such a secret and mitigated manner as not to be known to the board.

Another evil which reduced the purchasing value of the workmen's earnings was the custom of paying them in the villages at late hours on Saturday night or early on Sunday mornings, when no markets were available. This was also advertised in the newspapers as contrary to the wishes of the board, and individual employers guilty of the practice were written to in terms of remonstrance, and the evil thereby checked, although, perhaps, not thoroughly eradicated. Deductions from earnings in excess of the customary charges of the trade have been steadily discountenanced and suppressed. When the board was first founded [in 1860] it was generally considered a doubtful experiment. Several manufacturers were openly or covertly hostile to it ; some regarded it as utopian and impracticable ; others as likely to pry into the secrets of their business ; and some as derogatory to their position and independence. These objections, however, have been steadily disappearing, until at the present time there are only two or three who refuse to acknowledge its decisions; but these are as effectually governed by its regulations as its warmest supporters; and the resolutions of the board have been generally loyally responded to by both masters and workmen.

The discussions at the board have always been conducted in the most friendly spirit and orderly manner. There has never been the slightest contention as to who should fill the offices of president or vice-president. The workmen proposed a manufacturer as president, and the manufacturers a workman as vice-president. Whenever any breach of economic laws has been suggested by workmen outside the board, the operative delegates have always been the first to denounce it. The voices of reason and humanity have invariably had due weight with the delegates of both sections. And although both masters and workmen are accustomed to express their opinions of each other's individual and collective acts without the slightest reserve, no manufacturer or workman has ever been known to suffer from the free and honest expression of his views. One of the most evident results of this interchange of thought and opinion is, that the workman becomes better acquainted with the laws which govern trade and commerce, and with the influence of foreign competition; and the master learns to appreciate the difficulties of the workman, and to sympathise more with his trials and struggles to maintain and improve his position.

It is important to notice that the success of this system is more attributable to its preventive than its curative character. Nine-tenths of the matters arising in the trade, that would, if allowed to go on, produce dissensions and irritation, are never brought before the board, but are arranged by the interposition of the committee of enquiry, who, by taking prompt action, and by exercising a spirit of justice and conciliation, succeed generally in arriving at a satisfactory result; if unable to do so a reference is then made to the board. . . .

The facts which the board points to as the best proof of its success are: that during the six years of its existence no strike or lock-out has taken place, no personal attacks have been made, and no inflammatory handbills circulated. Never in the history of the trade has there existed so much good feeling betwixt employers and employed as at the present moment; and during the past two years, wherein labour has been scarce and agitation on the question of wages prevalent throughout England, the manufacturers in this branch of industry have been able to accept contracts without apprehension and execute them without delay.

(*e*) From the Evidence of A. J. Mundella. Tenth Report of the Royal Commission on Trade Unions (1867–1869), p. 76.

19,374. And you have had great experience of the representatives of the men in your part of England ? — Yes.

19,375. What sort of men have you found them to be ? — I will tell you what has been the effect of our board of arbitration. The very men that the manufacturers dreaded were the men sent to represent the workmen at the board. We found them the most straightforward men we could desire to have to deal with ; we have often found that the power behind them has been too strong for them ; they are generally the most intelligent men ; and often they are put under great pressure by workmen outside to do things which they know to be contrary to common sense, and they will not do them. They have been the greatest barriers we have had between the ignorant workmen and ourselves, and I know that is so. I have found it in my correspondence with trade union secretaries and leaders ; all over England I have found that so. I have known that they are opposed to most of the evils that pervade the trades unions, but there are some that are not so ; it is quite clear that this Commission has developed that.

(*f*) From the evidence of Sir Rupert Kettle. Fourth Report of the Royal Commission on Trade Unions (1867–1869), p. 26.

[The agreed rules] were then signed by the six delegates for the masters, by the six delegates for the men, and by myself as umpire, and in these rules the masters delegates were the future arbitrators for the masters, the mens delegates were the future arbitrators for the men, and I was the umpire ; and in order to make them binding upon men and binding upon masters, one of the provisions is that these rules shall be printed and posted up in every master builder's workshop in Wolverhampton, and that in any court, or before any arbitrator or umpire, unless a contract in writing is shewn, these shall be taken to be the contract between the masters and the carpenters and joiners employed in that establishment. These are posted up and the men have notice that these are the rules containing the terms of the contract of the hiring when a new man is taken into employment. . . .

In the course of the first year (1864, I think it was) Mr. Thomas Whittall, the secretary of the carpenters and joiners union, came to me upon other business connected with the working men in another relation of life, and he said that he thought an arbitration rule requiring upon all disputes that 13 persons should be brought together and that this somewhat troublesome process should be gone through was rather inconvenient that in minor differences the men hesitated to trouble the masters or to trouble me about it, and that the working carpenters would be very much obliged to me if I would turn my attention to some means by which disputes of a minor kind might be settled without the trouble and delay of an arbitration. During the first year I thought of the matter, and at the meeting next year to alter the rules we adopted another rule, a supplemental rule to the arbitration rule, called the conciliation rule, and this has been found in practice more useful than the arbitration rule. That conciliation rule is this, " That in case any trade dispute or difference of a private nature shall arise between any individual master and any individual workman or workmen, by which the general interests of the trade are not directly affected, then, in such case, before proceeding to arbitration under the last rule, the master shall nominate one of the hereinbefore appointed masters' arbitrators, and the workman or workmen of the hereinbefore appointed workmen's arbitrators, who shall, as soon as conveniently may be, meet together and endeavour, if possible, to arrange such private dispute or difference without proceeding to a formal reference, and in case they cannot so arrange such difference to the mutual satisfaction of both contending parties, the matter in dispute shall be determined by arbitration, under rule 1. as though no such meeting for conciliation had been held." They then had several meetings for conciliation under this rule, and I am very happy to say that, as I expected, there has not been one instance, in which they have not settled the dispute without being under the necessity to appeal to a formal arbitration.

12. THE FACTORY REFORM MOVEMENT

[By the end of the 1850s the cotton workers had stabilised their Trade Unions and had achieved a considerable degree of recognition of the rights of collective bargaining. The Factory Acts had been extended to a number of further trades; and in 1864 the first big extension outside the textile trades took place, with the passing of an Act applying to a number of dangerous trades, including pottery. There had, however, been no reduction of hours below the 10½ accepted by Shaftesbury in 1850, as an amendment of the Ten Hours Act of 1847 — the extra half-hour being conceded in return for improved provisions for enforcement, though the Short Time Committees had strongly objected to the concession. In 1867 the textile Unions launched a new campaign for the Eight Hours Day. They were not successful; but in that year a new Factory Act extended regulation to all factory trades. The textile workers, dissatisfied with their position, then organised a Factory Acts Reform Association (1869), which secured an amending Act in 1875.]

From *The Beehive*, February 23, 1867.

The following statement has been issued to the factory workers of Lancashire, Yorkshire, Cheshire and Derbyshire :—

" FELLOW WORKMEN,—At the delegate meeting, held at the Wheatsheaf Inn, Swan Street, Manchester, on the 10th day of February, the Reverend Joseph Rayner Stephens in the chair, when representatives from the card-room hands, spinners, and weavers of the above districts were present, the following was agreed to as the fundamental basis of the Association :—

" That this meeting of delegates is convinced that the time has arrived when, in consequence of the increased speed of machinery, the great addition to the number of mills, and other causes, a further limitation in the hours of factory labour has become indispensably necessary.

That the delegates now present resolve to agitate for such a measure of legislative restriction as shall secure a uniform Eight Hours' Bill in factories, exclusive of meal times, for adults, females and young persons; and that such Eight Hours' Bill have for its foundation a restriction upon the moving power.

That for the equitable adjustment of all disputes arising between factory workers and their employers, it is indispensably necessary that there should be a Court of Appeal, to which factory workers can resort, — This meeting therefore cordially supports the formation of boards of arbitration between employers and employed, and resolves to petition Parliament for a legislative enactment to that effect.

That the delegates here present resolve to form themselves into an association for the purpose of carrying out the above-named objects, to be called the Lancashire, Yorkshire, Cheshire and

Derbyshire Factory Workers Short Time and Arbitration Association. . . ."

13. THE UNITED KINGDOM ALLIANCE OF ORGANISED TRADES

[In January 1867 a renewed attempt was made by the Trade Unions, chiefly in the North of England, to create a federal organisation for common defence. The main purpose was not aggressive action, but concerted resistance to lock-outs and attempts to reduce wages. The Alliance was set up at Manchester, but had its headquarters at Sheffield. It was active in resisting attacks on wages during the next few years, but died away after 1870, when most of the large Unions transferred their allegiance to the Trades Union Congress. The Alliance was confined to trades which had well-established Trade Unions. Its secretary and leading personality was William Dronfield, the Sheffield compositor.]

From " Rules for the Government of the United Kingdom Alliance of Organised Trades " (1867), p. iii.

. . . Its primary *objects* are to render pecuniary and moral support to all Trades belonging to the Alliance, who may be exposed to the evils resulting from, or incident to, *Lock-outs*, which entail such an incalculable amount of misery and suffering on so many of our fellow-men, as well as on their unoffending wives and families; which are alike an outrage, not only to the most clearly defined and generally accepted principles of political and social economy, but are calculated seriously to injure the trade and commerce of the country generally.

The Executive of the Alliance believe that its objects can be accomplished in various ways — by bringing about and perpetuating a better understanding and closer intercourse amongst the trades at large, by the dissemination of reliable information, through the medium of its Quarterly Reports, on such topics as may be generally useful or interesting — and by a judicious exercise of the power invested in the Executive of using their best endeavours, when a Lock-out appears imminent, of averting such a disastrous calamity, by conciliating measures.

Failing in their efforts at conciliation, the Executive, with the sanction of the Judicial Council, will dispense with the pecuniary benefits provided by the Rules, which although not so large as might be desirable, will, nevertheless, be more than many trades received during the struggles they have lately been engaged in, and is, of course, intended only as *supplementary* to what the trade so locked-out may be able or willing to grant to its members for the time being. This, it is presumed, will be better than the present system of sending delegates and appeals throughout the country to solicit the pecuniary aid of the trades — a system alike expensive in its operations, and uncertain in its results — as witness the numerous appeals which have been made during the last year. And here it may be remarked that the Trades belonging to the Alliance will be saved the frequency of those appeals for extraneous aid, inasmuch as it is only fair to presume that as all Trades have an opportunity of joining the Alliance, on payment of an entrance fee of one halfpenny per member, and the half-yearly subscriptions of a like amount, that *they will refuse to grant relief to those Trades who do not embrace the opportunity of connecting themselves with the Alliance*, should such Trade be necessitated to appeal for pecuniary support in consequence of a *Lock-out*.

14. THE TRADES UNION CONGRESS

[The Trades Union Congress dates its foundation in 1868, when a Congress held at Manchester decided to set up a permanent organisation. There had, however, been a number of previous Conferences, beginning with the London Conference of 1864, called to concert measures for the amendment of the law of master and servant (see p. 552). In 1867 a Conference was to have been called by the London Trades Council to meet in London ; but the Council, alarmed by the outcry aroused by the Sheffield Outrages (see p. 558) and by the demands for repressive legislation, refused to call it. George Potter's rival body, the London Working Men's Association (see p. 540), then called the Conference, which was attended by delegates from most of the Northern Trade Unions, but not by the Amalgamated Societies, which set up as a rival body the Conference of Amalgamated Trades (see p. 564), and held aloof from the Manchester Congress of 1868. The following year the Congress appointed a Parliamentary Committee to take charge of Trade Union affairs between the annual Congresses ; and this body became, from 1871, when the Amalgamated Societies finally agreed to join it, the central representative organisation of the Trade Unions. It had, however, no authority to co-ordinate industrial action or control its affiliated Societies, being intended primarily as a means of lobbying for the fuller recognition of Trade Union rights and for the advancement of industrial legislation.]

(a) From *The Beehive*, 25th April, 1868. Circular from the Manchester Trades Council inviting delegates to the first Trades Union Congress.

To THE SECRETARY OF THE—

MANCHESTER, *April 16th*, 1868.

SIR,—You are requested to lay the following before your society. The vital interests involved, it is conceived, will justify the officials in convening a special meeting for the consideration thereof. The Manchester and Salford Trades Council, having recently taken into their serious consideration the present aspect of Trade Unions, and the profound ignorance which prevails in the public mind with reference to their operations and principles, together with the probability of an attempt being made by the Legislature, during the present session of Parliament, to introduce a measure which might prove detrimental to the interests of such Societies, unless some prompt and decisive action be taken by the working classes themselves, beg most respectfully to intimate that it has been decided to hold in Manchester, as the main centre of industry in the provinces, a Congress of the Representatives of Trades Councils, Federations of Trade, and Trade Societies in General. The congress will assume the character of the annual meetings of the social science association, in the transactions of which society the artisan class is almost entirely excluded : and papers, previously carefully prepared by such societies as elect to do so, will be laid before the Congress on the various subjects which at the present time affect trade societies, each paper to be followed by discussion upon the points advanced, with a view of the merits and demerits of each question being thoroughly ventilated through the medium of the public press. It is further decided that the subjects treated upon shall include the following :—

1. Trade Unions an absolute necessity.
2. Trade Unions and Political Economy.
3. The effect of Trade Unions on Foreign Competition.
4. Regulation of the Hours of Labour.
5. Limitation of Apprentices.
6. Technical Education.
7. Courts of Arbitration and Conciliation.
8. Cooperation.
9. The present inequality of the Law in regard to Conspiracy, Intimidation, Picketing, Coercion etc.

10. Factory Acts Extension Bill, 1867: the necessity of compulsory inspection, and its application to all places where women and children are employed.

11. The present Royal Commission on Trade Unions: how far worthy of the confidence of the Trade Union interest.

12. Legislation of Trade Societies.

13. The necessity of an Annual Congress of Trade Representative from the various centres of industry.

(b) From G. Howell, " The Conflicts of Capital and Labour " (1878), pp. 427-31.

TRADE-UNION CONGRESSES.

§ 26. The nearest approach to anything like federative action on the part of trade-unions is to be found in the annual trade-union congresses, which, from March 1871, have had a permanent committee, called the " Parliamentary Committee ", elected on the last day but one of each successive congress, whose duty it is to watch over all legislative matters affecting, directly or indirectly, the trade-unionists of the country, and to initiate such measures as from time to time may be thought necessary, either for the purposes of amending laws already in existence, repealing those which are considered detrimental to their interests, or placing others on the statute-book which they deem just and reasonable (p. 427).

. . . .

§ 29. . . . The most prominent topic at each of these early congresses was the unprotected state of trade-union funds, as shown by the then recent decision in the case of Hornby *v*. Close. . . . In addition, however, to this special and paramount object, papers were read, and discussion arose, on piece-work, hours of labour, the limitation of apprentices, the necessity for greater protection for the lives and limbs of those working in mines, the objects and uses of trade-unions, strikes and lock-outs, conciliation and arbitration, co-operation and industrial partnerships, national education, and, for the first time, the question of the direct representation of labour in Parliament. . . (p. 429).

§ 30. . . . Other subjects were, however, considered by this congress [March 1871], in addition to those above named, similar to those discussed at Birmingham [1869] and a still wider field was opened by discussions on the Mines' Regulation Bill, the truck system, and weekly payment of wages, employment of women and children in agriculture, the Factories and Workshops Acts, convict labour and free labour, taxation — imperial and local — waste lands, and unemployed labour, emigration, and the international fraternisation of labour (p. 431).

(c) From a Circular of the Trades Union Congress Parliamentary Committee, 1872.

. . . It is necessary to be borne in mind that these Congresses are essentially reserved for Trades Union Delegates, representing bona fide Trades Societies, Trades Councils, and similar bodies by whatever name they may happen to call themselves; and it is desirable that this fundamental characteristic shall be retained.

The only latitude which the Committee recommend is contained in No. 30 [*i.e.* Standing Order No. 30], which gives the power to invite persons, not delegates, to attend the sittings of the Congress, and it may be, to speak, so that those who from time to time identify themselves with the labour movement, whether in or out of Parliament, may be able to be present to give advice or aid in the great work to which we have addressed ourselves. . . .

XVIII
WORKING CLASS POLITICS, 1858–1867

INTRODUCTION

CHARTISM, as an organised movement, flickered out in 1858; but by that time a new movement for Reform was already on the way. The working classes in the North of England, for the most part, collaborated in this movement with the middle-class Radicals. The first big forward moves were made about 1858, the North-East Coast being well to the van with its Northern Reform Union, in which Sir Joseph Cowen, who became Radical M.P. for Newcastle-on-Tyne in 1865, and his son of the same name worked closely with the leaders of the miners and ironworkers. There were parallel movements in Yorkshire and Lancashire, with Abel Heywood and Ernest Jones taking a leading part in Manchester. In the South and Midlands the Trade Unions took a more independent line, the National Reform League, with headquarters in London, being mainly dominated by them, whereas the National Reform Union, centred on Manchester, was much more under middle-class Radical leadership. This did not prevent these bodies from working together for Reform; but there was within their collaboration a continual struggle for influence, the working-class leaders insisting on the need for Manhood Suffrage and the Ballot, whereas many of their allies were prepared to compromise on Household Suffrage without the Ballot. The agitation steadily gathered force during the 1860s, especially after Palmerston's death in 1865 had removed the main obstacle to the taking up of Reform by the Whigs. After the failure of Russell's Reform Bill in 1866 and the introduction of Disraeli's Bill in 1867, the Radicals in Parliament devoted themselves to eliminating the ' fancy franchises ' and making the best of the remainder of the Bill, while the working-class Reformers continued to demand Manhood Suffrage and the Ballot. The Bill, as finally passed, not only almost doubled the electorate, but also, by redistribution of seats, added greatly to the voting effectiveness of the working classes in the towns. It did not include the Ballot, which was conceded by the Liberal Government in 1872.

See " Short History ", Part II, chapter 4.
" Common People ", chapters 29 and 31.

1. THE NORTHERN REFORM UNION

[The Northern Reform Union, with headquarters at Newcastle-on-Tyne, was one of the first bodies to take up seriously the demand for Radical Reform after the decline of the earlier movements recorded in Section XV (see pp. 406). It was led by Joseph Cowen the younger, who owned *The Newcastle Chronicle* and was a staunch friend of the miners and ironworkers, whose powerful Unions took a large part in the campaign. Apart from Manhood Suffrage and the Ballot, its chief demand was for Financial Reform; but Cowen and his group were also keenly interested in continental revolutionary movements and in social reform. Cowen later took the chair at the meeting called by Hyndman, out of which the Democratic Federation developed in 1881.]

From *The Newcastle Chronicle*, March 12, 1858.

The Address of the Northern Reform Union to the People of Great Britain and Ireland.

. . . When therefore the " Northern Reform Union " seeks the attainment of Manhood Suffrage, and the protection of the vote by ballot, they only do so because they are deeply conscious of existing evils, for which it is hoped that an extended and free suffrage may provide a cure. . . .

To those who would pourtray [sic] the multiform mischiefs which have flowed upon the British people from the prolific source of oligarchical legislation, the only difficulty is selection. The giant mischief, however, is sufficiently prominent. Two words express it — *excessive taxation*. This is the fountain head; for a careful reflection shows us that under this head may be included almost every species of misgovernment existing in Great Britain. It is the great Upas-Tree, poisoning all beneath its shadow. Tyranny, in its grosser forms, has shrunk before the slow progress of public opinion. . . . Open Rapine can no longer be hazarded; she must now take the shape of taxation. Of British taxation, it may safely be said that nothing approaching to it is recorded in history. . . . When the means of comfort and independence, to this astounding extent, are torn from an industrious people, the consequences are the same whether the end be obtained by force or by fraud. These consequences are the establishment of a landed and monied oligarchy, who, without seeming to do so, in reality rule everything; the enriching of the few at the expense of the millions, and an aristocratic monopoly of every source of honour and emoluments that can possibly be monopolised — whilst the toiling masses, from whom all this comes, may be accurately likened to men placed upon a tread mill, who toil incessantly without advancing one step, but whose toil grinds abundance for those who set them there.

2. THE DEVELOPMENT OF THE REFORM MOVEMENT

[This memorandum by George Howell, the Secretary of the National Reform League, was written as a record of the development of the Reform agitation, mainly from the London angle. Howell (1833–1910) was a bricklayer. He became Secretary of the Trades Union Congress in 1872 (till 1876) and M.P. for Bethnal Green in 1885 (till 1895). A leading adherent of the ' Junta ', he took a prominent part in the struggle for Trade Union legalisation, and his books, " The Conflicts of Capital and Labour " (1877) and " Labour Legislation, Labour Movements, Labour Leaders " (1902), are important sources of information. His papers, including many vital papers and documents bearing on working-class history, are preserved in the Bishopsgate Institute.]

From the Howell Papers in the Bishopsgate Institute, London.

Reform League Letter Book, September, 24th, 1867 (George Howell's MS).

The following facts may aid you.

In the year 1859 a great agitation took place in London amongst the Building Trades for a reduction in their hours of labour from 10 hours to 9 hours per day.

This resulted in a lock out of about 20,000 workmen of the building trades. This agitation continued more or less through 1860 and in March 1861 another lock out occurred in consequence of the men refusing to adopt the hour system. The immediate result of this was to bring together a number of men who saw that the working class could get little advancement until they had more political power.

During 1862 great interest was evinced in the American War, the working classes as a rule defending the Federalists.

Many preliminary reform meetings took place under the " Reform Union ", " London Political Union " and the Ballot Society, but the most important move was being made by the leaders of Trades' Societies. Several manifestoes were published and circulated by them. In May, 1862, an attempt was made, in London, by a conference to inaugurate a movement but it went for a compromise and was unsuccessful.

In the latter part of 1862 English workmen began to express great sympathy with the movement of Garibaldi; this also assisted to produce political feeling in England. They formed a committee to welcome him to England.

On October 28th a meeting was held to establish a Political Association. It was called "The Trades Unionists' Manhood Suffrage and Vote by Ballot Association". This was the first great attempt of Trades Unions to take up politics.

The address to the People of England was written by Mr. George Howell and issued on November 18th, 1862.

The year 1863 opened with several meetings in favour of reform, but it relaxed for a time in consequence of the Political feelings on the American question. On January 28th an immense meeting took place in Exeter Hall, this was followed by the great Trades Union Meeting in St. James' Hall on February 26th at which John Bright Esq. M.P. presided. This meeting thoroughly committed Trades Unions to political movements. This was followed by other similar meetings, and also by some large meetings in favour of Poland. Throughout the remaining portion of the year Political meetings were held and evidences given that a great movement was at hand.

1864 opened quietly but men were still at work and on April 11th, a great Trades' procession met Garibaldi at the Nine Elms Station and escorted him through London. It was purely a political demonstration. Garibaldi had intended to go through England and visit many of the large towns but left London abruptly in consequence of political complications. The Working Men's Committee thereupon convened a meeting on Primrose Hill for April 23rd. This meeting the police dispersed after a stout resistance. It was at a meeting in the evening of the above date that Mr. Howell the present secretary of the Reform League broached the idea (that is propounded) of a *National Political Organisation*. This was warmly taken up by several present and did not after this entirely drop although no immediate action was taken.

Meanwhile the Trades' Unions' Association continued their work. On May 11th Mr. Gladstone delivered his famous reform speech in The House of Commons, this speech gave an immense impetus to the Reform Movement.

On May 17th, 1864, Mr. Beales occupied the chair at a meeting to organise for the franchise, and to protect the right of public meetings in the parks. At this meeting Mr. Gladstone was complimented for his adhesion to the Reform Cause.

On June 22nd, a great Metropolitan reform meeting took place at the Freemasons' Hall, Mr. Beales in the chair. Messrs. Rogers, Nicholay, Howell, Wilks, and others addressed the meeting.

This was followed by one in the Vestry Hall, St. Pancras, on the 25th at which meeting Mr. Washington Wilks fell dead on the platform whilst speaking. This was a sad blow to the Reform Movement, for Mr. Wilks was one of the leading spirits of the advance party. Meetings continued to be held during the remaining portion of the year, and in October preparation was made for a great meeting at which Mr. Bright was to preside. About this time the Working Men's International Association was established to watch over continental politics and to extend the hand of sympathy to the toilers on the continent. Meetings continued to be held in various parts of the country but the proposed meeting with Bright in the chair was abandoned. Thus ended 1864.

In February 1865 the suggestion by Mr. Howell at the Garibaldi meeting before mentioned was revived and [taken up by] Mr. Beales, the President of the League, with Mr. Mason Jones and many others. On February 23rd a meeting was held in St. Martin's Hall convened by circular at which the following resolution was passed :—That in order to secure to the working classes those political rights to which they are constitutionally entitled, this meeting do now form itself into an Association to be called ' The Reform League ', the objects to be as follows :

1st. To secure the extension of the Elective Franchise to every resident and registered adult male person of sound mind and unconvicted of crime.

2nd. To obtain for the voter the protection of the Ballot. After several addresses the meeting adjourned to the 16th of March. On this date the meeting reassembled at Radley's Hotel at which Mr. Bright, Mr. Morley and several leading Reformers attended. On March 23rd another meeting was held at St. Martin's Hall when the rules of the association was adopted. Mr. Beales was elected President and Mr. Howell Secretary. Then followed the election of the Council and the taking of permanent offices in Adelphi Terrace. Then on May 2nd was issued the Address to the People of England.

On May 13th a public inauguration took place at St. Martin's Hall . . . [writing here obliterated] . . . and public meeting took place at Manchester.

In June the secretary Mr. Howell wrote the Address to the Trades Unions, marked No. 3.,[1] and sent copies to all trades societies of England.

After the Election a second edition was issued with the simple alteration from the future to the past tense.

During this time the old associations were fused with the Reform League and all became united in one body. Now followed the work of organisation, opening branches and public meetings. On April 13th, 1866, was published the annual Report and Balance Sheet. Other publications followed. Then came the agitation all over the country for Gladstone's Reform Bill, and its defeat. And on July 23rd the Hyde Park Meeting and fighting for three days. The Agricultural Hall Meeting attended by 40,000 persons under one roof. Other great meetings all over the country followed which compelled the Tory Government to bring in a Reform Bill early in 1867. The rest you know.

3. THE MANHOOD SUFFRAGE AND VOTE BY BALLOT ASSOCIATION

[This Association, founded in 1862, was a purely working-class body, formed by the London Trade Unions associated with the London Trades Council after an attempt to set up a wider organisation, including the middle-class Radicals, had broken down because the middle-class groups were not prepared to accept the whole programme. The Manhood Suffrage and Vote by Ballot Association was later merged in the National Reform League.]

From *Reynolds' Newspaper*, November 23, 1862.

' Address of the Manhood Suffrage and Vote by Ballot Association.'

Our numbers and our position as skilled artisans of this country give us an influence which, if wisely directed, would greatly advance the interests of the toiling masses of our fellow countrymen in every direction. Hitherto, our efforts have been directed to the removal of one evil only, forgetting, or only partially remembering, that all the evils under which we suffer have a common origin — namely, an excess of political power in the hands of those holding a higher

[1] See p. 535.

social position. We do not wish you to relax one iota of your efforts in reference to the amelioration of our social condition. Our advice is to be more than ever united for the purpose of reducing the hours of labour, and for advancing its price. Nor do we wish to turn our trades societies into political organisations, to divert them from their social objects; but we must not forget that we are citizens, and as such should have citizens' rights. Recollect also that by obtaining these rights we shall be able more effectually to secure our legitimate demands as Unionists. Our object is, therefore, to create an organisation for the purpose of obtaining our rights as citizens; or, in other words, our just share of political power. These objects sought to be obtained by the present organisation are precise and definite — namely, registered manhood suffrage by the ballot. Upon these two great principles we take our stand, and invite the whole of the Trade Unionists of this country to cooperate with us until our agitation is crowned with success.

Let us work, work, work — united, consistently and persistently; and our voice will be heard within the walls of Parliament. The friends of progress there will support our demands, and Sovereign and people will, at no distant date, celebrate our victory.

4. THE TRADE UNIONS AND THE AMERICAN CIVIL WAR

[The Trade Unions and the Radical movement generally gave solid support to the cause of the North in the American Civil War. The distress caused by the war was mainly confined to the cotton districts; but there, too, the working-class organisations took their stand solidly on the anti-slavery side.]

(*a*) From *The Beehive*, March 28, 1863.

THE TRADES' UNIONS' EMANCIPATION MEETING.

St. James' Hall was on Thursday evening the scene of a remarkable demonstration. The *élite* of the working men of London — The Trades' Unionists of the Metropolis — assembled in their thousands proclaiming with one voice, in the name of the working men of England, their entire repudiation of any sympathy with the rebel slaveholders of the Southern States of America, adopting, at the same time, an address to President LINCOLN, expressive of their admiration at the firmness and vigour with which, in spite of discouragement from lukewarm friends, and the machinations of the traitors by whom he has been surrounded, he has upheld the cause of Union and Emancipation. Well and nobly have the working men of London redeemed the character of Englishmen, tarnished by the conduct of certain portions of the aristocracy and privileged classes, and a corrupt and venal press, following in the wake of the ever infamous *Times*.

(*b*) From G. J. Holyoake, " The History of the Rochdale Pioneers " (2nd Edition, 1867), chapter 17.

When the dangerous years (from 1861 to 1864) set in, we had *Times* correspondents writing from Rochdale. What they had to tell will be remarkable reading for many years to come. In 1862 the relief committees had not dispensed very much among the unemployed families. On December 19th of that year, the *Times* commissioner wrote from Rochdale, saying :—" It is never very easy to ascertain with any degree of accuracy the extent to which the unemployed have taxed their own resources to meet the calamity which has fallen upon them. The investments most preferred by the working classes vary in different towns. In some the savings bank is the favoured depository ; in others, building and benefit societies are the fashion ; and of late there has been a very general run on the co-operative associations. On this account, comparison of savings bank accounts will not always be a correct indication of what is going on. In several towns where I have inquired into the point I have found that the withdrawals in this year of distress very little exceed those of last year, and the explanation given was that the operatives had just begun to withdraw their deposits in order to invest them in this new movement. In Rochdale it may be said that the co-operative societies, which are on a very large scale, have absorbed pretty nearly the whole of the savings of the working classes. There are here three great concerns managed on this principle — the Store, the Corn Mill, and the Cotton Mill, representing among them a capital of close upon £140,000."

5. THE WELCOME TO GARIBALDI

[Robert Hartwell, a London printer and a former Chartist, was closely associated with the left wing of the London working-class movement, and became Secretary of the London Working Men's Association (see p. 540)

525

and one of the chief promoters of the movement for working class representation in Parliament. He was candidate for Stoke-on-Trent in 1868, but had to withdraw for lack of funds. The London Working Men's Association arose out of the Committee here mentioned, which organised the Garibaldi welcome. The Committee itself had grown out of the attempt to help the London builders in their struggles of 1859–1861.]

From *Reynolds' Newspaper*, April 17, 1864.

. . . Mr. Hartwell, one of the secretaries of the Working Men's Committee, comes forward and reads the following address from the Working Men's Committee, which was also in the course of its reading loudly cheered :—

"Illustrious Chief,—In the name of Britain's sons and daughters of toil, we bid you welcome to this metropolis. We hail you as the representative of a regenerated and united Italy, and for the love we bear to that beautiful land and its noble people, so long oppressed — but now, thanks to your devoted patriotism and indomitable courage, almost freed from the foreign oppressors, we bid you welcome. Your name is to us a household word, the symbol of liberty, associated with lofty daring, bold enterprise, and unselfish devotion to the cause of human progress; for your noble deeds we thank, love and welcome you; and in the name, the sacred name, of that liberty for which you have fought bled and won for the oppressed peoples, we give you a place — the first place in our hearts; and while doing so we cannot forget that there are many who have been associated with you in your glorious enterprises who are also deserving of our admiration and esteem, especially the illustrious Joseph Mazzini, who has done so much for Italy, freedom, and humanity. We therefore hope soon to be able to show our love for your co-workers. Accept then, dear brother, our heartfelt delight at seeing you in our midst; and expressing a fervent desire for the full realisation of your hopes, viz., your country's and the world's freedom, once more — in the unbounded fulness of our love for you and liberty — welcome.

Signed, on behalf of the working men of Great Britain's Metropolis, ROBERT HARTWELL
Secretary of the Working Men's Committee,
LONDON, *April* 11, 1864."

. . . . . .

When Garibaldi came forward to acknowledge the working men's address, he seemed bursting with emotion. At length overcoming his feelings with an effort, he stepped forward and said :—

" I wish to say to the workmen particularly that I am very grateful, and shall never in my life forget the welcome of a class to which I have the honour to belong. (Prolonged Cheers). I like to call my brothers the workmen of every part of the world."

6. THE INTERNATIONAL WORKING MEN'S ASSOCIATION

[The ' First International ' was set up in London in 1864, Karl Marx drafting its Address. Its General Council was drawn mainly from British Trade Union leaders and from foreign exiles in London. The British Trade Unionists were quite prepared to believe in the desirability of revolution on the continent, even though they had no wish for it in Great Britain. Some of them, especially Robert Applegarth, took a quite active part in its affairs. But they began to drop away as its revolutionary character became more evident, and Marx's support of the Paris Commune of 1871 in the manifesto on " The Civil War in France ", issued in the name of the I.W.M.A., accelerated the secessions. By 1872 the I.W.M.A. had lost most of its Trade Union support in Great Britain. The rump of its adherents then attempted to form a British Labour party in opposition to the reformist Labour Representation League (see p. 585); but the attempt was abortive, and the British Section speedily faded away.]

(*a*) From the Rules of the International Working Men's Association, 1864.

CONSIDERING,

That the emancipation of the working classes must be conquered by the working classes themselves; that the struggle for the emancipation of the working classes means not a struggle for class privileges and monopolies, but for equal rights and duties, and the abolition of all class rule;

That the economical subjection of the man of labour to the monopoliser of the means of labour, that is the sources of life, lies at the bottom of servitude in all its forms, of all social misery, mental degradation and political dependence;

That the economical emancipation of the working classes is therefore the great end to which every political movement ought to be subordinate as a means;

That all efforts aiming at that great end have hitherto failed from the want of solidarity between the manifold divisions of labour in each country, and from the absence of a fraternal bond of union between the working classes of different countries;

That the emancipation of labour is neither a local, nor a national, but a social problem, embracing all countries in which modern society exists, and depending for its solution on the concurrence, practical and theoretical, of the most advanced countries;

That the present revival of the working classes in the most industrious countries of Europe, while it raises a new hope, gives solemn warning against a relapse into the old errors, and calls for the immediate combination of the still discontented movements;

FOR THESE REASONS :—

The first International Working Men's Congress declares that the International Association and all societies and individuals adhering to it will acknowledge truth, justice, and morality, as the basis of their conduct towards each other, and towards all men, without regard to colour, creed or nationality;

This Congress considers it the duty of a man to claim the rights of a man and a citizen, not only for himself, but for every man who does his duty. No rights without duties, no duties without rights;

And in this spirit they have drawn up the following rules of the International Association :—

1. This Association is established to afford a central medium of communication and cooperation between Working Men's Societies existing in different countries and aiming at the same end; viz., the protection, advancement, and complete emancipation of the working classes. . . .

(*b*) From " Annual Report of the London Trades' Council ", May 1867, p. 2.

THE COUNCIL AND THE INTERNATIONAL ASSOCIATION.

During the year many questions of great importance have occupied the attention of the Council. One of these came from the International Association, asking the Council to co-operate with them in all matters affecting the interests of labour. A deputation attended a delegate meeting. The subject was well discussed, and the following resolution unanimously adopted :—

" That this meeting is of the opinion that the position of the working man can never be much improved, and is in immediate danger of being seriously depreciated, while the people of different countries have no regular intercommunication among themselves for the purposes of regulating the hours of labour and assimilating wages; and as the International Association affords the best facilities for bringing about that object, it is hereby resolved to co-operate with that association for the furtherance of all questions affecting the interests of labour at the same time continuing the London Trades' Council as a distinct and independent body as before."

It will from this be seen that steps have been taken which, if well followed up, will be the means of doing more good for the working community than all the isolated efforts can by any possibility do.

7. THE NATIONAL REFORM UNION

[The National Reform Union, formed in 1864 under mainly middle-class leadership, refused to commit itself to Manhood Suffrage, accepting instead a compromise by which lodgers, as well as householders, were to be admitted to the franchise, provided they were liable to pay the poor rate. The National Reform Union's programme included the Ballot and redistribution of seats. The Trade Unionists who had formed the Manhood Suffrage Association refused to compromise on this issue, and created the National Reform League as a counterblast to the N.R.U. Thereafter, Reform demonstrations were often marred by conflict between the rival groups, amendments in favour of Manhood Suffrage being sometimes carried against the platform from the floor, though in many cases the two groups worked together in meetings critical of the Bills introduced first by the Whigs and later by Disraeli.

(*a*) From " Report of Proceedings at the National Reform Conference, Manchester, May 1865 ", p. 19.

Mr. J. D. Morton, agent of the National Reform Union, read the following statement, which had been drawn up by the executive committee :—

" In November, 1861, the Leeds Working Men's Parliamentary Reform Association called a meeting of the reformers of Yorkshire and Lancashire to consider the position of the Liberal party. The gathering was a very successful one, though necessarily of a preliminary character. The result was the appointment of a committee to take steps to convene a National Reform Conference, in London, in the following spring, to decide upon a reform platform. In May, 1862, such a Conference was held, and was attended by some of the more advanced reform members of the House of Commons. A most animated debate took place, extending over two days. The good temper and discretion which distinguished that assembly were singularly remarkable, affording a triumphant answer to those who distrust the intelligence and judgment of the working classes. The issue of their deliberations was the adoption, with five dissentients, of the following resolution : That while the statements made in this Conference show the deep conviction of the people in favour of manhood suffrage, in which conviction a large proportion of the delegates fully sympathise, the Conference considers that the union of all classes of real reformers is essential to the attainment of any great improvement of the representation, and with this view it submits to the country the following programme as a basis of action :—Such an extension of the Franchise as will confer the suffrage upon every male person, householder or lodger, rated or liable to be rated for the relief of the poor, together with a more equitable distribution of seats, vote by ballot, and a limitation of the duration of parliament to three years. An executive committee was appointed to prepare a constitution embodying the above programme, and to submit it to a National Conference to be held in Manchester in the ensuing autumn.

Owing, however, to the cotton crisis, it was impracticable to hold a meeting earlier than April, 1864. On the 19th and 20th of that month a Conference took place in the Free-trade Hall, Manchester, where the executive committee presented their report, which was adopted by a large majority, there being only nine dissentients. The new society was designated the National Reform Union, and embraced the subjoined Constitution : 1. To obtain such an extension of the franchise as shall confer the parliamentary suffrage, in counties and boroughs, on every male person, householder or lodger, rated or liable to be rated for the relief of the poor. 2. To secure the free exercise of the franchise, by affording to the voter the protection of the ballot. 3. To procure an equal distribution of members of parliament, in proportion to population and property. 4. To establish more frequent opportunities for the expression of national opinion, by shortening the duration of parliament to three years.

The executive committee then appointed have, under the presidency of their long-tried friend, George Wilson, Esq.,[1] endeavoured to carry out the objects of the Union to the utmost of their power and resources. The details of their labours will be duly submitted to the members at the annual meeting of the National Reform

[1] George Wilson (1808–1870) had been Chairman of the Anti-Corn Law League. In 1867 he became Chairman of the Lancashire and Yorkshire Railway Company.

Union; suffice it at present to state that branch associations have been formed in some of the most populous districts throughout the country. It is now clear that the question of parliamentary reform has reached a crisis:—the executive have, therefore, deemed it expedient to convene the present Conference, to consider what steps can be taken to secure the cordial co-operation of all classes of reformers in the promotion of their common object at the next general election. The executive committee will submit resolutions for the consideration of the Conference, which they hope will meet with its concurrence, and contribute to that unity so essential at the present juncture."

(*b*) Leaflet issued by the National Reform Union (n.d.) [1866–1867].

CONSTITUTION

Title.

This Association shall be denominated the NATIONAL RE-FORM UNION.

Objects.

1. To obtain such an extension of the Franchise as shall confer the Parliamentary Suffrage, in Counties and Boroughs, on every male person, householder, or lodger, rated or liable to be rated for the relief of the poor.

2. To secure the free exercise of the Franchise, by affording to the voter the protection of the Ballot.

3. To procure an equal distribution of Members of Parliament, in proportion to population and property.

4. To establish more frequent opportunities for the expression of national opinion, by shortening the duration of Parliament to three years.

Means.

That the objects of the Reform Union shall be sought to be accomplished by means of Branch Associations, Lectures, Public Meetings, Annual Conferences, and by such other means of diffusing information as the General Executive may from time to time determine.

The active operations of the NATIONAL REFORM UNION commenced in 1864, and from that date to the present, not less than seven hundred and fifty Public Meetings on the Reform question have been held in connection with the Union in various towns in England. One hundred and thirty Branch Associations have been formed, more than five hundred thousand circulars and other publications have been distributed, twenty thousand cards of membership have been issued, and petitions have been presented to the House of Commons signed by upwards of five hundred and thirty-four thousand persons in favour of the late Government Reform Bill. During the winter of 1865 to 1866 the Executive have continued the agitation, and since September last more than five hundred Public Meetings have been held under the auspices of the Union in different parts of the Country.

8. THE NATIONAL REFORM LEAGUE

[The National Reform League was formed in 1865 in London, chiefly by the Trade Unionists who had set up the Manhood Suffrage and Vote by Ballot Association three years previously. It included a few middle-class supporters — among them its barrister President, Edmond Beales (1803–1881), who had been closely connected with various bodies active on the Radical side in foreign affairs, such as the Polish Exiles' Friends Society, the Emancipation Society, and the Garibaldi Welcome Committee. The National Reform League remained, however, a predominantly working-class organisation. It had many branches outside London, especially in the South and Midlands : it never gained any large following in the North.]

(*a*) From the Rules of the Reform League, 1865.

The following are the Rules of the League, as adopted at a Public Meeting held in St. Martin's Hall, on Thursday Evening, the 23rd of March :—

OBJECTS

1. To procure the extension of the elective franchise to every resident and registered adult male person of sound mind, and unconvicted of crime.

2. To obtain for the voter the protection of the Ballot.

MEANS

The League will endeavour to accomplish the above objects by means of branch associations, public meetings, lectures, conferences, requiring pledges from candidates, and such other means as the executive council may from time to time determine.

MEMBERS

All persons approving its objects, and contributing to its funds one shilling and upwards annually, or one penny monthly, shall be members of the League, and be furnished with printed tickets of membership.

MANAGEMENT

The affairs of the League shall be conducted by a president, vice-presidents, and an executive committee, with the assistance of secretaries and a treasurer.

The vice-presidents to have the option of sitting and voting at any meeting of the executive committee.

BRANCH OR AUXILIARY ASSOCIATIONS

1.—All members enrolled by branch associations shall be members of the League, and their names shall be regularly forwarded to the central executive. Cards of membership to be furnished at cost price, and numbered seriatim to facilitate registration.

2.—The chairman of branch associations shall have the option of sitting and voting at all meetings of the central executive.

3.—All branch associations shall have control over their own funds, the central executive not being in any way liable for the acts or responsibilities of branch associations.

4.—All branch associations shall have the sole management of local measures of agitation; but all business affecting the general interest of the movement, such as parliamentary and other national operations transacted in the name, and on behalf of the Reform League, shall be under the guidance of the central executive.

5.—All branch associations shall make such contributions to the general fund as their resources will permit, the central executive having the power, however, to make special appeals to any or all of the members of such branch associations on behalf of the general fund.

6.—All branch associations to be entitled to the publications of the League, at cost price, and to such assistance by way of lectures, deputations, etc., as the circumstances of the case will permit, according to the resources at the disposal of the central executive.

7.—That those reform associations throughout the country who cannot amalgamate with the League, but are nevertheless disposed to assist the League in its objects, may do so by contributing to the general fund.

(*b*) Address issued May 1865.

THE REFORM LEAGUE TO THE WORKING MEN OF GREAT BRITAIN AND IRELAND

FELLOW WORKMEN !

The Working Classes of our Country, the producers of its wealth, are in a degraded and humiliating position. We are denied those inherent rights which the working men of other countries possess, or are in a fair way to acquire ; and England — the beacon-light of freedom and progress in ages past — has now become stationary, if not retrogressive.

The Working Classes of Great Britain — the men who have fought her battles, manned her ships, tilled her soil, built up her manu-factures, trade and commerce, and carried her manners, customs, laws and civilisation to the four quarters of the globe — are denied the most essential privileges of citizens.

The Working Classes pay the great bulk of the taxes, but they are pertinaciously refused all share in the election of those who impose the taxes.

The Working Classes obey the laws, but are allowed no voice in electing the men who make the laws.

Can our country be truly safe and prosperous while so many of her children suffer such great injustice ?

Fellow Workmen ! Without representation in the Parliament of our country, we are powerless for the present, hopeless for the future. Taxation and Government without representation are tyranny, and the Many are at the mercy of the Few. Let us, there-fore — the entire body of unrepresented men in the three kingdoms — league ourselves together to carry into effect that fundamental principle of all genuine Reform and Self-Government—*MANHOOD SUFFRAGE* ; and with it, let us demand for our protection *THE BALLOT*, which the rich use for their own purposes but deny to others.

Let us contrive to set an example of respect for law and thereby give a dignified answer to all calumniators.

Above all, let us sink our individual differences in presence of our common grievance and thereby prove how earnest we are in the struggle for our rights !

Union is strength! Let us then march shoulder-to-shoulder towards our political enfranchisement ! The march may be long, but the victory is assured ; for when our opponents see us determined, persevering and united, they will no longer refuse our just demands. They are our countrymen, and time and reflexion will lead them to act justly toward us.

Fellow Workmen! Organise! Organise! Organise! Organise in your cities, towns, villages, parishes, and fields. *Enrol yourselves members of the Reform League!* Argue the question of your rights coolly, courageously, continually ; and avoid everything which countenances unholy compromise of a just principle. Take courage from the triumph of our brethren in America, and let us emulate their virtues and resolution, while constitutionally battling for our rights.

EDMOND BEALES, President.

CENTRAL OFFICE OF THE REFORM LEAGUE,
8, ADELPHI TERRACE, STRAND, W.C.
May 2nd, 1865.

(c) Address issued by the Reform League, June 1865.

TO THE TRADES' UNIONISTS OF THE UNITED KINGDOM.

FELLOW WORKMEN,

As a Trades Unionist, like yourselves, I desire to speak freely and frankly to you on behalf of Manhood Suffrage.

During the last few weeks you have been called upon to witness a General Election. About 1,000,000 of our fellow countrymen have had the " *privilege* " of recording their votes in the election of the " *Law Makers* " of Great Britain.

Out of this number only about 100,000 or one-tenth of the whole, belong to the *Working Class* of our population. Besides which there are about 6,000,000 of the adult males without *any* vote or direct voice in the great council of the nation.

Yet these " Law Makers " enact laws binding upon us all ; they impose taxes we all have to pay ; aye, and spend these taxes most improvidently. Yet we have no voice to advise, no power to check, any extravagance in the expenditure, or mismanagement in the government, or injustice in the laws.

The privileged classes in this country tell us that we have " no rights without duties ". This we admit. But they *impose duties* and *withhold* the *rights* : of this we complain. We obey the laws in common, let us have a voice in their enactment. We pay taxes far greater than the rich in *proportion* to the *means* we *have*, or our *property* to be *protected*, yet we are denied any voice in the *adjustment* of our *taxation*, or in the spending of our revenue.

The consequence is, that our laws are partial ; being made by a class, for a class ; and the taxation most oppressive upon those least able to bear it.

As Unionists we have just reason to complain, in as much as there are laws not yet repealed which bear heavily upon the workmen. For example, those relating to master and workmen. How often do we find some case which startles us by the manifest cruelty and injustice of the sentence. For if the case had been reversed, the employer defendant instead of the employed, it would have been dismissed. (*See evidence before the Committee of the House of Commons this Session.*)

How often have we found some of our greatest and most combined efforts rendered nugatory by some antique piece of legislation in the shape of an unrepealed Act of Parliament, or by some action taken by the *Home Office* ? Is it not fresh in your recollection that the Government lent soldiers to a private contractor at Chelsea to enable him to resist his workmen's demand ? Have they not done so at Plymouth ? Did they not do so at Aldershot ? And in how many cases have they given assistance where the men could not bring positive proof although they have felt morally certain ? Scotland Yard provided " pickets " in blue coats for a large number of buildings in London during the Builders' Strike and Lock-out. Yet we were condemned if we sent a private citizen (without citizen's rights) simply to inform workmen in the most friendly and civil manner that a trade dispute existed.

Bearing all this in mind, let us now demand our enfranchisement ; *not as a class*, but as subjects in the eye of the law, and as citizens of our common country, which we all love, all support, and all protect. You spend thousands of pounds annually to obtain some trifling advance in wages, and some small reduction in time ; and are compelled to fight for its maintenance over and over again, because no voice is heard in Labour's right in the " *Commons* ", or people's House.

Men stand there and vilify our class, our motives, and our actions, because they know we cannot be present to rebut their charges.

Let us once be able to maintain by the force of intellect and truth our rights as workmen, in that house, and depend upon it we shall rise in the social scale, and show that we can discharge our duties as well as exercise our rights.

But they tell us we are incapable of self-government, and unfit to be trusted!! This we deny. Our own organisations prove our power of government, our self-restraint, our financial ability and economy, and our law-making capabilities *likewise*. They show more, they prove that we understand justice, and are earnest in the protection of every member, whether he be assailed by an employer, or by a fellow-workman and brother Unionist. Your combinations are the most perfect in organisation and the most powerful in influence of any in the kingdom. Let us use them for our rights as citizens, and you will soon see the rights of labour respected and the workman benefitted thereby.

We seek not to overbalance political power by the substitution of one class influence for another. We seek it for all men without distinction; for, on the principle of Manhood Suffrage, protected by the ballot, class legislation as well as class representation will be no more.

Support, then, the Reform League in your various localities, and our next parliament will merit your gratitude and respect, by passing a Reform Bill at once comprehensive and just to the People.

I am, fellow workmen,

Yours in unity,

GEORGE HOWELL,

Secretary of the Reform League,

8, ADELPHI TERRACE, STRAND, W.C.

(*d*) From the Minute Book of the Reform League.

Executive Council Friday March 16th 1866.

Specially to Consider the Government Reform Bill.

OPENING BY MR BEALES.

1st. Mr Beales, the president, in opening the proceedings, gave an outline of the proposed Bill, and stated that he placed it in the hands of the meeting for discussion.

CORRESPONDENCE.

2nd. Letters were read from Prof. Beesly, Wm. Shaen Esq, Wm. Man Esq, Mark E. Marsden Esq., and H. S. Slack Esq.

advising the Council to support the Bill introduced by the Government, but not to relax its efforts for further reforms in accordance with its principles.

RESOLUTION.

3rd. Moved by Dr Perfitt, seconded by Mr Geo. W. Wheeler,

" That the Reform League deems it its duty to oppose the Reform Bill introduced by the Government in consequence of its not meeting the just expectations of the people."

AMENDMENT.

4th. Moved by Mr E. D. Rogers, Seconded by Mr Henriette,

" That this League protest against the insufficient provisions of the Government Reform Bill, but under the circumstances deem it right to support the Government against the Conservative and sham Liberal party in enabling such a Bill to pass, at the same time taking every means to procure substantial amendments in it, for the further extension of the franchise, during its discussion in Committee."

This amendment was opposed by the Revd. Mr Bonner, Mr McHeath and Mr Chas. Bubb. It was supported by Mr Richard Moore, Mr Wynne and Mr Lucraft.

5th. Mr Wynne handed the following amendment to the Chairman to read to the meeting : " That the League continue the advocacy of its own principles, without, directly or indirectly, opposing the Government Bill."

. . . .

EXECUTIVE MEETING, MARCH 20TH, 1866.

Adjourned from Friday last. Mr Beales presided as before ; he opened proceedings by reading the resolution and amendment of the previous meeting. Mr Odger wished to submit a resolution which he thought would reconcile all parties and preserve our own principles. The resolution having been read and a discussion thereon having taken place the following amended resolution was adopted with only five dissentients. Viz :—

" That this Council, whilst strictly adhering to the principle of Residential and Registered Manhood Suffrage as the only just, sound, permanent and satisfactory basis of representation for this country, and whilst protesting against the insufficient provisions of the Government Reform Bill now before Parliament, deem it their duty under the circumstances to support the Government against the combined Conservative and sham Liberal parties in enabling such Bill to pass."

EDMOND BEALES.

(e) From the Minute Book of the Reform League, 1867.

Date. Delegate Meeting, Sussex Hotel, Wednesday, February 27th, 1867.

Chairman. Edmond Beales, Esq. in the Chair. About 230 present.

The following resolutions were adopted after a long discussion :—

RESOLUTIONS.

1st. " That this meeting, composed of delegates from Trades, Friendly Temperance, and other Societies, and of Metropolitan branches of the Reform League, having duly considered the Government plan of Parliamentary Reform proposed by Mr. Disraeli, is of opinion that, as it is based upon a rating franchise, makes no provision for giving a vote to lodgers, and, in fact, contains no adequate provision for the full representation of the working classes, it is wholly unworthy of the support of this meeting, or of the true Liberal Party of this Country."

2nd. " That this meeting is further of opinion, that no measure of reform will sufficiently meet the just claims of the unrepresented classes which is not, without any subterfuge or evasion, based upon the true and constitutional principle of residential, registered Manhood Suffrage, protected by the Ballot ; and calls upon all sincere reformers to redouble their efforts in insisting upon these principles as the only final settlement of this question."

3rd. " That there be a great gathering of Metropolitan and Provincial Reformers on Good Friday in Hyde Park during the afternoon for the purpose of a Reform promenade and recreation."

4th. " That the Committee of the League be requested to convene a meeting in Trafalgar Square on Monday evening March 11th."

5th. " That unless a satisfactory prospect is held out in Parliament of the Working Classes being universally enfranchised upon the principles of the Reform League it will be necessary to consider the propriety of those classes adopting a universal cessation from labour until their political rights are conceded."

The question of Sunday Meetings was withdrawn.

Read and declared to be correct at a Council held March 6th, 1867.

J. BAXTER LANGLEY.

9. THE LONDON WORKING MEN'S ASSOCIATION

[The London Working Men's Association, headed by George Potter and Robert Hartwell, was the rival of the London Trades Council, and was opposed to the influence exercised on that body and on the National Reform League by the leaders of the Amalgamated Societies. It was the first body, after the Reform Act of 1867, to put forward plans for the widespread adoption of working-class candidates for Parliament.]

(*a*) From *The Beehive*, August 18, 1866.

. . . The Working Men's Association materially differs from any other existing society in its purposes. It is not merely a political or trades' society, but with part of their characteristics it comprehends a wider field than either of these organisations can reach. A political society has generally a definite object, and terminates on its attainment. A trades' society is necessarily confined to the interests of one special class, although it may heartily sympathise with the objects of all the industrial classes. In the pursuit of their business trade societies generally avoid politics, and political societies as certainly exclude trades' business from their proceedings, whilst this Association includes both departments, when matters arise of public and urgent importance. The need of some extensive organisation, not only for political or trade purposes, but for the attainment of social changes, is generally acknowledged.

(*b*) From *The Beehive*, June 2, 1866.

ADDRESS TO THE WORKING MEN OF ENGLAND.

FELLOW WORKMEN,—We invite you to join our association, established to watch over and promote the political and social interests of the industrious classes by means of the platform and the press. We believe there never was a time when, politically and socially, industrial interests stood in a greater need of a careful consideration and earnest support, and an association such as we hope with your aid to establish cannot fail in effecting a large amount of good. Amongst the many subjects to which the attention of such an association could be directed in addition to the Complete Enfranchisement of the People, we may enumerate the Reduction in the Hours of Labour; the Improvement in the Dwellings of Working Men; the Amendment or the Abrogation of those legislative acts affecting industry, passed in a time when the relation of Capital to Labour was little, if at all, understood, and which are therefore generally of a onesided and partial character; the Education of the Working Classes; the Organisation of Labour; and the removal of many other existing evils which have grown up and flourished under the evil influence of Class Legislation. We do not pretend that we shall be able to create a Utopia or bring about a Millenium where every man would be happy and contented, but we do believe that our united efforts may result in removing some and modifying others of the many social and political evils now existing. In appealing to our fellow workmen for their cooperation we use the term workmen in the broadest possible sense; we do not simply mean skilled artisans only, but include in that term clerks, shopmen, warehousemen, porters, and labourers of every description; all, in short, who live by the earning of wages. Neither will we refuse the honest cooperation of those of any other classes sincerely desirous of rendering us assistance in furtherance of our objects. In conclusion, therefore, we confidently ask the cooperation of all true friends of Progress; but especially do we call upon the thousands of our provident fellow workmen enrolled in the various trades, friendly and other organisations of working men to come forward and aid us in our good work, which has for its object the greatest possible amount of happiness for the greatest possible number of people.

We remain, Fellow Workmen, yours, in the cause of Progress,

On behalf of the Executive Committee,

GEORGE POTTER, President.

F. G. DAVIS, Treasurer.

R. HARTWELL, Secretary.

10. THE HYDE PARK MEETING, 1866.

[The Hyde Park incident, described in the first of these two extracts, was the culminating point in the Reform struggle, in that it helped to convince both the main political parties that Reform had to come and thus cleared the way for the Reform Act of the following year.]

(*a*) From Joseph Irving, " The Annals of Our Time ", 1871.

Entry for July 23, 1866.

Riot in Hyde Park, arising out of an official notice issued to prohibit its use by the Reform League for a great political demonstration. Early in the afternoon a notice signed by Sir Richard Mayne was extensively posted throughout London, stating that the park gates would be closed to the public at five o'clock. The Committee of the Reform League met in the afternoon to conclude their arrangements, and resolved not to abandon what they considered their line of duty. The numerous processions were to march with banners and music to the Marble Arch, where properly appointed persons would demand admittance on their behalf if necessary. By five o'clock thousands were standing near the chief entrances. The police were at first posted inside the gates ; but a few missiles, now a stone and then a stick, being thrown, the men were marched outside. A line of ordinary policemen, in a semicircle, stood before the gates, protected in front by mounted constables. As soon as the banners of the first procession were seen, a cheer was raised, and a space was opened for the leaders to pass along to the gates. Mr. Edmond Beales, Colonel Dickson, Mr. George Brooke, and other prominent members of the Reform League alighted from the foremost carriage, and, addressing the nearest mounted officer, Mr. Beales requested a quiet admittance to the Park : the officer told him he could not go in, and in answer to Mr. Beales' question, " Why ? " he said, " I have authority to prevent you." Mr. Beales asked who gave him the authority, and the reply was, " Our Commissioner." The leaders of the Reform party, thus repulsed, stepped back into their carriages amidst loud cheering and a little murmuring on the part of those whose curiosity would, perhaps, have been better satisfied had resistance been carried further. As much of the procession as could be organized in the dense mass, variously estimated at from a hundred to two hundred thousand persons, followed the carriages of the Committee towards Oxford-street, along which they proceeded. At length the head of the demonstration reached Trafalgar-square, where the speaking was brief, and confined to the proposing and seconding of two resolutions, urging the prosecution of lawful and constitutional means for the extension of the franchise, and thanking Mr. Gladstone, Mr. Bright, and others, for being faithful to the cause, while others had basely deserted it. While the leaders were marching to Trafalgar-square, more exciting work engaged the attention of the crowds who remained at Hyde Park. A large portion, finding a forcible entry by the gate prevented, moved westward, and in one bold dash smashed down the railings of the park in sight of the police, and entered the ground cheering and waving handkerchiefs. The railings at Park-lane were broken in about the same time, and in a few minutes several thousands had entered the park. Encounters between the police and mob now became rife, the former using their truncheons freely, and the latter stones and other missiles. Before long several prisoners and wounded persons were removed; and the most serious consequences were apprehended when a detachment of Foot Guards arrived, under the command of Colonel Lane Fox. The Guards were cheered by the mob, and took up a position near the gate, where they remained throughout. A body of the Life Guards soon after arrived, and were cheered in the same manner. They, however, galloped off to some other part of the park. When the police were left to themselves, they were again pelted and attacked by the mob, and one or two of their number unhorsed. After a series of charges against the mob the police were reinforced by a second detachment of Foot Guards, drawn up in front of the gate, and who, with the first detachment, received orders to be in readiness to fire should it become necessary. Encounters between the police and the mob then became less frequent, and finally quiet was restored when another body of Life Guards augmented the soldiery, and combined to help in removing the mob from the park.

(*b*) From *Reynolds' Newspaper*, July 29, 1866.

. . . The people have triumphed, in so far as they have vindicated their right to meet, speak, resolve, and exhort in Hyde-park. The men of London have shown by their behavior and achievements on Monday last that if Hyde-park be royal property it is also the people's property.

True, the gates were closed and guarded against them. They were not allowed to enter by the customary, the legal, and the constitutional way. But, then, they found out there were other ways than the legal, the constitutional and the customary way of effecting an entrance.

Yes, the gates of Hyde-park were closed against them, and, lo! in twenty minutes after, Hyde-park all round was one vast, wide, gaping gate. The ordinary gates were the only closed part of the fencing. Hyde-park became as open as a " common ". By the exercise of that natural and " constitutional " muscular and mental might which God has given them, they established their right to enter into their own park. By a long pull, a strong pull and a push all together, down went the iron railings and the stones in which they were fixed in hundreds of yards, so that in less time than it takes to tell the story, the iron barriers which excluded the people from Hyde-park were levelled to the ground, or inclined against the trees, for miles.

Then the people poured in hundreds of thousands into the park, and there, under the nose of Sir Richard Mayne, and before the masses of the bludgeon-brigade, and through scarlet lines of Foot Guards and Life Guards, with bayonets fixed and sabres drawn, were flanking the police, and ready to charge, a meeting was held, a chairman appointed, speeches made, and resolutions proposed, seconded, and carried.

11. THE REFORM ACT, 1867.

[Disraeli's Reform Bill, shorn of its ' fancy ' clauses, became law on August 15, 1867. It gave the franchise to £10 householders and lodgers paying £10 rent in the towns, and to householders of houses rented at £12 in the counties. It also provided for a large-scale redistribution of seats. The working-class Radicals were divided in their reception of it.]

(a) From *The Commonwealth*, January 12, 1867.

THE FORTHCOMING DEMONSTRATION AND THE TRADES' UNIONS.

It is impossible to award too much praise to those members of societies who have determined to swell the cry and actively engage in the settlement of the great question of political Reform. The opponents to the extension of political rights, have over and over again pointed to the apathy of these bodies, as a proof of the indifference of the working classes to the existence and purpose of organisations like unto the Reform League, and to that argument there was no replying, save, by the unfortunate plea that trade societies were not political bodies, a reply utterly at variance with truth and directly in opposition to the history of trade societies.

Trade organisations have repeatedly shown the fallacy of the argument, for their members have continually taken action against and also in favour of political measures affecting their interests, not only as workmen but as citizens. Social and political Reform are so intimately interwoven, that it is extremely difficult to distinguish the one from the other, and hence we have heard men object to being called politicians, while their entire action prove them to be political rather than social Reformers. . . .

That we do not attach too much importance to the latest addition to our ranks, or rather to the ranks of the Reform League, may be shown by the mere statement that among the associated bodies that have determined to take part in the forthcoming demonstration are to be found :—the Amalgamated Engineers, the Amalgamated Iron-founders, the Amalgamated Carpenters, the Amalgamated Cord-wainers, and the Operative Bricklayers. Some of the most numerous and influential, if not the most, of the entire trades. But above and beyond this, their decision *is sanctioned by the London Trades Council*, containing representatives from the great bulk of the London trades and indirectly representing the trades of the entire kingdom. It is impossible to calculate the moral weight and importance which their decision will give to all future doings of the Reform League. . . .

(*b*) From *The Commonwealth*, March 23, 1867.

[Resolutions carried at a meeting of the Reform League and Trades Delegates, following the introduction of Disraeli's Reform Bill.]

. . . Colonel Dickson moved the following resolution :—" That the plan of Reform proposed by the Government admits the justice and validity of the principle of residential manhood suffrage, advo-cated by the Reform League, by extending the franchise to house occupiers without reference to rent, but endeavours to fettle and paralyse the operation of such franchise by rating and excessive residence conditions, and the gross class injustice of dual voting; and that it is the duty of the League now to redouble its exertions to obtain the unrestricted exercise of the franchise by lodgers and all other occupiers ; or, in other words, residential manhood suffrage, with the protection of the ballot to secure the independence of the voter.' . . ."

Mr Merriman moved, Mr Henwood seconded, and it was agreed : " That the members of the Reform League residing in various cities and boroughs throughout the kingdom be invited to form them-selves forthwith into election committees for the following purposes :

1st. To secure the return at the next election, and at the least possible expense, of gentlemen now in Parliament, and either favourable to the principles of the League, or closely approximating thereto.

2nd. To ascertain the exact position of all professed Liberal M.P.'s who have not declared themselves in favour of the League programme, or of household suffrage for boroughs unfettered by ratepaying clauses, and supplemented by a liberal lodger franchise; and in the event of their declining to assist in demands of this extent, to take measures for replacing them by more advanced Reformers at the next election."

On the motion of Dr Perfitt, seconded by Mr Guedalla, the following resolution was carried : " That in furtherance of the cause of Reform it is essential that steps be immediately taken by the Reform League to call a national convention of delegates from the whole of the branches of the Reform League and other Reform associations, and trade, friendly and temperance societies in the United Kingdom, for the purpose of determining what more decided action shall be taken to ensure the full and complete enfranchisement of the people on the basis of the League."

(c) From *The Beehive*, October 5, 1867.

Reform Fete and Banquet, organised by the London Working Men's Association.

[At the Open Air Meeting :]

Mr Mark Price (of Manchester), then came forward and said : The working men hold this meeting here to-day to celebrate the passing of the Reform Bill, which they consider a Liberal triumph, and in a short time the friends of Lord Derby are to hold a banquet at Manchester to celebrate the same event which they consider a Tory triumph. I consider the opinions of the latter are nearer the truth. What has the bill done ? Has it given manhood suffrage ? No. It has given household suffrage, but it has coupled with that the condition that the enfranchised householders are to pay their own rates. What else is given by this bill, which some of us think will work the redemption of the working man ? What has it done for the working men of London ? Do you think that such of you as pay 4s. a week for your lodgings will get votes ? No, you will not get votes unless you pay 5s. a week. . . . Then, again, what has the bill done for that great industrious multitude — the agricultural labourers ? Will any one pretend that any portion of that body will be admitted to the franchise by the Reform Act. (Cheers). Household suffrage has given — what ? Why, it only affects the boroughs, and them in an infinitesimal degree, leaving out altogether more than half the whole country.

[At the Banquet :]

The chairman George Potter . . . As to the results of the Bill which they had met to celebrate, it must be productive of good to the country. It would admit several hundred thousand men to the rights of citizenship, who would bring their influence as electors to help those who were still without the franchise to obtain it. (Cheers). We have achieved a great triumph, but we have not achieved a final one. (Loud Cheers). All that is incomplete must be perfected. The narrowness of the franchise must be widened. The smallness of the redistribution scheme must be enlarged. The destruction of the popular voice must be restored. The protection of the vote must be secured by the Ballot, and bribery must be punished by imprisonment. . . .

XIX

THE LABOUR LAWS, 1867–1876

INTRODUCTION

FROM 1864, when the Trade Unions set on foot an agitation to secure the amendment of the law of master and servant, to 1875, when the Conspiracy and Protection of Property Act and the Employers and Workmen Act completed the new legal code dealing with Trade Unions and industrial relations, the Trade Union movement was engaged in a continuous struggle to win legal recognition of the rights of collective bargaining and of the equality of employers and workmen as parties to the contract of employment. The outcry that followed the Sheffield Outrages of 1806 — coinciding with the Fenian troubles in Ireland — seemed to threaten Trade Unionism with a renewal of legal repression; but the Unions, aided by able friends among the middle classes, such as Frederic Harrison and Thomas Hughes, were able to beat off the attacks and, in the end, to secure an adequate legal foundation both for their organisation and for the conduct of strikes and collective bargaining. They also won, in 1875, recognition of the equality of employers and workmen before the law. These concessions were obtained in turn from Liberal and from Conservative Governments. The Gladstone Government passed the Trade Union Act of 1871, which secured the legal basis of the movement, but coupled with it the penal clauses of the Criminal Law Amendment Act, which, despite speedy demonstration of their repressive effects, Gladstone refused to modify. It was left for Disraeli and the Conservatives both to repeal this Act and replace it by a less oppressive measure, and to put on the statute book the Employers and Workmen Act of 1875.

In this struggle, the Trade Unions were greatly aided by the votes gained by many of their members under the Reform Act of 1867. But, though this Act was passed by the Conservatives and many Trade Unionists voted for the Conservatives in 1874 in protest against the Criminal Law Amendment Act, thereafter the bulk of Trade Union votes were cast for the Liberals.

See " Short History ", Part II, chapters 5 and 6.
" Common People ", chapter 32.

1. THE LAW OF TRADE UNIONS AFTER 1825

[The Act of 1825 had given only a very narrow recognition of the right to combine, and it had remained difficult to carry on strikes without the risk, in one way or another, of running foul of the law. The attitude of the courts varied with the political atmosphere of the time ; and after Lord Melbourne's day there was no general attack on Trade Unions as such from Government quarters. But any act which could be represented as interfering with the right of any workman ' to dispose of his labour as he thought fit ' was liable to be treated by the law as a criminal conspiracy, and much weight was also put on the unlawfulness of the Trade Unions' interference with any employer's lawful business. The first of the following extracts, from a judgment of Mr. Justice Erle. in 1851, illustrates this attitude ; and his memorandum, drawn up sixteen years later for the Royal Commission, shows that his interpretation of the law had not changed.]

(a) From the summing up of J. Erle, in the case of Reg. *v.* Duffield (1851). Cox's " Criminal Cases ", vol. v, p. 431.

But, gentlemen, I think it would be most dangerous indeed if that rule of law, so in favour of workmen protecting their own interests, were at all construed to extend to that which is charged upon this indictment, and which the counsel for the prosecution supposes is made out by the evidence, and in respect of which your verdict is to be given ; that is to say : to suppose that workmen, who think that a certain rate of wages ought to be obtained, have a right to combine together to induce men, already in the employ of other masters, for the purpose of compelling those masters to raise their wages. The indictment charges in one class of the counts, and that to which I think your attention should be most prominently directed, that they conspired to obstruct Mr. Perry in the carrying out of his business, by persuading and inducing workmen, that had been hired by him, to leave his service in order to force him to change the mode of carrying on his business. There are no threats or intimidations supposed to have been used towards the workmen, but there is a class of counts founded upon that, and I take it to be perfectly clear in point of law, and I lay it down to you for the purpose of your verdict, that if that class of counts is made out you will find the defendants guilty upon that class of counts, that they conspired to obstruct Mr. Perry by persuading his workmen to leave him in order to induce him to make a change in the mode of conducing and carrying on his business.

(*b*) From the Eleventh Report of the Royal Commission on Trade Unions, (1867–1869), Memorandum by Sir William Erle on ' The Law relating to Trade Unions ', p. lxxi.

Furthermore, I think that there may also be unlawful restraint of trade without coercion by unlawful means, and without such obstruction or molestation as is last above mentioned.

I assume that the employer and the employed have each a right to a free course for free trade in labour, as above described. The supply of labour to the employer is stopped if the working man chooses to stop ; and assuming for the present that his act is lawful whenever he freely chooses so to do, still a party who induces him so to do may, in so doing (as it seems to me) infringe the rights of the employer to a free course for the supply of labour. I take the case of money paid to the working man to induce him to stop, in which the motive for so paying is malice towards the employer — that is, some corrupt or spiteful motive. I put aside money so paid from a motive of supposed interest, as in the case of some strikes, and assume it to be paid for the sole purpose of ruining the employer or destroying his manufacture. A question is thus raised, Does the law allow it ? I think not. A stop in the supply of labour is obviously a damage in every trade ; the causing of the stop is a restraint of trade ; and all restraint of trade is, as above stated, presumed to be unlawful until the contrary be shown. . . .

What has been said of gifts of money for the purpose of stopping supply of labour is true, mutatis mutandis, of persuasion for the same purpose. . . .

[*Ibid.* p. lxxii.]

As to combination, each person has a right to choose whether he will labour or not, and also the terms on which he will consent to labour, if labour be his choice. The power of choice in respect of labour and terms, which one person may exercise and declare singly, many after consultation may exercise jointly, and they may make a simultaneous declaration of their choice, and may lawfully act thereon for the immediate purpose of obtaining the required terms ; but they cannot create any mutual obligation having the legal effect of binding each other not to work or not to employ unless upon terms allowed by the combination. . . . Every party who chooses to put an end to it is thenceforward as free to claim his own terms for his labour, as if such arrangement had never been made. . . . A person can neither alienate for a time his freedom to dispose of his own labour or his own capital according to his own will, nor alienate such freedom generally and make himself a slave; it follows that he cannot transfer it to the governing body of a union.

2. THE MOLESTATION OF WORKMEN ACT, 1859

[This Act, which was the first to modify the legislation of 1825, was notable for the fact that it legalised ' peaceful picketing ' and gave the Trade Unions a clearer recognition of the right to combine. Its repeal in 1871, when the Criminal Law Amendment Act re-defined the offences of molestation, obstruction, and intimidation, was one of the principal grievances of the Unions; and the position was not fully restored in respect of picketing until the Trade Disputes Act of 1906 reinstated the right of ' peaceful persuasion '. The Conspiracy and Protection of Property Act, 1875, gave only the right to attend at a place for the purpose of communicating or receiving information, not that of ' peacefully persuading ' potential blacklegs to abstain from working. The Act of 1859 was largely due to the efforts of the National Association of United Trades for the Protection of Labour (see p. 469).]

From the Molestation of Workmen Act, 1859. (22 Vict. c. 34.)

An Act to amend and explain an Act of the sixth year of the reign of King George the Fourth, to repeal the Laws relating to the combination of Workmen, and to make other Provisions in lieu thereof. (19th April, 1859)

Whereas an Act was passed in the sixth year of the reign of King George the Fourth, intituled " An Act to repeal the Laws relating to the combination of Workmen, and to make other provisions in lieu thereof : " and whereas different decisions have been given on the construction of the said Act : Be it therefore declared and enacted . . . as follows :—

1. That no workman or other person, whether actually in employment or not, shall, by reason merely of his entering into an agreement with any workman or workmen, or other person or persons, for the purpose of fixing or endeavouring to fix the rate of wages or remuneration at which they or any of them shall work, or by reason merely of his endeavouring peaceably, and in a reasonable manner, and without threat or intimidation, direct or indirect, to persuade others to cease or abstain from work in order to obtain the rate of wages or the altered hours of labour so fixed or agreed

upon or to be agreed upon, shall be deemed or taken to be guilty of " molestation " or " obstruction ", within the meaning of the said Act, and shall not therefore be subject or liable to any prosecution or indictment for conspiracy. Provided always, that nothing herein contained shall authorize any workman to break or depart from any contract or authorize any attempt to induce any workman to break or depart from any contract.

3. THE LAW OF MASTER AND SERVANT

[The unfairness of the law of master and servant pressed heavily on all classes of workers, but most of all on the miners, against whom it was applied with the greatest frequency and rigour. If a workman broke his contract of service, the act was criminal, and punishable by imprisonment or fine, whereas breach by a master was only a civil wrong, giving rise to damages. It followed, in the then state of the law, that a master could give evidence in his own defence, whereas a workman, being charged with a criminal act, could not. Moreover, a workman could be summarily arrested on the order of a single justice, though (in England, but not in Scotland) he could, as an alternative, be summonsed to appear. Even so, he could be arrested if a magistrate thought he might not answer the summons. The campaign against the law was started by Alexander Macdonald, the Scottish Miners' leader, who enlisted Alexander Campbell, the old Owenite, Secretary of the Glasgow Trades Council. The Glasgow Trades Council convened the Trade Union Conference which met in London to deal with the question in 1864. It was very widely attended by representatives of all sections of the Trade Union movement, and has a fair claim to be regarded as the real beginning of the Trades Union Congress (see p. 514).

Of the speakers mentioned, George Odger (1813–1877, not 1820–1877 as is usually stated) was the best-known political leader of the London Trade Unionists; Daniel Guile (1814–1883) was the Secretary of the Ironfounders; Robert Applegarth (1834–1924) was Secretary of the Amalgamated Carpenters and Joiners; Thomas Connolly was the leader of the Stonemasons; Alexander Macdonald (1821–1881) was at the head of the newly formed National Miners' Association; William Dronfield was a compositor, and Secretary to the Sheffield Trades; Robert Austin was later General Secretary of the Engineers; George Potter was the leader of the London Building Trades; T. J. Dunning (1799– ?) was Secretary of the Bookbinders, and the doyen of the movement.

The Act of 1867 removed the ban on a workman giving evidence on his own behalf, and made summons, instead of arrest, the normal procedure; but it still left the master and the workman unequal parties, by retaining the criminal taint attached to breach of contract by a ' servant '.]

(a) From " Report of a Conference on the Law of Masters and Workmen under their Contract of Service " (1864), p. 5.

Mr. Strachan on behalf of the Glasgow Committee, explained the reason which had induced the workmen in Glasgow to initiate the movement which had resulted in the assembling of the present Conference. While the workmen both in England and Scotland were equally liable to be punished as *common felons* for a breach of their contract of service; in England it was competent to summon a workman to appear in Court to answer to any complaint against him, while in Scotland the Law made it imperative for the Magistrate on a complaint against a workman being laid before him, to issue his warrant for at once apprehending the workman and bringing him a prisoner into court. This law was found in practice to be most oppressive, workmen being in every instance apprehended without notice, and often sent to prison before either their families or friends were aware of the proceedings against them. With the view of obtaining an amendment of the law, a Committee had been formed in Glasgow, consisting of representatives from nearly all the trades in the city, and this committee had got prepared and printed a statement explanatory of the statute law affecting workmen under their contract of service. 15,000 copies of this statement had been circulated in Glasgow, Edinburgh, London, Liverpool, Sheffield, Bristol, Nottingham, Leeds, Newcastle and the Potteries, and through the society of Amalgamated Engineers, and the National Association of Miners. To give a national character to the move-ment, it was considered advisable to convene the present Con-ference; and, from the answers received from the places invited to send representatives, it was right to explain that, if there had been more time allowed, the representation would be at least double the number now present. Thereafter, the delegates having fully dis-cussed the present law affecting workmen under their contract of service, and considering that

Whereas the contract of service entered into between masters and their workmen is a mutual contract of a purely civil character, and in law and equity ought to be dealt with as such; and whereas in all questions which arise relating to a breach of such contract on the part of such masters they are treated simply as parties to a civil contract; and whereas in questions relating to a breach of such contract on the part of workmen they are treated not only as parties to a civil contract and liable as such, but in addition are liable to be proceeded against criminally under the statute 20 Geo II., cap. 19; 6 Geo III., cap. 25; and 4 Geo IV., cap. 34; and to be punished as *common felons* by imprisonment with hard labour, for a period not exceeding three months—

RESOLVED

Moved by Mr. Odger, London, seconded by Mr. Hides, Sheffield, and unanimously agreed to :—

That this unequal state of the law as to questions arising under contracts of service between masters and workmen is most unjust and oppressive as against the workmen, and ought to be repealed or amended.

Moved by Mr. Lang, Glasgow, seconded by Mr. Guile, London, and unanimously agreed to :—

That the rights and remedies of either master or workman, under their mutual civil contract of service, ought to be entirely of a civil character, and all provision of the Law attaching criminal consequences to a breach of such contract ought to be wholly repealed.

Moved by Mr. Applegarth, London, seconded by Mr. Connolly, London, and agreed to :—

That in any amendment of the Law, no favour should be given to either master or workmen, and whatever remedies are open to masters against their workmen should be open to workmen against their masters, so that both may be equally dealt with as to all questions arising under their mutual contract.

Moved by Mr. M'Donald, Holytown, Lanarkshire, seconded by Mr. Williams, Liverpool, and unanimously agreed to :—

That, in the amended law, power should be given to the court appointed to determine such question to direct the contract to be fulfilled on the part of either master or workman, or to relieve both or either of the parties of their obligations under such contracts and in all cases when the judge shall direct the contract to be fulfilled, he ought in his judgement, in order to that effect, to assess and determine the damages to be sustained by the one party, through the other party's failure to complete his contract as directed, and in the event of such failure, the judges shall order the party failing to make payment to the other party of the damages so as to be assessed and determined, and may issue his warrant to levy the same by distress and sale.

Moved by Mr. Dronfield, Sheffield, seconded by Mr. Austin, Sheffield, and unanimously agreed to :—

That, as the questions which arise between masters and workmen, under their contract of service, are at present in almost every instance tried and determined before justices who are themselves employers of labour, and, in consequence interested parties, it is desirable that the jurisdiction of the justices in all such questions should be transferred to some other tribunal.

Moved by Mr. Potter, London, seconded by Mr. Dunning, London, and unanimously agreed to :—

That a bill ought, with as little delay as possible, to be introduced into Parliament with the view of affecting an alteration of the Law in accordance with the preceding resolutions.

(b) From the Master and Servant Act, 1867. (30 & 31 Vict. c. 141.)

. . . . . .

4. Whenever the Employer or Employed shall neglect or refuse to fulfil any contract of service, or the Employed shall neglect or refuse to enter or commence his service, according to the contract, or shall absent himself from his service, or whenever any question, Difference, or Dispute shall arise as to the Rights or Liabilities of either of the Parties, or touching any Misusage, Misdemeanor, Misconduct, ill-treatment, or injury to the Person or Property of either of the Parties under any contract of service, the Party feeling aggrieved may lay an Information or Complaint in writing before a justice, magistrate, or sheriff, setting forth the Grounds of Complaint, and the amount of Compensation, Damage, or other Remedy claimed for the 'Breach or Non-Performance of such contract, or for any Misusage, Misdemeanor, Misconduct, Ill-treatment, or Injury to the Person or Property of the Party so complaining ; and upon such Information or Complaint being laid, the Justice, Magistrate, or Sheriff shall issue or cause to be issued a summons or citation to the Party so complained against, setting out the Grounds of Complaint, and the Amount claimed for Compensation, Damage, or other Remedy as set forth in the said Information or Complaint, and requiring such Party to appear, at the time and Place therein appointed, before two Justices or before a Magistrate, or before the

Sheriff, to answer the Matter of the Information or Complaint, so that the same may be then and there heard and determined.

. . . . . .

7. Wherever the Party complained shall neglect or refuse to appear to any summons or citation as aforesaid according to the provisions of this Act, a Justice, Magistrate, or Sheriff may, after due Proof on Oath of the Service of such Summons or Citation, issue a Warrant for the Apprehension of such Party in order to the hearing and determining of the Matter of the Information or Complaint.

. . . . . .

9. Upon the Hearing of any Information or Complaint under the Provisions of this Act two Justices, or the Magistrate or Sheriff, after due Examination either shall make an abatement of the whole or part of any Wages then already due to the Employed, or else shall direct the Fulfilment of the Contract of Service, with a Direction to the Party complained against to find forthwith good and sufficient security, by Recognizance or Bond, with or without Sureties, to the Satisfaction of a Justice, Magistrate or Sheriff, for the Fulfilment of such Contract, or else shall annul the Contract, discharging the Parties from the same, and apportioning the Amount of Wages due up to the completed Period of such Contract, or else where no Amount of Compensation or Damage can be assessed, or where pecuniary Compensation will not in the opinion of the Justices, Magistrate, or Sheriff meet the circumstances of the case, shall impose a Fine upon the Party complained against, not exceeding in Amount the sum of Twenty Pounds, or else shall assess and determine the amount of Compensation or Damage, together with the Costs, to be made to the Party Complaining, inclusive of the Amount of any Wages abated, and direct the same to be paid accordingly; and if the Order shall direct the Fulfilment of the Contract, and direct the Party complained against to find good and sufficient security as aforesaid, and the Party complained against neglect or refuse to comply with such Order, a Justice, Magistrate, or Sheriff may, if he shall think fit, by Warrant under his Hand, commit such Party to the Common Gaol or House of Correction within his Jurisdiction, there to be confined and kept until he shall so find Security, but nevertheless so that the term of Imprisonment, whether under One or several successive Committals, shall not exceed in the whole the Period of Three Months : Provided always, that the two Justices, Magistrate, or Sheriff may, if they or he think fit, assess and deter-

mine the amount of Compensation or Damage to be paid to the Party complaining, and direct the same to be paid, whether the Contract is ordered by them or him to be annulled or not, or, in addition to the annulling of the Contract of Service and Discharge of the Parties from the same, may, if they or he think fit, impose the Fine as hereinbefore authorized, but they or he shall not under the Powers of this Act have the Effect of annulling any Indenture or Contract of Apprenticeship that they or he might not have annulled or that would not have been annulled if this Act had not been passed.

11. Where on the Hearing of an Information or Complaint under this Act an Order is made for the Payment of Money and the same is not paid as directed, the same shall be recovered by Distress or Pounding of the Goods and Chattels of the Party failing to pay, and in default thereof by Imprisonment of such Party, according and subject to the Acts described in the Second Schedule to this Act; but no such Imprisonment shall be for more than Three Months, or be with Hard Labour.

14. Where on the Hearing of an Information or Complaint under this Act it appears to the Justices, Magistrate, or Sheriff that any Injury inflicted on the Person or Property of the Party Complaining, or the Misconduct, Misdemeanor or Ill-treatment complained of has been of an aggravated Character, and that such Injury, Misconduct, Misdemeanor has not arisen or been committed in the *bonâ fide* Exercise of a legal Right existing, or *bonâ fide* and reasonably supposed to exist, and further, that any pecuniary Compensation or other Remedy by this Act provided will not meet the Circumstances of the Case, then the Justices, Magistrate, or Sheriff may, by Warrant, commit the Party complained against to the Common Gaol or House of Correction within their or his Jurisdiction, there to be (in the Discretion of the Justices, Magistrate, or Sheriff,) imprisoned with or without Hard Labour, for any Term not exceeding Three Months.

16. Upon the hearing and determining of any Information or Complaint between Employer and Employed, and on any Appeal, under the Provisions of this Act, the respective Parties to the Contract of Service, their Husbands or Wives shall be deemed and considered as competent witnesses for all the Purposes of this Act.

4. THE SHEFFIELD OUTRAGES

[The Fearnehough affair was the culminating point in a series of violent acts done under the auspices of certain small craft Unions in the Sheffield cutlery trades. The main body of the Sheffield trades was in no way implicated, nor were similar practices discovered elsewhere, except among the brickmakers at Manchester. The news from Sheffield, however, was followed by a public outcry, reinforced by demands from many employers for the suppression of Trade Unions by law. The almost simultaneous foundation at Sheffield of the United Kingdom Alliance of Organised Trades (see p. 564) was taken as implicating it in the outrages ; and the Government was pressed to act. The consequence was the setting up of the Royal Commission on Trade Unions in 1867.]

(*a*) From " Trades Union Commission : Sheffield Outrages Inquiry " (1867), Report, pp. ix-x.

THE SAW GRINDERS' UNION

Thomas Fearnehough, a saw grinder, had long been obnoxious to the union. Having been a member of the union, he left it eight years ago, and shortly after joined again from fear of bodily harm. In 1865 he left the union a second time, and never rejoined it. He had been in the habit of working on his own tools instead of his master's (which was against the rules of the union), and at the time of this outrage he was working for Messrs. Slack, Sellars, and Co., who had a dispute with the saw handle makers. The saw grinders had in consequence been withdrawn, but Fearnehough had, notwithstanding the withdrawal of the grinders, persisted in working for the firm. Messrs. Slack, Sellars, and Co., aware of the danger which Fearnehough incurred by working for them, took power for him at Messrs. Butchers' wheel, to which there was no access except through a covered gateway which was carefully guarded. Fearnehough was therefore safe from being rattened.

Two or three months before October 1866, Henry Skidmore, secretary of the Saw Makers' Society, and Joseph Barker, secretary of the Saw Handle Makers' Society, called on Broadhead, and represented to him that Fearnehough was working for Messrs. Slack, Sellers, and Co, and thereby injuring the trade, and asked him " if something could not be done at him to stop him working ". They were aware that he could not be rattened at Butchers' wheel, but no plan was laid down by them by which Fearnehough was to be coerced, although they agreed to bear their share of the expense of compelling him to submit to the union. On the 8th October 1866 a can of gunpowder was exploded in the cellar under Fearnehough's house in New Hereford Street, in which he was then living with his family, consisting of two sons and a daughter. No one was hurt, but great damage was done to the house. Samuel Crookes was hired by Broadhead to commit this outrage, and was assisted by Joseph Copley, a member of the Saw Grinders' Union. A day or two after this occurrence, Barker and Skidmore, with the knowledge of Thomas Smith, Secretary of the Saw Makers' Union, paid Broadhead 7*l.* 10*s.*, the share of each union for the expense of committing the outrage. Joseph Barker found the money (the Saw Handle Makers' Union being then 18*l.* in debt to the Saw Makers' Union), and Smith credited Barker with the amount in the books of the Saw Makers' Union. The entry of the amount was passed over by the auditors without enquiry in the December following; this could not have been done if the audit had been carefully and honestly conducted.

A reward of £1,100 offered for the detection of the perpetrators failed to elicit any information.

The fact of these outrages having been done in the interest of the trade was well known to the union, and although in one or two instances individual members had protested against them, yet nothing like an investigation had been demanded, nor had there been any general vote of condemnation of these acts until the case of Fearnehough occurred, when public indignation was aroused, and then the outrage was denounced, and a reward was offered by the union for the detection of the offenders. The whole of the above offences were directed by Broadhead, and sums amounting to nearly £200 had been taken by him out of the funds of the union to pay the parties who committed them. Although these acts were not proved to have been directly authorised by the union, there must have been a knowledge, or at all events a well grounded belief, amongst its members that they were done, not only in the interests of their society, but through the agency of some one or more of their governing body, and we repeat that all the above outrages were promoted, encouraged, and connived at by the Saw Grinders' Union; and that the Hereford Street outrage was promoted and encouraged by the Saw Grinders', Saw Makers' and Saw Handle Makers' Unions. . . .

(*b*) From " Trades Union Commission: Sheffield Outrages Inquiry " (1867), Report, pp. vii-viii.

. . . The first subject which engaged our attention was that of " rattening ". Rattening is a mode of enforcing payment of contributions to and compliance with the rules of the Union. The wheel-bands, tool and other materials of a workman, are taken and held in pledge until he has satisfied the society by payment of his arrears, or by submitting to the rules which he has infringed. At first it was denied that the unions connived at this practice, but we had not proceeded far with our investigation, before it was admitted on all hands that rattening had been for a long time prevalent in the grinding trades, and in all trades connected with them.

It is fair to the unions to say, that in the majority of cases where the demands of the union have been complied with, and a payment of a small sum for the expenses of rattening has been made, the property taken has been restored.

Rattening is always done in the interests of the union, and very commonly by the direction of the secretary, who negotiates with the party rattened for the restitution of his property. In some cases a member of the union, without express authority, rattens another member who is known to have incurred the displeasure of the society, and takes his chance of having his act adopted by the union.

Recourse is seldom had to the police to recover property so taken away, but application is almost always made to the secretary immediately upon the loss of tools, etc, being discovered.

The practice of rattening is well known to be illegal, and persons detected in illegally taking away property have frequently been convicted and punished. The excuse offered by the unions for this system is, that, in the absence of legal powers, rattening affords the most ready means of enforcing payment of contributions and obedience to the rules of the union.

Many articles of Sheffield manufacture require for their completion the labour of various classes of workmen. For example, the manufacture of a saw requires the work of the sawgrinders, the saw makers, and the saw handle makers. All these workmen form separate branches of the saw trade and are in separate unions. These unions are, however, all amalgamated together for mutual support. In case of default by any member of any of the branches, or in case of a dispute with the masters, as the grinders' tools are the most easily abstracted, and as stopping the grinding stops the whole saw trade, the course commonly adopted is to ratten the grinders, although the dispute may be with the saw makers or saw handle makers, and on the matter being arranged, the other branches indemnify the grinders for their loss of time and for the expenses incurred. An attempt is often successfully made to saddle the whole cost of the rattening, as well as the cost of supporting the men while out of employment, upon the master, even where he is no party to the dispute, on the ground that he ought to have compelled his workmen to comply with the rules of the union.

The system of rattening has generally proved successful in effecting its object. If, however, the person rattened continues refractory, he commonly receives an anonymous letter warning him of the consequences of his obstinacy. If this warning is disregarded, recourse has been had to acts of outrage, the nature of which will be understood from a perusal of the cases actually investigated by us.

5. HORNBY *v.* CLOSE

[In 1867, the Boilermakers' Society had proceeded against the treasurer of its Bradford branch for wrongfully withholding £24, the property of the Society. Action had been taken, as was the practice of Trade Unions at the time, under the Friendly Societies Act of 1855 ; but the magistrates' court decided, and the Court of Queen's Bench confirmed on appeal, that a Trade Union, being at common law an unlawful Society in restraint of trade, was not entitled to the benefit of the Friendly Societies Act. This judgment, by putting all Trade Union funds in jeopardy, made the Trade Union leaders as eager for a new Trade Union Act as their opponents had been before.

The following year the Larceny and Embezzlement Act (known as Gurney's Act) made it possible for *criminal* proceedings to be taken against defaulting Trade Union officials, but did not cover *civil* action for the recovery of any sum due to the Union. This latter point was dealt with, and Lord Chief Justice Cockburn's judgment temporarily set aside, by the Trade Union (Protection of Funds) Act, 1869, which was passed to give *interim* protection pending legislation to be based on the Royal Commission's Reports.]

(*a*) From the Lord Chief Justice Cockburn's Judgment in Hornby *v.* Close, 2 Q.B. 153 (1867).

Cockburn, C. J.— I think that we ought not to hesitate for a moment in holding that the Magistrates were quite right in deciding that this society was not within the scope of the Friendly Societies' Act (18 & 19 Vict. I. 63) so as to give them jurisdiction. I quite agree with Mr. Mellish that if the main purpose of this society had been benevolent, or if it had been established for any of the objects specified in section 9. of the act, that the mere fact that one or two of its rulers went a little more or less in a different direction ought not to exclude it from the benefit conferred by the legislature. But in the present instance we find that the very purpose of the existence of this association is not merely for carrying out the objects of a benevolent society, properly so called, but those of a trades union. Now a trades union is generally understood to mean a combination of men who bind themselves not to work except upon certain conditions, and to support one another if they happen to be out of employment, in conformity with the wishes and interests of the body at large. I am very far from saying that a trades union constituted for such a purpose would bring those who compose it within the reach of the criminal law; but as trades unions, so far as they have come under my notice, have rules and regulations that operate in restraint of trade, I think that, just as in Hilton *v.* Eckersley, the combination of masters to employ only such workmen as have complied with certain conditions was held by the Exchequer Chamber (confirming the decision of this Court) to be not criminally illegal, but illegal in this sense, that the breach of an agreement relating to such a combination could not be enforced in a court of law; so here, where we have a society which appears to be constituted for the purpose of carrying out the object of a trades union, I think that it is illegal within the meaning of the decision in that case. Some of these rules are so much in restraint of trade, that were an action to be brought upon the contract or obligation to be implied from an assent to them, they would, without any doubt, be held to be in restraint of trade, so that the action could not be maintained. I think, therefore, that, for two reasons, it is impossible to hold that the case is within the 9th and 44th sections of the act 18 & 19 Vict. c. 63. In the first place, the purposes of a trades union are not purposes *analogous* to those of a friendly society, properly so called; and, secondly, although those who become parties to these arrangements may not be criminally responsible, and may obey any such rules and regulations which they think fit to impose upon themselves; yet these rules, being in restraint of trade, are by the law of the land illegal and cannot be enforced. The society is not established for a friendly object within the meaning of the act, and it cannot be said to be established for a purpose which is not illegal, so as to bring it within the terms of section 44. I think, therefore, that the Magistrates were right in deciding that the case did not come within the scope of the act of parliament.

(*b*) From an Act to amend the Law relating to Larceny and Embezzlement, July 31, 1868. (31 & 32 Vict. c. 116.)

Whereas it is expedient to provide for the better security of the Property of Co-partnerships and other joint beneficial Owners against Offences by Part Owners thereof, and further to amend the Law relating to Embezzlement : be it enacted as follows :

1. If any Person, being a Member of any Co-partnership, or being One or Two or more beneficial Owners of any Money, Goods, or Effects, Bills, Notes, Securities or other property, shall steal or embezzle any such Money, Goods, or Effects, Bills, Notes, Securities or other Property of or belonging to any such Co-partnership or to such joint beneficial Owners, every such Person shall be liable to be dealt with, tried, corrected, and punished for the same as if such Person had not been or was not a Member of such Co-partnership or One of such beneficial Owners.

2. All the Provisions of the Act passed in the Session of Parliament held in the eighteenth and nineteenth years of Her present Majesty's Reign, intituled *An Act for diminishing Expense and Delay in the Administration of Criminal Justice in Certain Cases*, shall extend and be applicable to the offence of Embezzlement by Clerks or Servants, or Persons employed for the Purpose or in the Capacity of Clerks or Servants, and the said Act shall henceforth be read as if the said Offence of Embezzlement had been included therein.

3. This Act shall not extend to Scotland.

(*c*) From an Act to protect the Funds of Trades Unions from Embezzlement and Misappropriation, August 9, 1869. (32 & 33 Vict. c. 61.)

Be it enacted . . . as follows :

1. An association of persons having rules, agreements or practices among themselves as to the terms on which they or any of them will or will not consent to employ or to be employed shall not, by reason only that any of such rules, agreements, or practices may operate in restraint of trade, or that such association is partly for objects other than the objects mentioned in the Friendly Societies Acts, be deemed, for the purposes of the twenty-fourth section of the Friendly Societies Act, 1855, for the punishment of frauds and impositions, to be a society established for a purpose which is illegal, or not to be a friendly society within the meaning of the forty-fourth section of the said Act.

2. This Act shall not continue in force after the last day of August one thousand eight hundred and seventy.

3. This Act may be cited as " The Trades Unions Funds Protection Act."

6. THE TRADE UNIONS AND THE ROYAL COMMISSION

[The outcry which followed the Sheffield affair caused consternation among the Trade Unions. The London Trades Council was asked to convene a National Conference to deal with the question, but refused, as the leaders of the Amalgamated Societies which dominated it were afraid that such a gathering might refuse their moderate leadership and antagonise parliamentary opinion. Instead, these leaders formed a Conference of Amalgamated Trades, and attempted to take the entire conduct of the Trade Union case into their own hands. The London Working Men's Association, however, called the National Conference in defiance of the L.T.C., and representatives came to it from most of the big Societies and Councils in the North. Consequently, two rival Trade Union leaders, Robert Applegarth for the Amalgamated Trades, and Thomas Connolly for the St. Martin's Hall Conference, were instructed to take charge of presenting the Trade Union case to the Royal Commission. Applegarth, who was on good terms with the Commissioners friendly to the Unions (Thomas Hughes and Frederic Harrison), got his way : Connolly speedily quarrelled with the Commissioners and was excluded from their sittings. But the Northern Unions remained suspicious of the London ' Junta ' until, in 1871, all sections united to oppose the Criminal Law Amendment Act (see p. 572).]

(*a*) From " Report of the Trades Conference held at St. Martin's Hall on March 5, 6, 7, 8, 1867 ", p. 29.

. . . The Trades' Delegates from the provinces understood from rumour that there was a misunderstanding betwixt certain of the Trades Associations of London. These they believed were formal, and personal only. The policy and influence of the law itself and arrangements good and bad, are held alike by both the London and provincial associations. The evil of the late law decision, and of the importance of the Trades' Union Inquiry Commission is held exactly alike by all. But whereas, some did act and some did not — some thought one set of men the most fit, and others thought otherwise ; and whereas things had been said and done, equally vexing and annoying on both sides, and after all, as it was but personalities and not principles that the London Trades really differed and quarrelled upon; the provincial delegates were desirous of carefully avoiding party personalities, and yet of uniting, if possible, the whole trades associations for their common interest. And while invited by certain persons to meet for general interests, the delegates did not intend in responding to ally themselves with preceding affairs, with which they had resolved to have nothing to do. But in order to avoid even the appearance of neglecting important trades whose interests they appreciated most highly, or of overlooking officials they were willing to pay due attention to, before a single act was taken to constitute the Conference, steps were taken by persons above the suspicion of sinister party objects to solicit the co-operation of the London Trades' Council in the general interest and subject of the Conference. Overtures were made to remove obstructions, and all that sincerity and honourable consideration required was done to secure a general unity of Trades' Union action. We regret to report that both private intercourse and a more public meeting of the delegates afterwards completely failed to conciliate the officials of the London Trades' Council to a general or common course of action. And what we regret still more to report is, that the objections were wholly and solely party and personal; and that these, so far as the Committee could find out, are, if true, really frivolous, unworthy and unimportant. . . .

(b) From a report of the St. Martin's Hall Conference, March 1867, in *The Beehive*, March 9, 1867.

Mr M'Donald said Mr Neate's Bill did not meet the wants of Trades Societies generally. He had seen that gentleman and had ascertained from him that his bill protected only the benevolent portion, but not the labour portion, of the funds of a society. (Cheers). It was therefore but a one-barrelled bill, and they must have a bill of a much broader character. Mr Neate's bill might protect those societies who, by fraudulent pretences, had obtained the sanction of the Registrar General to their rules, but not to trade combinations generally. (Hear).

Mr Connolly (Mason) said . . . [that his] society did not go sneaking to Tidd Pratt under false pretences. They called a spade a spade; they had a strike fund, and they called a strike a strike, not an out-of-work fund, in order to get the rules certified, as some societies had done. (Hear). It might suit those societies to be content with Mr Neate's Bill, but it did not suit the masons of England. (Hear).

7. THE ROYAL COMMISSION ON TRADE UNIONS,
1867-1869

[The Royal Commission, after producing interim reports on the Sheffield and Manchester affairs, settled down to its main task, and produced its main series of Reports in 1869. The Minority Report was drafted by Frederic Harrison, and was signed by him, Thomas Hughes, and the Earl of Lichfield.]

(*a*) From the Eleventh Report of the Royal Commission on Trade Unions (1869), p. xix.

LEGALITY OF TRADE UNIONS

. . . (58) No trades union, so far as our observation has extended, has attempted to give to the combination a wholly legal character by confining the application of its funds in support of men on strike to the limits within which alone combinations are legalised by the Act 6 Geo iv. c. 129. Unions contemplate generally the application of their funds to the support of men engaged in a strike for the purpose of enforcing some decision come to by the union in what they deem to be the interests of trade. Many such strikes would therefore be unlawful combinations at common law, and would not be relieved by the Statute. Again, the rules above adverted to, imposing restrictions not only on the members of the unions, but also on employers of labour in their mode of conducting their business — such, for example, as those relating to the number of apprentices to be employed, the taking of piecework, the working overtime, the working with men not members of the union, and the like — are either expressly adopted or tacitly acted upon more or less by nearly all the trades unions throughout the United Kingdom, and being what the law deems in restraint of trade, are such as to make those unions unlawful associations.

(59) It may be assumed, therefore, that the trades unions, with very few exceptions, have by their rules and proceedings, placed their funds more or less beyond the protection of the law; and they are not altogether relieved either by the Act (31 & 32 Vict. c. 116) giving remedies to associations in case of larceny by members thereof, or by the section in the Friendly Societies Act applicable to trade societies (18 & 19 Vict. c. 63, s. 44), since that section applies only to societies established for " any purpose which is not illegal ". This is a state of things which we think ought not to be allowed to continue; and we are brought, therefore, to the consideration of that

part of Your Majesty's Commission which directs us to suggest any improvements to be made in the law with respect to trades unions.

RIGHT TO COMBINE

(60) With regard to the general question of the right of workmen to combine together for determining and stipulating with their employer the terms on which only they will consent to work for him, we think that, provided the combination be perfectly voluntary, and that full liberty be left to all other workmen to undertake the work which the parties combining have refused, and that no obstruction be placed in the way of the employer resorting elsewhere in search of a supply of labour, there is no ground of justice or of policy for withholding such a right from the workmen. . . .

(61) In every bargain there is, more or less, a struggle between the buyer and the seller, the seller desiring to get as much as he can, and the buyer to pay as little as possible; but as between the employer and the workman, there is in general this advantage on the side of the employer, that he can more easily wait — i.e., can hold out longer than the workman. . . . It is to redress this inequality that the power of combining is justified by the promoters of trades unions.

(62) But upon the same principle and for a precisely similar reason, we think that whilst conceding to such workmen as desire to exercise it an extended right to combine against their employers, especial care should be taken that an equal right be secured to those workmen who desire to keep aloof from the combination, to dispose of their labour with perfect freedom as they severally think fit. The power of working, and consequently the value of a man's labour varies in different individuals according to their strength, their skill, and their industry. The workmen who think it for their advantage to combine together in the disposal of their labour are no more justified in constraining any other workman, who does not desire such association, to combine with them — to bring his labour into common stock as it were with theirs; and it is the more important that the law should protect the non-unionist workman in his right freely to dispose of his labour as he thinks best, because, standing alone, he is the less able to protect himself. . . .

PICKETING

(68) It has been shown in evidence that these rights are most liable to be interfered with by what is commonly known as the

system of " picketing ". Picketing consists in posting members of the union at all the approaches to the works struck against, for the purpose of observing and reporting the workmen going to or coming from the works, and of using such influence as may be in their power to prevent the workmen from accepting work there.

(69) It is alleged that instructions are given to the pickets to confine themselves to a mere representation of the case of the union promoting the strike, and to use argument and persuasion only, without resorting to violence, intimidation, or undue coercion. But although such instructions may be given, it is hardly in human nature that the pickets, who are interested parties and are suffering the privations incident to the strike, should always keep within the fair limits of representation and persuasion, when dealing with men whom they see about to undertake the work which they have refused, and who may thus render the strike abortive. Accordingly, experience shows, and the evidence before us leaves no doubt on our minds, that during the existence of a strike, workmen desirous to accept work are often subjected, through the agency of the pickets, to molestation, intimidation, and other modes of undue influence, and in effect are prevented from obtaining employment.

(70) So far as relates to members of the union promoting the strike, the pickets cannot be necessary if the members are voluntarily concurring therein; so far as relates to workmen who are not members of the union, picketing implies in principle an interference with their right to dispose of their labour as they think fit, and is, therefore, without justification; and so far as relates to the employer, it is a violation of his right of free resort to the labour market for the supply of such labour as he requires. . . .

(*b*) From the Eleventh Report of the Royal Commission on Trade Unions (1869), p. xxiv.

(82) The registration of trades unions might be effected through the Registrar of Friendly Societies, and it would be his duty to see that the rules and byelaws of a society claiming to be registered were unobjectionable — that is, not intended to promote the objects which we now proceed to specify as justifying in his opinion the refusal of registration.

(83) These objects are :

1. To prevent the employment or to limit the number of apprentices in any trade.

2. To prevent the introduction or to limit the use of machinery in any trade or manufacture.

3. To prevent any workman from taking a sub-contract, or working by the piece, or working in common with men not members of the union.

4. To authorise interference, in the way of support from the funds of the union, with the workmen of any other union when out on strike, or when otherwise engaged in any dispute with their employer, in any case in which such other union is an unconnected union.

(c) From the Eleventh Report of the Royal Commission on Trade Unions (1869), p. xxix.

DISSENT III

We, the undersigned, Commissioners appointed by Your Majesty, found ourselves reluctantly compelled to dissent from the foregoing Report, in which we are unable to concur for the following reasons :—

It is in our opinion essential to any serious amendment of the law relating to trades unions that the doctrine of the Common Law · whereby it is presumed that all combinations, whether of workmen or employers, are unlawful, and according to some authorities are punishable as conspiracies — a doctrine, we must observe, which has long had none but indirect effects — should be broadly and unequivocally rescinded.

We think that to rescind this rule, as it proposes, partially but not entirely, or abrogate it in words whilst keeping it in force by a series of intricate provisoes, none of which in our view could have any practical effect in preventing crime, would be to add fresh uncertainties to a very difficult branch of law, and to involve the association in latent liabilities without any compensating public good.

We are of opinion that no adequate ground has been shown for the continuance of special laws relating exclusively to the employment of labour. We think that no amendment of the law would have any effect in practice which did not deal with the wide but uncertain operation of the third section of the Statute of 6 Geo. iv c. 129, in the punishment of offences described under the general terms " intimidation ", " molestation ", and " obstruction ". In our view all offences of this class should be dealt with under the general criminal law, and we submit that it may be a question for further consideration whether any additional legislation is required to protect equally all classes of Your Majesty's subjects from personal molestation.

We are further of opinion that simple registration and protection for property should be equally accorded to all associations alike, whether of workmen or employers, with the sole condition of their proving themselves to be free from criminal designs. We are convinced that the greatest protection which could be given to the public would be the securing, by means of registration, publicity for the rules, and for the receipts and expenditure of all associations whatever ; whilst we think it a matter of justice that all property should be efficiently protected.

To the proposal to grant registration to societies on the terms of their subjecting their rules to a series of special conditions we are unable to give our assent. Whatever the rules of these voluntary associations be, on economic grounds, expedient or the contrary, we consider that it would be impolitic to exclude them from the pale of, and at the same time to free them from the responsibility to, the law. For these reasons we think that all associations might be permitted to acquire a simple right of registration, with protection for their funds, under no other condition than this, that they submitted their rules, together with their receipts and expenditure, to the Registrar, and satisfied him that they were free from anything of a criminal nature.

[The signatories to this note of dissent were Frederic Harrison, Thomas Hughes, and the Earl of Lichfield.]

8. THE TRADE UNION ACTS, 1871

[The Trade Union Act of 1871 went much nearer to the Minority than to the Majority recommendations of the Royal Commission, and gave the Trade Unions in most respects a fairly satisfactory legal status. But with it was coupled the Criminal Law Amendment Act, which, under pretence of being mainly a restatement of the existing law, created a series of ambiguous offences highly dangerous to Trade Union strike action. The Government had intended to include both measures in a single Act, but was induced by strong Trade Union pressure to divide the criminal from the other classes. This made it easier for the Trade Unions to agitate for the repeal of the Criminal Law Amendment Act without endangering the concessions gained in the Trade Union Act. The need for such an agitation caused the rival groups to drop their differences and concentrate on a common campaign. The Conference of Amalgamated Trades was wound up, and the ' Junta ' group threw its full strength in with the Trades Union Congress, which it was soon able to dominate.]

(*a*) From an Act to amend the Law relating to Trades Unions, June 29, 1871. (34 & 35 Vict. c. 31.)

Be it enacted . . . as follows.

PRELIMINARY

1. This Act may be cited as " The Trade Union Act, 1871 ".

CRIMINAL PROVISIONS

2. The purposes of any trade union shall not, by reason merely that they are in restraint of trade, be deemed to be unlawful so as to render any member of such trade union liable to criminal prosecution for conspiracy or otherwise.

3. The purposes of any trade union shall not, by reason merely that they are in restraint of trade, be unlawful so as to render void or voidable any agreement on trust.

4. Nothing in this Act shall enable any court to entertain any legal proceeding instituted with the object of directly enforcing or recovering damages for the breach of any of the following agreements, namely,

1. Any agreement between members of a trade union as such, concerning the condition on which any members for the time being of such trade union shall or shall not sell their goods, transact business, employ, or be employed :

2. Any agreement for the payment by any person of any subscription or penalty to a trade union :

3. Any agreement for the application of the funds of a trade union,—
   a. to provide benefits to members ; or
   b. to furnish contribution to any employer or workman not a member of such trade union, in consideration of such employer or workman acting in conformity with the rules or resolutions of such trade union ; or
   c. to discharge any fine imposed upon any person by sentence of a court of justice ; or

4. Any agreement made between one trade union and another ; or

5. Any bond to secure the performance of any of the above-mentioned agreements.

But nothing in this section shall be deemed to constitute any of the above-mentioned agreements unlawful.

5. The following Acts, that is to say,

1. The Friendly Societies Acts, 1855 and 1858, and the Acts amending the same;
2. The Industrial and Provident Societies Act, 1867, and any Act amending the same; and
3. The Companies Acts, 1862 and 1867,

shall not apply to any trade union, and the registration of any trade union under any of the said Acts shall be void, and the deposit of the rules of any trade union made under the Friendly Societies Acts, 1855 and 1858, and the Acts amending the same, before the passing of this Act, shall cease to be of effect.

.   .   .   .   .   .

9. The trustees of any trade union registered under this Act, or any other officer of such trade union who may be authorised so to do by the rules thereof, are hereby empowered to bring or defend, or cause to be brought or defended, any action, suit, prosecution, or complaint in any court of law or equity, touching or concerning the property, right, or claims to property of the trade union; . . .

(*b*) From an Act to amend the Criminal Law relating to Violence, Threats, and Molestation, June 29, 1871. (34 & 35 Vict. c. 32.)

Be it enacted . . . as follows:

1. Every person who shall do any one or more of the following acts, that is to say,

1. Use violence to any person or any property,
2. Threaten or intimidate any person in such manner as would justify a justice of the peace, on complaint made to him, to bind over the person so threatening or intimidating to keep the peace,
3. Molest or obstruct any person in manner defined by this section,

with a view to coerce such person,—

1. Being a master to dismiss or to cease to employ any workman, or being a workman to quit any employment or to return work before it is finished;

2. Being a master not to offer, or being a workman not to accept any employment or work ;

3. Being a master or workman to belong or not to belong to any temporary or permanent association or combination ;

4. Being a master or workman to pay any fine or penalty imposed by any temporary or permanent association or combination ;

5. Being a master to alter the mode of carrying on his business, or the number or description of any persons employed by him,

Shall be liable to imprisonment, with or without hard labour, for a term not exceeding three months.

A person shall for the purposes of this Act be deemed to molest or obstruct another person in any of the following cases ; that is to say,

1. If he persistently follow such person about from place to place :

2. If he hide any tools, clothes, or other property owned or used by such person, or deprive him or hinder him in the use thereof :

3. If he watch or beset the house or other place where such person resides or works, or carries on business, or happens to be, or the approach to such house or place, or if with two or more persons he follow such person in a disorderly manner in or through any street or road.

Nothing in this section shall prevent any person from being liable under any other Act, or otherwise, to any other or higher punishment than is provided for any offence by this section, so that no person be punished twice for the same offence.

Provided that no person shall be liable to any punishment for doing or conspiring to do any act on that ground that such act restrains or tends to restrain the free course of trade, unless such act is one of the acts herein-before specified in this section, and is done with the object of coercing as herein-before mentioned.

9. THE LONDON GAS STOKERS, 1872

[The dangers inherent in the Criminal Law Amendment Act were speedily made plain by the prosecution of the London Gas Stokers in 1872. A number of men were sentenced under the Act, and some of the leaders were prosecuted at common law for criminal conspiracy. The sentences aroused nation-wide Trade Union protests, and greatly strengthened the campaign for the repeal of the Act of 1871 and for a measure preventing the use of the common law doctrine of conspiracy against strikers or strike leaders.]

(a) From *The Illustrated London News*, December 14, 1872.

THE GAS STRIKE IN LONDON.

The strike of the gasworks' stokers, which came to an end last Tuesday evening, when the Imperial Gas Company allowed most of the men at Hackney to return to their employment, had continued ten days, since the previous Saturday week. It began at the Fulham station, the excuse being that a coke-backer had been discharged, for a manifest breach of duty, and another man, who was a non-unionist, had been put in his place. The disaffection spread from the Fulham to the St. Pancras station, and thence to the Haggerston station, where the men struck. It seems that about the middle of last month the directors of this company increased the wages of their workmen nearly 20 per cent. For twelve hours' work, either by day or by night, except on Sundays, between six a.m. and six p.m., scoopmen's wages were increased from 5s. to 5s. 11d., stokers to 5s. 6½d., coke-hole men to 4s. 7d., and coal stagers to 4s. 4d.; while the gangs employed on Sundays between six a.m. and six p.m. received a day and a half's pay for the twelve hours at the above scale. The men expressed themselves satisfied at the time. In the second instance last week, the stokers of the Chartered Gas Company, at Beckton, North Woolwich, turned out without the slightest notice, their avowed object being to enforce the reinstatement of the " union " man who had been discharged from the works of the Imperial Gas Company at Fulham. The men were receiving pay as follows :—Firemen, 38s. 9d. per week; scoopers, 38s. 9d.; stokers, 37s. 4d.; fire-rakers, 31s.; coal-wheelers, 28s. per week, with the addition of numerous indulgences and extra allowances. At the works of the Independent Gas-Light Company, Kingsland road, also, the stokers struck work, without previous notice, the only reason assigned being that they had orders to do so by the delegates of the Stokers' Union. A few weeks ago the wages of these men were increased to the extent of about 15 per cent, and with this increase they expressed themselves perfectly satisfied.

The several gas companies lost no time in engaging as many labourers as they could get to do their work; but the production of gas was much diminished; and, to save the lessening stock in the gasometers, they reduced the amount of supply to their customers, and to the street lamps. This occasioned some temporary inconvenience, in particular districts, on the evening of Tuesday week. In Westminster, every alternate street lamp was turned off; the St. James's Theatre was closed; and naphtha lamps were used in the Metropolitan and District Railway. Ludgate-hill station was lighted with carriage-lamps. There was a run upon the chandler's and oilmen's shops by many of the householders, and shopkeepers, who had been led to expect that they would be entirely deprived of gas at night, and that they must furnish themselves with other means of lighting up their premises. These apprehensions were, fortunately, not altogether realised by the event, as the supply of gas, which had begun on a low scale that evening, improved after nine-o'clock, thanks to the exertions of the company's directors and officers; but the scenes delineated by our Artist, in his sketch of what may be conceived the likely effects of such a deprivation as London was threatened with, cannot be accused of much exaggeration. At the Thames Police Court, on Monday, four of the men in the service of the Commercial Gas Company, at Stepney, were summoned for wilful and malicious breach of contract, and were each sentenced to six weeks' imprisonment. At the Woolwich Police Court, on Tuesday, six men of the Chartered Gas Company were committed for trial.

(b) From " The London Gas Stokers. A Report by the Committee of their trial for Conspiracy, of their Defence and of the Proceedings for their Liberation " (1873), p. 3.

THE GAS STOKERS DEFENCE COMMITTEE'S REPORT.

. . . We are not prepared to defend the course adopted by the London Gas Stokers for the redress of their grievances, but we felt it to be our duty to defend men, whoever they might be, against a prosecution for conspiracy for breach of contract, or alleged intimidation or molestation, when the Legislature had passed special acts for these offences. For breach of contract, the Master and Servants (1867) provides as a maximum three months' imprisonment, and even then the breach of contract must be of an aggravated character.

For molestation, or intimidation, the Criminal Law Amendment Act provides also a maximum of three months' imprisonment. At the time Government passed these Acts, and in answer to our protest against their severity, the defenders of the enactments assured us that, under these laws working men would know their position, and the greatest punishment they would receive for these offences would be three months' imprisonment. But in the case of the Gas Stokers' Strike, after the prosecutors had taken out something like five hundred summonses under the Master and Servants' Act, and had got a number of the men sentenced to six weeks' imprisonment with hard labour, they suddenly (and to our utter amazement) succeeded in committing seven of the men to the Central Criminal Court for conspiracy, thereby rendering them liable to two years' imprisonment. They were sentenced to twelve months for conspiring to do an act which others had actually committed, but received only six weeks' imprisonment.

The indignation exhibited by the public in consequence of this vindictive sentence, the able and masterly articles and letters it drew from the pens of gentlemen who are authorities on these questions; the startling manner in which it revealed the danger of such a law to the people's liberty whilst legitimately pursuing their industrial interests; the condemnation of the Judge by Government, in remitting eight months of the sentence, as well as some acknowledgement to the great trades who so generously and promptly supplied the committee with means to discharge the legal liabilities for their defence, and for the maintenance of their wives and families during the men's imprisonment, are sufficient reasons why the trades should have a record of the whole case.

The business of gas stoking does not require a great amount of skill, two months' practice is generally sufficient training for a man to become an ordinary workman, providing he has a constitution and a skin that will stand any amount of fire and severe physical exertion; therefore, it is not surprising that (with a constant overflowing supply of labouring men) workers of this class do not receive that amount of pay which such a dangerous and laborious occupation demands. (Their rate of wages will be found further on in this Report). Neither is it surprising, at a time when all classes of industry were getting the working hours reduced, that the gas stokers thought it time to move for shorter hours and higher wages. To some, the pay the men were receiving may seem fair for unskilled work, but it must be stated that the hours worked amounted to something like eighty per week, Sunday included. The only rest day (or Sabbath) they knew, was one day in each month; the consequence was, they determined to unite, and in August, and September, 1872, they entered into a vigorous agitation, formed a union — with many imperfections, certainly — but it had its effect in advancing their wages, and out of some twenty-five gas factories, fourteen of them closed their works between the hours of 6 a.m. and 6 p.m. on Sundays. But, as in all similar cases, they had leaders in the movement, and the companies began gradually weeding them out by discharging them. Had the men followed the advice given to them, viz., to provide the victims with the means of living until other employment was found, they might have been at this time a well-united body; but they did not maintain that even balance of mind, which can only be acquired by experience, so necessary for successfully conducting labour movements. . . .

10. THE LABOUR LAWS OF 1875–1876

[The Liberals refused to amend the laws passed by them in 1871. Disraeli, on coming to power after the election of 1874, set out to placate Trade Union opinion by agreeing to the repeal of the Criminal Law Amendment Act and its replacement by a law re-defining the notions of molestation, obstruction, and intimidation, and also re-stating the application of the notion of ' conspiracy ' to Trade Union affairs. The Conspiracy and Protection of Property Act was passed after a Report had been made by a Royal Commission on which Alexander Macdonald, then M.P. for Stafford, agreed to serve despite the decision of the Trades Union Congress to boycott its proceedings.

In the same year the law of master and servant was further amended by the Employers and Workmen Act, which made employers and workmen fully equal parties to a purely civil contract ; but certain criminal provisions relating to breach of contract in the public utility services or in circumstances likely to lead to loss of life or valuable property were inserted in the Conspiracy and Protection of Property Act. The right of peaceful picketing was only partly regained (see p. 579).

Finally, in 1876, a brief amending Act cleared up a point of bad drafting in the Trade Union Act of 1871, by making it clear that a Trade Union did not need to be unlawful at common law in order to secure the protection of the Statute. This amending Act became important subsequently because its defining clause was used in the Osborne Case to serve as a definition of the authorised scope of Trade Union activities.]

(a) From an Act for amending the Law relating to Conspiracy, and to the Protection of Property, and for other Purposes, August 13, 1875. (38 & 39 Vict. c. 86.)

Be it enacted . . . as follows :

1. This Act may be cited as the Conspiracy and Protection of Property Act, 1875.

2. This Act shall come into operation on the first day of September one thousand eight hundred and seventy-five.

CONSPIRACY AND PROTECTION OF PROPERTY

3. An agreement or combination by two or more persons to do or procure to be done any act in contemplation or furtherance of a trade dispute between employers and workmen shall not be indictable as a conspiracy if such act committed by one person would not be punishable as a crime.

Nothing in this section shall exempt from punishment any person guilty of a conspiracy for which a punishment is awarded by any Act of Parliament.

Nothing in this section shall affect the law relating to riot, unlawful assembly, breach of the peace, or sedition, or any offence against the State or the sovereign. . . .

4. Where a person employed by a municipal authority or by any company or contractor upon whom is imposed by Act of Parliament the duty, or who have otherwise assumed the duty, of supplying any city, borough, town, or place, or any part thereof, with gas or water, wilfully and maliciously breaks a contract of service with that authority or company or contractor, knowing or having reasonable cause to believe that the probable consequences of his so doing, either alone or in combination with others, will be to deprive the inhabitants of that city, borough, town, place, or part, wholly or to a great extent of their supply of gas or water, he shall on conviction thereof by a court of summary jurisdiction, or on indictment as herein-after mentioned, be liable either to pay a penalty not exceeding twenty pounds, or to be imprisoned for a term not exceeding three months with or without hard labour. . . .

5. Where any person wilfully and maliciously breaks a contract of service or of hiring, knowing or having reasonable cause to believe that the probable consequences of his so doing, either alone or in combination with others, will be to endanger human life, or cause serious bodily injury, or to expose valuable property whether real or personal to destruction or serious injury, he shall on conviction thereof by a court of summary jurisdiction, or on indictment as hereinafter mentioned, be liable either to pay a penalty not exceeding twenty pounds or be imprisoned for a term not exceeding three months, with or without hard labour.

. . . . . .

7. Every person who, with a view to compel any other person to abstain from doing or to do any act which such other person has a legal right to do or abstain from doing, wrongfully and without legal authority,—

1. Uses violence to or intimidates such other person or his wife or children, or injures his property ; or,
2. Persistently follows such other person about from place to place ; or
3. Hides any tools, clothes, or other property owned or used by such other person, or deprives him of or hinders him in the use thereof ; or
4. Watches or besets the house or other place where such other person resides, or works, or carries on business, or happens to be, or the approach to such house or place ; or,
5. Follows such other person with two or more other persons in a disorderly manner in or through any street or road,

shall, on conviction thereof by a court of summary jurisdiction, or an indictment as herein-after mentioned, be liable either to pay a penalty not exceeding twenty pounds, or to be imprisoned for a term not exceeding three months, with or without hard labour.

Attending at or near the house or place where a person resides, or works, or carries on business, or happens to be, or the approach to such house or place, in order merely to obtain or communicate information, shall not be deemed a watching or besetting within the meaning of this section.

(*b*) From the Employers and Workmen Act, 1875. (38 & 39 Vict. c. 90.)

3. In any proceeding before a county court in relation to any dispute between an employer and a workman arising out of or incidental to their relation as such (which dispute is hereinafter referred to as a dispute under this Act) the court may, in addition to any jurisdiction it might have exercised if this Act had not passed, exercise all or any of the following powers ; that is to say,

(1) It may adjust and set off the one against the other all such claims on the part either of the employer or of the workman, arising out of or incidental to the relation between them, as the court may find to be subsisting, whether such claims are liquidated or un-liquidated, and are for wages, damages, or otherwise ; and,

(2) If, having regard to all the circumstances of the case, it thinks it just to do so, it may rescind any contract between the employer and the workman upon such terms as to the apportionment of wages or other sums due thereunder, and as to the payment of wages or damages, or other sums due, as it thinks just; and

(3) Where the court might otherwise award damages for any breach of contract it may, if the defendant be willing to give security to the satisfaction of the court for the performance by him of so much of his contract as remains unperformed, with the consent of the plaintiff, accept such security, and order performance of the contract accordingly, or place either of the whole of the damages which would otherwise have been awarded, or some part of such damages.

The security shall be an undertaking by the defendant and one or more surety or sureties that the defendant will perform his contract, subject on non-performance to the payment of a sum to be specified in the undertaking.

Any sum paid by a surety on behalf of a defendant in respect of a security under this Act, together with all costs incurred by such surety in respect of such security, shall be deemed to be a debt due to him from the defendant; and where such security has been given in or under the direction of a court of summary jurisdiction, that court may order payment to the surety of the sum which has so become due to him from the defendant.

COURT OF SUMMARY JURISDICTION

4. A dispute under this Act between an employer and a workman may be heard and determined by a court of summary jurisdiction, and such court, for the purposes of this Act, shall be deemed to be a court of civil jurisdiction and in a proceeding in relation to any such dispute the court may order payment of any sum which it may find to be due as wages, or damages, or otherwise, and may exercise all or any of the powers by this Act conferred on a county court: Provided that in any proceeding in relation to any such dispute the court of summary jurisdiction—

(1) Shall not exercise any jurisdiction where the amount claimed exceeds ten pounds; and

(2) Shall not make an order for the payment of any sum exceeding ten pounds, exclusive of the costs incurred in the case; and

(3) Shall not require security to an amount exceeding ten pounds from any defendant or his surety or sureties.

PART II

Procedure.

8. A person may give security under this Act in a county court or court of summary jurisdiction by an oral or written acknowledgement in or under the direction of the court of the undertaking or condition by which and the sum for which he is bound, in such manner and form as may be prescribed by any rule for the time being in force, and in any case where security is so given, the court in or under the direction of which it is given may order payment of any sum which may become due in pursuance of security. . . .

9. Any dispute or matter in respect of which jurisdiction is given by this Act to a court of summary jurisdiction shall be deemed to be a matter on which that court has authority by law to make an order on complaint in pursuance of this Summary Jurisdiction Act, but shall not be deemed to be a criminal proceeding; and all powers by this Act conferred on a court of summary jurisdiction shall be deemed to be in addition to and not in derogation of any powers conferred on it by the Summary Jurisdiction Act, except that a warrant shall not be issued under that act for apprehending any person other than an apprentice for failing to appear to answer a complaint in any proceeding under this act, and that an order made by a court of summary jurisdiction under this act for the payment of any money shall not be enforced by : imprisonment except in the manner and under the conditions by this Act provided; and no goods or chattels shall be taken under a distress ordered by a court of summary jurisdiction which might not be taken under an execution issued by a county court.

A court of summary jurisdiction may direct any sum of money, for the payment of which it makes an order under this Act, to be paid by instalments, and may from time to time rescind or vary such order.

Any sum payable by any person under the order of a court of summary jurisdiction in pursuance of this Act, shall be deemed to be a debt due from him in pursuance of a judgment of a competent court within the meaning of the fifth section of the Debtors Act, 1865, and may be enforced accordingly; and as regards any such debt a court of summary jurisdiction shall be deemed to be a court within the meaning of the said section. . . .

(c) From the Trade Union Act (1871) Amendment Act, 1876. (39 & 40 Vict. c. 22.)

16. . . . The term "trade union" means any combination, whether temporary or permanent, for regulating the relations between workmen and masters, or between workmen and workmen, or between masters and masters, or for imposing restrictive conditions on the conduct of any trade or business, whether such combination would or would not, if the principal Act had not been passed, have been deemed to have been an unlawful combination by reason of some one or more of its purposes being in restraint of trade.

XX

POLITICAL MOVEMENTS, 1866–1875

INTRODUCTION

THE enactment of the Reform Act of 1867 made the working classes for the first time a considerable voting power in the urban constituencies, though not to any great extent in the counties. It was at once followed by the establishment of bodies designed to promote the election of working men to Parliament. The National Reform League was dissolved, but was replaced by the Labour Representation League. The General Election of 1868 came too soon for the working-class candidates to achieve any victories, though Ernest Jones came fairly near to success at Manchester, and Samuel Plimsoll, the seamen's advocate, was elected at Derby. By 1874 the movement had become better organised, and two of the miners' leaders were returned as the first 'working-men M.P.s'. The agitation for further electoral reform was carried on by the National Reform Union and by the reconstituted Northern Reform League in the North-East.

The years after 1867 were very fertile in industrial and social legislation. The Elementary Education Acts of 1870 and 1876, the Mines Acts of 1872, the Merchant Shipping Acts of 1873 and 1876, the Factory Acts of 1867, 1875, and 1878, the Public Health Acts of 1872 and 1875, the Housing Acts of 1868 and 1875, the Building Societies Act of 1874, the Friendly Societies Act of 1875, and the Industrial and Provident Societies Act of 1876 served, in addition to the Trade Union Acts and the amendments of the law of master and servant, as tokens of the attention paid by both the great parties to the new status of the working-class electors.

See " Short History ", Part II, chapter 4, and chapter 6, section 1.
" Common People ", chapters 29 and 31.

1. THE LONDON WORKING MEN'S ASSOCIATION AND THE GENERAL ELECTION OF 1868

[In November 1867 the London Working Men's Association issued a manifesto calling for a national movement to promote working-class representation in Parliament. It demanded the constitution of a ' Working

Men's Parliamentary Fund ', to be used for the support of approved working-class candidates, and it called upon Co-operative Societies, Trades Councils, and other working-class organisations to take common action in arranging to contest suitable seats. Partly as a consequence of this move, a number of working-class candidates made their appearance at the General Election of 1868. These included W. R. Cremer, of the Carpenters, at Warwick, Edward Owen Greening, the Co-operator, at Halifax, and William Newton, the Engineer, at Tower Hamlets (in conjunction with Edmond Beales, the Chairman of the National Reform League), and George Howell, of the National Reform League, at Aylesbury. In addition, Robert Hartwell was put up for Stoke-on-Trent, Alexander Macdonald for Kilmarnock, and G. J. Holyoake for Birmingham ; but all three had to withdraw for lack of funds. George Odger withdrew at Chelsea, under pressure from the middle-class Radicals. Charles Bradlaugh and F. R. Lees, the ' Temperance Chartist ', fought Northampton.]

From A. W. Humphrey, " A History of Labour Representation " (1912), p. 18.

THE LONDON WORKING-MEN'S ASSOCIATION TO THE PEOPLE OF ENGLAND ON THE DIRECT REPRESENTATION OF LABOUR IN PARLIAMENT

.   .   .   .   .   .

Providing a careful selection of working-class candidates be made, there is no reason why they should stand isolated as a class in Parliament any more than the special representatives of other interests now sitting there. . . . We believe that, after the first novelty of their appearance in the House has worn off, they will, insensibly and imperceptibly, blend with the other members in the performance of the usual duties expected from members of the Legislature. . . . We presume that the working-class candidate, in addressing a constituency, would do as all other candidates do — appeal to the electors generally and not to those of a particular interest. . . .

The working-men selected as candidates for the representation of industrial interests should hold enlarged views on all public questions. They should also be men who have been hard workers in the cause of industrial progress — not mere word-spinners — who have for years past made sacrifices, personal and pecuniary, for the cause they advocated. . . . They should be men whose general abilities, character, and demeanour should be such that no one of their colleagues, however aristocratic, should be ashamed to associate with them in Westminster Hall. There are hundreds of such working-men to be found. . . . The return of such men to Parliament would do much to disarm the hostility of the Tories to the further extension of the franchise and allay the fears of those timid Liberals who are afraid they have already gone too far, and would redound to the credit and honour of their constituencies.

The objects of the Association were then set out as follows under the heading " Our Platform ". *Political*: The extension of the franchise until it rests upon the basis of residential and registered manhood suffrage; protection of the ballot for the voter; a just and equitable redistribution of seats; a direct representation of industrial interests by the return of working-men to Parliament; abolition of Church rates; an improvement of the relation between landlord and tenant; the removal of those evils which have grown up and flourished under the influence of class legislation. *Social*: A national unsectarian system of education; legal protection for the funds of trade unions; a reduction of the hours of labour to the lowest minimum without injury to the power of production; the promotion of the co-operative system and co-partnership of industry; the adoption of measures to facilitate the improvement of the dwellings and workshops of the labouring classes; the promotion of emigration to the colonies.

2. THE LABOUR REPRESENTATION LEAGUE

[The National Reform League was at first intended to continue in existence after the Reform Act of 1867 had become law ; but it was later wound up, and the Trade Unions proceeded in 1869 to set up the Labour Representation League as an agency for promoting working-class candidatures. They did this partly in order to get the control away from the London Working Men's Association. The Labour Representation League was responsible for putting forward George Howell for Norwich at a by-election in 1871 ; but he withdrew in order not to split the Liberal vote. In 1874 there were a dozen Labour candidates, mostly supported by the L.R.L., and two seats were won (see p. 592). The Labour Representation League remained active until about 1880, and then disappeared.]

(*a*) Circular pasted into the Minute Book of the Reform League [September 1867].

THE REFORM LEAGUE

To the Branch Secretaries and other Officers throughout the United Kingdom.

GENTLEMEN,

It having been decided to continue our great work for Reform, not only till our Irish and Scotch friends have obtained their promised Reform Bills, but until we have the Ballot for the protection of the Voter, and also the entire removal of the rating clauses, and the enfranchisement of the toiling masses in County Constituencies upon the same basis as in Boroughs, we feel it our duty to urge upon you the necessity of renewing your annual subscriptions, and thereby place *a real power* in the hands of your local Committees.

We trust this appeal will receive an universal response from the entire of our members throughout the country.

We also entreat you to keep up regular meetings, if not so often as during the past two years, yet sufficiently often to sustain the interest of your members throughout the country.

Conversations and discussions can take place upon the doings of our General Council, as reported in the *Star* and other Papers every Thursday, and upon the documents issued from time to time by our Council, as for instance the enclosed programme of the Policy of the League.

I am Gentlemen,
Your obedient Servant,
GEORGE HOWELL
Secretary

By order of the Executive
8, ADELPHI TERRACE, W.C.

Note.—I desire personally to thank the whole of the Local Secretaries for their earnest and vigorous co-operation in the past, and trust that I shall be able to rely on you all, for active support in the future.

I am, yours truly,
GEORGE HOWELL.

September 18th, 1867.

(b) From a Leaflet issued by the Labour Representation League (n. d.) [1869].

RULES

1. This Association shall be called the LABOUR REPRE-SENTATION LEAGUE, and consist of working men and others desirous of securing the direct representation of labour in the Legislature.

2. The subscription to its funds shall be as under :—Working men, 1s. per annum. Persons who have been working men, but who

have passed into other occupations, ten shillings per annum. Honorary members not less than one guinea per annum.

3. The objects of the League shall be to prevent the continued exclusion of qualified working men from Parliament, School Boards, Municipal Councils, and other representative bodies; and to secure for the working people a fair share in the representation of the country. With a view to this end, it will promote throughout the kingdom the registration of working men's votes, without reference to their political opinions, its aim being to organise fully the strength of the operative classes as an electoral power. It will also consider and advocate all questions connected with the welfare of the nation, especially those affecting the interests of the Industrial Classes.

4. The LABOUR REPRESENTATION LEAGUE will also advocate such political, industrial and social questions as involve the well-being of the Working Classes. And beyond this, when deemed necessary, it will recommend and support candidates from other classes who have studied the great labour problem, and who are friendly to an equitable settlement of the difficult questions it involves.

5. It will be the duty of the League to take cognizance of all Parliamentary Bills proposing any alteration in the laws affecting the welfare of working men; to take such steps generally as may be expedient for the promotion of the interests of labour.

. . . . . .

16. Constituences and branches of the Labour Representation League shall forward to the Executive Council the names of such persons as they deem fit to represent labour in Parliament. The Executive Council shall keep a register of such names, and from these and such others as the Council may deem suitable they shall select such person as, by consultation with the constituency applying, may be deemed the most suitable candidate. The registry of names to be read at a summoned meeting of the General Council. In cases where branches of the League or Constituences shall prefer to elect a local or other candidate other than the candidate who may be submitted by the League, and shall notify whom they have chosen to the Executive, the Executive, if they feel satisfied that the selection has been fairly and honourably made, and that the candidate is a fitting representative of the principles of the League, shall have power to give to such candidate whatever support the League is capable of. In such constituences where branches of the League

exist, the members of such branches shall be summoned together when a candidate has to be selected to contest the representation. And when branches of the League do not exist, the Executive shall take whatever steps it may deem necessary to ascertain that the election has been made in a fair and open manner.

(*c*) " Address of the Labour Representation League to the Working Men Electors of the United Kingdom ", 1871.

FELLOW WORKING MEN,

We ask you to consider the following facts—

There are about twenty millions of persons in the United Kingdom belonging to the working classes. The comfort, the progress, the security, the happiness, of these millions depend to a great extent on the way they are legislated for in the House of Commons.

There are also in Great Britain ten millions or thereabouts of all other classes, viz : nobility, landed gentry, the various professions, employers of labour and others.

In the House of Commons there are 658 members, whose business it is to make the laws under which the whole of the people of all classes live. These 658 men are supposed to understand the circumstances of the various classes, and to shape their laws, so as to impartially promote the interests of all. Strange to say, however, every one of the 658 belongs to the middle and upper classes — Labour has not one direct representative — there is not in the House of Commons ONE MAN whose life has been spent in the workshop in intimate daily experience of the working man's trials, or who has been engaged in those struggles in connexion with labour, upon which he founds his hopes of future regeneration.

In connexion with this, let it be remembered that working men's questions are almost daily under consideration in that assembly, and some of them vitally affect their welfare. Amongst others, the great question of the poor laws. — Employment of children in workshops. — The truck system. — Regulation of mines. — The condition of the agricultural labourer. — Emigration. — Extravagant and wasteful expenditure in any department of the State.

In common fairness working men ought to be in a position to speak to the legislature and the nation on these questions. Surely some men of the working class ought to have an opportunity to explain the views of their fellow workers on matters of such seriousness ; to urge their demands and give shape to their requirements.

Working men; do not forget you can alter all this if you will. If you suffer any longer from such an injustice, the fault will be entirely your own. Determine to organise your numbers thoroughly; resolve to act unitedly, firmly and continuously. You are powerful by the suffrage, you will be invincible by the Ballot, and in the future you will not be trammelled by heavy legal expenses.

We call on you as a paramount and pressing duty, to return qualified men of your own order to Parliament. Give us your hearty cooperation and we pledge ourselves that this shall be done.

Establish branches of the League throughout the country; knit yourselves firmly together, and let us try if by united, friendly, and vigorous action we cannot break down a system of class exclusion from Parliament; injurious by its effects to the happiness of the mass of the people, and odious by the stamp of inferiority with which it brands the industrial population of these islands.

By order of the Executive Council.

Signed. ⎰ ROBERT M. LATHAM, President.
⎱ WILLIAM ALLAN, Treasurer.
⎰ LLOYD JONES, Secretary.

(d) From a Leaflet issued by the Labour Representation League, just before the General Election of 1874.

TO THE WORKING CLASS VOTERS OF THE UNITED KINGDOM.

FELLOW WORKERS,

The long-expected electoral struggle is at last upon us.

The two great political parties of the country are about to grapple with each other all over the kingdom; and as your aid will be invoked from both sides, it is necessary you should at once decide as to your course of action. . . .

There are at the present moment several Labour Candidates in the field, and we ask you earnestly, emphatically, and as you prize your rights as free citizens, to Vote for these without hesitation.

3. THE NORTHERN REFORM LEAGUE

[The Northern Reform League did not dissolve when the Act of 1867 became law, but soon reconstituted itself on a new basis, with the Northumberland and Durham Miners' Associations as its principal constituents. In conjunction with a specially created Miners' Franchise Union, it devoted itself to getting as many workmen as possible entered on the electoral rolls under the ' lodger franchise ' provisions of the Act, and it selected Morpeth for special attention, as a borough containing a large number of mining voters. Joseph Cowen, junior, its leader, won a safe seat at Newcastle-on-Tyne in a by-election in January 1874, caused by his father's death.]

From *The Newcastle Daily Chronicle*, October 27, 1873.

WINTER ARRANGEMENTS OF THE NORTHERN REFORM LEAGUE.

The Chairman [Mr. Joseph Cowen] said this was the first regularly summoned meeting of the Council of the League as re-constituted. As they were aware, upwards of eighteen months ago, a movement was made in the neighbourhood of Morpeth, for the purpose of getting the miners of that district placed upon the electoral roll. Out of that movement arose an agitation for the extension of the suffrage to the working men in the counties. From Northumberland that movement extended to Durham, and the immediate outcome of the efforts of the reformers in the two counties was the great demonstration which was held at Newcastle Town Moor, at Easter last. The committee who had charge of the arrangements of that meeting constituted themselves into a permanent association, in accordance with the resolution passed on that occasion. Since then the committee had been quietly but persistently organising a feeling in favour of reform in the two counties. In this they had met with a large measure of success, for the entire body of miners in connection with the Northumberland Union, and those connected with the Durham Union had joined the League in a body. With the support the association had got from the workmen in the different northern towns, it now represented a society of something like 50,000 members. It was thus probably the most powerful political organisation of working men that had been known in England of late years. Certainly they had never had such an organisation before in this district. . . .

4. THE TRADES UNION CONGRESS AND THE GENERAL ELECTION OF 1874

[The Trade Unions did all they could to make the amendment of the Labour Laws a test question for candidates at the General Election of

1874. This and the demand for a new Factory Act were the principal Trade Union issues. But the Congress also gave strong support to Samuel Plimsoll's agitation for a new Merchant Shipping Act to improve safety at sea and put forward proposals for various amendments in general criminal procedure. It confined itself to a narrow range of questions, and put forward no general working-class programmes.]

A Leaflet issued by the Trades Union Congress Parliamentary Committee, 1874.

GENERAL ELECTION

Electors everywhere are earnestly requested to put the following test questions to every candidate.

Will you vote for :—

1. Repeal of the Criminal Law Amendment Act.

2. Alteration of the Master and Servants Act, so that breach of contract shall not be a criminal offence.

3. Alteration of the law of conspiracy in accordance with the Bill introduced last session by the present Solicitor-General.

4. Reconstruction of the Small Penalties list, on the principle that imprisonment should only be used as a method of enforcing payment after failure of all other means, and as a last resort.

5. Consideration by Parliament of the important constitutional question of what limit should be placed upon the summary jurisdiction of magistrates, which deprives citizens of the right of trial by jury.

6. Enquiry by a Royal Commission as to the state of the laws and procedure relating to summary jurisdiction ; as to the way in which the law has been administered by qualified and unqualified magistrates ; and also as to the mode of their appointment and removal.

7. Reduction of the qualification of jurymen, to admit workmen to discharge the civic duties of jurymen.

8. Alteration of the law so that workmen or their families may be able to sue employers in the event of injury or death from accidents due to negligence.

9. A factory Nine Hours Bill for women and children.

10. An Act to prevent Truck by making compulsory weekly payments to workmen in the current coin of the realm.

11. An Act for the better protection of seamen's lives by preventing the sending of ill-found, and unseaworthy vessels to sea.

By order,
Trades' Union Congress Parliamentary Committee.

5. THE FIRST WORKMEN M.P.s.

[At the General Election of 1874 Alexander Macdonald, the miners' leader, was elected for Stafford, sharing the representation with a Conservative. Macdonald ran in association with a Liberal, against two Conservatives. At Morpeth, Northumberland, Thomas Burt, the local miners' leader, won in a straight fight with a Conservative for the single seat. He was strongly supported by the Northern Reform Union. The remaining Labour candidates were all beaten, though several polled well.]

(a) From A. Macdonald's ' Address to the Electors of Stafford ', 1874. Reprinted in A. W. Humphrey, " A History of Labour Representation " (1912), pp. 52-3.

TO THE ELECTORS OF STAFFORD.

GENTLEMEN,

As promised in a former notice, I beg now formally to state, for your consideration, some of the leading subjects that would claim my attention and support if returned by you to serve in Parliament.

The anomalous condition of the County Franchise cannot much longer be maintained, as it deprives a large portion of our fellow-citizens of the privilege that others possess. It would be my endeavour to get the Borough and County Franchise assimilated.

Following as a right, we would require a redistribution of seats. Any measure brought forward for that purpose would have my most cordial support, if just in its character and suited to the needs and requirements of the case.

Having long taken a deep interest in the question of Restricted Hours of Labour for Children, I would sedulously watch all matters pertaining to the extension and application of the Factory and Workshop Acts to such occupations as need to be brought within the provisions of these and similar Acts.

All questions affecting the interests of Capital and Labour would have my constant and undivided attention, believing, as I do, that it is only by a more peaceful relation of these interests that the greatness and strength of our country can be maintained.

With these views, I would support a measure for the total repeal of the Criminal Law Amendment Act, modification of the Master and Servants Acts, so as to remove the criminal clauses, a clear and defined Law of Conspiracy, and such other changes as would remove the limitation that now exists, which is alike injurious to employees and employed.

The present enormous taxation would also have my attention. I would support every effort made for real reduction. Pensions and sinecures would be most carefully watched.

The easy transfer of land, the abolition of the Game Laws, a peaceful foreign policy would have my cordial support, if returned.

As regards Local Government in Ireland, I am impressed with Mr. Butt's opinions, and would give them my hearty support.

Many other important matters, which I cannot touch upon here, I will personally, by public meeting and by visitation, explain at length then, and give such explanations as I hope may lead you to support me.

I have the honour to be, Gentlemen,
Your obedient servant,

HOLYTOWN, N.B.   ALEXANDER MACDONALD.
January 28th, 1874.

(*b*) From *The Newcastle Weekly Chronicle*, October 25, 1873.

TO THE ELECTORS OF THE BOROUGH OF MORPETH.

GENTLEMEN,—In response to a requisition, signed by 3,500 of your number, I offer myself as a candidate to represent your borough in the Commons' House of Parliament at the next election.

The constituency of Morpeth being largely composed of working men, questions affecting the interests of labour must necessarily have strong claims on the attention of your representative.

Since the laws of the country have in the past been made almost exclusively by employers and capitalists, many of them bear very oppressively and unjustly on the working classes. Among enactments of this character may be mentioned the Master and Servant Act, the Criminal Law Amendment Act, and the Law of Conspiracy. . . .

Believing, as I do, in the sovereignty of the people, I would give a vote to all sane persons of full age, who, not being paupers or criminals, are called upon to obey the laws and to fulfil the ordinary duties of citizenship. Popular Government will be very incomplete without a better apportionment of members to population, shorter Parliaments, and payments of representatives. I would, therefore, vote for all measures which have those objects in view.

Our national expenditure is enormous and requires prompt and vigorous retrenchment. The Geneva Arbitration, followed as it has been by the passing in the House of Commons of Mr. Richard's motion in favour of International Arbitration, is a hopeful sign of the times, and leads us to indulge the expectation that our extravagant and disgraceful war expenditure may, before long, be greatly diminished.

For many years I have been an advocate of National Education, free, unsectarian, and compulsory. No system can, in my opinion, be really national and effective without the recognition of these principles. The Education Act of 1870 is very defective, and should, I think, be amended in the direction I have indicated. The 25th. Clause of that Act, which provides for the payment of fees to denominational schools, is unjust, and ought to be at once repealed. I am in favour of perfect religious equality; and I hold that the state ought to have nothing to do with the teaching of any religious opinions whatever. Consequently I would vote for the disestablishment and disendowment of the Churches of England, Wales, and Scotland.

The land of the kingdom does not at present, in the opinion of competent authorities, produce near the quantity of food it might do if properly tilled. That the people may enjoy a better and cheaper supply of food, the waste lands of the country should, as far as possible, be cultivated, and the soil already under cultivation ought to be improved to the utmost extent attainable. In order that this may be done, our land laws, in my judgment, must be thoroughly reformed. The Game Laws, which are a relic of feudalism, are so iniquitous in character and so lamentable in results that any proposition to abolish them would have my hearty support. Nearly ten thousand convictions take place under them every year, and they entail an enormous loss to the community. These are sufficient reasons for sweeping them away.

Our national intemperance is a terrible curse. It is a prolific source of crime, lunacy, pauperism, and of consequent taxation. As a Radical, I am in favour of the people who suffer and pay the costs having a voice in controlling the liquor traffic. I should therefore vote in favour of the principle of the Permissive Bill — a principle which would empower the ratepayers to deal with the public sale of intoxicating drinks in a given district.

On these and on other subjects of present and prospective importance I shall, before the election, address public meetings in various parts of the borough.

I am, Gentlemen,
yours very respectfully

Newcastle-upon-Tyne
October 20, 1873.

Thomas Burt.

(c) From *The Newcastle Daily Chronicle*, January 10, 1874.

. . . Mr Burt thanked them heartily for this strong manifestation of their approval and confidence. If sent to the House of Commons, he had no wish to be sent as the representative of any class, however numerous, but as the representative of the people. On this point he held very decided opinions, and would never himself vote or speak in favour of any man, however capable, merely because he was a labour representative. They had themselves always complained, and justly complained, of class representation, and it would be highly improper and inconsistent on their part to act on the principles they condemned in others. He did not, however, wish to hide from them that his sympathies were, and would ever be, with the class to which he belonged — the great class which earned their bread by their manual labour. He should not, however, be so narrow and illiberal as to regard that class as being everything and everybody; but he should, as far as possible, lose sight of classes and try to represent, as far as his ability would allow, the people, who were greater than any class, for they embraced all. (Cheers).

6. THE NATIONAL REFORM UNION

[The National Reform Union continued in existence after 1867, and continued to agitate for electoral reform in the county constituencies, which had been left in the main unreformed. The county franchise was widened in 1884, and a further extensive redistribution of seats followed in 1885. The N.R.U. also took up other questions, especially that of the Land Laws, which were also the province of the Land Tenure Reform Association, founded by John Stuart Mill in 1870, and of James Harvey's Land and Labour League of 1867. George Potter became a lecturer for the National Reform Union after he had been driven from the editorship of *The Beehive* by the ' Junta ' group.]

From a Leaflet of the National Reform Union [1875].

Statement of Objects, as revised by the Conference held December 1875.

OBJECTS OF THE UNION

The Reform of the Representative System, by the extension of Household Suffrage to all householders in the counties, and the equalisation of electoral power.

Religious equality — involving the disestablishment and dis-endowment of the English and Scotch Established Churches, and the establishment of a National Unsectarian system of Education.

A thorough Revision of the Land Laws, so as to provide such systems of tenure as will promote the best cultivation of the soil, and secure a fair valuation of the land for the purposes of national taxation in proportion to its increased value.

Popular control over licenses for the Sale of Intoxicating Liquors.

XXI

INDUSTRIAL MOVEMENTS, 1870–1876

INTRODUCTION

THE great trade boom of the early 1870s brought with it a general increase of Trade Union activity and an extension of the movement to many groups hitherto unorganised. The engineers and builders were largely successful in winning the Nine Hours Day; and there was a big extension of Trade Union recognition and collective bargaining as a consequence of the Trade Union Act of 1871, as well as of the state of the labour market. The agricultural workers, who had been inactive since their repression in the 1830s, set up Unions in many parts of the country; and Joseph Arch, at the head of the largest of these, led a great agitation on their behalf. Samuel Plimsoll espoused the cause of the seamen, and secured the enforcement of the ' Plimsoll Line ' under the Merchant Shipping Act of 1876. Emma Paterson set on foot a movement to organise women workers outside the cotton trade, where they were already catered for. The forward movement lasted until about 1875, but was thereafter crushed out by the onset of the ' Great Depression ', which reached its lowest point in 1879. The new Unions, for the most part, disappeared, or were reduced to impotence; and even the Unions of the skilled crafts lost many members and were reduced to a strictly defensive policy. These conditions lasted until the big Trade Union revival of the late 1880s.

See " Short History ", Part II, chapter 6, sections 3 and 4.
" Common People ", chapter 32.

1. THE NINE HOURS MOVEMENT

[The Nine Hours Movement of the North-East Coast Engineers in 1870 and 1871 was a great working-class victory, won mainly by a rank-and-file movement among workers who were largely unorganised. The struggle was conducted by a hastily created Nine Hours League, under the leadership of John Burnett, subsequently Secretary of the Amalga-

597

mated Society of Engineers. The International Working Men's Association helped to defeat the employers' attempts to bring in blacklegs from the continent; and large subscriptions were raised in aid of the strike fund from Trade Unions all over the country, as well as from middle-class sympathisers. The Nine Hours Movement coincided in time with the big developments of Co-operative Production in the Tyneside area (see p. 459); and the Ouseburn Engineering Works ran as a Co-operative enterprise largely animated by the industrial struggle. The period was one of rapidly advancing trade prosperity, culminating in the boom of 1872–1873, which was especially marked in the constructional industries. The victory on the North-East Coast was followed by the concession of the nine-hours day in many other areas, and parallel victories were won in the building and in other industries.]

From " Amalgamated Society of Engineers. Abstract Report of the Council's Proceedings from June 1st, 1870, to December 31st, 1872 ", p. 184.

By reference to the last published Abstract of Council's Proceedings (page 98), a report will be found of a meeting of the Newcastle Central District Committee, wherein the nine hours system was mooted, but by a resolution it was not considered the proper time to move in the matter, beyond treating it as a question of so much importance that it was not to be lost sight of.

This meeting was held in June, 1870, and in the following April the engineering trade in Sunderland, on their own account, struck for the nine hours system.

It is now curious to peruse the tone of the meeting which was held there during the strike by the Newcastle Central District Committee : but if a calm view of the formidable obstacles which afterwards appeared in the Newcastle strike are taken into account, with the probability of defeat, it will at once be seen that such was only a prudent caution in dealing with so important a question.

The engineering firms in Sunderland granted the workmen the terms they asked, and therefore the system was inaugurated.

The movement then extended to Newcastle and resulted in one of the most memorable strikes on record. At first our society had difficulties to meet from the fact that upwards of 8,000 men had struck, whereas only 500 of them belonged to our society, and very few to any other. With wonderful celerity the men on strike joined the nine hours league, through which the dispute was contested and settled, our society rendering to the cause a generous support, and all the branches were strongly urged by the council to render all possible aid. Mr Cohn was dispatched at the society's expense to the Continent to intercept the foreign workmen that the employers were engaging; by making known to his countrymen the nature of the strike, many were induced by his energy and eloquence to relinquish their engagements, thereby reducing the number of those that did come to a minimum, and even those an inferior class of workmen. The contest went on, and the workmen ultimately triumphed. The press, to a large extent was favourable to the shortening of the hours of labour. They had witnessed and recorded the productive agencies of our country, and had concluded that the workmen could and ought to live by devoting fewer of the hours of their existence to the workshop. The same concessions that were made by the Newcastle employers to their workmen, were rapidly granted by others all over England and Ireland. In Scotland they went a step further and demanded 51 hours per week to be granted. The employers there offered 54 per week, and an advance of wages, but all honour to the men, they refused the money and firmly adhered to the shortening of the hours, which they ultimately obtained.

During the whole of the period the Council spent much of their time in advising and aiding our members and others all over the country in securing the shortening of the hours of labour.

The Council were repeatedly applied to to appeal to the members for a levy for the non-society men. This, however, they were under the necessity of refusing, inasmuch as the rule distinctly states the objects for which alone levies can be made. At the same time it must be borne in mind that they appealed to the branches for a renewal of the contingent fund, which was favourably responded to, and thereby enabled the Council to grant our members 5s. per week in addition to the ordinary donation benefit.

2. THE NINE HOURS BILL

[At the same time as the engineers and builders were winning the nine hours day by industrial action, the textile operatives were attempting to secure the passing of a Nine Hours Bill. The movement was again organised through Short Time Committee in the factory districts, including progressive employers and other sympathisers as well as Trade Unionists. In deference to Lord Shaftesbury's wishes, it was kept formally apart from the Trade Union movement, though the separation had not much reality. The Factory Act of 1875 did not concede the nine hours day; but a maximum working week of 56½ hours was established by law for women and young persons, and a great consolidating Act was passed in 1878.]

From the Trades Union Congress Parliamentary Committee's Report for the 1873 Congress, p. 3.

THE FACTORIES' NINE HOURS BILL.

The " Bill for the further restriction of the hours of labour of children, young persons, and females, in certain factories ", was in the charge of a special committee composed partly of unionists, and partly of non-unionists, as Lord Shaftesbury and others declared that they would not undertake a measure proposed in the interests of trade unions, as they were only a section of the people, whereas the Bill was based upon quite other grounds.

With this feeling your Committee had nothing whatever to do. They were anxious to see so good and useful a measure carried, by whosoever promoted.

As soon as the " Factory Workers' Short-time Committee " came to London, your committee, as in duty bound according to the resolution passed at the last Congress, and as advised by several leading men of the factory operatives, sought an interview with that committee and proffered their services in any way which those who had charge of the measure deemed most useful and expedient. Some members of the short time committee thought that even co-operation with the Congress Committee would be disastrous rather than useful; your Committee, therefore, withdrew.

The matter was, however, subsequently discussed by the factory delegates, and an intimation was given to the Secretary that our co-operation would be thankfully accepted.

Such co-operation was cheerfully rendered, not the slightest antagonism being in any way manifested on either side.

3. TRADE UNION PROGRESS

[The Parliamentary Committee of the Trades Union Congress, in its Reports for 1873 and 1874, was able to congratulate itself both on the very rapid growth of Trade Unionism and its extension to previously un-organised bodies of workers, including the agricultural labourers, and also on the absence of serious disputes in the well-organised trades. These, as long as the boom lasted, were able to win substantial concessions without the need to strike ; but the situation changed rapidly as trade conditions worsened after 1874. The miners especially became involved in bitter struggles against wage-reductions ; and Trade Unionism as a whole was put on the defensive, and lost all the vitality of the years after 1867. What has been called the ' Lib-Lab period ' really began, not in 1867, but during the years of depression which followed the boom of the early 1870s.]

(a) From the Trades Union Congress Parliamentary Committee's Report for the 1874 Congress, p. 1.

REPORT, 1873.

The year just closed has been unparalleled for the rapid growth and developement of Trade Unionism. In almost every trade this appears to have been the same, but it is specially remarkable in those branches of industry which had hitherto been but badly organised. It is not, however, in members only that this increase is observable, the funds have correspondingly increased, and this has gone on side by side with movements for increased pay and shorter hours of labour. . . .

(b) From the Trades Union Congress Parliamentary Committee's Report for the 1875 Congress, p. 1.

The year which has just closed has been an eventful one for Trades Unions in several respects.

The struggle of the Agricultural Labourers for an advance of wages, and for better conditions of labour, although not so successful as your Committee could have desired, was long, persistent, and intense, and in its results not without permanent advantage to that underpaid class of workmen. The better paid workmen of the towns nobly assisted them in their efforts to improve their own condition, and thus assisted in alleviating the distress and suffering of those locked out or on strike.

The Miners, the Ironworkers, and others, have also had severe struggles, chiefly to maintain advantages already won, with varying success.

But there has been a remarkable absence of strikes amongst the better paid Mechanics and Artisans. Much of this we believe to be due to their strong and healthy organisation — an evidence, to our thinking, that good, sound, and well-conducted Trades Associations do not conduce to strikes.

4. THE AGRICULTURAL LABOURERS

[The agricultural labourers' movement that was led by Joseph Arch began in Warwickshire in 1872 ; but for some time previously there had been local stirrings among the rural workers. The movement spread very rapidly, in face of bitter opposition from the farmers and from most of the local gentry and parsons. Though Arch's Agricultural Labourers' Union covered a number of counties, there were also a number of independent Unions which refused to link up with it. By 1874 the Unions had won substantial wage-concessions, though the cost in victimisation of active Union members had been high. As long as the boom held, it was usually easy for the victimised men to find work ; but they suffered much hardship through eviction from cottages tied to the farms. As the depression set in during the later 1870s, victimisation was renewed on a large scale, and the Unions began to disintegrate, losing many of their best members by emigration, which they actively promoted in order to reduce the supply of labour. Only in a few areas were the Unions still active by 1880, and thereafter they continued to fall away. There was no revival such as took place among the urban workers towards the end of the 1880s.]

(*a*) From " Joseph Arch : the Story of His Life, by Himself " (1898), pp. 86-90.

On the Good Friday of 1872, about six weeks after the formation of the Union, we held a great demonstration and tea meeting in the public hall, Portland Street, Leamington. It made a tremendous stir, and people came flocking and streaming in from miles round. Crowds of poor labourers with their wives and children marched into the town, headed by their village fife and drum bands. Leamington had never seen such a sight in all its born days ; and those who saw it and took part in it are not likely to forget it. Wellesbourne was to the fore as usual. John Lewis had seen to that. He was one of the very first men in the district to help set the Union going, and he was no laggard now. He sent messengers off to scour the neighbourhood, and he got a bell and went round like a town-crier, summoning the people to a tryst under the old chestnut tree at 8.30 a.m. on Good Friday morning. At the appointed time men and women came tramping up dressed in what of best they had. A poor best according to rich folk's notions no doubt, but smock frock and fustian jacket and shabby gown covered brave English hearts, beating high with hope of the good times coming. That little band of stiff and bent and battered men, stunted and toil-worn, with their thin and haggard wives, were no coneys — a sorry and a feeble folk. No ; they were strong in Union as they took the road this March morning, with stout and trusty John Lewis at their head. They marched away, singing this rhyme as they tramped into Leamington :

> " The farm labourers of South Warwickshire,
> Have not had a rise for many a year,
> Although bread has often been dear ;
> But now they've found a Union."

And so they had, as all the world was soon to know.

It was a busy day for me, if it was a proud one. I took the chair at the Organising Committee which sat in the room downstairs. They elected me organising secretary at a small salary, and Henry Taylor, a Leamington carpenter, was elected paid secretary, on the condition that he gave up any office he might hold in another Union, and joined ours. We wanted neither outsiders nor professional Trades Union men ; we knew our own business and we were determined from the outset to manage it in our own way. " Hands off ! " we said to any outside meddler who wanted to poke a finger into our Union pie. We then drew up the following Rules :—

1. The name of the Society shall be the " Warwickshire Agricultural Labourers' Union ".

2. Its object is to elevate the social position of the farm labourers of the county by assisting them to increase their wages ; to lessen the number of ordinary working hours ; to improve their habitations ; to provide them with gardens or allotments ; and to assist deserving and suitable labourers to migrate and emigrate.

3. In all questions of dispute about remuneration of labour, an attempt shall be made to decide such dispute by arbitration between the Union and the employers of labour.

4. The Board shall have power to make arrangements for arbitration as regards the price of labour ; to take charge of all disputes between employers and employed ; to make arrangements for supporting members when out of work ; to help labourers to migrate and emigrate ; to suspend, fine or expel any member who shall violate the society's regulations, and shall have such other powers as may be necessary to accomplish the objects of the Society, and shall avail itself of all requisite provisions under the Friendly Societies and Trades Unions Acts.

5. The Board shall hereafter decide how many hours, not exceeding ten, shall constitute a day's work, and all over-time shall be paid for at the rate of fourpence per hour, and all Sunday work shall be

paid for as overtime, except in such cases as the Union shall direct.

6. Labourers' work shall cease by four o'clock on Saturdays, except in such cases as the Union may direct.

7. The Board shall consist of one delegate, elected by each branch numbering not less than fifty members, and three members of the Leamington Trades' Union; but the last-mentioned members shall not have the power of voting.

8. The Board shall meet monthly at Leamington to transact the business of the Society, and special meetings may be convened by the secretary and chairman jointly at two days' notice; nine delegates to form a quorum.

Rule 9 provided for the election of a chairman, secretary, treasurer (who must find security), two trustees, and a professional auditor.

Rule 13 provided that there should be a yearly meeting at Leamington, at which the Board shall submit a report and balance sheet (audited) for approval.

The contributions to the Union were fixed at sixpence entrance fee, and twopence per week subscription.

We had got through a good afternoon's work by the time all was settled, and we had the evening meeting still before us. Oh, what a meeting that was !

Many of the Trade Unions took part in it, and nearly every tradesman in and around Leamington was there. The gentlemen of Warwickshire were conspicuous by their absence, but the people had been pouring in, and pouring in like a flood, till the hall was as full as it could hold; and then they overflowed into the street, and thousands more joined the overflow. They called for me to come out and address them; so out I came, and Forbes took the chair and we held a meeting there. When I stood up in my moleskins, I faced such a crowd of my fellow-creatures as I had never before set eyes on. It was a flood-tide of humanity which swayed and heaved as far as I could see in the gaslight; it extended right away down Windsor Street.

(b) From " Constitution and Rules of the National Agricultural Labourers' Union " (as revised 1874).

RULE 2.—OBJECTS.

1. To improve the general condition of farm and other Labourers in the United Kingdom by
    (a) Increasing their wages and lessening their hours of labour.

(b) To protect their trade interests, and to secure legal redress against oppression.

(c) To assist its members to migrate and emigrate.

2. To encourage the formation of Branch and District Unions, and to promote co-operation and communication between Unions already in existence.

(c) From *The Labourers' Union Chronicle*, March 14, 1874.

. . . The work of the leaders of the National Agricultural Labourers' Union may be contemplated as fourfold. First :—Combining and enlightening the whole peasantry. Secondly : Forwarding in every way wholesale emigration; to improve the condition of the long-suffering farm labourer, and give him an easy chance of prosperity and independence; and bring about vast political and social changes by reducing farm rents to a minimum, and increasing labourers' wages to a maximum by creating, as far as possible, an absolutely empty market of farm labourers. For the few that will be soon left, factory and farm will compete for, and the towns will carry them off by bidding the highest wages; and by these means we hope to facilitate the political agitations for the changes we aim at further. Thirdly. The assimilation of the county with the borough franchise — to give household and lodger suffrage to our farm labourers. And fourthly, to thoroughly destroy the English, Irish and Scottish land monopoly; to protect tenant farmers from game and eviction by no delusory palliatives — mere mockeries of protection and delusive shams, that only excite trust to betray it. We have laid down our programme, and we are satisfied that it is thoroughly practicable, and if once acted upon will work thoroughly for the protection of tenant farmers and farm labourers, and raise up a numerous small farm proprietary to bless England and the sister kingdoms with peace, and prosperity, and social advantages, many and valuable.

(d) From *The Labourers' Union Chronicle*, March 21, 1874.

. . . About 2,000 men are now in idleness and on the funds of the N.A.L.U. — some for asking for a rise in their wages — for the sin of asking, the right to do which is absolutely denied; — some have struck because, having asked for a rise by giving a week's notice to their employers, they are refused, for, as the farmers say, " it looks like ' meaking us ' "; — others and by far the greater number, are locked out because they are members of the Union, and they refuse to employ them unless they withdraw. . . .

(*e*) From " Songs for Singing at Agricultural Labourers' Meetings ", by Howard Evans. 85th Thousand. New and enlarged edition (n. d.).

THE MASTER AND I [1]

Tune — " *Bonnie Dundee* "

Says the master to me, — " Is it true, as I'm told,
Your name's on the books of the Union enrolled ?
I can never allow that a workman of mine
With wicked disturbers of peace should combine ;
I give you fair warning, mind what you're about,
I shall put my foot down on it, trample it out ;
On which side your bread's butter'd sure you can see,
So decide now at once for the Union or me."

Says I to the master, — " It's perfectly true
That I'm in the Union, — I'll stick to it, too !
And if between Union and you I must choose,
Why, I've plenty to win, and little to lose ;
For twenty years, mostly my bread has been dry,
And to butter it now, I shall certainly try ;
And though I respect you, remember I'm free —
No master in England shall trample on me."

Says the master to me, — " A word or two more —
We never have quarrelled on matters before ;
If you stick to the Union, 'ere long, I'll be bound,
You'll come and ask me for more wages all round.
Now I cannot afford more than two ' bob ' a day,
When I look at the taxes, and rent that I pay ;
And the crops are so injured by game, as you see,
If it is hard for you, it's hard also for me."

Says I to the master, — " I do not see how
Any need has arisen for quarrelling now ;
And though, likely enough, we shall ask for more wage,
I can promise you, we shan't get first in a rage ;
Your landlord mayn't think so, but I don't deny
Your taxes and rent are a great deal too high ;
But granted all that, — you've been both in the swim,
We are bound to squeeze you, — now you go and squeeze him."

---

[1] A somewhat different version of this poem is cited in Reg Groves's book, " Sharpen the Sickle : The History of the Farm Workers' Union ", 1949.

(*f*) From the Report of the Royal Commission on Agriculture, 1882. Minutes of Evidence, vol. iii, pp. 3 and 85.

Examination of Mr. J. Arch.

58,421. How do you set about ensuring the labourers getting higher wages ? — We have reduced the number of labourers in the market very considerably.

58,422. How have you reduced the number of labourers in the market ? — We have emigrated about 700,000 souls, men, women and children, within the last eight or nine years.

58,423. How have these 700,000 souls been emigrated; out of what funds ? — I went over to Canada, and I made arrangements with the Canadian Government to give them so much, and we found them so much from the funds of our trade.

58,424. That is, out of the funds of the association ? — Yes.

58,425. Then some of the labourers subscribed themselves in order to emigrate the rest; is that so ? — Yes.

.   .   .   .

60,354. (J. Arch) The 750,000 emigrants that have gone out have not all gone out directly under the auspices of our union, but indirectly. The emigration agents and the shipping companies have made our union a means to get into the various countries where our union has not gone, and they have by that means got a very large number of people to emigrate when there was free emigration to Canada.

5. THE UNSKILLED AND THE FORBIDDEN

[The boom of the 1870s brought with it the first attempt to organise a ' general labour ' Union of unskilled workers in all types of heavy employment. It also gave rise to attempts at organisation among black-coated workers, and to movements by postal employees to get their grievances voiced in Parliament, in face of the refusal of the Government to agree to any form of collective bargaining.]

(*a*) From the Rules of the General Labourers' Amalgamated Union, 1872.

1. This Society shall be called the GENERAL LABOURERS' AMALGAMATED UNION. It shall be composed of labourers who work in the following branches of industry, namely, all builders' labourers, including navvies, labourers who work in the iron trades

or other manufactories, such as gas works, brickfields, engineer shops and foundries, and all other unskilled labourers.

. . . .

4. The objects are first to procure for its members, by all honourable means, the full value for their labour; secondly, to diminish the hours of labour to such an extent as is consistent with man's moral and physical nature.

(*b*) From the Report of the Trades Union Congress (1874), p. 27.

POSTAL EMPLOYEES AND THEIR GRIEVANCES

Mr. Geo. Howell (secretary to the Parliamentary Committee) read a very interesting paper on the grievances of the postal employees, setting forth very explicitly their present position as compared with other working men. From it we take an extract. Mr. Howell adverted to the employees trying to ameliorate their condition; and of the little that was known by the public respecting the objects they sought, and the means by which they sought to obtain them. Their position was peculiar, and gave them a strong claim upon the sympathy and support of the members of the Congress. By the rules of the department the men were forbidden to hold public meetings to discuss their grievances, or take any action whatever for the purpose of removing them. The only course open to them was to apply to their immediate superior, with right to appeal.

6. THE WOMEN'S PROTECTIVE AND PROVIDENT LEAGUE

[The Women's Protective and Provident League, the pioneer body which set out to organise women workers outside the cotton and woollen industries, was founded by Emma Paterson (1848–1886) in 1874. Mrs. Paterson, who had been connected with the Working Men's Club movement and the Women's Suffrage Association, came into contact with women's Trade Unions on a visit to the United States, and returned to found a number of small women's Unions in the London area. She also founded the National Union of Working Women. She became a regular attendant at the Trades Union Congress and stood several times without success for the Parliamentary Committee. The League subsequently developed into the Women's Trade Union League, and helped to give birth to Mary Macarthur's National Federation of Women Workers.]

From " Women's Protective and Provident League. First Annual Report " (1875), p. 3.

The Committee of the Women's Protective and Provident League have pleasure in submitting their First Annual Report to Members and Friends of the League.

Appointment of Committee.

The Committee was appointed at a Conference convened to consider a proposal made in a paper previously privately circulated and published in the Labour News, that a national union should be formed for improving the " Position of Working Women ". The Conference was held on the 8th of July, 1874, Mr Hodgson Pratt in the chair, at the Quebec Institute, Lower Seymour Street. After full discussion of the question under consideration, the following resolutions were passed :—

1. That a Committee be appointed, to be entitled the Women's Protective and Provident Committee.

2. That one of the objects of the Association shall be to enable women earning their own livelihood to combine to protect their interests.

3. That it shall be one of the objects of the Association to provide a benefit fund for assistance in sickness and other contingencies.

. . . . . .

MODIFIED PLAN DECIDED ON FOR COMMENCE-MENT OF OPERATIONS

The question of the best mode of carrying out the resolutions passed at the conference was then discussed, and it was decided that it would not be advisable, in the first instance, to endeavour to form a national union managed from a centre, but to promote the formation of separate societies in the various trades in which women are employed, keeping in view, however, the desirability of ulti-mately promoting some kind of federation of the various societies.

It should be mentioned that the plan of a national union, sug-gested in the paper before referred to, was considered and adopted at a conference held in Bristol last August. This conference was attended by Mrs Paterson, who explained the action already decided on in London.

Whilst adhering to, and endeavouring to carry out, their resolu-tion as to the advisability of the formation of separate unions in the various trades, the Committee heartily wish success to the work undertaken in Bristol, and they have gladly offered to cooperate with its promoters. . . .

The Committee are particularly anxious to disclaim any views of antagonism towards the employers of female labour as a class; many employers are friendly to the movement from their own knowledge of the need for some provident organisation amongst their workpeople, and others may be expected to sympathise with its indirect tendency to relieve respectable tradesmen from the competition of dealers in " slop goods " of all kinds. The object of the League is to promote an *entente cordiale* between the labourer, the employer and the consumer; and revision of the contract between labourer and employer is only recommended in those cases in which the terms appear unreasonable and unjust to the dispassionate third party, the consumer, who pays the final price for the manufactured goods, and is certainly not interested in adding artificially to their cost.

Progress of the societies already formed.

The Society of Women employed in Bookbinding has enrolled, during the eight months of its existence, 270 members, and has accumulated from members' entrance fees and subscriptions, a fund of £80. In October, payment of sick and out of work benefits will commence.

The Society of Upholsterers, Dressmakers, Hat Makers and Shirt Makers are of much more recent establishment, but are steadily progressing.

The advantages afforded by the societies — other than the direct payment of benefits, not yet commenced, — have already become clearly apparent and are frequently acknowledged by the members. It may be well to give a summary of them.

Advantages.

1. The interchange of useful trade information, for which facilities are afforded by the frequent opportunities of meeting together.

2. The registration of demands for work and for workers. One of the most important uses of the societies — when they have been longer established — will probably be this saving of time and strength afforded to the members by this system of registration. Hitherto the women have been obliged to go through the trouble and fatigue of walking from shop to shop in search of work. Numerous applica-

tions for workwomen have been received from employers and managers. The rules of the societies require some testimony as to the competency, in their trade, of persons wishing to become members, and this is an advantage of which the employers are glad to avail themselves.

3. An advance of wages given in some few instances.

4. Facilities for ascertaining the opinions of women concerned in the operation of the Factory and Workshops' Act, as to whether the extension of such legislation is desirable. This is a question of great importance to the women, but they have seldom been consulted about it.

5. The developement of business habits and knowledge through the work of the societies.

7. THE PLIMSOLL LINE

[Samuel Plimsoll (1824–1898), known as ' the Sailors' Friend ', was M.P. for Derby from 1868 to 1880, and devoted himself in Parliament to improving the seamen's conditions, above all the legal provisions for safety. He denounced ' coffin-ships ' and demanded a ' load-line ' that would make for reasonable security. He published " Our Seamen " in 1872, courting actions for libel from the shipowners whom he outspokenly denounced. This led to the appointment of a Royal Commission, which resulted in 1875 in a Government Bill to amend the law. The Bill, in an improved form due largely to Plimsoll's efforts, became an Act in 1876.]

(a) From Samuel Plimsoll, " Our Seamen. An Appeal " (1872), pp. v-vi.

PREFACE

Everybody knows that there is a great loss of life on our coasts annually, and nearly everybody deplores it. I am sure that if the English public equally knew how much of this loss is preventible, and the means of preventing it, no long time would elapse before means would be taken to secure this end.

It is with the view of giving this information, so as to enable each person who reads these pages to pronounce with decision upon this question, that this pamphlet is submitted to the public.

I have kept steadily in mind the idea of writing to an individual, as otherwise I should not have had the courage to address the public in what (from its length alone) looks like a book. As to a portion of it, I (perhaps naturally) shrink a good deal from submitting it to the public. It seemed, however, in writing it, and still seems to me, to give weight to my testimony on behalf of the working men. I apologise to any of my friends who may feel annoyed, and who would doubtless have aided me had they known of the straits to which I was brought in the earlier part of my life in London; but I ask them to think what a grand and glorious thing it will be if, by *any* sacrifice, we can put a stop to the dreadful and the shameful waste of precious human life which is now going on.

I thank all those gentlemen in the east, in the west, in the north, in the south, and in London, who have so greatly assisted me for some years in my inquiries, but they would not thank me if I thanked them by name. They are, however, one and all, longing to tell to a Royal Commission all they have told to me — and more ; for then they would speak under the protection of the law, whereas now they have to depend upon my discretion.

I intended to treat the subject at greater length, describing surveys for continuation, restoration, and some other matters, but, fearing to make my Appeal too long — when nobody would read it — I have curtailed it : as the Illustrations, however, were printed, I have had a few of the most beautiful stitched in at the end.

(*b*) From George Howell, " Labour Legislation, Labour Movements, and Labour Leaders ", vol. ii, chapter 27. (2nd edition, 1905.)

10. *The Plimsoll and Seamen's Fund Committee.*

After the distribution of " Our Seamen " at the Leeds Congress in January, 1873, Mr. Plimsoll asked me to organise a workmen's committee to help him in the creation of a sufficiently strong public opinion to ensure the passing of his Bill, or secure the appointment of a Royal Commission to inquire into the subject. I consented. But I suggested something broader than a mere sectional committee of workers, as represented by the Trades Congress, for the question was of national importance. My consent being given, Mr. Plimsoll left the rest to me. At that time he thought that the whole expenses would have to be borne by himself ; he did not anticipate any large response to his " Appeal ", except in the shape of sympathy and in the irresistible demand for better conditions for poor Jack.

11. *Formation of the Committee.*

I consulted a number of persons in the ranks of labour and otherwise as to the character and extent of the committee, and as to its objects when constituted. Among others I consulted Mr. Thomas Hughes, M.P., and he suggested a general committee of all sections of the community, and that Lord Shaftesbury should be asked to become the chairman. . . .

12. *Constitution of Committee.*

I called upon Lord Shaftesbury to ask him to join the Committee, and to become chairman thereof. His lordship promised to attend and to become chairman, if the Committee so desired. The persons so suggested and selected were convened, when Lord Shaftesbury was elected chairman, Mr. Thomas Hughes, vice-chairman; Sir W. R. Farquhar, Bart., treasurer; and myself, secretary. . . . Funds poured in; committees were formed in Manchester and Sheffield forthwith, and in a number of other towns and ports subsequently. The movement spread, enthusiasm was unbounded; vast meetings were called together to champion the cause of the sailor. A wave of popular feeling swept over the country such as had never before been evoked in the cause of any section of the working class. The Press, the theatre, the music-hall, the pulpit, the platform were all enlisted in the cause of " Our Seamen ".

. . . .

25. *Unseaworthy Vessels Detained.*

" Although Mr. Plimsoll's Bill was defeated in 1873 the Government, as a result of the agitation, brought in a temporary Bill, which was carried." It " gave power to the Board of Trade to detain vessels which they had evidence to show were unseaworthy, whether from unseaworthiness or from overloading ". Under that Act 440 vessels were detained as unseaworthy within about a year, " only sixteen of which were found to be sufficiently seaworthy to be allowed to go to sea ".

. . . .

30. *Legislation in 1876.*

Early in the Session of 1876 the Government reintroduced their Merchant Shipping Bill. It was read a second time on February 17th without a division. On May 8th the Bill passed through Committee in the House of Commons. It was read a third time and sent to the House of Lords, where it passed through its several stages and became law by the Queen's assent. Of course some efforts were made to " improve the Bill " by emasculating it, but it did not suffer severely.

It was not all that was desired; still it was a great step. Mr. Plimsoll had won a signal victory.

.   .   .   .   .   .

32. *The Libel Actions.*

The actions for libel issued against Mr. Plimsoll and others that were threatened caused grave anxiety to the Committee and to Mr. Plimsoll's other friends in and out of Parliament. Every effort was made to avert the final issue of such in courts of law. Cases of criminal libel might have involved imprisonment if the allegations could not be legally substantiated. Civil actions for damages might have crippled his resources, if not caused actual financial disaster. Therefore earnest efforts were made in Parliament by mutual friends and outside of it by the Committee and others to avert trials in the courts. In one case, perhaps the gravest, Mr. Robert Applegarth was requested by some members of Parliament to interest himself in the matter and try to pave the way for a withdrawal of the action. He visited the port associated with the allegations and the consequent action, and he at least paved the way for an abandonment of that serious action. By means of those friendly interventions none of the actions were fought out in the courts of law, nor was Mr. Plimsoll called upon to pay any of the costs on the other side. As it was, the costs were very considerable, even as reduced by negotiations between the different firms of solicitors and the secretary of the Plimsoll Committee. The full costs before such reductions amounted to a much larger sum. The combined influence of Lord Shaftesbury, Mr. Thomas Hughes, M.P., Mr. A. J. Mundella, M.P., and others was of the greatest value in all those peaceful negotiations.

8. PROPOSALS FOR CLOSER FEDERATION

[The Alliance of Organised Trades having died out, and the Trades Union Congress having no authority to co-ordinate industrial action, proposals were put forward in 1874 for a renewed attempt to create a closer unity in the Trade Union movement. Proposals to convert the Trades Union Congress into an industrial federation being abortive, some of the larger Unions, headed by the Carpenters and Joiners and the Ironfounders, set on foot a more limited plan of federation in the metal and building trades, which had closely similar systems of apprenticeship and division between craft and craft and between skilled and less skilled workers. This project, like many others, came to nothing in the depression of the later 1870s.]

(*a*) From the Official Report of the Trades Union Congress, 1874, p. 9.

From the presidential address.

. . . The Government and the country knew that the committee elected by the working men's congress had power — but in his judgment that power might be very greatly increased. In the first place, it might be increased by a stronger federation amongst themselves — (Cheers) — and by making the committee a direct connecting link of the trades' unions of the country, instead of being simply the connecting link from congress to congress, as they were at present. What should hinder that congress from making the Parliamentary Committee the direct representative of all the trades' unions throughout the country ? His idea with reference to that subject was that the Parliamentary Committee, by direct contribution from the trades composing the congress, should constantly keep connected with those trades. (Hear, hear). As it was, they had no direct communication with any trade. They were simply appointed by one congress, and waited until the next congress came round, doing the work of Parliament in reference to legislation throughout the year.

(*b*) From " Proposed Rules for the Government of the Federation of Organised Trade Societies " (1875), p. 3.

During the autumn of 1874, the Councils of the Amalgamated Society of Carpenters and Joiners, the Amalgamated Ironworkers' Association, and the Boiler Makers' and Iron Shipbuilders' Society, being of opinion that some steps should be taken with the view of federating the various trade societies in the iron and building trades, instructed their general secretaries to conjointly issue an address calling attention to the importance of the question, and inviting societies interested in the movement to instruct their representatives to attend a meeting to be held during the sittings of the Liverpool Trades Union Congress.

A meeting of representatives of various societies in the iron and building trades was accordingly held at Liverpool on Thursday, January 21st, 1875, under the presidency of Mr Daniel Guile, of the Ironfounders' Society, when the desirability of forming a federation of trade societies was unanimously affirmed. It was considered advisable not to restrict the federation to any particular trades, but to extend it to all trade societies which are sufficiently well organised to become a source of strength, not of weakness to the federation.

The representatives whose names [1] are appended to this address, were appointed as a committee to draft a code of rules, and submit them for the consideration of the various trade societies.

It will be evident to those who attentively consider the events of the past two years that struggles between capital and labour will probably be conducted in future on a far more gigantic scale than we have hitherto witnessed. Our great national societies have, whenever they have been formed on a sound financial basis, rendered the employers in a local contest powerless to cut off the resources of their workmen. When men in any town have been on strike, funds have freely been supplied from other localities, under the direction of the central governing body of the society, remunerative employment has been found elsewhere for the men on strike, and the employers have been unable to successfully resist the influences brought to bear upon them by the national organisations of workmen.

Recent events clearly indicate that the employers have recognised the weakness of their position, and have determined on the formation of large and powerful organisations for mutual protection and assistance. Whilst their cry through the public press is Peace! Peace! their actions show that they are actively preparing for war. Assurance companies are being formed to subsidise capitalists in their contests with their workmen, and before long some particular trade will probably be selected as the object of attack, the employers in that trade being supported by the united strength of the federation, in an attempt to destroy the unions existing among the men.

In the face of our common danger, it behoves the trade societies of the country to present one united front, and to combine for the purpose of creating a common fund, available wherever an emergency may arise. . . .

[1] The names included Henry Broadhurst, Daniel Guile, George Howell, John Kane, Robert Knight, John E. Osborne, J. D. Prior, David Thomson.

INDEX

Index

Index

THE END

PRINTED IN GREAT BRITAIN BY
LOWE AND BRYDONE (PRINTERS) LIMITED, LONDON